Visual Analytics and Interactive Technologies:
Data, Text and Web Mining Applications

Qingyu Zhang
Arkansas State University, USA

Richard S. Segall
Arkansas State University, USA

Mei Cao
University of Wisconsin–Superior, USA

INFORMATION SCIENCE REFERENCE

Hershey · New York

Director of Editorial Content:	Kristin Klinger
Director of Book Publications:	Julia Mosemann
Acquisitions Editor:	Lindsay Johnston
Development Editor:	Joel Gamon
Typesetter:	Milan Vracarich, Jr.
Production Editor:	Jamie Snavely
Cover Design:	Lisa Tosheff

Published in the United States of America by
Information Science Reference (an imprint of IGI Global)
701 E. Chocolate Avenue
Hershey PA 17033
Tel: 717-533-8845
Fax: 717-533-8661
E-mail: cust@igi-global.com
Web site: http://www.igi-global.com

Library of Congress Cataloging-in-Publication Data

Visual analytics and interactive technologies : data, text, and web mining
applications / Qingyu Zhang, Richard Segall, and Mei Cao, editors.
    p. cm.
  Includes bibliographical references and index.
  Summary: "This book is a comprehensive reference on concepts, algorithms,
theories, applications, software, and visualization of data mining, text
mining, Web mining and computing/supercomputing, covering state-of-the-art of
the theory and applications of mining"-- Provided by publisher.
  ISBN 978-1-60960-102-7 (hardcover) -- ISBN 978-1-60960-104-1 (ebook) 1.
Data mining. I. Zhang, Qingyu, 1970- II. Segall, Richard, 1949- III. Cao,
Mei, 1969-
  QA76.9.D343V568 2011
  006.3'12--dc22
                        2010042271

British Cataloguing in Publication Data
A Cataloguing in Publication record for this book is available from the British Library.

All work contributed to this book is new, previously-unpublished material. The views expressed in this book are those of the authors, but not necessarily of the publisher.

List of Reviewers

Mieczysław A. Kłopotek, *Polish Academy of Sciences, Poland*
N. Ranga Suri, *Centre for Artificial Intelligence and Robotics, India*
P. Alagambigai, *Easwari Engineering College, India*
Daniel Rivero, *University of A Coruña, Spain*
Tri Kurniawan Wijaya, *Sekolah Tinggi Teknik Surabaya, Indonesia*
Tzu-Liang (Bill) Tseng, *The University of Texas at El Paso, USA*
Marko Robnik-Šikonja, *University of Ljubljana, Slovenia*
Alan Olinsky, *Bryant University, USA*
Roberto Marmo, *University of Pavia, Italy*
H. Hannah Inbarani, *Periyar University, India*
Carson Kai-Sang Leung, *The University of Manitoba, Canada*
R. Roselin, *Sri Sarada College for Women, India*
Riadh Hammami, *Université Laval, Canada*
Anca Doloc-Mihu, *Emory University, USA*
Mei Cao, *University of Wisconsin-Superior, USA*
Richard S. Segall, *Arkansas State University, USA*
Qingyu Zhang, *Arkansas State University, USA*

Table of Contents

Section 2
Applications of Mining and Visualization

Section 3
Visual Systems, Software and Supercomputing

Detailed Table of Contents

Section 1
Concepts, Algorithms, and Theory

Mieczysław A. Kłopotek, Polish Academy of Sciences, Poland & University of Natural and Human Sciences, Poland

Sławomir T. Wierzchoń, Polish Academy of Sciences & University of Gdańsk, Poland

Krzysztof Ciesielski, Polish Academy of Sciences, Poland

Michał Dramiński, Polish Academy of Sciences, Poland

Dariusz Czerski, Polish Academy of Sciences, Poland

The chapter focuses on how to best represent a typical document in a large collection of objects (i.e., documents). They propose a new measure of document similarity – GNGrank that was inspired by the popular idea that links between documents reflect similar content. The idea was to create a rank measure based on the well known PageRank algorithm which exploits the document similarity to insert links between the documents. Various link-based similarity measures (e.g., PageRank) and GNGrank are compared in the context of identification of a typical document of a collection. The experimental results suggest that each algorithm measures something different, a different aspect of document space, and hence the respective degrees of typicality do not correlate.

N N R Ranga Suri, Centre for Artificial Intelligence and Robotics, India

M Narasimha Murty, Indian Institute of Science, India

G Athithan, Centre for Artificial Intelligence and Robotics, India

The chapter highlights some of the important research issues that determine the nature of the outlier detection algorithm required for a typical data mining application. Detecting the objects in a data set with unusual properties is important since such outlier objects often contain useful information on abnormal behavior of the system or its components described by the data set. They discussed issues including methods of outlier detection, size and dimensionality of the data set, and nature of the target application. They attempt to cover the challenges due to the large volume of high dimensional data and possible research directions with a survey of various data mining techniques dealing with the outlier detection problem.

Chapter 3

The chapter proposes a meta-data engine for extracting external data in the Web for data warehouses that forms a bridge between the data warehouse and search engine environments. This chapter also presents a framework named the semantic web application that facilitates semi-automatic matching of instance data from opaque web databases using ontology terms. The framework combines information retrieval, information extraction, natural language processing, and ontology techniques to produce a viable building block for semantic web applications. The application uses a query modifying filter to maximize efficiency in the search process. The ontology-based model consists of a pre-processing stage aimed at filtering, a basic and then more advanced matching phases, a combination of thresholds and a weighting that produces a matrix that is further normalized, and a labeling process that matches data items to ontology terms.

Chapter 4

The chapter discusses VISTA as a Visual Clustering Rendering System that can include algorithmic clustering results and serve as an effective validation and refinement tool for irregularly shaped clusters. Interactive visual clustering methods allow a user to partition a data set into clusters that are appropriate for their tasks and interests through an efficient visualization model and it requires an effective human-computer interaction. This chapter entails the reliable human-computer interaction through dimensionality reduction by comparing three different kinds of dimensionality reduction methods: (1) Entropy Weighting Feature Selection (EWFS), (2) Outlier Score Based Feature Selection (OSFS), and (3) Contribution to the Entropy based Feature Selection (CEFS). The performance of the three feature selection methods were compared with clustering of dataset using the whole set of features. The performance was measured with popular validity measure Rand Index.

The chapter proposes a new technique of graph evolution based ANN and compares it with other systems such as Connectivity Matrix, Pruning, Finding network parameters, and Graph-rewriting grammar. Traditionally the development of Artificial Neural Networks (ANNs) is a slow process guided by the expert knowledge. This chapter describes a new method for the development of Artificial Neural Networks, so it becomes completely automated. Several tests were performed with some of the most used test databases in data mining. The performance of the proposed system is better or in par with other systems.

Chapter 6

The chapter focuses on several feature selection methods as to their effectiveness in preprocessing input medical data. Feature selection is an active research area in pattern recognition and data mining communities. They evaluate several feature selection algorithms such as Mutual Information Feature Selection (MIFS), Fast Correlation-Based Filter (FCBF) and Stepwise Discriminant Analysis (STEPDISC) with machine learning algorithm naive Bayesian and Linear Discriminant analysis techniques. The experimental analysis of feature selection technique in medical databases shows that a small number of informative features can be extracted leading to improvement in medical diagnosis by reducing the size of data set, eliminating irrelevant features, and decreasing the processing time.

Chapter 7

The chapter conceptually discusses the techniques to mine hidden information or knowledge which lies in data. In addition to the elaboration of the concept and theory, they also discuss about the application and implementation of data mining. They start with differences among data, information, and knowledge, and then proceed to describe the process of gaining the hidden knowledge, and compare data mining with other closely related terminologies such as data warehouse and OLAP.

Section 2
Applications of Mining and Visualization

Chapter 8

Chun-Che Huang, National Chi Nan University, Taiwan
Tzu-Liang (Bill) Tseng, The University of Texas at El Paso, USA
Hao-Syuan Lin, National Chi Nan University, Taiwan

The chapter applies rough set theory (RST), which is suitable for processing qualitative information, to induce rules to derive significant attributes for categorization of the patent infringement risk. Patent infringement risk is an important issue for firms due to the increased appreciation of intellectual property rights. If a firm gives insufficient protection to its patents, it may loss both profits and industry competitiveness. Rather than focusing on measuring the patent trend indicators and the patent monetary value, they integrate RST with the use of the concept hierarchy and the credibility index, to enhance application of the final decision rules.

Chapter 9

Marko Robnik-Šikonja, University of Ljubljana, Slovenia
Koen Vanhoof, University of Hasselt, Belgium

The chapter makes use of the ordinal evaluation (OrdEval) algorithm as a visualization technique to study questionnaire data of customer satisfaction in marketing. The OrdEval algorithm has many favorable features, including context sensitivity, ability to exploit meaning of ordered features and ordered response, robustness to noise and missing values in the data, and visualization capability. They choose customer satisfaction analysis as a case study and present visual analysis on two applications of business-to-business and costumer-to-business. They demonstrate some interesting advantages offered by the new methodology and visualization and show how to extract and interpret new insights not available with classical analytical toolbox.

Chapter 10

Alan Olinsky, Bryant University, USA
Phyllis Schumacher, Bryant University, USA
John Quinn, Bryant University, USA

The chapter entails the use of several types of predictive models to perform data mining to evaluate the student retention rate and enrollment management for those selecting a major in the Actuarial Science at a medium size university. The predictive models utilized in this research include stepwise logistic regression, neural networks and decision trees for performing the data mining. This chapter uses data mining to investigate the percentages of students who begin in a certain major and will graduate in the same major. This information is important for individual academic departments in determining how to allocate limited resources in making decisions as to the appropriate number of classes and sections to be offered and the number of faculty lines needed to staff the department. This chapter details a study that utilizes data mining techniques to analyze the characteristics of students who enroll as actuarial mathematics students and then either drop out of the major or graduate as actuarial students.

Chapter 11

H. Hannah Inbarani, Periyar University, India
K. Thangavel, Periyar University, India

The chapter proposes a robust Biclustering algorithm to disclose the correlation between users and pages based on constant values for integrating user clustering and page clustering techniques, which is followed by a recommendation system that can respond to the users' individual interests. The proposed method is compared with Simple Biclustering (SB) method. To evaluate the effectiveness and efficiency of the recommendation, experiments are conducted in terms of the recommendation accuracy metric. The experimental results demonstrated that the proposed RB method is very simple and is able to efficiently extract needed usage knowledge and to accurately make web recommendations.

Chapter 12

Roberto Marmo, University of Pavia, Italy

The chapter reviews and discusses the use of web mining techniques and social networks analysis to possibly process and analyze large amount of social data such as blogtagging, online game playing, instant messenger, etc. Social network analysis views social relationships in terms of network and graph theory about nodes (individual actors within the network) and ties (relationships between the actors). In this way, social network mining can help understand the social structure, social relationships and social behaviours. These algorithms differ from established set of data mining algorithms developed to analyze individual records since social network datasets are relational with the centrality of relations among entities.

Section 3
Visual Systems, Software and Supercomputing

Chapter 13

Carson Kai-Sang Leung, The University of Manitoba, Canada
Christopher L. Carmichael, The University of Manitoba, Canada

The chapter proposes an interactive visual analytic system called iVAS for providing visual analytic solutions to the frequent set mining problem. The system enables the visualization and advanced analysis of the original transaction databases as well as the frequent sets mined from these databases. Numerous algorithms have been proposed for finding frequent sets of items, which are usually presented in a lengthy textual list. However, the use of visual representations can enhance user understanding of the inherent relations among the frequent sets.

The chapter applies classification algorithm to image processing (e.g., mammogram processing) using genetic Ant-Miner. Image mining deals with the extraction of implicit knowledge, image data relationship, or other patterns not explicitly stored in the images. It is an extension of data mining to image domain and an interdisciplinary endeavor. C4.5 and Ant-Miner algorithms are compared and the experimental results show that Ant-Miner performs better in the domain of biomedical image analysis.

Chapter 15

The chapter develops SciDBMaker to provide a tool for easy building of new specialized protein knowledge bases. The exponential growth of molecular biology research in recent decades has brought growth in the number and size of genomic and proteomic databases to enhance the understanding of biological processes. This chapter also suggests best practices for specialized biological databases design, and provides examples for the implementation of these practices.

Chapter 16

The chapter discusses an Adaptive Image Retrieval System (AIRS) that is used as a tool for actively searching for information in large image databases. This chapter identifies two types of users for an AIRS: an end-user who seeks images and a research-user who designs and researches the collection and retrieval systems. This chapter focuses in visualization techniques used by Web-based AIRS to allow different users to efficiently navigate, search and analyze large image databases. Recent advances in Internet technology require the development of advanced Web-based tools for efficiently accessing images from tremendously large, and continuously growing, image collections. One such tool for actively searching for information is an Image Retrieval System. The interface discussed in this chapter illustrates different relationships between images by using visual attributes (colors, shape, and proximities), and supports retrieval and learning, as well as browsing which makes it suitable for an Adaptive Image Retrieval Systems.

Chapter 17

The chapter describes supercomputer as the fastest type of computer used for specialized applications that require a massive number of mathematical calculations. The term "supercomputer" was coined in

1929 by the New York World, referring to tabulators manufactured by IBM. These tabulators represent the cutting edge of technology, which harness immense processing power so that they are incredibly fast, sophisticated, and powerful. The use of supercomputing in data mining has also been discussed in the chapter.

Preface

Large volumes of data and complex problems inspire research in computing and data, text, and web mining. However, analyzing data is not sufficient, as it has to be presented visually with analytical capabilities, i.e., a chart/diagram/image illustration that enables humans to perceive, relate, and conclude in the knowledge discovery process. In addition, how to use computing or supercomputing techniques (e.g., distributed, parallel, and clustered computing) in improving the effectiveness of data, text, and web mining is an important aspect of the visual analytics and interactive technology. This book extends the visual analytics by using tools of data, web, text mining and computing, and their associated software and technologies available today.

This is a comprehensive book on concepts, algorithms, theories, applications, software, and visualization of data mining and computing. It provides a volume of coherent set of related works on the state-of-the-art of the theory and applications of mining and its relations to computing, visualization and others with an audience to include both researchers, practitioners, professionals and intellectuals in technical and non-technical fields, appealing to a multi-disciplinary audience. Because each chapter is designed to be stand-alone, readers can focus on the topics that most interest them.

With a unique collection of recent developments, novel applications, and techniques for visual analytics and interactive technologies, the sections of the book are Concepts, Algorithms, and Theory; Applications of Mining and Visualization; and Visual Systems, Software and Supercomputing, pertaining to Data mining, Web mining, Data Visualization, Mining for Intelligence, Supercomputing, Database, Ontology, Web Clustering, Classification, Pattern Recognition, Visualization Approaches, Data and Knowledge Representation, and Web Intelligence.

Section 1 consists of seven chapters on concepts, algorithms, and theory of mining and visualizations.

Chapter 1, *Towards the Notion of Typical Documents in Large Collections of Documents*, by Mieczysław A. Kłopotek, Sławomir T. Wierzchom, Krzysztof Ciesielski, Michał Dramiński, and Dariusz Czerski, focuses on how to best represent a typical document in a large collection of objects (i.e., documents). They propose a new measure of document similarity – GNGrank that was inspired by the popular idea that links between documents reflect similar content. The idea was to create a rank measure based on the well known PageRank algorithm which exploits the document similarity to insert links between the documents. Various link-based similarity measures (e.g., PageRank) and GNGrank are compared in the context of identification of a typical document of a collection. The experimental results suggest that each algorithm measures something different, a different aspect of document space, and hence the respective degrees of typicality do not correlate.

Chapter 2, *Data Mining Techniques for Outlier Detection*, by N. Ranga Suri, M Narasimha Murty, and G Athithan, highlights some of the important research issues that determine the nature of the outlier detection algorithm required for a typical data mining application. Detecting the objects in a data set with unusual properties is important; as such outlier objects often contain useful information on abnormal behavior of the system or its components described by the data set. They discussed issues including methods of outlier detection, size and dimensionality of the data set, and nature of the target application. They attempt to cover the challenges due to the large volume of high dimensional data and possible research directions with a survey of various data mining techniques dealing with the outlier detection problem.

Chapter 3, *Using an Ontology-based Framework to Extract External Web Data for the Data Warehouse*, by Charles Greenidge and Hadrian Peter, proposes a meta-data engine for extracting external data in the Web for data warehouses that forms a bridge between the data warehouse and search engine environments. This chapter also presents a framework named the semantic web application that facilitates semi-automatic matching of instance data from opaque web databases using ontology terms. The framework combines information retrieval, information extraction, natural language processing, and ontology techniques to produce a viable building block for semantic web applications. The application uses a query modifying filter to maximize efficiency in the search process. The ontology-based model consists of a pre-processing stage aimed at filtering, a basic and then more advanced matching phases, a combination of thresholds and a weighting that produces a matrix that is further normalized, and a labeling process that matches data items to ontology terms.

Chapter 4, *Dimensionality Reduction for Interactive Visual Clustering: A Comparative Analysis*, by P. Alagambigai and K. Thangavel, discusses VISTA as a Visual Clustering Rendering System that can include algorithmic clustering results and serve as an effective validation and refinement tool for irregularly shaped clusters. Interactive visual clustering methods allow a user to partition a data set into clusters that are appropriate for their tasks and interests through an efficient visualization model and it requires an effective human-computer interaction. This chapter entails the reliable human-computer interaction through dimensionality reduction by comparing three different kinds of dimensionality reduction methods: (1) Entropy Weighting Feature Selection (EWFS), (2) Outlier Score Based Feature Selection (OSFS), and (3) Contribution to the Entropy based Feature Selection (CEFS). The performance of the three feature selection methods were compared with clustering of dataset using the whole set of features. The performance was measured with popular validity measure Rand Index.

Chapter 5, *Database Analysis with ANNs by Means of Graph Evolution*, by Daniel Rivero, Julián Dorado, Juan R. Rabuñal, and Alejandro Pazos, proposes a new technique of graph evolution based ANN and compares it with other systems such as Connectivity Matrix, Pruning, Finding network parameters, and Graph-rewriting grammar. Traditionally the development of Artificial Neural Networks (ANNs) is a slow process guided by the expert knowledge. This chapter describes a new method for the development of Artificial Neural Networks, so it becomes completely automated. Several tests were performed with some of the most used test databases in data mining. The performance of the proposed system is better or in par with other systems.

Chapter 6, *An Optimal Categorization of Feature Selection Methods for Knowledge Discovery*, by Harleen Kaur, Ritu Chauhan, and M. A. Alam, focuses on several feature selection methods as to their effectiveness in preprocessing input medical data. Feature selection is an active research area in pattern recognition and data mining communities. They evaluate several feature selection algorithms such as Mutual Information Feature Selection (MIFS), Fast Correlation-Based Filter (FCBF) and Stepwise Discriminant Analysis (STEPDISC) with machine learning algorithm naive Bayesian and Linear Discriminant analysis techniques. The experimental analysis of feature selection technique in medical databases shows that a small number of informative features can be extracted leading to improvement in medical diagnosis by reducing the size of data set, eliminating irrelevant features, and decreasing the processing time.

Chapter 7, *From Data to Knowledge: Data Mining*, by Tri Kurniawan Wijaya, conceptually discusses the techniques to mine hidden information or knowledge which lies in data. In addition to the elaboration of the concept and theory, they also discuss about the application and implementation of data mining. They start with differences among data, information, and knowledge, and then proceed to describe the process of gaining the hidden knowledge, and compare data mining with other closely related terminologies such as data warehouse and OLAP.

Section 2 consists of five chapters on applications of mining and visualizations.

Chapter 8, *Patent Infringement Risk Analysis Using Rough Set Theory*, by Chun-Che Huang, Tzu-Liang (Bill) Tseng, and Hao-Syuan Lin, applies rough set theory (RST), which is suitable for processing qualitative information, to induce rules to derive significant attributes for categorization of the patent infringement risk. Patent infringement risk is an important issue for firms due to the increased appreciation of intellectual property rights. If a firm gives insufficient protection to its patents, it may loss both profits and industry competitiveness. Rather than focusing on measuring the patent trend indicators and the patent monetary value, they integrate RST with the use of the concept hierarchy and the credibility index, to enhance application of the final decision rules.

Chapter 9, *Visual Survey Analysis in Marketing*, by Marko Robnik-Šikonja and Koen Vanhoof, makes use of the ordinal evaluation (OrdEval) algorithm as a visualization technique to study questionnaire data of customer satisfaction in marketing. The OrdEval algorithm has many favorable features, including context sensitivity, ability to exploit meaning of ordered features and ordered response, robustness to noise and missing values in the data, and visualization capability. They choose customer satisfaction analysis as a case study and present visual analysis on two applications of business-to-business and costumer-to-business. They demonstrate some interesting advantages offered by the new methodology and visualization and show how to extract and interpret new insights not available with classical analytical toolbox.

Chapter 10, *Assessing Data Mining Approaches for Analyzing Actuarial Student Success Rate*, by Alan Olinsky, Phyllis Schumacher, and John Quinn, entails the use of several types of predictive models to perform data mining to evaluate the student retention rate and enrollment management for those selecting a major in the Actuarial Science at a medium size university. The predictive models utilized in this research include stepwise logistic regression, neural networks and decision trees for performing the data mining. This chapter uses data mining to investigate the percentages of students who begin in a certain major and will graduate in the same major. This information is important for individual academic departments in determining how to allocate limited resources in making decisions as to the appropriate number of classes and sections to be offered and the number of faculty lines needed to staff the department. This chapter details a study that utilizes data mining techniques to analyze the characteristics of students who enroll as actuarial mathematics students and then either drop out of the major or graduate as actuarial students.

Chapter 11, *A Robust Biclustering Approach for Effective Web Personalization*, by H. Hannah Inbarani and K. Thangavel, proposes a robust Biclustering algorithm to disclose the correlation between users and pages based on constant values for integrating user clustering and page clustering techniques, which is followed by a recommendation system that can respond to the users' individual interests. The proposed method is compared with Simple Biclustering (SB) method. To evaluate the effectiveness and efficiency of the recommendation, experiments are conducted in terms of the recommendation accuracy metric. The experimental results demonstrated that the proposed RB method is very simple and is able to efficiently extract needed usage knowledge and to accurately make web recommendations.

Chapter 12, *Web Mining and Social Network Analysis*, by Roberto Marmo, reviews and discusses the use of web mining techniques and social networks analysis to possibly process and analyze large amount of social data such as blogtagging, online game playing, instant messenger, etc. Social network analysis views social relationships in terms of network and graph theory about nodes (individual actors within the network) and ties (relationships between the actors). In this way, social network mining can help understand the social structure, social relationships and social behaviours. These algorithms differ from established set of data mining algorithms developed to analyze individual records since social network datasets are relational with the centrality of relations among entities.

Section 3 consists of five chapters on visual systems, software and supercomputing.

Chapter 13, *iVAS: An Interactive Visual Analytic System for Frequent Set Mining*, by Carson Kai-Sang Leung and Christopher L. Carmichael, proposes an interactive visual analytic system called iVAS for providing visual analytic solutions to the frequent set mining problem. The system enables the visualization and advanced analysis of the original transaction databases as well as the frequent sets mined from these databases. Numerous algorithms have been proposed for finding frequent sets of items, which are usually presented in a lengthy textual list. However, the use of visual representations can enhance user understanding of the inherent relations among the frequent sets.

Chapter 14, *Mammogram Mining Using Genetic Ant-Miner*, by Thangavel. K. and Roselin. R, applies classification algorithm to image processing (e.g., mammogram processing) using genetic Ant-Miner. Image mining deals with the extraction of implicit knowledge, image data relationship, or other patterns not explicitly stored in the images. It is an extension of data mining to image domain and an interdisciplinary endeavor. C4.5 and Ant-Miner algorithms are compared and the experimental results show that Ant-Miner performs better in the domain of biomedical image analysis.

Chapter 15, *Use of SciDBMaker as Tool for the Design of Specialized Biological Databases*, by Riadh Hammami and Ismail Fliss, develops SciDBMaker to provide a tool for easy building of new specialized protein knowledge bases. The exponential growth of molecular biology research in recent decades has brought growth in the number and size of genomic and proteomic databases to enhance the understanding of biological processes. This chapter also suggests best practices for specialized biological databases design, and provides examples for the implementation of these practices.

Chapter 16, *Interactive Visualization Tool for Analysis of Large Image Databases*, by Anca Doloc-Mihu, discusses an Adaptive Image Retrieval System (AIRS) that is used as a tool for actively searching for information in large image databases. This chapter identifies two types of users for an AIRS: an end-user who seeks images and a research-user who designs and researches the collection and retrieval systems. This chapter focuses in visualization techniques used by Web-based AIRS to allow different users to efficiently navigate, search and analyze large image databases. Recent advances in Internet technology require the development of advanced Web-based tools for efficiently accessing images from tremendously large, and continuously growing, image collections. One such tool for actively searching for information is an Image Retrieval System. The interface discussed in this chapter illustrates different relationships between images by using visual attributes (colors, shape, and proximities), and supports retrieval and learning, as well as browsing which makes it suitable for an Adaptive Image Retrieval Systems.

Chapter 17, *Supercomputers and Supercomputing*, by Jeffrey S. Cook, describes supercomputer as the fastest type of computer used for specialized applications that require a massive number of mathematical calculations. The term "supercomputer" was coined in 1929 by the New York World, referring to tabulators manufactured by IBM. These tabulators represent the cutting edge of technology, which harness immense processing power so that they are incredibly fast, sophisticated, and powerful. The use of supercomputing in data mining has also been discussed in the chapter.

All chapters went through a blind refereeing process before final acceptance. We hope these chapters are informative, stimulating, and helpful to the readers.

Qingyu Zhang
Arkansas State University, USA

Richard S. Segall
Arkansas State University, USA

Mei Cao
University of Wisconsin-Superior, USA

Acknowledgment

The publication of a book is a cooperative and joint effort and involves many people. We wish to thank all involved in the solicitation process of book chapters and the review process of the book, without whose support the book could not have been completed.

Special thanks and gratitude go to the publishing team at IGI Global, in particular to the development editor Joel Gamon and the acquisition editorial assistant Erika Carter, whose contributions throughout the process of the book publication have been invaluable.

We want to thank all the authors for their excellent contributions to this book. We are also grateful to all the reviewers, including most of the contributing authors, who served as referees for chapters written by other authors, and provided constructive and comprehensive reviews in the double-blind review process.

Qingyu Zhang
Arkansas State University, USA

Richard S. Segall
Arkansas State University, USA

Mei Cao
University of Wisconsin-Superior, USA

May 2010

Section 1
Concepts, Algorithms, and Theory

Chapter 1
Towards the Notion of Typical Documents in Large Collections of Documents

Mieczysław A. Kłopotek
Polish Academy of Sciences, Poland & University of Natural and Human Sciences, Poland

Sławomir T. Wierzchoń
Polish Academy of Sciences & University of Gdańsk, Poland

Krzysztof Ciesielski
Polish Academy of Sciences, Poland

Michał Dramiński
Polish Academy of Sciences, Poland

Dariusz Czerski
Polish Academy of Sciences, Poland

ABSTRACT

This chapter presents a new measure of document similarity – the GNGrank that was inspired by the popular opinion that links between the documents reflect similar content. The idea was to create a rank measure based on the well known PageRank algorithm which exploits the document similarity to insert links between the documents. A comparative study of various link- and content-based similarity measures, and GNGrank is performed in the context of identification of a typical document of a collection. The study suggests that each group of them measures something different, a different aspect of document space, and hence the respective degrees of typicality do not correlate. This may be an indication that for different purposes different documents may be important. A deeper study of this phenomenon is our future research goal.

DOI: 10.4018/978-1-60960-102-7.ch001

INTRODUCTION

The usual way to get an overview of a large collection of objects (e.g. documents) is to cluster them, and then to look for the representatives (or summaries) of the individual clusters. The objects are placed within a feature space (in case of documents, frequently features are the terms, and co-ordinates are e.g. tf-idf measure and the representatives are the centroids (or medoids) of clusters (Manning, Raghavan & Schütze, 2009).

There are some conceptual problems with such an approach in case of document collections. On one hand, one insists that text understanding is essential for proper clustering. Regrettably, application of the full-fledged text understanding methods for very large collections is not feasible so that some replacements have to be sought, therefore, in fact, the feature space approach is the dominant one.

The next problem is that with feature space approach a rigid weighting of features is imposed, whereas the natural language experience is that within the given group of related documents the meaning and so the importance of terms may drift. We proposed here a solution called contextual processing, where terms are re-weighted at stages of the clustering process (Ciesielski & Klopotek, 2006).

Then we have the issue of cluster relationships. Clusters formed are usually not independent. Hierarchical clustering surely does not cover all the possible kinds of relationships among clusters. For this reason we pledged for using competitive clustering methods like WebSOM, i.e. text document version of self organizing maps, (Kohonen, Kaski, Somervuo, Lagus, Oja, & Paatero, 2003), Growing Neural Gas, or GNG, of Fritzke (1997) or aiNet (an immunological method mimicking the idiotypical network) of de Castro & Timmis (2002)).

Finally, there is a problem of the centroid. The centroids are usually "averaged" documents, i.e. they represent a rather abstract concept. Averaged weights of documents may in fact not represent any meaningful document at all, and closeness to the centroid may say nothing about the importance of a document for the collection. Therefore, in our system we aim at a more realistic representative of a cluster. In this chapter we want to investigate two competing technologies:

- a histogram-based notion of document typicality
- a PageRank-like selection of "medoidal" documents.

The abovementioned concepts have been implemented and tested within our map-based search engine BEATCA[1] (Klopotek, Wierzchon, Ciesielski, Draminski & Czerski, 2007).

Subsequently we will explain these ideas in some extent. In particular within the chapter we will explain in detail the idea of contextual clustering, methodology behind identifying typical documents and medoidal documents and show results of empirical evaluation of relationships between traditional centroids, typical documents and medoidal documents.

BACKGROUND AND MOTIVATION

The Idea of Contexts

We have introduced the idea of contexts in the paper (Ciesielski & Klopotek, 2007).

For purposes of document retrieval we rarely encounter deep linguistic analysis. For massive collection, shallow analysis is applied at most, and term space representation is most frequently encountered. In this representation, instead of analyzing the text linguistically, distinct terms are identified and frequencies of their occurrence are counted. Then a space is imagined in which all distinct terms from all documents of the collection serve as dimension labels, and documents are treated as vectors in this space where the coordinate

$w_{t,d}$ for a given term t for a given document d is a function of the frequency with which this term occurs in the document and the collection. Then the execution of a query against the document collection is reduced to transforming the query text into a vector in the very same vector space and the similarity between each vector and the query is computed as a dot-product of the query vector and the document vector.

In the simplest case we assign $w_{t,d} = 1$, if the document contains at least one occurrence of term t, and $w_{t,d} = 0$ otherwise. Such a measure does not take into account the fact that a term used more frequently in the document is more important for it. So $w_{t,d} = count(t \text{ in } d)$, or to get a more flat dependence, $w_{t,d} = \log(count(t \text{ in } d)+1)$. This was still considered as not satisfactory, as it gave more weight to common words than to content-expressing ones. So the researchers came to the conclusion that a punishment for being a common word has to be included, so finally the so-called tf-idf (term frequency – inverse document frequency) measure was introduced (Manning, Raghavan & Schütze, 2009):

$$w_{t,d} = count(t \text{ in } d) * \log(cont(docs \text{ in collection})/count(docs \text{ containing } t)$$

With this formula the "general context" of a document becomes visible and more realistic query results are achieved. Still, to get rid of the impact of document length on the similarity measure, the vectors describing documents are normalized so that they are of unit length.

The text documents are not uniformly distributed in the space of terms. So usually, if a clustering algorithm is run with the above-mentioned similarity measure (dot product of document vectors) a collection would split into subsets of similar documents that are usually topically related.

At this point we come to a crucial insight. While looking at the similarity relations between documents within the clusters, the usual approach is to look at the documents from the perspective of the "general context". So if by chance documents from the field of medicine and computer science are present in the collection, then if one compares the medical documents, then their similarity is impaired by the fact that there are also computer science publications there. In our research we considered this as not appropriate and decided that for within group comparisons we will use not the general context, but rather the context of the group. So we redefined the tf-idf measure so that the representation of a document within the group, called "context" takes into account the group and not the whole collection.

By producing contextual models we operate simultaneously in two spaces: the space of documents and (extended) space of terms. The whole algorithm iteratively adapts: (a) documents representation, (b) description of contexts by means of the histograms, and (c) the degrees of membership of documents to the contexts as well as weights of the terms. As a result of such a procedure we obtain homogenous groups of documents together with the description fitted individually to each group.

Such an approach proved fruitful as it contributed to dimensionality reduction within the context and more robust behavior of subsequent document map generation process and incremental updates of document collection map (Ciesielski & Klopotek, 2007).

Competitive Clustering

The above-mentioned map of a document collection is to be understood as a flat representation (that is on a two-dimensional Euclidian plain) of the collection formed in such a way that documents similar in the term space will appear more closely on the document map. So called competitive clustering algorithms are usually used to form such a map. Competitive clustering algorithms, like WebSOM, GNG or aiNet, are attractive because of at least two reasons. First, they adaptively fit to the internal structure of the data. Second, they offer natural possibility of visualizing this structure by projecting high-dimensional input vectors to a two-dimensional grid structure (a map with composed of discrete patches, called cells). This map preserves most of the topological information of the input data.

Each cell of the map is described by so-called reference vector, or "centroid", being a concise characteristic of the micro-group defined by such a cell. These centroids attract other input vectors with the force proportional to their mutual similarity. In effect, weight vectors are ordered according to their similarity to the cells of the map. Further, the distribution of weight vectors reflects the density of the input space. Reference vectors of cells neighboring on the map are also closer (in original data space) to one another than those of distant cells.

Typical Document Issue

One of the major questions posed about document collections is how to summarize their content. For purposes of speedy analysis in clustering algorithms the centroids (or eventually medoids) in the term space are considered. Ciesielski & Klopotek (2007) proposed to extend this representation by taking into account histograms of term weights (as defined above) within the clusters.

The idea, why histograms are used, may be explained as follows: Note that the weight of a term in a document depends usually on three factors:

- the number of its occurrences in the document,
- the number of documents containing this term, and
- the length of the document.

The term which occurred several times in a short document and does occur in only a few other documents, is awarded by high weight, as it is characteristic for such a group. Terms that occur everywhere, or those occurring one time in a very long document, will have low weight.

The histogram then reflects the probability distribution that a particular term occurs with a given weight in the documents forming particular context. The terms, that have only low weights in the documents, are not important within the context. Those with strong share of high weight occurrences can be considered important in discriminating the documents within the context. Now, as "typical" we understand the document containing only those terms that are labeled as important for a given context.

Analogously to content terms, one can build histograms of the distribution of additional semantic attributes within the context and the "typical" document can be defined now as one sharing important (typical) semantic attributes with this context.

Whatever information is used, given the histogram profile of a cluster, typical documents are filtered out as those most similar to the profile.

Medoidal Document Issue

In a map-like environment there exist new possibilities to analyze links between documents, that may lead to inclusion of content information into rank computations in a PageRank manner. For example, we can consider GNG nodes like special type "pages" that are linked to one another according to the GNG links as well as to documents assigned to them. Beside a link to the GNG node containing it, a document may be deemed linked to other documents within the same GNG node via their "natural" hyperlinks. We introduce further links via similarity relationships. A document may be deemed linked to k-Nearest Neighboring documents within the same GNG node. These links may be considered as unidirectional. The reason for this is that the relation of "top ranked" similarity is not a symmetric relation, so that if A is most similar to B among all pages similar to A, then still B may be most similar to say C among all pages similar to B.

Due to the way the clustering of nodes is performed in our system, fuzzy-membership of documents may emerge, so that cross-links are possible.

With this link structure PageRank may be computed in the conventional way, providing with a kind of GNGrank. Note that co-occurrence of documents in queries may be a replacement for links also. In this way both hyperlinks and content information will be taken into account. The content information is translated into similarity among documents, and the links are a kind of locally thresholded similarity.

Under this view, the medoidal document within a cluster will be one with the highest GNGrank.

Let us subsequently look at this idea of GNG rank in more detail.

Overview of PageRank

Basic Idea Behind PageRank and its Variations

There exist a number of reasons why the pages on the Web are ranked according to a variety of criteria. One of particular interest to business is that of the likelihood of a page being visited. The earliest attempt to measure this likelihood is ascribed to the so-called PageRank (Brin, 1998) (a ranking method patented in the meantime in the USA, with over 4000 citations on CiteSeer). PageRank is a ranking method of web pages based on the link structure of the Web. The intuition behind this ranking is that important pages are those linked-to by many important pages.

The basic insight provided by an equivalently formulated PageRank is the probability that a randomly walking surfer will find himself on a given page. It is assumed that the surfer on a given page jumps with equal probability to any other page linked to by this page. With some fixed probability the surfer jumps to any other page on

the Internet. He jumps also anywhere from a page without outgoing links.

This model has an important implication from the business point of view: it tells where to place advertisement so that it is most likely visited.

The random walk model of PageRank has been widely criticized for not being realistic on one hand, and on the other its potential was appreciated so that other processes were modeled along its lines.

Hence a number of improvements have been proposed.

The personalized PageRank (Fogaras & Racz, 2004) assumes that the jump not following the links is performed not to arbitrary page, but rather to a [set of] preferred page[s], so that the random surfer remains within a vicinity of the pages he likes.

Another version of PageRank, Topical PageRank (Zhang, Zhang, & Li, 2008) closely related to the above modification relies on assignment of documents to particular topic of interest out of a limited list.

Query-dependent PageRank (Manaskasemsak & Rungsawang, 2004) sets a preference to pages containing some words from a query. It is argued that the QDPR for a given query can be computed approximately as a composition of QDPR for constituent terms of the query.

In this way, the PageRank for any topic of interest can be computed out of components.

The previous approaches assume that the surfer always moves forward. The RBS by Sydow (2005) includes the application of back-step option of the browser. In this way more realistic surfer behaviour is simulated. Also a comparison with the original PageRank may be an indication of a small world (PageRank trap) in the link structure.

Other extensions of PageRank include so-called EigenTrust (Kamvar, Haveliwala, Manning & Golub, 2003), a PageRank adjusted to trust management, in case that there are differentiating evaluations of links to various pages (unequal jump probabilities). The TrustRank (Gyongyi, GarciaMolina & Pedersen, 2004) assumes that each (or many) pages are assigned a value how good it is, and the rank computation takes it into account. For example, time is taken into account (older pages may be more rigorously discarded than newer ones). Value of a page may be estimated based on how one cares about it (number of dead links that are outgoing).

There exist other link-based methods for evaluation of Web page ranking, including HITS (Kleinberg, 1999), SALSA (Lempel & Moran, 2000), PHITS (Cohn & Hoffman, 2001) etc., that are based on other principles. HITS assigns two ranks to the page: hub (how good it is at pointing at authorities) and authority (how well it is referred to by hubs). SALSA is based on the idea of random walk both along the links and in the reverse direction (which is not feasible, but may provide interesting insights). PHITS estimates how probable the structure of links is given some set of (hidden) underlying topical structure of the internet.

The applications of PageRank go beyond links between Web Pages and include social links, e-commerce trust relationships etc.

However, content-oriented PageRank analogues, or generally combined content and link information based methods are not frequently investigated.

One of the earliest approaches was that of Cohn and Hoffman (2001) who merged probabilistic analogue of HITS and LSI (latent semantic analysis) into one framework. The basic idea was that background (hidden) topics drive both link insertion and text inclusion.

An overview of other methods can be found in (Chikhi, Rothenburger & AussenacGilles, 2008). Note that in some content-based systems the link information is used to extend the textual one via incorporation of so-called anchor text (the text between <a> and </a>, eventually the text around the link).

In this paper we intend to follow a different way. We suggest to derive "thematic" links from the document similarity. In some sense this may resemble the ideas of link prediction (Zhu, Hong & Hughes, 2002) on the Web (or more generally in social networks), as used e.g. in Web usage mining, in connection with recommender systems. We will, however, exploit the content-based clustering process itself (GNG clustering, aiNet clustering, WebSOM clustering etc.) to create a link structure, and not the reverse way.

Mathematical Foundations

The initial idea of the PageRank was that of a network of pipes through which "authorities" flow from one Web page to another. Two pages are connected by a (directed) pipe, if one contains a Web link to the other. The flow of authority is from the pointing page to one pointed at by the link.

It is assumed that the overall sum of authorities is equal to 1 and that the authority leaves a page in equal proportions for each outgoing edge.

So a connectedness matrix A (of size NxN), where N is the total number of pages) is defined in which $A_{ij}=1/k_j$ means that there is a link from page j to page i, with page j having k_j outgoing links. $A_{ij}=0$ means no link from j to i. Each column of A sums up to 1 (a comment on this below).

The vector of authority R of size Nx1 (R_j= authority of page j) would be then defined as

$$R=A * R$$

that is the (main) eigen-vector of the connectedness matrix A.

For uniqueness, the sum of elements of R should be equal 1, so that it can be considered as a probability distribution.

A random walk model of a surfer who enters a page and leaves it over any outgoing link with equal probability has been proposed as yielding page visit probability equal to the respective R vector component (Langville & Meyer, 2006).

The model had a couple of flaws, however. There are pages without outgoing links on the

Web (so that the sums of some columns are equal 0, and not 1), ones without ingoing links (so that their rank drops to 0, as well as of those pages that are pointed to solely by zero authority nodes), not all pages are linked together (there are isolated islands). Under these circumstances the R cannot be actually computed uniquely or cannot be computed at all (due to leak of authority).

So in fact, with the leak, the eigenvalue problem of the form

$$l\ R = A * R$$

is solved, l being the eigenvalue to be determined.

The model has been modified by adding an artificial "supernode". All pages are deemed to be linked to this node in both directions. The choice of outgoing link in the supernode is the same as elsewhere, but the rules for jumping to the supernode are different. First, each node having no outgoing page, has 100% probability of jumping to the supernode (An alternative interpretation is that a node without outgoing links is treated as one with outgoing links leading to all the other nodes). For other nodes, the jump to the supernode happens with the same ("decay") probability d for each node, not depending on the number of outgoing edges of the node.

So the formal model has been modified to

$$R = (1-d)A*R + D(S)$$

S is a Nx1 vector with elements of the form $S_j = 1/N$. D(S) is a "decay factor", that multiplies S_j with d if page j has at least one outgoing edge, and multiplying with 1 otherwise. R is the authority vector to be computed,

Here we have again the eigenvalue problem and we choose the solution in which R sums up to 1. Now the proper solution exists.

If we have a network in which each node has an outgoing edge[2] then in the above equation, D will consist only of ds, whatever the distribution

R (recall that R sums up to 1). Under these circumstances the above equation can be rewritten as

$$R = (1-d)A * R + d*S$$

Various modifications of the PageRank have been proposed. For example personalized PageRank, consists in departures from the uniform distribution of the S vector. Other, like RBS, add further matrices to this equation. Eigentrust on the other hand departs from uniform distribution of non-zero values in the columns.

Accelerating PageRank Computation

Note that parallel computation of PageRank has been subject of intensive research, e.g. (Kohlschtter, Chirita & Nejdl, 2006; Zhu & Li, 2005).

The feasibility of iterative PageRank computation stems from the fact that Web links are largely designed for purposes of navigation. So, as mentioned in (Kohlschtter, Chirita & Nejdl, 2006) about 93.6% of all non-dangling links are intra-host and 95.2% intra-domain ones.

PageRank parallelization is approached in two major ways:

- Exact Computations: Here, the web graph is initially partitioned into blocks, which may be either grouped randomly (e.g. P2P PageRank (Aberer & Wu, 2004) or lexicographically sorted by page (MIKElab PageRank (Manaskasemsak & Rungsawang, 2004) and Open System PageRank (Shi, Yu, Yang, & Wang, 2003)) or balanced on the grounds of the number of links (PETSc PageRank (Gleich, Zhukov & Berkhin, 2004)). Within blocks, standard iterative methods are applied in parallel.
- Approximations: The goal is not to compute the PageRank value as such, but rather a vector organized on the ground of

PageRank ideology, matching rather rank than value; two levels computations are typical: the outer-structure of page blocks (which are few) and the inner-structure of page blocks (which can be computed In parallel). Examples are the U-Model (Avrachenkov, Dobrynin, Nemirovsky, Pham & Smirnova, 2008), or HostRank/ DirRank (Eiron & McCurley, 2003).

PageRank: Overview of Applications

Recommender Systems

In an obvious way the abovementioned random walk model for PageRank and its modifications is directly applicable for recommendation purposes. The page with the highest PageRank would be recommended.

For example (Abbassi & Mirrokni, 2007) applies personalized PageRank to recommend pages based on weblogs, for which weblog graphs are constructed. In (Zhang, Zhang & Li, 2008), the Topical PageRank is used for a recommender system, which aims to rank products by analysing previous user-item relationships in order to recommend top-rank items to potentially interested users. Note that, as an alternative, also the HITS algorithm was used to recommend a top authority item among those returned by a query, and their parents and children in the link graph (Huang, Zeng & Chen, 2007).

Clustering

It is worth noting that link-based ranking algorithms have been used in the past to cluster objects (Andersen, Chung & Lang, 2007; Avrachenkov, Dobrynin, Nemirovsky, Pham & Smirnova, 2008; Gibson, Kleinberg & Raghavan, 1998). The "similar" objects have been identified as those with high ranks in the so-called personalized random walks (personalized PageRank (Avrachenkov, Dobrynin, Nemirovsky, Pham & Smirnova, 2008)), where the

decay jumps were performed towards the starting node instead of the "supernode".

GNGRANK

The aforementioned link structure allows for a convenient PageRank computation. As the content-based approach to creation of link structure and due to its special character, that allows for some more efficient computations, we will call the new computation method "GNGrank" (The GNGrank computation method is in some broad terms similar to web block structure based methods, but there are some distinct computational advantages used)

Random Walk Under the Document Map Concept

It has to be acknowledged that the basic random walk model of PageRank has a number of unrealistic assumptions about the behavior of an Internet user.

On one hand, it is intuitively obvious, though not thoroughly investigated, that the presence of search engines changes the information retrieval behavior. The user starts his search with queries to a search engine. Then he usually enters a couple of top results corresponding to the query. So it is in fact the content similarity that generates a kind of link information between the documents, and not their inter-links alone.

Second, the user does not follow just any of the outgoing links but rather those related to his interest (text around the link plays a role). So one can say, as already explored in Topical PageRank (Zhang, Zhang & Li, 2008), that a multi-topic document splits into subdocuments in the sense of the membership to topical areas.

So we assume the following random walk behavior: The surfer pursues some topic of interest so he queries the search engine. The search engine returns him some page proposals as well as some kind of document space structure (for example a document map, or a GNG etc.) Documents and elements of the visible structure may be called nodes. In each step the surfer enters one of the nodes, and then leaves it either to the supernode (the search engine query mechanism) if he looses his interest in the formulated topic (with the probability d), and otherwise he follows a topical link weighting equally all of them. The topical link may be the similarity link between documents, a jump from the document to the collection (structural node), a jump from a collection to a similar collection, from the collection to one of its documents.

In this way we assume that the user does not follow a random link if he changes the topic of interest. Rather we assume that he follows links with changed topic to the extent as the topic drift in documents impacts changes of his interest.

Some Inspiring PageRank Properties

Now let us investigate some important properties of the PageRank, that may prove useful when designing a computational algorithm. Let us consider two networks Net_A and Net_B without any links between them. Let A be the connection matrix of the first one, and B - of the second one. Let R_A be the solution to the equation

R_A=(1-d)A * R_A+d*S_A

with {S_A}j=1/dim(A) being the number of rows/columns in the rectangular matrix A, and let R_B be the solution to the equation

R_B=(1-d)B * R_B+d*S_B

{S_B}j=1/dim(B).

Now let us ask, what would be the PageRank of the nodes if we put both of the networks together into a single network Net_AB where there are no links between both subnetworks.

First let as assume that in both networks there are no nodes without outgoing edges. Obviously, we can get R_AB as a weighted combination of R_A, R_B, multiplying both with their share in the number of nodes in Net_AB. This exercise shows first that the amount of authority in the independent subnets depends on the size of these subnets. Second that for independent components the PageRank can be computed separately, and then composed. Third, we can expect that for loosely coupled components the behaviour can be similar.

We shall be alerted at this point by the fact that we assume no nodes without outgoing edges. But what if there are such the nodes in one or both of the networks? Recall that sometimes the nodes without outgoing links are treated as if linked to all the other nodes. When we join two networks, then the networks will not be isolated any more because the virtual "outgoing links" of zero-outdegree nodes of one subnetwork will now point to nodes of the other subnetwork, and hence the authority will flow between them in a complex way, so that the above simple determination of R_AB does not hold.

Let us consider still another class of graphs: Let Net_A, Net_B be subnets of the network Net and let there be no links from Net_B to Net_A, and none of the Net nodes is without outgoing edges. So let us look for the PageRank in Net – see also (Langville & Meyer, 2006) for a related analysis. It can be easily derived that to compute PageRank for the Net_A part of the network, we can summarize the whole subnetwork Net_B into a single node (with multiple links from the supernode) and then compute PageRank for Net_A separately. As soon as this is obtained, Net_B PageRank can be computed from the original PageRank equation by fixing values for the Net_A network (with appropriate normalization).

This actually means that for networks with a DAG (directed acyclic graph) like structure, or decomposable into DAG like components a simplified method of PageRank computation may be applied. Again the assumption of absence of nodes without outgoing edges is crucial.

Last not least let us discuss a tempting property of the PageRank computation. If we look at a node, then with the random walk model the difference between the amount of authority ingoing minus the outgoing is equal 0. So if we take a subnetwork and take into account the balancing within the subnetwork, then the amount of authority entering the subnetwork minus the amount leaving it as a whole is equal zero.

So why not replace the subnetwork with a single special node to simplify the computations in a structural manner. The first obstacle is that the subnetwork can have more than 1 outgoing edge, and the amount of authority leaving it via individual links may differ and also is not proportional to any quantity, because its distribution depends on internal subnetwork structure and the total amount of authority entering it from outside (Recall that the modified formulation of PageRank is not an intrinsic eigenvalue problem). So we might be tempted to consider subnetworks with single outgoing link to outside. But we still have the problem that we cannot estimate the share of PageRank kept outside of the subnetwork, so that we would not know how to normalize during the computation.

So let us for a moment resign from the assumption of the supernode in the network. Then we have the aforementioned property, that if a vector R is a solution to the original PageRank equation, then R*c, where c is a constant, is also a solution.

As we found the DAG property a useful one, let us consider the possibilities of turning a network with loops into a DAG. Let j0 be a node belonging to a loop. We can follow the flow of a unit of authority leaving it (we can think of the node being attached to a source of unit authority, and run a kind of Pagerank computation). In the end only a fraction f returns to j on its ingoing looping edge. If we would now remove the edge entering j and would multiply the outgoing authority with (1+f), then the overall PageRank would remain

unchanged. Repeating this procedure till there is no lop, we will obtain a PageRank equivalent DAG. This exercise does not pay off for networks with many loops, but it is still a useful insight.

Let us then return to the issue of structural evaluation of PageRank. Assume that a subnetwork has a single entry and a single exit node. Then, if the authority is not leaking out (via nodes without exit), the whole subnetwork can be replaced by a single node for computations of the overall network PageRank, and then the PageRank of the subnetwork can be computed. In case that there are more than one exits from the subnetwork, we can proceed in the following way. We first compute the PageRank for the subnetwork assuming that all the exits of the subnetwork are connected to the single entry of it. Then the subnetwork is replaced by a special node distributing its outputs in proportions as it was computed for the outgoing edges. The PageRank for the whole network is computed and then the PageRank in the subnetwork is set proportionally to the result of the special node. This is permitted because whatever the solution to the PageRank problem, the solutions on the subnetwork are proportional to one another.

GNGrank Computations

Now we will introduce our GNGrank algorithm. So let us turn back to the network model of the GNG random surfer. Here all the nodes have outgoing edges. Furthermore, let us assume for simplicity that the documents belong to only one structural group (no fuzzy membership).

Let us consider a network with the following structure: There is a node X and a subnetwork Y such that there are bidirectional links between X and every element of Y, and the remaining network Z connected eventually to X, but not to Y. If the number of links between X and Y by far outnumbers the number of links between X and the rest of the network (that is Z), then for GNGrank (PageRank) computations within Y we nearly do not need to know anything about links from X to Z. So if we would have the PageRank of X, we could compute the Pageranks in Y. This actually mimics the situation in which Y is a context network and X plus Z form the between-contexts-network.

So the computation of the ranking function can be executed for subdivided matrices: first for the between-contexts-network, then within each context network. For purpose of better reliability, several iterations of these steps should be performed.

Fuzzy GNG Rank

As already indicated in the Topical PageRank Zhang's paper (Zhang, Zhang & Li, 2008), there exist possibly documents that belong to several topical areas and within them they may be of different importance. The proposal of Zhang et al. went into the direction to maintain different PageRanks for different topical areas, reflecting the membership to them via appropriate changes to the flow of authority from the supernode for different topical areas, as well as by assigning topics to outgoing links and letting the random surfer choose first if he wants to jump to the supernode with a fixed probability, if he wants to follow a topical link with a fixed probability or if he jumps to any outgoing link, changing the topic at the same time.

Note that under that approach the issue of a separation of groups of documents on the same subject may influence a coherent estimate of document importance because of impact of link structure of the intermediate documents on paths between them. The basic difference between their approach and ours is that the link structure in our case is inserted after the split into topics and therefore documents on the same topic are linked together in the process of replacement of similarity with links. In the previous section, we have assumed, however, that a single document belongs to a single topic.

A natural question arises how to approach fuzzy memberships to some topical groups when computing the GNGRank. The accompanying problem is the interpretation of such a computational method.

We took the path of splitting the multi-topic node into separate sub-nodes. Each sub-node participates in the whole network creation process as a separate entity, so that links to nodes in respective topical clusters are created as if we had to do with separate documents. When it comes to the GNGrank computation, sub-nodes are also treated separately. However, in order not to hype the importance of a document, the amount of authority flowing from the supernode is split between the sub-nodes proportionally to their degree of membership, so that each document obtains in all the same amount.

We assume that the surfer remains focused when he enters such a page. This means that when entering a document in a given cluster, he will leave it towards other nodes of the same cluster. Such an assumption is justified by the overall context: in a map-based search engines the documents are close to the current one that appear in the same cluster. This assumption simplifies the computations.

Another decision to be taken is whether or not the links from a pointing page in the given cluster should be weighted according to the degree of membership of the linked-to documents or not.

The semantic issue behind is whether or not the creator of a document says that a link from this document leads to a multi-topical document or not. Typically it is not the case. So we decided that no re-weighting of links will be carried out.

GNG Rank Computed in Parallel

Note that though it may not be a critical issue, but the GNGrank may be computed in a predominantly parallel manner - the computations for each cluster may be carried out independently, and later higher

Table 1.

path length no. paths	**1** 352768	**2** 3556549	**3** 15448638	**4** 27821446	**5** 29469374	**6** 24165593	**7** 17837069	**8** 14137074
path length no. paths	**9** 12793356	**10** 12038525	**11** 11179144	**12** 10242330	**13** 9199232	**14** 8119975	**15** 6981941	**16** 5808284
path length no. paths	**17** 4657051	**18** 3546328	**19** 2561140	**20** 1748737	**21** 1139234	**22** 715155	**23** 440237	**24** 267108
path length no. paths	**25** 160251	**26** 94421	**27** 53833	**28** 29027	**29** 14508	**30** 6758	**31** 2899	**32** 1139
path length no. paths	**33** 406	**34** 131	**35** 37	**36** 10	**37** 2			

level (GNG level) GNGrank may be computed in the second stage.

EXPERIMENTS

The Issue for Investigations

The concept of GNGrank has two different aspects: On one hand it constitutes still another attempt to propose a remedy for the original PageTank concept of a non-thinking surfer. We want to reflect the natural structure of the document collection when ranking the surfer.

The other issue is that we replace intrinsic link information with the similarity information. In the literature it is frequently claimed that links on the Web are inserted keeping the topic (topical closeness) which is exploited for example in topical crawlers. So theoretically, if we remove links and replace them with similarity links, we would expect that the PageRank computed for intrinsic links and for "similarity links" should be somehow related.

Let us investigate to what extend this relationship holds.

Dataset Description

For our investigations we downloaded KDDCup 2003 dataset and processed it with our BEATCA system.

KDDCup 2003 dataset consists of 29555 papers from arXiv.org, submitted between 1992 and 2003. The textual content is either the LaTeX source of each paper (without additional files and figures) or only its abstract, together with arXiv submission date, revised date(s), title and paper authors. Beside textual content, the complete citation graph for the hep-th papers, obtained from SLAC/SPIRES, is available. Each node in the graph is labeled by its unique identifier. As it is stated at http://www.cs.cornell.edu/projects/kddcup/index.html, "revised papers may have updated citations. As such, citations may refer to future papers, i.e. a paper may cite another paper that was published after the first paper". However, majority of the directed citation links is concordant with chronological order of papers submission dates.

Citation Graph: Shortest Paths Statistics

Statistics of the shortest paths in the citation graph are presented in Table 1. These paths will be used in the next section to create three aggregated measures of paper prominence.

There are 352768 directed links (path length = 1) in the citation graph. The longest path has length equal to 37, but one can notice that the mode value of the path length distribution is 5. Longer paths are becoming gradually less frequent. Both of these observations are somewhat coherent

Table 2.

link type	link count	avg. cosine distance	std. cosine distance
same GNG cell	33419	90,94%	14,32%
adjacent GNG cell	59819	92,58%	12,36%
other GNG cells	259569	94,39%	10,58%

with small-world phenomenon. Another remark is that older papers have more chances (a priori) to be cited within given dataset than newer papers (there are no "dangling citations" in this datasets, i.e. we have only citations between papers included in the 1992-2003 arXiv snapshot).

Citation Measures

We have constructed three aggregated statistics to measure paper importance within the citations graph.

First measure is just the total number of citations for a given paper **d**. It is equal to the number of direct links pointing to this paper. Later on we call this measure **citDirect(d).**

Second measure is similar, but it counts also the size of the second-order neighbourhood in the citations graphs:

$$cit2^{rd}order(d) = citDirect(d) \sum_{d':d'-cites-d} citDirect(d')$$

The last citation statistics counts the weighted total of the citations. Each neighbourhood order (i.e. shortest path length, cf. Table 1) has weight $1/(2^\wedge order)$, where order is equal to the shortest path length between the two papers

$$citTotal(d) = \sum_{d'\in D-\{d\}} 2^{-shortestPathLength(d,d')}$$

For documents not linked by any path in the citation graph, shortestPathLength(d,d') is equal to infinity, thus they do not affect citTotal value.

Content Similarity vs. Citation Links

We have also compared information brought by textual content clustered via GNG with the citation graph structure. We split citation links into three categories, on the basis of GNG-induced clustering (see Table 2). First type consists of the citations among documents, which were clustered into one GNG cell. Second type are citations documents laying in adjacent GNG cells (i.e. cells linked by a direct edge in GNG graph). All other links are put into third category.

One can notice, that 10% of all citations lie within the same GNG cell. Another 20% of citations lie within neighbouring cells. The average cosine distance between content of papers linked those three types of citations vary slightly (and the variance is in agreement with distance in GNG graph). However, the difference is rather small, and average cosine distance in all cases is high (above 90%).

We have also compared average textual content distance (i.e. 1 - cosine similarity between vector-space representations of arXiv papers) among documents linked by a direct citation and documents not linked directly. The result is presented in Figure 1. One can see, that documents which are not linked are also almost orthogonal (average distance oscillates near maximal value 1). However, almost half of the linked documents (right-hand side of the plot) is also nearly orthogonal. The similarity among non-orthogonal, linked documents (left-hand side) has exponential distribution.

Figure 1.

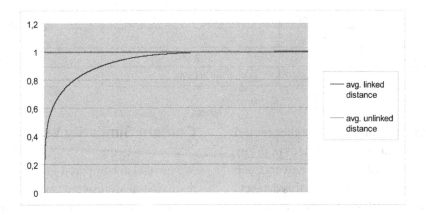

Rank Correlations between Measures

We have computed Spearman's rank correlation between various measures of document importance, especially GNGRank (as defined in this paper, that is based on GNG clustering and document similarity), PageRank (link-based measure), three paper citation statistics, distance to the nearest GNG-cluster centroid and histogram-based cluster typicality measure (see Table 3).

Three citation statistics have strong correlations: 0.946 (cit2ndorder and citTotal), 0.939 (citDirect and cit2ndorder) and 0.862 (citDirect and citTotal). Also PageRank correlates highly with all three citation statistics: 0.889 (citDirect), 0.843 (cit2ndorder) and 0.822 (citTotal). On the other hand, as we noticed earlier, there is little or no correlation between information brought by citation links and textual content. This observation is also supported by the lack of correlation between PageRank and any of content-based measure (GNGRank, centroidDistance, histogramDistance). Neither of these correlations exceeds 0.13. Correlation between GNGRank and two other content-based measures (centroidDistance, histogramDistance) is too low to be considered significant.

Table 3.

	gngrank	pagerank	centroiddist	direct citations	citations 2nd order	weighted total citations
gngrank	1	-0.00957	-0.17424	0.02178	0.0157	-0.00315
pagerank	-0.00957	1	-0.09413	0.8893	0.8439	0.82209
centroid dist	-0.17424	-0.09413	1	-0.22668	-0.22724	-0.17358
Direct citations	0.02178	0.8893	-0.22668	1	0.93989	0.86262
citations 2nd order	0.0157	0.8439	-0.22724	0.93989	1	0.94688
weighted total citations	-0.00315	0.82209	-0.17358	0.86262	0.94688	1
histogram distance	0.02379	0.12950	-0.35745	0.13664	0.11699	0.10107

CONCLUSION

The result of our investigations may appear at first glance a bit surprising: There is apparently no correlation between the textual content information and the link information. They constitute apparently different worlds.

But at a second glance these results seem to be plausible for a couple of reasons:

- the collection we investigated is a set of scientific papers (abstracts in fact); one would tend to avoid accusations someone's other work (plagiarism) so the citation links are per definition to absolutely different texts; even if we took the complete tezxts, the word-based similarity didn't improve
- the links between the documents were (due to their nature) nearly acyclic, whereas the similarity based links of GNGrank could be and were cyclic.
- Undoubtedly the similarity links were bounded to GNG cells, while the citation links could go outside of cell boundaries; but even within the cells the correlation between GNGrank and PageRank was occurring seldomly (in some of cells only),
- The number of similarity links was bounded (to 5) within this experiment, while the number of citation links could go into hundreds (the number of outgoing links), apparently from some overviews of the research subfield.

So we can conclude that GNGrank reflects a totally different aspect of a data collection than PageRank does. Also we can say that similarity and link occurrence are unrelated at the level of single documents and come into appearance at the level of large document groups.

We can then say that while intrinsic linkage between documents can say about the authoritativeness of a document, it is totally useless when identifying typical documents of a collection. For this latter task similarity based methods need to be applied. The GNG rank may be one of them.

FURTHER RESEARCH

Since content and link information are apparently complementary sources of information, we should try to exploit them at least in the following way:

- define a combined measure of document similarity, based on both content and links,
- try to establish the reason, why there are documents not linked but similar in content and vice-versa,
- identify documents that are promoted by the various measures of document simuilarity.

A number of hypotheses are open in the last case, including unawareness, too high number of similar documents to cite, a careful way to write documents on the same subject avoiding similarity to other on the same topic etc. Possibly one can tell what is the case when exploring statistics of the document collection and of its sections (histograms etc.).

REFERENCES

Abbassi, Z., & Mirrokni, V. S. (2007). A recommender system based on local random walks and spectral methods. In WebKDD/SNAKDD '07: Proceedings of the 9th WebKDD and 1st SNAKDD 2007 workshop on Web mining and social network analysis (pp. 102-108). New York, NY, USA.

Aberer, K., & Wu, J. (2004). Using siterank for p2p web retrieval. Technical report. Swiss Fed. Institute of Technology.

Andersen, R., Chung, F., & Lang, K. (2007). Local partitioning for directed graphs using PageRank. WAW2007 [Springer-Verlag.]. *Lecture Notes in Computer Science, 4863,* 166–178. doi:10.1007/978-3-540-77004-6_13

Avrachenkov, K., Dobrynin, V., Nemirovsky, D., Pham, S. K., & Smirnova, E. (2008). Pagerank based clustering of hypertext document collections. In SIGIR '08: Proceedings of the 31st annual international ACM SIGIR conference on Research and development in information retrieval (pp. 873-874), New York, NY, USA.

Brin, S. (1998). The anatomy of a largescale hypertextual web search engine. In Computer Networks and ISDN Systems (pp. 107-117).

Broder, A. Z., Lempel, R., Maghoul, F., & Pedersen, J. (2004). Efficient PageRank approximation via graph aggregation. In WWW Alt. '04: Proceedings of the 13th international World Wide Web conference on Alternate track papers & posters (pp. 484-485), New York, NY, USA.

Chikhi, N.F., Rothenburger, B., & AussenacGilles, N. (2008). Combining link and content information for scientific topics discovery. IEEE International Conference on Tools with Artificial Intelligence (pp. 211-214). Dayton, OH, USA.

Ciesielski, K., & Klopotek, M. A. (2006). Text data clustering by contextual graphs. In Todorovski, L., Lavrac, N., & Jantke, K. P. (Eds.), *Discovery Science (DS2006), LNAI 4265* (pp. 65–76). Barcelona, Spain: SpringerVerlag. doi:10.1007/11893318_10

Ciesielski, K., & Klopotek, M.A. (2007). Towards adaptive web mining: Histograms and contexts in text data clustering. In M.R. Berthold and J. ShaweTaylor, editors, Intelligent Data Analysis (IDA2007), LNCS 4723 (pp. 284-295). SpringerVerlag. Ljubljana, Slovenia.

Cohn, D., & Hofmann, T. (2001). The missing link a probabilistic model of document content and hypertext connectivity. In *Advances in Neural Information Processing Systems (Vol. 13).* The MIT Press.

de Castro, L. N., & Timmis, J. (2002). *Artificial Immune Systems: A New Computational Intelligence Approach.* Springer Verlag.

Eiron, N., & McCurley, K. S. (2003). Analysis of anchor text for web search. In SIGIR '03: Proceedings of the 26th annual international ACM SIGIR conference on Research and development in informaion retrieval (pp. 459-460). New York, NY, USA.

Eiron, N., McCurley, K. S., & Tomlin, J. A. (2004). Ranking the web frontier. In WWW '04: Proceedings of the 13th international conference on World Wide Web, (pp. 309-318). ACM Press. New York, NY, USA.

Fogaras, D. I., & Racz, B. (2004). Towards scaling fully personalized PageRank. In Proceedings WAW 2004, (pp. 105-117).

Fritzke, B. (1997). A selforganizing network that can follow nonstationary distributions. In ICANN '97: Proceedings of the 7th International Conference on Artificial Neural Networks, (pp. 613-618). SpringerVerlag.

Gibson, D., Kleinberg, J., & Raghavan, P. (1998). Inferring web communities from link topology. In HYPERTEXT '98: Proceedings of the ninth ACM conference on Hypertext and hypermedia: links, objects, time and space--structure in hypermedia systems, (pp. 225-234). ACM. New York, NY, USA.

Gleich, D., Zhukov, L., & Berkhin, P. (2004). *Fast parallel PageRank: A linear system approach. Technical report, Yahoo!* Research Labs.

Gyongyi, Z. GarciaMolina, H., & Pedersen, J. (2004). Combating web spam with trustrank. Technical Report 200417. Stanford InfoLab.

Huang, Z., Zeng, D., & Chen, H. (2007). A comparison of collaborative filtering recommendation algorithms for ecommerce. *IEEE Intelligent Systems*, *22*(5), 68–78. doi:10.1109/MIS.2007.4338497

Kamvar, S. D., Haveliwala, T., Manning, C., & Golub, G. (2003). *Exploiting the block structure of the web for computing PageRank. Technical report*. Stanford University.

Kamvar, S.D., Schlosser, M.T., & GarciaMolina, H. (2003). The eigentrust algorithm for reputation management in p2p networks. In Proceedings of the Twelfth International World Wide Web Conference, (pp. 640-651). ACM Press.

Kleinberg, J. (1999). Authoritative sources in a hyperlinked environment. In Journal of the ACM, 46 (pp. 604632).

Klopotek, M., Wierzchon, S., Ciesielski, K., Draminski, M., & Czerski, D. (2007). *Conceptual Maps of Document Collections in Internet and Intranet. Coping with the Technological Challenge*. Warszawa, Poland: IPI PAN Publishing House.

Kohlschtter, C., Chirita, R., & Nejdl, W. (2006). Efficient parallel computation of PageRank. In Proc. of the 28th European Conference on Information Retrieval.

Kohonen, T., Kaski, S., Somervuo, P., Lagus, K., Oja, M., & Paatero, V. (2003). *Selforganization of very large document collections. Technical report*. Helsinki, Finland: University of Technology.

Kopak, R. W. (1999). *Functional link typing in hypertext. ACM Computing Surveys*. New York, NY, USA: ACM Press.

Langville, A., & Meyer, C. D. (2006). *Google's Pagerank and Beyond: The Science of Search Engine Rankings*. Princeton, Oxford: Princeton University Press.

Lempel, R., & Moran, S. (2000). The stochastic approach for linkstructure analysis (salsa) and the tkc effect. In Proceedings of the Ninth International Conference on the World Wide Web.

Manaskasemsak, B., & Rungsawang, A. (2004). Parallel PageRank computation on a gigabit pc cluster. In AINA '04: Proceedings of the 18th International Conference on Advanced Information Networking and Applications, page 273. IEEE Computer Society. Washington, DC, USA.

Manning, Ch. D., & Raghavan, P. (2009). *Schütze, H. An Introduction to Information Retrieval*. Cambridge: Cambridge University Press.

Richardson, M., & Domingos, P. (2002). The intelligent surfer: Probabilistic combination of link and content information in PageRank. In Advances in Neural Information Processing Systems 14 (pp. 14411448). Cambridge, MA: MIT Press. Department of Computer Science and Engineering, University of Washington, USA.

Sankaralingam, K., Sethumadhavan, S., & Browne, J. C. (2003). Distributed PageRank for p2p systems. In Proc. of the 12th IEEE Intl. Symp. on High Performance Distributed Computing (HPDC).

Shi, S., Yu, J., Yang, G., & Wang, D. (2003). Distributed page ranking in structured p2p networks. Parallel Processing, International Conference.

Sydow, M. (2005). Approximation quality of the rbs ranking algorithm. In Intelligent. *Information Systems*, *2005*, 289–296.

Wang, Y., & DeWitt, D. J. (2004). Computing PageRank in a distributed internet search system. In VLDB '04: Proceedings of the Thirtieth international conference on Very large data bases (pp. 420-431). VLDB Endowment.

Zhang, L., Zhang, K., & Li, C. (2008). *A topical PageRank based algorithm for recommender systems* (pp. 713–714). In SIGIR.

Zhu, J., Hong, J., & Hughes, J. G. (2002). Using markov models for web site link prediction. In HYPERTEXT '02: Proceedings of the thirteenth ACM conference on Hypertext and hypermedia, (pp. 169-170). ACM Press. New York, NY, USA.

Zhu, Y., & Li, X. (2005). Distributed PageRank computation based on iterative aggregationdis-aggregation methods. In Proc. of the 14th ACM international conference on Information and knowledge management (pp. 578-585).

KEY TERMS AND DEFINITIONS

(GNG) Growing Neural Gas: A new concept in neural computing developed mainly by B. Fritzke (1997). A GNG is a kind of structural clustering of objects occurring in an incremental process. Each time an object is presented, its proximity to existing clusters is computed and a link is added or strengthened between the winner and the second choice. A node with too high diversity is split. Links are aging in the process and may vanish if not strengthened. As a result one obtains a set of clusters and links between them with weights indicating how close the clusters are to one another.

Citation Graph: A graph reflecting relationship between e.g. papers. A paper is a node in the graph and there is a link from paper j to paper k if paper k is cited by paper j.

Document Context: In this chapter the group of documents to which a document belongs. Context membership impacts the way how terms are weighted in the document, and in consequence also its measures of similarity to other documents.

Document Similarity: A measure how close the content of two documents is. Usually the similarity measures are based on frequency of occurrence of words (terms) in both documents. A deeper linguistic analysis is rarely performed. Co-occurrence in both documents can be weighted by the importance of the terms in the whole collection of documents or in a group they belong to. One can compare the similarity by computing the dot product of weights of terms in the documents.

Histogram-Based Similarity: Given a group of document, we can approximate the distribution of weights of a term in the documents by a histogram. When computing similarity between groups, instead of the traditional dot product of vectors of weights, comparing groups, one can use measures of histogram similarities for each term.

PageRank: A method of measuring importance of pages in a hypertext network. It is essentially the main eigenvector of a properly defined connectivity matrix.

Term Weight in a Document: The weight of a term in a document is usually a function of the frequency with which it occurs in the document (increasing) and with its frequency in the collection (decreasing). Usually, after computing the weights for a document, they are normalized so that e.g. the sum of squares of the weights is equal to 1.

ENDNOTES

[1]   BEATCA – Bayesian and Evolutionary Approach to Textual Content Analysis
[2]   When there are nodes without outgoing links, we can do this transformation given that we replace them with nodes that have outgoing links to all the other nodes of the network

Chapter 2
Data Mining Techniques for Outlier Detection

N N R Ranga Suri
Centre for Artificial Intelligence and Robotics, India

M Narasimha Murty
Indian Institute of Science, India

G Athithan
Centre for Artificial Intelligence and Robotics, India

ABSTRACT

Among the growing number of data mining techniques in various application areas, outlier detection has gained importance in recent times. Detecting the objects in a data set with unusual properties is important as such outlier objects often contain useful information on abnormal behavior of the system described by the data set. Outlier detection has been popularly used for detection of anomalies in computer networks, fraud detection and such applications. Though a number of research efforts address the problem of detecting outliers in data sets, there are still many challenges faced by the research community in terms of identifying a suitable technique for addressing specific applications of interest. These challenges are primarily due to the large volume of high dimensional data associated with most data mining applications and also due to the performance requirements. This chapter highlights some of the important research issues that determine the nature of the outlier detection algorithm required for a typical data mining application. The research issues discussed include the method of outlier detection, size and dimensionality of the data set, and nature of the target application. Thus this chapter attempts to cover the challenges and possible research directions along with a survey of various data mining techniques dealing with the outlier detection problem.

DOI: 10.4018/978-1-60960-102-7.ch002

INTRODUCTION

The recent developments in the field of data mining have lead to the outlier detection process mature as one of the popular data mining tasks. Due to its significance in the data mining process, outlier detection is also known as outlier mining. Typically, outliers are data objects that are significantly different from the rest of the data. Outlier detection or outlier mining refers to the process of identifying such rare objects in a given data set. Although rare objects are known to be fewer in number, their significance is high compared to other objects, making their detection an important task. The general requirement of this task is to identify and remove the contaminating effect of the outlying objects on the data and as such to purify the data for further processing. More formally, the outlier detection problem can be defined as follows: given a set of data objects, find a specific number of objects that are considerably dissimilar, exceptional and inconsistent with respect to the remaining data (Han, 2000). A number of new techniques have been proposed recently in the field of data mining to solve this problem. This chapter mainly deals with these techniques for outlier detection and highlights their relative merits and demerits.

Many data mining algorithms try to minimize the influence of outliers or eliminate them all together. However, this could result in the loss of important hidden information since one person's noise could be another person's signal (Knorr, 2000). Thus, the outliers themselves may be of particular interest, as in the case of fraud detection, where they may indicate some fraudulent activity. Besides fraud detection, financial applications and niche marketing and network intrusion detection are other applications of outlier detection, making it an interesting and important data-mining task. Depending on the application domain, outlier detection has been variously referred to as novelty detection (Markou, 2003a), chance discovery (McBurney, 2003), or exception mining (Suzuki,

2000), etc. A related field of research is activity monitoring with the purpose of detecting illegal access. This task consists of monitoring an online data source in the search for unusual behavior (Fawcett, 1999).

Much of the research related to outlier detection has evolved in the context of anomaly detection. An anomaly is something that is different from normal behavior. Though anomalies are often considered as noise, they could be deemed as the early indicators of a possible major adverse effect. Thus, detection of anomalies is important in its own right and also due to the increasing number of applications like computer network intrusion detection (Chandola, 2009; Lazarevic, 2003), fraud detection, astronomical data analysis (Chaudhary, 2002), etc. In most of the cases, anomaly detection is intended to understand evolving new phenomena that is not seen in the past data. A standard method for detecting anomalies is to create a model of the normal data and compare the future observations against the model. However, as the definition of normality differs across various problem domains, the problem of anomaly detection turns out to be a more challenging and involved process. A generic computational approach is to look for outliers in the given data set. Some research efforts in this direction can be found in (Lazarevic, 2003; Sithirasenan, 2008), in the context of network intrusion detection.

There have been various definitions in the literature for outliers that were proposed in different research contexts. A popular one among them, given by (Hawkins, 1980), is to define an outlier as an observation that deviates so much from other observations as to arouse suspicion that it is generated by a different mechanism. The presence of an outlying object in a data set shows itself in some form or the other. For example, data objects P and Q in Figure 1(a) are outliers, which is obvious from a visual examination. However, in cases where the objects like P_1 and P_2 in Figure 1(b) are present in a data set, identifying them as outliers requires some extra effort. Also, depending

Figure 1. Sample outliers depicted in two example scenarios

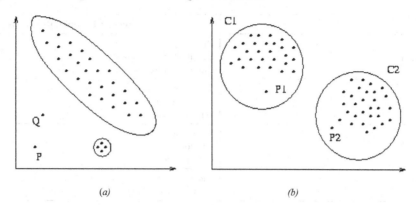

(a)   (b)

on the relative position and grouping of outliers in a data set, some specialized techniques are required for their detection.

The early research in the field of outlier detection has been based on statistical methods (Barnett and Lewis, 1994). The literature in this field defines an outlier as an observation, which appears to be statistically inconsistent with the remainder of the data set. The statistical methods are parametric methods that assume a known underlying distribution or statistical model of the given data. According to these methods, outliers are those objects that have low probability of belonging to the statistical model. However, these approaches are not effective even for moderately high dimensional spaces. Also, finding the right model is often a difficult task in its own right.

A survey on various outlier detection methodologies can be found in (Hodge and Austin, 2004). The authors of this paper have brought out various forms of outlier detection problem in different application settings. In addition to the anomaly detection problem, they have also discussed the use of outlier detection in medicine, pharmacology, etc. The methodologies discussed in this paper are categorized into three types depending on the experimental setting of the detection method. The paper basically dwells on two fundamental considerations for selecting a suitable methodology for outlier detection: (i)

selecting an algorithm that can accurately model the data distribution and (ii) selecting a suitable neighborhood of interest for an outlier. Basically the survey brought out in this paper talks about various neural network-based and machine learning-based methods, besides some statistical methods. Towards the end, the authors discuss a few hybrid methods for outlier detection.

Similarly, an introductory material on outlier detection is presented as a book chapter in (Ben-Gal, 2005). The author explains the taxonomy of various outlier detection methods, which are categorized as parametric and non-parametric techniques. The focus is mainly on different statistical methods for univariate and multivariate outlier detection. A short discussion on data mining methods is also included along with a brief comparison of various outlier detection methods.

Though various surveys on outlier detection talk about some of the fundamental aspects of the popular methodologies, they have not fully explored the important research issues concerning the application domains. These issues have attracted the attention of researchers in recent times. It is important to understand these issues and develop techniques addressing the challenges posed by them. Thus, the purpose of this chapter is to focus on these frequently encountered research challenges and also provide a survey of some of the latest techniques addressing them. Also, a

Table 1. Research issues in outlier detection

Research Issues	Specific Research Directions
1. Method of Detection	Distance-based Methods Density-based Methods Clustering-based Methods
2. Nature of the Detection Algorithm	Supervised Detection Un-supervised Detection Semi-supervised Detection
3. Nature of the Underlying Data Set	Numerical Data Categorical Data Mixed Data
4. Size and Dimension of the Data Set	Large Data High Dimensional Data
5. Nature of the Application	Stream Data Applications Time Series Applications

number of new techniques for outlier detection have been proposed recently, making it important to survey the current status of this field.

Section 2 brings out various research issues that are considered significant in outlier detection. It provides a comprehensive survey of various research efforts made in the recent past addressing each one of the research issues. A discussion on current research trends related to these research issues is presented in Section 3. Experimental results on some benchmark data sets are provided in Section 4 to demonstrate the process of outlier detection. Finally, this chapter is concluded with some remarks and future directions of research in Section 5.

RESEARCH ISSUES IN OUTLIER DETECTION

As outlier detection finds applications in diverse domains, choosing an appropriate detection method is not a trivial task. Also, various applications deal with varying type of data in terms of the nature, dimensionality and size. Frequently, the requirements of the detection method are specific to the nature of the application. Thus, the researchers dealing with these applications are often faced with new technological challenges in finding efficient solutions. Various research issues that are of significance to outlier detection are depicted in Table 1. A detailed discussion on these research issues is presented here.

Method of Detection

Though there are a number of methods for detecting outliers in a given dataset, no single method is found to be the universal choice. Depending on the nature of target application, different applications require use of different detection methods.

According to the taxonomy brought out in (Ben-Gal, 2005), the outlier detection techniques can be broadly divided into parametric and non-parametric varieties. The statistics-based methods that assume a model for a given data are the parametric variety. Typically, the user has to model a given data set using a statistical distribution, and data objects are determined to be outliers depending on how they appear in relation to the postulated model. On the other hand, most of the non-parametric methods rely on a well-defined notion of distance to measure the separation between two data objects. The non-parametric variety includes distance-based, density-based, and clustering-based methods. These non-parametric

Figure 2. A Taxonomy of the outlier detection methods

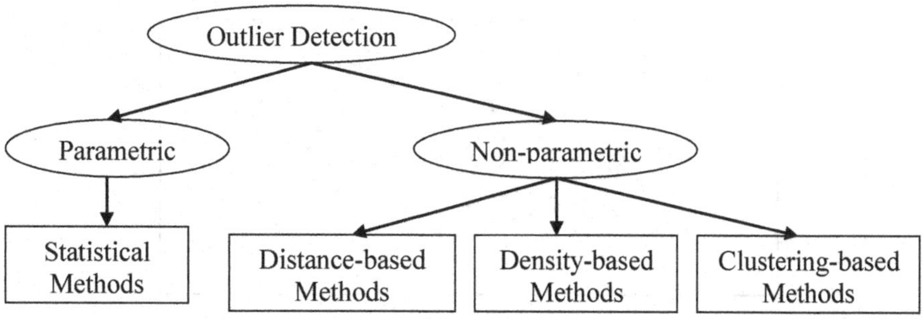

methods are also known as the data mining methods. A taxonomy of the existing outlier detection methods is shown in Figure 2.

Distance-Based Methods

The distance-based methods are one of the early techniques that were proposed for outlier detection under the data mining variety. In order to overcome the problems associated with statistical methods, a distance-based method was proposed in (Knorr, 1998) using a simple and intuitive definition for outliers. According to this method, an object in a data set is an outlier with respect to the parameters k and d if no more than k objects in the data set are at a distance of d or less from that object. A simple nested-loop algorithm is presented in this work, which requires $O(rN^2)$ computations in worst-case scenario, where r is the dimension of the data and N is the number of data objects. This way of finding outliers does not need a priori knowledge of data distributions that the statistical methods do. However, this algorithm requires the user to specify a distance threshold d to determine outliers.

Addressing the high computational cost of this algorithm, a novel formulation for distance-based mining of outliers was proposed in (Ramaswami, 2000) which is based on the distance to the kth nearest neighbor of a data object. Intuitively, this distance is a measure of how much of an outlier a data object is. For example, referring to Figure 1(a), object P is a much stronger outlier than Q. In essence, this technique ranks each object based on its distance to its kth nearest neighbor. The user can get a desired number of outliers from the ranked list of outliers. In order to overcome the quadratic time complexity of the nested-loop algorithm, the authors propose a cell-based approach for computing outliers. They use the micro-clustering phase of BIRCH algorithm (Zhang, 1996) to quantise the space in near linear time. In subsequent efforts, a modified scheme measuring the average distance to the k-nearest-neighbors of a data object was proposed in (Knorr, 2000) to detect a desired number of top ranked outliers.

In a similar effort, a simple nested loop algorithm, with quadratic time complexity in worst case, is found to give near linear time performance when the data is presented in random order (Bay, 2003). The authors also use a pruning rule in addition to randomizing the input. A novel distance-based algorithm to detect the top ranked outliers of a large and high-dimensional data set was proposed in (Angiulli, 2005). Given an integer k, this algorithm finds the weight of a point defined as the sum of the distances separating it from its k-nearest-neighbors. It avoids the distance computation of each pair of objects by using the space-filling curves to linearize the data set. The data objects with high weights are considered as outliers in this algorithm.

To summarize, various definitions proposed for distance-based outliers by different methods are listed below.

Figure 3. Difference between various distance-based outlier definitions

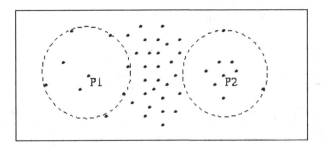

- Outliers are those objects for which there are fewer than a designated number of other objects present within a designated distance *d* (Knorr, 1998; Bay, 2003).
- Outliers are the top ranked objects whose distance to the kth nearest neighbor is large (Ramaswamy, 2000).
- Outliers are the top ranked objects whose average distance to the *k*-nearest-neighbors is large (Knorr, 2000; Angiulli, 2005).

All of the above definitions are based on identifying the nearest neighbors of a data object so as to determine the objects with only a few neighbors as outliers. Though the underlying principle is the same, the set of outliers generated by these definitions could be potentially different. This observation is depicted in Figure 3, in which both the objects P_1 and P_2 have 8 nearest neighbors each shown inside the dashed circles. However, they may not get assigned the same outlier rank using the above methods. The advantages of distance-based methods are that no explicit distribution needs to be defined to determine unusualness, and that they can be applied to any feature space for which a distance measure can be defined.

Density-Based Methods

To deal with the local density problems of the distance-based methods, the density-based approaches have been developed. A density-based method was proposed in (Breunig, 2000), which relies on a novel density measure named as the Local Outlier Factor (LOF). The LOF measure was introduced based on the notion of local outlier that defines the likelihood of a data object being an outlier. This notion of outliers is based on the same theoretical foundation of density-based clustering DBSCAN (Ester, 1996). The key idea of this work is to determine the outlying degree of any object by the clustering structure in a bounded neighborhood of the object. Thus, the LOF of a data object is defined as the average of the ratios of its density to the density of its nearest neighbors. The LOF of an object depends on the local density of its neighbors and the data objects with high LOF are identified as outliers. Figure 4 gives an example scenario involving some density-based outliers. Using the nearest neighbor based methods, object P_1 may not be detected as an outlier as it has some objects in its proximity, while P_2 gets detected as an outlier as all it neighbors of are far away. However, the LOF-based detection finds both P_1 and P_2 as outliers as both of them get high LOF values.

The computation of LOF values for all the objects in a data set requires a large number of *k*-nearest-neighbors searches and can be computationally expensive. When dealing with large data sets, most objects are usually not outliers. Considering this fact, it is useful to provide users with the option of finding only the desired number of top ranked data objects, which are most likely to be local outliers according to their LOF values. Based on this simplification, a method

Figure 4. Illustration of density-based outliers

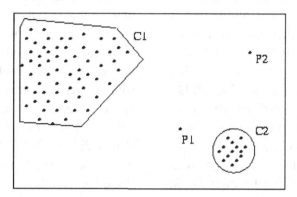

was proposed in (Jin, 2001) using the concept of micro-clusters from BIRCH (Zhang, 1996) introduced to compress the data. A cut-plane solution for overlapping data was also proposed in this work to deal with the overlapping in the micro-clusters.

Many extensions to LOF have been proposed in the literature. One such extension method named as Local Correlation Integral (LOCI) was proposed in (Papadimitriou, 2003) for finding outliers in large, multidimensional data sets. This method works based on a novel measure called the multi-granularity deviation factor (MGDF), using which any data object whose MGDF value deviates much from the local averages is considered as an outlier. The MGDF measure was defined to cope with local density variations in the feature space and for detecting both isolated outliers as well as outlying clusters, such as cluster C_2 shown in Figure 4. This method seems appealing, as it provides an automatic data driven cut-off for determining outliers by taking into account the distribution of distances between pairs of objects. A novel local distribution based algorithm (LDBOD) was proposed in (Zhang, 2008), which attempts to find local outliers. From the local distribution of the data points of interest, this algorithm extracts three features namely local-average-distance, local-density, and local-asymmetry-degree. Local outliers are detected from the viewpoint of local distribution characterized by these features. Though it is simi-

lar to LOF, the use of local-asymmetry-degree improves over the discriminating power of LOF in detecting outliers.

Clustering-Based Methods

The clustering-based approaches for outlier detection are motivated by the unbalanced distribution of outliers versus normal objects in a given data set, as outliers represent a very low fraction of the total data. Thus, clustering-based outlier detection tends to consider clusters of small sizes as clustered outliers. A clustering algorithm, named BIRCH, for dealing with large data was proposed in (Zhang, 1996) which can handle outliers. Similarly, various other clustering algorithms like the density-based clustering DBSCAN (Ester, 1996), and ROCK (Guha, 1999) can also detect outliers present in a data set. However, outlier detection is not the main purpose of these algorithms, as their primary concern is to find clusters in the given data.

A two-phase algorithm to detect outliers is presented in (Jiang, 2001), which makes use of a modified *k*-means algorithm to cluster the data and then find the outliers. According to this algorithm, small clusters are regarded as outliers, using minimum spanning trees. However, a measure for identifying the degree of each object being an outlier was not presented. Furthermore, the procedure for distinguishing small clusters from the rest is not addressed in this algorithm. Addressing these issues, a new cluster-based outlier detection method was proposed in (He, 2003). This method uses the Cluster-Based Local Outlier Factor (CBLOF) measure for identifying the physical significance of an outlier. The CBLOF of an object is measured by both the size of the cluster that the object belongs to and the distance between the object and its closest big cluster. To capture the spirit of local outliers proposed in (Breunig, 2000), the cluster-based outliers should satisfy that they are local to some specific clusters. For example, referring to Figure 1(b), object P_1 is local to cluster C_1 and P_2 is local to C_2. Thus, the objects P_1 and P_2 turn out to be cluster-based local outliers.

An outlier detection method based on hierarchical clustering technique was proposed in (Loureiro, 2004) for data cleaning applications. The usefulness of this method was established by identifying erroneous foreign trade transactions in data collected by the Portuguese Institute of Statistics. As the non-hierarchical clustering techniques would spread the outliers across all clusters during cluster initialization, they are not considered as stable as the hierarchical clustering based detection. Similarly, an improved single linkage hierarchical clustering-based method was proposed in (Almeida, 2007), which is based on a self-consistent outlier reduction approach. This method can deal with data sets comprising diluting clusters, i.e., clusters that possess scattered objects in their periphery. A novel algorithm that works in linear time in the number of objects was proposed in (Ceglar, 2007) using quantization and implied distance metrics. This algorithm includes a novel direct quantization procedure and discovers outlying clusters explicitly. It requires only two sequential scans for analyzing disk resident datasets, as it does not perform object level comparisons and only stores the cell counts.

A recent technique called as density-based subspace clustering for outlier detection was proposed in (Assent, 2007). Basically, subspace clustering aims at finding clusters in any subspace of a high-dimensional feature space and hence may result in some overlapping clusters in different subspaces. However, the proposed technique defines outliers with respect to maximal and non-redundant subspace clusters. A more recent technique is detecting cluster-based outliers using LDBSCAN, which is a local density based spatial clustering algorithm (Duan, 2009). This technique gives importance to the local data behavior and detects outliers using the LOF-based computation. It defines a new measure called cluster-based outlier factor (CBOF), which captures the essence of cluster-based outliers. The higher the CBOF of a cluster is, the more abnormal that cluster would be. It is claimed that this technique outperforms LOF in identifying meaningful and interesting outliers.

To summarize, the advantage of the clustering-based approaches is that they do not have to be supervised. Moreover, clustering-based techniques are capable of being used in an incremental mode, i.e., after learning the clusters, new data objects can be inserted into the system and tested for outliers.

Nature of the Detection Algorithm

Data mining techniques that have been developed for outlier detection are based on both supervised and unsupervised learning. Supervised learning methods (Torgo, 2003; Joshi, 2004) typically build a prediction model for rare objects based on labeled data, and use it to classify each object as being an outlier or a normal object. These approaches may suffer from problems of strong unbalanced class distributions, which may adversely affect the performance of the classification models (Weiss, 2001). The major disadvantages with supervised data mining techniques include the necessity to have labeled data and the inability to detect new classes of rare objects. On the other hand, unsupervised learning methods typically do not require labeled data and detect outliers as data objects that are very different from the normal data based on some measure. The success of these methods depends on the choice of similarity measures, feature selection and weighting, etc. These methods suffer from a possible high rate of false positives, as previously unseen data are also recognized as outliers.

Outlier detection algorithms of both predictive (supervised) and direct (unsupervised) varieties exist in the literature. Supervised neural networks and decision trees are two common forms of predictive outlier analysis. A neural networks-based technique, named as replicator neural networks, is proposed in (Harkins, 2002) for outlier detection. This approach is based on the observation that the trained neural network will reconstruct some small number of objects poorly, which can be considered as outliers. A detailed survey on the use of neural networks for outlier detection is presented in (Markou, 2003b). While supervised neural networks require numerical data, a decision tree-based method (Skalak, 1990) identifies simple class boundaries in categorical data. Direct techniques, which include statistical, proximity (distance), density and clustering based techniques, refer to those applications in which labeled training sets are unavailable. Although typically more complex than predictive techniques, direct methods are less constrained, as discovery is not dependent upon pre-defined models.

The exact nature of an outlier detection algorithm could be determined based on the nature of the dataset at hand. In general, the method of detection considered impacts the nature of the algorithm to be used. Supervised measures determine similarity based on class information, while data-driven measures determine similarity based on the data distribution. In principle, both these ideas can be combined to develop hybrid methods.

Nature of the Underlying Data Set

A dataset may be having objects described using attributes that are purely numerical or a mix of numerical and categorical attributes. Detecting outliers in numeric data is a fairly well addressed

problem, while detecting outliers in categorical data has gained prominence only recently. (Das, 2007; Ghoting, 2004). It is important to take into account the occurrence frequencies of different attribute values, while defining a proximity measure for these data objects. Recent research in this direction has resulted in defining some data driven similarity measures (Boriah, 2008) useful in defining methods for detecting outliers in categorical data.

The replicator neural networks based method (Harkins, 2002) is one of the early methods used with categorical data. Subsequently, a cluster-based outlier detection method was proposed in (He, 2003) extending the concept of local outliers. A fast greedy algorithm for outlier mining was proposed in (He, 2006) based on the concept of entropy of a given categorical data set. According to this algorithm, a data object that has maximum contribution to the entropy of the data set is selected as an outlier. However, this algorithm requires a number of scans over the data set. Addressing this issue, an algorithm was presented in (Koufakou, 2007) using the attribute value frequencies (AVF) of a given data set. Each data object is assigned an AVF-score and objects with low scores are considered as outliers. Further research in dealing with categorical data is being reported only recently. Thus, there is a lot of scope for developing effective and efficient algorithms for dealing with categorical data sets.

Size and Dimension of the Data Set

Most applications today deal with large volumes of high dimensional data making it a computationally challenging task. Many of the techniques developed for outlier detection have been extended to deal with large data sets in some way. An outlier detection technique named as SNIF was proposed in (Tao, 2006) which can accommodate arbitrarily large datasets through prioritized flushing. Priorities are assigned based on the likelihood that an object will be an outlier or not with relatively few neighbors. Other such work includes the RBRP (Recursive Binning and Re-Projection) technique (Ghoting, 2006), which iteratively partitions the dataset and thus limits comparisons of distance. However, efforts on detecting outliers in high dimensional data are still being explored for developing efficient techniques.

Most of the outlier detection methods are based on a nearest neighbors density estimate to determine the objects in low probability regions as outliers. For efficiently determining the nearest neighbors of a data object, spatial indexing structures such as KD-tree (Bentley, 1975), X-tree (Berchtold, 1996) have been used by some researchers. For low-dimensional data sets, use of various indexing structures can work extremely well and potentially scales as $N logN$, if the index tree can find an example's nearest neighbors in $log N$ time. However, these indexing structures break down as the dimensionality increases. For instance, a variant of the X-tree was used in (Breuing, 2000) to do nearest neighbor search and it was found that the index only worked well for low dimensions, less than five. Sequential scanning over the index tree has been recommended for high-dimensional data.

Many algorithms attempt to detect outliers by computing the distances in full dimensional space. However, it is stated in (Beyer, 1999; Aggrawal, 2001) that in very high dimensional spaces, the data is very sparse and the concept of similarity may not be meaningful anymore. Thus, in high dimensional spaces, similarity based detection can flag each data object as a potential outlier. Also, many methods tend to miss out some outliers that are embedded in some subspaces, which cannot be explored when working with the entire feature space for detection. Addressing the curse of dimensionality, a new method (Aggrawal, 2001) was proposed using low-dimensional projections to find outliers in the projected space. This method considers a data object to be an outlier, if it is present in a local region of abnormally low density in some lower dimensional projec-

tion space. Subsequently, another technique was proposed in (Aggarwal, 2005), which deals with high dimensional applications effectively by using an evolutionary search technique. This technique works almost as well as a brute-force implementation over the search space in terms of finding projections with very negative sparsity coefficients, but at a much lower computational cost. Thus, it has advantages over simple distance based outliers, which cannot overcome the effects of the curse of dimensionality. In a similar effort, another method using multiple projections onto the interval [0,1] with Hilbert space filling curves was proposed in (Angiulli, 2002). According to this method, each successive projection improves the estimate of an example's outlier score in the full-dimensional space.

A novel feature bagging approach for detecting outliers in very large, high dimensional data was proposed in (Lazarevic, 2005), employing an ensemble of outlier detection algorithms. Every algorithm uses a small subset of features that are randomly selected from the original feature set. As a result, each outlier detector identifies different outliers and also assigns an outlier score to every data object. The individual detector scores are then combined to find the overall outliers in the given data set. It is worth noting here that the problem of combining outlier detection algorithms however differs from that of classifier ensembles.

Nature of the Application

Though the application area is not as serious a concern as the other aspects discussed above, it also influences the method employed for outlier detection. For the applications requiring real time response, the detection algorithms must be as quick as possible. In case of applications that are evolving in nature, the outlier detection algorithms must account for this characteristic. In some cases where accuracy is of primary concern, the same has to be ensured in developing a suitable outlier detection technique.

Many of the recent applications deal with data streams, where data arrive incrementally over time. Detecting outliers in stream data poses another challenge, as one cannot keep the entire data in memory for the outlier detection computations. As regards the applications that operate on disk resident data sets is concerned, cluster-based outlier detection methods or the methods using quantization with a few scans over the dataset (Ceglar, 2007) are the suitable choices. A latest technique dealing with data streams detects distance-based outliers under the sliding window model (Angiulli, 2010). This model is appropriate as stream monitoring applications are usually interested in analyzing the most recent behavior. The notion of one-time outlier query is introduced in this technique in order to detect outliers in the current window at arbitrary points in time.

Time series data is another prominent application variety. One such frequently encountered time-series data application is analyzing financial market data. As this analysis has direct bearing on the economic growth and further monetary policies, it assumes importance. However, financial market data is often affected by either missing or erroneous data objects, or unknown external events which can have a large impact on individual objects (Gutierrez, 2008). Detecting those suspicious objects as outliers is difficult using informal inspection and graphical displays.

CURRENT RESEARCH TRENDS

Existing outlier detection algorithms are not effective in dealing with data sets having non-homogeneous object densities. Clustering-based outlier detection algorithms are the known best methods to handle such applications. However, these methods also cannot properly detect the outliers in case of noisy data, unless the number of clusters is known in advance. Addressing these issues, a novel unsupervised algorithm for outlier detection was proposed in (Yang, 2008). This algorithm uses the Expectation Maximization (EM) algorithm to fit a Gaussian Mixture Model (GMM) to a given data set with a Gaussian centered at each data object. The outlier factor of a data object is then defined as a weighted sum of the mixture proportions with weights representing the similarities to other data points. This outlier factor is thus based on the global properties of the data set, as opposed to the strictly local property of most existing approaches for outlier detection.

As brought out in the previous section, the dimensionality of the underlying data set has been a serious concern in outlier detection. Addressing this aspect, a new technique for dealing with high dimensional data sets was described in (Zhang, 2006). In contrast to the conventional outlier detection techniques, this technique aims at detecting outlying subspaces that assumes significance given the current scenario of various detection methods. Outlying subspace detection is formally defined as: given a data object, find the subspaces in which this object turns out to be an outlier. These objects under study are called query points, which are usually the data that the users are interested in. A method for example-based outlier mining in high dimensional feature spaces was initially proposed in (Zhu, 2005). The basic idea of this method is to find the outlying subspaces of the given example outliers, from which more outliers that have similar outlier characteristics can be found. Using this method, outlier detection is to be performed only in those detected outlying subspaces leading to a substantial performance gain. Detecting outlying subspaces can also help in better characterizing the detected outliers as to which outlying subspaces they belong to. A novel distance-based technique using distance distribution clustering was proposed in (Niu, 2007). This technique uses a new distance-based characterization for outliers. It tries to find outliers by clustering in the distribution difference space rather than in the original feature space.

Another evolving research direction is the use of semi-supervised learning techniques for outlier detection. Traditional learning methods use only labeled data, which require the efforts of experienced human annotators. On the other hand, unlabeled data may be relatively easy to collect, but there has been few ways to use them. Semi-supervised learning (Zhu, 2009) can improve the accuracy using supervision of some labeled data compared to that of unsupervised learning, while reducing the need for expensive labeled data. A semi-supervised outlier detection method was proposed in (Gao, 2006). This method uses an objective function that punishes poor clustering results and deviation from known labels as well as restricts the number of outliers. The outliers are found as a solution to the discrete optimization problem regarding the objective function. The basic idea involved in this method is to capture the clustering of the normal objects with the aid of labeled objects and remaining objects turn out to be outliers. Thus, the use of known outliers prevents misclassifying the outliers as normal objects.

Addressing the issue of many recent data sets having both categorical and numerical attributes, OutRank (Muller, 2008) is an algorithm proposed for ranking outliers in heterogeneous (mixed attribute) high dimensional data. Starting from the most unusual objects with respect to the objects in the data set, the ranking can be studied up to a user specified point. This algorithm uses novel scoring functions to assess the deviation of these objects from the rest of the data as determined by subspace clustering analysis. Similarly, a fast outlier detection strategy was proposed in (Koufakou, 2010) to deal with distributed high-dimensional data with mixed attributes. This distributed algorithm requires only one round of communication, as nodes need only to exchange their local models once, in order to construct the global model. In the mixed attributes space, the deviating behavior of an object may be seen in either categorical space or continuous space or both. This algorithm consists of two phases. The first phase constructs a model, while the second phase detects the outliers using the constructed

model. The computation of the outlyingness score for each object makes use of the idea of an itemset from the frequent itemset mining literature.

The development of Support Vector Machines (SVMs) for data mining tasks has its contribution for outlier detection as well. One of the early SVM-based methods for novelty detection was proposed in (Scholkopf, 1999). Subsequently, the research community dealing with outlier detection showed much interest in using SVM-based methods. An unsupervised technique for anomaly detection was proposed in (Li, 2006) using a new kind of kernel function. The kernel function used is a simple form of the p-kernel, the 1-dimensional case in the one-class SVM.

A summary of the literature on various research issues discussed in this chapter relating to outlier detection is presented below in Table 2 for a quick and ready reference.

EXPERIMENTAL RESULTS

To bring out the usefulness of various outlier detection methods discussed above, this section presents the experimental results obtained on a few benchmark data sets from the UCI Machine Learning repository (Asuncion, 2007). As pointed out earlier, the data sets can be of numerical or categorical varieties. One dataset each corresponding to these two varieties is considered in this experimentation. The experimental results obtained with a few numerical data sets using a distance-based outlier detection algorithm are furnished first, followed by the results on a categorical data set.

The general practice in outlier detection is to determine the degree of outlyingness of each data object using a detection method and arrange the data objects in decreasing order of their degree of outlyingness. This process is also referred to as outlier ranking by some authors in the literature. To evaluate a detection algorithm, we count the number, q, of known outliers present among the

Table 2. Summary of the literature on various research issues in outlier detection

Research Issue	Related Literature
1. Method of Detection	Knorr, 1998; Ramaswami, 2000; Knorr, 2000; Bay, 2003; Angiulli, 2005; Niu, 2007; Breunig,2000; Jin, 2001; Papadimitriou, 2003; Zhang, 2008; Zhang, 1996; Ester, 1996; Guha, 1999; Jiang, 2001; He, 2003; Loureiro, 2004; Almeida, 2007; Ceglar, 2007; Assent, 2007; Duan, 2009; Scholkopf, 1999; Li, 2006;
2. Nature of the Detection Algorithm	Skalak, 1990; Harkins, 2002; Markou, 2003a; Torgo, 2003; Joshi, 2004; Yang, 2008; Gao, 2006; Zhu, 2009;
3. Nature of the Underlying Data Set	Harkins, 2002; He, 2003; Ghoting, 2004; Das, 2007; He, 2007; Koufakou, 2007; Boriah, 2008; Muller, 2008; Koufakou, 2010;
4. Size and Dimension of the Data Set	Bentley, 1975; Berchtold, 1996; Beyer, 1999; Aggarwal, 2001; Aggarwal, 2005; Lazarevic, 2005; Zhu, 2005; Tao, 2006; Ghoting, 2006; Zhang, 2006;
5. Nature of the Application	Ceglar, 2007; Gutierrez, 2008; Angiulli, 2010;

top p objects of the ranked outlier sequence, where p is the total number of known outliers in that data set. Then, the accuracy of the detection algorithm is given by q/p. This evaluation method establishes a common framework for comparison of various detection methods for their performance.

Experimentation with Numerical Data

The Orca program (Bay, 2003) is considered to demonstrate the process of outlier detection on numerical data. The Orca program is a distance-based method that uses the distance from a given object to its nearest neighbors to determine its unusualness. This program is available on the Internet for free use by non-profit institutions for educational and research purposes.

Experimentation on some small data sets (Iris and Wine) (Asuncion, 2007) is provided here for better understanding. The Iris data set consists of 150 data objects belonging to 3 different classes: Iris-setosa, Iris-versicolor and Iris-virginica. Each class contains 50 objects described using 4 continuous attributes. To make it suitable for outlier detection and to introduce imbalance in the size, every 10th object of the Iris-virginica class is considered, thus making it only 5 objects of this class present in the data set of 105 objects. The small class objects are considered as outliers and the rest 100 objects are considered as normal. Performance of the Orca program on detecting these outliers is shown in Table 3. The indices of the top p objects in the ranked outlier sequence are shown here. The indices corresponding to the

Table 3. Experimental results on numerical data sets using Orca program

Sl. No.	Data Set	Class-wise Objects Distribution	Number of Objects	Num of Outliers (p value)	Indices of Top p Objects Detected by Orca	Accuracy of Detection (q/p)
1	Iris	Setosa: 1 to 50 (50) Versicolor: 51 to 100 (50) Virginica: 101 to 105 (5)	105	5	**101**, 42, **104**, **103**, 16	3/5 (60.0%)
2	Wine	Class 1: 1 to 59 (59) Class 2: 60 to 130 (71) Class 3: 131 to 136 (6)	136	6	**131**, 122, **135**, **133**, 74, 96	3/6 (50.0%)

Table 4. Sample results of outlier detection in categorical data

Top Portion (p value)	Detection by the Greedy Algorithm	Detection by the AVF Algorithm
4	4/39 (10.26%)	4/39(10.26%)
8	7/39 (17.95%))	7/39 (17.95%)
16	15/39 (38.46%)	14/39 (35.9%)
24	22/39 (56.41%)	21/39 (53.85%)
32	27/39 (69.23%)	28/39 (71.79%)
40	33/39 (84.62%)	32/39 (82.05%)
48	36/39 (92.31%)	36/39 (92.31%)
56	**39/39 (100%)**	**39/39 (100%)**

known outliers among these objects are shown in bold face.

The Wine data set consists of 178 data objects belonging to 3 different classes, described using 13 numerical attributes. Class-wise distribution of these objects is: Class 1 – 59, Class 2 – 71 and Class 3 – 48. For the purpose of outlier detection, every 8th object of Class 3 is only retained by removing all other objects of this class. These 6 objects of Class 3 are considered as outliers and the other 130 objects are considered as normal, making it a total of 136 objects in the data set. The performance of the Orca program on this data set is shown in Table 3.

Experimentation with Categorical Data

We implemented two recent algorithms, namely the Attribute Value Frequency (AVF) algorithm (Koufakou, 2007) and the Greedy algorithm (He, 2006) for experimenting on categorical data. The Wisconsin breast cancer data set (Asuncion, 2007) has been considered in this experimentation. It is a categorical data set described using 10 categorical attributes. It consists of 699 data objects belonging to two different classes with labels 2 (benign) and 4 (malignant). All the objects with missing values have been removed from this data. Using the data preprocessing method described

in (He, 2006), we retained every sixth malignant object in the set. As mentioned above, the objects belonging to the smallest class are considered as outliers. According to this notation, there are 39 (8%) malignant objects considered as outliers and 444 (92%) benign objects considered as normal objects in the processed data.

Given in Table 4 are the results obtained using the AVF algorithm and the Greedy algorithm on this data set. To demonstrate the capability of these methods in detecting outliers, the number of known outliers detected by them corresponding to various top portions (p values) of ranked outlier sequence is shown in different rows of this table. The reader can understand that corresponding to the value $p=56$, both these methods could predict all the 39 known outliers (malignant objects) in the data set. However, for the other reported values of p, these two methods have slight difference in their detection performance as evident from Figure 5.

CONCLUSION AND FUTURE DIRECTIONS

Most existing work on detecting outliers comes from the field of statistics. The statistical methods have largely focused on data that is univariate, and data with a known distribution. Thus, their applicability to large real-world data is restricted, as the

Figure 5. Performance comparison on Wisconsin Breast Cancer data set

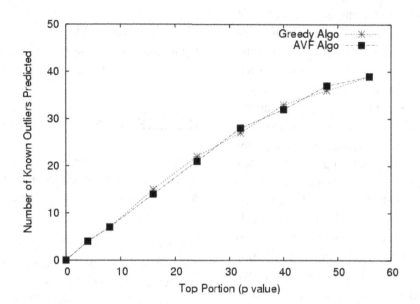

real-world data most of the time is multivariate with unknown distribution. The vast majority of work that refers to outliers is merely interested in developing modeling techniques that are robust to their presence. This means that outliers are not the focus of these modeling techniques, in contrast to the theme of this chapter. However, due to the increasing interest in the field of data mining, the non-parametric methods have evolved as better choices over the traditional statistical methods. The development of non-parametric approaches to outlier detection, based on the distance of a data object to its nearest neighbors, has spurred the data mining community towards developing more efficient algorithms for addressing the problem. The clustering-based approaches are the unsupervised mechanisms to determine the clustered outliers, based on the size of the resulting clusters. Though the distance-based methods based on *k*-nearest-neighbors detection are the most popular ones, clustering-based methods like the *k*-means and some variants of hierarchical clustering are also well known in the research community.

With the growing demand for efficient and scalable algorithms for data mining tasks, a similar requirement is seen for detecting outliers in large and high dimensional data sets. This chapter has presented a survey on various techniques available in the literature and the challenges faced by the researchers in this field. The method of detection is a key research issue that influences the outcome of outlier detection. Different methods are found to have varying capabilities in dealing with various applications. Likewise, the nature of the detection algorithm defines the basic detection logic, which can unearth outliers of varying characteristics. For any given application, the underlying data set is another key issue, as it determines the data related issues like size, dimensionality and its nature. In addition to these issues, this chapter has also dealt with the issue of the nature of the application itself. Different applications are of different nature requiring specialized methods that suite their inherent characteristics. It has also emphasized the need for developing efficient algorithms targeting the specific challenges brought out here. For the sake of completeness, some of the latest algorithms corresponding to various detection methods have been discussed.

As brought out in the previous sections, the dimensionality of the data remains an issue requiring special attention. Though some of the recent techniques have been developed addressing this issue, more efficient methods are required to deal with applications, where the dimensionality is simply explosive. Examples of this variety are the applications dealing with text data. Techniques dealing with projected subspaces or outlying subspaces are probably the best directions to look at. Many of the recent data mining applications have to process the data obtained through multiple data sources connected through a network. Such data keeps arriving continuously and this streaming nature of the data is another interesting research direction that is being pursued actively. Efficient management of stream data and detection of outliers in such data is a non-trivial task. One another issue of interest is dealing with mixed attributes data for outlier detection. Methods that can combine the numerical and categorical data in an innovative way are very much needed. As far as the method of detection is concerned, there are a few recent hybrid methods that leverage the advantages of several individual outlier detection methods. Such useful combinations of the basic methods need to be explored further.

In our ongoing research work, we considered the problem of finding outliers in mixed attribute data sets. The emphasis is on developing a hybrid method that can detect outliers in stream data generated by a networked application environment. A novel characterization of outliers and their detection using a clustering-based method for categorical data is under progress. It includes a new formulation for defining the outlier score of an object. This new outlier score is expected to capture objects having infrequent attribute values as well as objects with unusual behavior local to a cluster. The effectiveness of this method is being evaluated experimentally.

ACKNOWLEDGMENT

The authors would like to thank Director, CAIR for facilitating and supporting the research work reported in this paper.

REFERENCES

Aggarwal, C. C., & Yu, P. S. (2001). Outlier detection for high dimensional data. In *ACM SIGMOD International Conference on Management of Data* (pp.37-46).

Aggarwal, C. C., & Yu, P. S. (2005). An effective and efficient algorithm for high-dimensional outlier detection. *The VLDB Journal, 14,* 211–221. doi:10.1007/s00778-004-0125-5

Almeida, J. A. S., Barbosa, L. M. S., Pais, A. A. C. C., & Formosinho, S. J. (2007). Improving hierarchical cluster analysis: A new method with outlier detection and automatic clustering. *Chemometrics and Intelligent Laboratory Systems, 87,* 208–217. doi:10.1016/j.chemolab.2007.01.005

Angiulli, F., & Fassetti, F. (2010). Distance-based outlier queries in data streams: the novel task and algorithms. *Data Mining and Knowledge Discovery, 20*(2), 290–324. doi:10.1007/s10618-009-0159-9

Angiulli, F., & Pizzuti, C. (2002). Fast outlier detection in high dimensional spaces. In *the sixth European conference on the principles of data mining and knowledge discovery*, (pp.15-26).

Angiulli, F., & Pizzuti, C. (2005). Outlier mining in large high-dimensional data Sets. *IEEE Transactions on Knowledge and Data Engineering, 17*(2), 203–215. doi:10.1109/TKDE.2005.31

Assent, I., Krieger, R., Muller, E., & Seidl, T. (2007). Subspace outlier mining in large multimedia databases. In *Dagstuhl Seminar Proceedings on Parallel Universes and Local Patterns.*

Asuncion, A., & Newman, D. J. (2007). *UCI Machine Learning Repository*. Retrieved from http://www.ics.uci.edu/~mlearn/MLRepository. html. Irvine, CA: University of California, School of Information and Computer Science.

Barnett, V., & Lewis, T. (1994). *Outliers in Statistical Data*. New York: Wiley.

Bay, S., & Schwabacher, M. (2003). Mining distance-based outliers in near linear time with randomization and a simple pruning rule. In *ACM SIGKDD* (pp. 29-38).

Ben-Gal, I. (2005). Outlier Detection. In Maimon, O., & Rockack, L. (Eds.), *Data Mining and Knowledge Discovery Handbook: A Complete Guide for Practitioners and Researchers* (pp. 1-16). Amsterdam: Kluwer Academic Publishers. doi:10.1007/0-387-25465-X_7

Bentley, J. L. (1975). Multidimensional binary search trees used for associative searching. *Communications of the ACM, 18*(9), 509–517. doi:10.1145/361002.361007

Berchtold, S., Keim, D., & Kreigel, H. P. (1996). The X-tree: an index structure for high-dimensional data. In *the 22nd International Conference on Very Large Databases,* (pp. 28-39).

Beyer, K., Goldstein, J., Ramakrishnan, R., & Shaft, U. (1999). When is nearest neighbor meaningful? In *the 7th International Conference on Database Theory* (pp. 217-235).

Boriah, S., Chandola, V., & Kumar, V. (2008). Similarity measures for categorical data: a comparative evaluation. In *SIAM International Conference on Data Mining,* (pp. 243-254).

Breunig, M., Kriegel, H., Ng, R., & Sander, J. (2000). LOF: Identifying density-based local outliers. In the *ACM SIGMOD International Conference on Management of Data* (pp.93-104).

Ceglar, A., Roddick, J. F., & Powers, D. M. W. (2007). CURIO: A fast outlier and outlier cluster detection algorithm for large datasets. In Ong, K. L., Li, W., & Gao, J. (Ed.), *Conferences in Research and Practice in Information Technology, Vol. 84, The Second International Workshop on Integrating AI and Data Mining*. Gold Coast, Australia: Australian Computer Society, Inc.

Chandola, V., Banerjee, A., & Kumar, V. (2009). Anomaly Detection: A Survey. *ACM Computing Surveys, 41*(3), 15:1-15:58.

Chaudhary, A., Szalay, A. S., Szalay Er, S., & Moore, A. W. (2002). Very fast outlier detection in large multidimensional data sets. In *ACM SIGMOD Workshop in Research Issues in Data Mining and Knowledge Discovery* (pp. 45-52).

Das, K., & Schneider, J. (2007). Detecting anomalous records in categorical datasets. In *the 13th ACM SIGKDD International Conference on Knowledge Discovery and Data Mining* (pp. 220-229), San Jose, USA.

Duan, L., Xu, L., Liu, Y., & Lee, J. (2009). Cluster-based outlier detection. *Annals of Operations Research, 168,* 151–168. doi:10.1007/s10479-008-0371-9

Ester, M., Kriegel, H. P., Sander, J., & Xu, X. (1996). A density-based algorithm for discovering clusters in large spatial databases. In *ACM SIGKDD International Conference on Knowledge Discovery and Data Mining* (pp. 226-231).

Fawcett, T., & Provost, F. (1999). Activity monitoring: noticing interesting changes in behavior. In S. Chaudhuri, & D. Madigan, (Ed.), *5th ACM SIGKDD International Conference on Knowledge Discovery and Data Mining (KDD),* (pp. 53-62).

Gao, J., Cheng, H., & Tan, P. N. (2006). Semi-supervised outlier detection. In *the ACM SIGAC Symposium on applied computing* (pp. 635-636). New York: ACM Press.

Ghoting, A., Otey, M. E., & Parthasarathy, S. (2004). LOADED: link-based outlier and anomaly detecting in evolving data sets. In *International Conference on Data Mining* (pp. 387-390).

Ghoting, A., Parthasarathy, S., & Otey, M. (2006). Fast Mining of distance-based outliers in high-dimensional datasets. In *SIAM International Conference on Data Mining (SDM'06),* (pp. 608-612). Bethesda, MA: SIAM.

Guha, S., Rastogi, R., & Kyuseok, S. (1999). ROCK: A robust clustering algorithm for categorical attributes. In *International Conference on Data Engineering (ICDE'99)* (pp. 512-521).

Gutierrez, J. M. P., & Gregori, J. F. (2008). *Clustering techniques applied to outlier detection of financial market series using a moving window filtering algorithm.* Unpublished working paper series, No. 948, European Central Bank, Frankfurt, Germany.

Han, J., & Kamber, M. (2000). *Data Mining: Concepts and Techniques.* San Francisco: Morgan Kaufman Publishers.

Harkins, S., He, H., Williams, G. J., & Baxter, R. A. (2002). Outlier detection using replicator neural networks. In Y. Kambayashi, W. Winiwarter & M. Arikawa (Ed.), *the 4th International Conference on Data Warehousing and Knowledge Discovery (DaWak'02),* LNCS, Vol. 2454 (pp. 170-180). Aixen-Provence, France: Springer.

Hawkins, D. (1980). *Identification of Outliers.* London: Chapman and Hall.

He, Z., Xu, X., & Deng, S. (2003). Discovering cluster-based local outliers. *Pattern Recognition Letters, 24,* 1641–1650. doi:10.1016/S0167-8655(03)00003-5

He, Z., Xu, X., & Deng, S. (2006). A fast greedy algorithm for outlier mining. In *PAKDD'06* (pp. 567-576).

Hodge, V., & Austin, J. (2004). A survey of outlier detection methodologies. *Artificial Intelligence Review, 22*(2), 85–126. doi:10.1023/B:AIRE.0000045502.10941.a9

Jiang, M. F., Tseng, S. S., & Su, C. M. (2001). Two-phase clustering process for outliers detection. *Pattern Recognition Letters, 22,* 691–700. doi:10.1016/S0167-8655(00)00131-8

Jin, W., Tung, A. K. H., & Han, J. (2001). Mining top-n local outliers in large databases. In *KDD'01* (pp. 293-298).

Knorr, E., & Ng, R. (1998). Algorithms for mining distance-based outliers in large data sets. In *the 24th International conference on Very Large Databases (VLDB),* (pp. 392-403).

Knorr, E., Ng, R., & Tucakov, V. (2000). Distance-based outliers: algorithms and applications. *The VLDB Journal, 8,* 237–253. doi:10.1007/s007780050006

Koufakou, A., & Georgiopoulos, M. (2010). A fast outlier detection strategy for distributed high-dimensional data sets with mixed attributes. *Data Mining and Knowledge Discovery, 20*(2), 259–289. doi:10.1007/s10618-009-0148-z

Koufakou, A., Ortiz, E. G., Georgiopoulos, M., Anagnostopoulos, G. C., & Reynolds, K. M. (2007). A Scalable and Efficient Outlier Detection Strategy for Categorical Data. In *the 19th IEEE International Conference on Tools with Artificial Intelligence,* (pp. 210-217).

Lazarevic, A., Ertoz, L., Kumar, V., Ozgur, A., & Srivastava, J. (2003). A comparative study of Anomaly detection schemes in network intrusion detection. In *SIAM International Conference on Data Mining.*

Lazarevic, A., & Kumar, V. (2005). Feature bagging for outlier detection. In *KDD'05* (pp. 157-166).

Li, K., & Teng, G. (2006). Unsupervised SVM based on p-kernels for anomaly detection. In *the IEEE International Conference on Innovative Computing, Information and Control* (pp. 59-62), Beijing, China.

Markou, M., & Singh, S. (2003a). Novelty detection: A review – Part 1: Statistical approaches. *Signal Processing, 83*(12), 2481–2497. doi:10.1016/j.sigpro.2003.07.018

Markou, M., & Singh, S. (2003b). Novelty detection: A review – Part 2: Neural network based approaches. *Signal Processing, 83*(12), 2499–2521. doi:10.1016/j.sigpro.2003.07.019

McBurney, P., & Ohsawa, Y. (2003). *Chance discovery, Advanced Information Processing*. Berlin: Springer.

Muller, E., Assent, I., Steinhausen, U., & Seidl, T. (2008). OutRank: Ranking outliers in high dimensional data. In *IEEE ICDE 2008 Workshops: The 3rd International Workshop on Self-managing Database Systems (SMDB)*, (pp. 600-603), Cancún, México.

Niu, K., Huang, C., Zhang, S., & Chen, J. (2007). ODDC: Outlier detection using distance distribution clustering. In Washio, T. (Eds.), *PAKDD 2007 Workshops: Emerging Technologies in Knowledge Discovery and Data Mining, 4819* (pp. 332–343). Berlin: Springer. doi:10.1007/978-3-540-77018-3_34

Papadimitriou, S., Kitawaga, H., Gibbons, P., & Faloutsos, C. (2003). LOCI: Fast outlier detection using the local correlation integral. In *International Conference on Data Engineering,* (pp. 315-326).

Patcha, A., & Park, J. M. (2007). An overview of anomaly detection techniques: Existing solutions and latest technological trends. *Computer Networks, 51*, 3448–3470. doi:10.1016/j.comnet.2007.02.001

Ramaswami, S., Rastogi, R., & Shim, K. (2000). Efficient Algorithms for Mining Outliers from Large Data Sets. In *ACM SIGMOD International Conference on Management of Data,* (pp. 427-438). New York: ACM Press.

Scholkpof, B., Williamson, R., Smola, A., Taylor, J. S., & Platt, J. (1999). Support vector method for novelty detection. In *the Advances in Neural Information Processing Systems (NIPS),* (pp.582-588). Cambridge, MA: MIT Press.

Sithirasenan, E., & Muthukkumarasamy, V. (2008). Substantiating security threats using group outlier detection techniques. In *IEEE GLOBECOM,* (pp. 2179-2184).

Skalak, D., & Rissland, E. (1990). Inductive learning in a mixed paradigm setting. In *the 8th National Conference on Artificial Intelligence,* (pp. 840-847). Boston: AAAI Press / MIT Press.

Suzuki, E., & Zytkow, J. (2000). Unified algorithm for undirected discovery of exception rules. In *PKDD'00,* (pp. 169-180).

Tao, Y., Xiao, X., & Zhou, S. (2006). Mining distance-based outliers from large databases in any metric space. In *the 12th ACM SIGKDD International Conference on Knowledge Discovery and Data Mining* (394-403). Philadelphia: ACM Press.

Torgo, L., & Ribeiro, R. (2003). Predicting outliers. In Lavrac, N., Gamberger, D., Todorovski, L., & Blockeel, H. (Eds.), *Principles of Data Mining and Knowledge Discovery, LNAI 2838* (pp. 447–458). Springer.

Wiess, G., & Provost, F. (2001). *The Effect of Class Distribution on Classifier Learning: An Empirical Study*. Unpublished Technical Report ML-TR-44, Department of Computer Science, Rutgers University.

Yang, X., Latecki, L. J., & Pokrajac, D. (2008). Outlier detection with globally optimal exemplar-based GMM. In *SIAM International Conference on Data Mining (SDM'08)* (pp. 145-154).

Zhang, J., & Wang, H. (2006). Detecting outlying subspaces for high-dimensional data: the new task, algorithms, and performance. *Knowledge and Information Systems, 10*(3), 333–355. doi:10.1007/s10115-006-0020-z

Zhang, T., Ramakrishnan, R., & Livny, M. (1996). Birch: An efficient data clustering method for very large databases. In *the ACM SIGMOD International Conference on Management of Data* (pp. 103-114), Montreal, Canada: ACM Press.

Zhang, Y., Yang, S., & Wang, Y. (2008). LDBOD: A novel distribution based outlier detector. *Pattern Recognition Letters, 29*, 967–976. doi:10.1016/j.patrec.2008.01.019

Zhu, C., Kitagawa, H., & Faloutsos, C. (2005). Example-based robust outlier detection in high dimensional datasets. In *the IEEE International Conference on Data Mining (ICDM'05),* (pp. 829-832).

Zhu, X., & Goldberg, A. (2009). *Introduction to Semi-Supervised Learning*. San Francisco: Morgan and Claypool Publishers.

KEY TERMS AND DEFINITIONS

Data Mining: The process of identifying valid, novel, potentially useful and ultimately understandable patterns in large data sets.

Ensemble Methods: The methods that use multiple models to obtain better predictive performance than is possible from any of the constituent models.

Example-Based Outlier Mining: Given a set of outlier examples, finding additional outliers from the data set that exhibit similar outlier characteristics.

Outlier Mining: A data mining task aiming to find a specific number of objects that are considerably dissimilar, exceptional and inconsistent with respect to the majority objects in the input data sets.

Outlying Subspaces: An outlying subspace is the subspace that contains predominantly objects that display outlier characteristics.

Semi-Supervised Learning: A special form of machine learning that uses a large amount of unlabeled data together with some labeled data, to build better learning models.

Subspace: The space spanned by a subset of features or attributes of a data set.

Chapter 3
Using an Ontology–Based Framework to Extract External Web Data for the Data Warehouse

Charles Greenidge
University of the West Indies, Barbados

Hadrian Peter
University of the West Indies, Barbados

ABSTRACT

Data warehouses have established themselves as necessary components of an effective Information Technology (IT) strategy for large businesses. In addition to utilizing operational databases data warehouses must also integrate increasing amounts of external data to assist in decision support. An important source of such external data is the Web. In an effort to ensure the availability and quality of Web data for the data warehouse we propose an intermediate data-staging layer called the Meta-Data Engine (M-DE). A major challenge, however, is the conversion of data originating in the Web, and brought in by robust search engines, to data in the data warehouse. The authors therefore also propose a framework, the Semantic Web Application (SEMWAP) framework, which facilitates semi-automatic matching of instance data from opaque web databases using ontology terms. Their framework combines Information Retrieval (IR), Information Extraction (IE), Natural Language Processing (NLP), and ontology techniques to produce a matching and thus provide a viable building block for Semantic Web (SW) Applications.

DOI: 10.4018/978-1-60960-102-7.ch003

INTRODUCTION

Data warehouses have established themselves as necessary components of an effective IT strategy for large businesses. Modern data warehouses can be expected to handle up to 100 terabytes or more of data (Berson & Smith, 1997; Devlin, 1998; Inmon, 2002; Imhoff et al., 2003; Schwartz, 2003; Day, 2004; Peter & Greenidge, 2005; Winter & Burns, 2006; Ladley, 2007). In addition to the streams of data being sourced from operational databases, data warehouses must also integrate increasing amounts of external data to assist in decision support. It is accepted that the Web now represents the richest source of external data (Zhenyu et al., 2002; Chakrabarti, 2002; Laender et al., 2002), but we must be able to couple raw text or poorly structured data on the Web with descriptions, annotations and other forms of summary meta-data (Crescenzi et al, 2001).

In an effort to ensure the availability and quality of external data for the data warehouse we propose an intermediate data-staging layer called the Meta-Data Engine (M-DE). Instead of clumsily seeking to combine the highly structured warehouse data with the lax and unpredictable web data, the M-DE we propose mediates between the disparate environments.

In recent years the Semantic Web (SW) initiative has focused on the production of "smarter data". The basic idea is that instead of making programs with near human intelligence, we rather carefully add meta-data to existing stores so that the data becomes "marked up" with all the information necessary to allow not-so-intelligent software to perform analysis with minimal human intervention (Kalfoglou et al, 2004). The Semantic Web (SW) builds on established building block technologies such as Unicode, Uniform Resource Indicators (URIs), and Extensible Markup Language (XML) (Dumbill, 2000; Daconta, Obrst & Smith, 2003; Decker et al, 2000). The modern data warehouse must embrace these emerging web initiatives.

In order to overcome the many technical challenges that remain before the Semantic Web (SW) can be adopted, key problems in Data Retrieval (DR), Information Retrieval (IR), Knowledge Representation (KR) and Information Extraction (IE), must be addressed (Silva and Rocha, 2003; Manning et al., 2008; Horrocks et al., 2005; Zaihrayeu et al., 2007; Buitelaar et al., 2008). The rise of the Web, with its vast data stores, has served to highlight the twin problems of Information Overload and Search (Lee et al., 2008). To address these limitations smarter software is needed to sift through increasing Web data stores, and the data itself must be adequately marked-up with expressive meta-data to assist the software agents. A major hindrance to the full adoption of the SW is that much data is in a semi-structured or unstructured form and lacking adequate meta-data (Abiteboul et al., 1999; Embley et al., 2005; Etzioni et al., 2008). Without the existence of robust meta-data there is no opportunity for SW inferencing mechanisms to be deployed.

To overcome this hindrance new web tools are being developed, with SW technologies already integrated into them, which will facilitate the addition of the necessary mark-up (Dzbor & Motta, 2006; Shchekotykhin et al., 2007). Beyond this there is an Information Extraction issue that must be tackled so that older web data, or data currently managed by older tools, can be correctly identified, extracted, analysed, and ultimately semantically marked up. In traditional Artificial Intelligence (AI) (Russell & Norvig, 2003) much work has been done in the field of ontological engineering where there is an attempt to model concepts of the real world using precise mathematical formalisms (Holzinger et al., 2006; Sicilia, 2006; Schreiber & Aroyo, 2008).

Mapping web data to domain ontologies allows several Information Extraction issues to be directly addressed. We use a variety of techniques to make sense of the structure and meaning of the Web data, ultimately providing a match to a domain ontology. In particular the WordNet lexical database

(Gomez-Perez et al., 2004; Euzenat & Shvaiko, 2007; Fellbaum, 1998) is used to facilitate some basic matching activities. We also make use of current search engine capability in our ontology mapping process. Allowing search engine inputs helps us to align the matching process with data as it exists online, rather than as construed in some selectively crafted catalog which may not be representative of web data (Schoop et al., 2006).

In this chapter we propose a model which provides mechanisms for sourcing external data resources for analysts in the data warehouse. We also propose the Semantic Web Application (SEMWAP) framework which addresses the issues inherent in using the Web as the source of external data, and which facilitates semi-automatic matching of instance data from opaque web databases using ontology terms.

The rest of the chapter is organized as follows. In the next section we provide the background to the topic, including the appropriate literature review. This is followed by the main section in which we discuss the issues, controversies, and problems involved in using the Web as an external data source. We suggest the ontology approach as one way of solving the problem, and provide the relevant algorithm. The remaining sections provide the directions for future research and the conclusion, respectively.

BACKGROUND

Data Warehousing

Data warehousing is an evolving IT strategy in which data is periodically siphoned off from multiple heterogeneous operational databases and composed in a specialized database environment in which business analysts can pose queries. Traditional data warehouses tend to focus on historical/archival data but modern data warehouses are required to be more nimble, utilizing data which becomes available within days of creation in the operational environments (Schwartz, 2003; Imhoff et al., 2003; Strand & Wangler, 2004; Ladley, 2007). Data warehouses must provide different views of the data, allowing users to produce highly summarized data for business reporting. This flexibility is supported by the use of robust tools in the data warehouse environment (Berson & Smith, 1997; Kimball & Ross, 2002). One of the characteristics of data warehousing is that it relies on an implicit acceptance that external data is readily available. A major challenge in data warehousing design is that it should ensure the purity, consistency, and integrity of the data entering the data warehouse.

External Data and Search Engines

External data is an often ignored but essential ingredient in the decision support analysis that is performed in the data warehouse environment. Relevant sources such as trade journals, news reports and stock quotes are required by data warehouse decision support personnel when reaching valid conclusions based on internal data (Inmon, 2002; Imhoff et al., 2003). External data, if added to the data warehouse, may be used to put into context data originating from operational systems. The Web has long provided a rich source of external data, but robust Search Engine (SE) technologies must be used to retrieve this data (Chakrabarti, 2002; Sullivan, 2000). In our model we envisage a cooperative nexus between the data warehouse and search engines.

Search Engines continue to mature with new regions, such as the Deep Web, now becoming accessible (Bergman, 2001; Wang & Lochovsky, 2003; Zillman, 2005). The potential of current and future generations of SEs for harvesting huge tracts of external data cannot be underestimated. Our model allows a naïve (business) user to pose a query which can be modified to target the domain(s) of interest associated with the user. The SE acts on the modified query to produce results,

Figure 1. Semantic Web essentials

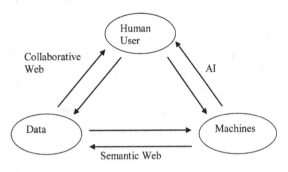

which are then formatted for the requirements of the data warehouse.

The Semantic Web

The Semantic Web is an initiative to augment the World Wide Web in such a way as to make it more accessible to machines. The term machine denotes user programs, software agents and other forms of automated processes (Chen, 2004; Antoniou & van Harmelen, 2008). Much work has been done to ensure the viability of the SW (Shadbolt et al., 2006; Schoop et al., 2006; Horrocks et al., 2005). In particular work has progressed in enabling Web technologies such as XML, Resource Description Framework (RDF), and ontologies (Ding et al., 2007; Powers, 2003; Lacy, 2005; Gruber, 1993). Additional relevant information about these enabling technologies is available in (Greenidge, 2009). Figure 1 highlights the essence of the Semantic Web initiative.

Work has also been done to enable Semantic activities to be mapped over the current Web by utilizing tools such as Magpie (Dzbor et al., 2003) - a SW browser, RitroveRAI (Basili et al., 2005) - a Semantic indexer of multimedia news, and Haystack (Quan et al., 2003) - a tool for easing end user manipulation of onerous RDF constructs. In the area of ontology construction and manipulation notable efforts include the Protégé tool (Noy et al., 2000) and the Ontolingua server,

KAON, WebODE and OntoEdit (Bozsak et al., 2002; Gomez-Perez et al., 2004).

The SW seeks to achieve several goals, including promoting greater interoperability between software agents, enhancing Web Information Retrieval, improving search capability and relieving information overload. In the short term, the area to benefit the most from the SW initiative is the development of XML. XML helps to address some interoperability concerns on the Internet, and provides a tree structure which lends itself to processing by a plethora of algorithms and techniques (Draper et al., 2001; Harold, 2003).

In the medium term, the SW is spurring research in a variety of areas including NLP, Search, IR, knowledge representation, data extraction and ontological engineering. The SW has encouraged the production of tools to both produce and manage meta-data. RDF, an XML-based dialect, in its simplest incarnations seeks to reduce the semantic gap left by XML by imposing a few more semantically useful constructs which, while not bridging the gap, takes us a few steps closer.

There are several challenges in handling data from the Web. First, we note that from a database perspective much data is seen as unstructured or semi-structured, and a major problem in the SW initiative is how to convert such data into coherent information which can be incorporated in a data warehouse, say.

The verbose and visually complex contents of even small XML documents pose many challenges for human authoring. To this end, XML tools and editors have been developed to hide complexity for human authors while preserving the computational exigencies afforded by a tree structure. Tools are also needed to handle RDF, an essential but unfriendly technology, which enables simple statements to be made.

Another challenge is the latency of data on the Web. In many cases the data may exist in a database somewhere but have been archived away from direct access on a homepage. In the case where the webpage content has been generated dynamically, the latency problem becomes even more acute. Still another issue is that of the authority of the website. If two websites contain contradictory information, then the one that is more reputable, accurate, and authoritative is the preferred one.

Ontologies and Their Application

A number of approaches precede, and have influenced, our ontology-based framework. Handwritten wrappers are a first approach to IE on the Web but the well known limitations of such approaches are robustness and scalability hurdles (Crescenzi et al., 2001; Shen et al., 2008). Wrappers tend to target structural page layout items rather than conceptual page content parameters which are less likely to change over time. The literature on ontology- driven IE on the Web is rather sparse, however, there is a growing body of literature which grapples with ontology-based matching of data on the Web (Hassell et al., 2006; Embley et al., 1998; Isaac et al., 2007).

Work done on Dutch collections show that simple Jaccard based measures (Euzenat & Shvaiko, 2007) can give adequate results. Holzinger (Holzinger et al., 2006) again dealt with table extraction issues without relying on HTML tags explicitly. Hu and Qu (Hu & Qu, 2007) studied simple matches between a relational schema and an (OWL-based) ontology, ultimately constructing the MARSON system for performing these mappings. Shchekotyhin (Shchekotykhin et al., 2007) argued about the general unsuitability of traditional Natural Language Processing (NLP), IE, and clustering techniques for ontology instantiation from web pages and proposes an ontology modeling system for the identification/extraction of instance data from tabular web pages.

MAIN FOCUS OF THE CHAPTER

The Model 1: The Meta-Data Engine

We now examine the contribution of our model. In particular we highlight the Query Modifying Filter (QMF), Search Engines submission and retrieval phases, and meta-data engine components. The approach taken in our model aims to maximize the efficiency in the search process. A query modification process is desirable due to the intractable nature of composing queries. We also wish to target several different search engines with our queries. We note that search engines may independently provide special operators and/or programming tools (Google API, for example) to allow for tweaking of the default operations of the engine. Thus the QMF (labeled filter in figure 2) may be used to fine tune a generic query to meet the unique search features of a particular search engine. We may need to enhance terms supplied by a user to better target the domain(s) of a user. Feedback from the meta-data engine can be used to guide the development of the QMF.

The use of popular search engines in our suite guarantees the widest possible coverage by our engine. The basic steps in the querying process are

1. Get user's (naïve) query.
2. Apply QMF to produce several modified, search engine specific queries.
3. Submit modified queries to their respective search engines.
4. Retrieve results and form seed links.
5. Use seed links and perform depth/breadth first traversals using seed links.
6. Store results from step 5 to disk.

Architecture

To ensure that our proposed system functions effectively, the following issues pertaining to both

Figure 2. Query and Retrieval in Hybrid Search Engine

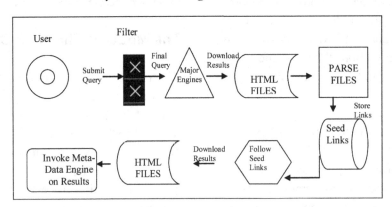

the data warehouse and SE environments must be addressed:

1. Relevance of retrieved data to a chosen domain.
2. Unstructured/semi-structured nature of data on the web.
3. Analysis and Generation of meta-data.
4. Granularity.
5. Temporal Constraints (for example, time stamps and warehouse cycles).
6. Data Purity.

Our model bridges the disparate worlds of the data warehouse and the Web by applying maturing technologies while making key observations about the data warehouse and search engine domains. The model addresses the problematic and incongruous situation in which highly structured data in the data warehouse would be brought in contact with web data which is often unstructured or semi-structured.

A standard SE ordinarily consists of two parts: a crawler program, and an indexing program. Meta-search engines function by querying other search engines and then ranking combined results in order of relevance. In our model we take the meta-search approach instead of initiating a separate crawler and then utilize the meta-data engine components to assume the role of an indexing

program. The Meta-Data Engine (M-DE) forms a bridge between the data warehouse and search engine environments. The M-DE in Figure 3 provides an interface in which poorly structured or semi-structured data becomes progressively more structured, through the generation of meta-data, to conform to the processing requirements of the data warehouse.

The architecture of the M-DE allows for a variety of technologies to be applied. Data on the Web covers a wide continuum including free text in natural language, poorly structured data, semi-structured data, and also highly structured data. Perversely, highly structured data may yet be impenetrable if the structure is unknown, as in the case with some data existing in Deep Web databases (Wang & Lochovsky, 2003; Zillman, 2005).

We now examine Figure 3 in detail. Logically we divide the model into four components - namely, Filter, Modify, Analyze, and Format. The Filter component takes a query from a user and checks that it is valid and suitable for further action. In some cases the user is directed immediately to existing results, or may request a manual override. The Modify component handles the task of query modification to address the uniqueness of the search criteria present across individual search engines. The effect of the modifications is to maximize the success rates of searches across

Figure 3. Meta-Data Engine Operation

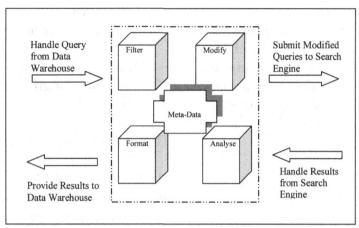

the suite of search engines interrogated. The modified queries are then sent to the search engines and the returned results are analyzed to determine structure, content type, and viability. At this stage redundant documents are eliminated and common web file types are handled including.HTML,.doc,.pdf,.xml and.ps.

Current search engines sometimes produce large volumes of irrelevant results. To tackle this problem we must consider semantic issues, as well as structural and syntactic ones. Standard IR techniques are applied to focus on the issue of relevance in the retrieved documents collection. Many tools exist to aid us in applying both Information Retrieval (IR) and Data Retrieval (DR) techniques to the results obtained from the Web (Baeza-Yates & Ribeiro-Neto, 1999; Zhenyu et al, 2002; Daconta et al, 2003).

Semantic Issues

In the Data Warehouse much attention is paid to the retention of retain the purity, consistency and integrity of data originating from operational databases. These databases take several steps to codify meaning through the use of careful design, data entry procedures, and database triggers. One promising avenue in addressing the issue of relevance in a heterogeneous environment is the use

of formal, knowledge representation constructs known as Ontologies. These constructs have again recently been the subject of revived interest in view of Semantic Web initiatives. In our model we use a domain-specific ontology or taxonomy in the format module to match the results terms and hence distinguish relevant from non-relevant results (Guarino & Giaretta, 1995; Decker et al, 2000; Chakrabarti, 2002; Kalfoglou et al, 2004; Hassell et al, 2006; Holzinger et al, 2006).

Data Synchronization

Data entering the data warehouse must be synchronized due to the fact that several sources, including the Web, are utilized. Without synchronization the integrity of the data may be compromised. There is also the issue of the time basis of information including page postings, retrieval times, page expiration dates, and so on. Calculating the time basis of information on the Web is an inexact science and can sometimes rely on tangential evidence. Some auxiliary time basis indicators include Internet Archives, Online Libraries, web server logs, content analysis and third party reporting. For instance content analysis on a date field in a prominent position relative to a heading may reveal the publication date.

Analysis of the M-DE Model

The model seeks to relieve information overload as users may compose naïve queries which will be augmented and tailored to individual search engines. When results are retrieved they are analyzed to produce the necessary meta-data which allows for the integration of relevant external data into the warehouse.

Benefits of this model include

- Value-added data.
- Flexibility.
- Generation of meta-data.
- Extensibility.
- Security.
- Independence (both Logical & Physical).
- Reliance on proven technologies.

This model extends the usefulness of data in the data warehouse by allowing its ageing internal data stores to have much needed context in the form of external web-based data. Flexibility is demonstrated since the M-DE is considered a specialized component under a separate administration and queries are tailored to specific search engines. Relevant descriptors of stored data are as important as the data itself. This meta-data is used to inform the system in relation to future searches.

The logical and physical independence seen in the tri-partite nature of the model allows for optimizations, decreases in development times, and enhanced maintainability of the system. The model bolsters security by providing a buffer between an unpredictable online environment and the data warehouse.

Limitations

Some obvious limitations of the model include

- Inexact matching and hence skewed estimations of relevance.
- Handling of granularity.

- Need to store large volumes of irrelevant information.
- Manual fine-tuning required by system administrators.
- Handling of Multimedia content.
- Does not directly address inaccessible "Deep Web" databases.

The Ontology Approach

The limitations of the M-DE model provide the motivation for a new (or enhanced) model. In this section we introduce the ontology-based model. We propose a framework which incorporates techniques from web search, NLP, IR, IE and traditional AI, to tackle the IE problem of unstructured and semi-structured web data. Such a framework produces labels based on a mapping between a user-supplied ontology and web data instances (Buitelaar et al., 2008; Jurafsky & Martin, 2009).

Our approach consists of the following:

1. A pre-processing stage aimed at filtering and ensuring that data is in a form suitable for later stages.
2. A basic matching phase where rudimentary matching is performed on primarily structural and lexical considerations.
3. A more advanced matching phase making use of web search and IR techniques.
4. A combination of thresholds and a weighting, producing a matrix which is further normalized.
5. A labeling process which matches data items to ontology terms.

Our framework utilizes the English version of the WordNet lexical database for a part of the matching process. The framework makes use of general purpose search engines and, therefore, some level of redundancy and/or irrelevant web data can be expected.

The Model 2: The Semantic Web Application (SEMWAP) Framework

To realize the full potential of the SW we need building block technologies for the SW corresponding to the roles played by HTML in the current Web. True building block technologies for the SW must simultaneously address structural, syntactic, and semantic issues.

Our SEMWAP framework is designed to facilitate Information Extraction and Data Extraction on the Semantic Web (Feldman & Sanger, 2007; Wong & Lam, 2009). Data Extraction is required since all data released on the Web is not in a pure form, and also lacks meta-data. Data extraction provides the scope to retrieve data stored in diverse formats, for example, tabular data codified with the HTML <table> tag. The framework incorporates the well known Semantic Web stack schematic (Horrocks et al., 2005) to meet the goals of machine readability which are central to the realization of the full potential of the SW. The Semantic Web stack consists of at least the following nine distinct layers: (a) URI & Unicode, then (b) XML and namespaces, (c) RDF M&S., (d) RDF Schema, (e) Ontology, (f) Rules, (g) Logic, (h) Proof and (i) Trust. Digital Signatures and encryption complete the stack by enabling layers (c) to (h). The journey from the lowest layer to the highest takes us through structural, syntactic and semantic considerations.

Our framework is relevant to several layers found in the SW stack. The Information Extraction component of our model seeks to utilize pre-existing ontologies to semi-automatically map data entities to ontology terms.

Data Staging

Data staging allows for data to be moved to a specialized environment where it can be massaged into a form suitable for subsequent processing modules. The data staging layer provides a mechanism in which data that is to be analyzed can be aligned with other data sets. It allows for the addition of vital meta-data to data selected as candidates for further processing.

The data staging layer supports the activity of scientifically sampling larger data sets to produce smaller yet representative data sets. The overall effect is to produce results in a timely manner without sacrificing the quality of the results. The data staging area also provides a location where we may perform conversions from one file type to another, for example a.PDF to HTML.

Label Pre-Processing

In the data staging layer we were concerned about the purity, integrity, and consistency of our data across data sets. In the label pre-processing layer we seek to focus on readying data for eventual matching by our labeling algorithm. This involves reducing the scope/type of data items so that they fall into smaller categories which are suitable for processing by the labeling algorithm. We argue that there must be logical independence between the data staging layer and the label pre-processing layer, since the goals of the label pre-processing layer are unique to the particular type of ontology mapping that must occur. For each domain, the label pre-processing layer will be altered to match the expectations of that particular domain.

Ontology Mapping

The goal of our ontology mapping algorithm is to map data fields to terms in the ontology which indicates how closely a match has been made. On the SW ontologies are important as a way of representing knowledge and allowing reasoning to occur on this knowledge in an automated fashion. Given that the ontologies are well designed and have accurately modeled real-world concepts, we can use them to determine the suitability of data we have collected from websites for use in the data warehouse. Data that is closely related to our domain of interest produces high correlations

Figure 4. Simplified Ontology

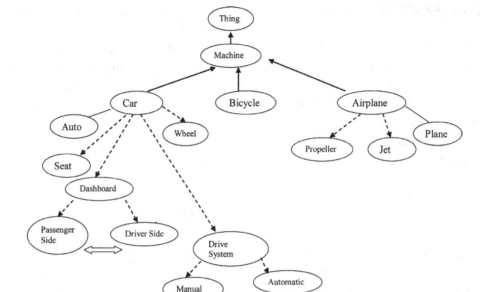

when we compare it with the terms, concepts, and relationships as seen in our domain ontology. Figure 4 is an example of a simplified ontology.

To aid in distinguishing word senses we use a trigram approach (Manning & Schutze, 1999), where we do not take a data field in isolation but combine it with its two nearest neighbors before doing a comparison. In the case where the data fields are simple one-word, one-token entities this approach corresponds to an approach commonly taken in NLP where we try to gather indication of word sense by examining nearby words.

If we are dealing with data fields consisting of phrases, sentences, paragraphs and larger texts, then the trigram approach we take can be seen in terms of co-occurrence where n > 0. Ultimately, a number of distinct terms found in the data set should cluster around terms in the ontology. Matching the ontology terms to data is a sophisticated undertaking, but if the ontology is well modeled and the data is reasonably pure and representative of the domain, then we expect that the underlying categories will emerge when we do the matching process. To reduce the possibility of errors in our labeling, a normalization process is performed on the matrix containing the values obtained by the matching process.

Benefits of SEMWAP

Our model enjoys the following benefits:

1. It addresses a major hurdle currently impeding the development of the SW - namely, how to leverage current structured, semi-structured, or unstructured data so that it can be used on the SW. In actuality only a tiny fraction of the Web data has been marked-up using RDF or similar technologies. Without this special meta-data the ontology-driven

inferencing mechanisms are of little use and the goals of the SW will not be realized.

2. It proposes an incremental approach to the problem of information extraction (IE) from web pages. It is not possible to know beforehand both the quality and reliability of web data in relation to our ontology matching process, so there must be parameters which can be varied to take into account the fact that data sets from the Web are of varying quality.

3. It is completely transparent, and at each stage can be tested or fine tuned independently of the other stages.

4. It enjoys a high degree of flexibility due to its modular design. The reliance on current technologies is a definite strength, and newer technologies may be incorporated as needed.

Weaknesses of SEMWAP

Some drawbacks to our framework include:

1. The memory intensive nature of the framework – natural language processing tools tend to hog memory due to the large numbers of syntactic, lexical, morphological, and semantic considerations.

2. The potentially slow response when processing large numbers of web pages means that the framework may be better suited to off-line, non-interactive environments.

3. An implicit reliance on well designed ontologies, but no way of automatically verifying the quality of the ontologies being utilized. If terms are not descriptive and distinct, then it is very hard to discern appropriate labels for the data, even if a human expert is available to perform this task.

4. The semi-automatic nature of the framework means that it may require human intervention in cases where data-rich and data-poor extremes frustrate the efforts of the labeling algorithm.

The Detailed SEMWAP Mapping Algorithm

In the previous section we introduced the SEMWAP framework and its many characteristic features. However, in this section we provide more information leading up to the detailed algorithm.

Noise Reduction

The sources of noise in Web documents are manifold. The presence of so many diverse technologies and structural layouts within HTML documents, and so little strict data validation controls, means that errors can easily creep into an HTML document unnoticed, introducing noise. Many web pages draw their content and structure from back-end databases which are often not open to direct public scrutiny and may contain subtle errors or inaccurate information, further contributing to the Web noise phenomena. Great emphasis is often placed on a homepage with decreasing attention paid to pages deeper in the site's hierarchy.

To combat the presence of noise, we propose a naïve Bayes classifier (Russell & Norvig, 2003) at the very beginning of our strategy. The filtering of the Web documents so that non-essential data is excluded will lighten our processing load in later stages and enhance the quality of results achieved by our system.

Database Sampling

Although there is a data sparsity problem in natural language processing, merely adding more data will not help. There is need when processing the data to recognize that quality is just as important as quantity. Since much of the data on the Web can never be fixed permanently, it is better to take representative samples of the data and work with those rather than processing larger volumes. Database sampling reduces the quantity of the data that must be processed. In this paper we recognize the need for a variety of sampling approaches

(Greenidge, 2009) to better capture the specific kinds of information found on the Web.

Trigram Generation

Trigrams have long been used in NLP (Manning & Schutze, 1999). This idea is that individual words cannot be correctly interpreted except by the surrounding text. Some words have multiple meanings (senses). For example, "bank" can have different meanings based on the context in which it is used. If three tokens (words) are selected, we have a trigram model. Trigrams seek to exploit the fact that adjacent units (words, phrases, sentences, or paragraphs) often bear some relationship to each other and can be used to mutually interpret each other. In our model we recognize that there is need to contextualize individual units in any matching process, and so we grab adjacent units of data, compose a trigram and check if the results are helped by the composition. In the database world since logically related data must often be presented in a physically close way (that is, on the same screen or report), we expect that physically adjacent data on database-generated websites will bear some logical correspondence as well. By designing our model to embrace groups of three physically ordered units we expect to gain some benefits from any logical relatedness that may exist among some units. The trigram model will only capture relatively simple co-occurrence relations in the data rather than complex intra-document ones.

Bag-of-words

It is important when analyzing texts to be able to distinguish constituent parts beginning at individual characters, then individual words, phrases, sentences, and paragraphs. Often we are concerned about relationships between words or groups of words. A bag-of-words is a collection of words in which duplication may occur, and in which order is not important. For example, 'the', 'cat',

'sat', 'on', 'the', 'mat' is a bag-of-words in which 'the' occurs twice. To ascertain the relationships between words or groups of words (bags-of-words) we need a lexicon. We utilize the Princeton WordNet lexical database to identify words, their meanings, and interrelationships.

WordNet allows us to specify parts of speech information when querying their lexical database. By constructing queries based on bag-of-words data and ontology terms we can use the existence of synonymy and other relationships in the Word-Net database to provide a basic lexical mapping between ontology terms and data terms. WordNet also allows us to construct bag-of-words based on the words found in both the data fields and the ontology elements. We can then apply standard similarity methods such as Jaccard's coefficient (Euzenat & Shvaiko, 2007) to determine similarity at a lexical level. To compensate for data entry errors ("noise") in the data we may also add similarity methods such as the Levenshtein method (Manning & Schutze, 1999) to detect similarity at the structural level.

Building Similarity Matrix R

Similarity matrices are used in NLP to capture correspondences between matching terms, indicating how similar these terms are. Dissimilar terms may indicate that no relatedness exists or that more sophisticated analysis is required to discover any latent relatedness. Among the variety of techniques that can be applied to discover several different types of similarity are similarity in basic structure (character level), similarity in morphology (word root level), and similarity in meaning (word sense level). We use WordNet in constructing our similarity (relevance) matrix R.

Matching Process and Weightings

The matching process proceeds by using the trigram terms and querying a search engine with these terms to produce a document set. This document set is then used to calculate a term frequency–inverse document frequency (tf-idf) (Baeza-Yates & Ribeiro-Neto, 1999) based on the occurrence of the corresponding ontology term for the trigram in the document set. If there are x data terms there will be x unique trigrams that can be generated (by allowing a wrap around in the last terms in the row). The matrix R will consist of y ontology terms, giving a total of x * y calculations to be done. We store these values in a matrix called M. To calculate values for matrix M we will combine results based on

a.   the tf-idf of the ontology term in retrieved documents,
b.   evidence of ontology term in linking text (that is, within HTML anchor tags)
c.   popularity of pages containing ontology term, using search engine backlink counts.

For each value obtained we apply a scaling factor to weight these values, also we weight the overall sum obtained based on the height of the ontology term in its tree structure. The weighting for the ontology term is such that nodes near the root of the tree are given a lesser weighting than nodes in the leaves. We also take the size of the tree into account, with ontology terms from trees with more nodes having a heavier weighting than those with fewer nodes. The formula used in the calculation is as follows:

ComputedValue = Weighting-of-ontology-term * (v1*v2*v3),

where v1,v2,v3 are scaled values computed by matches from retrieved documents. The computed value is then applied to those three cells in the matrix which correspond to the data fields used to generate that specific trigram. The process is repeated until all computed values have been obtained for all trigrams and all the cells in matrix M have been updated. Figure 5 shows the steps

in the algorithm where the various matrices are generated

Label Assignment

To aid in distinguishing word senses we use the trigram approach. The higher the calculated value, the better the match – however, this leads to several possible ways of labeling since the mapping is done on a trigram by trigram basis. In the worst case we may find, that for a particular ontology term, that all the data fields score low in the mapping process, suggesting that for those terms the data fields are only weakly correlated.

In the best case we may have several strong matches of a majority of our ontology terms, and these matches may be distributed in such a way that one data field is strongly correlated to one ontology term. Such a situation suggests that both data fields and ontology terms are well delineated with little overlap between them. This is the idealized situation that is unlikely to occur because in the real world concepts are inextricably linked to each other - that is, there is usually a level of semantic overlap. Since our algorithm takes a hierarchical ontology tree into account when weighing values in the mapping process, data that does not naturally exhibit this property may degrade the mapping process.

If we have a one-to-one mapping between a data field and an ontology term we may adopt an approach in which we label the data field based on its highest scoring across ontology terms. If we find that a given data field scores high with respect to two or more ontology terms then we have to consider how to select one term from out of this set of candidate terms, or how to combine terms and generate a label based on this composite ontology concept. Thus in an m-to-n matching process situation, where m>>n, we see that there may be a high level of redundancy in the data set, the ontology may be inadequately constrained, or the matching process itself may need refinement. The case where n >>m is the unusual situation in

Figure 5. SEMWAP Matrices

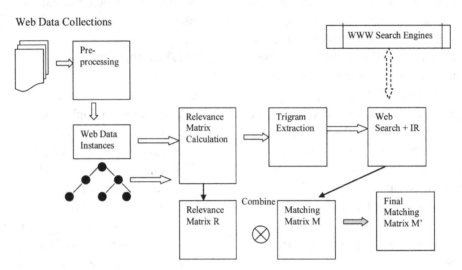

which relatively few data fields match our ontology terms. Such a situation may occur if the ontology itself is unusually large or detailed, while the number of correlated data fields is relatively small.

Normalization Process and Adjustments

The goal of normalization is to reduce the effects of the trigram overlap by eliminating outlier values. This pragmatic approach recognizes that in practice some data fields will be tied very strongly to the ontology while others may be only marginally relevant. Having obtained a relevance matrix R and trigram matched matrix M we compute the dot product of R and M and divide by 3 (to reduce the effects of trigram overlap) to produce a normalized matrix M' (see figure 6). The matching process may be performed in the following ways:

a. Eliminate from consideration values falling below a particular threshold.
b. Choose to label the data term with the ontology field for which it has the largest valid value. The end result may be that several fields in the data are labeled with a particular ontology field.

c. Selectively delete from further consideration ontology labels as they are mapped so that the ontology terms mapped to individual data terms maintain a 1:1 relationship.

Analysis and Anomaly Detection

Our framework performs matches between data instances and ontology terms, and it is expected that well defined ontology terms will match data instances, provided that they are from closely-related domains. If there is too little or too much labeling we should perform further analysis. To assist in such analysis and refinement the whole process is repeated over a new set of data terms. Data on the web is notoriously noisy and so we expect some level of erroneous data despite our best processing efforts. We can use robust clustering algorithms (Feldman & Sanger, 2007; Chakrabarti, 2003) and unsupervised learning techniques (Doan et al., 2003; Wong & Lam, 2009) to detect the existence of implicit associations in the data.

A potential problem to be addressed is how to treat cases where a large number of data fields remain unmatched. It may be an indication that further fine tuning and normalization is neces-

Figure 6. SEMWAP Framework Algorithm

SEMWAP Framework Algorithm

Input: set W of web documents, set O of ontology terms ordered hierarchically as a tree
Output: set Ω matchings between web-instance data and ontology terms, where $|\Omega| = n$.

0. Initial selection of S from W, $S \phi W$, such that Γ is satisfied – Γ is a selection primitive, e.g. Bayes classifier.

1. For each record $i = 1..n$, and keywords $x = 1..m$, let there be pre-preprocessing giving $t_{i,x}$ such that $t_{i,x} \phi T$, where T is the set of terms found in S (i.e. extraction of keywords).
2. 2. Further reduction of initial terms, giving τ_i such that $\tau_i \phi p_i$, where $p_i = \{t_{i,1} ... t_{i,m}\}$, such that E is satisfied – E is a selection primitive. Let $|\tau_i| = j$.

3. **for** $i \leftarrow 1$ to n **do**

4. for record I, examine data terms $\tau_{i,1}$ to $\tau_{i,j}$ (that is, keywords) from the previous step, generate trigrams consisting of $D_{i,k}$, $D_{i,k+1}$, $D_{i,k+2}$, where k, k+1, k+2 denote consecutive data terms in $\tau_{i,1}$ to $\tau_{i,j}$ and $D_{i,k}$ is the kth data term in record i. The list of data terms is treated as being circular for the purpose of trigram generation. Store the set of trigrams Θ in a vector V.
5. Construct similarity matrix R between ontology terms in O and data terms ($\tau_{i,1}$ to $\tau_{i,j}$) using WordNet relationships and similarity measures. Values in R are positive real values in the range 0..1.
6. Use trigrams in V to perform web searches and store related retrieved web documents in vector F.
7. Construct matching matrix M between ontology terms in O and data terms ($\tau_{i,1}$ to $\tau_{i,j}$) by searching for the ontology terms in retrieved web results in F, and applying tf-idf in retrieved texts, and linking texts, and using backlink count of pages pointed to by anchors with ontology term. This result is weighted based on the height of the ontology term $o \, \varepsilon \, O$ in the tree.
8. Perform the operation $M' = R + M$, where + means combining and normalizing the two matrices to produce positive real values in the range 0..1.
9. Perform matchings in which numeric values in M' are examined – matches occur when the largest row values intersect with the largest column values.
10. Output matching results to Ω.

11. **end for**

12. Analyze results in Ω – clustering algorithms may be applied to highlight groupings and allow for fine tuning of system parameters

sary or that there is a strong relationship between these specific data items and the ontology under consideration. Another anomalous case is when one data field is assigned multiple labels from the ontology. This event suggests that too broad a range of ontology terms is being matched and may indicate that the data term is very general with respect to the ontology, or that the ontology itself may be too loosely defined.

FUTURE RESEARCH DIRECTIONS

We are already considering the rise of newer modes of external data sources on the web such as blogs and RSS feeds. These may well become more important than the ezines, online newspapers, and electronic forums of today. Search Engine technology is continuing to mature and heavy investments by commercial engines like Yahoo!, Google, and MSN are starting to yield results. We expect that future searches will handle relevance, multimedia, and data on the Deep Web with far greater ease. Developments on the Semantic Web and, in particular, in the area of Ontological Engineering, will allow web-based data to be far more transparent to software agents. The data warehouse environment will continue to evolve, having to become more nimble and more accepting of data in diverse formats, including multimedia. The issue of dirty data in the warehouse must be tackled, especially as the volume of data in the warehouse continues to mushroom (Kim, 2003).

Currently ontology development is very manual and skill intensive (Hepp, 2007), and therefore large complex ontologies that model real world concepts are difficult to design. On the other hand, small simplistic ontologies can be produced easily but will not scale or facilitate complex business interactions. What we need is a mechanism to assimilate existing ontologies and combine feature sets into newer ontologies in a simple and time efficient manner.

The major features of SEMWAP have been codified into the java-based prototype, called SODL, in which several experiments have been conducted to validate the efficacy of our approach. The results should appear in a subsequent publication (Peter & Greenidge, 2009).

CONCLUSION

The model presented in this chapter seeks to promote the availability and quality of external data for the data warehouse through the introduction of an intermediate data-staging layer, the meta-data engine, which mediates between the disparate environments of the data warehouse and the Web. Key features are the composition of domain specific queries which are further tailor made for individual entries in the suite of search engines being utilized. The ability to disregard irrelevant data through the use of Information Retrieval

(IR), Natural Language Processing (NLP), and/ or Ontologies is also a plus. Furthermore the exceptional independence and flexibility afforded by our model will allow for rapid advances as niche specific search engines and more advanced tools for the warehouse become available.

In our chapter we present the SEMWAP framework which utilizes a combination of IR, IE, NLP, and AI techniques to achieve Information Extraction from web data. These techniques are recognized to be essential to the full realization of the SW vision and are the subject of intense research activities. Our framework forms a basic building block template which can be used in the construction of IE-aware modules for SW Applications. The vision will reach maturity when large quantities of automatically generated data, in the form of meta-data, can be coupled with sophisticated reasoning mechanisms.

Our framework aims at reducing the difficulties by making it easier to use existing web data stores for SW purposes by proposing mappings between existing web data and pre-defined ontological categories. The framework is suitable for researchers, Web database practitioners, SW engineers, and business analysts. Researchers may seek to utilize the framework to compare Web datasets and provide measurements as to how closely selected sites may be similar/aligned across domains. Web database practitioners may utilize the framework to better understand the underlying data models of target web sites.

REFERENCES

Antoniou, G., & van Harmelen, F. (2008). *A Semantic Web Primer*. Cambridge, MA: Massachusetts Institute of Technology.

Baeza-Yates, R., & Ribeiro-Neto, B. (1999). *Modern Information Retrieval*. Boston: Addison-Wesley.

Basili, R., Cammisa, M., & Donati, E. (2005). RitroveRAI: A web application for semantic indexing and hyperlinking of multimedia news. In *Fourth International Semantic Web Conference 2005 (ISWC 2005), LNCS 3729 (pp. 97-111),* Galway, Ireland. Berlin: Springer.

Bergman, M. (2001, August). The deep Web:Surfacing hidden value. BrightPlanet. *Journal of Electronic Publishing, 7*(1). Retrieved from http://beta.brightplanet.com/ deepcontent/tutorials/DeepWeb/index.asp. doi:10.3998/3336451.0007.104

Berners-Lee, T., Hendler, J., & Ora, L. (2001). The Semantic Web. *Scientific American, 284*(5), 34. doi:10.1038/scientificamerican0501-34

Berson, A., & Smith, S. J. (1997). *Data Warehousing, Data Mining and Olap*. New York: McGraw-Hill.

Bozsak, E., Ehrig, M., Handschuh, S., Hotho, A., Maedche, A., Motik, B., et al. (2002). Kaon - towards a large scale Semantic Web. In *Third International Conference on E-Commerce and Web Technology, EC-Web 2002* (pp.304–313), Aix-en-Provence, France.

Buitelaar, P., Cimiano, P., Frank, A., Hartung, M., & Racioppa, S. (2008). Ontology-based information extraction and integration from heterogeneous data sources. *International Journal of Human-Computer Studies, 66*(11), 759–788. doi:10.1016/j.ijhcs.2008.07.007

Chakrabarti, S. (2003). *Mining the Web: Discovering Knowledge from Hypertext Data*. San Francisco, CA: Morgan Kaufmann Publications/ Elsevier.

Chen, A. (2004, 7/5/2004). Semantic Web is 2 steps closer. *eweek.com* 21(27), 46.

Crescenzi, V., Mecca, G., & Merialdo, P. (2001). *ROADRUNNER: Towards Automatic Data Extraction from Large Web Sites*. Paper presented at the 27th International Conference on Very Large Databases, Rome, Italy.

Daconta, M. C., Obrst, L. J., & Smith, K. T. (2003). *The Semantic Web: A Guide to the Future of XML, Web Services, and Knowledge Management*. Chichester, UK: Wiley.

Day, A. (2004). Data Warehouses. *American City and County, 119*(1), 18.

Decker, S., van Harmelen, F., Broekstra, J., Erdmann, M., Fensel, D., & Horrocks, I. (2000). The Semantic Web: The Roles of XML and RDF. *IEEE Internet Computing, 4*(5), 63–74. doi:10.1109/4236.877487

Ding, L., Kolari, P., Ding, Z., Avancha, S., Finin, T., & Joshi, A. (2007). Using ontologies in the Semantic Web: A survey. In Sharman, R., Kishmore, R., & Ramesh, R. (Eds.), *Ontologies: A handbook of Principles, Concepts and Applications in Information Systems* (*Vol. 14*, pp. 79–113). Berlin: Springer-Verlag.

Draper, D., Halevy, A. Y., & Weld, D. S. (2001). The nimble xml data integration system. In *17th International Conference on Data Engineering (ICDE 01),* (pp. 155–160).

Dzbor, M., Domingue, J., & Motta, E. (2003). Magpie: Towards a Semantic Web browser. In *International Semantic Web Conference 2003 (ISWC 2003)*.

Dzbor, M., & Motta, E. (2006). Study on integrating semantic applications with magpie. In Euzenat, J., & Domingue, J. (Eds.), *AIMSA 2006, LNAI 4183* (pp. 66–76).

Dzbor, M., Motta, E., & Stutt, A. (2005). Achieving higher level learning through adaptable Semantic Web applications. *International Journal of Knowledge and Learning, 1*(1/2), 25–43. doi:10.1504/IJKL.2005.006249

Embley, D., Tao, C., & Liddle, S. (2005). Automating the extraction of data from html tables with unknown structure. *Data & Knowledge Engineering, 54*(1), 3–28. doi:10.1016/j.datak.2004.10.004

Etzioni, O., Banko, M., Soderland, S., & Weld, D. S. (2008). Open information extraction from the web. *Communications of the ACM, 51*(12), 68–74. doi:10.1145/1409360.1409378

Euzenat, J., & Shvaiko, P. (2007). *Ontology Matching*. Berlin: Springer-Verlag.

Feldman, R., & Sanger, J. (2007). *The Text Mining Handbook: Advanced Approaches in Analyzing unstructured Data*. New York: Cambridge University Press.

Gomez-Perez, A., Fernando-Lopez, M., & Corcho, O. (2004). *Ontological Engineering: with examples from the areas of Knowledge Management, e-Commerce and the Semantic Web*. London: Springer-Verlag.

Greenidge, C. A. (2009). *SEMWAP: An Ontology-Based Information Extraction Framework for Semantic Web Applications*. Unpublished doctoral dissertation, University of the West Indies, Cave Hill, Barbados.

Harold, E. R. (2003). *Processing XML with Java: A guide to SAX, DOM, JDOM, JAXP and TrAX*. Boston: Addison-Wesley.

Hassell, J., Aleman-Meza, B., & Arpinar, I. B. (2006). *Ontology-Driven Automatic Entity Disambiguation in Unstructured Text*. Paper presented at the ISWC 2006, Athens, GA, USA.

Hepp, M. (2007). Possible ontologies: How reality constrains the development of relevant ontologies. *IEEE Internet Computing, 11*(1), 90–96. doi:10.1109/MIC.2007.20

Holzinger, W., Krupl, B., & Herzog, M. (2006). Using ontologies for extracting product features from web pages. In *ISWC 2006,* LNCS, Athens, GA, USA.

Horrocks, I., Parsia, B., Patel-Schneider, P., & Hendler, J. (2005). Semantic Web architecture: Stack or two towers? In *Principles and Practice of Semantic Web Reasoning* (pp. 37–41). PPSWR. doi:10.1007/11552222_4

Hu, W., & Qu, Y. (2007). Discovering simple mappings between relational database schemas and ontologies. In K. Aberer (Ed.), *International Semantic Web Conference, LNCS Vol. 4825,* Busan, Korea. Berlin: Springer.

Imhoff, C., Galemmo, N., & Geiger, J. G. (2003). *Mastering Data Warehouse Design: Relational and Dimensional Techniques*. New York: John Wiley & Sons.

Inmon, W. H. (2002). *Building the Data Warehouse* (3rd ed.). New York: John Wiley & Sons.

Isaac, A., van der Meij, L., Schlobach, S., & Wang, S. (2007). An empirical study of instance-based ontology matching. In K. Aberer (Ed.), *International Semantic Web Conference, Vol. 4825,* pp. 253–266, Busan, Korea.

Jurafsky, D., & Martin, J. H. (2009). *Speech and Language Processing: An Introduction to Natural Language Processing, Computational Linguistics, and Speech Recognition* (2nd ed.). Upper Saddle River, NJ: Pearson, Prentice Hall.

Kalfoglou, Y., Alani, H., Schorlemmer, M., & Walton, C. (2004). *On the emergent Semantic Web and overlooked issues*. Paper presented at the 3rd International Semantic Web Conference (ISWC'04).

Kim, W. (2003). A Taxonomy of Dirty Data. *Data Mining and Knowledge Discovery*, *7*, 81–99. doi:10.1023/A:1021564703268

Kimball, R., & Ross, M. (2002). *The Data Warehouse Toolkit: The Complete Guide to Dimensional Modeling* (2nd ed.). New York: John Wiley & Sons.

Lacy, L. W. (2005). *OWL: Representing Information Using the Web Ontology Language*. Bloomington, IN: Trafford Publishing.

Ladley, J. (March 2007). Beyond the Data Warehouse: A Fresh Look. *DM Review Online*. Available at http://dmreview.com

Laender, A. H. F., Ribeiro-Neto, B. A., da Silva, A. S., & Teixeira, J. S. (2002). A Brief Survey of Web Data Extraction Tools. *SIGMOD Record*, *31*(2), 84–93. doi:10.1145/565117.565137

Lee, H.-T., Leonard, D., Wang, X., & Loguinov, D. (2008). Scaling to 6 billion pages and beyond. In *WWW2008*. Beijing, China: Irlbot.

Manning, C. D., Raghavan, P., & Schutze, H. (2008). *Introduction to Information Retrieval*. Cambridge, UK: Cambridge University Press.

Manning, C. D., & Schutze, H. (1999). *Foundations of Statistical Natural Language Processing*. Cambridge, MA: MIT Press.

Noy, N. F., Ferguson, R. W., & Musen, M. A. (2000). The knowledge model of Protégé-2000: Combining interoperability and flexibility. In: Dieng, R., Corby, O. (eds), *12th International Conference in Knowledge Engineering and Knowledge Management (EKAW'00)*, Juan-Les-Pins, France, (pp. 17-32).

Peter, H., & Greenidge, C. A. (2005). Data Warehousing Search Engine. In Wang, J. (Ed.), *Encyclopedia of Data Warehousing and Mining* (*Vol. 1*, pp. 328–333). Hershey, PA: Idea Group Publishing.

Peter, H. & Greenidge, C.A. (2009). Validation of an ontology-based Framework for the Semantic Web. (*Journal of Web Semantics*).

Powers, S. (2003). *Practical RDF*. Sebastopol, CA: O'Reilly Media.

Quan, D., Huynh, D., & Karger, D. R. (2003). Haystack: A platform for authoring end user Semantic Web applications. In *12th International WWW Conference 2003*.

Ross, M. (2006, Oct.). Four Fixes Refurbish Legacy Data Warehouses. *Intelligent Enterprise*, *9*(10), 43–45. Available at http://www.intelligententerprise.com.

Russell, S., & Norvig, P. (2003). *Artificial Intelligence: A Modern Approach* (2nd ed.). Upper Saddle River, NJ: Prentice Hall.

Schoop, M., De Moor, A., & Dietz, J. L. (2006). The pragmatic web: A manifesto. *Communications of the ACM*, *49*(5), 75–76. doi:10.1145/1125944.1125979

Schreiber, G., & Aroyo, L. (2008). Principles for knowledge engineering on the web. In *16th International Conference on Knowledge Engineering: Practice and Patterns*, LNAI, Acitrezza, Italy. Berlin: Springer-Verlag.

Schwartz, E. (2003). Data Warehouses Get Active. *InfoWorld*, *25*(48), 12–13.

Shadbolt, N., Berners-Lee, T., & Hall, W. (2006). The Semantic Web revisited. *IEEE Intelligent Systems*, *21*(3), 96–101. doi:10.1109/MIS.2006.62

Shah, U., Finin, T., Joshi, A., Cost, R. S., & Mayfield, J. (2002). *Information Retrieval on the Semantic Web*. Paper presented at the Tenth International Conference on Information and Knowledge Management (CIKM 2002), McLean, VA.

Shchekotykhin, K., Jannach, D., Friedrich, G., & Kozeruk, O. (2007). Allright: Automatic ontology instantiation from tabular web documents. In K. Aberer (Ed.), *International Semantic Web Conference*, (LNCS 4825, pp. 466–479), Busan, Korea, Berlin: Springer.

Shen, W., DeRose, P., McCann, R., Doan, A., & Ramakrishnan, R. (2008). Toward best-effort information extraction. In *ACM SIGMOD International Conference on the Management of Data*, Vancouver, Canada

Sullivan, D. (2000). *Search Engines Review Chart*. Retrieved June 10, 2002, from http://searchenginewatch.com

Wang, J., & Lochovsky, F. H. (2003). Data extraction and label assignment for Web databases. *WWW 2003 Conference*, Budapest, Hungary.

Wong, T.-l., & Lam, W. (2009). An unsupervised method for joint information extraction and feature mining across different web sites. *Data & Knowledge Engineering, 68*(1), 107–125. doi:10.1016/j. datak.2008.08.009

Zaihrayeu, I., Sun, L., Giunchiglia, F., Pan, W., Ju, Q., Chi, M., & Huang, X. (2007). From web directories to ontologies: Natural language processing challenges. In *ISWC/ASWC 2007, LCNS 4825, Busan, Korea*. Berlin: Springer-Verlag.

Zillman, M. P. (2005). *Deep Web research 2005*. Retrieved from http://www.llrx.com/features/deepweb2005.htm

ADDITIONAL READING

Abiteboul, S., Buneman, P., & Suciu, D. (1999). *Data on the Web: From Relations to Semistructured Data and XML*. San Francisco, CA: Morgan Kaufmann.

Chakrabarti, S. (2002). *Mining the web: Analysis of Hypertext and Semi-Structured Data*. New York: Morgan Kaufman.

Devlin, B. (1998). Meta-data: The Warehouse Atlas. *DB2 Magazine, 3*(1), 8-9.

Doan, A., Madhavan, J., Domingos, P., & Halevy, A. Y. (2003). Ontology matching: A machine learning approach. In Stabb, S., & Studer, R. (Eds.), *Handbook on Ontologies in Information Systems*. Springer-Verlag.

Dumbill, E. (2000). The Semantic Web: A Primer. Retrieved Sept. 2004, 2004, from http://www.xml.com/pub/a/2000/11/01/semanticweb/index.html

Embley, D., Campbell, D., Jiang, Y., Liddle, S., Ng, Y., Quass, D., & Smith, R. (1998). A conceptual modeling approach to extracting data from the web. In *17th International Conference on Conceptual Modeling.*

Fellbaum, C. (Ed.). (1998). *Wordnet: An Electronic Lexical Database*. Cambridge, MA: MIT Press.

Gruber, T. (1993). A translation approach to portable ontology specifications. *Knowledge Acquisition, 5*(2), 199–220. doi:10.1006/knac.1993.1008

Guarino, N., & Giaretta, P. (1995). *Ontologies and knowledge bases towards a terminological clarification*. Amsterdam: IOS Press.

Sicilia, M.-A. (2006). Meta-data, semantics and ontology: Providing meaning to information sources. *International Journal of Meta-data. Semantics and Ontologies, 1*(1), 83–86. doi:10.1504/IJMSO.2006.008773

Silva, N., & Rocha, J. (2003). Complex Semantic Web ontology mapping. *Web Intelligence and Agent Systems, 1*(3-4), 235–248.

Strand, M., & Wangler, B. (June 2004). Incorporating External Data into Data Warehouses – Problem Identified and Contextualized. *Proceedings of the 7th International Conference on Information Fusion,* Stockholm, Sweden, 288-294.

Winter, R., & Burns, R. (2006, Nov.). Climb Every Warehouse. *Intelligent Enterprise, 9*(11), 31–35. Available at http://www.intelligententerprise.com.

Zhenyu, H., Chen, L., & Frolick, M. (2002, Winter). Integrating Web Based Data Into A Data Warehouse. *Information Systems Management, 19*(1), 23–34. doi:10.1201/1078/43199.19.1.20 020101/31473.4

KEY TERMS AND DEFINITIONS

Data Warehouse: A subject-oriented, integrated, time-variant, non-volatile collection of data used to support the strategic decision-making process the enterprise. It is the central point of data integration for business intelligence.

Deep Web: Denotes those significant but often neglected portions of the web where data is stored in inaccessible formats that cannot be readily indexed by the major search engines. In the literature the term *"Invisible Web"* is sometimes used.

External Data: Data originating from other than the operational systems of a corporation.

Metadata: Data about data; in the data warehouse it describes the contents of the data warehouse.

Ontology: A method of representing items of knowledge (for example, ideas, facts, things) in a way that defines the relationships and classifications of concepts within a specified domain of knowledge.

Operational Data: Data used to support the daily processing a company does.

Semantic Web: Area of active research in which XML based technologies are being used to make web data "smarter" so that it can be readily handled by software agents.

Chapter 4

Dimensionality Reduction for Interactive Visual Clustering:
A Comparative Analysis

P. Alagambigai
Easwari Engineering College, India

K. Thangavel
Periyar University, India

ABSTRACT

Visualization techniques could enhance the existing methods for knowledge and data discovery by increasing the user involvement in the interactive process. VISTA, an interactive visual cluster rendering system, is known to be an effective model which allows the user to interactively observe clusters in a series of continuously changing visualizations through visual tuning. Identification of the dominating dimensions for visual tuning and visual distance computation process becomes tedious, when the dimensionality of the dataset increases. One common approach to solve this problem is dimensionality reduction. This chapter compares the performance of three proposed feature selection methods viz., Entropy Weighting Feature Selection, Outlier Score Based Feature Selection and Contribution to the Entropy Based Feature Selection for interactive visual clustering system. The cluster quality of the three feature selection methods is also compared. The experiments are carried out for various datasets of University of California, Irvine (UCI) machine learning data repository.

DOI: 10.4018/978-1-60960-102-7.ch004

INTRODUCTION

The interactive clustering methods allow a user to partition a dataset into clusters that are appropriate for their tasks and interests. Even though a large number of clustering algorithms (Jain, Murty & Flynn, 1999) have been developed, only a small number of cluster visualization tools (Cook, et. al, 1995) are available to facilitate users understanding of the clustering results. Visualization techniques could enhance the current knowledge and data discovery methods by increasing the user involvement in the interactive process. The existing visual approaches use the result of clustering algorithm as the input for visualization system. Current visual cluster analysis tools can be improved by allowing users to incorporate their domain knowledge into visual displays that are well coordinated with the clustering result view (Tory & Moller, 2004; Hinnerburg, Keim & Wawryniuk, 1999).

Existing tools for cluster analysis (Jain, Murty & Flynn, 1999) are already used for multidimensional data in many research areas including financial, economical, sociological, and biological analyses. One of the troubles with cluster analysis is that evaluating how interesting a clustering result is to researchers is subjective, application-dependent, and even difficult to measure. This problem generally gets worse when dimensionality and number of items grows.

All feature selection algorithms broadly fall into two categories: (i) the filter approach and (ii) the wrapper approach (Dy & Broadly, 2000). The filter approach basically pre-selects the dimensions and then applies the selected feature subset to the clustering algorithm. The wrapper approach incorporates the clustering algorithm in the feature search and selection. There has been a wide variety of feature selection procedures proposed in recent years (Dy & Broadly, 2004; Pierre, 2004).

VISTA, an interactive visual cluster rendering system, is known to be an effective model, which invites human into the clustering process (Chen & Liu, 2004). When the dimensionality of the dataset increases, identification of the dominating dimensions for visual tuning and visual distance computation process becomes tedious. One common approach to solve this problem is dimensionality reduction. This study compares the performance of three proposed feature selection methods for interactive visual clustering system. The first method called Entropy Weighting Feature Selection (EWFS) is a wrapper approach in which the relevant dimensions are obtained by identifying the weight entropy of dimensions during the automatic clustering process, for instance K-Means (Alagambigai, Thangavel & Karthikeyani Vishalakshi, 2009).

The second method namely Outlier Score based Feature Selection (OSFS) is a filter method which is independent of clustering algorithm (Alagambigai & Thangavel, 2009). In this approach, the relevant features are identified by exploring individual features of the given dataset in boxplot model. The features that have maximum outlier score are considered as irrelevant features and they are eliminated. The identified relevant features are then used in the visual cluster rendering system. The third method, Contribution to the Entropy based Feature Selection (CEFS) works with "filter" approach (Thangavel, Alagambigai & Devakumari, 2009). In this approach, the relevant features are identified for visual tuning according to its contribution to the entropy (CE) which is calculated on a leave-one-out basis. The experiments are carried out for various datasets of UCI machine learning data repository in order to achieve the efficiency of the feature selection methods.

The rest of the paper is organized as follows. In section 2, the background and related works are described. The issues and challenges are discussed in section 3. The proposed work is discussed in section 4. The experimental analysis is explored in section 5. Section 6 concludes the paper with direction for future research work.

BACKGROUND

Interactive Clustering

Clustering is a common technique used for unsupervised learning, for understanding and manipulating datasets (Jain, Murty & Flynn, 1999). It is a process of grouping the data into classes or clusters so that the objects within clusters have high similarity in comparison to one another, but are very dissimilar to objects in other clusters. Cluster analysis is based on a mathematical formulation of a measure of similarity. Generally the clustering algorithms deals with the following issues (i) The definition of similarity of data items (ii) The characteristics of clusters including size, shape and statistical properties (iii) The computation cost and error rate of the result (Chen & Liu, 2004). Many clustering algorithms are proposed regarding these issues (Guha, Rastogi & Shim, 1998). Most of earlier clustering research has been focused on automatic clustering process and statistical validity indices. All the clustering algorithms include K-Means almost exclude human interaction during the clustering process. Human experts do not monitor the whole clustering process and the incorporation of domain knowledge is highly complicated. In reality, no clustering algorithm is completed, until it is evaluated, validated and accepted by the user. This leads to the need of interactive clustering, which allows the user to participate in the clustering process. The quality of clusters is evaluated and refined by the user.

Interactive clustering methods allow a user to partition a data set into clusters that are appropriate for their tasks and interests. In general, there will be a single best clustering (or possibly several local maxima), which depend on the similarity metric used for clustering, the particular objective function being optimized by the clustering algorithm, and the search method (Sourina & Liu, 2004). In practice, however, the "best" clusters may also depend on the user's goals and interests. For example, when performing clustering in a collection of student data, an admissions officer may be looking for patterns in student performance, whereas a registrar might want to track enrollment patterns for different course offerings. The appropriate clusters will not be the same for these two users. An automated clustering method might find one of these clustering, but not both.

Visualization is known to be most intuitive method for validating clusters, especially clusters in irregular shape and it can improve the understanding of the clustering structure. Visual representations can be very powerful in revealing trends, highlighting outliers, showing clusters and exposing gaps (Chen & Liu, 2006). To incorporate visualization techniques, the existing clustering algorithms use the result of clustering algorithm as the input for visualization system. The drawback of such approach is that it can be costly and inefficient. The better solution is to combine two processes together, which means to use the same model in clustering and visualization. This leads to the necessity of interactive visual clustering.

Visualization is defined by ware as "a graphical representation of data or concepts" which is either an "internal construct of the mind" or an "external artifact supporting decision making". Visualization provides valuable assistance to the human by representing information visually. This assistance may be called cognitive support. Visualization can provide cognitive support through a number of mechanisms such as grouping related information for easy search and access, representing large volumes of data in a small space and imposing structure on data and tasks can reduce time complexity, allowing interactive exploration through manipulation of parameter values (Tory & Moller, 2004). The visualization of multidimensional data can be categorized in to either static or dynamic visualization. The static visualization displays the data with fixed set of parameters, while dynamic cluster visualization allows the user to adjust a set of parameters, resulting in a series of continuously changing visualization. Visualization has been used routinely in data mining as a presentation tool to generate initial views, navigate data with complicated structures and convey the results of an analysis (Wong, 1999). In most existing data mining tools visualization is only used during two particular steps of the process. View the original data in one step and to view results in one of the last step (Boudjeloud & Poulet, 2005).

Visualization has been categorized in to two major areas: i) scientific visualization –which involves scientific data with an inherent physical component. ii) Information visualization – which involves abstract nonspatial data. There has been a wide variety of information visualization techniques were used in data mining (Keim, 2002). The early research on information visualization is Scatter plots, Parallel coordinates and RadViz. The purpose of the Scatterplot is to project two data attributes along the x and y axes of a cartesian coordinate system. The parallel coordinate system maps a k-dimensional data or object space onto 2D display by drawing k equally spaced axes parallel to one of the display axes.

Star coordinate (Kandogan, 2001) is an interactive information visualization model that treat dimensions uniformly, in which data are represented coarsely and by simple and more space efficient points, resulting in less cluttered visualization for large data sets. Interactive Visual Clustering (IVC) (DesJardins, MacGlashan & Ferraioli, 2007) combines spring-embedded graph layout techniques with user interaction and constrained clustering. VISTA (Chen & Liu, 2004) is a recent information visualization model utilizes star coordinate system provide similar mapping function like star co-ordinate systems.

Dimensionality Reduction

Dimension reduction and attribute selection aims at choosing a small subset of attributes that is sufficient to describe the data set. It is the process of identifying and removing as much as possible the irrelevant and redundant information.

Sophisticated attribute selection methods have been developed to tackle three problems: reduce classifier cost and complexity, improve model accuracy (attribute selection), and improve the visualization and comprehensibility of induced concepts (Lei, 2004).

At the pre-processing and post-processing phase, feature selection / extraction (as well as standardization and normalization) and cluster validation are as important as the clustering algorithms. Feature selection is a process that selects a subset of original features. The optimality of a feature subset is measured by an evaluation criterion. Finding, an optimal feature subset is usually intractable (Kohavi & John, 1997) and many problems related to feature selection have been shown NP-hard (Blum & Rivest, 1992). The feature selection process consists of four basic steps: subset generation, subset evaluation, stopping criterion and result validation. The subset generation deals with search procedure that produces candidate feature subsets for evaluation based on certain search strategy. Each candidate subset is evaluated and compared with the previous best one according to certain evaluation criteria. The process of subset generation and evaluation is repeated until a given stopping criterion is satisfied. Finally, the selected subsets are necessarily validated.

All feature selection algorithms fall into three categories: (i) the filter approach and (ii) the wrapper approach and (iii) hybrid model. The wrapper model uses the predictive accuracy of a predetermined mining algorithm to determine the goodness of a selected subset. It is computationally expensive for data with a large number of features. The filter model separates feature selection from classifier learning and relies on general characteristics of the training data to select feature subsets that are independent of any mining algorithms. The hybrid model attempts to take advantage of the two models by exploiting their different evaluation criteria in different search stages.

VISTA-Visual Cluster Rendering System

Chen and L. Liu (Chen & Liu, 2004) proposed a dynamic visualization model; VISTA provides an intuitive way to visualize clusters with interactive feedbacks to encourage domain experts to participate in the clustering revision and cluster validation process. It allows the user to interactively observe potential clusters in a series of continuously changing visualizations through α mapping. More importantly, it can include algorithmic clustering results and serve as an effective validation and refinement tool for irregularly shaped clusters. The VISTA system has two unique features. First, it implements a linear and reliable visualization model to interactively visualize the multi-dimensional datasets in a 2D star-coordinate space. Second, it provides a richest set of user-friendly interactive rendering operations, allowing users to validate and refine the cluster structure based on their visual experience as well as their domain knowledge. The VISTA model consists of two linear mappings: max-min normalization followed by α-mapping. The max-min normalization is used to normalize the columns in the datasets so as to eliminate the dominating effect of large-valued columns.

The α - mapping maps k dimensional points onto two dimensional visual spaces with the convenience of visual parameter tuning. The α-mapping has two important properties: (i) since α-mapping is linear, it does not break clusters and the gaps in visualization are the real gaps in the original space. (ii) α-mapping provides dimension-by-dimension rendering.

The VISTA model adopts star coordinates (Kandogan, 2001). A k-axis 2D star coordinates is defined by an origin $\vec{o}(x_o, y_o)$ and k coordinates $S_1, S_2, \ldots, S_k$. The k coordinates are equidistantly distributed on the circumference of the circle C, where the unit vectors are $\vec{S}_i = (\cos(2\pi i/k), \sin(2\pi i/k)), i = 1, 2, 3, \ldots, k$

. The radius c of the circle C is the scaling factor to the entire visualization. Changing c will change the effective size and the detailed level of visualization. Let a 2D point $Q(x,y)$ represent the mapping of a k-dimensional max-min normalized (with normalization bounds [-1, 1]) data point $P(x_1, x_2, \ldots, x_k)$ on the 2D star coordinates. $Q(x,y)$ is determined by the average of the vector sum of the k vectors, $\alpha_i \bullet x_i \bullet \vec{S}_i$ (i = 1, 2,..., k), where α_i's are the k adjustable parameters. This sum can be scaled by the radius c.

Two kinds of visual rendering methods were used in VISTA model, one is unguided rendering and the other is guided. The unguided rendering is performed by marking clusters based on the information obtained via dynamic and interactive exploration. In guided rendering the class labels obtained by clustering algorithms acting as "landmarks" for visual clustering.

VISTA interactive clustering process consists of the following steps:

- Exploring the given data set in VISTA visualization model.
- Finding clusters with α- mapping.
- After getting clusters, labeling is performed by free hand drawing.
- The outliers are handled by boundary extension method.

In this proposed work, the basic frame work of VISTA model with max-min normalization followed by α-mapping is applied for clustering and the outliers are labeled as members of the nearby clusters.

Related Work

Clustering of large data bases is an important research area with a large variety of applications in the data base context. Missing in most of the research efforts are means for guiding the clustering process and understand the results, which is especially important if the data under consideration is high dimensional and has not been collected for the purpose of being analyzed. Visualization technology may help to solve this problem since it allows an effective support of different clustering paradigms and provides means for a visual inspection of the results (Hinnerberg, 1999). Since a wide range of users for different environment utilize the visualization models for clustering, it is essential to ease the human computer interaction. One way to ease the human computer interaction is to provide minimum number of features for clustering and analysis. There is large variety of visualization models are proposed during the past decade, but very few are deals with exploring the dataset with minimum features.

The goal of feature selection for clustering is to find the smallest feature subset that best uncovers "interesting natural" grouping (clusters) from data set. Feature selection has been extensively studied in the past two decade. Even though feature selection methods are applied for traditional automatic clustering, visualization models are not utilizing them much. This motivates us for the proposed framework.

The issues about feature selection for unsupervised learning can be found in (Dy & Broadly, 2004). Dy & Broadly (2004) proposed a wrapper based feature selection for unsupervised learning which wraps the search around Expectation-Maximization clustering algorithm. Jouve & Nicoloyannis (2005) proposed "filter feature selection method for clustering" which is consequently completely independent of any clustering algorithm. The feature selection is based upon the use of two specific indices that allow assessing the adequacy between two sets of features.

Sparity is an accompanying phenomenon of high dimensional data. When clustering is applied to sparse data, a special treatment called subspace clustering is required. The subspace clustering aims at finding clusters from subspaces of data instead of entire data space. The major challenge of subspace clustering, which makes its distinctive

from traditional clustering, is the simultaneous determination of both clustering memberships of objects and the subspace of each cluster. According to the ways of clustering, the subspace clustering methods are divided as hard subspace clustering in which exact subspaces of different clusters are identified and soft subspace clustering where clustering performed in the entire data space and different weight values are assigned to different dimensions of clusters during clustering process. Subspace clustering (or projective clustering) is very important for effective identification of patterns in a high dimensional data space which receives great attention in recent years. The recent survey (Jing, Michael, & Huang, 2007) offers a comprehensive summary on the different applications and algorithms of subspace clustering.

Domeniconi, et. al (2004) proposed an algorithm that discovers clusters in subspace spanned by different combinations of dimensions via local weighting of dimensions. The method associates to each cluster in weight vector, whose values capture the relevance of dimensions within the corresponding clusters. Jing, Michael, & Huang (2007) proposed a new K-Means type algorithm for clustering high-dimensional objects in subspaces. They extend the K-Means by adding an additional step to the K-means which automatically compute the weights of all dimensions in each cluster and use the weight values to identify the subsets of important dimensions that categorize different clusters.

Interactive Clustering differs from traditional automatic clustering in such a way that it incorporates user's domain knowledge into the clustering process. There are wide variety of interactive clustering methods are proposed in recent years (DesJardins, MacGlashan & Ferraioli, 2007; Hinnerberg, 1999). DesJardins, MacGlashan & Ferraioli (2007) presented a novel approach called Interactive Visual Clustering (IVC). In this approach, the relational data is initially displayed using a spring-embedded graph layout. The user can then move group of instances to different places on the screen in order to form initial clusters. A constrained clustering algorithm is applied to generate clusters that combine the attribute information with the constraints implied by the instances that have been moved. Chen & Liu (2004) proposed VISTA model, an intuitive way to visualize clusters. This model provides a similar mapping like star coordinates, where a dense point cloud is considered a real cluster or several overlapped clusters.

VISUAL CLUSTERING: ISSUES AND CHALLENGES

For data mining to be effective, it is important to include the human in the data exploration process and combine the flexibility, creativity, and general knowledge of the human with the enormous storage capacity and the computational power of today's computers. Visual data exploration aims at integrating the human in the data exploration process, applying its perceptual abilities to the large data sets available in today's computer systems. The basic idea of visual data exploration is to present the data in some visual form, allowing the human to get insight into the data, draw conclusions, and directly interact with the data. Visual data mining techniques have proven to be of high value in exploratory data analysis and they also have a high potential for exploring large databases. In addition to the direct involvement of the user, the main advantages of visual data exploration over automatic data mining techniques from statistics or machine learning are,

- Visual data exploration can easily deal with highly inhomogeneous and noisy data
- Visual data exploration is intuitive and requires no understanding of complex mathematical or statistical algorithms or parameters.

As a result, visual data exploration usually allows a faster data exploration and often provides better results, especially in cases where automatic algorithms fail. In addition, visual data exploration techniques provide a much higher degree of confidence in the findings of the exploration (Keim & Ward, 2007).

Considering visualization as a supporting technology in data mining, four possible approaches are stated in (Thuraisingham, 1999). The first approach is the usage of visualization technique to present the results that are obtained from mining the data in the database. Second approach is applying the data mining technique to visualization by capturing essential semantics visually. The third approach is to use visualization techniques to complement the data mining techniques. The fourth approach uses visualization technique to steer mining process.

There has been a wide variety of visualization models proposed to handle the first two approaches such as scatter plots, etc. whereas a very few visualization models deals with the third and fourth approaches. To present the results of data mining process, variety of static visualization models are proposed in recent years. It is commonly believed that static visualization is not sufficient for visualizing clusters (Keim, 2002) and it has been shown that clusters can hardly be preserved in a static visualization. The dynamic visualization overcome these difficulties, by allowing the user to adjust a set of parameters, resulting in a series of continuously changing visualization (Chen & Liu, 2006).

In general, the visual data exploration usually follows a three step procedure process called information seeking mantra: Overview first, zoom and filter and then details-on-demand (Keim, 2004). To explore the result and identify the patterns this three step process is sufficient, where to complement data mining technique through visualization and to steer the mining process a high level of Human-Computer interaction is required. This could be achieved through domain knowledge.

Domain knowledge plays a critical role in the clustering process. It is the semantic explanation to the data groups, which may be different from the structural clustering criteria. Domain knowledge can be represented in various forms in Artificial intelligence (Chen & Liu, 2004). The domain knowledge could come from the specific properties of the application, the experimental results, or any hypotheses that the application holds. In this paper, we utilize the domain knowledge which obtained by analyzing the individual dimension.

In the original version of VISTA-visual clustering system, for the clustering process the domain knowledge can be simply represented as a few labeled instances. This method is inefficient because identifying class labels for large dataset required automatic algorithms which usually increase the computation cost and time. Instead of that, a proposed work focusing on the role of dimensions in forming the clusters.

Even though visualization techniques have advantages over automatic methods, it brings up some specific challenges such as (i) Limitation in visibility (ii) Visual bias due to mapping of dataset to 2D/ 3D representation (iii) Easy-to-use visual interface operations (iv) Reliable Human-computer interaction. Although each of these issues has been studied, there is surprisingly little research on how to improve the Human-Computer interaction. However VISTA address all the issues effectively, it brings out some limitation in Human-Computer interaction. Since VISTA has been proved as a dynamic interactive visual cluster rendering system, the challenges exists in finding the clusters by adjusting the α values of the visually domination dimensions. In order to achieve that, VISTA provides a rich set of visual rendering, which enables the user to find dominating dimensions, so as to observe the dataset from different perspectives, and to distinguish real clusters from cluster overlaps in continuously changing visualization.

The following are the rules applied in VISTA for visual rendering,

- Render the visualization in an order of dimension, such as in counter-clockwise direction, beginning at the dimension 0.
- When rendering the visualization in an order of dimension, fine the main contributing dimensions and maximizes their α values either to 1 or -1, to separate all clusters as possible.
- Use minor contributing dimensions to polish the clusters, which increases the cluster cohesion.
- The non-contributing dimensions move all points together and theses are omitted during visual rendering.

Guided by the above specified simple visual rendering rules, a trained user can easily find satisfactory visualization. When combined with the cluster labels that are generated by automatic clustering algorithms (for example, the K-Means algorithm), the rendering becomes even easies. The VISTA mapping is adjustable by α_i. By tuning α_i continuously, the user can see the influence of ith dimension on the cluster distribution through a series of smoothly changing visualizations, which usually provides important clustering clues. The dimensions that are important for clustering will cause significant changes to the visualization as the corresponding α values are continuously changed. Even though the visual rendering is completed within minutes, the sequential rendering becomes tedious when the number of dimensions is large. In most of the cases, the continuous change of α leads to different patterns, may resulting in incorrect clusters. And in some of the data sets, the user gets confusion with identifying the visually dominating dimensions, since the α variation is very small. In such cases, the incorporation of domain knowledge is essential. Particularly if domain knowledge assist the normal users then the whole clustering process i.e "clustering – validation/evaluation" becomes easier. This motivates the applicability of dimensionality reduction for visual clustering in VISTA. In general any visualization system is a human-computer, brings the following constraints,

- Human eyes cannot distinguish very small visual differences, so a visualization system should not use very small visual differences to carry any information.
- Human eyes have difficulty to handle a display with overwhelmingly rich visual features, which makes understanding and extraction of information difficult and hurt the motivation of visualization.

The visual data mining is different form scientific visualization and is having the following characteristics: wide range of users, wide choice of visualization techniques and important dialog function. The users of scientific visualization are scientists and engineers who can endure the difficulty in using the system for little at most, whereas a visual data mining must have the possibility that the general persons uses widely and so on easily.

To address all the above specified problems, we propose three dimensionality reduction methods for interactive visual clustering system. All the three methods are aimed to perform efficient visual clustering through dimensionality reduction. The visual clustering process is carried out based on the individual characteristics of the dimension not with labeled instance. This makes whole clustering process to be more effective. Since, irrelevant dimensions are reduced; the visual gap between the clusters could be obtained easily, which make the understanding and extraction of clusters easy. Since the number of dimensions is less, number of iterations in the process of computing visual distance is reduced resulting in efficient and reliable Human-computer interaction.

DIMENSIONALITY REDUCTION FOR VISUAL CLUSTERING

In this section, three different feature selection methods are proposed for visual clustering.

Entropy Weighting Feature Selection (EWFS)

The basic idea of the EWFS is to identify important dimensions based on their contribution in forming the clusters. EWFS is using wrapper approach to find the relevant features. The step by step procedure of EWFS is shown in Figure 1. Initially the data set is clustered by using any centroid based partitioning clustering algorithms for instance K-Means.

Based on the clustering results, the weight entropy of dimensions is identified using (3). The weight entropy for a dimension in a cluster is inversely proportional to the dispersion of the values from the center in the dimension of the cluster. Since the dispersions are different in different dimensions of different cluster, the weight entropies for different clusters are different. The high weight indicates a small dispersion in a dimension of the cluster. Therefore, that dimension is more important in forming the cluster (Jing, Michael, & Huang, 2007). If the entire set of dimensions are equally participating in the formation of clusters, then

$$\gamma_1 = \gamma_2 = . \quad . \quad . \quad = \gamma_k \qquad (5)$$

where γi is the threshold value of weight entropy of ith dimension. If the dimensions are not contributing much in the formation of clusters, the weight entropy gets the least value which is usually less than the threshold γ. The dimensions which have least weight entropy (i.e) entropy less than γ makes a large dispersion in the visualization and moves all data points together in a single

Figure 1. Entropy Weighting Feature Selection Algorithm

Input : n Data set with underlying Distribution
Output : K Partitions of Data sets

Step 1: Cluster each datasets by K-Means and obtain class labels.

Step 2: Apply the following formula to find the weight entropy of dimension for each cluster (Jiang, Tang & Zhang, 2004)

$$\lambda_{li} = \frac{1}{\sum_{i=1} \left[\frac{\sum_{j} \omega^{\eta}_{lj}(z_{li}-x_{ji})^2}{\sum_{j} \omega^{\eta}_{lj}(z_{li}-x_{ji})^2} \right]^{1/(\beta-1)}} \tag{1}$$

Subject to

$$\sum_{l=1} \omega_l = 1, \quad 1 \le j \le n \quad \text{if } j^{th} \text{ object belonging to the } l^{th} \text{ cluster , else} \tag{2}$$
$$= 0$$

$$\sum_{i=1} \lambda_i = 1, \quad 1 \le l \le k, \quad 0 \le \lambda_{li} \le 1 \tag{3}$$

Where $n, k,$ and m are the number of objects, clusters and dimensions respectively.

λ_i = weight for the ith dimension in the lth cluster.
ω_{lj} = degree of membership of the jth object belonging to the lth cluster.
x_{ji} = value of ith dimension in the jth object.
z_{li} = value of the ith component of the lth cluster.
β (>1) and $\eta (\ge)$ are two parameters greater than 1.

Step 3: Eliminate the dimensions whose weight entropy is less than the threshold γ since it is not contributing much to the cluster, where $\tag{4}$

$$\text{Threshold,} \quad \gamma = \frac{1}{\text{No. of dimensions}}$$

Step 4: Explore only the selected dimensions in VISTA.

Step 5: Perform interactive visual clustering with α- tuning until satisfactory results.

direction, does nothing in the visual clustering. Hence it is eliminated for further refinement of clusters. Similarly the dimension with large weight entropy makes a small dispersion either towards the center of the cluster or away from it, depends on the corresponding value of α. This dimension is very important in forming the cluster. Hence it is included for visual clustering. The elimination of irrelevant dimensions makes the identification of the dominating attributes for visual tuning and visual distance computation process easier. Specifically it eases the human-computer interaction.

Outlier Score Based Feature Selection (OSFS)

The main objective of the outlier score based feature selection method is to increase the performance of visual cluster rendering system by selecting only the relevant feature, such that identification of the dominating attributes for visual tuning and visual distance computation process becomes easier. Here, the popular statistical tool boxplot is applied to seek the irrelevant features. OSFS method doesn't require any automatic algorithm to find the relevant feature, thus it is filter approach.

The basic idea of this feature selection method is to identify the features which have high outlier score. The outlier score of individual feature is obtained based on the occurrence of extreme outlier in it. Initially the individual feature of the given dataset is explored in boxplot and the number of mild outliers and extreme outliers are computed. The Boxplot is a graphical display where the outliers appear tagged. Two types of outliers are distinguished: mild outliers and extreme outliers. An observation x is declared an extreme outlier if it lies outside of the interval $(Q_1 - 3 \times IQR, Q_3 + 3 \times IQR)$ where Q_1 is the 25th quartile & Q_3 is the 75th quartile and IQR is called as the interquartile range. An observation x is declared a mild outlier if it lies outside of the interval $(Q_1 - 1.5 \times IQR, Q_3 + 1.5 \times IQR)$. The numbers 1.5 and 3 are chosen by comparison with a normal distribution. In this proposed work, boxplots are used to identify extreme outliers of the individual attributes in the given data set. Let M_i represents the number of mild outliers for ith feature and E_i represents the number of extreme outliers for ith feature. Let the outlier score (OS_i) of feature ith is defined as

$$OS_i = \frac{E_i}{M_i + E_i} \tag{6}$$

Let us define the average of all extreme outliers to be AVE and then we distinguish the features in to two groups as,

- OS_i > AVE features with maximum outlier score, hence eliminated.
- OS_i < AVE features with minimum outlier score, hence considered as relevant features and included for visual clustering.

Contribution to the Entropy Based Feature Selection (CEFS)

The Contribution to the Entropy based Feature Selection identifies the important dimensions according to its contribution to the entropy (CE) by a leave-out basis. The step by step procedure is shown in Figure 2. Features with high CE lead to entropy increase; hence they are assumed to be very relevant. The features of the second group i.e features with average contribution do not change the entropy of the dataset and hence they can be filtered out without much information loss. The third group includes features that reduce the total Singular Value Decomposition (SVD) - entropy (usually C < 0). Such features may be expected to contribute uniformly to the different instances, and may just as well be filtered out from the analysis. The relevant features are then applied to VISTA model for clustering process.

EXPERIMENTAL ANALYSIS AND DISCUSSION

The objective of the experiments is to examine the quality of the clusters before and after applying the proposed feature selection methods in VISTA model.

Experimental Setup

The proposed algorithms have been implemented and tested with fifteen benchmark numeric

Figure 2. Contribution to the Entropy based Feature Selection

Input : n Data set with underlying Distribution
Output : K Partitions of Data sets

Step 1: Find the Contribution to the entropy (Vayshavsky, et. al., 2004; Wall, Rechtsteiner & Rocha, 2003) of the ith feature as

$$CE_i = E(A_{nXm}) - E(A_{nXm-1}]) \qquad (7)$$

Where the Entropy

$$E = -\frac{1}{\log(N)} \sum_{j=1}^{N} V_j \log(V_j) \qquad (8)$$

And the normalized relative values

$$V_j = \frac{S_j^2}{\sum_k S_k^2} \qquad (9)$$

Where S_j^2 is the eigen values of the nXn matrix $A A^i$

Step 2: Sort the features based on their contribution to the entropy..

Step 3: Group the features as
   i). $CE_i > C$, features with high contribution
   ii). $C > CE_i > C$ features with average contribution
   iii). $CE_i < C$ features with low (usually negative) contribution
   Where C = Average (CE)

Step 4: Eliminate the dimensions with average and negative contribution, since they
      are irrelevant.

Step 5: Explore only the selected dimensions in VISTA.

Step 6: Perform interactive visual clustering with α- tuning until satisfactory results.

datasets available in the UCI machine learning data repository (Merz & Murphy, 1998). The information about the datasets is shown in Table 1. The comparative analysis of the feature selection methods with visualization is illustrated with Australian dataset. The feature selection is carried out with test data (20% of original dataset) for dataset whose instance is greater than 10000.

Evaluation Methodology

The quality of clusters is measured in terms of Homogeneity/Separation (H/S) ratio, Rand Index as proposed by (Jiang, Tang & Zhang, 2004). The Homogeneity measures the similarity of data objects in the clusters, whereas the Separation measures the dissimilarity between every pair of

Table. 1. Details of Datasets

S. No	Data Set	No. of Attributes	No. of Classes	No. of Instances
1	Hepatitis	19	2	155
2	Australian	14	2	690
3	Breast Cancer	32	2	569
4	Dermatology	34	6	366
5	Ionosphere	34	2	351
6	Pima	8	2	768
7	Sonar class	60	2	208
8	Mammographic	6	2	961
9	Spam Base	57	2	4601
10	Gamma	10	2	19020
11	Bupa	6	2	345
12	Gene Expression Data	37	2	7457
13	Web Log Data	145	2	250
14	Image Segmentation	16	7	2100
15	SPECTF Heart	44	2	267
16	Wine	12	3	178

clusters. The Rand index is based on the agreement between clustering results and the "ground truth".

Comparative Analysis

Australian Dataset

Australian Dataset concerns with credit card applications. This dataset is interesting because there is a good mix of attributes continuous, nominal with small numbers of values, and nominal with larger numbers of values. This data set also has missing values. Suitable statistical based computation is applied for finding the missing values. Australian Dataset has two classes with class distribution of 44.5% for class A and 55.5% for class B. Since the K-Means clustering results are highly sensitive to the initial centroid selection, the weight entropy of dimensions in forming the clusters may vary.

For experimental purpose, initial centroid is selected by using the following two methods: (i) random selection (ii) sampling, where the initial centroids are selected using preliminary clustering phase on random 10% sub sample of the given data. The preliminary phase is itself initialized using 'sample'. The weight entropy of individual clusters obtained by K-Means with random selection is shown in Figure 3. It is observed that the contributions of dimension in forming the two clusters are almost similar, except in one or two dimensions. The experimental results show that the dimensions 2, 3, 5, 7, 10, 13 and 14 have weight entropy less than γ for cluster 1 and dimensions 2, 3, 5, 13 and 14 have weight entropy which is less than γ for cluster 2. Based on this, dimensions 2, 3, 5, 7, 10, 13 and 14 are found to be irrelevant, hence omitted for interactive visual clustering. Only dimensions with weight entropies greater than γ are then applied in to VISTA.

The visualization of Australian data with the entire set of dimensions after the α tuning is shown in Figure 4a) and the visualization of clusters with only the relevant dimensions obtained from EWFS shown in Figure 4b) with $\alpha_i = 0.5$. From the visualization results, it is observed the distribution of points in the clusters obtained by the proposed

Figure 3. Weight entropy vs. clusters

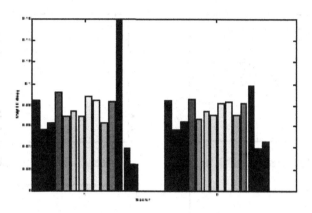

method is similar to that of the original clusters obtained by using the original sample, whereas the visual distance between the clusters is high in Figure 4b). And the visualization with feature selection doesn't need α tuning. This is an interesting scenario found in Australian dataset, makes the clustering process to be very simple. Similar kind of result found in Bupa dataset also. Figure 4 c) shows the visualization of Australian dataset with OSFS and Figure 4 d) shows the visualization of CEFS method. EWFS selects the following features: 1, 4, 6, 8, 9, 11, 12 and OSFS selects 12 features such as 1, 2, 3, 4, 5, 6, 8, 9, 10, 11, 12, 13. The CSFS eliminates only one feature.

From the results, it is observed that all the three method selects the following features 1, 4, 6, 8, 9, 11, 12. And feature 14 found to be irrelevant in all the three cases. When analyzing the value distribution of individual attributes of Australian Dataset, features 7 and 14 are found with maximum outliers. Hence eliminating features with extreme univariate outliers i.e features 14 and 7 improves the cluster quality. The feature selection retains the Best cluster quality with respect to the original set and improves the Average cluster quality. Since, the number of features is less than 14, the number of iteration for visual distance computation is reduced. Thus eases the human-computer interaction. The number of

features selected using the three feature selection methods are shown in Table 2.

From Table 2 it is observed that CEFS method selects very less number of features for Hepatitis and Breast Cancer Dataset. For Bupa and Wine Dataset CEFS selects only 2 features for visual clustering. This is not adequate for exploring the dataset in VISTA. If the number of features is greater than three VISTA explores the dataset well. And EWFS selects less number of features for Australian dataset. The OSFS method selects the features in the range of 14.28% to 41.17% that is quite high when comparing with other feature selection method. Medical datasets Pima and Breast cancer does not contain extreme outliers, so OSFS utilize all the features for clustering. For most of the datasets OSFS method selects large amount of features, since it deals with only the extreme outliers. The selection of EWFS is completely depends on the automatic algorithm applied. Since in this proposed work K-Means is used for clustering, the result of EWFS is completely dependent on the selection of initial centroid. The resultant cluster quality of EWFS, OSFS and CEFS are shown in Table 3 and 4.

Figure 4. Visualization of Australian data set

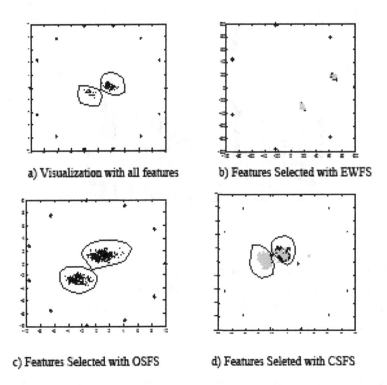

a) Visualization with all features   b) Features Selected with EWFS

c) Features Selected with OSFS   d) Features Seleted with CSFS

Table. 2. Results of Feature Selection methods

Datasets	No. of Features in Original Dataset	No. of Features Selected		
		EWFS	OSFS	CEFS
Hepatitis	19	15	12	4
Australian	14	7	12	13
Breast Cancer	32	24	32	5
Dermatology	34	31	20	33
Ionosphere	34	33	33	16
Pima	8	4	8	5
Sonar class	60	32	30	28
Mammographic	6	4	4	4
Spam Base	57	48	14	3
Gamma	10	3	10	10
Bupa	6	4	6	2
Gene Expression Data	37	35	11	37
Web Log Data	145	82	113	30
Image Segmentation	16	7	3	14
SPECTF Heart	44	4	44	17
Wine	13	10	13	2

Table. 3. Rand Index Comparison of EWFS, OSFS and CEFS with respect to Whole Features

Datasets	VISTA with Entire dimension		VISTA with Selected Features using EWFS		VISTA with Selected Features using OSFS		VISTA with Selected Features using CEFS	
	Best	*Avg*	*Best*	*Avg*	*Best*	*Avg*	*Best*	*Avg*
Hepatitis	57.24	54.30	65.97	63.24	57.24	54.30	65.97	63.24
Australian	75.22	69.99	75.22	74.09	75.22	74.09	75.22	75.22
Breast Cancer	53.21	53.21	53.23	53.18	53.21	53.21	53.21	53.21
Dermatology	74.06	72.06	76.01	76.01	76.27	76.27	73.46	73.46
Ionosphere	51.14	51.14	51.14	50.83	51.06	51.06	51.14	50.83
Pima	50.44	50.44	50.58	50.58	50.44	50.44	50.58	50.58
Sonar class	50.30	48.12	51.67	50.22	51.67	51.00	51.35	50.97
Mammographic	63.81	63.81	64.14	64.14	64.14	64.14	63.92	63.92
Bupa	50.44	50.44	51.09	51.09	50.44	50.44	-	-
Image Segmentation	72.44	70.12	72.00	72.56	72.21	71.0	70.56	69.20
SPECTF Heart	62.90	62.90	62.90	62.90	62.90	62.90	62.90	62.90
Wine	84.93	84.24	85.6	85.6	84.93	84.24	-	-

CONCLUSION

Interactive visual clustering methods allow a user to partition a data set into clusters that are appropriate for their tasks and interests through an efficient visualization model and it requires an effective Human-computer interaction. In this chapter, we obtained the reliable human-computer interaction through dimensionality reduction. Three different kinds of dimensionality reduction methods were compared. The performance of the three feature selection methods were compared with clustering of dataset using the whole set of features. The performance was measured with popular validity measure Rand Index.

From this comparative analysis, the study concludes some remarks:

- The results presented in this chapter show that in general the best index values for visual clustering through EWFS, OSFS, CSFA are always closer to or sometimes better than clustering with the whole set of features. Thus feature selection improves or retains the cluster quality.

- Since the number of features selected is less, the number of iterations in visual distance computation is reduced. This makes the whole clustering process to be reliable to the user.

- Since the non contributing features are eliminated, identification of the dominating dimensions for visual tuning is much easier, thus makes the α tuning process in VISTA to be effective.

- More importantly the feature selection method eases the Human-computer interaction.

- Among the three feature selection methods, OSFS is a very simple and doesn't require any additional algorithm. Since it is interactive technique, considered as flexible method.

- The EWFS is utilizing the clusters obtained by K-Means algorithm to select the features. The feature set obtained using EWFS is completely dependent on the clustering algorithm.

Table. 4. Homogeneity/Separation Comparison of EWFS, OSFS and CEFS with respect to Whole Features

Datasets	VISTA with Entire dimension		VISTA with Selected Features using EWFS		VISTA with Selected Features using OSFS		VISTA with Selected Features using CEFS	
	Best	*Avg*	*Best*	*Avg*	*Best*	*Avg*	*Best*	*Avg*
Hepatitis	0.4487	0.4311	0.3948	0.3787	0.4775	0.4694	0.3127	0.3127
Australian	0.4836	0.4836	0.4836	0.4836	0.4836	0.4836	0.4836	0.4836
Breast Cancer	0.2203	0.2203	0.2203	0.2203	0.2236	0.2203	0.2203	0.2203
Ionosphere	0.3725	0.3725	0.3814	0.3814	0.3776	0.3776	0.3814	0.3814
Pima	0.4894	0.4894	0.4991	0.4991	0.4894	0.4894	0.4991	0.4991
Sonar class	0.4146	0.4168	0.4774	0.4774	0.4674	0.4774	0.464	0.4774
Mammographic	0.4239	0.4239	0.2602	0.2602	0.2602	0.2602	0.2602	0.2602
Spam Base	0.7685	0.7601	0.7685	0.7601	0.7278	0.7278	0.7685	0.7601
Gamma	0.2276	0.2276	0.2276	0.2276	0.2276	0.2276	0.2276	0.2276
Bupa	0.2152	0.2152	0.0817	0.0817	0.2152	0.2152	-	-
Gene Expression Data	0.1350	0.1350	0.1350	0.1350	0.1211	0.1211	0.1350	0.1350
Web Log Data	0.2816	0.2816	0.2816	0.2816	0.2910	0.2910	0.2711	0.2711
Image Segmentation	0.2968	0.3010	0.3400	0.361	0.3511	0.3511	0.3407	0.3500
SPECTF Heart	0.4244	0.4244	0.4244	0.4244	0.4244	0.4244	0.4244	0.4244
Wine	0.3106	0.3106	0.3233	0.3233	0.3411	0.3411	-	-

FURTHER RESEARCH DIRECTION

Since VISTA require an efficient Human-computer interaction in finding the right clusters, techniques need to be introduced to improve the visualization model. And the identification of relevant features with different criteria needs future research.

ACKNOWLEDGMENT

The second author expresses his thanks to University Grants Commission for financial support (F-No. 34-105/2008, SR).

REFERENCES

Alagambigai, P., & Thangavel, K. (2009). Feature Selection for Visual Clustering, In *Proceedings of International Conference on Advances in Recent Technologies in Communication and Computing, IEEE Computer Society*, (pp.498-502).

Alagambigai, P., Thangavel, K., & Karthikeyani Vishalakshi, N. (2009). Entropy Weighting Feature Selection for Interactive Visual Clustering. In *Proceedings of 4th International Conference on Artificial Intelligence,* (pp. 545-557).

Blum, A. L., & Rivest, R. L. (1992). Training a 3-node neural networks is NP-complete. *Neural Networks*, (5): 117–127. doi:10.1016/S0893-6080(05)80010-3

Boudjeloud, L., & Poulet, F. (2005). Visual Interactive Evolutionary Algorithm for High Dimensional Data Clustering and Outlier Detection. In Carbonell, J. G., & Siekmann, J. (Eds.), *Advances in Knowledge Discovery and Data Mining* (pp. 426–431). Berlin: Springer Berlin. doi:10.1007/11430919_50

Chen, K., & Liu, L. (2004). VISTA - Validating and Refining Clusters via Visualization. *Information Visualization*, 4, 257–270. doi:10.1057/palgrave.ivs.9500076

Chen, K., & Liu, L. (2006). iVIBRATE: Interactive Visualization-Based Framework for Clustering Large Datasets. *ACM Transactions on Information Systems*, *24*, 245–294. doi:10.1145/1148020.1148024

Cook, D. R., Buja, A., Cabrea, J., & Harley, H. (1995). Grand Tour and Projection pursuit. *Journal of Computational and Graphical Statistics*, *23*, 155–172. doi:10.2307/1390844

DesJardins, M., MacGlashan, J., & Ferraioli, J. (2007). *Interactive Visual Clustering* (pp. 361–364). Intelligent User Interfaces.

Domeniconi, C., Papadopoulos, P., Gunopulos, D., & Ma, S. (2004). Subspace Clustering of High Dimensional Data. In *Proc. SIAM Int'l Conf. Data Mining*, (pp.31-35).

Dy, J. G., & Broadly, E. C. (2000). Interactive Visualization and Feature selection for Unsupervised Data. In *Proceedings of 6th ACM SIGKDD International Conference on Knowledge Discovery and data Mining*, (pp.360-364). New York: ACM Press.

Dy, J. G., & Broadly, E. C. (2004). Feature Selection for unsupervised learning. *Journal of Machine Learning Research*, *5*, 845–889.

Guha, G. Rastogi., R. & Shim, K. (1998). CURE: An efficient clustering algorithm for large databases. In *Proc. of the ACM SIGMOD*, (pp.73-84).

Hinnerburg, A., Keim, D., & Wawryniuk, M. (1999). HD-Eye: Visual Mining of High–Dimensional Data. *IEEE Computer Graphics and Applications*, *19*(5), 22–31. doi:10.1109/38.788795

Jain, A. K., Murty, M. N., & Flynn, P. J. (1999). Data Clustering: A Review. *ACM Computing Surveys*, 264–323. doi:10.1145/331499.331504

Jiang, D., Tang, C., & Zhang, A. (2004). Cluster analysis for gene expression data: a survey. *IEEE Transactions on Knowledge and Data Engineering*, *16*(11), 1370–1386. doi:10.1109/TKDE.2004.68

Jing, L., & Michael, K., Ng., & Huang, J. Z. (2007). An Entropy Weighting k-Means Algorithm for Subspace Clustering of High-Dimensional Sparse Data. *IEEE Transactions on Knowledge and Data Engineering*, *19*(8), 1026–1041. doi:10.1109/TKDE.2007.1048

Jouve, P., & Nicoloyannis, N. (2005). A filter feature selection method for clustering, In *ISMIS*, (pp. 583-593). Berlin: Springer.

Kandogan, E. (2001). Visualizing Multi-dimensional Clusters, Trends and outliers using star co-ordinates. In *Proceedings of ACM KDD*, (pp. 107-116).

Keim, D., & Ward, M. (2007). Visualization. In Berthold, M., & Hand, D. J. (Eds.), *Intelligent Data Analysis: An Introduction* (pp. 403–429). Berlin: Springer.

Keim, D. A. (2002). Information visualization and Visual Data mining. *IEEE Transactions on Visualization and Computer Graphics*, *7*(1), 1–8. doi:10.1109/2945.981847

Keim, D. A., Panse, C., Sips, M., & North, S. C. (2004). Visual data mining in large geospatial point sets. *IEEE Computer Graphics and Applications*, *24*, 36–44. doi:10.1109/MCG.2004.41

Kohavi, R., & John, G. H. (1997). Wrappers for Feature Subset Selection. *Artificial Intelligence*, *97*(1-2), 273–324. doi:10.1016/S0004-3702(97)00043-X

Merz, C. J., & Murphy, P. M. (1998). *UCI Repository of Machine Learning Databases*. Irvine, CA: University of California. Retrieved from http://www.ics.uci.eedu/~mlearn/

Sourina, O., & Liu, D. (2004). Visual interactive 3-dimensional clustering with implicit functions. *Proceedings. of the IEEE Conference on Cybernetics and Intelligent Systems, 1*(1-3), 382–386.

Thangavel, K., Alagambigai, P., & Devakumari, D. (2009). Improved Visual Clustering through Unsupervised Dimensionality Reduction, Goebel, R., Siekmann, J. & Wahlster, W. (Ed.), *Rough Sets, Fuzzy Sets, Data Mining and Granular Computing, (LNCS 5908)*, (pp. 439-446). Berlin: Springer.

Thuraisingham, B. (1999). *DataMining: Technologies, Techniques, Tools and Trends* (pp. 42–48). Boca Raton, FL: CRC press.

Tory, M., & Moller, T. (2004). Human Factors in Visualization Research. *IEEE Transactions on Visualization and Computer Graphics, 10*(1), 72–84. doi:10.1109/TVCG.2004.1260759

Vayshavsky, R., Gottlieb, A., Linial, M., & Horn, D. (2004). Noval Unsupervised Feature Filtering of Biological Data. In *Text Mining and Information Extraction* (pp. 1–7). Oxford, UK: Oxford University Press.

Wall, M., Rechtsteiner, A., & Rocha, L. (2003). Singular value Decomposition and Principal Component Analysis. In Berrar, D., Dubitzky, W., & Granzow, M. (Eds.), *A Practical approach to Microarray Data Analysis* (pp. 91–109). Amsterdam: Kluwer. doi:10.1007/0-306-47815-3_5

Wong, P. C. (1999). Visual Data Mining. *IEEE Computer Graphics and Applications, 19*(5), 20–21. doi:10.1109/MCG.1999.788794

KEY TERMS AND DEFINITIONS

Dimensionality Reduction: It is the process of identifying and removing as much as possible the irrelevant and redundant information.

Entropy Weighting Feature Selection: Entropy Weighting Feature Selection (EWFS) is a wrapper approach in which the relevant dimensions are obtained by identifying the weight entropy of dimensions during the automatic clustering process, for instance K-Means.

Feature Selection: Feature selection is a process that selects a subset of original features. The optimality of a feature subset is measured by an evaluation criterion.

Information Visualization: Visual representation of abstract nonspatial data.

Interactive Visual Clustering: Interactive clustering methods allow a user to partition a data set into clusters that are appropriate for their tasks and interests through visualization.

Outlier Score Based Feature Selection: Outlier Score based Feature Selection (OSFS) is a filter method which is independent of clustering algorithm where the relevant features are identified by exploring individual features of the given dataset in boxplot model. The features that have maximum outlier score are considered as irrelevant features and they are eliminated.

Subspace Clustering: The subspace clustering aims at finding clusters from subspaces of data instead of entire data space.

Chapter 5
Database Analysis with ANNs by Means of Graph Evolution

Daniel Rivero
University of A Coruña, Spain

Julián Dorado
University of A Coruña, Spain

Juan R. Rabuñal
University of A Coruña, Spain

Alejandro Pazos
University of A Coruña, Spain

ABSTRACT

Traditionally, the development of Artificial Neural Networks (ANNs) is a slow process guided by the expert knowledge. This expert usually has to test several architectures until he finds one suitable for solving a specific problem. This makes the development of ANNs a slow process in which the expert has to do much effort. This chapter describes a new method for the development of Artificial Neural Networks, so it becomes completely automated. Since ANNs are complex structures with very high connectivity, traditional algorithms are not suitable to represent them. For this reason, in this work graphs with high connectivity that represent ANNs are evolved. In order to measure the performance of the system and to compare the results with other ANN development methods by means of Evolutionary Computation (EC) techniques, several tests were performed with problems based on some of the most used test databases in Data Mining. These comparisons show that the system achieves good results that are not only comparable to those of the already existing techniques but, in most cases, improve them.

DOI: 10.4018/978-1-60960-102-7.ch005

INTRODUCTION

One of the most widely used techniques in Data Mining are Artificial Neural Networks (ANNs). They are very used in Data Mining because of their ability to solve problems related to different aspects such as classification, clustering or regression (Haykin, 1999). These systems are, due to their interesting characteristics, powerful techniques used by the researchers in different environments (Rabuñal, 2005).

ANNs are systems that try to emulate the behaviour of the nervous system. Therefore, as the biological nervous system is composed by a high number of neurons connected between them, an ANN is also composed by several artificial neurons with a high connectivity. Even each artificial neuron performs a very easy mathematical function with the inputs that it received from other neurons or from the environment, the result of a high number of neurons connected between them can be a very complicated function. In fact, ANNs are universal approximators: any mathematical function can be reproduced by means of using ANNs.

However, the development of ANNs is not an easy task. This process can be divided into two parts: architecture development and training and validation. The architecture development determines not only the number of neurons of the ANN, but also their connectivity. The training will determine the connection weights for such architecture. This second step is automatically performed by different training algorithms. However, the first step, architecture development, given that the architecture of the network depends on the problem to be solved, is usually performed by the use of a manual process, meaning that the expert has to test different architectures until he finds the one that returns the best results.

Therefore, if the expert wants to develop an ANN to solve a specific problem, he will have to design several networks and train several times each network (due to the stochastic nature of the training algorithms) in order to determine which one of these architectures is the best one. This is a slow process due to the fact that architecture determination is a manual process, although techniques for relatively automatic creation of ANNs have been recently developed.

This work presents a new technique that automatically develops ANNs, so that no human participation will be needed. This technique is a modification of the Genetic Programming (GP) algorithm in order to allow it to evolve graphs instead of trees.

BACKGROUND

Genetic Programming

GP (Koza, 92) is based on the evolution of a given population. Its working is similar to a GA. In this population, every individual represents a solution for a problem that is intended to be solved. The evolution is achieved by means of the selection of the best individuals – although the worst ones have also a little chance of being selected – and their mutual combination for creating new solutions. This process is developed using selection, crossover and mutation operators. After several generations, the population is expected to contain some good solutions for the problem.

The GP encoding for the solutions is tree-shaped, so the user must specify which are the terminals (leaves of the tree) and the functions (nodes that have children) for being used by the evolutionary algorithm in order to build complex expressions. These can be mathematical (including, for instance, arithmetical or trigonometric operators), logical (with Boolean or relational operators, among others) or other type of even more complex expressions.

The wide application of GP to various environments and its consequent success are due to its capability for being adapted to numerous different problems. Although the main and more direct application is the generation of mathematical expressions (Rivero, 2005), GP has been also used in others fields such as filter design (Rabuñal, 2003), knowledge extraction (Rabuñal, 2004), image processing (Rivero, 2004), etc.

Using Evolutionary Computation Techniques for the Development of ANNs

The development of ANNs has been widely treated with very different techniques in AI. The world of evolutionary algorithms is not an exception, and proof of it is the large amount of works that have been published is this aspect using several techniques (Nolfi, 2002; Cantú-Paz, 2005). These techniques follow the general strategy of an evolutionary algorithm: an initial population with different types of genotypes encoding also different parameters – commonly, the connection weights and/or the architecture of the network and/ or the learning rules – is randomly created. Such population is evaluated for determining the fitness of every individual. Subsequently, the population is repeatedly induced to evolve by means of different genetic operators (replication, crossover, mutation) until a certain termination parameter has been fulfilled (for instance, the achievement of an individual good enough or the accomplishment of a predetermined number of generations).

As a general rule, the field of ANN generation using evolutionary algorithms is divided into three main groups: evolution of weights, architectures and learning rules.

The evolution of weight starts from an ANN with an already determined topology. In this case, the problem to be solved is the training of the connection weights, attempting to minimise the network failure. Most of training algorithms, as backpropagation (BP) algorithm (Rumelhart, 1986), are based on gradient minimisation, which presents several drawbacks (Sutton, 1986). The main of these disadvantages is that, quite frequently, the algorithm gets stuck into a local minimum

of the fitness function and it is unable to reach a global minimum. One of the options for overcoming this situation is the use of an evolutionary algorithm, so the training process is done by means of the evolution of the connection weights within the environment defined by both, the network architecture, and the task to be solved. In such cases, the weights can be represented either as the concatenation of binary values or of real numbers on a genetic algorithm (GA) (Greenwood, 1997). The main disadvantage of this type of encoding is the permutation problem. This problem means that the order in which weights are taken at the vector might cause that equivalent networks might correspond to completely different chromosomes, making the crossover operator inefficient.

The evolution of architectures includes the generation of the topological structure. This means establishing the connectivity and the transfer function of each neuron. The network architecture is highly important for the successful application of the ANN, since the architecture has a very significant impact on the processing ability of the network. Therefore, the network design, traditionally performed by a human expert using trial and error techniques on a group of different architectures, is crucial. In order to develop ANN architectures by means of an evolutionary algorithm it is needed to choose how to encode the genotype of a given network for it to be used by the genetic operators.

At the first option, direct encoding, there is a one-to-one correspondence between every one of the genes and their subsequent phenotypes (Miller, 1989). The most typical encoding method consists of a matrix that represents an architecture where every element reveals the presence or absence of connection between two nodes (Alba, 1993). These types of encoding are generally quite simple and easy to implement. However, they also have a large amount of inconveniences such as scalability (Kitano, 1990), the incapability of encoding repeated structures, or permutation (Yao, 1998).

In comparison with direct encoding, there are some indirect encoding methods. In these methods, only some characteristics of the architecture are encoded in the chromosome and. These methods have several types of representation.

Firstly, the parametric representations represent the network as a group of parameters such as number of hidden layers, number of nodes for each layer, number of connections between two layers, etc (Harp, 1989). Although the parametric representation can reduce the length of the chromosome, the evolutionary algorithm performs the search within a restricted area in the search space representing all the possible architectures. Another non direct representation type is based on a representation system that uses the grammatical rules (Kitano, 1990). In this system, the network is represented by a group of rules, shaped as production rules that make a matrix that represents the network.

The growing methods represent another type of encoding. In this case, the genotype does not encode a network directly, but it contains a set of instructions for building up the phenotype. The genotype decoding consists on the execution of those instructions (Nolfi, 2002), which can include neuronal migrations, neuronal duplication or transformation, and neuronal differentiation.

Another important non-direct codification is based on the use of fractal subsets of a map. According to Merrill (1991), the fractal representation of the architectures is biologically more plausible than a representation with the shape of rules. Three parameters are used to specify each node in an architecture: a border code, an input coefficient and an output code.

One important characteristic to bear in mind is that all those methods evolve architectures, either alone (most commonly) or together with the weights. The transfer function for every node of the architecture is supposed to have been previously fixed by a human expert and is the same for all the nodes of the network –or at least, all the nodes of the same layer–, despite of the fact that such function has proved to have a significant impact on network performance (DasGupta, 1992). Only few methods that also induce the evolution of the transfer function have been developed (Hwang, 1997).

With regards to the evolution of the learning rule, there are several approaches (Turney, 1996), although most of them are only based on how learning can modify or guide the evolution and also on the relationship among the architecture and the connection weights. There are only few works focused on the evolution of the learning rule itself.

ANN DEVELOPMENT WITH GRAPH EVOLUTION

ANNs are very complex structures with a very high connectivity. This is very complicated to represent in traditional codification schemes. Even previous works show that ANNs can be represented as trees and therefore the GP algorithm can be used to automatically evolve ANNs, the representation is still far from the representation of the ANNs: as a highly connected graph.

This is the reason why this work proposes a method that can perform the automatic development of graphs by means of an Evolutionary Algorithm (EA). This work is a step forward in the codification types, since traditional GAs have a binary or real-value string as codification, and GP has a tree-shaped codification. This work goes further and proposes an EA with a codification with the shape of graphs.

Since traditional tree codification used in GP is very similar to graphs, this new graph-based EA is based on GP. The difference is the codification, and, therefore, some genetic operators had to be modified too in order to allow them to work with graphs instead of trees. The operators were changed in this way:

- The creation algorithm must allow the creation of graphs. This means that, at the moment of the creation of a node's child, this algorithm must allow not only the creation of this node, but also a link to an existing one in the same graph, without making cycles inside the graph.

- The crossover algorithm must allow the crossover of graphs. This algorithm works very similar to the existing one for trees, i.e. a node is chosen on each individual to change the whole subgraph it represents to the other individual. Special care has to be taken with graphs, because before the crossover there may be links from outside this subgraph to any nodes on it. In this case, after the crossover these links are updated and changed to point to random nodes in the new subgraph.

- The mutation algorithm has been changed too, and also works very similar to the GP tree-based mutation algorithm. A node is chosen from the individual and its subgraph is deleted and replaced with a new one. Before the mutation occurs, there may be nodes in the individual pointing to other nodes in the subgraph. These links are updated and made to point to random nodes in the new subgraph.

With these modifications, the genetic operators allow the evolution of graphs. However, these algorithms must also follow two common restrictions in GP: typing and maximum height. The GP typing property (Montana, 1995) means that each node will have a type and will also provide which type will have each of its children. This property provides the ability of developing structures that follow a specific grammar. The maximum height is a restriction of the complexity of the graph, not allowing the creation of very large graphs that could lead to obtaining too big ANNs with over-fitting problems. These two restrictions are applied on the genetic operators making the resulting graphs follow these restrictions.

In order to allow this algorithm to evolve graphs, it is necessary to specify the terminal and function sets, i.e., the nodes that can be part of the graph. With them, the evolutionary system must be able to build correct graphs that represent ANNs. For each node, the user has to specify its type, the number of children and the types of its children. Therefore, the first thing to do is to define the types that are going to be used. These types are the following:

- TNET. This type identifies the network. It is only used in the root of the graph.
- TNEURON. This type identifies a node (or sub-graph) as a neuron, whether it is hidden, ouput or input.
- TREAL. This type identifies a node (or sub-graph) as a real value. It is used to indicate the value of the connection weights: a node that has this type will be either a floating point constant or an arithmetical sub-graph that defines a real value.

With just these three types, it is now possible to build networks. However, the set of terminals and functions is more complicated. The description is the following:

- ANN. Node that defines the network. It appears only at the root of the graph and has the same number of descendants as the network expected outputs, each of them a neuron (therefore, each of them must have a TNEURON type).
- n-Neuron. Node that identifies a neuron with n inputs. This node has 2*n descendants. The first n descendants will be other neurons, either input or hidden ones (with TNEURON type). The second n descendants will be arithmetical sub-graphs. These sub-graphs represent real values (with TREAL type). These values corre-

Table 1. Summary of the operators to be used in the graph

Node	Type	Num. Children	Children type
ANN	TNET	Num. outputs	TNEURON,..., TNEURON
n-Neuron	TNEURON	2*n	TNEURON,..., TNEURON REAL,..., TREAL
n-Input	TNEURON	0	-
+,-,*,%	TREAL	2	TREAL
[-4.4]	TREAL	0	-

spond to values of the respective connection weights of the input neurons – the first descendants – of this neuron.

- n-Input neuron. Nodes that define an input neuron which receives its activation value from the input variable n. These nodes have a TNEURON type, and they do not have any children.
- Finally, the arithmetic operator set {+,-,*,%}, where % stands for the operation of protected division (returns 1 if the divisor is 0). This set generates the values of connection weights: sub-graphs of the n-Neuron nodes that perform operations among constants in order to obtain new values. Since real values are also needed for such operations, they have to be introduced by means of the addition of random constants to the terminal set in the range [-4, 4] as recommended in previous works (Fahlman, 1988).

An overview of the operators used here can be seen on Table 1.

The execution of the graph performs the creation of the ANN: each n-Neuron node will make the creation of one neuron and links to connected neurons, each n-Input node connects an input neuron to another neuron, and an arithmetical subgraph sets the value of a weight. An example of this can be seen on Figure. 1.

It is important to keep in mind that, during the creation of a neuron and in the process of creating

or referencing children neurons, a neuron can appear several times as input of another neuron. In this case, a new input connection from that neuron to the other is not established, but instead the existing connection weight is modified and the weight value of the new connection is added. Therefore, a common situation is that an "n-Neuron" operator is not referencing n different neurons, but instead it is possible to have neurons repeated, especially if n has a high value. It is necessary to limit the n value, to determine which is the maximum number of inputs that a neuron can have. A high value will surely make the described effect: an effective use will not be made of all those input, but instead some of them will be repeated. However, a high value also guarantees a possibly high number of inputs.

Once a graph is evaluated, the genotype is turned into a phenotype, i.e., a network with fixed weight values that can now be evaluated instead of having to be trained. The evolutionary process requires the assignment of a fitness value to each genotype. This fitness value will be the result of the evaluation of the network with the pattern set that represents the problem. In this case, the result of this evaluation is the Mean Square Error (MSE) of the difference between the network outputs and the desired ones.

However, this error value which is taken as fitness value has been modified to make the system generate simple networks. For that reason, it has been penalized with a value which is added to this error. This value is a penalization value multiplied by the number of neurons of the network. In this

Figure 1. Graph and its resulting network

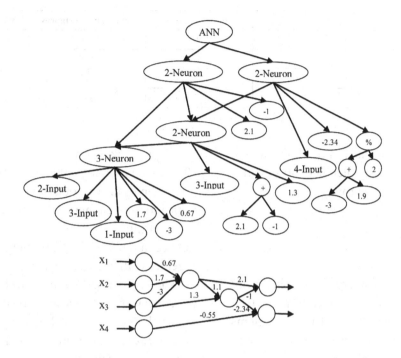

way, and given that the evolutionary system has been designed to minimize a value error, if a value is added to the fitness value, it will cause a bigger network to obtain a worse fitness value. This means that the appearance of simple networks is preferred because this added penalization value is proportional to the number of ANN neurons. The final fitness calculus is the following:

$$fitness = MSE + N*P$$

where MSE is the mean square error of the network on the training pattern set, N is the number of neurons of the network, and P is the penalization value to the number of neurons, with a low value. By giving a worse fitness value to a network with more neurons but with identical functioning, the system looks for simple systems with few neurons.

The system described in this work has two different parameter sets. Firstly, those parameters that affect the behaviour of the GP algorithm: crossover rate, mutation probability, etc. Secondly, those parameters of the system that limit the complexity of the resulting networks returned by the system. There are three parameters in this last set:

- Graph height. Although this parameter can be seen as a GP parameter, it has considerable influence on the system behaviour by limitating the deepness of the graphs generated by the system. Therefore, it limits the size of the resulting networks.
- Maximum number of inputs for each neuron. This parameter sets the maximum value of n for the n-Neuron nodes, where n stands for the number of inputs that neuron will have. The function set will be added with nodes going from 2-Neuron until n-Neuron.
- Penalization to the number of neurons. As explained above, this parameter establish-

Table 2. Summary of the problems to be solved

	Number of inputs	Number of instances	Number of outputs
Breast Cancer	9	699	1
Iris Flower	4	150	3
Heart Cleveland	26	303	1
Ionosphere	34	351	1

es a penalization and as a result the system tries to develop simpler networks with a lower number of neurons.

RESULTS

This technique has been used for solving problems of different complexity taken from the UCI (Asuncion & Newman, 2007). All these problems are knowledge-extraction problems from databases where, taking certain features as a basis, it is intended to perform a prediction about another attribute of the database. A small summary of the problems to be solved can be seen at Table 2.

Several experiments have been performed in order to evaluate the system performance. The values taken for the parameters at these experiments were the following:

• Population size: 1000 individuals.
• Crossover rate: 95%
• Mutation probability: 4%
• Selection algorithm: 2-individual tournament.
• Graph maximum height: 5
• Maximum inputs for each neuron: 9

Table 3 shows a comparison of the results obtained for different penalization values. For these experiments, the databases values have been normalized between 0 and 1 and the patterns divided into two parts for each problem, taking the 70% of the database for training and using the remaining 30% for validation purposes.

The penalization values range from very high (0.1) to very small (0.00001 or 0). High values only enables the creation of very small networks with a subsequent high error, and low values lead to overfitting problem. This overfitting can be noticed at the table in the training error decrease together with a test error increase.

The number of neurons as well as of connections that were obtained at the resulting networks is also shown in Table 2. Logically, such number is higher as the penalization decreases. The results correspond to the MSE obtained after both, the training and the validation of every problem. As it can be observed, the results clearly prove that the problems have been satisfactorily solved and, as far as penalization parameter is concerned, low values are preferred for the creation of networks. These low values in the penalization parameter allow the creation of networks large enough for solving the problem, avoiding overfitting, although it should be changed for every problem.

This table also shows that the networks obtained have a low number of neurons and connections. Obviously, the number of neurons and connections is higher as the penalization decreases.

In order to evaluate its performance, the system presented here has been compared with other ANN generation and training methods. In these new experiments, the parameters described above were used, as well as a penalization of 0.00001.

When comparing classification algorithms, the most used method is cross validation (Stone, 1978) for estimating the accuracy of the algorithms, and then using t-tests to confirm if the results are significantly different. In the cross validation method,

Table 3. Comparison of the results with different penalization values

		0.1	0.01	0.001	0.0001	0.00001	0
Breast Cancer	Neurons	1.8	2.05	3.95	7.35	9.6	8.95
	Connections	7.85	8.5	16.95	31.95	40.45	37.15
	Training	0.0706	0.0214	0.0200	0.0191	0.0167	0.0181
	Validation	0.0316	0.0129	0.0126	0.0131	**0.0122**	**0.0122**
Iris Flower	Neurons	3	3.55	11.25	22.15	30.4	30
	Connections	8.05	8.9	32.65	56.95	83.56	81.35
	Training	0.0825	0.0748	0.0457	0.0283	0.0280	0.0306
	Validation	0.0904	0.0813	0.0515	0.0305	**0.0283**	0.0321
Heart Cleveland	Neurons	1	1.05	4.2	5.95	9.4	10.05
	Connections	4.5	5.05	19.2	27.95	42.05	45.6
	Training	0.1123	0.1114	0.0929	0.0858	0.0832	0.0844
	Validation	0.1467	0.1439	0.1408	0.1399	0.1402	**0.1384**
Ionosphere	Neurons	1	2	7.1	13.05	17.35	16
	Connections	4.45	9.7	38.45	62.3	80.9	75.7
	Training	0.119074	0.083277	0.053061	0.0503	0.0457	0.0449
	Validation	0.116165	0.092259	0.074564	0.0698	0.0699	**0.0670**

the data set D is divided into k non overlapping sets D_1, ..., D_k (k-fold cross validation). In each i iteration (that varies from 1 to k), the algorithm trains with the $D\backslash D_i$ set and a test is carried out in D_i. However, some studies have shown that the comparison of algorithms using these t-tests in cross validation leads to what is known as type I error (Herrera, 2004).

In (Dietterich, 1998) the performance of the k-fold cross validation method was analyzed, combined with the use of a t-test. In this work, it was proposed to modify the used statistic and it was justified that it is more effective to do k/2 executions of a 2-fold cross validation test, with different permutations of the data, than performing a k-fold cross validation test. As a solution between test accuracy and calculation time, it was proposed to perform 5 executions of a cross validation test with k=2, resulting in the name 5x2cv. In each one of the 5 iterations, the data is divided randomly into two halves. One half is taken as input of the algorithm, and the other one is used to test the final solution, meaning that

there are 10 different tests (5 iterations, 2 results for each one) (Herrera, 2004).

In (Cantú-Paz, 2005) the 5x2cv method is used to compare different techniques based on evolutionary methods in order to generate and train ANNs. In that work, the results that are presented are the arithmetic means of the accuracies obtained in each one of the 10 results generated by this method. These values are taken as basis for comparing the technique described in this work with other well-known ones. Each one of these 10 test values were obtained after the training with the method described in this work.

That work also shows the average times needed to achieve the results. Not having the same processor that was used, the computational effort needed for achieving the results can be estimated. This effort represents the number of times that the pattern file was evaluated. The computational effort for every technique can be measured using the population size, the number of generations, the number of times that the BP algorithm was applied, etc. This calculation var-

Table 4. Architectures used

	Inputs	Hidden	Outputs	BP Epochs
Breast Cancer	9	5	1	20
Iris Flower	4	5	3	80
Heart Cleveland	26	5	1	40
Ionosphere	34	10	1	40

ies for every algorithm used. All the techniques that are compared with the work are related to the use of evolutionary algorithms for ANN design. Five iterations of a 5-fold crossed validation test were performed in all these techniques in order to evaluate the precision of the networks. These techniques are the following:

- Connectivity Matrix.
- Pruning.
- Finding network parameters.
- Graph-rewriting grammar.

In all these techniques, in order to evaluate the accuracy of each network generated by any of these methods, 5 iterations of a 5-fold cross validation test are performed, which have a notable influence on the computational effort needed to achieve the results presented.

The connectivity matrix technique is based on representing the topology of a network as a binary matrix: the element (i,j) of the matrix has a value of 1 if a connection exists between i and j, and zero if there is no connection. A genetic algorithm with binary codification can be easily used because the chromosome is easily obtained by linking the matrix rows together (Belew, 1991). In this case, the number of hidden neurons indicated in Table 4 is used, and connections have been allowed between inputs and outputs, meaning that the length of the chromosomes is l = (hidden + outputs)*inputs + hidden*outputs. A multipoint crossover was used with a probability of 1.0 with l/10 crossover points and a mutation rate of 1/l. The population had a size of individuals with a

minimum of 20. The algorithm was stopped after 5 generations without improving on the best solution or if a maximum of 50 generations was achieved.

The pruning technique is based on a representation similar to the previous one. However, the method is different. It begins with a totally connected network (Reed, 1993), which is trained by means of the BP algorithm according to the parameters in Table 4. When this trained network is obtained, the evolutionary algorithm is executed. The evaluation function of each individual consists on deleting from the previously trained network those weights whose value in the connectivity matrix is equal to 0. The resulting ANN is evaluated with the training set, with no further training. The networks begun with the topologies shown in Table 4, with the same configuration of parameters used in the previous case.

The finding of the network parameters is a different approach because in this case an evolutionary algorithm is used to find the general designing and training parameters of the networks (Belew, 1991; Marshall, 1991). In this case, these parameters are the number of hidden neurons, the BP algorithm parameters, and the initial interval of the weights. The chromosome's longitude was 36 bits, divided in the following way:

- 5 bits for the learning rate and the coefficient β of the activation function, in the [0,1] interval.
- 5 bits for the number of hidden neurons, in the [0,31] interval.
- 6 bits for the number of BP epochs.

Table 5. Parameters of the techniques used for the comparisons

	Matrix	Pruning	Parameters	Grammar
Chromosome length (L)	N	N	36	256
Population size	⌊3√L⌋	⌊3√L⌋	25	64
Crossover points	L/10	L/10	2	L/10
Mutation rate	1/L	1/L	0.04	0.004

N = (hidden+output)*input + output*hidden

- 20 bits for the upper and lower values of the initial weights interval (10 bits for each value), and their intervals were [-10, 0] and [0, 10] respectively.

The evaluation of an individual consists on the construction of the network, its initialization and its training according to the parameters. The population had 25 individuals and was randomly initialized. The algorithm used a two-point crossover with a probability of 1.0 and a mutation rate of 0.04. As in the rest of the experiments, a two-individual tournament selection algorithm without replacements was used and the execution was stopped after 5 generations with no change in the best solution or after having reached a limit of 50 generations.

Finally, the graph-rewriting grammar (Kitano, 1990) consists on a connectivity matrix which represents the network. As opposed to the previous cases, the matrix is not codified directly in the chromosome, but instead a grammar is used to generate the matrix. The chromosome only has rules which turn each element of the matrix into sub-matrixes with size 2x2. In this grammar, there are 16 terminal symbols that are matrices with size 2x2, and 16 non-terminal symbols. The rules have the n→m form, where n is one of the non-terminal symbols, and m is a non-terminal 2x2 matrix. There is a starting symbol and the number of steps is determined by the user.

The chromosome contains the 16 rules in the following manner: it contains the 16 right sides of the rules because the left side is implicit in the

position of the rule. To evaluate the fitness of an individual, the rules are decodified and a connectivity matrix is constructed by means of the same rules. The network, which is trained by means of BP, is generated from this matrix.

For the application in these problems, the number of steps is limited to 8, meaning that the results are networks with a maximum number of 256 elements. The size of the chromosome, therefore, is 256 bits (4 2x2 binary matrices for each one of the 16 rules). The population size is 64 individuals, with a multi-point crossover with a probability of 1.0 and 1/10 crossover points and a mutation rate of 0.004. The algorithm was stopped after 5 generations with no improvement in the best individual or after 50 generations.

Table 5 shows the parameter configuration used by these techniques. The execution was stopped after 5 generations with no improvement or after 50 total generations.

The results obtained with these 4 methods, in comparison with the method described in this work, can be seen in Table 6. In this table, each square corresponds to a particular problem with a particular technique. Three different values are shown: on the left, the accuracy value obtained in (Cantú-Paz, 2005); below, the computational effort needed to obtain that value with that particular technique; and on the right side, the value of the accuracy obtained with the presently described technique and corresponding to the result obtained with that computational effort value. If the computational effort needed for each technique is lower than 2,000,000 fitness function execu-

Table 6. Comparison with other methods

	Matrix		Pruning		Parameters		Grammar	
Breast Cancer	96.77	96.27	96.31	95.79	96.69	96.27	96.71	96.31
	92000		4620		100000		300000	
Iris Flower	92.40	95.49	92.40	81.58	91.73	95.52	92.93	95.66
	320000		4080		400000		1200000	
Heart Cleveland	76.78	81.11	89.50	78.28	65.89	81.05	72.8	80.97
	304000		7640		200000		600000	
Ionosphere	87.06	88.34	83.66	82.37	85.58	87.81	88.03	88.36
	464000		11640		200000		600000	
Average	88.25	90.30	90.46	84.50	84.97	90.16	87.61	90.32

tions, the accuracy value shown by the technique described in this work will be the one that corresponds to that effort. However, if the effort is greater, the shown accuracy value will correspond to the value obtained after 2,000,000 fitness function executions.

This table also shows a small overfitting problem. This is due to the fact that the system has been left to training up to a certain number of fitness function evaluations. This usually leads to overfitting the training set when it keeps training for a long time.

CONCLUSION

This work presents a new technique that allows the evolution of graphs based on GP. In order to adapt GP for graph evolution, modifications were done in the creation, crossover and mutation operators. With these modifications, the system can evolve any kind of graphs with the nodes specified by the user.

In this chapter, this graph evolution system was used to automatically evolve ANNs. These are very complex structures with very high connectivity and therefore their codification with the shape of graphs seemed to be suitable. Moreover, this system does not allow only the obtaining of ANNs, but also their simplification. The adding

of a penalization parameter forces the system to look for simple networks. Results show that the networks obtained have a low number of neurons and connections.

The system described in this chapter was also compared with other systems in order to evaluate its performance. In this comparison, the 5x2cv algorithm was used, and this system was compared with other ANN generation and training systems. Results show that the performance of the system described here is as good as the rest of the techniques, and better in many cases.

FUTURE TRENDS

Once this system is described and tested, new research lines are open.

First, a future line of works in this area could be the study of the system parameters in order to evaluate their impact on the results from different problems.

Another interesting research line consists on the integration of a constant optimization system in the evolutionary model. After the execution of some generations of the evolutionary graph development system, the constant optimisation system could be run in order to change the values of the constants of the system. After this optimisation is done, the evolutionary system keeps running for another certain number of generations until the optimisation system is executed again. A GA could be used as this optimisation system. This whole hybrid system could be seen somehow similar to a Lamarckian strategy. As the graph evolution system is being used for ANN generation, this constant optimisation would be, in practice, a training of the ANNs being generated.

ACKNOWLEDGMENT

The development of the experiments of this paper was made thanks to the support of the "Centro de Supercomputación de Galicia (CESGA)".

The Cleveland heart disease database was available thanks to Robert Detrano, M.D., Ph.D., V.A. Medical Center, Long Beach and Cleveland Clinic Foundation.

REFERENCES

Alba, E., Aldana, J. F., & Troya, J. M. (1993). Fully automatic ANN design: A genetic approach. In *Proc. Int. Workshop Artificial Neural Networks (IWANN'93),* (LNCS 686, pp. 399-404). Berlin: Springer-Verlag.

Asuncion, A., & Newman, D. J. (2007). *UCI Machine Learning Repository.* Irvine, CA: University of California, School of Information and Computer Science.

Belew, R., McInerney, J., & Schraudolph, N. (1991). Evolving networks: using the genetic algorithm with connectionist learning. In *Proceedings of the Second Artificial Life Conference,* (pp. 511-547). New York: Addison-Wesley.

Cantú-Paz, E., & Kamath, C. (2005). An Empirical Comparison of Combinatios of Evolutionary Algorithms and Neural Networks for Classification Problems. *IEEE Transactions on Systems, Man, and Cybernetics. Part B, Cybernetics,* 915–927. doi:10.1109/TSMCB.2005.847740

DasGupta, B. & Schnitger, G. (1992). *Efficient approximation with neural networks: A comparison of gate functions.* Dep. Comput. Sci., Pennsylvania State Univ., University Park, Tech. Rep.

Dietterich, T. G. (1998). Approximate statistical tests for comparing supervised classification learning algorithms. *Neural Computation, 10*(7), 1895–1924. doi:10.1162/089976698300017197

Fahlman, S. (1988). Faster-learning variantions of back-propagation: An empirical study. In D.S. Touretzky, G. Hinton, T. Sejnowski, (Eds.), *Proceedings of the 1988 Connectionist Models Summer School,* (pp. 38-51). San Mateo, CA: Morgan Kaufmann.

Greenwood, G. W. (1997). Training partially recurrent neural networks using evolutionary strategies. *IEEE Transactions on Speech and Audio Processing, 5,* 192–194. doi:10.1109/89.554781

Harp, S. A., Samad, T., & Guha, A. (1989) Toward the genetic synthesis of neural networks. In J.D. Schafer, (Ed.), *Proc. 3rd Int. Conf. Genetic Algorithms and Their Applications,* (pp. 360-369). San Mateo, CA: Morgan Kaufmann.

Haykin, S. (1999). *Neural Networks* (2nd ed.). Englewood Cliffs, NJ: Prentice Hall.

Herrera, F., Hervás, C., Otero, J., & Sánchez, L. (2004). Un estudio empírico preliminar sobre los tests estadísticos más habituales en el aprendizaje automático. In Giraldez, R., Riquelme, J. C., & Aguilar, J. S. (Eds.), *Tendencias de la Minería de Datos en España, Red Española de Minería de Datos y Aprendizaje (TIC2002-11124-E)* (pp. 403–412).

Hwang, M. W., Choi, J. Y., & Park, J. (1997). Evolutionary projection neural networks. In *Proc. 1997 IEEE Int. Conf. Evolutionary Computation, ICEC'97*, (pp. 667-671).

Kim, J.-H., Choi, S.-S., & Moon, B.-R. (2005). Normalization for neural network in genetic search. In *Genetic and Evolutionary Computation Conference*, (pp. 1-10).

Kitano, H. (1990). Designing neural networks using genetic algorithms with graph generation system. *Complex Systems*, *4*, 461–476.

Koza, J. R. (1992). *Genetic Programming: On the Programming of Computers by Means of Natural Selection*. Cambridge, MA: MIT Press.

Marshall, S. J., & Harrison, R. F. (1991). Optimization and training of feedforward neural networks by genetic algorithms. In *Proceedings of the Second International Conference on Artificial Neural Networks and Genetic Algorithms*, (pp. 39-43). Berlin: Springer-Verlag.

Merrill, J. W. L., & Port, R. F. (1991). Fractally configured neural networks. *Neural Networks*, *4*(1), 53–60. doi:10.1016/0893-6080(91)90031-Y

Miller, G. F., Todd, P. M., & Hedge, S. U. (1989) Designing neural networks using genetic algorithms. In *Proceedings of the Third International Conference on Genetic algorithms*, (pp. 379-384). San Mateo, CA: Morgan Kaufmann.

Montana, D. J. (1995). Strongly typed genetic programming. *Evolutionary Computation*, *3*(2), 199–200. doi:10.1162/evco.1995.3.2.199

Nolfi, S., & Parisi, D. (2002). Evolution of Artificial Neural Networks. In *Handbook of brain theory and neural networks* (2nd ed., pp. 418–421). Cambridge, MA: MIT Press.

Rabuñal, J. R., & Dorado, J. (2005). *Artificial Neural Networks in Real-Life Applications*. Hershey, PA: Idea Group Inc.

Rabuñal, J. R., Dorado, J., Pazos, A., Pereira, J., & Rivero, D. (2004). A New Approach to the Extraction of ANN Rules and to Their Generalization Capacity Through GP. *Neural Computation*, *16*(7), 1483–1523. doi:10.1162/089976604323057461

Rabuñal, J.R., Dorado, J., Puertas, J., Pazos, A., Santos, A. & Rivero, D. (2003). Prediction and Modelling of the Rainfall-Runoff Transformation of a Typical Urban Basin using ANN and GP. *Applied Artificial Intelligence*.

Reed, R. (1993). Pruning algorithms – a survey. *IEEE Transactions on Neural Networks*, *4*(5), 740–747. doi:10.1109/72.248452

Rivero, D., Rabuñal, J. R., Dorado, J., & Pazos, A. (2004). Using Genetic Programming for Character Discrimination in Damaged Documents. In *Applications of Evolutionary Computing, EvoWorkshops2004: EvoBIO, EvoCOMNET, EvoHOT, EvoIASP, EvoMUSART, EvoSTOC (Conference proceedings)*, (pp. 349-358).

Rivero, D., Rabuñal, J. R., Dorado, J., & Pazos, A. (2005). *Time Series Forecast with Anticipation using Genetic Programming* (pp. 968–975). IWANN.

Rumelhart, D. E., Hinton, G. E., & Williams, R. J. (1986). Learning internal representations by error propagation. In Rumelhart, D. E., & McClelland, J. L. (Eds.), *Parallel Distributed Processing: Explorations in the Microstructures of Cognition* (pp. 318–362). Cambridge, MA: MIT Press.

Stone, M. (1978). Cross-validation: A review. *Matemastische Operationsforschung Statischen. Serie Statistics*, *9*, 127–139.

Sutton, R. S. (1986). Two problems with backpropagation and other steepest-descent learning procedure for networks. In *Proc. 8th Annual Conf. Cognitive Science Society*, (pp. 823-831). Hillsdale, NJ: Erlbaum.

Turney, P., Whitley, D., & Anderson, R. (1996). Special issue on the baldwinian effect. *Evolutionary Computation*, *4*(3), 213–329.

Yao, X. (1999). `Evolving artificial neural networks. *Proceedings of the IEEE*, *87*(9), 1423–1447. doi:10.1109/5.784219

Yao, X., & Liu, Y. (1998). Toward designing artificial neural networks by evolution. *Applied Mathematics and Computation*, *91*(1), 83–90. doi:10.1016/S0096-3003(97)10005-4

KEY TERMS AND DEFINITIONS

Area of the Search Space: Set of specific ranges or values of the input variables that constitute a subset of the search space.

Artificial Neural Networks: A network of many simple processors ("units" or "neurons") that imitates a biological neural network. The units are connected by unidirectional communication channels, which carry numeric data. Neural networks can be trained to find nonlinear relationships in data, and are used in applications such as robotics, speech recognition, signal processing or medical diagnosis.

Back-Propagation Algorithm: Learning algorithm of ANNs, based on minimising the error obtained from the comparison between the outputs that the network gives after the application of a set of network inputs and the outputs it should give (the desired outputs).

Data Mining: The application of analytical methods and tools to data for the purpose of identifying patterns, relationships or obtaining systems that perform useful tasks such as classification, prediction, estimation, or affinity grouping.

Evolutionary Computation: Solution approach guided by biological evolution, which begins with potential solution models, then iteratively applies algorithms to find the fittest models from the set to serve as inputs to the next iteration, ultimately leading to a model that best represents the data.

Genetic Programming: Machine learning technique that uses an evolutionary algorithm in order to optimise the population of computer programs according to a fitness function which determines the capability of a program for performing a given task.

Genotype: The representation of an individual on an entire collection of genes which the crossover and mutation operators are applied to.

Phenotype: Expression of the properties coded by the individual's genotype.

Population: Pool of individuals exhibiting equal or similar genome structures, which allows the application of genetic operators.

Search Space: Set of all possible situations of the problem that we want to solve could ever be in.

Chapter 6
An Optimal Categorization of Feature Selection Methods for Knowledge Discovery

Harleen Kaur
Hamdard University, India

Ritu Chauhan
Hamdard University, India

M. Afshar Alam
Hamdard University, India

ABSTRACT

With the continuous availability of massive experimental medical data has given impetus to a large effort in developing mathematical, statistical and computational intelligent techniques to infer models from medical databases. Feature selection has been an active research area in pattern recognition, statistics, and data mining communities. However, there have been relatively few studies on preprocessing data used as input for data mining systems in medical data. In this chapter, the authors focus on several feature selection methods as to their effectiveness in preprocessing input medical data. They evaluate several feature selection algorithms such as Mutual Information Feature Selection (MIFS), Fast Correlation-Based Filter (FCBF) and Stepwise Discriminant Analysis (STEPDISC) with machine learning algorithm naive Bayesian and Linear Discriminant analysis techniques. The experimental analysis of feature selection technique in medical databases has enable the authors to find small number of informative features leading to potential improvement in medical diagnosis by reducing the size of data set, eliminating irrelevant features, and decreasing the processing time.

DOI: 10.4018/978-1-60960-102-7.ch006

INTRODUCTION

Data mining is the task of discovering previously unknown, valid patterns and relationships in large datasets. Generally, each data mining task differs in the kind of knowledge it extracts and the kind of data representation it uses to convey the discovered knowledge. Data mining techniques has been applied to a variety of medical domains to improve medical decision making. The sheer number of data mining techniques has the ability to handle large associated medical datasets, which consist of hundreds or thousands of features. The large amount of features present in such datasets often causes problems for data miners because some of the features may be irrelevant to the data mining techniques used. To deal with irrelevant features data reduction techniques can be applied in many ways, by feature (or attribute) selection, by discretizing continuous feature-values, and by selecting instances. There are several benefits associated with removing irrelevant features, some of which include reducing the amount of data (i.e., features). The reduced factors are easier to handle while performing data mining, and is capable to analyze the important factors within the data.

However, the feature selection has been an active and fruitful field of research and development for decades in statistical pattern recognition (Mitra, Murthy, & Pal, 2002), machine learning (Liu, Motoda, & Yu, 2002; Robnik-Sikonja & Kononenko, 2003) and statistics (Hastie, Tibshirani, & Friedman, 2001; Miller, 2002). It plays a major role in data selection and preparation for data mining. Feature selection is the process of identifying and removing irrelevant and redundant information as much as possible. The irrelevant features can harm the quality of the results obtained from data mining techniques; it has proven that inclusion of irrelevant, redundant, and noisy attributes in the model building process can result in poor predictive performance as well as increased computation.

Moreover, the feature selection is widely used for selecting the most relevant subset of features from datasets according to some predefined criterion. The subset of variables is chosen from input variables by eliminating features with little or no predictive information. It is a preprocessing step to data mining which has proved effective in reducing dimensionality, removing irrelevant data, increasing learning accuracy, and improving comprehensibility in medical databases. Many methods have shown effective results to some extent in removing both irrelevant features and redundant features. Therefore, the removal of features should be done in a way that does not adversely impact the classification accuracy. The main issues in developing feature selection techniques are choosing a small feature set in order to reduce the cost and running time of a given system, as well as achieving an acceptably high recognition rate. The computational complexity of categorization increases rapidly with increasing numbers of objects in the training set, with increasing number of features, and increasing number of classes. For multi-class problems, a substantially sized training set and a substantial number of features is typically employed to provide sufficient information from which to differentiate amongst the multiple classes. Thus, multi-class problems are by nature generally computationally intensive. By reducing the number of features, advantages such as faster learning prediction, easier interpretation, and generalization are typically obtained.

Feature selection is a problem that has to be addressed in many areas, especially in data mining, artificial intelligence and machine learning. Machine learning has been one of the methods used in most of these data mining applications. It is widely acknowledged that about 80% of the resources in a majority of data mining applications are spent on cleaning and preprocessing the data. However, there have been relatively few studies on preprocessing data used as input in these data mining systems.

In this chapter, we deal with more specifically with several feature selection methods as to their effectiveness in preprocessing input medical data. The data collected in clinical studies were examined to determine the relevant features for predicting diabetes. We have conducted feature selection methods on diabetic datasets using the MIFS, FCBF and STEPDISC scheme and demonstrate how it works better than the single machine approach.

This chapter is organized as follows: Section 3, we discuss the related works. Section 4 discusses the existing feature selection approaches. Experimental analysis study is presented in section 5. Conclusions are presented in the last section. We shall now briefly review some of the existing feature selection approaches.

REVIEW OF FEATURE SELECTION APPROACHES

There are several studies on data mining and knowledge discovery as an interdisciplinary field for uncovering hidden and useful knowledge (Kim, Street, & Menczer, 2000). One of the challenges to effective data mining is how to handle immensely vast volumes of medical data. If the data is immensely large then the number of features to learning algorithms can make them very inefficient for computational reasons.

As previously mentioned, feature selection is a useful data mining tool for selecting sets of relevant features from medical datasets. Extracting knowledge from these health care databases can lead to discovery of trends and rules for later diagnostic purposes. The importance of feature selection in medical domain is found in Kononenko, Bratko, & Kukar (1998) and Kaur et al. (2006) worked in applied data mining techniques i.e. association rule mining in medical data items.

The profusion in data collection by hospitals and clinical laboratories in recent years has helped in the discovery of many disease associated factors,

such as diagnosing the factors related to patient's illness. In this context, Kaur and Wasan (2009) proposed experience management can be used for better diagnosis and disease management in view of the complexity. Thus, the complexity of data arrives as the number of irrelevant or redundant features exists in the medical datasets (i.e., features which do not contribute to the prediction of class labels). At this point, we can efficiently reduce the complex data by recognizing associated factors related with disease.

The performance of certain learning algorithms degrades in the presence of irrelevant features. In addition, irrelevant data may confuse algorithms making them to build inefficient classifiers while correlation between features sets which causes the redundancy of information and may result in the counter effect of over fitting. Therefore, it is more important to explore data and utilize independent features to train classifiers, rather than increase the number of features we use. Feature selection can reduce the dimensionality of data, so that important factors can be studied well for the hypothesis space and allows algorithms to operate faster and more effectively.

Feature selection in medical data mining is appreciable as the diagnosis of the disease could be done in this patient-care activity with minimum number of features while still maintaining or even enhancing accuracy (Abraham, Simha, & Iyengar, 2007). Pechinizkiy, has applied classification successfully for number of medical applications like localization of a primary tumor, prognostics of recurrence of breast cancer, diagnosis of thyroid diseases, and rheumatology (Richards, Rayward-Smith, Sonksen, Carey, & Weng, 2001). Statistical pattern recognition has been studied extensively by (Miller, 2002). Impressive performance gain by reducing the irrelevant features in feature selection has been studied (Langley, 1994; Liu & Motoda, 1998; Dy & Brodley, 2000; Dash, Liu, & Motoda, 1998). Moustakis and Charissis, surveyed the role of machine learning in medical decision making and provided an extensive literature review.

Although Feature Selection literature contains many papers, few feature selection algorithms that have appeared in the literature can be categorized in two classes, according to the type of information extracted from the training data and the induction algorithm (John, Kohavi, & Pfleger, 1994). However, we could only find a few studies related to medical diagnosis using data mining approaches. Several publications have reported performance improvements for such measures when feature selection algorithms are used. Detailed survey of feature selection method can be found in (Langley, 1994; Dash & Liu, 1997).

Recently, more attention has been received by feature selection because of enthusiastic research in data mining. Aha & Bankert, 1995, have considered the specific survey of forward and backward sequential feature selection algorithms and their variants. The feature selection algorithms for classification and clustering, comparing different algorithms with a categorizing framework based on different search strategies, evaluation criteria, and data mining tasks, reveals un attempted combinations, and provides guidelines in selecting feature selection algorithms with an integrated framework for intelligent feature selection has been proposed by (Liu & Yu, 2005). The new method that combines positive and negative category and feature set is constructed. Chi-square, correlation coefficient has being used for comparison in feature selection method by (Zheng, Srihari, & Srihari, 2003).One of the oldest algorithms used for selecting the relevant feature is branch and bound (Narendra & Fukunaga, 1977). The main idea of the algorithm is to select as few features as possible and to place a bound on the value of the evaluation criterion. The select as few features as possible and to place a bound on the value of the evaluation criterion. It starts with the whole set of features and removes one feature at each step. The bound is placed in order to make the search process faster. Branch and bound (BB) is used when the evaluation criterion is monotonous. (Krishnapuram, Harternink, Carin, & Figueiredo,

2004; Chen & Liu, 1999) has studied the best subset of features for prediction by reducing the number of features which are irrelevant or redundant ones. The irrelevant data decreases the speed and reduces the accuracy of mining algorithm. (Kirsopp & Shepperd, 2002) have also analyzed the application of feature subset selection to cost estimation reaching. This has led to the development of a variety of techniques for selecting an optimal subset of features from a larger set of possible features. Finding an optimal subset is usually intractable (Kohavi & John, 1997).

The interesting topic of feature selection for unsupervised learning (clustering) is a more complex issue, and research into this field is recently getting more attention in several communities (Varshavsky et al., 2006).

Recently, Dy and Brodley, 2000a, Devaney and Ram, 1997, Agrawal et al., 1998, have studied feature selection and clustering together with a single or unified criterion. Thus feature selection in unsupervised learning aims to find a good subset of features that forms high quality of clusters for a given number of clusters.

Recent advances in computing technology in terms of speed, cost, as well as access to tremendous amounts of computing power and the ability to process huge amounts of data in reasonable time has spurred increased interest in data mining applications to extract useful knowledge from data.

FEATURE SELECTION ALGORITHMS

The feature selection method is developed as an extension to the recently proposed maximum entropy discrimination (MED) framework. MED is described as a flexible (Bayesian) regularization approach that subsumes, e.g., support vector classification, regression and exponential family models. In general, feature selection algorithms fall into categories

1. the filter approach and
2. the wrapper approach
3. Embedded approach (Kohavi & John, 1997), (Liu & Setiono, 1996).

The filter model relies on general characteristics of the training data to select predictive features (i.e., features highly correlated to the target class) without involving any mining algorithm (Duch, 2006). The assessments of features are based on independent general characteristics of the data. Filter methods are preprocessing methods which attempt to assess the merits of features from the data, ignoring the effects of the selected feature subset on the performance of the learning algorithm by computing the correlation.

Some filter methods are based on an attempt to immediately derive non redundant and relevant features for the task at hand (e.g., for prediction of the classes) (Yu & Liu, 2004). Filter techniques are computationally simple, fast and can easily handle very high-dimensional datasets. They are independent of the classifier so they need to perform only once with different classifiers. Filter methods are independent of the classification algorithm. Among the pioneering filter methods, and very much cited, are focused (Almuallim & Dietterich, 1991) it searches for all possible feature subsets, but this is applicable to only few attributes and Relief is used to compute ranking score of every feature (Kira & Rendell, 1992).

The wrapper model uses the predictive accuracy of a predetermined mining algorithm to give the quality of a selected feature subset, generally producing features better suited to the classification task. It generally searches for features better suited to the mining algorithm, aiming to improve mining performance, but it also is more computationally expensive (Langley, 1994; Kohavi & John, 1997) than filter models. These methods assess subsets of variables according to their usefulness to a given predictor. They conduct a search for a good subset by using the learning algorithm as part of the evaluation function. Chen et al., 2005

has presented the application of feature selection using wrappers to the problem of cost estimation. However, it is computationally expensive for high-dimensional data (Blum & Langley, 1997).

Embedded methods: they perform variable selection as part of the learning procedure and are usually specific to given learning machines. Examples are classification trees, regularization techniques (e.g. lasso). Embedded techniques are specific for given learning algorithm and search for an optimal subset of features, which are in built into classifier. They are less computationally expensive.

There are various ways to conduct feature selection. We introduce some often used methods conducted by analyzing the statistical properties of the data.. There are different ways to implement feature selection, depending on the type of data. In this chapter, we have evaluated feature selection techniques such as Fast-Correlation Based Filter (FCBF), Mutual information feature selection (MIFS) and Stepwise Discriminant Analysis (SDA).

In Fast correlation based filtering technique (FCBF) (Yu & Liu, 2003) is the irrelevant features are identified and filtered out. The FCBF (Fast Correlation-Based Filter) algorithm consists of two steps, first features are ranked by relevance which is computed as the symmetric uncertainty with respect to target attribute; it also discards the irrelevant features which have score below defined threshold. The second step is called redundant analysis in which the features are identified using an approximate Markov blanket configured to identify for a given candidate feature whether any other feature is both

i. More correlated with the set of classes than the candidate feature and
ii. More correlated with the candidate feature than with the set of classes.

If both conditions are satisfied, then the candidate feature is identified as a redundant feature and is filtered out. The correlation factor is used to measure the similarity between the relevant and irrelevant factors. For feature X with values x_i and classes Y with values y_i are treated as random variables. The linear coefficient is defined as:

$$P(X,Y) = \frac{\sum_i \left(xi - \overline{xi} \right)\left(yi - \overline{yi} \right)}{\sqrt{\sum_i \left(xi - \overline{xi} \right)^2 \sum_i \left(yi - \overline{yi} \right)^2}}$$

where, X and Y are linearly dependent if (X, Y) is equal to ± 1; if P takes the value +1 or -1 then the variables are completely correlated. If the value of correlation is zero then they are completely uncorrelated.

Stepwise discriminant analysis is the feature selection technique to find the relevant subset with determination of addition and removal of feature (Afifi & Azen, 1972). In this process the significance level of each feature is found with analysis of discriminant function. Stepwise selection begins with no variables in the model. The initial variable is then paired with each of the other independent variables one at a time; the success is measured with discriminant until the rate of discrimination improves. In the stepwise manner it founds the best discriminatory power. The discriminant function is calculated with Mahalanobis D2 and Rao's V distance function.

Mutual information feature selection (MIFS) (Battiti, 1992) is the quantity to measure mutual dependencies in between two random features. It maximizes the mutual information between the selected features and the classes, while minimizing the interdependence among the selected features. For columns that contain discrete and discretized data entropy measured is used.

The mutual information between two random variables can be specified as I (M;N) between the set of feature values M and the set of classes N. I

(M;N) measures the interdependence between two random variables M and N. It can be computed as follows:

$$I \left(M; N \right) = H \left(N \right) - H \left(N \mid M \right)$$

The entropy H (N) measures the degree of uncertainty entailed by the set of classes N, and can be computed as

$$H \left(N \right) = -\sum_{n \varepsilon N} p(n) \log p(n)$$

The remaining entropy in between M and N is measured as

$$H \left(N \mid M \right) = -\sum_{n \varepsilon N} \sum_{m \varepsilon M} p(m, n) \log p(n \mid m)$$

The mutual information in between the two discretizied random features are defined as

$$I \left(M; N \right) = \sum_{n \varepsilon N} \cdot \sum_{m \varepsilon N} \cdot p(m,n) \times \log \frac{p(m, n)}{p(m)p(n)}$$

If the data is continuous random the mutual information is defined as

$$I \left(M; N \right) = \int_{n \varepsilon N} \int_{m \varepsilon M} p(m,n) \times \log \frac{p(m, n)}{p(m)p(n)} \, dm \, dn$$

The drawback of the MIFS algorithm is that it does not take into consideration the interaction between features. It has been proved that choosing features individually does not lead to an optimal solution.

RESULTS

Data mining technology has become an essential instrument for medical research and hospital Management. Numerous data mining techniques are applied in medical databases to improve medical decision making. Diabetes affects between 2% and 4% of the global population (up to 10% in the over 65 age group), and its avoidance and effective treatment are undoubtedly crucial public health and health economics issues in the 21st century. There has been extensive work on diabetic registries for a variety of purposes. These databases are extremely large and have proved beneficial in diabetic care. Diabetes is a disease that can cause complications such as blindness, amputation and also in extreme cases causes cardiovascular death. So, the challenge for the physicians is to know which factors can prove beneficial for diabetic care.

Evaluation Techniques

The aim of this research was to identify significant factors influencing diabetes control, by applying feature selection in diabetic care system to improve classification and knowledge discovery. The classification models can be used to determine individuals in the population with poor diabetes control status based on physiological and examination factors.

The study focuses on feature selection techniques to develop models capable of predicting qualified medical opinions. The techniques used are Fast-Correlation Based Filter (FCBF), Mutual information feature selection (MIFS), and Stepwise discriminant analysis (STEPDISC) filtering techniques. The models are compared in terms of their performances with significant classifier. Moreover each model reveals specific input variables which are considered significant. In, this study we compare the effectiveness of different feature sets chosen by each technique are tested with two different and well-known types of

classifiers: a probabilistic classifier (naive Bayes) and linear discriminant analysis. These algorithms have been selected because they represent different approaches to learning and for their long standing tradition in classification studies. As stated previously, Feature Selection can be grouped into filter or wrapper depending on whether the classifier is used to find the feature subset.

In this chapter for the filter model, we have used consistency and correlation measures; for the wrapper-method, standard classifiers have been applied: Naive Bayes, to find the best suitable technique for diabetic care in feature selection.

The Naïve Bayes technique depends on the famous Bayesian approach following a simple, clear and fast classifier (Witten & Frank, 2005). It has been called 'Naïve' due to the fact that it assumes mutually independent attributes. The data in Naïve Bayes is preprocessed to find the most dependent categories. This method has been used in many areas to represent, utilize, and learn the probabilistic knowledge and significant results have been achieved in machine learning. The Naïve Bayesian technique directly specific input variables with the class attribute by recording dependencies between them.

We have used the tanagra toolkit to experiment with these two data mining algorithms. The tanagra is an ensemble of tools for data classification, regression, clustering, association rules, and visualization. The toolkit is open source software issued under the General Public License (GNU).

The diabetic data set has 403 rows and 19 attributes from 1046 subjects who were interviewed in a study to understand the prevalence of obesity, diabetes, and other cardiovascular risk factors in Central Virginia for African Americans. It contains the basic demographics for each patient, that is, patient id, age, race, height, weight, hip size, waist size, stabilized glucose, high density lipoprotein, glycosolated Hemoglobin and the symptoms presented when the patient first came to the emergency room, as well as the emergency room diagnosis these features were continuous.

Table 1. Error Rate Using Naïve Bayes classifier

Before filtering		After using FCBF	
MIN	1	MIN	0.8
MAX	1	MAX	0.8
Trial	**Error rate**	**Trial**	**Error rate**
1	1	1	0.8
2	1	2	0.8
3	1	3	0.8

Whereas gender, frame and location were taken as discrete attributes.

An Illustrative Application Domain: Experiment I

We now introduce an example that will be used to illustrate the concept of feature selection methods in spatial data mining. In this study the diabetic dataset was used to examine the Naïve Bayes technique using FCBF and MIFS filtering. We have found that error rate before and after feature selection on naïve classifier. The whole training dataset is used for analysis.

The error rate before the feature selection was 1%, whereas the analysis suggests that error rate got reduced 0.8% after the Fast-Correlation Based Filtering technique was applied, and they are shown in Table 1. We observe that the FCBF feature selection process improves the accuracy of the Naive Bayes classifier. In order to determine the number of features in the selected model, a five-fold cross validation was carried. Cross

validation is an estimate of a selected feature set's performance in classifying new data sets. Of course domain knowledge is crucial in deciding which attributes are important and which are not. Therefore, it was used to determine the best number of features in a model. In a five-fold cross validation, a training data set was divided into two equal subsets. Each subset took turns to be the subset, to determine accuracy of data. The classification error rate or fitness of individual feature was obtained and thus that feature can be decided to be added or removed from the feature subset used.

In Table 2 the overall cross validation is use to measure the error rate of Naïve Bayes classifier. Table 3 shows the error rate using cross validation in Fast-Correlation Based Filtering technique was applied. We have found that FCBF increases the efficiency of Naïve Bayes classifier, by removing the irrelevant and redundant information.

In this case, we used Mutual information feature selection (MIFS) filtering technique with

Table 2. Cross validation on Naïve Bayes

Error rate			1			
Values prediction			**Confusion matrix**			
Value	**Recall**	**1-Precision**		**Female**	**Male**	**Sum**
Female	0	1	Female	0	9	9
Male	0	1	Male	6	0	6
			Sum	6	9	15

Table 3. Cross Validation after FCBF

Error rate			0.8			
Values prediction			Confusion matrix			
Value	Recall	1-Precision		Female	Male	Sum
Female	0	0.6667	Female	2	6	8
Male	0	1	Male	5	0	5
			Sum	7	6	13

Table 4. Naïve Bayes classifier

Error rate			0.4333			
Values prediction			Confusion matrix			
Value	Recall	1-Precision		female	male	Sum
Female	0.3333	0.5556	Female	4	8	12
Male	0.7222	0.381	Male	5	13	18
			Sum	9	21	30

Naïve Bayes classifier. The continuous attributes are chosen part of analysis using gender as a target attribute. The MDLPC technique was applied to continuous attributes into ordered discrete one. We then insert the Naïve Bayes classifier and error rate was determined by cross validation. The cross Validation was applied for 5 trials and 2 folds. The table was analyzed for rows and columns. Table 4 shows the error rate before filtering technique was applied on Naïve Bayes classifier. Table 5 error rate after MIFS feature selection was applied on Naïve Bayes classifier. We have found that the error rate of Naïve Bayes classifier improves after MIFS filtering technique is applied.

Third analysis was conducted using linear discriminant analysis prediction technique to stepwise discriminant analysis (STEPDISC) filtering technique, to evaluate the efficiency of datasets. Classification of data is analyzed using linear discriminant technique, we perform the stepwise discriminant analysis on the training data sets, and about 19 features were selected by the stepwise selection process. Bootstrap was carried out to measure the efficiency number of features in a selected model. Bootstrap re-samples the available data at random with replacement; we estimated error rate by bootstrap procedure for selected feature set's performance for classifying new data sets. Therefore, it was used to determine

Table 5. MIFS on Naïve Bayes

Error rate			0.2			
Values prediction			Confusion matrix			
Value	Recall	1-Precision		female	male	Sum
Female	0.75	0.25	Female	9	3	12
Male	0.8333	0.1667	Male	3	15	18
			Sum	12	18	30

Table 6. Bootstrap in Linear Discriminant analysis

Error Rate		Error Rate after stepwise discriminant analysis	
.632+ bootstrap	0.4682	.632+ bootstrap	0.1426
.632 bootstrap	0.4682	.632 bootstrap	0.122
Resubstitution	0.4286	Resubstitution	0
Avg. test set	0.4912	Avg. test set	0.193
Repetition	**Test Error**	**Repetition**	**Test Error**
1	0.4912	1	0.193
Bootstrap	**Bootstrap+**	**Bootstrap**	**Bootstrap+**
0.4682	0.4682	0.4682	0.1426

the best number of features in a model. The 4 features were chosen by stepwise selection process. If the F statistic has lower value than the threshold value the feature gets excluded, if F statistic has higher value the feature gets added to the model. Table 6 shows the error rate with 25 replication after STEPDISC is performed.

The classification performance is estimated using the normal procedure of cross validation, or the bootstrap estimator. Thus, the entire feature selection process is rather computation-intensive. The accuracy of the classifier has improved with the removal of the irrelevant and redundant features. The learning models efficiency has improved by; alleviating the effect of the curse of dimensionality; enhancing generalization capability; speeding up learning process; improving model interpretability. It has also benefited medical specialists to acquire better understanding of data by analyzing related factors. Feature selection, also known as variable selection, feature reduction, and attribute selection or variable subset selection.

The spatial distribution of attributes sometimes shows the distinct local trends which contradict the global trends. For example, the maps in Figure 1 show the data was significant taken from Virginia State of Louisa and Buckingham country. It is interesting to note that there statistical difference in the two population, as noted that population of Louisa has more significant increase in the level of cholesterol as compared to Buckingham. We have also found that level of cholesterol is higher in males rather than females.

The above spatial distribution represents the number of cases in Stabilized Glucose level with respect to age in Louisa and Buckingham. This is most vivid in Figure 2 where the distribution represents that people of Louisa has more frequent chances of having diabetes as compared to population of Buckingham. The people of Louisa of age group (years) between 35 to 45 are having active chances of carrying diabetes as compared to Buckingham. Thus Male age group has more chances of having diabetes. For example, later on we show how to build rule induction from diabetic dataset.

Experiment II

Rule induction is a data mining process for acquiring knowledge in terms of if-then rules from training set of objects which are described by attributes and labeled by a decision class. Rule Induction Method has the potential to use retrieved cases for predictions. Initially, a supervised learning system is used to generate a prediction model in the form of "IF <conditions> THEN <conclusion>" style rules. Rule Induction Method has the potential to use retrieved cases for predictions. The rule antecedent (the IF part) contains one or more conditions about value of

Figure 1. Indicated areas shows the level of cholesterol in Virginia State of Louisa and Buckingham country

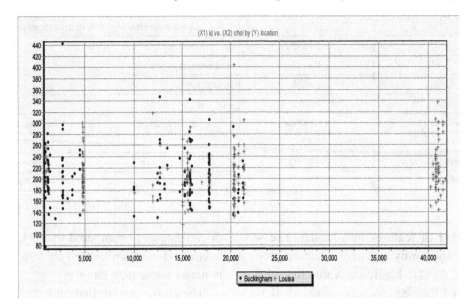

predictor attributes where as the rule consequent (THEN part) contains a prediction about the value of a goal attribute. The decision making process improves if the prediction of the value of a goal attribute is accurate. IF-THEN prediction rules are very popular in data mining; they represent discovered knowledge at a high level of abstraction. Algorithms for inducing such rules have been mainly studied in machine learning and data mining. In the health care system it can be applied as follows: In this method we adopted pre

Figure 2. Indicated areas of Stabilized Glucose level people of Louisa Vs Buckingham

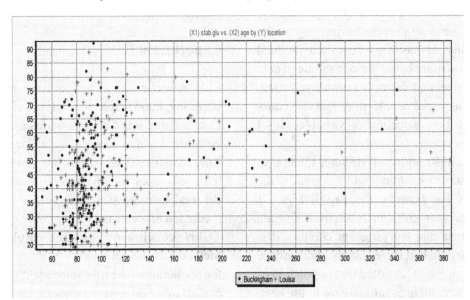

Example 1.

```
If_then_rule induced in the onset of diabetic in adult
If Sex = Male OR Female
    AND Frame= LARGE
    AND Cholestrol>200, then
    Diagnosis = chances of diabetic increases.
```

classification technique which is represented as logical expressions of the following form:

(Symptoms) (Previous--- history) ------- > (Cause--- of --- disease)

Using this technique, the attribute weight, sex, age, cholesterol, frame and amount produced the best results.

We have applied this technique with some knowledge of domain which can be used as decision making in healthcare. This method will predict whether the person has chances of diabetic or not. As usually happens, this study can be used as a stepping stone for further research in other Data Mining methods like Support Vector Machines and Rough Sets which enjoy good reputation for their classification capabilities remain to be tested in terms of performance and explanatory power.

CONCLUSION

We have investigated several feature selection algorithm in medical datasets, to determine number of essential feature subsets. Simulations were done on comparing the full feature set, reduced feature sets and randomly selected feature sets. The result shows that smaller datasets maintain the prediction capability with a lower number of attributes than the original datasets. Although our result shows that classifiers error rate improves after the filtering technique is applied and reduces the processing time of classifier. Also the wrapper mode is better than the filter mode but it is more computationally expensive. We will extend this work to further datasets and different cost estimation problems in different classifier.

Example 2.

```
If_then_rule induced in the diagnosis of diabetic in blood
If glycosolated heamoglobin ≥ 7.0 and waist ratio> 48 and age>50, then
      the record is pre-classified as "positive diagnosis"
            else if glycosolated heamoglobin < 2.0 and waist ratio<36, then
                  the record is pre-classified as "rare chances of diabetic"
            else
                  ignore the record
            end if
```

REFERENCES

Abraham, R., Simha, J. B., & Iyengar, S. S. (2007). Medical Data mining with a new algorithm for feature selection and Naïve Bayesian Classifier. In *Proceedings of IEEE International Conference on Information Technology*, (pp. 44-49).

Afifi, A. A., & Azen, S. P. (1972). *Statistical Analysis: A computer oriented approach*. New York: Academic Press, Inc.

Agrawal, R., Gehrke, J., Gunopulos, D., & Raghavan, P. (1998). Automatic subspace Clustering of high dimensional data for data mining applications. In *Proceedings of the ACM SIGMOD International Conference on Management of Data*, (pp. 94-105), Seattle, WA.

Aha, D. W., & Bankert, R. L. (1995). A Comparative Evaluation of Sequential Feature Selection Algorithms. In *Proceedings of the Fifth International Workshop on Artificial Intelligence and Statistics*, (pp. 199-206), Florida, USA.

Almuallim, H., & Dietterich, T. G. (1991). Learning with many irrelevant features. In *Proceedings of the Ninth Nat. Conf. on Artificial Intelligence*, (pp. 547-552), Anaheim, CA. Cambridge, MA: MIT Press.

Battiti, R. (1994). Using mutual information for selecting features in supervised neural net learning. *IEEE Transactions on Neural Networks*, 537. doi:10.1109/72.298224

Blum, A. L., & Langley, P. (1997). Selection of relevant features and examples in machine learning. *Artificial Intelligence*, *97*(1-2), 245–271. doi:10.1016/S0004-3702(97)00063-5

Chen, K., & Liu, H. (1999). Towards an evolutionary algorithm: Comparison of two feature selection algorithms. In *Proceedings of Congress on Evolutionary Computation*.

Chen, Z., Menzies, T., Port, D., & Boehm, B. (2005). Finding the right data for software cost modeling. *IEEE Software*, *22*, 38–46. doi:10.1109/MS.2005.151

Dash, M., & Liu, H. (1997). Feature selection methods for classifications. *Intelligent Data Analysis: An International Journal*, *1*(3).

Dash, M., Liu, H., & Motoda, H. (2000). Consistency based Feature Selection. In *Proceedings of Pacific-Asia Conf. on Knowledge Discovery and Data Mining (PAKDD)*, (pp. 98–109).

Devaney, M., & Ram, A. (1997). Efficient Feature Selection in conceptual Clustering. In *Proceedings of the 14th International Conference on Machine Learning*, (pp. 92-97). San Francisco: Morgan Kaufmann, http://cc.gatech.edu/aimosaic/students/markd/papers/icml-97/icml-97.pdf

Duch, H. (2006). Filter methods. In Guyon, I., Gunn, S., Nikravesh, M., & Zadeh, L. (Eds.), *Feature extraction, foundations and applications: Studies in Fuzziness and Soft Computing* (pp. 89–118). Berlin: Physica-Verlag, Springer.

Dy, J. G., & Brodley, C. E. (2000). Feature Subset Selection and Order Identification for Unsupervised Learning. In *Proceedings of the Seventeenth International Conference on Machine Learning*, (pp. 247-254), Stanford University, CA.

Dy, J. G., & Brodley, C. E. (2000a). Visualization and interactive feature selection for unsupervised data. In *Proceedings of the 6th ACM SIGKDD International Conference on Knowledge Discovery & Data Mining (KDD-00)*, (pp. 360-364).

Hastie, T., Tibshirani, R., & Friedman, J. H. (2001). *The Elements of Statistical Learning: data mining, inference, and prediction*. New York: Springer. Retrieved from Http://eric.univ-lyon2.fr/~ricco/tanagra/en/tanagra.html.

John, G. H., Kohavi, R., & Pfleger, K. (1994). Irrelevant Features and the Subset Selection Problem. In *Proceedings of the 11th Int. Conf. on Machine Learning.*

Kaur, H., & Wasan, S. K. (2009). An Integrated Approach in Medical Decision Making for Eliciting Knowledge, Web-based Applications in Health Care & Biomedicine. In Lazakidou, A. (Ed.), *Annals of Information System (AoIS).* Berlin: Springer.

Kaur, H., Wasan, S. K., Al-Hegami, A. S., & Bhatnagar, V. (2006). *A Unified Approach for Discovery of Interesting Association Rules in Medical Databases, Advances in Data Mining,* (LNAI 4065, pp. 53-63). Berlin: Springer-Verlag.

Kim, Y., Street, W., & Menczer, F. (2000). Feature selection for unsupervised learning via evolutionary search. In *Proceedings of the Sixth ACM SIGKDD International Conference on Knowledge Discovery and Data Mining,* (pp. 365–369).

Kira, K., & Rendell, L. (1992). The feature selection problem: traditional methods and a new algorithm. In *Tenth National conf. on AI,* (pp.129-134). Cambridge, MA: MIT Press.

Kirsopp, C., & Shepperd, M. (2002). Case and Feature Subset Selection in Case Based Software Project Effort Prediction. In *Proceedings of 22nd SGAI Int'l Conf. Knowledge Based Systems and Applied Artificial Intelligence.*

Kohavi, R., & John, G. (1997). Wrappers for feature subset selection. *Artificial Intelligence, 97*(1-2), 273–324. doi:10.1016/S0004-3702(97)00043-X

Kononenko, I., Bratko, I., & Kukar, I. (1998). Application of machine learning to medical diagnosis. In Michalski, R. S., Bratko, I., & Kubat, M. (Eds.), *Machine Learning and Data Mining: Methods and Applications* (pp. 389–408). Chichester, UK: Wiley.

Krishnapuram, B., Harternink, A. J., Carin, L., & Figueiredo, M. A. T. (2004). A bayesian approach to joint feature selection and classifier design. *IEEE Transactions on Pattern Analysis and Machine Intelligence,* 1105–1111. doi:10.1109/TPAMI.2004.55

Langley, P. (1994). Selection of relevant features in machine learning, In *Proceedings of the AAAI Fall Symposium on Relevance.* New Orleans: AAAI Press.

Liu, H., & Motoda, H. (1998). *Feature Selection for Knowledge Discovery and Data Mining.* Norwell, MA: Kluwer Academic Publishers.

Liu, H., Motoda, H., & Yu, L. (2002). Feature selection with selective sampling. In *Proceedings of the Nineteenth International Conference on Machine Learning,* (pp. 395–402).

Liu, H., & Setiono, R. (1996) A probabilistic approach to feature selection - a filter solution. In *Proceedings of the Thirteenth International Conference on Machine Learning (ICML),* (pp. 319–327). San Francisco, CA: Morgan Kaufmann Publishers.

Liu, H., & Yu, L. (2005). Towards integrating feature selection algorithm for classification and clustering. *IEEE Transactions on Knowledge and Data Engineering, 17*(4), 491–502. doi:10.1109/TKDE.2005.66

Miller, A. (2002). *Subset Selection in Regression.* Boca Raton, FL: Chapman & Hall/CRC.

Mitra, P., Murthy, P. A., & Pal, S. K. (2002). Unsupervised feature selection using feature similarity. *IEEE Transactions on Pattern Analysis and Machine Intelligence, 24*(3), 301–312. doi:10.1109/34.990133

Moustakis, V., & Charissis, G. (1999). Machine learning and medical decision making. In *Proceedings of Workshop on Machine Learning in Medical applications, Advance Course in Artificial Intelligence-ACAI99*, Chania, Greece, (pp. 1-19).

Narendra, P. M., & Fukunaga, K. (1977). A Branch and Bound Algorithm for Feature Subset Selection. *IEEE Transactions on Computers*, 917–922. doi:10.1109/TC.1977.1674939

Pechinizkiy, M., Tsymbal, A., & Puuronen, S. (2004). PCA-based Feature Transformations for Classification: Issues in Medical Diagnostics. In R. Long (Eds.), *Proc of 17th IEEE Symposium on Computer-Based Medical Systems*, Bethesda, MD, (pp. 535-540).

Richards, G., Rayward-Smith, V. J., Sonksen, P. H., Carey, S., & Weng, C. (2001). Data mining for indicators of early mortality in a database of clinical records. *Artificial Intelligence in Medicine, 22*, 215–231. doi:10.1016/S0933-3657(00)00110-X

Varshavsky, R., Gottlieb, A., Linial, M., & Horn, D. (2006). Novel unsupervised feature filtering of biological data. *Bioinformatics (Oxford, England), 22*(14), 507–513. doi:10.1093/bioinformatics/btl214

Witten, I. H., & Frank, E. (2005). *Data Mining: Practical machine learning tools and techniques*, (2nd Ed.). San Francisco: Morgan Kaufmann.

Yu, L., & Liu, H. (2003). Feature selection for high-dimensional data: A fast correlation-based filter solution. In *Proceedings of the 12th International Conference on Machine Learning (ICML-03)*, Washington, DC, (pp. 856–863). San Francisco, CA, Morgan Kaufmann.

Yu, L., & Liu, H. (2004). Efficient feature selection via analysis of relevance and redundancy. *Journal of Machine Learning Research, 5*, 1205–1224.

Zheng, Z., Srihari, R., & Srihari, S. (2003). A feature selection framework for text filtering. In *Proceedings of Third IEEE International Conference on Data Mining* (ICDM), November 19-22, (pp. 705- 708).

KEY TERMS AND DEFINITIONS

Data Mining: Is the task of discovering previously unknown, valid patterns and relationships from large datasets.

Fast Correlation-Based Filter (FCBF): Is a fast correlation-based filter algorithm designed for high-dimensional data and has been shown effective in removing both irrelevant features and redundant features.

Feature Selection: Is a preprocessing technique used in data mining tasks. It is the process of selecting a subset of features from the original set of available features. Feature selection is also well known as attribute reduction.

Mutual Information Feature Selection (MIFS): Is a feature selection method to select a subset of the considered features.

Naive Bayes: Is a simple probabilistic classifier based on applying Bayes' theorem (or Bayes's rule) with strong independence (naive) assumptions.

Stepwise Discriminant Analysis (STEP-DISC): Is a stepwise discriminant analysis method to select a subset of the quantitative variables.

Wrapper: This approach evaluates the relevance of features by using a classifier and relevant subsets of features are selected.

Chapter 7
From Data to Knowledge:
Data Mining

Tri Kurniawan Wijaya
Sekolah Tinggi Teknik Surabaya, Indonesia

ABSTRACT

This chapter will discuss a very useful technique to get (or to mine) a hidden information or knowledge which is lie in our data namely, data mining, which is a powerful and automatic (or semi-automatic) technique. Not only about the concept and theory, this chapter will also discuss about the application and implementation of data mining. Firstly, the authors will talk about data, information, and knowledge, whether they are different or not. After understand the term, they will discuss about what data mining is and what the importance of it. Second, they describe the process of gaining the hidden knowledge, how it is done, from the beginning until presenting the result. The authors will go through it step by step. In the next section, they will discuss about the several different tasks of data mining. In addition, to get a better understanding, the authors will compare data mining with other terminology which closely related so called data warehouse, and OLAP. For the last, but not the least, as stated before, this chapter will tell us about the real implementation of data mining in several different areas.

DOI: 10.4018/978-1-60960-102-7.ch007

INTRODUCTION

Data, Information and Knowledge

Before discussed any further about data mining, it is better for us to describe first what are data, information, and knowledge.

According to Palace (1996), Data are any facts, numbers, or text that can be processed by a computer. Recently, there are huge growing amounts of data in different formats and different databases. This includes:

- Operational or transactional data, data that are obtained from sales, cost, inventory, payroll, and accounting.
- Non-operational data, data are obtained from forecasting, industry, and macro-economic data.
- Metadata, that is data about the data itself, such as logical database design or data dictionary definitions

From data we can get information, which is the patterns, associations, or relationships among all the data. For example, from the analysis of point of sale transaction we can obtain information about which products are sold and when.

Furthermore, information can be converted into knowledge about historical patterns and future trends. For instance, the monthly information from the point of sale transaction can be analyzed to understand the consumer buying behavior. As a consequence, the retailer could determine which promotional effort is worth, or which products are going to be advertised more than the others.

What Data Mining is

In his books, Berson (2000) stated that data mining is an automated process of detecting relevant patterns in database. In his books, Berson gave an interesting example about how finding a pattern could be useful: suppose that there is a pattern that showed that married males with children tend to drive a sports car compared to married males without children then this pattern would indeed valuable and quite surprising for the marketing manager.

When discovering patterns in data, the process itself should be automatic or (usually) semiautomatic. The patterns discovered must be meaningful such that they lead to some advantage. Moreover, useful patterns allow us to make nontrivial predictions on new data. There are two approaches for the expression of a pattern (Witten & Frank, 2005): as a black box whose innards are effectively incomprehensible and as a transparent box whose construction reveals the structure of the pattern. Both, we are assuming, make good predictions. The difference between them is on their structure, whether their structure represent the pattern that can be examined and analyzed or not. In other words, we interested in patterns that also explain something about the data itself.

In order to understand data mining better, Palace (1996) gave a good example about data mining, data mining software and analysis. There are retailers that used the data mining capacity of Oracle software to analyze buying patterns of their customers. It is found that when men bought diapers on Thursdays and Saturdays, many of them also buy beer. After some analysis, it is revealed that these men typically did their weekly grocery shopping on Saturdays. On Thursdays, however, they only bought a few items. The retailers concluded that these men purchased the beer to have it available for the upcoming weekend. Then the retailers could use this newly discovered information in various ways to increase revenue. For example, we could sell beer and diapers at full price on Thursday as well as move the beer display next to the diaper display.

Data mining is also about solving problems by analyzing data in databases. For example, we want to figure out about the loyalty of our customer in a highly competitive marketplace. A database of customer, along with customer profiles, could be a good starting point. First we could analyze the behavior of the former customers, distinguishing the loyal ones from the customer who likely to switch to another products. Once the distinguished characteristics are found, we could use these characteristics to identify the present customer. This specific group can be targeted for a special treatment. Using the same techniques, we can also identify customers who might be attracted to another product, or another offers.

However, data mining is not a magic. For many years, experts have manually "mined" databases, looking for statistically significant patterns. Data mining is similar with when the analyst uses statistical and machine learning techniques to predict the patterns. Recently, technologies automate the mining process, integrate it with data warehouse and then present the result to the user (we will discuss more about data mining and data warehouse in section 4). Even though data mining become a very powerful and excellent technique that does not mean statistical analysts is not needed anymore. The absence of data mining just simply could not eliminate them. Analysts could bring values and analysis together with their experience that could not be delivered by data mining. Analysts are still needed to preprocess the data, decide which mining technique will be used, assess and interpret the model from the outcome of the mining process.

In data mining, data is stored electronically and then the search process is done automatically by the computer. Since a long time, economists, forecasters, and business users already have the idea to find patterns from their data automatically which then can be used for prediction or decision making. As the world grows in complexity and then overwhelming us with the data it generates, the chance of data mining to complete its task is increased. The possibility of finding interesting patterns from our data is increased. Thus data mining becomes everyone's hope for finding the patterns inside the data. In the end, data mining can lead us to new insights and, in particular settings, to gain competitive advantages.

Why Data Mining is Needed

Data mining now is used in for wide purposes in many different fields. Retailers, insurance, banking industries, medical community and many others use data mining to enhance their business process informatively:

- Retailers can use information collected through many programs, such as: shoppers' club cards, frequent flyer points, contests etc. to evaluate the how effective their advertisement or marketing strategy.
- The insurance and banking industries use data mining applications to assist in risk assessment (e.g., credit scoring). Insurance and banking could built a model that is able to assess whether a customer is in a high credit risk or not.
- The medical community can use data mining to predict how effective a medicine will be.
- Telephone or internet service providers can use data mining to classify which customer is likely to be a loyal customer and which customer is likely to switch to a competitor. A special treatment then is used to the customers that belong to the latter category.

Another reason why data mining is needed is that nowadays, with all of the data we have, we lack of experts that are able to transfer the huge amount of data into useful knowledge. The statement of Naisbitt (1984), "we are drowning in information but starved for knowledge", also supports several factors that fueled the ongoing noticeably growth in the field of data mining and knowledge discovery:

- The dramatic increased in the number of data that we have
- Data warehouse, which enable the company to access to a reliable database.

- The capability to access data from web navigation and intranets is increased
- The competitive pressure to increase market share in a globalize economy
- The rapid development of the commercial data mining software
- The significance improvement in computing power and storage capacity

DISCOVERING KNOWLEDGE FROM DATA

Recently, the notion of finding useful patterns in data has been given a variety of names, including data mining, knowledge extraction, information discovery, information harvesting, data archaeology, and data pattern processing. However, the complete process of finding the knowledge from data is named as knowledge discovery in databases to emphasize that knowledge is the end product of a data-driven discovery.

In this case, we are interesting in a term Knowledge Discovery in Databases (KDD). KDD is the complete process of discovering (useful) knowledge from data, whereas data mining refer to only one of step of the discovery process. As we discussed in the previous section, data mining is the application of specific algorithms for extracting patterns from data.

This section is intended to distinguish between these two popular notions (KDD and data mining), that data mining is only a step in the whole KDD process. The additional steps in the KDD process, such as problem definition, data preparation, and evaluate and interpret the result obtained are essential to ensure that the correctness and the usefulness of the knowledge that is derived.

Problem Definition

A KDD project starts with an understanding of the (business) problem. An understanding about the domain and the relevant prior knowledge has to be developed and the goal of the (KDD) process has to be established first. Experts (from different related fields) work together to define the project requirements and objectives from business point of view.

Without problem understanding, no technique or algorithm is going to provide us with a good result, even the sophisticated ones. Without the prior knowledge we will not be able to identify the problems that we are trying to solve. The prior knowledge is also important when we want to prepare the data for mining, or interpret the results correctly. In order to get the best result, we also have to make the objective as clear as possible, depending on our specific goal. For example, for the different purposes (but sound similar) "increasing the response rate" or "increasing the value of a response," we will have to build a very different model.

Data Preparation

After having a clear understanding about what the problem is, in the next phase we have to prepare the data that we would like to discover the knowledge from. In this phase, data is improved multiple times. Preparing the data by selecting tables, records, and attributes, are typical tasks in this phase. The meaning of the data is not changed. Please noticed that this process is also important and will have a big impact in our result. Like we already know before, garbage in, garbage out. This phase actually is divided into several steps:

- Data exploration: domain experts, who understand the meaning of the metadata, collect, describe, and explore the data. They also identify the quality and the problems of the data.
- Creating a target data set: selecting a data set, or focusing on a subset of variables or data samples, on which discovery is to be performed. Creating a new derived attributes, for example, an average value of

some number or amount is also allowed in this steps.

- Data cleaning and preprocessing: removing noise and handling missing data fields, including find the strategies and techniques to cope with them.
- Data reduction and projection: decide the features of the data depend on the objective of the task and different algorithm or transformation methods used in this phase to reduce the number of variables that are being considered.

Modeling

Modeling is about matching the goals of the KDD process that we derived from problem definition to a particular data mining method, for example: classification, association, clustering, and so on (see section 3 for data mining methods).

Next, we do an exploratory analysis, model and hypothesis selection: we choose the data mining algorithm(s) and selecting method(s) to be used for mining process. This process also includes deciding which models and parameters (as well another settings that might be required later) are appropriate and matching a particular data mining method with the overall criteria of the problem definition (for example, the end user might be more interested in understanding the model than its predictive capabilities).

Mining

This phase is an essential process where intelligent methods are applied in order to extract the meaningful patterns. This is the phase which people called "data mining". In other words, we are interesting in searching for patterns of interest in a particular representational form or a set of such representations, including classification rules or trees, association rules, and clustering. The correctness of performing the tasks in the preceding steps is also the key point of success for the mining phase. The various techniques and methods for this phase will be discussed more detailed in the next section.

In the mining phase, the interaction with the user or a knowledge base may also be built. The interesting findings might be presented to the user and stored as the new knowledge to the previous knowledge base. Since data mining is only one step from the entire process, this phase can also be repeated according to the requirement. However, one may argue that this process is the important one because it reveals the hidden pattern/knowledge inside our data.

Although data mining is just a step in the knowledge discovery process, however, in many industries and research community, "data mining" is more popular than "KDD" (Han, 2006). People often use the term data mining to resemble the whole process of KDD.

Result Interpreting and Evaluation

Next is about interpreting the mined patterns/knowledge. In this phase, there is also a possibility to return to the preceding steps for further iteration. However, this phase actually consist of the visualization or result presentation of the extracted pattern/knowledge.

In many cases after interpretation and evaluation, if the mining result does not satisfy the expectations, we could return to the modeling phase (or even the data preparation phase) and rebuild the model, for example by changing its parameters, until optimal values are achieved.

Knowledge Presentation

We use the mining results (discovered knowledge) by exporting the results into database tables or into other applications (for example: spreadsheets) for further actions or present the knowledge directly. We documenting it and reporting it to the one who need this result (our customer). In this phase, checking and resolving potential conflicts with the previous knowledge is also needed.

Just to close this section, generally the most of KDD projects has focused on the mining process. However, the other steps are also important (and probably more important) for a successful application of KDD in practice. Doing the mining process without appropriate prior steps can be a dangerous activity that easily leading to the discovery of meaningless and invalid patterns. In addition, the KDD process can involve significant iteration and can contain loops between any two steps.

DATA MINING TASKS

This section will be devoted to data mining, which according to many, is the most interesting steps in KDD process. Different methods and techniques are needed to find the different kinds of patterns. In this section, we differentiate tasks in data mining into several categories: classification, association, clustering, prediction, summarization and trend analysis. Each category serves different purposes.

Classification

Classification task aim to identify to which group each individual belongs to. Each group has its own characteristics that distinguished it from the others. This task can be used to predict the new individual as well as understand the existing data. For example, one may interested to predict whether a new customer can be classified as the customer that is likely to respond to an offer that come by direct mail campaign, or a phone call.

Data mining form the groups (for classification) by creating a model using already classified data or cases. These classified data/cases may come from an historical database. They may also come from an experimental data which samples already tested in the real world and then the results is used to create the classifier. For example: a company sent an offer by mail to a sample of its potential customer, then the result from this mailing is used to built the classification model for the entire customer. However, there also could be the case that experts are hired to classify the unclassified data. Then, the result from them is used as the basic for the classification model.

Several examples of classification tasks:

- Banking: determining whether a person is in a high-credit risk.
- Medical: diagnosing a disease given the symptoms.
- Advertising: determining the best way to advertise a product given the product specification.
- Language: determining the topic/field of an article.
- Education: determining whether a student is able to finish his/her thesis in the given time based on his/her academic record.
- Security: classifying a terrorist given the behavior or financial condition of a particular person.

Recently, there are many algorithms to do classification task. Some of them are: K-Nearest Neighbor, ID3, Naive Bayes classification, and Backpropagation (Artificial Neural Network).

Association

Association is the discovery of togetherness or the connection of objects. An association rule reveals the associative relationships among objects, that is the likelihood of a set of objects appear together with other objects. For example, in a retail database, we may find a rule that "bread" is associated with "chocolate", denoted as "bread → chocolate". It states that if customer buys bread, he or she very likely also buys a "chocolate."

Association task could be very useful for retailer, marketing, advertising, logistic management, etc. For example, a supermarket manager that found that people tend to buy bread together with chocolate could take an advantage of it. Store personnel then place the chocolate near the bread to promote the sale of both. They may even discount one to attract the customer for buying the other, since these shoppers now will be "saving money."

Several well-known association algorithms are: Apriori algorithm, FP-Growth, Fast algorithm, Eclat, and GUHA.

Clustering

Clustering is a process that dividing our data into groups of similar objects. Each group, called cluster, consists of objects that are similar each other and different to objects of other groups. According to Fayyad, Shapiro, and Smyth (1996), clustering is also a common descriptive task where one seeks to identify a set of categories (or clusters) to describe the data. The categories found can be mutually exclusive, hierarchical, or even overlapping categories.

Clustering aims to find categories/groups that are different from each other, whereas each member of the groups must be similar to each other. Unlike classification, we do not know what the clusters will be when we start, or by which attributes the data will be clustered. Consequently, experts from the field should interpret the resulting cluster. In many cases, it is also necessary to exclude a particular variable or even several variables based on an analysis or observation that stated that they are irrelevant (with the objectives) variables.

There are many clustering algorithm nowadays in data mining: K-Means, PAM, CURE, DEN-CLUE, DBSCAN, WaveCluster, etc.

Prediction

The main purpose of the prediction task is to determine what will likely happen in the future. It is similar to classification, in the sense that prediction built the model from the previous knowledge and then applies the model to the new input. Here are some examples of the prediction task:

- Predicting the average of students' grade on a particular course based on the students' background
- Predicting the price of a stock several weeks ahead
- Predicting the number of the attendance on the next football match
- Predicting the increase of traffic accident in the next year
- Predicting the increase of sales in the next month based on the sales history from previous years
- Predicting whether a new product will succeed in the market based on product characteristic and company history

There are many methods we can use to do prediction tasks, such as: traditional statistical methods, simple linear regression and correlation, multiple regression, and neural network, decision tree, and k-nearest neighbor methods. In addition, any of the methods and techniques used for classification may also be used, under appropriate circumstances, for prediction.

Trend Analysis

Trend analysis predicts unknown future values based on a time-series data. Time series data are records accumulated over time. For example, a company's sales, a customer's credit card transactions, and stock prices are all time series data.

Like classification and prediction, it uses known results (previous knowledge) to guide its results. Models must take into account the distinctive properties of time, especially the hierarchy of periods (including such varied definitions as the five- or seven-days work week, the thirteen-"month" year, etc.), the effect of the public holidays, arithmetic operation on date, and possibly consideration about how much of the past is still relevant.

In trend analysis, a model or a function is constructed to simulate the behavior of the object to predict future behavior. For example, a trend analysis could provide a CEO of a company an estimation of this year company's profit (possibly with the estimated annual increasing rate) based on the financial condition and last year's profit.

Trend analysis also includes identifying patterns in evolution of our observation, such as its ups and down, or peaks and valleys (Sumathi & Sivanandam, 2006). The increasing or decreasing streaks of an observation (for example: exchange rates of US dollar to euro) is an example of matching and changing trends problem that can also be handled using trend analysis. By comparing two or more objects historical changing curves or tracks, similar and dissimilar trends can be discovered and help us to understand the behavior of our observation as well. Analyzing company's sales and profit figures is the popular example for this objective.

DATABASE VS DATA MINING

This section will discuss two important notions in database which closely related to data mining: data warehouse and online analytical processing. However, this section will be started with an overview of database and its challenges that are relevant with data mining.

Database

With the increasing use of database in a company nowadays, the problem related to it become more complex day by day. One of the most difficult problems to deal with is that the data are stored in several different locations (Bianchi, 2009). Furthermore, the problem turn to be more complicated when each database (in each location) is built based on the preference, experience, style,

assumption and perspective of the local manager. It makes the queries difficult to be done from the outside.

From section 1 we know that data mining is the process of analyzing data and then extracts the meaningful knowledge or information. Technically, with respect to our database, data mining aims to find correlations or patterns among fields in large relational databases. In addition, data mining is also one of the best ways to illustrate the difference between data and information; data mining transforms data into information.

Data Mining and Data Warehousing

Data warehouse comes as a solution to the problem above. Data warehouse aims to join data located in separated databases. Data warehousing also means that we should collect and manage historical data from variety sources without errors, duplicating, or missing data. As the data sources might be always change, data warehouse also must be updated.

In most cases, the data that would be used in a KDD process of a company need to be extracted from the data warehouse first, because usually each department in a (big) company has its own database. There is some real benefit if our data is already part of a data warehouse. Actually, the problems of cleansing data for a data warehouse and for data mining are very similar. If the cleaning process has already been done for the data warehouse, then it most likely needs not to be cleansed again for the mining purposes.

The data mining database (database that we use to store the data for KDD process) may be a logical database rather than a physical subset of our data warehouse. If the DBMS (Database Management System) of our data warehouse does not support addition demand for the mining process that it would be better to separate the data mining database from the data warehouse. However, a data warehouse is not a requirement for data mining. Creating a large data warehouse that join data from many different sources, handle duplicating and missing data actually could be very time-consuming and costly. If that is the case, we could mine data from one or more transactional databases by extract the data into a read-only database first.

Data Mining and Online Analytical Processing (OLAP)

Many ask about what OLAP is and how it is different from data mining. OLAP is a decision support tools. However, OLAP is more than just a traditional query and report tools. OLAP used to answer why certain things are true.

Here is how it works: The user forms a hypothesis about a certain relationship and verifies it with a series of queries against the data. The analyst might first hypothesize that people with low incomes are bad credit risks and analyze the database with OLAP to verify this assumption. If the hypothesis were not proved by the data, the analyst might then look at high debt as the determinant of risk. If the data did not support this hypothesis (again), the analyst might then try debt and income together as the best predictor of bad credit risks. So, informally speaking, the OLAP analyst generates a series of hypothetical patterns and relationships and uses queries to the database to verify (or disprove) them.

OLAP analysis is essentially a deductive process. But what happens if the number of variables being analyzed is in hundreds or even thousands? Surely, it becomes much more difficult and time-consuming to find a good hypothesis.

OLAP is different from data mining because in data mining we use the data itself to reveal the interesting pattern, whereas OLAP only verify the hypothetical patterns. Data mining is essentially an inductive process. For example we found that there is an analyst that wanted to discover the risk factor for loan used a data mining tool. Suppose that the result from the data mining tool was people with high debt and low income were bad credit risks. However, the data mining tool might

go beyond that and also reveal that age is also an important factor of risk, something that the analyst even did not think about. We can imagine that if the analyst used OLAP, as long as the analyst did not think about age, there will be no "age" in the determinant factor of risk.

Despite of their difference, data mining and OLAP could complement each other. Before the analyst go further with the discovered patterns/ knowledge (from data mining), the analyst could use OLAP to be aware of the implication of using the discovered patterns/knowledge. The OLAP tool can allow the analyst to answer those kinds of questions. Furthermore, OLAP is also useful in the early stages of the knowledge discovery process because OLAP can help us explore our data, for instance by focusing attention on important variables, identifying exceptions, or finding interactions. This is important because the better we understand your data, the more effective the knowledge discovery process will be.

DATA MINING APPLICATIONS

There are many data mining applications as well as data mining tools that release in the market. After discussed about the concept, theory and many related-things about data mining, this section is intended to give real examples of the data mining implementation in the real world.

In this section we will discussed about two data mining tools that are very well-known: Intelligent Miner from IBM and Enterprise Miner from SAS and a data mining tools that enriched with visualization: Miner3D. As stated earlier, all of them are data mining tools i.e. tools that assist its user to conduct data mining process. The next example is the real implementation of data mining in WalMart and BBC. Implementation in WalMart shows us how data mining have an important role in everyday transaction data of the one of the biggest store in US, whereas in implementation in BBC, data mining showed its strength in prediction. The last but not the least, it is about how data mining being used to help airlines improved its flight security. CAPPS II is a data mining application that helps airlines to do screening process over its passenger.

Intelligent Miner (IBM)

IBM Corporation was developing data mining solutions "Intelligent Miner for Data" for a number of years using its resources of research laboratories from the United States (e.g., Watson Research, Almaden Research) and around the world (e.g., ECAM in France, Boblingen in Germany). Of course, the result of these efforts is a suite of sophisticated software solutions that encompass applied and fundamental research in the areas of artificial intelligence, machine learning, linguistics analysis, and knowledge discovery.

The Intelligent Miner supports a variety of data mining tasks, including discovery of associations and sequential patterns in transactions (market basket analysis) and trend analysis (stock market analysis), customer classification/profiling, clustering, and predicting values (IBM, 2002). A retailer might determine groups of customers that will respond to a new offer, or discover the opportunity of cross-selling using the Intelligent Miner. An insurance company might use the Intelligent Miner with claims data to isolate likely fraud indicators. However, the richness of the algorithms and the variety of customization options make Intelligent Miner user interface more suitable to an expert user than to a novice (Berson, 2000).

Enterprise Miner (SAS)

SAS Enterprise Miner is one of the formidable players in the data mining tools market. It leverages a significant power and influence of SAS statistical modules. SAS Enterprise Miner is designed to be used both by novice and expert users. Its GUI interface is data-flow driven, and it's easy to understand and use (SAS, n.d.).

SAS Enterprise miner is already completed with a number of data mining algorithms. It supports market-basket analysis, classification, predictive modeling, customer profiling and a range of statistical analyses for econometric time series, operations research, and many others (Berson, 2000).

SAS leveraged its considerable expertise in statistical analysis software to develop a full-function, easy-to-use, reliable, and manageable system. The wide range of modeling options and algorithms, well-designed user interface, capability to leverage existing data stores, and large market share in statistical analysis (allowing a company to acquire an incremental SAS component rather than a new tool), may all result in SAS taking a leading position in the data mining marketplace.

Miner3D

Miner3D is a data mining application that focused in the data visualisation and exploration. As its name sounds, it provides 3D visualization of the data for its user. Miner3D allowed us to analyze and explore data and create a chart and graphics in a customizable manner. In fact, Miner3D can be useful in trend analysis, cluster identification, or in the process of determining the relationship in our data. According to its specification, Miner3D could be very useful for practitioners and researchers in bank and investment analysis, sales managers, pharmaceutical and biotechnology, process engineering, geologist, or others that need the help of visualisation to understand and analyze their data.

WalMart

WalMart already used data mining to enhance its customer and supplier relationship. Almost every day, from its (around) 2,900 stores, Wal-Mart processes a huge numbers of data (about 7.5 terabyte of data). Wal-Mart tracked buying trends shelf by shelf and item by item. They improve both, their market grasp and supplier relationship. Which is more surprising, even in 1995, WalMart computers have processed over 1 million complex data queries (The Gale Group Inc. (2002)).

Moreover, WalMart allows more than 3,500 suppliers, to access data on their products and perform data analyses. Their suppliers then use the data to discover the buying patterns of customers in each local store. Based on this information, the suppliers manage the local store inventory and try to identify new marketing opportunity.

BBC

BBC use Clementine (a data mining tools produced by SPSS) that predict the audience share that a proposed new TV program would achieve given it was transmitted at a particular time (Hunter, 2001). This appears to be an ideal data mining project or implementation; the BBC has years of historical data showing what audience share watched each program.

However, the context of a TV program is quite complex. The project was carried out with around one year's viewing data. Based on this data, the system learn and then was able to predict the audience share with a similar accuracy compared to trained BBC staff. The model was able to predict the audience share within plus or minus four percent. It was not assumed to be particularly accurate, but the BBC was pleased. The prediction had similar accuracy to their best program planner's estimates. It took two years for these planners to become experts; with data mining the same accuracy is achieved in a few seconds.

CAPPS II

CAPPS or Computer Assisted Passenger Pre-Screening System is a data mining system that is run by an airline to prevent terrorism. CAPPS II is the next version of CAPPS that provides a high tech method of Passenger Profiling and has

an ability to build a more sophisticated airline passenger watch list.

According to the United States General Accounting Office report in 2004, the followings are how CAPPS II works.

1. Passengers who booking a flight will be asked for their full name, address, phone number and date of birth.
2. The private-sector security firms that is hired by the government will be given the passenger information and they will run this information against commercial database and assign a certainty value of who the passenger is based on the information given by the passenger.
3. Next, the score/value sent to the government. The government then checked it again against FBI, intelligence, or other watch list.
4. As the outcome, the passenger will be assigned a colour secretly: green, yellow, and red. Green means no threat; the passenger will experience a normal screening. Yellow means the passenger will have an additional screening process such as metal detectors. Red means the passenger will not allowed getting on the plane, in fact, the passenger will have a visit with law enforcement.

SUMMARY

In this chapter we already know what data mining really is and how it is become more important day by day. However, the most important idea is the whole process itself that called knowledge discovery in databases (KDD). Without a deep understanding in every single step of KDD, a project in finding knowledge from data will not be succeed and end up with frustration. From problem definition, data preparation until presenting the results, each of them has their unique role that strongly related each other.

In short, data mining is very promising. It offers us a capability to uncover the hidden yet valuable information that rely on our database. Together with its different kind of tasks e.g. classification, association, clustering, prediction, and trend analysis data mining have proved that it is really useful in many areas such as: retail, banking, broadcasting, security, etc. Researches and applications about data mining have grown rapidly in the decades. As strong and powerful tools, and applicable in many area, data mining will still continue to enjoy its popularity in the next years.

REFERENCES

Berson, A., Smith, S., & Thearling, K. (2000). *Building Data Mining Applications for CRM.* New York: McGraw-Hill Professional.

Bianchi, L. M. (2009). Databases and Data Mining. *Computer, Information and Society.* York University. Retrieved November 10, 2009 from http://www.yorku.ca/lbianchi/nats1700/lecture14.html

Fayyad, U., Piatetsky-Shapiro, G., & Smyth, P. (1996). From data mining to knowledge discovery in databases. *AI Magazine, 17,* 37–54.

Foong, D. L. Y. (2002). A Visualization-Driven Approach for Strategic Knowledge Discovery. In Fayyad, U. (Ed.), *Information Visualization in Data Mining and Knowledge Discovery.* San Fransisco, CA: Morgan Kaufmann.

Hunter, A. (2001). Data Mining. *Knowledge Management,* (July/August). Retrieved November 19, 2009 from http://www.cs.ucl.ac.uk/staff/a.hunter/tradepress/

IBM. (2002). *Using Intelligent Miner for Data.* Armonk, NY: IBM Corporation.

Larose, D. T. (2004). *Discovering Knowledge in Data: An Introduction to Data Mining.* New York: Wiley-Interscience.

Naisbitt, J. (1984). *Megatrends.* New York: Grand Central Publishing.

Palace, B. (1996). What is Data Mining. *Data Mining Technology Note prepared for Management 274A Anderson Graduate School of Management at UCLA.* Retrieved November 15, 2009 from http://www.anderson.ucla.edu/faculty/jason.frand/teacher/technologies/palace/datamining.htm

SAS. (n.d.). *Data mining with SAS® Enterprise Miner™.* Retrieved November 19, 2009 from http://www.sas.com/technologies/analytics/datamining/miner/

Sumathi & Sivanandam. (2006). *Introduction to Data Mining and Its Applications.* Berlin: Springer-Verlag.

The Gale Group Inc. (2002). Data Mining and Walmart. In *Computer Sciences, Encyclopedia.com.* Retrieved November 20, 2009 from: http://www.encyclopedia.com/doc/1G2-3401200510.html

United States General Accounting Office. (2004). *Computer-Assisted Passenger Prescreening System Faces Significant Implementation Challenges.* Report to Congressional Committees, GAO, Report GAO-04-385, Washington DC 20548. Retrieved November 10, 2009 from http://www.gao.gov/new.items/d04385.pdf

Witten, I. H., & Frank, E. (2005). *Data Mining Practical Machine Learning Tools and Techniques.* San Fransisco, CA: Morgan Kaufmann.

KEY TERMS AND DEFINITIONS

Associations: Data mining task to discover the connection of individuals.

Classification: Data mining task to identify to which group the new individual belongs to.

Clustering: Data mining task to divide the data into groups of similar individuals.

Data Mining: A method/process needed to find interesting patterns from data.

Data: Any facts, numbers, or text that can be processed further.

Database: A collection of data.

Knowledge Discovery: The complete process needed to extract information/patterns from data, including: problem definition, data preparation, data mining, data modeling and result evaluation.

Knowledge: Useful information/pattern gathered from data.

Prediction: Data mining task to determine what will likely happen in the future.

Trend Analysis: Data mining task to predict the future values based on a time-series data.

Section 2
Applications of Mining and Visualizations

Chapter 8
Patent Infringement Risk Analysis Using Rough Set Theory

Chun-Che Huang
National Chi Nan University, Taiwan

Tzu-Liang (Bill) Tseng
The University of Texas at El Paso, USA

Hao-Syuan Lin
National Chi Nan University, Taiwan

ABSTRACT

Patent infringement risk is a significant issue for corporations due to the increased appreciation of intellectual property rights. If a corporation gives insufficient protection to its patents, it may loss both profits from product, and industry competitiveness. Many studies on patent infringement have focused on measuring the patent trend indicators and the patent monetary value. However, very few studies have attempted to develop a categorization mechanism for measuring and evaluating the patent infringement risk, for example, the categorization of the patent infringement cases, then to determine the significant attributes and introduce the infringement decision rules. This study applies Rough Set Theory (RST), which is suitable for processing qualitative information to induce rules to derive significant attributes for categorization of the patent infringement risk. Moreover, through the use of the concept hierarchy and the credibility index, it can be integrated with RST and then enhance application of the finalized decision rules.

DOI: 10.4018/978-1-60960-102-7.ch008

INTRODUCTION

Patent infringement litigation occurs when a firm detects other firm's action to imitate or duplicate an invention without acquiring a license to do so. This legal issue has attracted a great deal of attention due to the increased importance of formal intellectual property rights protection, as well as the changing economic and legal importance of different instruments for such protection. These have created significant challenges for U.S. intellectual property rights policy (Graham and Mowery, 2003). Due to the high cost of research and development for a new patent application and for the patent maintenance fees, it is critical for a company to categorize the infringement risk for each patent development process. In addition, for the patent assignee, early provision of patent risk categorization aims at maximizing recoverable infringement damages during litigation (James, 2005). These patent damage awards have become an increasingly important feature of business strategy in the USA over the past 20 years (Jerry and Gregory, 2006).

Previous of patent studies have analyzed patent information and citation number, for example, patent analysis (Levitas *et al.*, 2006; Breitzman and Thomas, 2002), patent classification (Lai and Wu, 2005; Makarov, 2004), patent management (Stembridge and Corish, 2004; Reitzig 2004), and patent strategy planning (Knight, 2001; Gelle and Karhu, 2003). In addition some studies have attempted to analyze patent litigation cases. For instance, Lai and Che (2009) proposed a revolutionary valuation model for the monetary legal value of patents. Juan (1997) studied patent infringement, focusing on an index of patent rights. Some other studies have compared patent counts and patent citations to R&D expenditures and/or survey data in order to assess the efficacy of patent indicators (Acs and Audretsch, 1989; Duguet and MacGarvie, 2005). Technology licenses and publications have been utilized to a lesser extent as comparable measures of knowledge diffusion (Andrew, 2009). However, none of these studies categorized the infringement risk for each patent. In addition, qualitative information may involve in the patent documents. For example, inducting significant attributes and decision rules based on patent titles or property claims may be useful information for categorization.

To categorize patent infringement, this study focuses on analyzing historical patent documents to derive significant attributes from infringement patents and induce decision rules for the current patent development process. The rough set approach, which is suitable for processing qualitative information (Tseng and Huang, 2007), derives significant attributes and induce rules through the analysis of patent infringement cases. However, the previous RS approach does not handle attributes that are involved in the concept hierarchy, and also does not measure the evidence level of the credible index for the reduct.

In this study, a heuristic approach based on rough set theory is developed that creates credible infringement risk categorization by analyzing infringement patent information.. The proposed solution approach, first, analyzes attributes related to hierarchical information from the collected data sets and selects the highest class by calculating the modified credible index. Second, at the reduct generation stage, aggregation of the attributes and outcomes and induction of the decision rule are performed. Finally, at the rule extraction stage, the significant attributes and decision rules are inducted to categorize the infringement risk.

The rest of this study in this chapter is organized as follows. The "Background" section reviews the literatures in patent infringement and rough set theory, while the "Solutions and Recommendations" section proposes the solution approach. A study demonstrating the proposed approach to support risk-management and patent infringement is illustrated in the "Case Study" section and the "Conclusion" section summarizes the study. Using the aforementioned approach, a corporation can categorize patent risk for the possibility of infringement and reduce lost profits due to patent infringement. Moreover, the decision rules of patent infringement risk can also be developed. Business industry can utilize these rules to determine which patents have higher probability of being infringed, which patents are highly competitive, and which patents and categories require major capital investment for research and development.

BACKGROUND

Patent Infringement

In a legal context, infringement refers to the violation of a law or a right. This includes intellectual property infringements such as copyright infringement, patent infringement and trademark infringement. Patent infringement has attracted a great deal of research due to the increased importance of formal intellectual property rights protection, as well as the changing economic and legal issues of different instruments for such protection. Together, these create significant challenges for U.S. intellectual property rights policy (Graham and Mowery, 2003).

Patent infringement is a type of intellectual property damage that results when competing manufacturers imitate successful innovations or adapt them to their own use (Helpman, 1993). When patent infringement occurs, the original company loses the revenue from manufacturing the product and the original investment in the patent, as well as competitive advantage from the patent. For the patent owner, early provision of patent notice can help maximize recoverable infringement damages during litigation (James, 2005).

Recent surveys have found that financial executives rank risk management is as one of their most important objectives (Kenneth *et al.*, 1993). Patents are a knowledge asset in corporations, which have to invest huge amounts of money for the development process, including registration and maintenance fees in the patent office. However, in the past, the risk management concentrated on finance or the project risk (Kenneth *et al.*, 1993).

Previous Literature on Patent Infringement

The topic of patent infringement includes two issues (Table 1): (1) influences directly/indirectly resulted from patent indicators, and (2) the monetary values affected by patents (Lai and Che, 2009).

To detect patent infringement, analysis of previous patent documents is necessary (Lanjouw & Schankerman, 2001). Numerous studies have been made in the field of patent analysis to understand the relationship between technological development and economic growth (Penrose, 1951; Taylor and Sillberston, 1973), the assessment of the research and innovation process in a national and international context (Bosworth, 1984; Paci and Sassu, 1997). Referring to a technology indicator, patents are studied for the estimation of the trend and degree of technology development in some specific patents or industries from the perspective of company policy (Archibugi and Pianta, 1996; Ashton and Sen, 1988; Liu and Shyu, 1997). In addition, patent documents may have qualitative information that was not included in the analysis by previous studies. To deal with the qualitative information and determine significant features and decision rules, this study applies Rough Set Theory (RST), as presented next.

Rough Set Theory

Rough Set Theory (RST) was developed by Pawlak (1982) to classify imprecise, uncertain, or incomplete information or knowledge expressed by data acquired from experience. Rough Set Theory is a mathematical approach to managing vague and uncertain data or problems related to information systems, indiscernible relations and classifications, attribute dependence and approximation

Table 1. Two issues of patent infringement

Issues	Reference	Description
The influences directly/indirectly resulted from patent indicators.	Hirschey and Richardson (2001)	Scientific measures of the quality of inventive output are useful and country-specific influenced indicators of the economic value tie to patenting activity.
	Hereof, Schererc, and Vopel (2003)	The number of prior arts and the citations received are positively related to patent value
	Hirschey and Richardson (2004)	Patent citation information may indeed help investors judge the future profit-earning potential of a firm's scientific discoveries.
	Von Wartburg, Teichert, and Rost (2005)	This paper proposed a methodological reflection and application of multi-stage patent citation analysis for the measurement of inventive progress.
	Choy, Kim, and Park (2007)	This paper employed patent analysis in cross impact analysis of syntheses and interactions between various technologies and expected to help practitioners to forecast future trend and to develop better R&D strategies.
	Silverberg and Verspagenb (2007)	This paper focused on the analysis of size distributions of innovations by using patent citations as one indicator of innovation significance.
	Chiu and Chen (2007)	This paper proposed an objective scoring system for patents from the licensor side using the AHP to value patents for new products being developed by an actual enterprise.
	Park and Park (2004)	This paper proposed a valuation method that generates monetary value, rather than score or index, based on the structural relationship between technology factors and market factors.
The monetary values affected by patents.	Hereof and Hoisl (2007)	This paper described the characteristics of the German Employees' Inventions Act and discussed which incentives it creates by a survey of 3350 German inventors to test hypotheses regarding this institution, and finally concluded that the law creates substantial monetary rewards for productive inventors.
	Van Trieste and Vis (2007)	This paper focused on valuating a patent on cost-reducing process improvements from the viewpoint of the patent holding firm by considering the relevant cash flows that result from owning the patent, wherein the patent value was determined by licensing fees, royalty income, and competitive advantage resulting from the patent and patent maintenance costs.

accuracy, reduct and core attribute sets, as well as decision rules (Shyng et al., 2005). In RST, by using the data analysis concepts of "reduct" and "core" (Pawlak, 1982), the patterns or internal structures of a set of condition-decision and data records can be easily reduced and extracted as a set of minimal rules without any prior knowledge. The philosophy of RST is based on the assumption that every object in a universe of discourse can be associated with some information, such as data or knowledge. Thus, objects that are characterized by the same information are indiscernible, that is similar, according to the available information about them (Wang and Li, 2004).

The major reason for applying rough set approach for rule induction is the qualitative nature

of the data which makes it difficult to analyze by standard statistical techniques (Heckerman et al. 1997; Simoudis et al. 1996). RST has been applied to areas such as fault diagnosis (Zhang et al 2009; Shen *et al*, 2000), interval data clustering (Doumpos *et al*, 2009; Malcolm and Michael, 2001), supply chain management (Gaudreault *et al*, 2009; Liang and Huang, 2006), image analysis (Xiao and Zhang, 2008; Bartłomiej *et al*, 2008), knowledge acquisition (Qian *et al*, 2008; Jerzy, 1988), manufacturing quality control (Huang *et al*,2008; Tseng *et al*, 2004), customer relationship management (Tseng and Huang, 2007; Pawan *et al*, 2005). In this study, RST is applied to induct rules which aim at classify the infringement risk of patents.

MAIN FOCUS OF THE CHAPTER

Issues, Controversies, Problems

Two issues are concerned in this study:

1. There have been few research only attempts to develop a categorization for patent infringement risk, specifically to develop a credible index, such as a categorization matrix to enhance the object evidence, which refers to concept hierarchy. In addition, previous studies have not categorized significant attributes and rules in patent analysis in order to categorization patent infringement. Patent documents may have qualitative information that was not included in the analysis by previous studies.

2. In the rough set approach, reduct generation is determined by the attribute selection after measuring the upper and lower approximation (Pawlak, 1997). The reducts are established by the roughness value. However, these conventional reduct generation approaches can not guarantee that the categorization of a decision table is credible since the reducts do not have enough evidence of the result relationship. Fortunately, the availability of certain background knowledge, such as conceptual hierarchies, can improve the efficiency of the discovery process and the quality of categorization. For example, stronger regularities can be discovered at high concept levels and expressed in concise terms. Thus, it is often necessary to generalize low level primitive data in databases with relatively high level concepts for effective data mining.

Solutions and Recommendations

This solution approach focuses on how RST, together with conceptual hierarchical, and condition constraints can be used cooperatively to create high quality rule-based models. The solution approach includes presenting characteristics of patent infringements, introducing rough set techniques to determine the optimal level of each patent attribute for credible categorization, and developing a structural approach for the discovery of credible generalized and preference-based patent infringement decision rules. The discovery process is performed by heuristic approaches, and the patent infringement domain rules are finally evaluated.

Characteristics of Patent Infringement

In this section, a general decision table for the representation of the relationship between condition attributes and decision attributes is used. Patent information can provide significant condition attribute and decision attributes for the patent infringement risk. In Table 2, the element (e_{ij}) denotes the value of attribute (A_j) that an object (tuple) (X_i) contains, while O_k depicts the different decision attributes of the corresponding tuple. In addition, the number of values and weights are incorporated in this table.

An intelligent agent collects the patent infringement cases, including patent attributes, like "patent date" or "patent IPC code", etc. Since "whether some patent attributes have a hierarchy in the decision table" is the focus of this study, the concept of the hierarchy framework is introduced next.

Concept hierarchies are discussed in Kim (1990), Ziarko (1994) and Chen et al. (1996). Two examples of concept trees are introduced in this section: the patent date (see Figure 1) and the IPC code level (see Figure 2). The values on the left (e.g., level 0) label the depth of the tree, and the leaf values in a tree cover all possible values of the corresponding attribute.

To determine the most possible value combination, the DCmax is introduced. The maximum value for the degree of categorization (classifica-

Table 2. Fundamental structure of a decision table

j i		Condition attribute (A$_j$)						Decision category (Ok) (attribute)	
		1	2	3	.	.	m		
O	1	11	12	13			1m	(Grouped with the same outcome)	1
b	2	21	22	23			2m		1
j	3	31	32	33			3m		2
e	.	.	.	.	.	.			.
c	.	.	.	.	.	.			.
t	.	.	.	.	.	.			.
(X$_i$)		n1	n2	nl			nm		P
Set of values Weight		1	2	3			m	Note: condition domain:C decision domain:D object domain:T	
		1	2	3			m		

Figure 1. Concept tree for patent date

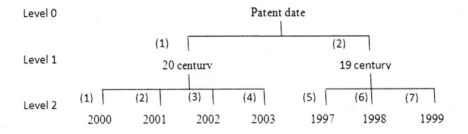

Figure 2. Concept tree for IPC code

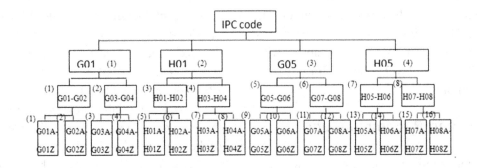

tory complexity) for a subset E of condition domain C, is defined as:

$$DCmax = \prod_{j \in E} card\left(V_j\right)$$

where V_j is the number of values of condition attributes, the function "card" yields set cardinality, and DCmax indicates the upper bound of classificatory complexity.

Level Search Based on Credibility Measurement

A categorization is a partition of the instance space into equivalence classes based upon the condition attributes. Pawlak (1991) and Quinlan (1993) applied inductive algorithms to categorize data. To be credible, a categorization must provide decisions which should be adequately supported by evidence. Three relevant factors of credibility are used in the literature: coverage, consistency, and evidence of each decision.

In general, it is obvious that selecting a higher level concept for each attribute should increase coverage and support of each decision but not valuable rules since the rules are too general. Moreover, the decision table may be inconsistent since some of the data collected may be conflicting. Since the categorization measurement in terms of the credibility index is based on consistent data, all of the inconsistent data should be eliminated.

Three indexes related to credibility and resolution:

Credibility index (CI(i)) and total credibility index (TCI):

$$CI\left(i\right) = \left(\frac{1}{DC-\left(q\right)}\right) \times \left(1 - \left|P(D|C(j)) - F(\bar{D})\right|\right)$$

(1)

$$TCI = \sum_{i=1}^{n} CI(i)$$

(2)

where: q is the number of inconsistent classes; DC is the degree of categorization of the decision table; P(D|C(j)) is the probability of the decision "D" specified by the class C(j); $F(\bar{D})$ is the theoretical fraction of D.

This index is used to confirm each categorization's credibility, and the smaller the difference between D and C(j), the higher the value of the credibility index. The higher credibility index is the higher modified credibility index.

Modified credibility index (MCI(j)) and total modified credibility index (TMCI):

$$MCI(i) = CI(i) \times (no\_of\_object)_i$$

(3)

$$TMCI = \sum_{i=1}^{n} MCI(i)$$

(4)

where $(no\_of\_object)_i$ is the number of objects that support the decision rule i

As the concept hierarchy is decreasing (i.e., less number of levels covered), the modified credibility index will change as the coverage is expanding. A higher MCI results in higher evidence of the categorization. The credibility reduct is determined based on wheather the highest categorization is identified.

Resolution index (RI):

$$RI = \sum_{j=1}^{m} L(j)$$

(5)

where: L(j) is the level of j-th attribute;

m is the number of condition attributes.

Whenever the level of concept hierarchical is generalized/specified, the resolution index must be recalculated since the lower RI indicates stronger support for the credibility.

Algorithm 1.

```
Step 1. Initialization
        B ←— NULL  and ConResult ←— NULL
Step 2. Select qualified categorizations
      For (i =0; i≤m; i++)
        For each level V_ir (r = N_i-1;i≤0;i--)
          Compute TMCI for each categorization
          If  TMCI of a categorization > T*
            Then  B ←— The categorization
            Else  B ←— NULL
          Endif
        Endfor
      Endfor
Step 3. Determine set of final desired categorizations
      ConResult ←— B - {The categorization which violate the constraints or
contain low value of RI}
```

The procedure presented next is applied to determine credible categorizations. Condition attributes are generalized by climbing their concept tree and one attribute is selected for generalization in each iteration. In this approach, the TMCI directs the algorithm. The decision table with its TMCI greater than the threshold value is defined as a credible categorization. The results of all combinations at the level of each attribute for credible categorization are determined by this procedure.

Level-Search Procedure

Input:

1. D: The infringement decision table have the attribute of patent;
2. C_i: The concept hierarchy corresponding to D;
3. N_j: The number of levels of each C_j;
4. V_{jr}: Level number r in the $N_j (0 \leq r \leq N_{j-1})$;
5. T*: Threshold value to determine the qualified categorization;
6. B: Basket of the value set

Output: ConResult: Set of final desired categorizations

Output: ConResult: Set of final desired categorizations (see Algorithm 1)

An alternative approach to determining categorizations is to normalize TMCI in the range [0,1] since decision-makers are more comfortable with this scale in determining the threshold value. For computing the resolution index (RI), an alternative approach is to assign a different weight for each attribute and recalculate the RI. If several categorization credibility indexes (TMCI) are equivalent, the highest RI should be selected.

Discovery of Credible Generalized and Preference Based Decision Rules

In this part, decision rules based on credible categorizations are discussed. In Figure 3, if the condition attributes do not contain the concept hierarchies, go to step 3 to generate a set of selected condition attributes to compute the TMCI. Step 4 checks whether the set is empty or not. Step 5 selects TMCI values that are higher than the

Figure 3. The solution approach for determining credible decision rules

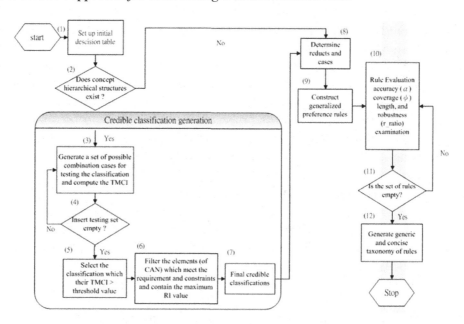

threshold value. In the final step, the credibility has been decided.

According to rough set theory, I = {U, A} is an information system, where U is a finite set of objects and A is a finite set of attributes. A set of its values Va is associated with every attribute a ∈ A. Assuming A = C ∪ D, B ⊂ C, where B is a subset of C; the positive region POSB(D) = {x ∈ U: [x]B ⊂ D} can be defined. The positive region POSB(D) includes all objects in U which can be classified into classes of D, in the knowledge B. The degree of dependency between B and D can

be defined as $K\left(B,\ D\right)\ =\ \dfrac{\mathrm{card}\left(\mathrm{POS_B}K\left(D\right)\right)}{\mathrm{card}\left(\mathrm{POS_C}K\left(D\right)\right)}$

, where card yields the set cardinality. In general, if K(B, D) = K(C, D), and K(B, D) ≠ K(B-{a}, D), for any a ∈ B hold; then B is a reduct of C. Since reduct (B) preserves the degree of dependency with respect to D and reduct (B) is a minimal subset, any further removal of condition attributes will change the degree of dependency. The following procedure for determining the

reducts and cases is adopted from the Pawlak (1991).

The reduct generation procedure is presented next.

Input: A decision table T classified into C and D
Output: The reducts (see Algorithm 2)

Note that the represents the objects where each A_j attribute contains V_{ij}, while $\left[V_{ik}\right]_{O_{K|i}}$ includes the objects with each $O_{k|i}$ outcome (decision) attribute containing V_{ik} In order to find dispensable attributes, the examination of each attribute of the object is required. One might also have to drop one attribute at a time and check whether the intersection of the remaining attributes is still included in the decision attribute.

Next, identification of the reducts with desired condition attributes from a data set is discussed. The direct use of the result provided by reduct generation algorithm may lead to many reducts containing condition attributes that are not meaningful. A strength index is introduced in order to identify meaningful reducts, and a reduct with a

Algorithm 2.

```
Step 1. Initialization: List all object in T
Step 2. Generation reducts for each object
        For (i =1 ; i ≤ n ; i++)
            For (j =1 ; j ≤ m; j++)
```
$$\text{If } \left(\left[V_{ij}\right]_{Aj} \subset \left[V_{ik}\right]_{o_{K|i}}\right)$$
```
                Then the reducts for  X  is formed
                                       i
                Else
                For (j =1 ; j ≤ m; j++)
```
$$\text{If } \left(C \cap A_{j}^{[V_{ij}]_{Aj}} \subset \left[V_{ik}\right]_{o_{K|i}}\right)$$
```
                    Then the reducts for X  is formed
                                          i
                    Else the reducts forX  is not formed
                                         i
                Endfor
            Endfor
        Endfor
Step 3. Termination: Stop and output all object reducts
```

higher strength index is preferred over a reduct with a lower index. Note that comparison of the reducts is restricted to the same decision attribute and the number of attributes selected in the reducts.

The strength index of reduct f is defined as follows:

$$SI(f) = \sum_{j=1}^{m} v_j W_j x\ n_f \tag{6}$$

where: f is the reduct number, $f = 1,..., n$;

$v_j = 1$ if condition attribute j is selected, 0 otherwise ($A_j = $ "x")

n_f is the number of identical reducts f

In general, a rule is a combination of the values of some attributes such that the set of all objects matching it is contained in the set of objects labeled with the same class. In order to simplify the decision table, value-reducts of the attributes illustrated in the previous section should be determined. Denote rule r_i as an expression:

$$r_i: (A_{i1} = u_{i1}) \wedge (A_{i2} = u_{i2}) \vee ... \wedge (A_{in} = u_{in}) \rightarrow (O = u_d) \tag{7}$$

where: $u_{i1}, u_{i2},..., u_{in}$, and u_d are the value contents of the attributes; set $\{\vee, \wedge, \rightarrow\}$ of connectives are disjunction, conjunction, implication, respectively

Basically, a set of specific decision rules (reducts) forms a reduced information system. Each rule corresponds to exactly one equivalence class of the original system. In other words, a set of those decisions rules (reducts) can be represented in a concise form (rule).

The proposed rule-extraction algorithm provides an effective tool for the generation of concise decision rules. To facilitate the rule-extraction process, the concept of a case is introduced. A case represents a set of reducts with the same number of attributes and the same outcome. The same case number might be assigned to more than one object and in general, the reducts of the same case are merged. More details are provided in the next section. Furthermore, the concept of extracting the best reducts is incorporated into

Algorithm 3.

```
Input:
R:  The origin reduct table of object.
Procedure:
Calculate the case number of each object in R
Create the table T₁ of all the reduct and sort by the case number
Select reduct from the T₁

For
IF the reduct number is large than object number then
      check the identified of the reduct.
IF the reduct(i) can be identify by reduct(i+1) then merge to the T₂  and se-
lect next reduct.
Else add the reduct to the T₂
Next reduct
Select one of the valid merge reduct in the T₂
For
   IF the reduct number is large than object then
     Check the identified of the reduct.
   IF the reduct(i) can be identify by reduct(i+1) then merge to the T₃ and se-
lect next reduct.
Next reduct
Select all the final merge rule in the T₃
Termination: Stop and output the results.
```

this algorithm. The quantitative information associated with each object is used to confirm the rules. The "weak" rules, i.e., those supported by only a few examples, are considered here as less important. Lastly, the final generalized relations are transformed into decision rules and the rules aggregation (simplification of decision rules) is also performed by this algorithm.

The Rule-Extraction Algorithm (REA) is presented next. (see Algorithm 3)

Evaluation of Decision Rules

Four performance measures are introduced: accuracy index, coverage index, length index, and robustness ratio.

The accuracy index is used to identify categorization accuracy of original data set. The coverage index is used to verify the rule of the rule set. Accuracy index $\alpha_R(D)$ and coverage index $\Psi_R(D)$ (Tsumoto, 1997):

$$\alpha_R\left(D\right) = \frac{\left|[x]_R \cap D\right|}{\left|[x]_R\right|}, \; and \; 0 < \alpha_R\left(D\right) \leq 1 \quad (8)$$

$$\Psi_R\left(D\right) = \frac{\left|[x]_R \cap D\right|}{\left|D\right|}, \; and \; 0 < \Psi_R\left(D\right) \leq 1 \quad (9)$$

where: $|A|$ denotes the cardinality of set A, $\alpha_R(D)$ denotes the accuracy of R (e.g., $e_{ij} = v_{ij}$, in a decision table) as to categorization of D, and $\Psi_R(D)$ denotes a coverage, respectively. In addition, $\alpha_R(D)$ measures the degree of the sufficiency of a proposition, R → D, while $\Psi_R(D)$ measures the degree of necessity of a proposition, D → R.

Length index refers to the count of the attributes. Length index (LI) and robustness ratio (r_ratio) for rule j:

$$LI(i) = \sum_{j=1}^{m} e_{ji} = no\_of\_attribute\ in\ rule\ i,$$

and $e_{ji} \neq$ "x" in the decision table $\qquad$ (10)

r_ratio(i) = no_of_the_rule-*i* /

$$\sum_{i=1}^{n}(no\_of\_the\_rule_i)\quad(11)$$

In general, rules with fewer attributes are preferred, and the robustness ratio is used to indicate a measure of confidence. A higher robustness ratio indicates clearer evidence of the categorization.

Case Study

The ABC Inc. is a professional IT OEM firm producing professional software associated with different disciplines and it owns 1,242 patents. To date, the infringement risk has not been categorized in patent development. To apply the solution approach in this study, the Intelligent Infringement Risk Evaluation (IIRE) platform is developed and the patent infringement data sets are collected from a court database and text-mining technology or other cluster algorism are used to cluster the possible attributes. The attributes were based on other studies are: (a) patent date (Levine, 1987), (b) patent title (Kuijk and Lobeck, 1984), (c) critical patent (Rupprecht, 1994), (d) license fee (Kamien *et al*, 1988), (e) product property (Verhaegen *et al*, 2009), (f) IPC code level (Foglia, 2007), patent claims (Saiki *et al*, 2006), inventor education (Mariani et al, 2007) and of registration country (Chen, 2008). After identification by the experts, two disjoint infringement domains are determined: (i) Infringement patent information and (ii) the infringement case information. For example; "patent title relevance" and "critical patent" are in domain I, while domain II attributes

include "license fee", "product property", and "IPC code level." In addition, the two decision attributes used to evaluate the infringement risk (g), infringement and patent function (h), are in the data set. The attributes are qualitative except for "d" and "f". Their domain usually consists of a limited number of values which are quantitative or linguistic terms. In addition, the domains of some attributes cannot be ordered, such as, "a", "b", "c", "e", "g", "h".

In the platform, a data set file is uploaded (Figure 4) and the initial decision table of the patent infringement risk categorization is viewed in Figure 5. Patent risk infringement categorization's attribute to the condition table and the result to the outcome table are determined in Figure 6. An object of the decision table refers to a patent which has been infringed.

In the condition table, patent date has 6 possible values and the patent title relevance has 2 possible values. The maximum degree of categorization is DCmax = $7 \times 2 \times 2 \times 2 \times 2 \times 16 =$ 1792. In this categorization, 6 equivalence classes are illustrated with the coverage of 6/1792 = 0.33%.

In the categorization shown in the Decision Table, only two attributes involve concept hierarchies, PD and ICL, which are represented in the first and sixth column. Note that a categorization is credible if all possible combinations of condition attributes can be covered in the decision table and each decision is supported by as many input instances as possible. The degree of categorization (DC) should represent the details of decision rules.

Find all of the categorization of the infringement. Establish the matrix of CI (credible index) and MCI (modified credible index) (see Figure 7). The credibility index of the first tuple in the Figure 7 is

$$CI = (\frac{1}{1792}) \times (1 - \left| \frac{5}{12} - \frac{1}{6} \right|)$$
$$= 4.2E-4, MCI = CI * 6(number\ of\ object)$$
$$= 2.5E-3$$

Figure 4. The imported data

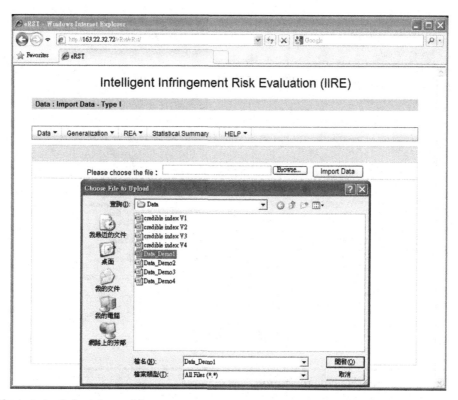

Figure 5. The original decision table

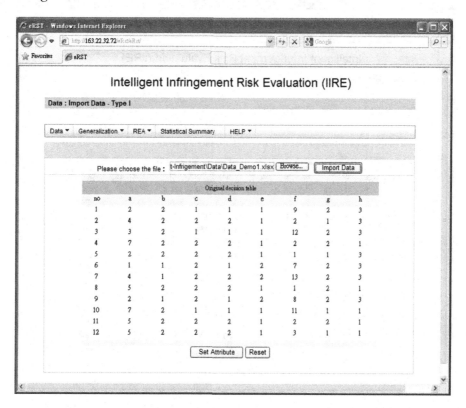

Figure 6. The attribute set

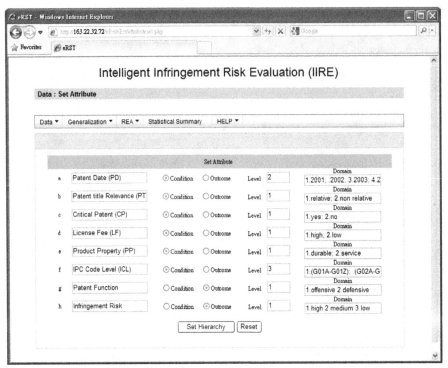

Figure 7. Example of a credible categorization

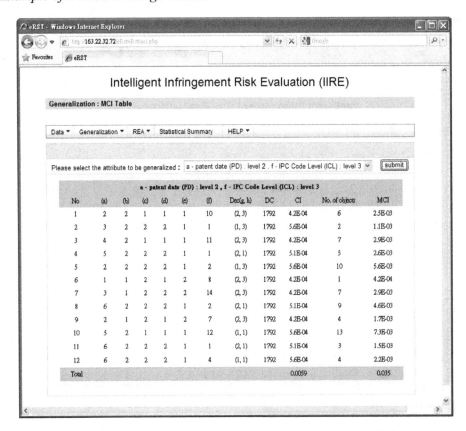

and the Resolution index (RI) is equal to 9. Since the total MCI is not acceptable, the generalization process is implemented next.

During the generalization of patent date (PD) level from level 3 to level 2, the instances ($\underline{5}$, 2, 2, 2, 1, $\underline{1}$, (2,1)), ($\underline{6}$, 2, 2, 2, 1, $\underline{2}$, (2,1)) and ($\underline{6}$, 2, 2, 2, 1, $\underline{1}$, (2,1)) were combined to form the ($\underline{2}$, 2, 2, 2, 1, $\underline{1}$, (2,1)) instance in Figure 8. Since the degree of categorization (DC) decreased and no inconsistent decisions occurred, the TMCI increased from 0.035 to 0.234. Note that the RI of Figure 8 is equal to 7.

However, during this generalization of the ICL, the decision does not remain consistent. For example, ($\underline{2}$, 2, 2, 2, 1, $\underline{1}$, (2,1)) and ($\underline{2}$, 2, 2, 2, 1, $\underline{1}$, (1,1)) in Figure 8 are in conflict. These two tuples should be removed and the results are presented in Figure 9. The value of DC in Figure 9 becomes 127 (=128-1). The increase of TMCI is not guaranteed as its value should be determined by the number of consistent tuplets and the degree of categorization (DC). In this case, the number of consistent tuplets and the value of DC decrease. However, the TMCI increases due to the weak impact of inconsistent instances on its value. Here, the value of RI is 6.

Consider the decision table shown in Figure 9 as the input to the level-search algorithm. The first row represents the state of generalization from the concept hierarchy contained attributes (e.g., (a) and (f)); and the first column includes the state of non-hierarchy contained attributes (e.g., (b), (c), (d), and (e)). The resulting credible categorization (TMCI) of all combinations of the levels for each attribute is also illustrated in Figure 10. Note that the original table (Figure 7) corresponds to the bottom of the first column of Figure 10.

Through computation of the aforementioned algorithm, the credibility (TMCI) can be assessed for each categorization and the combinations are listed in Figure 10. For a threshold value equal to 1, the shadowed cells in Figure 10 are the elements in CAN, for example, a1b0c0d0e0f3, a0b0c0d0e0f3,

etc. Obviously, a1b0c0d0e0f0 corresponds to the highest value but it is not a valuable categorization since the value of RI is 1.

After the requirements for each attribute have been determined, the elements of CAN are restricted to rows (1), (2), (5), (6), (9), (10), (13) and columns (5), (6), (7). After comparing the RI of each element, the seven categorizations marked in bold font were selected, {a1b0c0d0e0f3, a1b1c0d0e0f2, a1b0c1d0e0f2, a1b0c0d0e1f2, a1b1c1d0e0f1, a1b1c0d0e1f1 and a1b0c1d0e1f1}, all of which have an RI value of 4. Note that generalizing to the root of the concept tree is equivalent to removing the corresponding condition attribute. Finally, the summary of the TMCI based on a_0, a_1 and a_2 is represented in Figure 11.

An alternative approach to determine categorization is to normalize the TMCI in the range [0, 1] since decision-makers are more comfortable with this scale in determining the threshold value. For computing the resolution index (RI), an alternative approach is to assign a different weight for each attribute and recalculate the RI. If several categorization credibility indexes (TMCI) are equivalent, the highest RI should be selected.

In the previous section, seven categorizations were selected. Here, expertise is required to select the final categorization to generate the rules. Based on the domain expert's judgment, attribute b is highly correlated to attribute e and attribute d has a less significant impact on decision attributes. Therefore, the categorization - a1b0c1d0e1f1 (Figure 10) is selected. Note that attributes b and d are removed since they are at level 0 of the concept tree. Finally, the reducts of attributes equivalent to a set of generalized rules are determined as below (Figure 12). The weights are also assigned to the attributes a, c, e, and f (Figure 12).

The decision table in Figure 12 represents the final categorizations. After performing the reduct search procedure, the list of resulting value reducts for Figure 12 is obtained (see Figure 13). The heuristic procedure is applied to determine the reducts.

Consider Table 3, which includes the data from object 1 in Figure 13 expanded with a column indicating the number of objects and a row containing weights associated with the attributes.

The strength index for the three reducts with outcome (2, 3) is as follows:

Reduct 1, SI(1) = (1.0 x 1 + 1.0 x 0 + 0.9 x 1 + 0.6 x 1) x 13 = 32.5

Reduct 2, SI(2) = (1.0 x 1 + 1.0 x 1 + 0.9 x 0 + 0.6 x 1) x 13 = 33.8

Reduct 3, SI(3) = (1.0 x 1 + 1.0 x 1 + 0.9 x 1 + 0.6 x 0) x 13 = 37.7

A higher value of the strength index implies that the corresponding reduct is preferable. In this case reduct 3 with SI(1) = 37.7 is preferred over reduct 1 and reduct 2.

Before executing the rule extraction algorithm, a case number is created in the Table 4, where S is the case number determined by outcome and total number of attributes contained in the reduct. This represents a set of reducts with the same number of attributes and the same outcome. The same case number might be assigned to more than one object. In general, the reducts of the same case are merged.

Next, consider the value reducts in Figure 13. After the rule-extraction algorithm was performed, the list of resulting concise rules was derived (see Table 5 and Table 6). The heuristic algorithm was used to determine the concise rules.

The four performance measures computed for the data in Figure 12 and Table 5 are summarized in Table 6. The concise decision rules are presented in Figure 14.

In Figure 14, performance measures of the decisions rules are illustrated. First, "accuracy" represents how accurate the rule performs based on empirical data while "coverage" indicates how many incidences can be covered by the rule. Second, "length" is the count of the attributes in the rule. Finally, the r_ratio emphasizes the confidence of the rule.

In this case study, the company inducts the decision rules from the historical data. Four rules associated to measure the patent infringement risk are identified. The decision rules can help determine which patents plan to be extended or terminated. The R&D manager is able to choose desired patents with low risk to prevent from infringement. With effective risk management, the company can allocate resources optimally and can be more competitive in industry.

FUTURE RESEARCH DIRECTIONS

Future research can emphasize on collecting additional patent infringement data and cases and establishing an infringement rule database to fathom what features contribute more in high risk patent infringement. Exploration of the patent infringement risk categorization in different industry domains is also desired to pursue. Furthermore, future efforts can be invested in developing a weighted hierarchy framework to improve credibility of the rules.

CONCLUSION

In this study, a methodology to induce infringement rules based on a credible index was proposed. Litigation data was collected from the court database and used to analyze the desired attributes. The credible categorization is determined by the coverage, consistency and evidence of each decision. The level-search procedure was applied to determine credible categorizations. The contribution of the credible categorization approach included providing exact required information. At the rule extraction stage, each strength index is computed according to each decision rule. Finally, the decision rules for patent infringement risk were developed. Businesses and industries can use this findings to determine which patents are more likely to be infringed, which patents

Figure 8. Example of generalization of the patent date and the IPC code

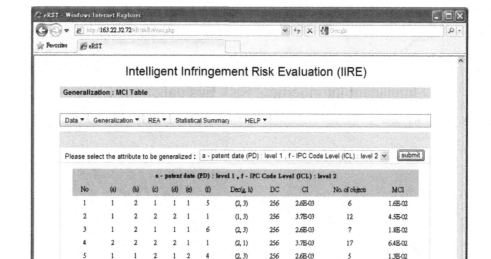

Figure 9. Example of generalization of the IPC code from the original table

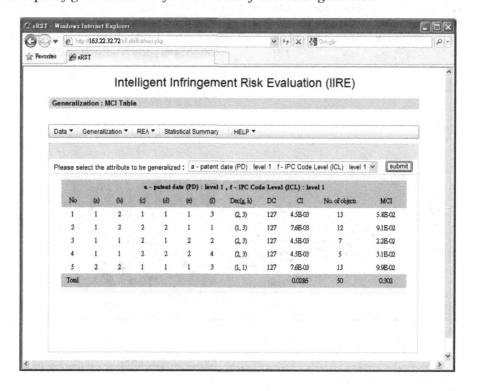

Figure 10. TMCI of the combination of the levels for all attributes

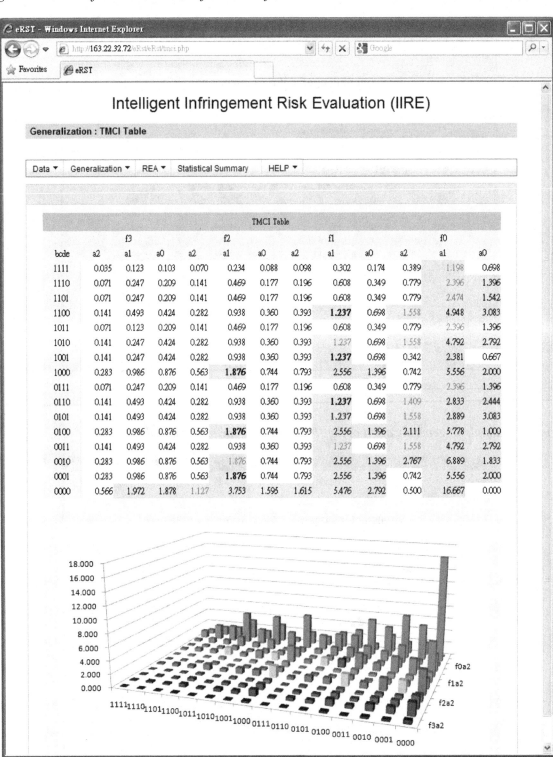

TMCI Table

bcode	f3 a2	f3 a1	f3 a0	f2 a2	f2 a1	f2 a0	f1 a2	f1 a1	f1 a0	f0 a2	f0 a1	f0 a0
1111	0.035	0.123	0.103	0.070	0.234	0.088	0.098	0.302	0.174	0.389	1.198	0.698
1110	0.071	0.247	0.209	0.141	0.469	0.177	0.196	0.608	0.349	0.779	2.396	1.396
1101	0.071	0.247	0.209	0.141	0.469	0.177	0.196	0.608	0.349	0.779	2.474	1.542
1100	0.141	0.493	0.424	0.282	0.938	0.360	0.393	**1.237**	0.698	1.558	4.948	3.083
1011	0.071	0.123	0.209	0.141	0.469	0.177	0.196	0.608	0.349	0.779	2.396	1.396
1010	0.141	0.247	0.424	0.282	0.938	0.360	0.393	1.237	0.698	1.558	4.792	2.792
1001	0.141	0.247	0.424	0.282	0.938	0.360	0.393	**1.237**	0.698	0.342	2.381	0.667
1000	0.283	0.986	0.876	0.563	**1.876**	0.744	0.793	2.556	1.396	0.742	5.556	2.000
0111	0.071	0.247	0.209	0.141	0.469	0.177	0.196	0.608	0.349	0.779	2.396	1.396
0110	0.141	0.493	0.424	0.282	0.938	0.360	0.393	**1.237**	0.698	1.409	2.833	2.444
0101	0.141	0.493	0.424	0.282	0.938	0.360	0.393	**1.237**	0.698	1.558	2.889	3.083
0100	0.283	0.986	0.876	0.563	**1.876**	0.744	0.793	2.556	1.396	2.111	5.778	1.000
0011	0.141	0.493	0.424	0.282	0.938	0.360	0.393	1.237	0.698	1.558	4.792	2.792
0010	0.283	0.986	0.876	0.563	1.876	0.744	0.793	2.556	1.396	2.767	6.889	1.833
0001	0.283	0.986	0.876	0.563	**1.876**	0.744	0.793	2.556	1.396	0.742	5.556	2.000
0000	0.566	1.972	1.878	1.127	3.753	1.595	1.615	5.476	2.792	0.500	16.667	0.000

Figure 11. Statistical summary of the TMCI based on a_0, a_1 and a_2

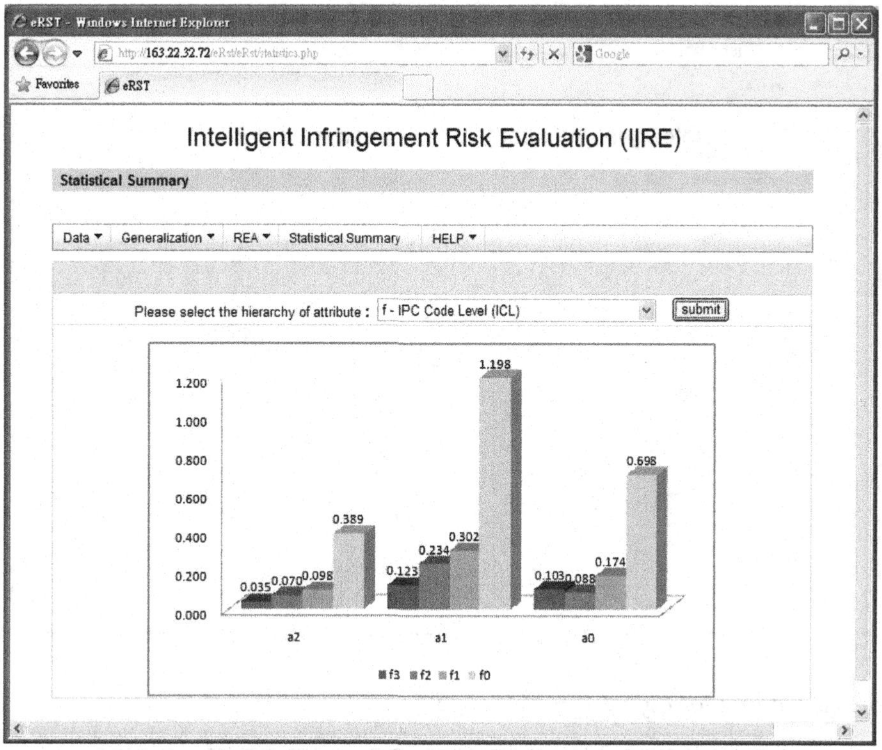

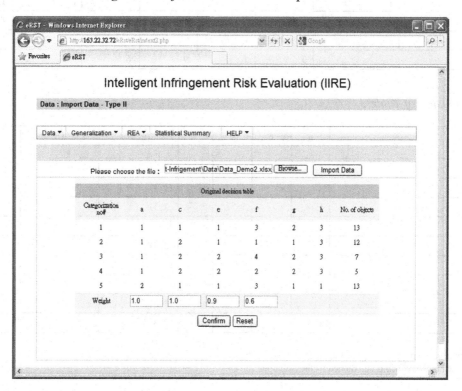

Figure 12. Final credible categorization from the level-search procedure

Figure 13. Value of reducts for the data in Figure 12

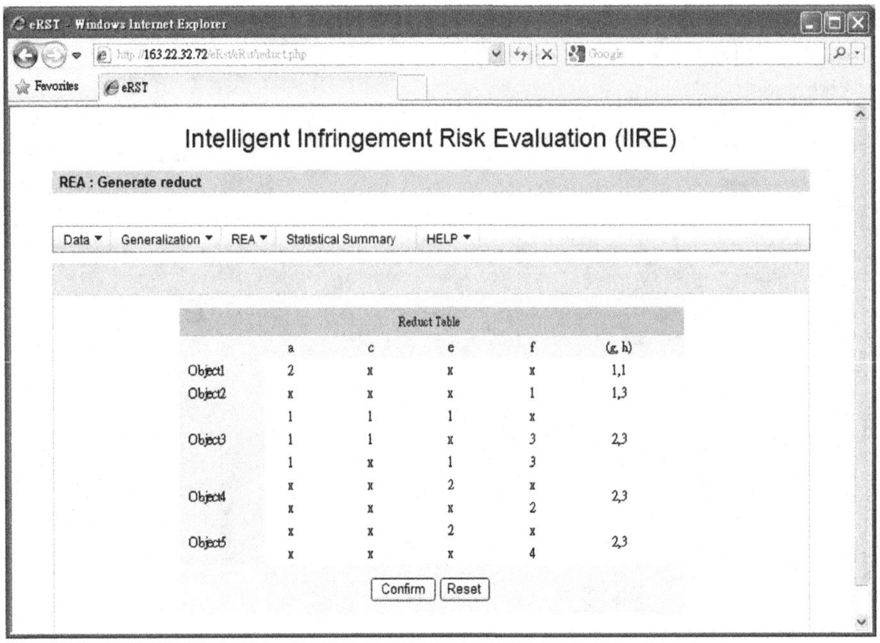

Table 3. Expanded data set for object 1 in Figure 13

Categorization No#.	Reduct No.	a	c	e	f	(g, h)	No. of objects
	1	1	x	1	3	(2, 3)	13
1	2	1	1	x	3	(2, 3)	13
	3	1	1	1	x	(2, 3)	13
Weight wj		0	.0	.9	.6		

Table 4. Extension of Table 3

Categorization No#.	a	c	e	f	(g, h)	Ui	S
5	2	x	x	x	(1, 1)	1	1
2	x	x	x	1	(1, 3)	1	2
	1	x	1	3	(2, 3)		
1	1	1	x	3	(2, 3)	3	4
	1	1	1	x	(2, 3)		
3	x	x	2	x	(2, 3)	1	3
	x	x	x	4	(2, 3)		
4	x	x	2	x	(2, 3)	1	3
	x	x	x	2	(2, 3)		
Note: (1) Ui: total number of attributes contained in the reduct i; (2) S: case number which is determined by the outcomes and Ui.							

142

Table 5. Final value reducts

No#.	T(1)	Reduct No.	a	c	e	f			Selected Weight	No. of Objects	a	c	e	f	Merged Objects	T(2) T(3)	Rule No.
5	1	1	2	x	x	x	(1,1)	1	1	13	2	x	x	x		1	1
2	2	1	x	x	x	1	(1,3)	2	0.6	12	x	x	x	1		2	2
3	3	1	x	x	2	x	(2,3)	3	1	7							
		2	x	x	x	4	(2,3)		0.6		x	x	2	x	3 & 4	3	3
4	4	1	x	x	2	x	(2,3)	3	1	5							
		2	x	x	x	2	(2,3)		0.6								
		1	1	x	1	3	(2,3)		2.5								
1	5	2	1	1	x	3	(2,3)	4	2.6	13	1	1	1	x		4	4
		3	1	1	1	x	(2,3)		2.9								
W			1	1	0.9	0.6											

Table 6. Resulting concise rules

$a_2 \rightarrow g_1 h_1$
$f_1 \rightarrow g_1 h_3$
$(a_1\ c1\ e_1) \vee c2 \rightarrow g_2 h_3$

Figure 14. Final decision rules based on the infringement patent data sets and performance measures of the decisions rules

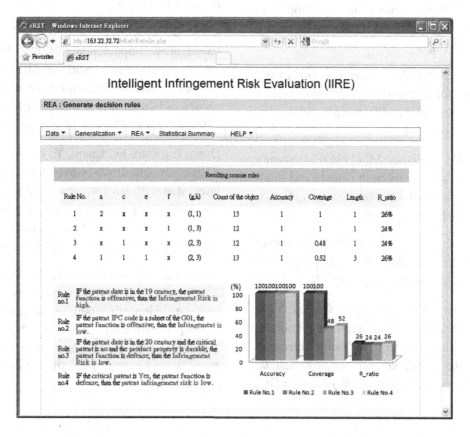

are highly competitive, which patent categories require major budget investments for research and development.

ACKLOWLEDGMENT

This work was partially supported by funding from the Nation Science Council of the Republic of China (NSC 98-2410-H-260-011-MY3, NSC-95-3114-P-260-001).

REFERENCES

Acs, Z. j., & Audretsch, D. B. (1989). Patents as a measure of innovative activity. *Kyklos*, *42*(2), 171–180. doi:10.1111/j.1467-6435.1989. tb00186.x

Andrew, J. N. (2009). Measuring knowledge spillovers: What patents, licenses and publications reveal about innovation diffusion. *Research Policy*, *38*(6), 994–1005. doi:10.1016/j. respol.2009.01.023

Andrew, K. (2001). Rough Set Theory: A Data Mining Tool for Semiconductor Manufacturing. *IEEE Transactions on Electronics Packaging Manufacturing*, *24*(1).

Archibugi, D., & Pianta, M. (1996). Measuring technological change through patents and innovation surveys. *Technovation*, *16*(9), 451–468. doi:10.1016/0166-4972(96)00031-4

Ashton, W. B., & Sen, R. K. (1988). Using patent information in technology business planning I. *Research-Technology Management*, *31*(6), 42–46.

Bello, R., Nowe, A., Caballero, Y., Gomez, Y., & Vrancx, P. (2005). A model based on ant colony system and rough set theory to feature selection. In *Proceedings of the 2005 conference on Genetic and evolutionary computation*, Washington DC.

Bosworth, D. L. (1984). Foreign patent flows to and from the United Kingdom. *Research Policy*, *13*(2), 115–124. doi:10.1016/0048-7333(84)90010-6

Breitzman, A., & Thomas, P. (2002). Using patent citation analysis to target/value M&A candidates. *Research technology management*, *45*(5), 28-36.

Chen, M. S., Han, J., & Chu, Y. P. S. (1996). Data Mining: An Overview from a Database Perspective. *IEEE Transactions on Knowledge and Data Engineering*, *8*(6), 866–883. doi:10.1109/69.553155

Chen, Q. (2008). The effect of patent laws on invention rates: Evidence from cross-country panels. *Journal of Comparative Economics*, *36*(4), 694–704. doi:10.1016/j.jce.2008.05.004

Chiu, Y. J., & Chen, Y. W. (2007). Using AHP in patent valuation. *Mathematical and Computer Modelling*, *46*(7-8), 1054–1062. doi:10.1016/j. mcm.2007.03.009

Choy, C., Kim, S., & Park, Y. (2007). A patent-based cross impact analysis for Quantitative estimation of technological impact: the case of information and Communication technology. *Technological Forecasting and Social Change*, *74*(8), 1296–1314. doi:10.1016/j.techfore.2006.10.008

Dong, L., Xiao, D., Liang, Y., & Liu, Y. (2008). Rough set and fuzzy wavelet neural network integrated with least square weighted fusion algorithm based fault diagnosis research for power transformers. *Electric Power Systems Research*, *78*(1), 129–136. doi:10.1016/j.epsr.2006.12.013

Doumpos, M., Marinakis, Y., Marinaki, M., & Zopounidis, C. (2009). An evolutionary approach to construction of outranking models for multi-criteria classification: The case of the ELECTRE TRI method. *European Journal of Operational Research*, *199*(2), 496–505. doi:10.1016/j. ejor.2008.11.035

Duguet, E., & Macgarvie, M. (2005). How well do patent citations measure flows of Technology? Evidence from French innovation surveys. *Economics of Innovation and New Technology, 14*(5), 375–393. doi:10.1080/1043859042000307347

Foglia, P. (2007). Patentability search strategies and the reformed IPC: A patent office perspective. *World Patent Information, 29*(1), 33–53. doi:10.1016/j.wpi.2006.08.002

Gaudreault, J., Frayret, J. M., & Pesant, G. (2009). Distributed search for supply chain coordination. *Computers in Industry, 60*(6), 441–451. doi:10.1016/j.compind.2009.02.006

Gelle, E., & Karhu, K. (2003). Information quality for strategic technology planning. *Industrial Management & Data Systems, 103*(8), 633–643. doi:10.1108/02635570310497675

Ginarte, J. C., & Park, W. G. (1997). Determinants of patent rights: A cross-national study. *Research Policy, 26*(3), 283–301. doi:10.1016/S0048-7333(97)00022-X

Graham, S., & Mowery, D. C. (2003). Intellectual property protection in the software industry. In Cohen, W., & Merrill, S. (Eds.), *Patents in the knowledge-based economy: proceedings of the science, technology and economic policy board*. Washington, DC: National academies press.

Hausman, J., & Leonard, G. K. (2006). Real options and patent damages: the legal treatment of non-infringing alternatives, and incentives to innovate. *Journal of Economic Surveys, 20*(4), 493–512. doi:10.1111/j.1467-6419.2006.00258.x

Heckerman, D., Mannila, H., Pregibon, D., & Uthurusamy, R. (1997). *Proceedings of the Third International Conference on Knowledge Discovery and Data Mining*. Menlo Park, CA: AAAI press.

Helpman, E. (1993). Innovation, imitation, and intellectual property rights. *Econometrica, 61*(6), 1247–1280. doi:10.2307/2951642

Hereof, D., & Hoisl, K. (2007). Institutionalized incentives for ingenuity-patent value and the german employees. *Inventions Act. Research Policy, 36*(8), 1143–1162.

Hereof, D., Schererc, F. M., & Vopel, K. (2003). Citations, family size, opposition and the value of patent rights. *Research Policy, 32*(8), 1343–1363. doi:10.1016/S0048-7333(02)00124-5

Hirschey, M., & Richardson, V. J. (2001). Valuation effects of patent quality: A Comparison for Japanese and US firms. *Pacific-Basin Finance Journal, 9*(1), 65–82. doi:10.1016/S0927-538X(00)00038-X

Hirschey, M., & Richardson, V. J. (2004). Are scientific indicators of patent quality Useful to investors? *Journal of Empirical Finance, 11*(1), 91–107. doi:10.1016/j.jempfin.2003.01.001

Huang, C. C., Fan, Y. N., Tseng, T. L., Lee, C. H., & Huang, H. F. (2008). A hybrid data mining approach to quality assurance of manufacturing process. *IEEE International Conference on Fuzzy Systems*.

Huang, C. C., & Tseng, T. L. (2004). Rough set approach to case-based reasoning application. *Expert Systems with Applications, 26*(3), 369–385. doi:10.1016/j.eswa.2003.09.008

Jensen, R., & Shen, Q. (2007). Fuzzy-Rough Sets Assisted Attribute Selection. *IEEE Transactions on Fuzzy Systems, 15*(1), 73–89. doi:10.1109/TFUZZ.2006.889761

Jerzy, W. G. (1988). Knowledge acquisition under uncertainty — a rough set approach. *Journal of Intelligent & Robotic Systems, 1*(1), 3–16. doi:10.1007/BF00437317

Kamien, M. I., Tauman, Y., & Zang, I. (1988). Optimal license fees for a new product. *Mathematical Social Sciences*, *16*(1), 77–106. doi:10.1016/0165-4896(88)90006-6

Kenneth, A. F., Scharfstein, D. S., & Stein, J. C. (1993). Risk management: coordinating corporate investment and financing policies. *The Journal of Finance*, *48*(5), 1629–1658. doi:10.2307/2329062

Kim, W. (1990). *Introduction to Object-Oriented Databases*. Cambridge, MA: MIT Press.

Knight, H. (2001). *Patent strategy for researchers and research managers. New York*. Jackson: Wiley.

Kuijk, Ad. J.G. van & Lobeck, M. A. (1984). A model title page for patent specifications. *World Patent Information*, *6*(1), 24–31. doi:10.1016/0172-2190(84)90020-6

Lai, K. K., & Wu, S. J. (2005). Using the patent co-citation approach to establish a new patent classification system. *Information Processing & Management*, *41*(2), 313–330. doi:10.1016/j.ipm.2003.11.004

Lai, Y. H., & Che, H. C. (2009). Modeling patent legal value by Extension Neural Network. *Expert Systems with Applications*, *36*(7), 10520–10528. doi:10.1016/j.eswa.2009.01.027

Lanjouw, J. O., & Schankerman, M. (2001). Characteristics of Patent Litigation: A Window on Competition. *The Rand Journal of Economics*, *32*(1), 129–151. doi:10.2307/2696401

Levine, L. O. (1987). Patent activity by date of application — Estimating recent applications in the U.S. patent system. *World Patent Information*, *9*(3), 137-139.

Levitas, E. F., McFadyen, M. A., & Loree, D. (2006). Survival and the introduction of new technology: a patent analysis in the integrated circuit industry. *Journal of Engineering and Technology Management*, *23*(3), 182–201. doi:10.1016/j.jengtecman.2006.06.008

Liang, W. Y., & Huang, C. C. (2006). Agent-based demand forecast in multi-echelon supply chain. *Decision Support Systems*, *42*(1), 390–407. doi:10.1016/j.dss.2005.01.009

Lingras, P., Hogo, M., Snorek, M., & West, C. (2005). Temporal analysis of clusters of supermarket customers: conventional versus interval set approach. *Information Sciences*, *172*(1-2), 215–240. doi:10.1016/j.ins.2004.12.007

Liu, S., & Shyu, J. (1997). Strategic planning for technology development with patent analysis. *International Journal of Technology Management*, *13*(5-6), 661–680. doi:10.1504/IJTM.1997.001689

Makarov, M. (2004). The process of reforming the International Patent Classification. *World Patent Information*, *26*(2), 137-141.

Malcolm, J. B., & Michael, J. P. (2001). Variable precision rough set theory and data discretisation: an application to corporate failure prediction. *Omega*, *29*(6), 561–576. doi:10.1016/S0305-0483(01)00045-7

Mariani, M., & Romanelli, M. (2007). Stacking" and "picking" inventions: The patenting behavior of European inventors. *Research Policy*, *36*(8), 1128–1142. doi:10.1016/j.respol.2007.07.009

Mogee, M. E. (1991). Using patent data for technology analysis and planning. *Research-Technology Management*, *34*(4), 43–49.

Paci, R., & Sassu, A. (1997). International patents and national technological specialization. *Technovation*, *17*(10), 25-38.

Park, Y., & Park, G. (2004). A new method for technology valuation in monetary legal value: procedure and application. *Technovation*, *24*(5), 387–394. doi:10.1016/S0166-4972(02)00099-8

Pawlak, Z. (1982). Rough sets. *International journal of computer and information sciences*, *11*(5), 341-356.

Pawlak, Z. (1991). *Rough sets Theoretical aspects of reasoning about data*. Dordrecht: Kluwer Academic Publishers.

Pawlak, Z. (1997). Rough set approach to knowledge-based decision. *European Journal of Operational Research, 99*(1), 48–57. doi:10.1016/S0377-2217(96)00382-7

Penrose, E. (1951). *The Economic of the International Patent System*. Baltimore, MD: John Hopkins Press.

Predki, B., Słowiński, R., Stefanowski, J., Susmaga, R., & Wilk, S. (2008). ROSE - Software Implementation of the Rough Set Theory. *Lecture Notes in Computer Science, 1424*, 605–608. doi:10.1007/3-540-69115-4_85

Predki, B., Słowiński, R., Stefanowski, J., Susmaga, R., & Wilk, S. (2008). ROSE - Software Implementation of the Rough Set Theory. *LNCS, 1424*, 605–608.

Qian, Y., Liang, J., & Dang, C. (2008). Converse approximation and rule extraction from decision tables in rough set theory. *Computers & Mathematics with Applications (Oxford, England), 55*(8), 1754–1765. doi:10.1016/j.camwa.2007.08.031

Quinlan, J. R. (1993). *Programs for Machine Learning*. Los Altos, CA: Morgan Kaufmann.

Reitzig, M. (2004). Improving patent valuations for management purposes—validating new indicators by analyzing application rationales. *Research Policy, 33*(6-7), 939–957. doi:10.1016/j.respol.2004.02.004

Reitzig, M. (2004). Improving patent valuations for management purposes – Validating new indicators by analyzing application rationales. *Research Policy, 33*(6-7), 939–957. doi:10.1016/j.respol.2004.02.004

Rupprecht, K. (1994). CD-ROMs for publication of patents: A critical review. *World Patent Information, 16*(4), 216–219. doi:10.1016/0172-2190(94)90006-X

Saiki, T., Akano, Y., Watanabe, C., & Tou, Y. (2006). A new dimension of potential resources in innovation: A wider scope of patent claims can lead to new functionality development. *Technovation, 26*(7), 796–806. doi:10.1016/j.technovation.2005.06.002

Shen, L., Francis, E., Tay, H., Qu, L., & Shen, Y. (2000). Fault diagnosis using Rough Sets Theory. *Computers in Industry, 43*(1), 61–72. doi:10.1016/S0166-3615(00)00050-6

Shyng, J. Y., Wang, F. K., Tzeng, G. H., & Wu, K. S. (2005). Rough set theory in analyzing the attributes of combination values for the insurance market. *Expert Systems with Applications, 32*(1), 56–64. doi:10.1016/j.eswa.2005.11.002

Silverberg, G., & Verspagenb, B. (2007). The size distribution of innovations Revisited: An application of extreme value statistics to citation and value Measures of patent significance. *Journal of Econometrics, 139*(2), 318–339. doi:10.1016/j.jeconom.2006.10.017

Simoudis, E., Han, J., & Fayyad, U. (1996). In *Proceedings of the Second International Conference on Knowledge Discovery and Data Mining*. Menlo Park, CA: AAAI press.

Soong, J. W. (2005). *Patent Damage Strategies and The Enterprise License: Constructive Notice, Actual Notice, No Notice*, Duke L. & Tech. Rev. 0002.

Stembridge & Corish. (2004). Patent data mining and effective patent portfolio management. *Intellectual Asset Management, 8*, 30–35.

Taylor, C. T., & Silberston, Z. A. (1973). *The Economic Impact of the Patent Systems: a Study of the British Experience*. London: Cambridge University Press.

Tseng, T. L., & Huang, C. C. (2007). Rough set-based approach to feature selection in customer relationship management. *Omega, 35*(4), 365–383. doi:10.1016/j.omega.2005.07.006

Tseng, T. L., Jothishankar, M. C., & Wu, T. T. (2004). Quality control problem in printed circuit board manufacturing—An extended rough set theory approach. *Journal of Manufacturing Systems, 23*(1), 56–72. doi:10.1016/S0278-6125(04)80007-4

Van Trieste, S., & Vis, W. (2007). Valuing patents on cost-reducing technology: A case study. *International Journal of Production Economics, 105*(1), 282–292. doi:10.1016/j.ijpe.2006.04.019

Verhaegen, P. A., D'hondt, J., Vertommen, J., Dewulf, S., & Duflou, J. R. (2009). Relating properties and functions from patents to TRIZ trends. [Design Synthesis]. *CIRP Journal of Manufacturing Science and Technology, 1*(3), 126–130. doi:10.1016/j.cirpj.2008.09.010

Von Wartburg, I., Teichert, T., & Rost, K. (2005). Inventive progress measured by Multi-stage patent citation analysis. *Research Policy, 34*(10), 1591–1607. doi:10.1016/j.respol.2005.08.001

Wang, Q. H., & Li, J. R. (2004). A rough set-based fault ranking prototype system for fault diagnosis. *Engineering Applications of Artificial Intelligence, 17*(8), 909–917. doi:10.1016/j.engappai.2004.08.013

Xiao, H., & Zhang, X. (2008). Comparison studies on classification for remote sensing image based on data mining method. *WSES Transactions on Computers, 7*(5), 552–558.

Zhang, Z., Shi, Y., & Gao, G. (2009). A rough set-based multiple criteria linear programming approach for the medical diagnosis and prognosis. *Expert Systems with Applications, 36*(5), 8932–8937. doi:10.1016/j.eswa.2008.11.007

Ziarko, W. P., & Van Rijsbergen, C. J. (1994). *Rough Sets, Fuzzy sets and Knowledge Discovery*. New York: Springer-Verlag.

ADDITIONAL READING

Aggarwal, N. & Walden, Eric A. (2007). The problem of distributed intellectual property bundles: a transaction cost perspective. *Proceedings of the ninth international conference on Electronic commerce*, Minneapolis, MN, USA.

Bit, M., & Beaubouef, T. (2008). Rough set uncertainty for robotic systems. *J. Comput. Small Coll., 23*(6), 126–132.

Choy, C., Kim, S., & Park, Y. (2007). A patent-based cross impact analysis for Quantitative estimation of technological impact: the case of information and Communication technology. *Technological Forecasting and Social Change, 74*(8), 1296–1314. doi:10.1016/j.techfore.2006.10.008

Ghoula, N., Khelif, K., & Dieng-Kuntz, R. (2007). Supporting Patent Mining by using Ontology-based Semantic Annotations. *Proceedings of the IEEE/WIC/ACM International Conference on Web Intelligence*, IEEE Computer Society.

Graham, S., & Mowery, D. C. (2003). Intellectual property protection in the software industry. *in patents in the knowledge-based economy: proceedings of the science, technology and economic policy board., Wesley cohen and steven merrill, eds. National academies press*, Washington

Grimes, S., Alkadi, G., & Beaubouef, T. (2009). Design and implementation of the rough relational database system. *J. Comput. Small Coll., 24*(4), 88–95.

Harris, C. G. Foster, S., Arens, R. & Srinivasan, P. (2009). On the role of classification in patent invalidity searches. *Proceeding of the 2nd international workshop on Patent information retrieval*, Hong Kong, China.

Huang, C. C., & Tseng, T. L. (2004). Rough set approach to case-based reasoning application. *Expert Systems with Applications, 26*(3), 369–385. doi:10.1016/j.eswa.2003.09.008

Jerzy, W. G. (1988). Knowledge acquisition under uncertainty — a rough set approach. *Journal of Intelligent & Robotic Systems, 1*(1), 3–16. doi:10.1007/BF00437317

Kim, Y., Tian, Y., & Jeong, Y. (2009). Automatic discovery of technology trends from patent text. *Proceedings of the 2009 ACM symposium on Applied Computing,* Honolulu, Hawaii.

Li, X., Chen, H., Zhang, Z., & Li, J. (2007). Automatic patent classification using citation network information: an experimental study in nanotechnology. *Proceedings of the 7th ACM/ IEEE-CS joint conference on Digital libraries,* Vancouver, BC, Canada.

Mogee, M. E. (1991). Using patent data for technology analysis and planning. *Research-Technology Management, 34*(4), 43–49.

Nanba, H., Fujii, A., Iwayama, M., & Hashimoto, T. (2008). The patent mining task in the seventh NTCIR workshop. *Proceeding of the 1st ACM workshop on Patent information retrieval,* Napa Valley, California, USA.

Pawlak, Z. (1982). Rough sets, *International journal of computer and information sciences, 11*(5), 341-356.

Pawlak, Z. (1991). *Rough sets Theoretical aspects of reasoning about data.* Dordrecht: Kluwer Academic Publishers.

Pawlak, Z. (1997). Rough set approach to knowledge-based decision. *European Journal of Operational Research, 99*(1), 48–57. doi:10.1016/ S0377-2217(96)00382-7

Predki, B., Słowiński, R., Stefanowski, J., Susmaga, R., & Wilk, S. (2008). ROSE - Software Implementation of the Rough Set Theory. *Lecture Notes in Computer Science, 1424,* 605–608. doi:10.1007/3-540-69115-4_85

Reitzig, M. (2004). Improving patent valuations for management purposes – Validating new indicators by analyzing application rationales. *Research Policy, 33*(6-7), 939–957. doi:10.1016/j. respol.2004.02.004

Samuelson, P. (2007). Software patents and the metaphysics of Section 271(f). *Communications of the ACM, 50*(6), 15–19. doi:10.1145/1247001.1247018

Shyng, J. Y., Wang, F. K., Tzeng, G. H., & Wu, K. S. (2005). Rough set theory in analyzing the attributes of combination values for the insurance market. *Expert Systems with Applications, 32*(1), 56–64. doi:10.1016/j.eswa.2005.11.002

Stembridge & Corish (2004). Patent data mining and effective patent portfolio management. *Intellectual asset management, 8,* 30-35.

Tan, S., Wang, Y., & Cheng, X. (2007). Text Feature Ranking Based on Rough-set Theory. *Proceedings of the IEEE/WIC/ACM International Conference on Web Intelligence,* IEEE Computer Society.

Tseng, T. L., & Huang, C. C. (2007). Rough set-based approach to feature selection in customer relationship management. *Omega, 35*(4), 365–383. doi:10.1016/j.omega.2005.07.006

Ziarko, W. P., & Van Rijsbergen, C. J. (1994). *Rough Sets, Fuzzy sets and Knowledge Discovery*. New York: Springer-Verlag.

KEY TERMS AND DEFINITIONS

Accuracy Index: An index used to identify categorization accuracy of the original data set.

Categorization: A partition of the instance space into equivalence classes based upon the condition attributes.

Credible Index: An index used to confirm credibility of each categorization.. The smaller the difference between "decision attribute" and "condition attribute," the higher the value of the credibility index. The higher credibility index is correlated to the higher modified credibility index.

Patent Infringement: A type of intellectual property damage that results when competing manufacturers imitate successful innovations or adapt them to their own use.

Reduct: The minimum data content necessary to represent an object.

Resolution Index: An index to indicate the level of concept hierarchical. After the hierarchy is generalized or specified, the resolution index must be recalculated since the lower resolution index indicates stronger support for the credibility.

Risk Analysis: It is a scientifically based process of evaluating hazards and the likelihood of exposure to those hazards, and then estimating the resulting public health impact.

Rough Set Theory: A theory was developed by Pawlak (1982) to classify imprecise, uncertain, or incomplete information or knowledge expressed by data acquired from experience. It is a mathematical approach to managing vague and uncertain data or problems related to information systems, indiscernible relations and classifications, attribute dependence and approximation accuracy, reduct and core attribute sets, as well as decision rules.

Strength Index: An index introduced in order to identify meaningful reducts. A reduct with a higher strength index is preferred over a reduct with a lower index.

Chapter 9
Visual Survey Analysis in Marketing

Marko Robnik-Šikonja
University of Ljubljana, Slovenia

Koen Vanhoof
Hasselt University, Belgium

ABSTRACT

The authors present a use and visualization of the ordinal evaluation (OrdEval) algorithm as a promising technique to study questionnaire data. The OrdEval algorithm is a general tool to analyze data with ordinal attributes, including surveys. It has many favorable features, including context sensitivity, ability to exploit meaning of ordered features and ordered response, robustness to noise and missing values in the data, and visualization capability. The authors select customer (dis)satisfaction analysis, an important problem from marketing research, as a case study and present visual analysis on two practical applications: business-to-business and costumer-to-business customer satisfaction studies. They demonstrate some interesting advantages offered by the new methodology and visualization and show how to extract and interpret new insights not available with classical analytical toolbox.

DOI: 10.4018/978-1-60960-102-7.ch009

BACKGROUND

In recent years we have observed large changes in economy in general and marketing in particular as a result of internet expansion, globalization, and ubiquitous information availability. One of the scientific fields which gained momentum as a result of this was data analysis under various names: statistics, data mining, machine learning, intelligent data analysis, knowledge discovery. Many new data analysis techniques emerged which exploit availability of more and different data from several sources, and increased computational power of nowadays computers. Some examples of these techniques are support vector machines, text analytics, association rules, ensemble techniques, subgroup discovery, etc. These techniques have been accepted into analytics' standard toolbox in many disciplines: genetics, engineering, medicine, vision, statistics, marketing, etc.

The *OrdEval* algorithm (Robnik-Šikonja & Vanhoof, 2007) is a novel analytical tool which emerged in data mining context aiming to evaluate the importance and the impact of various factors in the given data (e.g., survey). For example, in the analysis of customer satisfaction data for a particular product/service, OrdEval can determine the importance of each product's feature to the overall customer's satisfaction, and also indicate the thresholds where satisfaction with the individual feature starts having a strong positive or negative impact on the overall satisfaction. The output of OrdEval are probabilistic factors indicating the probability that increase/decrease in the individual feature or the feature's value will have impact on the dependent variable. The intuition behind this approach is to approximate the inner workings of the decision process taking place in each individual respondent, which forms the relationship between the features and the response. If such brain introspection would be possible one could observe a causal effect that the change of a feature's value has on the response value. By measuring such an effect we

could reason about the importance of the feature's values and the type of the attribute. Also, we could determine which values are thresholds for change of behavior. While this is impossible, OrdEval algorithm uses the data sample and approximates this reasoning. For each respondent it selects its most similar respondents and makes inferences based on them. For example, to evaluate the effect an increase in a certain feature value would have on the overall satisfaction, the algorithm computes the probability for such an effect from the similar respondents with increased value of that feature. To get statistically valid and practically interesting results the overall process is repeated for a large enough number of respondents, and weighted with large enough number of similar respondents.

Feature (attribute) evaluation is an important component of many machine learning tasks, e.g. feature subset selection, constructive induction, decision and regression tree learning. Scores assigned to attributes during evaluation, also provide important information to the domain expert trying to get an insight into the problem domain. In this chapter we are interested in a subclass of feature evaluation, namely evaluation of conditionally strongly dependent ordinal attributes where each of the individual attribute's values may be dependent on other attributes in a different way. The problem of feature (attribute) evaluation has received a lot of attention in the literature. There are several measures for evaluation of attributes' quality. For classification problems the most popular are e.g. Gini index (Breiman et al., 1984), gain ratio (Quinlan, 1993), MDL (Kononenko, 1995), and ReliefF (Kononenko, 1994; Robnik-Šikonja and Kononenko, 2003). The first three are impurity based and measure quality of attribute according to the purity of class value distribution after the split on the values of that attribute. They evaluate each attribute separately, are not aware of the ordering of the attribute's values and cannot provide useful information for each individual value of the attribute. ReliefF on the other hand is context sensitive (by measuring how the attribute separates similar instances) and could be adapted to handle ordered attributes (by changing the definition of its similarity measure), but cannot provide information for each value separately and does not differentiate between the positive and negative changes of the attribute and their impact on the class value. By converting ordered nominal attributes into numeric ones we could use RReliefF, a regression version of ReliefF (Robnik-Sikonja and Kononenko, 2003) which, at the cost of assuming linear ordering, naturally handles positive and negative changes of an attribute, but cannot separate between positive and negative impact on a class value; also the extraction of information for each individual attribute's value is not possible in the RReliefF.

A typical approach in practical marketing research of customer (dis)satisfaction is to define a number of features of the product/service and then to conduct a survey on a representative sample of customers where the customers rate their satisfaction with each of the features and also express their overall (dis)satisfaction. While all types of captured answers (features) can be integrated with our approach, we are interested only in those questions of the survey which correspond to the product/service features. We consider them attributes in our data set and the overall (dis)satisfaction corresponds to the class value. The goal of feature analysis in marketing research is manifold:

1. identify features which influence the overall (dis)satisfaction most,
2. identify type of features: marketing research differentiates mostly between three types of important features:
    a. *Basic features* are taken for granted by customers. High score in these features does not significantly increase the overall satisfaction, while a low score usually causes dissatisfaction.
    b. *Performance features* are important features not taken for granted; they

usually have a positive correlation with overall satisfaction: the higher the score the bigger the effect on the overall satisfaction,
    c. *Excitement features* usually describes properties of product/service which are normally not very important to the users, but can cause excitement (and boost in satisfaction) if the score is very high.
3. identify those attribute values (thresholds) which have positive/negative impact on overall satisfaction, and
4. identify typical behavior patterns of attribute values:
    a. *upward reinforcement*: the value of a feature has a positive effect on overall satisfaction,
    b. *downward reinforcement*: the value of a feature has a negative effect on overall satisfaction,
    c. *anchoring*: the value of a feature acts as an anchor on overall (dis)satisfaction and prevents its change,
    d. *compensation* is a type of behavior characteristic for subsets of features, namely low score in one of the features is compensated with high score in one or more others.

There are many different feature evaluation algorithms in data mining which can evaluate, rank and/or select the most informative features (goal 1). For problems with highly dependent features as is predominantly the case in the marketing research, the most suitable heuristics are probably ReliefF (Robnik-Sikonja & Kononenko, 2003) and CM (Hong, 1997). Other goals (2-4) remain mostly untouched by current work in machine learning and data mining.

The motivation and contribution of this chapter is to demonstrate how OrdEval works, how its output can be visualized and adapted to include information relevant for practitioners. As a means for this we use a marketing context and present application of OrdEval on two costumer (dis) satisfaction studies.

ORDEVAL APPROACH

OrdEval algorithm can be used for analysis of any data where the dependent variable has ordered values, meaning that it is also suitable for surveys where answers are given in the graded manner. The methodology uses conditional probabilities called 'reinforcement factors' as they approximate the upward and downward reinforcement effect the particular feature value has on the dependent attribute. For each value of the feature we obtain estimates of two conditional probabilities: the probability that the response value increases given the increase of the feature value (upward reinforcement), and the probability that the response value decreases given the decrease of the feature value (downward reinforcement). To take the context of other features into account, these probabilities are computed in the local context, from the most similar instances. The visualization of these factors gives clear clues about the role of each feature, the importance of each value and the threshold values. To understand the idea of OrdEval algorithm, the feature should not be treated as a whole. Rather we shall observe the effect a single value of the feature may have.

We use a notation where each of the n learning instances I is represented by an ordered pair (x,y), where each vector of attributes x consists of individual attributes A_i, $i=1,...,a$, (a is the number of attributes) and is labeled with one of the ordered class values y_j, $j=1,...,c$ (c is the number of class values) $y_1 < y_2 < ... < y_c$. Each discrete ordered attribute A_i has values 1 through m_i (m_i is the number of values of attribute A_i). We use $y(I)$ in a functional form when we refer to the class value of the t-th instance and $I_{t,i}$ when we refer to the value of the attribute A_i for the t-th instance. We write $p(y_j)$ as the probability of the class value y_j.

To explain the idea of the approach we need some definitions. Let R be a randomly selected observation and S the observation most similar to it. Let j be the value of the feature A_i at observation R. We observe the necessary changes of response value and features (A_i with value j in particular) which would change S to R. If these changes are positive (increase of response and/or feature values), let us define the following probabilities.

- $P(A_{i,j}^p)$ is a probability that j (the value of feature A_i at R) is larger than the value of feature A_i at its most similar observation S. By estimating $P(A_{i,j}^p)$ we gather evidence of the probability that the similar observation S has lower value of A_i and the change of S to R is positive.

- $P(C_{i,j}^p A_{i,j}^p)$ is a probability that both the response as well as j (the value of feature A_i at R) are larger than the response and feature value of its most similar observation S. With $P(C_{i,j}^p A_{i,j}^p)$ we estimate the probability that positive change in both the response and A_i value of similar instance S is needed to get the values of R.

Similarly, for negative changes which would turn S into R (decrease of response and/or feature values), we define $P(A_{i,j}^n)$ and $P(C_{i,j}^n A_{i,j}^n)$. The outputs of the algorithm are two factors, upward and downward reinforcement, computed for each value of each feature. These factors measure the upward/downward trends exhibited in the data. The upward reinforcement of the i-th feature's value j is defined as

$$U_{i,j} = P(C_{i,j}^p \mid A_{i,j}^p) = \frac{P(C_{i,j}^p A_{i,j}^p)}{P(A_{i,j}^p)} \qquad (1)$$

This factor reports the probability that a positive response change is caused by the positive feature change. This intuitively corresponds to the effect the positive change in a feature's value has on the response. Similarly the downward reinforcement is defined as

$$D_{i,j} = P(C_{i,j}^n \mid A_{i,j}^n) = \frac{P(C_{i,j}^n A_{i,j}^n)}{P(A_{i,j}^n)}, \qquad (2)$$

and reports the effect the decrease of attribute's value has on the decrease of the class' value. The $U_{i,j}$ and $D_{i,j}$ factors are efficiently estimated by the OrdEval algorithm which we present below in a simplified form intended for easier comprehension.

Input: for each respondent a vector of feature values and the overall score

Output: $U_{i,j}$ and $D_{i,j}$ for all features i and their values j

1. *for* all features i and their values j initialize $A_{i,j}^p$, $A_{i,j}^n$, $C_{i,j}^p A_{i,j}^p$, $C_{i,j}^n A_{i,j}^n$ to 0
2. *for* pre-specified number of respondents
3. randomly select a respondent R
4. find k nearest respondents closest to R
5. *for* each closest respondent S and each features i

update weights of $A_{i,j}^p$, $A_{i,j}^n$, $C_{i,j}^p A_{i,j}^p$, $C_{i,j}^n A_{i,j}^n$ as follows:

6. *if* feature value of S is lower than j increment $A_{i,j}^p$,
7. *if* both feature and overall score value of S are lower than j increment $C_{i,j}^p A_{i,j}^p$,
8. *if* feature value of S is higher than j increment $A_{i,j}^n$,
9. *if* both feature and overall score value of S are higher than j increment $C_{i,j}^n A_{i,j}^n$
10. *for* all features i and their values j compute

11. $U_{i,j} = C_{i,j}^p A_{i,j}^p \, / \, A_{i,j}^p$ and $D_{i,j} = C_{i,j}^n A_{i,j}^p \, / \, A_{i,j}^n$

The algorithm assumes that the cause of the differences in overall score are the differences in the attributes' values and gives these values some credit for that, but only if the sign of the differences in class and attribute is the same. It first sets counters of (co)occurring changes to zero (line 1). Than it randomly selects a respondent R (line 3) and searches for its k nearest respondents (line 4). For each of these most similar respondents it updates the counters for all the features depending on the overall scores and feature values of the randomly selected respondent and the near respondents (lines 5 - 9): if the feature value of the near instance is lower than the value of the random instance (line 6) then the change is positive and we update $A_{i,j}^p$, for the value j of the given feature i (j is the value of feature i for respondent R). If additionally the overall score of the similar respondent is lower than the score of the random respondent (line 7) then the change in both overall score and feature is positive and we update $C_{i,j}^p A_{i,j}^p$, for given feature i and its value of random respondent j. Similarly we do for negative changes in feature and overall score (lines 8-9). We repeat the whole process (lines 2 - 9) for a pre-specified number of iterations. Conservatively we can set this number to be equal to the number of respondents, but we get useful results even if we run only a few iterations (e.g., logarithm of the number of respondents). Finally the upward and downward enforcement factors for all the values of attributes are computed as conditional probabilities (lines 10-11).

The increments depend on the values of attribute A_i at the random instances R and its near instance S. The simplest form of update function $w(R,S)$ (see Eq. (3)) takes into account only the number of nearest instances k. The idea is to average the results of k nearest instances.

$$w(R, S) = \frac{1}{k} \qquad (3)$$

In our work we use value $k=10$ as this is the default value of most k-nearest neighbor classification studies. Depending on the nature of the problem other values could be more suitable, but this is not the topic of this work. For discussion see (Duda et al., 2001). A more sophisticated version of the updated function takes also the distance between the instances into account: closer instances should have greater impact. Exponentially decreasing weighted contribution of instances ranked by distance is recommended by Robnik-Šikonja and Kononenko (2003). See this reference for detailed explanation of this issue.

Missing entries which frequently occur in these types of problems can simply be excluded from computation. The similarity of instances is computed as Manhattan distance over all the attributes:

$$d(I_t, I_u) = \sum_{i=1}^{a} \mathrm{diff}(A_i, I_t, I_u). \qquad (4)$$

The single attribute distance for two instances I_t and I_u is computed with the function $\mathrm{diff}(A_i, I_t, I_u)$. For ordinal attributes, when we do not have better domain knowledge available we can assume linear ordering:

$$\mathrm{diff}(A_i, I_t, I_u) = \frac{|I_{t,i} - I_{u,i}|}{m_i - 1}, \qquad (5)$$

where m_i is the number of values of feature A_i.

The computational complexity of the algorithm is of the order $O(m \cdot n \cdot a)$. The main computational burden within each of the m iterations is the search for the nearest instances (line 4), for which we have to compute the distances to all the instances in $O(n \cdot a)$ steps. If the number of features is low we can reduce this computation by the use of smart data structures (for example k-d trees or R-trees) or we can investigate performance of approximate k-nearest neighbors algorithms (Duda et al., 2001). Each iteration of the algorithm is independent and here we see a path to parallelization of the algorithm.

Our algorithm does not cover all the information which could be extracted with the help of class and feature value changes in the nearest neighbor context. Important aspect could also be hidden in the amount of positive and negative changes resulting from no changes in attribute's value. This could be a useful hint about the coherency in the data, noise, overall importance of the attribute, as well as the amount of dependency between the attributes. Also important is the anchoring effect uncovered by our algorithm, but this remains as further work.

Illustrative Example

To show the behavior and usability of the algorithm we first define a simple artificial problem which is motivated by the Behavioral Decision Theory, stating that there are several distinct manners according to which marketing stimuli can be used during the formation of product attitude (Einhorn & Hogarth, 1981).

Our data set is described by six important and two irrelevant features. The important features correspond to different feature types from the marketing theory: two basic features (B_{weak} and B_{strong}), two performance features (P_{weak} and P_{strong}), two excitement features (E_{weak} and E_{strong}), and two irrelevant features ($I_{uniform}$ and I_{normal}). The values of all features are randomly generated integer values from 1 to 5, indicating for example score assigned to each of the features by the survey's respondent. The dependent variable for each instance (class) is the sum of its features' effects, which we scale to the uniform distribution of integers 1-5, indicating, for example, an overall score assigned by the respondent.

$$C = b_w(B_{weak}) + b_s(B_{strong}) + p_w(P_{weak})$$
$$+ p_s(P_{strong}) + e_w(E_{weak}) + e_s(E_{strong})$$

The effects of attributes are as follows.

Basic features are taken for granted by customers; a high score in these features does not significantly increase the overall score, while a low score has a decreasing effect on dependent variable. We define two variants of basic features, one with weaker and another with stronger negative impact:

$$b_w(A) = \begin{bmatrix} -2 & ; A \leq 2 \\ 0 & ; A \geq 3 \end{bmatrix}, \quad b_s(A) = \begin{bmatrix} -4 & ; A \leq 3 \\ -2 & ; A = 4 \\ 0 & ; A = 5 \end{bmatrix}.$$

Performance features have a positive correlation with the overall score: the higher the value of the attribute the bigger the effect on the overall score. We define the performance effects as

$$p_w(A) = \begin{cases} -3 & ; A = 1 \\ -2 & ; A = 2 \\ 0 & ; A = 3 \\ 2 & ; A = 4 \\ 3 & ; A = 5 \end{cases}, \quad p_s(A) = \begin{cases} -5 & ; A = 1 \\ -3 & ; A = 2 \\ 0 & ; A = 3 \\ 3 & ; A = 4 \\ 5 & ; A = 5 \end{cases}.$$

Excitement features describe properties of product/service which are normally not very important to the users, but can cause excitement if the score is very high. We define two grades of excitement effect as

$$e_w(A) = \begin{bmatrix} 0 & ; A \leq 4 \\ 1 & ; A = 5 \end{bmatrix}, \quad e_s(A) = \begin{bmatrix} 0 & ; A \leq 4 \\ 4 & ; A = 5 \end{bmatrix}.$$

We generated 1000 instances for this data set. While the value distribution and the independence of features are unrealistic, note that we have experimented also with more realistic distributions as well as with different types of correlation, but the results and conclusions remain unchanged. The upward and downward reinforcement factors the OrdEval algorithm returned for this data set are probabilities whose direct interpretation and analysis is of course possible, but visualization makes it easier.

The slope visualization proposed by Robnik-Sikonja & Vanhoof (2007) (upward and downward reinforcement are represented with the steepness of the line segment between two consecutive feature values) is unusual for marketing research practitioners and, as we argue below, does not convey all the information necessary for this specific field. We therefore propose a marketing friendly visualization of the OrdEval results on Fig. 1, which contains results for each feature separately.

The eight subgraphs are a sort of bar charts with addition of confidence intervals. For each graph a left-hand side contains downwards reinforcements for each feature score separately. Upwards reinforcement factors for all the scores are represented on the right-hand side of each graph. Before we explain the results let us give a motivation for box-and-whiskers graphs on top of each reinforcement bar.

There are two problems with these reinforcement factors in general and also when used in marketing:

- Imbalanced value distribution: it is quite common that for certain features some scores are almost non-existent (e.g., extremely low score of a basic feature is very rare - such a customer, would probably change the supplier), and also the reverse might be true, namely on a scale 1-5 it is not uncommon that almost all the scores are 4 and 5. Such imbalance also has consequences for reinforcement factors, since

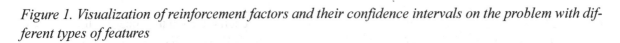

Figure 1. Visualization of reinforcement factors and their confidence intervals on the problem with different types of features

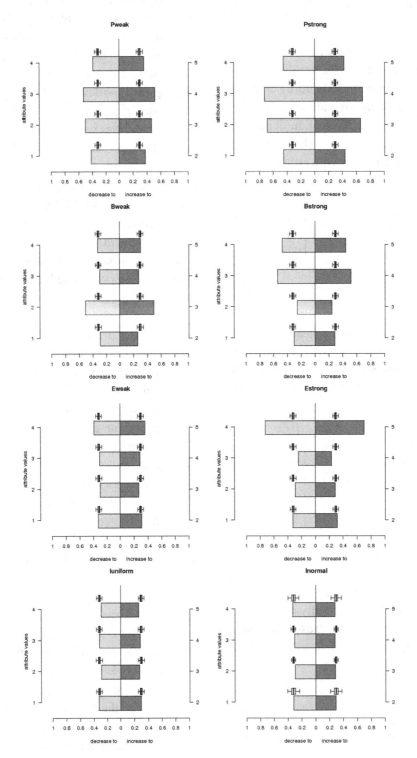

the probability of the increased/decreased overall score might be an artifact of the skewed distribution of values.

- Lack of information about significance of the reinforcement factors: the user does not know what expected range of a certain reinforcement factor is and weather the computed score is significantly different from the uninformative feature.

To solve both problems we compute confidence intervals for each reinforcement factor. Since we cannot assume any parametric distribution and have to take the context of a similar respondent into account we construct bootstrap estimates and form confidence intervals based on them (Efron & Tibshirani, 1993). We proceed as follows:

1. for each feature we construct e.g. n=200 features with bootstrap sampled values from the original feature (alternatively the values can be randomly shuffled), we call these features normalizing features,

2. when searching similar respondents we only take original features into account, but we estimate also the reinforcement factors of randomly constructed features,

3. for each reinforcement factor $U_{i,j}$ and $D_{i,j}$ (upward and downward reinforcement for each value of each feature) we perform a statistical testing based on bootstrap estimates.

   a. the null hypothesis states that the reinforcement factor is uninformative, i.e., it is equal to the median of its random normalizing features

   b. the alternative hypothesis is one-sided, as we are interested if the reinforcement of the original feature is larger than the random normalizing reinforcement

   c. set fixed confidence level, e.g. $\alpha=0.05$

   d. sort the reinforcement factors of random normalizing features in ascending order

   e. if the reinforcement factor of the original feature is larger than $n(1-\alpha)$th sorted factor we can reject the null hypothesis, and assume that the computed reinforcement contains significant information

4. the sorted reinforcement factors are the source of information for box-and-whiskers plot: the box is constructed from the 1st and 3rd quartile, middle line is median, while the whiskers are $100\alpha/2$ and $100(1-\alpha)/2$ percentiles (e.g. 2.5 and 97.5 percentiles) giving the borders of confidence interval (e.g., 95% confidence interval).

On. Fig. 1 reinforcement factors reaching beyond the box-and-whiskers therefore contain significant information. Since the way we construct confidence intervals is not sensitive to the number of instances, these intervals are valid even for low number of scores. We can observe that the algorithm has captured the important landmarks of the features:

- for performance features P_{weak} and P_{strong} (two graphs in the top row) all the upward and downward reinforcements are significant, and the relative length of the bars is roughly proportional to the difference between impacts of the values,

- for basic feature B_{weak} (left-hand graph in the second row) the thresholds at values 2 and 3 (increasing feature from 2 to 3 strongly increases the overall score, and decreasing this feature from 3 to 2 strongly decreases the overall score),

- for basic attribute B_{strong} (right-hand graph in the second row) the upward thresholds at values 3 and 4 and downward reinforcement thresholds 4 and 5,

- for excitement features E_{weak} and E_{strong} (third row graphs) the jump from 4 to 5 and back is detected, in upward and downward enforcement, respectively. The reinforcements are larger for E_{strong} as expected,

- irrelevant random features $I_{uniform}$ and I_{normal} have no significant values (bottom row).

Note that only the reinforcement for the thresholds we have defined, are significantly larger than the boundaries of confidence intervals defined by the normalization features.

The properties of the used approach relevant to our study in particular, and in more general terms, to the analysis of arbitrary survey at large, are manifold. Firstly, there is substantial *context sensitivity*. Typically the features are highly conditionally dependent upon the response and have to be evaluated in the context of other features. OrdEval is intrinsically contextual and assumes neither independence nor some fixed distribution of the features. The context of other features is handled through the distance. By using different distance measures and different features in the calculation of the distance, we are even in a position to use different contexts, e.g., we could use some background socio-economic information to calculate the similarity of respondents. Secondly, there is the *ability to handle ordered features and ordered response* and to use the information the ordering contains. The order of attribute's values contains information which is comparable but not the same as values of numerical features, e.g., values poor, good, very good, excellent are ordered in expressing certain attitude but this ordering is not necessarily linear. Thirdly, we have *awareness of the meaning implied by the ordering* of the answers and the positive (negative) correlation of changes between feature values and the response (e.g., if the value of the feature increases from poor to good, we have to be able to detect both positive and negative correlation to the change of the overall response value). Fourthly, OrdEval has the *ability to handle each value of the feature separately*, e.g., for some features the value of good and very good have identical neutral impact on the response, value poor may have a strong negative,

and value excellent a highly positive impact. We are able to observe and quantify each feature's values separately and thereby identify important thresholds. Next to that, *visualization* of the output allows experts to use it as a powerful exploratory data analysis tool, e.g., to identify type of features and the impact of their individual values. Also, *the output is in the form of probabilities*. Probability theory is commonly used and therefore the results in form of probabilities are comprehensible and interpretable by a large audience and can also be used operationally. Finally, we have *fast computation* and *robustness to noise and missing values*. A study of the family of the algorithms similar to OrdEval has shown that feature evaluation is possible and reliable even for extremely noisy data (Robnik-Sikonja & Kononenko, 2003).

Case Study: Customer Satisfaction Analysis In Marketing

Over the last forty years, consumer (dis)satisfaction has taken a prominent position in the marketing research literature (e.g. Anderson, 1973; Anderson and Sullivan, 1993; Cardozo, 1965; Churchill and Surprenant, 1982). This attention is justified since consumer (dis)satisfaction (directly or indirectly) impacts upon repurchase intention (Szymanski and Henard, 2001), consumer retention (Anderson, 1994; Mittal and Kamakura, 2001) and eventually upon firm performance (Anderson et al., 1994). Consumer (dis)satisfaction is a summarizing response that results from a consumer's post-consumption cognitive and affective evaluation of a product or service performance given pre-purchase expectations (Anderson and Sullivan, 1993; Oliver, 1993; Tse and Wilton, 1988).

Focusing on the antecedents of consumer (dis) satisfaction, two main issues dominate today's discourse: the expectancy-disconfirmation theory and the nature of the relationship between consumer (dis)satisfaction and its antecedents.

First, the expectancy-disconfirmation paradigm is a dominant framework for explaining consumer (dis)satisfaction (Oliver, 1997; Szymanski and Henard, 2001). In its basic format, the model proposes that consumers' overall (dis)satisfaction response is the result of two cognitive processes (Oliver, 1997). In the first, consumers form pre-purchase expectations on the performance of a product or service. In the second, consumers evaluate the actual performance of the product and compare this perceived performance to their expectations. If performance meets expectations, consumers experience confirmation of their expectations. If performance is greater than expected, they experience positive disconfirmation; if performance is less than expected, consumers experience negative disconfirmation (see Oliver (1997) and Yi (1991) for reviews).

Secondly and related to the first is the debate on the nature of the relationship between consumer (dis)satisfaction and its antecedents. Initially, the effects of the antecedents and in particular of attribute-level performance on consumer (dis) satisfaction were assumed linear and symmetric (Mittal et al., 1998; Sethi and King, 1999; Spreng et al., 1996). Only recently, marketing scholars have questioned this double assumption on the basis of economic and psychological theory as well as on a better empirical insight in the satisfaction response function (Anderson and Sullivan, 1993).

The presented attribute evaluation method attempts to extend the knowledge on the relationship between consumer (dis)satisfaction and its main antecedents. More specifically, we try to quantify and visualize the relationship between attribute-level (dis)satisfaction and overall (dis) satisfaction.

We report performance of our methods on one recent business-to-business (B2B) and one recent consumer-to-business (C2B) customer satisfaction study. For the business-to-business study the product involved is a high-tech product. Requirements are specified by the customer; the product is produced and delivered on demand. The whole process from order to delivery can take two or three months. The database provides the satisfaction scores of customers, who are active and have on-going orders. They reported their (dis) satisfaction with 11 product/service attributes as well as their overall satisfaction with the product. Overall satisfaction and attributes were measured on a 5-point scale. This data set is small (less than 100 records).

The consumer-to-business study is based on a study of a main European player in the entertainment sector. The survey is hierarchically organized. Satisfaction has been measured as general (overall satisfaction), on different dimensions (like personnel, administration, communication, etc.) and on aspects of the dimensions (like personnel friendliness, clearness of invoice, etc.). Dimensions and aspects are measured on a 10-point scale. The data set contains over 4000 instances.

Due to confidentiality we cannot go into details or give all the results. Therefore we will give some examples from both data sets. The chosen attributes/dimensions are attributes/dimensions that occur in most customer satisfaction data sets.

We report on the findings and types of behavior our algorithm can discover and give some relations to marketing literature. The visualization proposed by Robnik-Šikonja & Vanhoof (2007) conveys the information with the slope of the line segments between attribute values. The upward and downward reinforcement numbers represent the steepness of the line segment between two consecutive feature values (coefficient of the straight line between the two values) e.g., 0 is horizontal line, 1 corresponds to 45 degrees angle (the maximum), $0.5 \approx 26.6$ degrees angle, etc. We visualize U_{ij} and $D_{i,j}$ for all the values of one attribute in a single graph on the left-hand side of Figure 2. Feature values are displayed on horizontal axis, and the cumulative enforcement (sum of reinforcements up to the particular value) on the vertical axis. Upward reinforcement factors cover the upper part of the graph and downward reinforcement factors reside in the lower part of the graph. Arrows indicate the direction of the change. Beside slopes note also the total cumula-

Figure 2. The results for "price" in C2B data set. The left-hand side visualizes the reinforcement factors with the slope of line segment, and the right hand side gives additional information with bar charts and confidence intervals

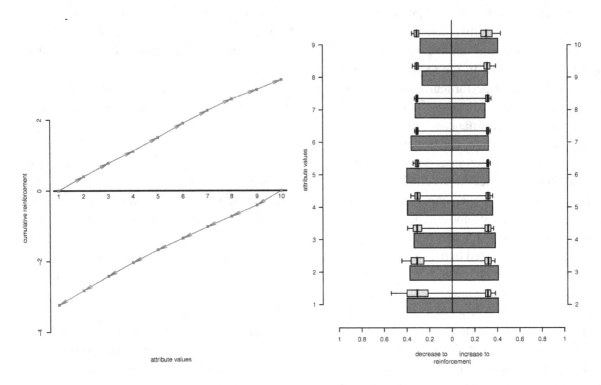

tive height of the slopes as it is indicative of the overall importance of the feature.

For a real world data set it is of course irrational to expect so clear distinctions between features as evident for our toy data in Fig. 1. In reality we find the same characteristics as predicted by theory (basic, performance, and excitement features) but less clearly expressed, or expressed only for some, usually most frequent, values.

We first look at the results obtained for "price" (Figure 2) from C2B study. The reinforcement factors are presented on the left-hand side with the slope of line segment, and on the right hand side with bar charts. If we only look at the left-hand side we see a clear picture of performance feature and the managerial conclusion would be that for all costumers the better the satisfaction with price the better the overall satisfaction, so

with price we can clearly regulate the overall satisfaction. The right-hand side graph gives much more precise information. First, the human eye is not sensitive enough to the angle of the line segment slope; therefore it is difficult to see even quite large differences. Additional benefit of confidence intervals is also clearly visible, namely for upward reinforcement only increases from values 1, 2, 3, and 4 are significantly larger (at 95% level) than the score obtained by random permutation of values. For downward reinforcement the significant values are 7, 6, and 5. The managerial consequences are clear: if management wants to increase the satisfaction of the customers the price reduction will have effect only on the least satisfied customers (scores 1, 2, 3, 4). On the other hand price increase will decrease overall satisfaction for a group of respondents

Figure 3. The results for "product quality" in B2B data set. The left-hand side shows reinforcement factors with confidence intervals, while the right-hand side shows the same information, but significant values are indicated with a different shade

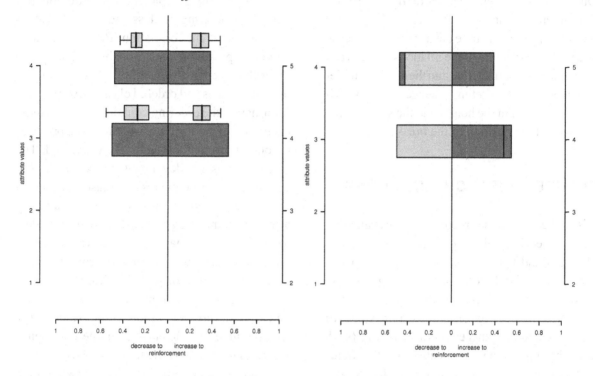

who claim medium price satisfaction. Similar conclusions are possible for other attributes and allow much more focused and precise managerial decisions as with classical statistical approaches, e.g., linear regression.

Besides "price" several other attributes in B2C and B2C study can also be classified as performance attributes, e.g., "information about promotions", or "communication", where for several values an increase (decrease) of the attribute level influences satisfaction (dissatisfaction).

Several attributes show a very similar pattern to a basic attribute. The example given is "product quality" (Figure 3) from B2B study.

A basic attribute behaves like a threshold or stepwise function: it creates (dis)satisfaction when (not) fulfilled. For example 'quality of the product' (Figure 3) is a basic requirement that obtains the quality level 3 or higher. Only these values

are presented in the study which is not surprising (customers dissatisfied with the product quality at this level would change the supplier). We can observe that only increase from 3 to 4 significantly influences satisfaction and a decrease from 5 to 4 significantly influences dissatisfaction.

Prospect theory in general and its assumptions of loss aversion and diminishing sensitivity in particular (Einhorn and Hogarth, 1981; Mittal and Kamakura, 2001) proposes an asymmetric S-shaped relationship between attribute-level performance and overall (dis)satisfaction. Indeed, it has been observed that the marginal contribution of attribute-level performance on overall (dis) satisfaction decreases with its size and that losses have more impact than gains. This is confirmed by evidence and theory on memory accessibility: negative information is more perceptually salient, is given more weight, and creates a stronger response than positive information (Mittal and Kamakura, 2001; Peeters and Czapinski, 1990). Our results show higher values for the downward reinforcement than for upward reinforcement. All these figures demonstrate clearly the asymmetric and non-linear nature of the relationship between consumer (dis)satisfaction and the attribute under consideration. Marketing managers are specifically interested in the height and the shape of the curves and the position of the breakpoints.

FUTURE RESEARCH DIRECTIONS

It is our belief, that the ordered attribute evaluation can be used in fields other than marketing. The algorithm and its visualizations can be useful in any survey analysis where the answers are graded. So far we have used only part of information hidden in the difference between class and feature values of similar instances. Other effects in marketing (such as anchoring) and new applications in other fields may demand definition of additional factors and development of novel visualization techniques.

For example, survey data collection is one of the most important sources of socio-demographic data and its quality is of key importance for informed policy-decision making. The design of survey questionnaires (visual appearance, structural organization, and wording) for collecting socio-demographic data is one of the most important factors affecting the quality of the data. We believe that OrdEval could be efficient in testing and evaluating the wording of survey questions based on experimental or post-survey data in the socio-demographic research. Due to OrdEval properties it is possible to adapt this analytical approach to test and evaluate survey questionnaires where many of the key survey variables are using ordinal scales.

CONCLUSION

OrdEval algorithm exploits the information hidden in the ordering of class and attribute values and their inherent correlation. Based on nearest neighbor paradigm and probability theory the algorithm is context sensitive, able to handle ordered attributes and ordered classes, aware of the information the ordering contains, able to handle each value of the attribute separately, and provides output which can be effectively visualized. The visualizations we developed turned out highly useful in our marketing research case study. From a data mining point of view the paper has adapted a general methodology for analysis of ordered data to the specifics of marketing. OrdEval algorithm possesses also other favorable properties like output in the form of probabilities, fast computation, robustness to noise and missing values, and a possibility of parallelization. Additionally it is possible to efficiently compute confidence intervals for reinforcement factors. For example imbalanced value distribution is quite a common phenomenon but it has severe consequences for reinforcement factors, since the probability of the increased/decreased overall score might be an artifact of the skewed distribution of values. Another such obstacle is information about the significance of the reinforcement factors: the user does not know what the expected range of a certain reinforcement factor is and weather computed score is significantly different from the uninformative feature. By computing distribution independent confidence intervals we provide information on reliability of the reinforcement scores which give them practical importance and enables confident decision making. Additionally the proposed visualization of the reinforcement factors enables detection of (non)linearity, (a) symmetry, threshold values and significance of the results.

This paper also has technical implications for academic research on costumer (dis)satisfaction. Extracting the kind of knowledge we discussed in the present study is not self-evident. In marketing research, the potential of the ordered attribute evaluation to unravel the decision-making heuristics of customers when 'deciding' on a certain level of (dis)satisfaction seems to outperform that of more traditional statistical models. This is due to the power of the method to allow for non-linear and asymmetric effects as well as to the fact that researchers should not a priori postulate the roles the different attributes will take. Although the algorithm appears analytically complex, it may yield parsimonious results. This paper illustrates and confirms earlier advice that managers should identify the 'optimal' performance level for each attribute. The goal should be to optimize, not to maximize attribute-level performance at a level where the payoff in terms of overall customer (dis) satisfaction is maximized. This optimal level can be determined by analyzing the different figures offered by our method. As such, the OrdEval algorithm can be a valuable technical contribution to the analysis of this particular task.

REFERENCES

Anderson, E. W. (1994). Cross-category variation in customer satisfaction and retention. *Marketing Letters*, *5*(January), 19–30. doi:10.1007/BF00993955

Anderson, E. W., Fornell, C., & Lehmann, D. (1994). Customer satisfaction, market share and profitability: Findings from Sweden. *Journal of Marketing*, *58*(July), 63–66.

Anderson, E. W., & Sullivan, M. (1993). The antecedents and consequences of customer satisfaction for firms. *Science*, *12*(2), 125–143.

Anderson, R. E. (1973). Consumer dissatisfaction: The effect of disconfirmed expectancy on perceived product performance. *JMR, Journal of Marketing Research*, *10*(February), 38–44. doi:10.2307/3149407

Breiman, L., Friedman, J. H., Olshen, R. A., & Stone, C. J. (1984). *Classification and Regression trees*. Belmont, CA: Wadsworth, Inc.

Cardozo, R. N. (1965). An experimental study of customer effort, expectations, and satisfaction. *JMR, Journal of Marketing Research*, *2*(August), 244–249. doi:10.2307/3150182

Churchill, G. A. J., & Surprenant, C. (1982). An investigation into the determinants of consumer satisfaction. *JMR, Journal of Marketing Research*, *19*, 491–504. doi:10.2307/3151722

Duda, R. O., Hart, P. E., & Stork, D. G. (2001). *Pattern Classification* (2nd ed.). New York: John Wiley & Sons.

Efron, B., & Tibshirani, R. J. (1993). *An Introduction to Bootstrap*. New York: Chapman & Hall.

Einhorn, H. J., & Hogarth, R. M. (1981). Behavioral decision theory: Processes of judgement and choice. *Annual Review of Psychology*, *32*, 53–88. doi:10.1146/annurev.ps.32.020181.000413

Hong, S. J. (1997). Use of contextual information for feature ranking and discretization. *IEEE Transactions on Knowledge and Data Engineering*, *9*(5), 718–730. doi:10.1109/69.634751

Kononenko, I. (1994). Estimating attributes: analysis and extensions of Relief. In De Raedt, L., & Bergadano, F. (Eds.), *Machine Learning: ECML-94* (pp. 171–182). Berlin: Springer Verlag.

Kononenko, I. (1995). On biases in estimating multi-valued attributes. In *Proceedings of the International Joint Conference on Artificial Intelligence (IJCAI'95)*, (pp. 1034–1040). San Francisco: Morgan Kaufmann

Mittal, V., & Kamakura, W. (2001). Satisfaction, repurchase intention, and repurchase behavior: Investigating the moderating effect of customer characteristics. *JMR, Journal of Marketing Research*, *38*(February), 131–142. doi:10.1509/jmkr.38.1.131.18832

Mittal, V., Ross, W. J., & Baldasare, P. (1998). The asymmetric impact of negative and positive attribute-level performance on overall satisfaction and repurchase intentions. *Journal of Marketing, 62*(January), 33–47. doi:10.2307/1251801

Oliver, R. L. (1993). Cognitive, affective and attribute bases of the satisfaction response. *The Journal of Consumer Research, 20*, 418–430. doi:10.1086/209358

Oliver, R. L. (1997). *Satisfaction: A Behavioral Perspective on the Consumer*. New York: McGraw-Hill.

Peeters, G., & Czapinski, J. (1990). Positive-negative asymmetry in evaluations: The distinction between affective and informational negativity effect. *European Review of Social Psychology, 1*, 33–60. doi:10.1080/14792779108401856

Quinlan, J. R. (1993). *C4.5: Programs for Machine Learning*. San Francisco: Morgan Kaufmann.

Robnik-Šikonja, M., & Kononenko, I. (2003). Theoretical and empirical analysis of ReliefF and RReliefF. *Machine Learning Journal, 53*, 23–69. doi:10.1023/A:1025667309714

Robnik-Šikonja, M., & Vanhoof, K. (2007). Evaluation of ordinal attributes at value level. *Data Mining and Knowledge Discovery, 14*, 225–243. doi:10.1007/s10618-006-0048-4

Sethi, V., & King, R. (1999). Nonlinear and noncompensatory models in user information satisfaction measurement. *Information Systems Research, 10*(1), 87–96. doi:10.1287/isre.10.1.87

Spreng, R. A., McKensey, S., & Olshavsky, R. (1996). A reexamination of the determinants of consumer satisfaction. *Journal of Marketing, 60*(July), 15–32. doi:10.2307/1251839

Szymanski, D. M., & Henard, D. (2001). Consumer satisfaction: A meta-analysis of the empirical evidence. *Journal of the Academy of Marketing Science, 29*(1), 16–35.

Tse, D. K., & Wilton, P. (1988). Models of consumer satisfaction formation: An extension. *JMR, Journal of Marketing Research, 25*(May), 204–212. doi:10.2307/3172652

Yi, Y. (1991). A critical review of consumer satisfaction. In Zeithaml, V. A. (Ed.), *Review of Marketing* (pp. 68–123). Chicago: American Marketing Association.

ADDITIONAL READING

Ben-David, A. (1995). Monotonicity maintenance in information-theoretic machine learning algorithms. *Machine Learning, 19*, 29–43. doi:10.1007/BF00994659

Breiman, L. (2001). Random Forests. *Machine Learning Journal, 2001*(45), 5–32. doi:10.1023/A:1010933404324

Brijs, K. Unravelling country-of-origin: Semiotics as a theoretical basis for a meaning-centred approach towards country-of-origin effects. PhD thesis, University of Hasselt, 2006. URL http://hdl.handle.net/1942/1819.

Cardoso, J. S., & da Costa, J. F. P. (2007). Learning to classify ordinal data: The data replication method. *Journal of Machine Learning Research, 8*, 1393–1429.

De Loof, K., De Baets, B., & De Meyer, H. (2008). On the random generation of monotone data sets. *Information Processing Letters, 107*, 216–220. doi:10.1016/j.ipl.2008.03.007

Demšar, J. (2006). Statistical comparison of classifiers over multiple datasets. *Journal of Machine Learning Research, 7*, 1–30.

Guyon, I., & Elisseeff, A. (2003). An introduction to variable and feature selection. *Journal of Machine Learning Research, 3*, 1157–1182. doi:10.1162/153244303322753616

Jacobsson, H. (2005). Rule extraction from recurrent neural networks: A taxonomy and review. *Neural Computation*, *17*(6), 1223–1263. doi:10.1162/0899766053630350

Kononenko, I., & Kukar, M. (2007). *Machine Learning and Data Mining, Introduction to Principles and Algorithms*. Horwood Publishing.

Leban, G., Zupan, B., Vidmar, G., & Bratko, I. (2006). VizRank: data visualization guided by machine learning. *Data Mining and Knowledge Discovery*, *13*(2), 119–136. doi:10.1007/s10618-005-0031-5

Madigan, D., Mosurski, K., & Almond, R. G. (1997). Graphical explanation in belief networks. *Journal of Computational and Graphical Statistics*, *6*(2), 160–181. doi:10.2307/1390929

Možina, M., Demšar, J., Kattan, M. W., & Zupan, B. Nomograms for visualization of naive bayesian classifier. In J.F. Boulicaut, F. Esposito, F. Giannotti, D. Pedreschi (Eds.), *Knowledge Discovery in Databases: Proceedings of PKDD*, pp. 337–348, Springer, 2004. A. Niculescu-Mizil & R. Caruana, Predicting good probabilities with supervised learning. In L. De Raedt & S. Wrobel (ed.), *Proceedings of the 22nd International Machine Learning Conference*, ACM Press, 2005 B. Poulin, R. Eisner, D. Szafron, P. Lu, R. Greiner, D.S. Wishart, A. Fyshe, B. Pearcy, C. Macdonell, J. Anvik. Visual explanation of evidence with additive classifiers. In *Proceedings of AAAI'06*. AAAI Press, 2006

Robnik-Šikonja, M., Brijs, K., & Vanhoof, K. Ordinal evaluation: A new perspective on country images. In P. Perner, editor, *Advances in Data Mining. Proceedings of 9th Industrial Conference, ICDM 2009*, volume 5633 of *Lecture Notes in Computer Science*, pages 261–275. Springer, 2009.

Robnik-Šikonja, M., Cukjati, D., & Kononenko, I. (2003). Comprehensible evaluation of prognostic factors and prediction of wound healing. *Artificial Intelligence in Medicine*, *29*, 25–38. doi:10.1016/S0933-3657(03)00044-7

Robnik Šikonja, M., & Kononenko, I. (2008). Explaining classifications for individual instances. *IEEE Transactions on Knowledge and Data Engineering*, *20*, 589–600. doi:10.1109/TKDE.2007.190734

Titsias, M. K., & Likas, A. (2003). Class conditional density estimation using mixtures with constrained component sharing. *IEEE Transactions on Pattern Analysis and Machine Intelligence*, *25*(7), 924–928. doi:10.1109/TPAMI.2003.1206521

Waegeman, W., De Baets, B., & Boullart, L. (2008). ROC analysis in ordinal regression learning. *Pattern Recognition Letters*, *29*, 1–9. doi:10.1016/j.patrec.2007.07.019

KEY TERMS AND DEFINITIONS

Attribute Evaluation: A data mining procedure which estimates the utility of attributes for given task (usually prediction). Attribute evaluation is used in many data mining tasks, for example in feature subset selection, feature weighting, feature ranking, feature construction, decision and regression tree building, data discretization, visualization, and comprehension.

Context of Attributes: In a given problem the related attributes, which interact in the description of the problem. Only together these attributes contain sufficient information for classification of instances. The relevant context may not be the same for all the instances in given problem.

Evaluation of Ordered Attributes: For ordered attributes the evaluation procedure should take into account their double nature: they are nominal, but also behave as numeric attributes. So each value may have its distinct behavior, but values are also ordered and may have increasing impact.

Feature Subset Selection: Procedure for reduction of data dimensionality with a goal to select the most relevant set of features for a given task trying not to sacrifice the performance.

Feature Weighting: Under the assumption that not all attributes (dimensions) are equally important feature weighting assigns different weights to them and thereby transforms the problem space. This is used in data mining tasks where the distance between instances is explicitly taken into account.

Non-Myopic Attribute Evaluation: An attribute evaluation procedure which does not assume conditional independence of attributes but takes context into account. This allows proper evaluation of attributes which take part in strong interactions.

Ordered Attribute: An attribute with nominal, but ordered values, for example, increasing levels of satisfaction: low, medium, and high.

Chapter 10
Assessing Data Mining Approaches for Analyzing Actuarial Student Success Rate

Alan Olinsky
Bryant University, USA

Phyllis Schumacher
Bryant University, USA

John Quinn
Bryant University, USA

ABSTRACT

One way to enhance the likelihood that more students will graduate within the specific major that they begin with is to attract the type of students who have typically (historically) done well in that field of study. This chapter details a study that utilizes data mining techniques to analyze the characteristics of students who enroll as actuarial students and then either drop out of the major or graduate as actuarial students. Several predictive models including logistic regression, neural networks and decision trees are obtained. The models are then compared and the best fitting model is determined. The regression model turns out to be the best predictor. Since this is a very well understood method, it can easily be explained. The decision tree, although its underpinnings are somewhat difficult to explain, gives a clear and well understood output. Not only is the resulting model a good one for predicting success in the major, it also allows us the ability to better counsel students.

DOI: 10.4018/978-1-60960-102-7.ch010

INTRODUCTION

One of the significant issues confronting higher education is the area of enrollment management with specific attention paid to student retention. In an analogous way, on the departmental level, university faculty and administration members are often interested in determining what percentage of students who begin in a certain major will eventually graduate in the same major. This information is important for individual departments in determining how to allocate limited resources in making decisions as to the appropriate number of classes and sections to offer and the number of faculty lines needed to staff the department. It is also important for admissions departments in deciding which students to target for specific programs and majors and for enrollment management in addressing student retention.

One way to enhance the likelihood that more students will graduate within the specific major that they begin with is to attract the type of students who have typically (historically) done well in that field of study. This chapter will detail a study that utilizes data mining techniques to analyze the characteristics of students who enroll as actuarial mathematics students and then either drop out of the major or graduate as actuarial students.

BACKGROUND

In a previous paper (Schumacher et al., in press). data mining techniques were applied in a study that investigated the likelihood that incoming college freshmen majoring in Actuarial Mathematics (AM) will graduate in this major. The study applied data mining to an earlier study which predicted success using only traditional logistic regression. The original study contained data spanning seven years of incoming university freshmen who started as AM majors in the years 1995-2001 (Smith and Schumacher, 2006).

There have been other recent studies utilizing the various techniques of data mining applied to issues within higher education. For example, in one comprehensive paper (Davis et al., 2008), predictive models were generated for three important educational concerns: student retention, student enrollment and donor giving. In another study (Herzog, 2006), used logistic regression, decision trees and neural nets to predict student retention and degree completion time for new and transfer students. Similarly, student retention was analyzed through six-year graduation predictive models which were developed with the use of various data mining techniques (Campbell, 2008). Furthermore, data mining methods, including neural nets and random forests were applied to an investigation (Vandamme et al., 2007) of academic success among first year college students. A data mining approach to predicting the disposition of admitted students as enrollees or nonenrollees was completed in another investigation (Antons and Maltz, 2006). There are additional papers involving applications of data mining within a university setting which are cited in the previous study (Schumacher et al., in press).

Since the goal of the original study was to predict whether or not a student graduated in the major, this became the target variable. The input variables included gender, math and verbal SAT scores, percentile rank in high school class and percentile rank on a department mathematics placement test. These variables were chosen from among data available from the admissions department collected from incoming students because they were know to be relevant to forecasting the student's grade point average in their concentration (Smith and Schumacher, 2005). The variable high school rank in class did have more missing values than high school GPA, which was available and could have been used. However, rank in class had previously been shown to be a better predictor of student success in the 2005 study and so was used in the 2006 and the 2010 studies as well.

The data mining procedures used in the previous study included logistic regression, decision trees and neural networks. The main conclusion drawn from this study was that these three approaches provided similar results with respect to predictive ability but that the decision trees had the additional advantage of treating cases with missing data without imputation. It was further concluded that if one technique was to be specified, then the pruned tree appeared to be the best choice in that it provided a simple set of rules to follow and avoided over-fitting of the data, that is, the phenomena of obtaining an exceptionally well fitting model that is not applicable to new data.

ANALYSIS OF ACTUARIAL SUCCESS RATE

In this chapter, we will extend the analysis of the initial paper in several ways using SAS™ Enterprise Miner (2006) 5.3 (EM5.3). We have obtained four more years of data, beyond the original study, so that we can enhance the predictability of the original models by adding this data to the existing data set. The addition of new observations will allow us to partition the data and therefore obtain better assessments of the models using the validation data. We will also add an ensemble model prior to the model comparison. Moreover, we will investigate more ways to assess and compare the various models, by considering lift charts, and receiver operating characteristic (ROC) curves. Finally, we will utilize our best chosen model to score the data for students currently enrolled as actuarial majors.

Data

As mentioned above, the variable of interest in this study and therefore the variable to be predicted is whether or not a student, who started as a freshman in the AM major eventually graduated in the same major. Therefore this is the target variable in the data analysis that follows. It is a binary variable, MAJOR with value =0: failure to graduate as an AM major, and value = 1: successful completion of the major. In order to be consistent and utilize the previous data, the predictor or input variables used are: GENDER, MSAT (math SAT score), VSAT (verbal SAT score), RANK (percentile rank in class), and TEST (percentile score on a mathematics placement test). The original study included 201 observations. Since that time, 127 observations have been added, increasing the data set to 328, still not an extremely large data set but larger than the original study. This will allow us to partition the data into a training and validation set which was not done in the original study. The addition of a validation set will allow us to measure the fit of the model with data that were not used to obtain the model. This is clearly an improvement over the original study.

The combined data set, consisting of 6 variables and 328 observations, includes all students starting as AM majors in the years 1995- 2005. It is the data that will be used in the following analysis. We also have a set of 119 observations of the same variables for current juniors and seniors, who were AM freshman in 2006 and 2007. We will use this final set of observations for scoring. After scoring the data we will check how well we are doing by considering a success at this time as being currently still enrolled in the AM major.

Process Flow Diagram

The Process Flow Diagram, presented below in Figure 1, illustrates the order of the procedures that were run in SAS Enterprise Miner to analyze the data set and to predict successful completion of the AM major with data mining techniques. Procedures are run in SAS Enterprise Miner through the use of such diagrams or streams, as is also the case in other data mining programs like SPSS Clementine. A stream, which is similar to a computer programming flow chart, is made up of a series of nodes connected by arrows. The

Figure 1. Process Flow Diagram

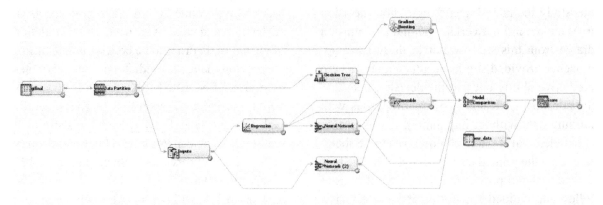

nodes indicate the procedure to be run whereas the arrows indicate the flow of the procedure. The set of procedures in SAS makes up a Data Project and the diagram is created in a project panel where the user manages the data sources and the procedures.

We have used SAS Enterprise Miner for our analysis which uses the mnemonic SEMMA (Sample, Explore, Modify, Model, and Assess) for the various components available for the overall analysis. Each individual procedural node is selected from within these categories and placed on the diagram. As can be observed in Figure 1, the stream used to execute the procedures in our study starts with a source node to read the data, followed by a data partition node to separate the data into training and validation data sets. Next an imputation node is added to estimate missing values. The imputation node flows into three of four forecasting techniques: a stepwise regression, and two neural networks one of which utilizes the data which is output from the regression. A fourth prediction procedure, a decision tree, follows directly from the data partition since it does not need to have missing values replaced. An ensemble model is connected to the four models and is used to combine the output from the other models into one model. These five models are then connected to a model comparison node which

is used to measure the effectiveness of all of the models and it is used to help in choosing the most appropriate model. Finally, the new data for testing the model is added in a new data source node and it and the model comparison node are connected to a scoring node which allows us to test or score the model with the new data. Each of these procedures will be explained more fully below.

The space in which this diagram appears is also called the diagram workspace and within this space the diagrams are not only created but they are also edited and run. As one runs the various procedures, indicated by the rectangles (nodes) a small green check appears at the right hand bottom corner indicating that procedure has been run. The arrows in the process flow diagram indicate the order in which the procedures should be run. Once a node is added to the diagram, the procedure can be run by clicking on the node and selecting to run the procedure. All previous connecting nodes will then be run with the procedure.

(It should be noted that a gradient boosting node appears in the process flow. This node was used in an additional research study and will be briefly discussed later in the future research section of the paper (Olinsky, 2010).

Data Source

The first node in a typical data analysis stream is the data source node which brings the data into the program for analysis. Only SAS data sets can be input by a data source node. We obtained the data for our study in an EXCEL data file. We needed to convert this data to a SAS data file in order to be able to analyze it with EM5.3. Once the data was converted we could then use it as a data source. Once a SAS data set is entered into the diagram as a data source, one utilizes a data source wizard to check the data and see that the variables are coded correctly as binary, nominal, ordinal, or interval. When a data set is read into Enterprise Miner, it is assigned to one of these categories but it is necessary to check to see if the assignments are correct. At this point it is also necessary to indicate which variable is to be used as the target or response variable. In our case this is the variable MAJOR, which is binary and indicates whether or not the student is an AM graduate. GENDER is also a binary variable and the remaining variables used for prediction variables are all coded as interval variables. If one is working with a large data set and only interested in some of the variables, it is possible at this step to reject any variables in the data set which are not going to be used for the study.

Data Partition

After entering and editing our data source, we created a data partition, with 75% of the data used for obtaining the various predictive models, and 25% of the data reserved as a validation set used to improve the model and which also can be used for model assessment. It is actually possible with very large data sets to partition the data into three sets, a training set, a validation set and a testing set. Although our data set had been enlarged since the original study, we felt that we still did not have enough data to obtain three sets. The 75/25 split that we chose left us a large enough set to

obtain reasonable models. The typical default is split is 40% training, 30% validation and 30% testing. However, even with a smaller data set, it is very important to have a validation set. The validation data is essential to avoid overtraining of the model and to help assess the fit of the models in the absence of a testing set. The data may be split by different techniques including simple random sampling, stratified sampling or cluster sampling. We chose to use the simple random sampling method.

Imputation

Following the data partition node we ran an impute node, which imputes missing data, prior to the regression and neural network nodes. The imputation node is used to replace the missing values with estimates. Without estimating the missing data, we would have lost a significant number of cases. The missing data can be replaced by different methods including the default of replacing missing values with the average of all values of the variable for quantitative variables and the mode for qualitative values, which was the method that we used. We could have chosen several other techniques such as a tree-based imputation method for interval values or a distribution based method for class variables. We placed the impute procedure to replace the missing data in the process flow diagram prior to the neural network and logistic regression nodes. It should be noted that decision trees have their own method for handling missing values. This is the reason that the node for imputation of missing values flows from the data partition to the neural network and the regression procedure nodes but not into the classification tree node.

Decision Tree

Directly following the data partitioning, we ran a decision tree, which is able to handle the missing data and therefore need not be attached to the imputation node. Decision trees are a very popular data mining tool for prediction of a target variable. The results are presented as trees which are visually attractive and easy to interpret and explain. The decision node actually uses regression to classify and predict a dependent variable, in this case, successful completion of the major. The output of the decision tree is composed of a diagram of a tree with nodes and branches with rules for splitting the data at each of the nodes. There are different methods for splitting the data which can be done automatically or interactively with the analyst making the decision where the split should occur. Since the trees, which often yield an excellent fitting model, can grow very large and be overly intricate and difficult to interpret, they are typically pruned back by reducing the number of branches and leaves. This can be done either manually or by for example, Enterprise Miner's default pruning method which makes use of the withheld validation sample. There are three methods in EM5.3 which can be used as splitting criteria for a categorical target variable. They include chi-square, logworth, entropy, and GINI. We used the GINI method because it seemed to work well with our data set. Because we had so few independent variables, it was not necessary to obtain a pruned tree.

Logistic Stepwise Regression

Logistic regression describes the relationship between a dichotomous dependent variable and a set of predictor variables. The predictor variables may be either numerical or categorical (dummy variables). This model is used for the prediction of the probability of the occurrence of an event by fitting data to a logistic curve. With a given numerical cutoff (often 0.5), cases with probabilities above this value are categorized as a 1 (success) while cases below this value are classified as a 0 (failure). When one runs a regression node in EM5.3, the target variable is detected and a logistic regression is run if it is binary and a linear regression is run if it is interval. Since our target

variable, MAJOR, is a binary variable, logistic regression is the appropriate choice. We chose to use the step-wise regression model since we were interested in which of our input variables were the most useful predictors of success as an actuarial major.

Neural Networks

In addition to the regression, we also ran two neural networks, one was run directly from the imputed data and the second of the neural networks utilized the variables selected by the stepwise regression and therefore was connected by a flow arrow from the regression node. A Neural Network gets its name from the fact that it works something like a human brain in the way it processes information. That is, it simulates many interconnected processing units which are said to resemble neurons. These processing units are usually arranged in layers, an input layer, where the input data are presented; one or more hidden layers, where the values are re-generated; and an output layer, from which the result is eventually relayed. The units are connected with varying connection weights. It is essentially a regression but the regression may be non-linear. The network considers individual inputs, generates a prediction for each record, evaluating the predictions and making adjustments to the weights whenever it makes an incorrect prediction. This process is repeated over and over, with continual improvements until one or more of the stopping criteria have been met. (SPSS, 2006)

A caveat, especially true with the use of neural networks, deals with overfitting in which the neural network, which can map nonlinear relationships, is trained to fit the training data extremely well. However, it is then possible that the resulting model is a poor predictor with new data. This is usually avoided in larger datasets by using training, validation, and even test portions of the dataset. Again, since this procedure is used for prediction, it is appropriate to use it with the actuarial data. With the addition of a validation set created by the data partition, we were able to compare the fit of the validation set and the training set to check for overfitting. The simplest neural net is equivalent to running a linear regression. As the network becomes more complex with hidden nodes, allowing for a better fit, it may actually be equivalent to a non-linear regression. One drawback of the neural net is that one cannot interpret the coefficients, which is a problem if we are interested in how the independent variables influence the dependent variable.

Ensemble Model

Next in our process flow, all four of the prediction procedures were connected to an Ensemble node which provides a new model by combining the predictions from the previous models. This is typically done in EM5.3 by averaging. As pointed out in the EM training manual, the ensemble model is only more accurate than the individual models if the individual models disagree. (SAS Enterprise Miner 5.3: Course Notes, 2009)

Model Comparison

The next node in our process flow is a model comparison node, which provides a comparison and assessment of the various models. The four models and the ensemble model are all connected to this node in order that the most appropriate model can be chosen. The output from this comparison includes tables and charts, such as lift charts which describe and compare the usefulness of the models.

Scoring Node

In order to test the model selected by the model comparison procedure and in the absence of a testing data set the new data for our current juniors and seniors is now added to the data flow as a second data source node in order to test the model. The scoring node accomplishes this and is the last node

in our process flow. One can see, with reference to the process flow diagram, that the new data source node and the model comparison node flow into the scoring node. The data to be scored comes from the new data source and the model used to score the data is the model which is selected as best by the model comparison procedure.

RESULTS

Decision Tree Results

The output from the Decision Tree procedure is presented below in Figure 2. First, it should be reiterated that the sample size of 328 observations which we have been able to compile thus far is still not large enough to provide a sufficient size validation set when partitioning the data to allow a good comparison with the training data set. However, it was still important that we create a validation set in order to compare how well the model fits with data that were not used to create the model. The fact that the validation data set is so much smaller that the training data set with the 25%/75% split may play a role in the fact that the validation and training results are not as close as would be expected with a larger sample. Nevertheless, the results are very nteresting and as can be seen in the diagram easy to read and interpret.

According to this model, the most important factor in determining whether a student completes the major is his/her score on our entering mathematics placement exam. As shown in the first split in the tree, considering the validation data, if a student obtains a score of 70 or higher, there is a 57.7% chance that student will complete the major. Whereas, if a student does not achieve that score, he or she has approximately a 65.5% chance of not completing the major. Clearly, the mathematics placement test is an important predictor of success in the major. The next split in the tree indicates that for those with 70 or higher on the exam, the Math SAT score is the next most im-

Figure 2. Decision Tree Output

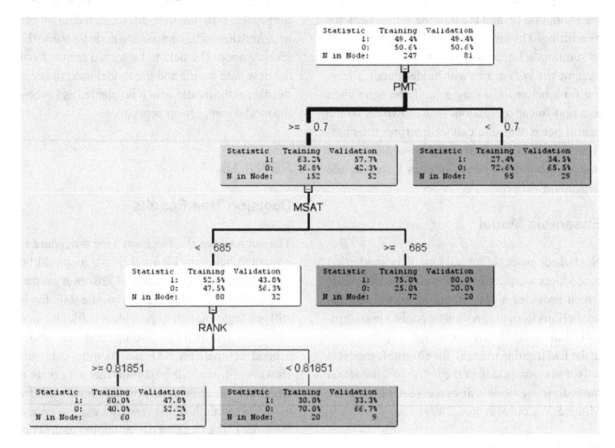

portant criterion for success in the AM major. Of those with a score of 685 or higher, 80% of those in the validation were predicted to complete the major, while of those with a score below 685, about half will not complete the major. The final split indicates then that for those with a Math SAT below 685, rank in high school becomes important. For those students who had a rank in high school class below 81.85%, approximately 60% do not complete the major, while for those with a rank of 81.85% or higher, approximately one half will complete the major. These results actually do not agree completely with our prior results which had a smaller data set and no validation set. In the previous study, math SAT was the highest predictor, followed by rank in class and then placement test score. Although the order of the significant

predicting variables is different, the same three variables do appear in the final output.

Each of the models produces as part of the output a cumulative lift chart. We have included a picture of the cumulative lift chart for the decision tree model. In examining the lift chart, we focus on the validation plots. The lift chart indicates that if we sort our model predictions in decreasing probability of completing the major, that we find, for example, at the top 20th percentile, we have approximately 60% more majors than if we selected a random sample of 20% of the students. This is interesting but would be much more meaningful in a marketing scenario where we are trying to predict more positives than negatives. In our situation, we are concerned with not making errors in predicting both success and failure.

Figure 3. Decision Tree Cumulative Lift Chart

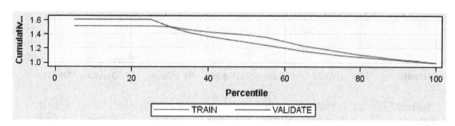

The results of the decision tree are further explained by the classification table which occurs in Table 1. Focusing on the results from the validation set, 52 out of 81 or 64.20% of the students are correctly classified. For the 43 who are predicted to complete the AM major by the neural network model, 27 or 62.79% were correctly classified and for the 38 predicted to not finish, 25 or 65.79% were correctly classified.

Logistic Stepwise Regression Results

The results of the stepwise regression are presented below in Figure 4. The output presented is the last step in the stepwise regression procedure. Since the procedure was run following imputation of missing values, the input variables included along with GENDER, the other variables with missing values imputed which were automatically renamed by the program as IMP_MSAT, IMP_VSAT, IMP_RANK, and IMP_PMT. The target variable is again MAJOR. The variables in this final step are the independent variables which were chosen in order of level of significance as predictors of success in the major. Since this is a step-wise regression, the fact that a variable

does not appear in the final step does not mean that it is not correlated to the target variable but that it might have been dropped because it had a high correlation with another variable which does appear in the final predicting variables. It can be seen that the most significant predicting variable is the imputed Math SAT score, with a significant p-value of 0.0013, followed by a second significant predictor the imputed math placement score, with a p-value of 0.0106. These two variables therefore emerge as the best predictors of success in the AM major according to this model.

The estimates of the regression coefficients appear in the next to the last column in the output. Since both values are positive, increases in Math SAT score and increases in placement test scores indicate an increase in the predicted probability of success in the major. The odds ratios represent the exponentiation of the coefficients of the model. The estimates of the odds ratios for the predictor variables appear at the bottom of the output. These ratios indicate the increase in the odds of completing the major for each one unit increase in the value of the predictor variable. The odds ratio of 1.008 for the MSAT score indicates that for each 1 point increase in the Math SAT score, the odds of a student completing the major

Table 1. Decision Tree Classification Results

	Predicted AM Majors	Predicted to Drop	Total
Correct	27	25	52
Incorrect	16	13	29
Total	43	38	81

Figure 4. Stepwise Logistic Regression Output

```
                    Analysis of Maximum Likelihood Estimates

                              Standard      Wald              Standardized
    Parameter      DF  Estimate    Error  Chi-Square  Pr > ChiSq   Estimate   Exp(Est)

    Intercept      1   -7.1070    1.5271    21.66      <.0001                   0.001
    IMP_MSAT       1    0.00833   0.00260   10.28       0.0013      0.3009      1.008
    IMP_PMT        1    2.2395    0.8759     6.54       0.0106      0.2448      9.389


        Odds Ratio Estimates

                        Point
    Effect            Estimate

    IMP_MSAT            1.008
    IMP_PMT            9.389
```

increase by 0.8 percent. The placement score odds of 9.383 indicate an increase of the odds of completing the major by 838% for each additional percentage point in the students rank on the placement exam.

The results of the regression are further explained by the classification table which occurs in Table 2. Focusing on the results from the validation set, 58 out of 81 or 71.60% of all students are correctly classified. For the 45 predicted to complete the AM major by the neural network model, 31 or 68.89% were correctly classified and for the 36 predicted to not finish, 27 or 75% were correctly classified.

Neural Network Results

One neural network procedure was run from the data which was output directly from the impute node. It therefore used all of the variables with missing values imputed. A second neural net was run using the results of the step-wise logistic regression. The reason for running a neural network following a regression is to reduce the dimensionality and give the neural net a better chance of convergence. However, in this case, since only two variables were output from the regression and we only had five independent variables to start with, there was no added benefit to the model by using the regression node first. We know this by looking the model comparison which will be discussed later.

Table 2. Logistic Regression Classification Results

	Predicted AM Majors	Predicted to Drop	Total
Correct	31	27	58
Incorrect	14	9	23
Total	45	36	81

Table 3. Initial Neural Network Weights

N	Parameter	Estimate	Gradient Objective Function
		Optimization Start Parameter Estimates	
1	IMP_MSAT_H11	0.381430	-0.002900
2	IMP_PMT_H11	0.271467	-0.010792
3	IMP_RANK_H11	0.291735	0.003861
4	IMP_VSAT_H11	-1.713889	0.004815
5	IMP_MSAT_H12	-0.320307	0.006068
6	IMP_PMT_H12	-1.031278	-0.012689
7	IMP_RANK_H12	-0.832053	0.010696
8	IMP_VSAT_H12	1.229476	0.006839
9	IMP_MSAT_H13	1.218358	0.013218
10	IMP_PMT_H13	0.075420	0.024612
11	IMP_RANK_13	0.238440	0.005467
12	IMP_VSAT_H13	-1.759124	0.005626
13	IMP_GENDER0_H11	0.915266	0.023131
14	IMP_GENDER0_H12	-0.017996	-0.005780
15	IMP_GENDER0_H13	2.019399	-0.008500
16	BIAS_H11	0.875424	-0.023340
17	BIAS_H12	0.367736	-0.002507
18	BIAS_H13	1.168478	0.002344
19	H11_MAJOR1	-2.808040	0.006537
20	H12_MAJOR1	-1.696647	-0.006424
21	H13_MAJOR1	1.746010	0.000852
22	BIAS_MAJOR1	0.646581	0.010833

The NEURAL Procedure

Value of Objective Function = 0.5606883961

We have provided some of the resulting output from the neural network node which flowed from the impute node. In order to illustrate the format of the output from a Neural Network, we have chosen to include the starting weights which are provided in Table 3. Unlike regression, these weights do not have a simple meaningful interpretation. They are the weight estimates assigned to the units and hidden units in the neural network.

The interpretation of the neural network is better explained by the classification table which occurs in Table 4. Focusing on the results from the validation set, 53 out of 81 or 65.43% are correctly classified. For the 42 predicted to complete the AM major by the neural network model, 27 or 64.29% were correctly classified and for the 39 predicted to not finish, 26 or 66.67% were correctly classified. Therefore the neural network was equally accurate at predicting those who completed the major and those who did not.

The diagram in Figure 5, also part of the neural network output, illustrates the importance of

Table 4. Neural Network Classification Table

	Predicted AM Majors	**Predicted to Drop**	**Total**
Correct	27	26	53
Incorrect	15	13	28
Total	42	39	81

Figure 5. Training of the Neural Network

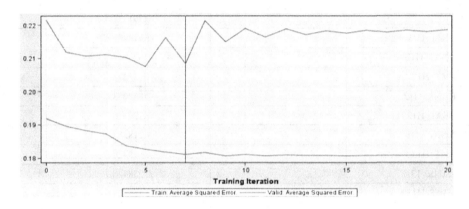

having a validation data set when running a neural network. It plots the average squared error at each iteration of the neural network for both the training and the validation set. As can be seen from this picture, the training set improves in accuracy as the iterations increase. This is what was referred to earlier as "overfitting." However, the results of the validation data set show that beyond a certain, in this case around 7 iterations, the error actually increases and then levels off. The neural network therefore is terminated at the iteration which minimizes the average square error for the validation data set, thus avoiding the problem of "overfitting".

Ensemble Node Output

The classification table from the ensemble node is presented below in Table 5. Focusing on the results from the validation set, 53 out of 81 or 65.43% are correctly classified. For the 42 predicted to complete the AM major by the ensemble method, 27 or 64.29% were correctly classified and for the 39 predicted to not finish, 26 or 66.67% were correctly classified.

The remainder of the output from this model is a combination of the previous models. The only other pertinent output from this model includes the cumulative lift charts. The lift charts are part of the individual output for every model but they

Table 5. Ensemble Classification Table

	Predicted AM Majors	**Predicted to Drop**	**Total**
Correct	27	26	53
Incorrect	15	13	28
Total	42	39	81

Figure 6. Results from Model Comparison Node

USE ▼	MODEL	MODELDESCRIPTION	TARGET	_VMISC_	_MISC_	_ASE_	_VASE_
Y	Reg	Regression	MAJOR	0.283951	0.336032	0.21334	0.197821
	Ensmbl	Ensemble	MAJOR	0.345679	0.294355	0.190745	0.202039
	Neural2	Neural Net...	MAJOR	0.345679	0.271255	0.181043	0.208362
	Neural	Neural Net...	MAJOR	0.358025	0.327935	0.202814	0.215205
	Tree	Decision Tr...	MAJOR	0.358025	0.299595	0.206414	0.222698

also appear as multiple graphs in the model comparison output. We have chosen, therefore to include the comparison lift chart later when we discuss the comparison of the models.

Model Comparison

The output from the model comparison node is used to identify the best model. This can be done by different criteria, such as misclassification rate and average square error, which are produced as part of a table in the output. In addition to the table, the model comparison node produces cumulative lift charts and ROC charts.

A piece of the output table is provided in Figure 6 below. As can be seen in this partial output, the Regression model has the lowest misclassification rate for the validation data set (VMISC) which was set as a goal in the model. In addition, the average squared error for the validation data set (VASE) is also the lowest for the regression model. Therefore the EM5.3 program has selected the regression model as the best which is indicated by its position as the first model in the output. Since it is chosen as the best model, it will automatically be used it for scoring new data.

We next look at the ROC charts and cumulative lift charts for our models. We can see that the charts include the four prediction models and the ensemble node which was added as an additional model. This ensemble model works best when the other models, which comprise this model, differ to a reasonable extent. In the lift charts the best procedure is the one with the highest lift as was defined and discussed earlier in

relation to the decision tree. It should be noted in Figure 7 that, in focusing our attention on the validation data sets, regression does yield the highest lift until approximately the 15th percentile. Then the ensemble node provides the best lift until approximately the 35th percentile. Regression then dominates until about the 65th percentile.

In addition to cumulative lift charts, Receiver Operating Characteristics (ROC) charts are a useful technique for comparing models and visualizing their performance. The combined ROC charts are presented in Figure 8.

In the ROC charts one should again focus on validation data set and note the area below the curves with the largest area being best. This should agree to a large extent with the cumulative lift charts. Here, the results are in agreement with the lift charts with the best model being the regression followed by the ensemble model. This result is further clarified by the model comparison output by the data in Table 6, which measures the area below the curve.

Scoring New Data Output

After completing this project, we were provided with new data. The new observations are from students who are now in their junior or senior year who started as AM majors and are now well established as actuarial majors or in other majors. To further test the model, we scored these students as if we didn't know their major. Scoring is accomplished in the process flow by combining the results of the model comparison, which exports the

Figure 7. Combined Cumulative Lift Charts from Model Comparison Node

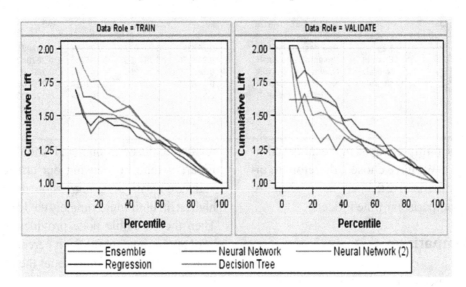

best model (in this case, the regression model), and the new dataset into a scoring node. The scoring node then predicts the probability of success in the major for these students. Based on the default cutoff point of .5, all individuals with probabilities above .5 are categorized as successful actuarial majors, those below .5 as non-actuarial majors. We then compared these results to the known results,

as to whether or not the students were still AM majors or not, and developed the following classification table (similar to earlier ones). The results of our scoring this new dataset are explained by the classification table which occurs in Table 7. Seventy-five out of 119 or 63.03% are correctly classified. For the 86 predicted to complete the AM major, 63 or 73.26% were correctly classi-

Figure 8. ROC charts

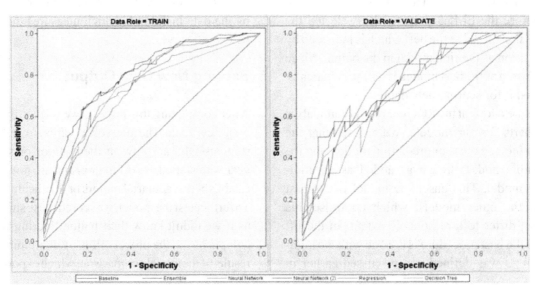

Table 6. ROC Indexes

Statistics	Reg	Ensmbl	Neural2	Neural	Tree
Valid: Roc Index	0.780	0.752	0.746	0.710	0.687

fied and for the 33 predicted to not finish, 12 or 36.36% were correctly classified. Apparently, we were better able to predict majors than non-majors.

It should also be pointed out that, if we had this new data sooner, we could have added it to the original data source and created a test partition in addition to the training and validation datasets.

CONCLUSION AND FUTURE RESEARCH

Our goal was to create a viable model for predicting whether an individual student, who begins his/her studies in actuarial math, actually is successful in completing this major or switches to another major. It appears that the regression model is the best predictor. Since this is a very well understood method, it can easily be explained. The decision tree, although its underpinnings are somewhat difficult to explain, would give a clear and well understood output. The neural network would be the most difficult to explain. However, whichever model works best would be our choice.

Not only is this model a good one for predicting success in the major, it also allows us the ability to better counsel students. However, it should be cautiously applied. It would be a more serious error for us to predict non-success for a student

who might well be able to achieve a successful completion of the major than predicting success for a student who eventually changes majors or drops out. The reason that incorrectly predicting a student to be a nonmajor is a more serious problem is because that the actuarial major requires a specific sequence of courses that other majors at the university do not usually take. If a student does not start as an actuarial major during their first year, then decides to become one later, they either have to double up on their coursework or spend an extra semester or two as a student. On the other hand, a student who begins as an actuarial student, but then switches to another major, can generally have the mathematics courses in the actuarial curriculum applied to their new major. To this end, future models might well use carefully determined decision weights to accommodate the ramifications of the two types of errors.

We thought that the Math SAT exam would be a good predictor of success in actuaral math. However, we were surprised that our own mathematics placement test, which is given to all of our incoming freshman, would also be an excellent predictor. Another caveat, however, would be that the stepwise regression might have omitted an important predictor which is highly correlated with one of our resulting significant predictors.

Table 7. Classification Results from Scoring New Students

	Predicted AM Majors	Predicted to Drop	Total
Correct	63	12	75
Incorrect	23	21	44
Total	86	33	119

Another suggestion for future investigation would be to include modifying the default cutoff point of the .5 probability for separating cases into predictions of success versus failure. SAS EM5.3 has added a new experimental cutoff node which allows one to simulate the process for different possible cutoff values. In addition, we plan on exploring the use of gradient boosting, which is now available in the latest version of Enterprise Miner, to improve the accuracy of classification trees. One of the authors has started to study the use of gradient boosting in predictive modeling (Olinsky, 2010). The procedure is defined in the AAEM manual in the following way:

Gradient boosting is a boosting approach that resamples the data set several times to generate results that form a weighted average of the resampled data set. Tree boosting creates a series of decision trees which together form a single predictive model. A tree in the series is fit to the residual of the prediction from the earlier trees in the series. This residual is defined in terms of the derivative of a loss function. For squared error loss with an interval target the residual is simply the target value minus the predicted value. Each time the data is used to grow a tree and the accuracy of the tree is computed. The successive samples are adjusted to accommodate previously computed inaccuracies. Because each successive sample is weighted according to the classification accuracy of previous models, this approach is sometimes called stochastic gradient boosting.

Boosting is defined for binary, nominal, and interval targets. Like decision trees, boosting makes no assumptions about the distribution of the data. For an interval input, the model only depends on the ranks of the values. For an interval target, the influence of an extreme value theory depends on the loss function. The Gradient Boosting node offers a Huber M-estimate loss which reduces the influence of extreme target values. Boosting

is less prone to overfit the data than a single decision tree, and if a decision tree fits the data fairly well, then boosting often improves the fit. (AAEM, 2009)

In the future, we also plan on adding more students to our dataset and further refining our model in accordance with our aforementioned thoughts.

REFERENCES

Antons, C. M., & Maltz, E. N. (2006). Expanding the role of Institutional Research at small private universities: A case study in Enrollment Management using Data Mining. *New Directions for Institutional Research, 131*(Fall), 69–81. doi:10.1002/ir.188

Applied Analytics Using SAS Enterprise Miner (AAEM) 5.3: Course Notes (2009).

Campbell, J. D. (2008). *Analysis of Institutional Data in Predicting Student Retention Utilizing Knowledge Discovery and Statistical Techniques.* Unpublished doctoral dissertation, Northern Arizona University.

Davis, C. M., Hardin, J. M., Bohannon, T., & Oglesby, J. (2008). Data Mining applications in higher Education. In K. D. Lawrence, S. Kudyba & R. K, Klimberg (Eds.) *Data Mining Methods and Applications* (pp. 123-147). Boca Raton, FL: Auerbach Publications.

Enterprise Miner, S. A. S. (2006). *SAS Enterprise Miner software, Version 5.2 of the SAS System for Windows.* Cary, NC: SAS Institute Inc.

Herzog, S. (2006). Estimating student retention and degree-completion time: Decision Trees and Neural Networks vis-à-vis Regression. *New Directions for Institutional Research, 131*(Fall), 17–33. doi:10.1002/ir.185

Olinsky, A., Kennedy, K., & Kennedy, B. (2010). *Assessing Gradient Boosting in the Reduction of Misclassification Error in the Prediction of Success of Actuarial Majors*. NEDSI 2010 Proceedings, March 2010.

Schumacher, P., Olinsky, A., & Quinn, J. (in press). A comparison of Logistic Regression, Neural Networks, and Classification Trees predicting success of actuarial students. *Journal of Education for Business*.

Smith, R., & Schumacher, P. (2005). Predicting success for actuarial students in undergraduate mathematics courses. *College Student Journal*, (39): 165–177.

Smith, R., & Schumacher, P. (2006). Academic attributes of college freshmen that lead to success in actuarial studies in a business college. *Journal of Education for Business*, (81): 256–260. doi:10.3200/JOEB.81.5.256-260

SPSS. (2006). *15.0 Command Syntax Reference*. Chicago: SPSS Inc.

Vandamme, J. P., Meskens, N., & Superby, J. F. (2007). Predicting academic performance by Data Mining methods. *Education Economics*, *15*(4), 405–419. doi:10.1080/09645290701409939

KEY TERMS AND DEFINITIONS

Actuarial Mathematics: The discipline that applies mathematical and statistical methods to assess risk in the insurance industry

Data Imputation: The process of replacing missing data in databases; especially useful in regression and related models, less so in decision trees.

Data Mining: The process of finding patterns in large datasets.

Decision Tree: One of the most popular classification algorithms in current use in Data Mining

Logistic Regression: The statistical technique used for the prediction of the probability of the occurrence of an event by fitting data to a logistic curve.

Neural Network: A technique based on the observed behavior of neurons and used in predicitve modeling.

Predictive Modeling: The process by which a model is created or chosen to try to best predict the probability of an outcome; includes techniques of logistic regression, decision trees, and neural networks.

Student Retention: The process of retaining students once they are accepted into your institution

Chapter 11
A Robust Biclustering Approach for Effective Web Personalization

H. Hannah Inbarani
Periyar University, India

K. Thangavel
Periyar University, India

ABSTRACT

Web recommendation or personalization could be viewed as a process that recommends the customized web presentations or predicts the tailored web contents to web users according to their specific need. The first step in intelligent web personalization is segmenting web log data into web user sessions for constructing user model. These segments are later used to recommend relevant URLs to old and new anonymous users of a web site. The knowledge discovery part can be executed offline by periodically mining new contents of the user access log files. The recommendation part is the online component of a usage-based personalization system. In this study, we propose a robust Biclustering algorithm to disclose the correlation that exists between users and pages. This chapter proposes a Robust Biclustering (RB) method based on constant values for integrating user clustering and page clustering techniques which is followed by a recommendation system that can respond to the users' individual interests. To evaluate the effectiveness and efficiency of the recommendation, experiments are conducted in terms of the recommendation accuracy metric. The experimental results have demonstrated that the proposed Biclustering method is very simple and is able to efficiently extract needed usage knowledge accurately for web page recommendation.

DOI: 10.4018/978-1-60960-102-7.ch011

1. INTRODUCTION

Web Mining specifies three domains: web content mining, web structure mining and web usage mining. The last domain is the most popular one in the area of recommendation(Claypool et al., 2001). Web usage mining, also known as web log mining, aims to discover user patterns from the data stored in server logs or browser logs while surfing the web system. Most of these efforts have been proposed to discover web usage patterns using various data mining or machine learning techniques to model and understand web user activity (Haibin Liu et.al, 2000). The mined knowledge can improve the design of web pages, and develop adaptive usage scenarios more efficiently and effectively.

Web usage mining consists of three steps, i.e. data collection and preprocessing, pattern mining as well as knowledge application. Feature selection is a preprocessing step in data mining, and it is very effective in reducing dimensions, reducing the irrelevant data, increasing the learning accuracy and improving comprehensiveness. Log files usually contain nonessential information from the analytical point of view. Thus the first data pre-processing step is the selection of features. The output of the pre-processing phase must be divided into sessions (Hannah Inbarani et al., 2007). These feature selection algorithms are used for selecting significant attributes for describing a session which is suitable for pattern discovery phase.

Pattern mining draws upon the methods and algorithms developed from several fields such as statistics, data mining, machine learning and pattern recognition. The usage mining tasks can involve the discovery of association rules, sequential patterns(Mamata Jenamani et al., 2002) page view clusters(Mobasher, 2002) transaction clusters(Hannah Inbarani et al., 2009) or any other pattern discovery method from user transactions.

The aim of web recommendation is to find the most matched user access pattern to the active user session, which is derived from web usage mining, and to recommend a list of pages that the users might be interested in, via referring to the visiting preferences of the chosen usage pattern. To perform recommendations efficiently and effectively, there are a variety of machine learning algorithms that have been well studied and developed, and can be used in web recommendation (Guandong Xu, 2008).

Basically, there are two kinds of technologies to carry out personalization recommendation: association rules and cluster analysis (TAN Xiaoqiu et al., 2006).

In this chapter, we present and experimentally evaluate a new technique, based on integrated clustering of both user transactions and of page views, in order to discover user and page biclusters of users and pages that can be effectively used by recommender systems for real-time web personalization.

The main contribution of this chapter is to propose Robust Biclustering (RB) algorithm for page recommendation. The proposed algorithm performs simultaneous clustering of users and pages to provide more accurate recommendations.

The rest of this chapter is organized as follows. Section 2 describes the Background Section 3 describes the Methodology for Recommendation process. Section 4 summarizes the related work and Experimental results are given in Section 5. Finally, Section 6 concludes this chapter with observations from the experimentation.

2. BACKGROUND

The stages of page recommender systems include preprocessing, segmenting web log data into web user sessions, and learning a usage model from this data. The usage model can come in many forms: from the modeling used in collaborative filtering, that simply stores all other users' information and then relies on K Nearest Neighbors to provide recommendations from previous history of neighbors or similar users, to a set of frequent

Figure 1. System Architecture

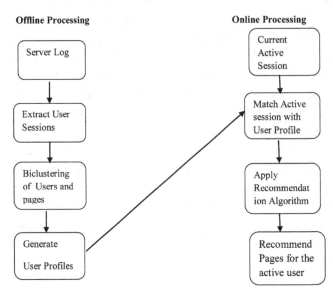

itemsets and associations, to a set of clusters of the user sessions, and resulting web user profiles or summaries(Olfa Nasraoui, 2003).

Web clustering can involve either users grouping of users who exhibit similar browsing patterns or pages grouping of pages having related content based on information derived from different sources. Specifically, user clustering approaches can be based on usage data and create groups of users with similar browsing behaviour (Pallis G., Angelis. L and Vakali A.,2007). On the other hand, in web page clustering approaches, information can be extracted from pages content(Hammouda, K.M and Kamel, M.S., 2004) and usage data (Sophia G. Petridou et al., 2008). Moreover, the clustering results may be beneficial for a wide range of applications such as websites' personalization (Nasraoui et al., 2008), web caching and prefetching (Li et al., 2007), search engines, (Hui et al., 2006) and Content Delivery Networks (Pallis G. et al., 2006). In addition, the clustering results can contribute to the enhancement of recommendation engines (Chi, C-C et al., 2008) and to the design of collaborative filtering systems (Srinivasa et al., 2004).

A number of different approaches to web page prediction have been proposed, including collaborative filtering (CF) (Goldberg et al.,1992), Markov models (Sarukkai, 2000), association rule mining (Mamata Jenamani et al., 2002), clustering (Fu et al., 1999). One research area that has recently contributed for this problem is web mining. In this work, Biclustering is proposed for page recommendation.

3. METHODOLOGY

Web personalization system based on web usage mining discovers web usage profiles, followed by a recommendation system that can respond to the users' individual interests. The Recommendation system architecture is specified in Figure 1.

The Recommendation Process consists of four major steps.

i.   Preprocessing,
  ii.Biclustering of users and pages
  iii.   User Profiling,
  iv.   Page Recommendation

Figure 2. Sample Web Log file

218.248.30.146 - - [21/Nov/2009:03:10:51 +0530]	"POST /make_slides.php HTTP/1.1" 200 740
216.104.15.130 - - [21/Nov/2009:03:20:37 +0530]	"GET /messengerplus.php HTTP/1.0" 200 15202

3.1 Preprocessing

Data cleaning operation is performed as defined in (Doru Tanasa and Brigitte Trousse 2004), which removes image files and style sheet files. The access log of a web server is a record of all files (URLs) accessed by users on a web site. Each log entry consists of the information components such as remotehost, Authuser, date,time, URL request, status and bytes.

The sample entries in the web log file are listed in Figure 2.

In the next step, using user session identification process, user sessions are identified and Session Matrix is created. User Access Matrix A = $\{a_{ij}\}$ where a_{ij} =1 if page j has been visited by user i otherwise it is set to zero. The weight associated with each visited page is represented by Wt = $\{wt_{ij}\}$ where each entry in the weight matrix specifies the number of hits on a specific page as defined in (Claypool M., 2001). For each user, the weight vector of each navigational session is represented as a sequence of visited pages with corresponding weights $\{wt_{11}, wt_{12}, wt_{13},...,wt_{1n}\}$ where wt_{ij} denotes the weight for a page j visited in i^{th} user session.

3.2. User Profiling

User profiling is the process of collecting information about the characteristics, preferences, and activities of a web site's visitors. This can be accomplished either explicitly or implicitly. Explicit collection of user profile data is performed through the use of online registration forms, questionnaires, and the like. The methods that are applied for implicit collection of user profile data vary from the use of cookies or similar technologies to the analysis of the users' navigational behavior that can be performed using web log mining techniques (Jian-Guo Liu et al., 2004).

In the web domain and especially in e-commerce, user profiling has been developed significantly because Internet technologies provide easier means of collecting information about the users of web site, which in the case of e-business sites are potential customers(Jian-Guo Liu et al., 2004). An efficient and effective algorithm for web recommendations is the user profiling approach, which is on a basis of collaborative filtering techniques, a kind of commonly used algorithms in recommender systems.

Mobasher B. et al., (2002) have proposed a potentially effective method for the derivation of profiles from transaction clusters. In this work, Profile Aggregations based on Clustering Transactions (PACT) method is proposed to generate aggregate profiles based on the centroids of each transaction cluster. However the centroid of each cluster may represent the different groups of pages without much correlation. Hence in this chapter, biclustering approach is proposed to generate profiles which represent the implicit relationship that exists between the pages and users.

3.3.1. Discovery of Aggregate Profiles Based on Biclustering

In this proposed method, for each bicluster, the weight of each page view is computed by the ratio of the mean weight value of pages in the bicluster. In generating the usage profiles, low-support pageviews (i.e. those with mean value below a certain threshold α) are filtered out.

Figure 3. Building user profile based on Biclustering

[**Input**] : A set of biclusters NB
[**Output**] : A set of user profiles UP$_j$ j = 1,2, .., NB
  Step 1 : Apply Biclustering algorithm fo
           simultaneously
  Step 2 : For each bicluster j, Calculate mean weights of the pages visited by users   in
           the bicluster.
  Step 3 : For each page P$_i$ within the bicluster, if the mean weight is greater than the
           threshold μ,

$$UP_j = UP_j \; U \; P_i$$

  Step 4 : Sort the pageviews with their weights in descending order and output the
           user profile UP$_j$.

3.4 Recommendation Process

Web Personalization aims to provide intelligent online services such as web recommendations, based on past web user navigation patterns. Web personalization can be accomplished in four different ways: Manual decision rule, collaborative filtering, content based filtering, and web usage mining. The most promising approach is web usage mining, which mines web logs to extract useful patterns concerning the users' navigational behavior(Mamata Jenamani et. al.,2002). Most of the page recommender systems are mainly based on user and page clustering techniques. However user and page clustering techniques are one sided approaches which cannot discover possible correlations between web pages and user groups. Hence this chapter proposes Biclustering approach for page recommendation.

3.4.1 Need for Biclustering Approach for Page Recommendation

The first step in intelligent web personalization is clustering web log data into web user sessions for constructing user model. These session clusters are later used to recommend relevant URLs to old and new anonymous users of a web site.

The limitations of traditional user/page clustering approaches such as K-Means are

- Puts each user in exactly one cluster
- Different preferences, of the user are not taken into account for the process of assigning the user to clusters.
- Number of clusters must be given as input

Collaborative filtering approach finds other users with similar tastes to the current user and recommends what they have liked to that user. Traditional collaborative filtering requires explicit user participation for providing his/her interest to the pages(Breese et al., 1998 and Chein-Shung Hwang et al., 2001). However, despite their success, the explicit ratings may suffer from some limitations, such as additional user effort, user behavior alteration and data sparsity. To overcome such problems, several researchers (Claypool 2001, Parsons J et al., 2004) have investigated the use of implicit interest indicators. An important implicit indicator of the user's navigation path is the time spent or number of hits on different pages. In this chapter, number of hits on different pages is used as an implicit indicator of page rating since implicit rating can be used for the analysis of any web site.

Regarding Recommendation approaches, there exist two main approaches: (a) User-Based (UB), which recommends pages on similarity between users; and (b) Page- Based(PB)(Sarwar B. Karypis et al., 2006), which recommends pages

Figure 4. Biclustering Based Recommendation

Input : Recommendation Threshold α, a set of user profiles generated from the Biclusters and a current session S

Output: Recommendation vector R.

Step 1 : Generate integrated User and Page Biclusters using Biclustering algorithm.
Step 2 : Generate User profiles using the method specified in section 2
Step 3 : Compute the similarity between user's sub session vector and the user Profiles generated .
Step 4 : Sort each row of the similarity matrix in descending order based on weights
Step 5 : Recommend pages in Top K biclusters if weight > Threshold α

based on correlation between pages. User-Based approaches identify users whose interests are similar to an active user and recommends items they like. However, they suffer from serious scalability problems which make them unsuitable for on-line processing. On the other hand, page based approaches suggest pages that are most similar to the set of pages the active user has accessed. User-based (UB) CF is proposed in (Resnick et al., 1994) which forms neighborhoods based on similarities between users. Then, UB recommends to the test user, the most frequent items in the formed neighborhood.

In web usage mining, both UB and PB are one-side approaches, in the sense that they examine similarities either only between users or only between items, respectively. This way, they ignore the clear duality that exists between users and items. Furthermore, UB and PB algorithms cannot detect partial matching of preferences, because their similarity measures consider the entire set of items or users, respectively. However, two users may share similar preferences only for a subset of items.

Our attention in this chapter is focused on specific Biclustering techniques for the discovery of the relevant components of user and page clusters. Recommendation process consists of two components. In the offline component, user and page biclusters are discovered using Biclustering algorithms. In the online component of the system, the Web server keeps track of the active server session as the user's browser makes HTTP requests.

The recommendation engine considers the active server session in conjunction with the discovered patterns to provide personalized content based on the similarity between the current session and the discovered biclusters. Only the top N hyperlinks with weight larger than the given threshold value is considered for recommendation.

Biclustering based Recommendation procedure is specified in Figure 4. The similarity between test user u and user profile UP_j is calculated using cosine similarity as defined in (Bamshad Mobasher, 2002). It is obvious that similarity values range between [0,1].

In CB approach, the Weighted Frequency (WF) of a page p in a bicluster b, is defined as the mean weight of pages in the recommended biclusters.

$$WF(P_i, B_k) = Wt(U_i, P_j) / \sum Wt(U_i, P_j) \text{ if } U_i \in B_k \text{ and } P_j \in B_k$$

for i= 1,2,..,m, j= 1,2,..,n k= 1,2,..,NB

where m- Number of users, n- Number of pages and NB-number of biclusters

In order to provide recommendations, we have to find the biclusters containing users with preferences that have strong partial similarity with the test user. This stage is executed online and consists of two basic operations:

- The formation of test users' neighborhood, i.e., to find the K nearest biclusters.
- The generation of the top-N recommendation list of pages

For User and page clustering algorithms, Top N weighted scoring algorithm proposed in (Guandong Xu, 2008) is used for Recommendation.

4. RELATED WORK

4.1 Biclustering Approach

The biclustering, in data mining, is referred to the process of simultaneously finding clusters on the rows and columns of a matrix (Cheng Y. et al., 2000). There are several approaches to deal with the biclustering problem. Many different algorithms for biclustering have already been proposed in the literature (Sheng Q. et al., 2001 and Tang et al., 2001). In short, these methods can be classified by (*i*) the type of biclusters they find; (*ii*) the structure of these biclusters; and (*iii*) the way the biclusters are discovered.

The type of the biclusters is related to the concept of similarity between the elements of the matrix. For instance, some algorithms search for constant value biclusters, while others search for coherent values of the elements or even for coherent evolution biclusters (Pablo A. et al., 2007).The structure of the biclusters can be of many types. There are single bicluster algorithms, which find only one bicluster in the center of the matrix; the exclusive columns and/or rows, in which the biclusters cannot overlap in either columns or rows of the matrix; arbitrary positioned, overlapping biclusters and overlapping biclusters with hierarchical structure. The way the biclusters are discovered refers to the number of biclusters discovered per run. Some algorithms find only one bicluster, others simultaneously find several biclusters and some of them find small sets of biclusters at each run. The algorithm proposed in this chapter finds a set of pages in the bicluster simultaneously followed by set of users in the bicluster.

4.2 Biclustering for Web Usage Mining

By analyzing the characteristics of the clusters, web designers may understand the users better and may provide more suitable, customized services to the users. Regarding web usage clustering algorithm, there exist two main approaches: User clustering which clusters users based on their similarity and Page clustering which creates page clusters based on similarity between pages (Qinbao Song et al., 2006, Tang C. et al., 2001 and Xiao J. et al., 2001). Instead of performing only user clustering, we perform simultaneous clustering of users and pages which correspond to group of users that exhibit highly correlated ratings on groups of pages. User clustering and page clustering algorithms cannot detect partial matching of preferences because their similarity measures consider the entire set of users or pages respectively.

The simultaneous clustering of users and pages discovers biclusters which correspond to group of users which exhibit highly correlated ratings on groups of pages. In this chapter two Biclustering algorithms are proposed to extract user profiles by integrating user clustering and pages clustering techniques. Therefore, this research explores a new user profiling method integrating user clustering and page clustering techniques.

4.3 Robust Biclustering Approach(RB)

The Robust Biclustering (RB) Algorithm works as follows: In the first step, distinct patterns of the session matrix are extracted. Given that A is made up of L distinct patterns, Pattern Matrix P can be expressed as $P = p_{lj}$ where l is the number of distinct patterns and $j = 1,2,.., n$ and n is the number of pages. The distinct patterns are extracted using Hadamard product (Roger Horn, 1994). In the second step, one can identify the pages accessed by two users simultaneously by

Figure 5. Biclustering(Ses,m,n,BP,BU,NB)

```
Input :  Session Matrix Ses(m,n)
         NU- Number of users
         n – Number of pages
         minp –Minimum number of pages allowed in a bicluster
Output :  NB Biclusters
NB =0; /*     Index of bicluster

Identify distinct patterns of Ses and store it in Matrix P

   /* P – set of distinct patterns
   /* L is the number of distinct patterns in Ses
   Step 1 :  Extract all the L distinct Patterns  using Hadamard product.
   Step 2:  Place all the pages in the extracted Pattern 1 in Bicluster BPi,  l=1,2,..,L
   Step 3 : If the Extracted pattern exists is user session , Place user j in Bicluster BUi
                                     for   j = 1,2,..,m and  i = 1,2,..,L
   NB= L  / Number of Biclusters is set to Number of Distinct Patterns
   Output NB        /* Number of biclusters
   Output BU and BP /* Users and Pages in each Bicluster
```

performing element wise product of plj and a_{ij} thereby forming the bicluster.

The main goal of the RB algorithm is to find all possible biclusters. The required input to RB is the minimum number of pages in a bicluster. The default minimum value is taken as 2. Hence RB algorithm finds a large number of overlapping biclusters. The degree of overlapping can be reduced by increasing the minimum number of pages in the bicluster.

4.4 Simple Biclustering(SB)

In this Biclustering algorithm, the similarity between users is obtained using Jaccard coefficient as defined in (Daxin Jiang et. al., 2004) and the biclusters are obtained from the submatrix by elementwise Hadamard product of row vectors as defined in (Alain B. Techagang et. al., 2005). The proposed algorithms allow overlapping to some extent based on threshold value given.

The degree of overlapping in this algorithm can be controlled by threshold α. As the value of α is increased, degree of overlapping reduces. Though SB produces minimum number of biclusters that are inclusion maximal, SB is not efficient in terms of memory and time as illustrated in

section 4. It consumes large amount of memory space and so it is not suitable for large data sets.

5. EXPERIMENTAL EVALUATION

5.1. Experimental Setup

Data Source

We used the access logs from www.bbminfo.com for our experiments. After preprocessing and removing references by web spiders, image files and style sheet files, a total of 6244 transactions are produced using the transaction identification process. The total number of URLs representing pageviews is 145 and we eliminated the pageviews appearing in less than 0.25% of the transactions. Approximately 25% of these transactions are randomly selected as the testing set, and the remaining portion is used as the training set for page recommendation. The total number of remaining pageview URLs in the training and the evaluation sets is 83.

Figure 6. Simple Biclustering(Ses,m,n,BP,BU,NB)

Input : Session Matrix Ses(m,n)
          m- Number of users
          n – Number of pages

Output : NB Biclusters

Step 1 : Find similarity between users and construct similarity matrix
Step 2 : If similarity between user I and user J > α
               Place user I and j in a new bicluster
               Find the Hadamard product of Ses_i and Ses_j
               Add the pages in the Resultant pattern to bicluster
          End
Step 3 : If the page pattern of any 2 biclusters are same,
               Merge those 2 biclusters

Output NB   /* Number of biclusters
Output BU and BP /* Users and Pages in each Bicluster

5.2. User Profiles

User profiling on the web consists of studying important characteristics of the web visitors. The biclustering process is an important step in establishing user profiles. Some of the discovered user profiles obtained using Robust Biclustering algorithm is summarized in Table 1. These sample user profiles are obtained as per the method specified in section 3.

5.3 Evaluation Metrics

For measuring the performance of the proposed algorithm, widely accepted metrics from information retrieval is used in this chapter. For a test user that receives a top-N recommendation list, let R denote the number of relevant recommended pages.

The F-measure is defined as the harmonic mean of precision and recall as given in. In the recommender evaluation literature the F-measure is often referred to as

$$F - \text{Measure} = \frac{2*\text{precision}*\text{Recall}}{\text{Precision}+\text{Recall}} \quad (1)$$

Table 1. Sample User Profiles

Bicluster	Pageviews	Weight
1	/support.html /travels/Package.html /travels/spots.html	1 0.7687 0.7261
2	/bbmsoftsolutions/web.html /help.html /support.html	1 0.3928 0.3457
3	bbmsoftsolutions/ecommerce.html /help.html /support.html /bbmsoftsolutions/services.html /index.html /services/services.html	1 0.7222 0.7222 0.5000 0.5000 0.5000

Table 2. Symbols

Symbol	Description
K	Number of Biclusters Recommended
N	Number of Recommended pages
nn	Number of pages in the Active session window

$$E - Measure = \frac{1}{\alpha * \left(\dfrac{1}{Precision}\right) + (1-\alpha)*\left(\dfrac{1}{Recall}\right)}$$

(2)

The parameter α controls the trade-off between precision and recall. In this work, α is taken 0.6.

5.4 Parameter Setting

The maximum size of the recommendation list is set to 10 and the minimum number of pages and users in a bicluster is set to 2. The implicit rating obtained from the hits of users are stored as weights and the weight of each page in the bicluster is determined from mean weights of pages visited by all the users in the bicluster. The weights are normalized so that the range of weights fall from 0 to 1. In E-measure, the value of α is taken as 0.6. Table 2 summarizes the symbols that are used in the sequel.

5.5 Recommendation Results of Robust Biclustering

The recommendation engine takes a collection of user profiles as input and generates a recommendation set by matching the current user's activity against the discovered patterns. We use a fixed-size sliding window over the current active session to capture the current user's history depth. Thus, the sliding window of size n (n <= number of pages) over the active session allows only the last n visited pages to influence the recommendation value of items in the recommendation set. This sliding window is called as active session window.

In each iteration, each transaction t in the evaluation set was divided into two parts. The first *n* page views were used for generating recommendations, whereas, the remaining portion of t (target set) was used to evaluate the generated recommendations. For the recommendation process we chose a session window size of 2. The recommendation results are given in Table 3 for the sample path.

5.6 Performance Analysis for Robust Biclustering

The required input of the algorithm is minimum number of pages to be included in the bicluster. In order to discover the best biclusters it is important to fine-tune this input variable. For the 100 K data set, we examine the performance of F- metric and E-Meric versus different values for *minp* where *minpis* the minimum allowed number of pages in a bicluster, Figure 7 depicts the average numbers of pages in a bicluster, which increases with increasing *minp*.

In the following, the comparative results for effectiveness are shown. Figure 8 Illustrates the values of F- measure and E-Measure for varying values of *minp*. As illustrated in the figure, the best performance is attained for n = 2. As minimum number of biclusters are recommended which are

Table 3. Recommendation Results for a Typical User Navigation Path

Pages of Active User session	Recommended Web pages	Recommendation score
/bbm/index.html	bbmsoftsolutions/web.html	0.4512
/services/services.html	hr/employment.html	0.5218
/bbmsoftsolutions/services.html	/bbmsoftsolutions/multimedia.html	0.5477
	/bbm/contact.html	0.5492

Figure 7. Average number of pages in the bicluster for 100 k data set for various values of minp

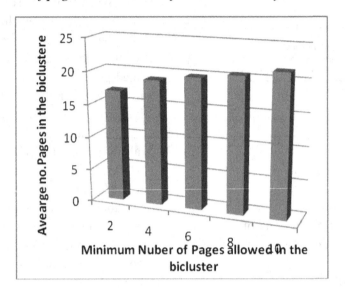

very similar to the current active session, the values of F-Measure and E-Measure remains increased.

RB finds all possible biclusters. It is obvious that this characteristic generates overlapping biclusters. The number of overlapping biclusters can be enormously large. To avoid this, we can set minimum number of pages to be included in a bicluster with respect to the desired overlapping degree.

5.7 Performance Analysis for Simple Biclustering

In the following, we show the comparative results for effectiveness. Figure 9 Illustrates the values of F1 measure and E-Measure for varying values of *minp*. As shown, the best performance is attained for n = 2. As minimum number of biclusters are recommended which are very similar to the cur-

Figure 8. Number of Recommended Biclusters versus F-Measure and E-Measure For RB

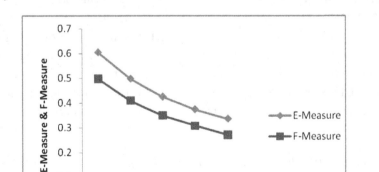

Figure 9. Number of Recommended Biclusters versus F-Measure and E-Measure for SB

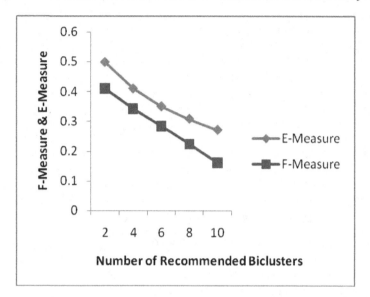

rent active session, the values of F-Measure and E-Measure remains decreased.

5.8 Comparative Results for Effectiveness

In this section, the performance of RB with SB are compared for page recommendation. The parameters, are tuned as follows: the size of the recommendation list (N, default value 10), and the size of training set (default value 75%). The test set consists of all remaining users, i.e., those not in the training set. Users in the test set are the basis for measuring the examined metrics. The performance comparison of RB and SB using E-Measure for various data set sizes 1000, 2000, 3000, 4000 and 5000 are illustrated in Figure 10. It can be observed from the figure that the performance of RB is better than the performance of SB.

Fig. 10 shows the values of E-Measure for various sizes of data set and Figure 11 shows the values of F-Measure for various sizes of data set.

6. FUTURE RESEARCH DIRECTIONS

The limitation of conventional Biclustering algorithm is the biclusters may *overlap*, which means that several users or pages of the session matrix may participate in multiple biclusters. The degree of overlapping is not taken into account for each user and for each page in the bicluster. Hence Fuzzy sets can be included in the biclustering approach to capture the overlapping between user's interests.

7. CONCLUSION

In this chapter a new personalized recommendation method is proposed, which is applied to web log mining by integrating user and page clustering techniques to improve web personalized Recommendation. The accuracy of the proposed algorithm is computed using recommendation measures. Our extensive experimental results illustrate the effectiveness and efficiency of the proposed algorithm.

Figure 10. E-Measure for RB and SB

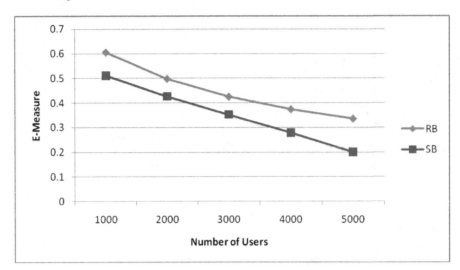

Figure 11. F-Measure for RB and SB

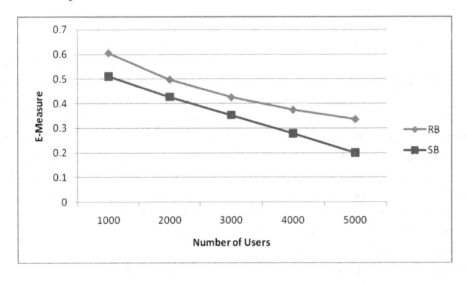

REFERENCES

Breese, J., Heckerman, D., & Kadie, C. (1998). Empirical analysis of predictive algorithms for collaborative filtering. In *Proceedings of the Uncertainty in Artificial Intelligence Conference*, (pp. 43–52).

Cheng, Y., & Church, G. M. (2000). Biclustering of expression data. In *Proceedings. of the eighth International Conference on Intelligent Systems for Molecular Biology*, (pp. 93–103).

Chi, C.-C., Kuo, C.-H., & Lu, M.-Y. % Tsao, N-L. (2008). Concept-based pages recommendation by using cluster algorithm. In *Proceedings of Eighth IEEE International Conference on Advanced Learning Technologies*, 1–5 July, Santander, Spain, (pp.298–300).

Claypool, M., Le, P., Wased, M., & Brown, D. (2001). Implicit Interest Indicators. In *Proceedings of sixth international conference on Intelligent User Interfaces* (pp. 33–40). New York: ACM Press. doi:10.1145/359784.359836

de Castro, P. A. D., de França, F. O., Ferreira, H. M., & Von Zuben, F. J. (2007). Applying Biclustering to Perform Collaborative Filtering. In *Seventh IEEE International Conference on Intelligent Systems Design and Applications,* (pp. 421-426).

Eirinaki, M., & Vazirgiannis, M. (2003). Web Mining for Web Personalization. *ACM Transactions on Internet Technology*, *3*(1), 1–27. doi:10.1145/643477.643478

Fu, Y., Sandhu, K., & Shih, M. (1999). Fast Clustering of Web Users Based on Navigation Patterns. In *Proceedings of World Multiconference on Systemics, Cybernetics and Informatics (SCI/ISAS'99)*, (5), 560-567.

Geyer-Schulz, A., & Hahsler, M. (July 2002). Evaluation of Recommender Algorithms for an Internet Information Broker based on Simple Association Rules and on the Repeat-Buying Theory, In B. Masand, M. Spiliopoulou, J. Srivastava, O. Zaïane, (Eds.), *Proceedings of WEBKDD'2002* (pp. 100-114). Edmonton: Canada.

Goldberg, D., Nichols, D., Oki, B. M., & Terry, D. (1992). Using Collaborative Filtering to Weave an Information Tapestry. *Communications of the ACM*, *35*(12), 61–70. doi:10.1145/138859.138867

Hammouda, K. M., & Kamel, M. S. (2004). Efficient phrase-based document indexing for Web document clustering. *IEEE Transactions on Knowledge and Data Engineering*, *16*(10), 1279–1296. doi:10.1109/TKDE.2004.58

Horn, R. (1994). *Topics in Matrix Analysis*. Cambridge, UK: Cambridge University Press.

Hui, Z., Bin, P., Ke, X., & Hui, W. (2006). An efficient algorithm for clustering search engine results. In *2006 International Conference on Computational Intelligence and Security*, November, Guangzhou, China, (pp. 1429–1434).

Hwang, C.-S., & Chen, Y.-P. (2006). Fuzzy Collaborative Filtering for Web Page Prediction. In *Proceedings of JCIS Advanced Intelligent Systems Research,* (pp. 11-16).

Inbarani, H., & Thangavel, K. (2009). Mining and Analysis of Clickstream Patterns. In *Foundations of Computational, Intelligence - Data Mining, Studies in Computational Intelligence* (pp. 3–27). Berlin: Springer.

Inbarani, H., Thangavel, K. & Pethalakshmi. (2007). A Rough Set Based Feature Selection for web usage mining. In *Proceedings of the International Conference on Computational Intelligence and Multimedia Applications* (ICCIMA 2007),1, (pp. 33-38).

Jenamani, M., Mohapatra, P. K. J., & Ghose, S. (2002). Online Customized Index Synthesis in Commercial Web Sites. *IEEE Intelligent Systems*, 20–27. doi:10.1109/MIS.2002.1134358

Jiang, D., Tang, C., & Zhang, A. (2004). Cluster Analysis for Gene Expression Data: A Survey. *IEEE Transactions on Knowledge and Data Engineering*, *11*(16), 1370–1386. doi:10.1109/TKDE.2004.68

Li, H.-Y., Xie, C.-S., & Liu, Y. (2007). A new method of pefetching I/O requests. In *International Conference on Networking, Architecture and Storage*, July, Guilin, China, (pp. 217–224).

Liu, H., & Keselj, V. (2007). Combined mining of Web server logs and web contents for classifying user navigation patterns and predicting users' future requests. *Data & Knowledge Engineering*, *2*(61), 304–330. doi:10.1016/j.datak.2006.06.001

Liu, J.-G., & Wu, W.-P. (2004). Web Usage Mining For Electronic Business Applications. In *Proceedings of the Third International Conference on Machine Learning and Cybernetics,* Shanghai, (2), 1314-1318.

Mobasher, B. (2002). Discovery and Evaluation of Aggregate Usage Profiles for Web Personalization. *Data Mining and Knowledge Discovery, 6,* 61–82. doi:10.1023/A:1013232803866

Mobasher, B., Cooley, R., & Srivastava, J. (1999). Creating adaptive web sites through usage-based clustering of urls. In *IEEE Knowledge and Data Engineering Workshop (KDEX'99),* (pp. 19-25).

Nasraoui, O., & Petenes, C. (2003). Combining Web Usage Mining and Fuzzy Inference for Web site Personalization. In *proceedings of WebKDD workshop,* (pp. 37-46).

Nasraoui, O., Soliman, M., Saka, E., Badia, A., & Germain, R. (2008). A web usage mining framework for mining evolving user profiles in dynamic websites. *IEEE Transactions on Knowledge and Data Engineering, 2*(20), 202–215. doi:10.1109/TKDE.2007.190667

Pallis, G., Angelis, L., & Vakali, A. (2007). Validation and interpretation of web users' sessions clusters. *Information Processing & Management, 5*(43), 1348–1367. doi:10.1016/j.ipm.2006.10.010

Pallis, G., & Vakali, A. (2006). Insight and perspectives for content delivery networks. *Communications of the ACM, 1*(49), 101–106. doi:10.1145/1107458.1107462

Parsons, J., Ralph, P., & Gallagher, K. (2004). Using Viewing Time to Infer User Preference in Recommender Systems. In *Proceedings of AAAI Workshop on Semantic Web Personalization,* (pp. 52-63).

Perkowitz, M., & Etzioni, O. (2000). Towards adaptive web sites: conceptual framework and case study. *Artificial Intelligence, 118,* 245–275. doi:10.1016/S0004-3702(99)00098-3

Petridou, S. G., Koutsonikola, V. A., Vakali, A. I., & Papadimitriou, G. I. (2008). Time Aware Web Users Clustering. *IEEE Transactions on Knowledge and Data Engineering, 5*(20), 653–667. doi:10.1109/TKDE.2007.190741

Resnick, P., Iacovou, N., Suchak, M., Bergstrom, P., & Riedl, J. (1994). Grouplens: An open architecture for collaborative filtering on netnews. In *Proceedings of the Computer Supported Collaborative Work Conference,* (pp. 175–186).

Sarukkai, R. R. (2000). Link Prediction and Path Analysis Using Markov Chains. In *Proceedings of the 9th International World Wide Web Conference on Computer networks,* (pp. 377-386). Amsterdam: North-Holland Publishing.

Sarwar, B., Karypis, G., Konstan, J., & Riedl, J. (2001). Item-based collaborative filtering recommendation algorithms. In *Proceedings of the WWW Conference,* (pp. 285–295).

Sheng, Q., Moreau, Y., & De Moor, B. (2003). Biclustering micrarray data by Gibbs sampling. *Journal of Bioinformatics, 19*(2), 196–205.

Song, Q., & Shepperd, M. (2006). Mining web browsing patterns for E-commerce. *Computers in Industry,* 622–630. doi:10.1016/j.compind.2005.11.006

Srinivasa, N., & Medasani, S. (2004). Active fuzzy clustering for collaborative filtering. In *Proceedings of IEEE International Conference on Fuzzy Systems,* July, Budapest, Hungary, (pp. 1607–1702).

Tan, X., Yao, M., & Xu, M. (2006). An Effective Technique for Personalization Recommendation Based on Access Sequential Patterns. In *IEEE Proceedings of Asia-pacific conference on Services computing*.

Tang, C., Zhang, L., Zhang, I., & Ramanathan, M. (2001). Interrelated two-way clustering: an unsupervised approach for gene expression data analysis. In *Proceedings of the 2nd IEEE Int. Symposium on Bioinformatics and Bioengineering*, (pp. 41–48).

Xiao, J., Zhang, Y., Jia, X., & Li, T. (2001). Measuring Similarity of Interests for Clustering web-Users. In *Proceedings Of the 12th Australian Database Conference*, (pp. 107-114).

Xu, G. (2008). *Web Mining Techniques for Recommendation and Personalization*. Ph.D thesis.

Chapter 12
Web Mining and Social Network Analysis

Roberto Marmo
University of Pavia, Italy

ABSTRACT

Research on social networks has advanced significantly due to wide variety of on-line social websites and very popular Web 2.0 application. Social network analysis views social relationships in terms of network and graph theory about nodes (individual actors within the network) and ties (relationships between the actors). Using web mining techniques and social networks analysis it is possible to process and analyze large amount of social data (such as blogtagging, online game playing, instant messenger etc.) and by this to discover valuable information from data. In this way, we can understand the social structure, social relationships and social behaviors. This new approach is also denoted as social network mining. These algorithms differ from established set of data mining algorithms developed to analyze individual records, because social network datasets are called relational due to centrality of relations among entities. This chapter also sets out a process to apply web mining.

DOI: 10.4018/978-1-60960-102-7.ch012

Figure 1. An example of social network: individuals on nodes and links represent relationships

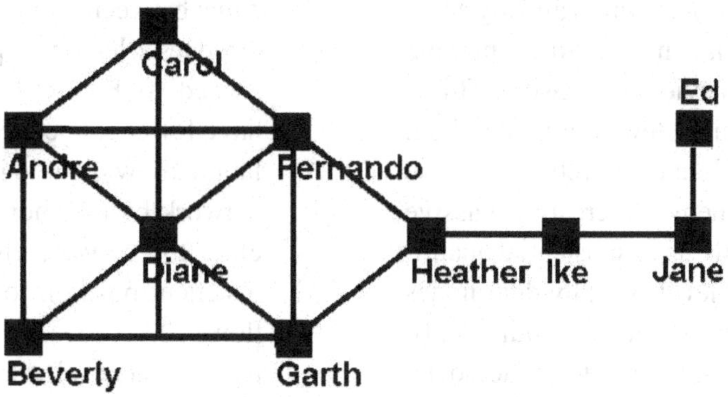

INTRODUCTION

A social network is a social structure made of individuals (organizations, company etc.) also called nodes, which are connected by links represent relationships and interactions between individuals, a rich relational interdependency and content for mining. Figure 1 shows an example of social network.

Online social network focuses on building on Internet communities of people who share interests and/or activities, who are interested in exploring the interests and activities of others or who are interested to communicate, interact and share. So, they are very popular Web 2.0 application. Some well-known social networking websites are: Facebook as general network, LinkedIn and Viadeo as business social network, Flickr about photo sharing etc. Thus, social network is a relevant part of human life (Fu, 2007; Goth, 2008).

This chapter describes how to use web mining techniques and online social networks analysis to obtain analysis regarding user profile and behaviour, information suitable for marketing, sociology etc. The analysis are focused on web resources such as user content, network structures, user behaviour on network website and how user creates its network

This chapter is structured as follows: section 1 presents social network analysis, section 2 presents web mining algorithms and techniques can be used for social networks analysis, section 3 presents techniques and process, section 4 discusses some applications. Finally, future challenges and research directions are explained.

SOCIAL NETWORK ANALYSIS

Social network analysis (SNA) is a mathematical technique developed in modern sociology, in order to understand structure and behaviour between members of social systems, to map relationships between individuals in social network, also to serve up business intelligence on the ties. Social network analysis is related to network theory and graph theory, so the network topology helps to determine a network's usefulness to its individuals. It is possible to classify objectives in: static to find community structures, dynamic to monitor community structure evolution and to spot abnormal individuals or abnormal time-stamps.

Evaluation of people location in network, that is the centrality of a node, is relevant to understand networks and their participants. These measures provided by social network analysis give us insight into the various roles and groupings: who are the connectors, leaders, bridges, isolates, the clusters existing and who is in them, who is in the kernel of network and who is on the periphery.

Social network analysis is descriptive rather than predictive, because it is built with only a few global parameters, so it is not useful for making prediction of future behaviour of network. This is due to networks availability, few information about each node and lack of data. In Web 2.0 age we have very large social networks creating massive quantities of data and we have substantial quantities of information at level of individual nodes suitable to build statistical models of individuals. The relevant difficult regards how to extract social data from a set of very different communication resources (Jin, 2007; Matsuo, 2007).

Adjacency matrix is a simply way to represent a network by representing which vertices of a graph are adjacent to which other vertices: if person i and j are connected with one direct link we have (i,j)=1 and (i,j)=0 otherwise. Using matrix algebra on adjacency matrix it is possible to evaluate some numerical properties useful for SNA, such as computing the intensity of relation between person (Kolaczyk, 2009; Scott, 2000; Wasserman, 1994) based on:

- degree: number of ties or relations for person, related to Figure 1 Diane has the most direct connections in the network, making hers the most active node in the network, she is a connector or hub in the network
- betweenness: lying between each other pairs of persons, related to Figure 1 Diane has many direct ties, Heather has few direct connections compared to average in network, Heather is between two important sub-network or cluster and she plays a broker role in network, but she is a single point of failure so this is a risk because Ike and Jane would be cut off from information and knowledge in Diane's cluster, so a person like Heather holds a lot of power over the outcomes in network
- flow centrality is similar to betweenness centrality, except that we consider all paths instead of considering only the shortest paths between pairs of nodes
- closeness: length of paths to other person, related to Figure 1 Fernando and Garth have fewer connections than Diane, but relation allow them to access all the nodes in network by the shortest paths. so they are close to everyone else and they are in an excellent position to monitor the network flow
- network centralization: a very centralized network is dominated by one or few central nodes that can become a point of failure, in fact if these nodes are removed or damaged, the network quickly fragments into unconnected sub-networks; related to Figure 1 Diane is an example of central node
- network reach: the shorter paths in network are more important, related to Figure 1 Fernando and Garth can reach everyone else in three steps or less
- boundary spanners: nodes that connect their cluster to others have high network metrics, related to Figure 1 Fernando, Garth, and Heather are boundary spanners because are more central in network than their neighbours whose connections are only local
- peripheral nodes can be connected to networks not currently mapped in order to create a new information flow, related to Figure 1 Ike and Jane receive very low centrality scores in this mapped network, but they may be contractors toward another not mapped networks
- dynamism of the network due to changing edges and the strengths of association of the nodes.

Another goals of SNA regards to explain the observed network in a predictable manner, identification of subgroup, inferring real-world connections and discovering, labelling, characterizing communities. (Adamic, 2007).

Topic identification of flowing textual data can be used to cluster the social network, five classical methods for topic identification are: topic unigram based on counting the number of occurrence of each word, cache model, topic perplexity, TFIDF classifier, weighted model used for sparse data like email based on computing scores of topics so highest score value determines the topic (Bigi, 2001).

Information Visualization is also a relevant topic and suitable visual technique for social network analysis. In fact, visualization of social networks provides an easily understood of the structure of networks, distribution of nodes, links between nodes and clusters and groups (Card, 1999; Heer, 2005; Spence, 2000) to benefit from the power of both human visual perception and computing. The social graph as Figure 1 shows you and your friends, the networks they belong to, and the social cliques they are part of. It is possible to see who is central to a particular group and which friends are connectors between two groups. An example of software for visualization is TouchGraph Facebook Browser available on www.touchgraph.com/TGFacebookBrowser.html that lets you see how your friends are connected on network Facebook, it is possible to explore the friend network by graphing photos from friend's photo album.

Relevant visualization tools for social network support a wide range of visualization options and a support for calculating structural graph properties, including interactive views, but they are limited to uni-modal graph representations.

MINING TECHNIQUES

Several techniques for learning statistical models have been developed recently by researchers in machine learning and data mining. Actually focus is on statistical challenges raised by relational data, so denoted because the relations among in-terrelated people are central, distinguishing from meaning of data stored in relational databases because while relational databases can represent relational data, relational data can also be represented and accessed in other ways (Jensen, 2002; Scott, 2000).

Web mining regards application of data mining techniques to discover patterns and extracting useful information from web site (Chakrabarti, S. 2003). According to different target and data resources, web mining techniques can be classified into:

- web usage mining is the process of finding out what users are looking for on web site to define the navigation patterns of users
- web structure mining is the process of using graph theory to analyse the node and connection structure of a web site. in order to improve navigation
- web content mining explores and discovers useful information from text, image, audio or video data in the web.

Graph mining can handle thousands of nodes and millions of edges in a graph using a specific set of algorithms tailored to extracting knowledge from massive graph data structure (Chakrabarti D., 2006). Graph mining and social network analysis regards graphs, so they share many concepts and ideas, but some of the algorithms in use in SNA (such as combinatorial optimizations) become impractical for large datasets. Graph mining community have not worked on social roles or the power of nodes, due to the different semantics of the datasets analyzed.

The goal of process mining is to extract a structured process description about processes from transaction logs created by set of information regarding real executions (Aalst. 2004a; Agrawal, 1998; Grigori, 2001; Sayal, 2002). Process mining can be used to construct models that explain some aspect of the behavior registered. The focus is on the various process activities and their dependencies, deriving roles and other organizational entities. Regarding social network analysis, the focus is on: the relation between person or groups of person acting in the process (Aalst, 2004b). Metrics proposed for mining organizational relations are based on: (possible) causality, joint cases, joint activities, special event types (e.g., delegation).

Visual data mining is a collection of interactive reflective methods that support visual exploration of data sets by dynamically adjusting parameters to see how they affect the information being presented, moreover it offer the luxury of being able to make observations without preconception. Also above mentioned, a social network can be represented by a graph, so visual data mining is useful tool to explore the network about task as finding group of closest people. Invenio (Singh, 2007) is a tool for visual mining of socials that integrates a wide range of interactive visualization options. Invenio interactively explore multimodal, multi-relational social networks and it also supports construction of views using both database operations and basic graph mining operations.

Software MiSoN (Aalst, 2004a) has been developed to discover relationships between individuals from a range of enterprise information systems including workflow management systems such as Staffware, InConcert, and MQSeries, ERP systems, and CRM systems. Based on the event logs extracted from these systems MiSoN constructs sociograms that can be used as a starting point for SNA.

COMBINED APPROACH

Assembling social network analysis and web mining give us an innovative level of detail in social network analysis useful for new understanding, predictions, use in decision-making, viral marketing.

Social network website is, however, a classic website so web mining techniques and log

data extracted from webserver can be adopted to improve user navigation by web administrator.

In case of social network analysis, web mining techniques can be re-classified as follows:

- web usage mining is useful to transform usage data and user communication on network into relational data (Nowson, 2007), as example we can calculate the closeness of blog users (Tseng, 2005)
- web structure mining is useful to extract the links from many source of information (WWW link, email etc.) for extracting and constructing social network between users and other basic information suitable for social network analysis
- web content mining explores and discovers users0 reading interests and favourite content.

Typically it is usually necessary to utilize all three types of web mining and techniques together.

There are many different kinds of web mining techniques. The two relevant techniques are clustering and association rule mining and they can be combined using visualization (Tseng, 2005).

Clustering covers a wide class of methods to locate relevant information and organize it in an intelligible way, such as to find group of closest people in a network. Clusters have more desirable properties such as the weight of edges across different clusters are much smaller. This task is normally achieved by using a visualization technique in case of small social network, clustering can be used with a large network. A *k*-way hierarchical spectral clustering algorithm with heuristics to balance cluster sizes for social network analysis is discussed in (Kurucz, 2009).

Association rule mining, so called marketbasket analysis, can help discover the hidden relationships between nodes and it provide information in the form of if-then statements. These rules are computed from the data an, compared to if-then rules of logic, are provided with probabilistic measures, such as: "if Fernando knows Heather and also knows Diane then " or Fernando read Diane's blog and also see Ike's video, numeric parameters are: support 0.8 and confidence 0.6". This approach is helpful for the application after social networks analysis, such as recommendation systems or information filtering systems (Mishne, 2007).

The paper (Jin, 2007) expand the existing techniques for social network mining from the Web and apply them to obtain a social network for different entities. Two types of networks are investigated: firms and artists. Two technical improvements are made: relation identification and threshold tuning. Evaluations and effectiveness of these methods are discussed.

A new mining problem consists of finding periodic subgraphs in dynamic social networks to discover interaction patterns that occur at regular time intervals. The paper (Mayank Lahir, 2008) propose an efficient and scalable algorithm to find subgraphs that takes imperfect periodicity into account, a potential applications of periodic behavior analysis can be detection of predictable behavior.

A typical process to combine web mining and online social networks analysis includes (Hsien Ting, 2008):

1. selection of data analysis targets: email, video, blog, status update etc.
2. selection of online social networks analysis
3. data collected from log server and preparation
4. selection and combination of web mining techniques
5. results presentation and visualization
6. results interpretation and action.

The point (3) is very difficult because it is very hard to obtain data from administrators of social network. The required data can be collected in several ways like questionnaires, interviews and observations also by keep looking of flowing data in the web (Lauw, 2005) monitor the state of the network, based on time, location or both of them (Lauw, 2005). About point (6) some actions regards suggest two persons to create a contact, to invite a person to be more sociable, to invite a person to write more post on blog. Due to daily use of social network, this process can be a continuous process.

APPLICATIONS

It is possible to design viral marketing (that is, a recommendation from a friend or other trusted source has the credibility that advertisements lack) project to maximize positive word-of-mouth among customers and to achieve much higher profits compared to discarding interactions among customers and the corresponding network effects, as marketing does (Domingos, 2005; Leskovec, 2007). Therefore, we can try to look at certain online groups and predict whether the group will flourish or disband.

Using blog-specific properties it is possible to improve opinion retrieval effectiveness (Mishne, 2007). Blog timestamps are used to increase the retrieval scores of blog posts published near the time of a significant event, an inexpensive approach to comment amount estimation is used to identify the level of opinion expressed in a post (a message written on a blog), query-specific weights are used to change the importance of spam filtering for different types of queries. Each technique is based on a property of the blog-space and it is implemented with a simple mechanism.

ArnetMiner is a social network about researcher profiles and publications available at www.arnetminer.org (Tang, 2008) to provide services for managing academic information. Several key issues in extraction and mining are discussed: extraction of a researcher social network from the existing Web, integration of the publications from existing digital libraries, expertise search on a given topic, association search between researchers.

An advertisement according to user favorites and interests by mining his/her interactions in social networks is a desiderable chance. In paper (Zadeh, 2008) social network users are categorized based on the topic exchanges by them in the network, these topics are discovered by mining of flowing data in that environment, considering that these topics shows the user willing. Metrics are: environment's users amount, popularity and amount of time that user spend on that place. So, relevant advertisements will be represented to them increasing probability to accept the desired advertisement over traditional method at lowered cost.

The paper (Zhou, 2009) discusses a architecture solution by analyzing users' static attribute and interaction of BBS (Bulletin Board System) to mine what kinds of attitudes they show to others and what kind of relationship between them using mining technology, to establish users' social network, and to find out the key figures in networks. Construction of data sources, analysis of the static attribute information of personnel, analyze of members' interaction, network organizations are discussed.

Other application regards detection of emerging phenomena of community structure in social networks, anti web spamming, content quality, finding risky terroristic groups and business purposes specially viral marketing (Richardson, 2002), advertise management (Yang, 2006), community discovery (Zhou, 2007; Yang, 2007), email and instant messenger mining (Bird, 2006; Domingos, 2005; Staab, 2005).

FURTHER CHALLENGES

Problems are due to agent with local view of the network and direct interaction only with neighbours. Algorithmic challenges regard: large-scale networks, linear algorithms typically unfeasible due to network size, network is dynamic in many cases. Some trends regard accurate description of communities of interest in network based on collection and processing of statistics over past interactions.

Specific problem of maintaining individual privacy in studies of social networks is very relevant, because while much of the research on large-scale social systems has been carried out on public data, richest sources of social interaction information come from e-mail, instant messaging, or phone communication by strong expectations of privacy. A compromise between such availability and protection of privacy of the individuals must be adopted. Standard approaches consists on anonymization: the names of individuals are replaced with meaningless unique identifiers, in this way the network structure is maintained and private information has been deleted.

The book (Aggarwal, 2008) proposes a number of techniques to perform the data mining tasks in a privacy-preserving way.

The intersection of social network analysis and ontology emergence create a fertile ground for semantic social network research.

CONCLUSION

This paper describes extraction mining methods useful to social network analysis. How to combine different types of web mining techniques is also an open issue. This research field is very interested due to a moltitude of applications and actuality of online social network in real life.

REFERENCES

Adamic, L. A., & Adar, E. (2007). Friends and Neighbors on the Web. *Social Networks*, *25*, 211–230. doi:10.1016/S0378-8733(03)00009-1

Aggarwal, C. C., & Yu, P. S. (Eds.). (2008). *Privacy-Preserving Data Mining Models and Algorithms*. Berlin: Springer.

Agrawal, R., Gunopulos, D., & Leymann, F. (1998). Mining Process Models from Workflow Logs. In *Proceedings of Sixth International Conference on Extending Database Technology*, (pp. 469–483).

Bigi, B., Brun, A., Haton, J.-P., Smaïli, K., & Zitouni, I. (2001) A comparative study of topic identification on newspaper and e-mail. In *Proceedings of String Processing and Information Retrieval Conference (SPIRE2001)*, (pp. 238).

Bird, C., Gourley, A., Devanbu, P., Gertz, M., & Swaminathan, A. (2006). Mining email social networks in postgres. In *MSR '06: Proceedings of the 2006 international workshop on Mining software repositories*, (pp. 185-186). New York: ACM Press.

Card, S. K., Shneiderman, B., & Mackinlay, J. D. (1999). *Readings in information visualization: using vision to think*. San Francisco: Morgan Kaufmann.

Chakrabarti, D., & Faloutsos, C. (2006). Graph Mining: Laws, Generators, and Algorithms. *ACM Computing Surveys*, *38*(1).

Chakrabarti, S. (2003). *Mining the Web: Discovering Knowledge from Hypertext Data*. San Francisco: Morgan Kaufmann Publishers.

Domingos, P. (2005). Mining Social Networks for Viral Marketing. *IEEE Intelligent Systems*, *20*(1), 80–82.

Fu, F., Chen, X., Liu, L., & Wang, L. (2007). Social dilemmas in an online social network: the structure and evolution of cooperation. *Physics Letters. [Part A]*, *371*, 58–64. doi:10.1016/j.physleta.2007.05.116

Goth, G. (2008). Are Social Networking Growing Up? *IEEE Distributed Systems Online*, *9*(2), 3. doi:10.1109/MDSO.2008.4

Grigori, D., Casati, F., Dayal, U., & Shan, M. (2001). Improving Business Process Quality through Exception Understanding, Prediction, and Prevention. In *Proceedings of 27th International Conference on Very Large Data Bases (VLDB '01)*, (pp. 159–168).

Heer, J., & Boyd, D. (2005) Vizster: Visualizing Online Social Network. In *Proceedings of 2005 IEEE Symposium*, (pp.32-39).

Jensen, D., & Neville, J. (2002). *Data mining in social networks*. National Academy of Sciences Symposium on Dynamic Social Network Analysis.

Jin, Y. Z., Matsuo, Y., & Ishizuka, M. (2007). Extracting social networks among various entities on the web. In *Proceedings of the Fourth European Semantic Web Conference* (pp. 251-266). Berlin: Springer.

Kolaczyk, E. D. (2009). *Statistical analysis of network data: methods and models*. Springer.

Kurucz, M., Benczúr, A. A., Csalogány, K., & Lukács, L. (2009). Spectral Clustering in Social Networks, In *Proceedings of WebKDD/SNA-KDD 2007* (pp. 1–20).

Lahiri, M., & Berger-Wolf, T. Y. (2008). Mining Periodic Behavior in Dynamic Social Networks. In *Proceedings of Eighth IEEE International Conference on Data Mining* (pp. 373-382).

Lauw, H., Lim, E.-P., Pang, H., & Tan, T.-T. (2005). Social network discovery by mining spatio-temporal events. *Computational & Mathematical Organization Theory*, *11*(2), 97–118. doi:10.1007/s10588-005-3939-9

Leskovec, J., Adamic, L. A., & Huberman, B. A. (2007). The dynamics of viral marketing. *ACM Transactions on the Web*, *1*(1), 1–39. doi:10.1145/1232722.1232727

Matsuo, Y., Tomobe, H., & Nishimura, T. (2007). Robust Estimation of Google Counts for Social Network Extraction. In *Proceedings of Twenty Second Conference on Artificial Intelligence* (pp. 1395-1401).

Mishne, G. (2007). Using Blog Properties to Improve Retrieval. In *Proceedings of International Conference on Weblogs and Social Media (ICWSM 2007)*, Boulder, CO.

Nowson, S., & Oberlander, J. (2007). Identifying More Bloggers: Towards large scale personality classification of personal weblogs. In *Proceedings of International Conference on Weblogs and Social Media (2007)*, Boulder, CO.

Richardson, M., & Domingos, P. (2002). Mining Knowledge-Sharing Sites for Viral Marketing. In *Proceedings of 8th ACM SIGKDD International Conference on Knowledge Discovery and Data Mining*, (pp. 61-70).

Sayal, M., Casati, F., Dayal, U., & Shan, M. (2002). Business Process Cockpit. In *Proceedings of 28th International Conference on Very Large Data Bases (VLDB'02)*, (pp. 880–883).

Scott, J. (2000). *Social Network Analysis: A Handbook* (2nd ed.). New York: Sage Publications.

Singh, L., Beard, M., Getoor, L., & Blake, M. B. (2007). Visual mining of multi-modal social networks at different abstraction levels. In *Proceedings of 11th International Conference Information Visualization (IV '07)*, (pp. 672-679).

Spence, R. (2000). *Information visualization: design for interaction*. Reading, MA: Addison Wesley.

Staab, S., Domingos, P., Mike, P., Golbeck, J., Ding, L., & Finin, T. (2005). Social Networks Applied. *IEEE Intelligent Systems*, *20*, 80–93. doi:10.1109/MIS.2005.16

Tang, J., Zhang, J., Yao, L., & Li, J. (2008). Extraction and Mining of an Academic Social Network. In. *Proceedings of World Wide Web Conference, 2008*, 1193–1194.

Ting, H. (2008). Web Mining Techniques for Online Social Networks Analysis, In *Proceedings of International Conference on Service Systems and Service Managemen*, (pp. 1-5).

Tseng, B. L., Tatemura, J., & Wu, Y. (2005). Tomographic Clustering to Visualize Blog Communities as Mountain Views. In *Proceedings of World Wide Web Conference 2005*.

van der Aalst, W., & Song, M. (2004b). Mining Social Networks: Uncovering Interaction Patterns in Business Processes. In *Proceedings of International Conference on Business Process Management*, (pp. 244–260).

van der Aalst, W., Weijters, A., & Maruster, L. (2004a). Workflow Mining: Discovering Process Models from Event Logs. *IEEE Transactions on Knowledge and Data Engineering*, *16*(9), 1128–1142. doi:10.1109/TKDE.2004.47

Wasserman, S., & Faust, K. (1994). *Social Network Analysis: Methods and Applications*. Cambridge: Cambridge University Press.

Yang, C. C., & Ng, T. D. (2007). Terrorism and Crime Related Weblog Social Network: Link, Content Analysis and Information Visualization. In *Proceedings of IEEE International Conference on Intelligence and Security Informatics*, (pp. 55–58).

Yang, W.-S., Dia, J.-B., Cheng, H.-C., & Lin, H.-T. (2006). Mining social networks for targeted advertising. In *Proceedings of the 39th Annual Hawaii International Conference on System Science (HICSS '06)*, (vol. 6, pp. 137a).

Zadeh, P. M., & Moshkenani, M. S. (2008). Mining Social Network for Semantic Advertisement. In *Proceedings of Third International Conference on Convergence and Hybrid Information Technology*, (pp. 611-618).

Zhou, D., Councill, I., Zha, H., & Giles, C. (2007) Discovering Temporal Communities from Social Network Documents. In *Proceedings of 7th IEEE International Conference on Data Mining (ICDM 2007),* (pp. 745-750).

Zhou, L., Ding, J., Wang, Y., Cheng, B., & Cao, F. (2009). The Social Network Mining of BBS. *Journal of Networks*, *4*(4), 298–305. doi:10.4304/jnw.4.4.298-305

KEY TERMS AND DEFINITIONS

Adjacency Matrix: To represent a network by representing which vertices of a graph are adjacent to which other vertices.

Business Social Network: Social networking sites for businesses.

Information Visualization: Techniques for visual representation of large-scale collections of non-numerical information.

Social Data: Information created by members of social network, such as blogtagging, online game playing, photo tagging, instant messenger etc.

Social Graph: Chart that illustrates interconnections among people and organizations in a social network.

Social Network: A social structure made of individuals (organizations, company etc.) also called nodes, which are connected by links represent relationships and interactions between individuals.

Social Network Analysis: Mathematical technique developed to understand structure and behaviour between members of social system, to map relationships between individuals in social network.

Social Networking: Grouping of individuals into specific groups or communities.

Social Network Mining: Application of data mining on data from social network.

Viral Marketing: A new trend on marketing, based on the fact that a recommendation from a friend or other trusted source has the credibility that advertisements lack.

Section 3
Visual Systems, Software
and Supercomputing

Chapter 13
iVAS:
An Interactive Visual Analytic System for Frequent Set Mining

Carson K.-S. Leung
The University of Manitoba, Canada

Christopher L. Carmichael
The University of Manitoba, Canada

ABSTRACT

Nowadays, various data, text, and web mining applications can easily generate large volumes of data. Embedded within these data is previously unknown and potential useful knowledge such as frequently occurring sets of items, merchandise, or events. Hence, numerous algorithms have been proposed for finding these frequent sets, which are usually presented in a lengthy textual list. However, "a picture is worth a thousand words". The use of visual representations can enhance user understanding of the inherent relations among the frequent sets. Although a few visualizers have been developed, most of them were not designed for visualizing the mined frequent sets. In this chapter, an interactive visual analytic system called iVAS is proposed for providing visual analytic solutions to the frequent set mining problem. The system enables the visualization and advanced analysis of the original transaction databases as well as the frequent sets mined from these databases.

DOI: 10.4018/978-1-60960-102-7.ch013

INTRODUCTION

Due to advances in technology, large volumes of data can be easily generated. Examples of these data include structured data in relational or transactional databases, as well as semi-structured data in text documents or the World Wide Web. Embedded within these data is potentially useful knowledge that professionals, researchers, students, and practitioners want to discover. This calls for *data mining* (Frawley et al., 1991), which aims to search for implicit, previously unknown and potential useful information or knowledge from large volumes of data. A common data mining task is *frequent set mining* (Agrawal et al., 1993), and it analyzes the data to find frequently occurring sets of items. These frequent sets serve as building blocks for many other data mining tasks such as the mining of association rules, correlation, sequences, episodes, emerging patterns, web access patterns, maximal frequent patterns, closed frequent patterns, and constrained patterns (Agrawal & Srikank, 1994; Bayardo, 1998; Pasquier et al., 1999; Pei et al., 2000; Lakshmanan et al., 2003; Leung et al., 2007; Leung, 2009). Moreover, these frequently occurring sets of items can be used in the mining tasks like classification (e.g., associative classification (Liu, 2009)). Frequent sets can also answer many questions that help users to make important decisions for real-life applications in different domains such as health care, bioinformatics, social science, as well as business. For example, knowing the sets of frequently purchased merchandise helps store managers to make intelligent business decisions like item shelving, finding the sets of popular elective courses helps students to select the combination of courses they wish to take, and discovering the sets of frequently occurring patterns in genes helps professionals and researchers to get a better understanding of certain biomedical or social behaviours of human beings.

As frequent set mining has played important roles in many data mining tasks and has contributed to various real-life applications, it has drawn attention of many researchers. This explains why numerous frequent set mining algorithms (Han et al., 2007; Cheng & Han, 2009) have been proposed since the introduction of the frequent set mining problem (Agrawal et al., 1993). Most of these algorithms return the mining results in textual forms such as a very long unsorted list of frequent sets of items. However, presenting a large number of frequent sets in such a conventional lengthy list does not lead to ease of understanding. As a result, users may not easily discover the useful knowledge that is embedded in the large volumes of data.

It is well known that "a picture is worth a thousand words". As visual representation matches the power of the human visual and cognitive system, having a visual representation of the frequent sets makes it easier for users (e.g., professionals, researchers, students, practitioners) to view and analyze the mining results when compared to presenting a lengthy textual list of frequent sets of items. This leads to *visual analytics*, which is the science of analytical reasoning supported by interactive visual interfaces (Thomas & Cook, 2005; Keim et al., 2009). Since numerous frequent set mining algorithms (which analyze large volumes of data to find frequent sets of items) have been proposed, what we need are interactive systems for visualizing the mining results so that we could take advantages of both worlds (i.e., combine advanced data analysis with visualization).

Among the existing visualization systems, many of them were built to visualize data other than the mining results. For those that were built for visualizing the mining results, they mostly show the results for other data mining tasks—such as groups of similar objects (for clustering), decision trees (for classification), and rules (for association rule mining)—rather than frequently occurring sets of items (for frequent set mining). Hence, an objective of this chapter is to propose an *interactivevisualanalyticsystem* called *iVAS* for effective visualization and advanced analysis of large volumes of data and the frequent sets of items mined from these data.

In general, iVAS visually presents each transaction in the database (the input of the knowledge discovery process) and each frequent set of items in the mining results (the output of the knowledge discovery process) as a horizontal line in a two-dimensional space. By doing so, iVAS reduces unnecessary bends and avoids crossover of lines. Moreover, iVAS is equipped with interactive features and analytical capabilities so that users can easily perceive, relate, and conclude in the knowledge discovery process. Specifically, it follows the visual analytics mantra (Keim et al., 2006): "Overview first, zoom and filter, details on demand". To elaborate, iVAS shows an *overview* of the transaction database so that users can gain insight about the distribution of items in the database, allows users to express their interests and *filter* out the uninteresting data, and finally provides users with interactive features to *zoom in* and *zoom out* examining the *details* of the interesting data at different resolutions. Afterwards, iVAS further analyzes the data automatically to discover useful knowledge in the form of frequent sets of items. The proposed iVAS shows an *overview* of these mined frequent sets so that users can gain insight about the distribution of the mining results, allows users to express their interests and *filter* out the uninteresting sets, and provides users with interactive features to *zoom in* and *zoom out* exploring the interesting frequent sets at different resolutions so that users can obtain more *details* on the discovered knowledge (i.e., the mined frequent sets).

This chapter is an extension of our previously published paper (Leung & Carmichael, 2009). New materials in this chapter include (a) presentation of the visual analytics of database transactions, (b) descriptions on some additional interactive features for visual analytics of the mined frequent sets, (c) case studies on how to apply iVAS to various data mining applications,

as well as (d) discussions on the applicability of iVAS to text mining and web mining applications.

The remainder of this chapter is organized as follows. We first provide a historical perspective on relevant data mining, frequent set mining, and visualization techniques. Then, we focus on our proposed interactive visual analytic system (iVAS). We explain how it represents database transactions and frequent sets as horizontal lines in a two-dimensional space, detail its interactive features for conducting visual analytics, and illustrate how iVAS can be applied to various real-life applications (e.g., exploring a social network via communication patterns, examining popular courses). We also outline our plan for future extension of iVAS, and summarize the key features of iVAS in the conclusion.

BACKGROUND

Developing effective visualization systems has been the subject of many studies. Examples of data visualization systems include Spotfire (Ahlberg, 1996), VisDB (Keim & Kriegel, 1996), independence diagrams (Berchtold et al., 1998), and Polaris (Stolte et al., 2002). These systems provide features to arrange and display data in various forms. For example, VisDB provides users with pixel-oriented techniques, parallel coordinates, and stick figures for exploring large volumes of data. Polaris provides a visual interface to help users to formulate complex queries against a multi-dimensional data cube. However, the majority of these systems are not connected to any data mining engine, let alone were they designed to display the mining results. In contrast, our proposed iVAS allows users to visualize and analyze the data as well as the mining results (in the form of frequent sets of items).

Besides the above systems for visualizing data, there are also systems that were designed to visualize the results of various data mining tasks such as classification, clustering, and association rule mining. For example, Ankerst et al. (1999) proposed a visual framework, which allows users to participate in the building of decision trees. Koren and Harel (2003) designed a visualization method for cluster analysis and validation. Schreck et al. (2008) used interactive Kohonen Maps to perform visual cluster analysis on trajectory data. AViz (Han & Cercone, 2000) discretizes numeric attributes, and visualizes the mined two-dimensional association rules as a collection of two-dimensional planes in a three-dimensional space. ARVis (Blanchard et al., 2007) uses a rule-focusing methodology, which is an interactive methodology for the visual post-processing of association rules, to perform constraint-based association rule mining. Each of the mined rules is represented by an object consisting of a sphere perched on top of a cone. Note that all these systems visualize the results of classification, clustering, or association rule mining; our proposed iVAS visualizes the results of another data mining task—namely, frequent set mining.

Among the systems that were built for visualizing association rules, some of them can be used for visualizing frequent sets. For instance, Yang (2005) designed a system mainly to visualize association rules in a two-dimensional space consisting of many vertical axes. Such a system can also be used to visualize frequent sets. In his system, all domain items are sorted according to their frequencies and are evenly distributed along each vertical axis. A frequent set consisting of k items (also known as a k-itemset) is then represented by a curve that extends from one vertical axis to another connecting k such axes. The thickness of the curve indicates the frequency of the frequent set. However, such a representation suffers from the following problems:

- The use of thickness only shows the *relative* (but not the *exact*) frequency of the frequent set. Comparing the thickness of curves is not easy.

- Since domain items are sorted and *evenly* distributed along the axes, users only know some items are more frequent than the others, but cannot get a sense of how these items are related to each other in terms of their exact frequencies (e.g., whether item a is twice as frequent as, or just slightly more frequent than, item b).

In contrast, Munzer et al. (2005) presented the PowerSetViewer (PSV), which was designed to visualize frequent sets. The PSV provides users with guaranteed visibility of frequent sets in the sense that the pixel representing a frequent set is guaranteed to be visible by highlighting such a pixel. However, multiple frequent sets mined from large volumes of data may be represented by the same pixel.

Recently, we (Leung et al., 2008a) proposed a frequent itemset visualizer (FIsViz), which aims to visualize frequent sets. FIsViz represents each frequent set by a polyline (which is a continuous line composed of one or more line segments) in a two-dimensional space. The location of the polyline explicitly indicates the exact frequency of the frequent set. While FIsViz enables users to visualize the mining results (i.e., frequent sets) for many real-life applications, users may require more effort to be able to clearly visualize frequent sets when the number of frequent sets is huge. The problem is caused by the use of polylines for representing frequent sets because the polylines can be bent and/or can cross over each other. Consequently, one may encounter some difficulties in distinguishing one polyline (representing a frequent set) from another.

To deal with this problem, we developed WiFIsViz (Leung et al., 2008b) and FpViz (Leung & Carmichael, 2009). Among them, WiFIsViz uses two half-screens to visualize the mined frequent sets. Specifically, the left half-screen gives the frequency information of the frequent sets, and the right half-screen shows the relationships among the frequent sets. In contrast, FpViz uses a full-

Figure 1. The representation of some database transactions in iVAS

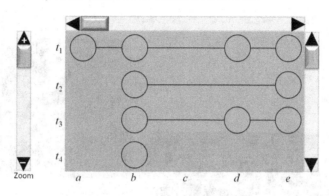

screen to visualize the mined frequent sets. As a preview, our proposed iVAS, on the other hand, can be used for visualizing not only the mined frequent sets (the output of the knowledge discovery process) but also the database transactions (the input of the knowledge discovery process).

IVAS: AN INTERACTIVE VISUAL ANALYTIC SYSTEM

In this section, we present our interactive visual analytic system (iVAS), which helps users to analyze the data for finding frequent sets of items (which are also known as *frequent itemsets*). The system follows the visual analytic mantra: It first gives users an overview, then allows users to zoom and filter, and finally provides users with details on demand.

Interactive Mining of Frequent Sets of Items with iVAS

Given a database of n transactions, we propose an interactive visual analytic system—called iVAS—to provide users with an overview so that they can gain some insight about the distribution of data. Specifically, iVAS displays the contents of the transaction database in a two-dimensional space. The x-axis shows the domain items, and the y-axis shows the transaction IDs. A transaction

containing k items is then represented by k circles, and these circles are linked by a horizontal line. With this representation, users can easily spot the presence or absence of some domain items in each database transaction. For instance, the presence of a circle at (x, t_y)-location implies that transaction t_y contains item x. Conversely, the absence of a circle from $(x', t_{y'})$-location implies that transaction $t_{y'}$ does not contain item x'. Let us consider a database containing five domain items a, b, c, d and e. Suppose the first transaction t_1 of the database contains four items a, b, d and e. Then, iVAS represents t_1 by a horizontal line connecting four circles that are located at (a, t_1), (b, t_1), (d, t_1) and (e, t_1). Similarly, suppose the next three transactions t_2, t_3 and t_4 of the database contain two items b & e, three items b, d & e, and only one item b, respectively. Figure 1 shows how our iVAS represents these four transactions. From the figure, one can easily observe the following:

- Items a, b, d and e are present in some of these transactions.
- In particular, item b occurs very frequently.
- Item c is absent from all four transactions.

To give an overview, iVAS squeezes all the horizontal lines and fits them onto a single screen. Such a visual representation helps users to gain some insight about the data distribution, especially for datasets following certain distribution. An

Figure 2. A snapshot of iVAS showing a seasonal database

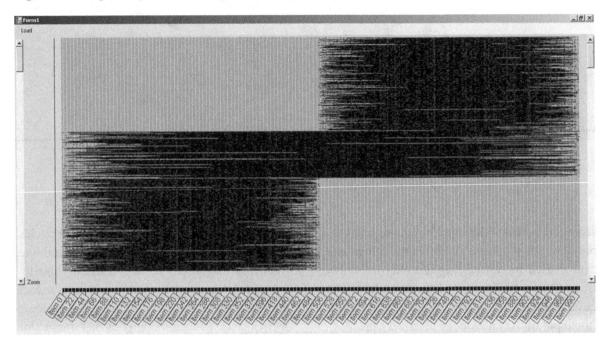

example of these datasets is a seasonal database, in which certain items appear in some portions of the database and some other items appear in other portions of the database (e.g., ski jackets, snow boots, and winter gloves are often purchased together in the winter, whereas swimwear, beach towels, and sandals are often purchased together in the summer). See Figure 2 for a snapshot showing large volumes of data in a seasonal database.

To draw an analogy, the overview gives users a "world map" showing the overall distribution of domain items in the database transactions. However, to obtain more detailed information, users need to zoom in and read the "street map". Hence, iVAS provides users with a *resolution slider*, which enables users to zoom in to or to zoom out from certain regions of the screen. When zooming out, users see an overview of the data on one screen; when zooming in, users get the details about the data split onto multiple screen space. To allow users to view the information across multiple screen space, iVAS provides users with (a) a *vertical scrollbar* for visualizing dif-

ferent transactions and (b) a *horizontal scrollbar* for visualizing different domain items. With the zoom-in view, users can obtain more details about the data in the database.

With this zoom-in view or with the overview (i.e., the zoom-out view), iVAS allows users to interactively select some domain items and/or transactions of interest. For example, users can draw a box in the overview to enclose those items and/or transactions in some dense regions of the screen (e.g., a region representing some winter transactions) for further analysis. Alternatively, users can click on the domain items (on the *x*-axis) and/or the transaction IDs (on the *y*-axis) shown in the zoom-in view to interactively select some specific items and/or transactions. By doing so, iVAS filters out the items and/or transactions that are uninteresting to users. For a real-life example, a store manager, who wants to put a promotion campaign on a specific brand of snow boots, can specify that he wants to explore only those transactions taking place in the month of December and containing a specific brand of snow boots for further analysis.

In addition, iVAS also provides users with details on demand, which consists of techniques that provide more details whenever users request them. The key idea is that, when users hover the mouse over a horizontal line or a circle, iVAS shows the contents (i.e., items within the transaction represented by circles on that line). For instance, when users hover the mouse over the second horizontal line in Figure 1 representing a transaction that contains two items, iVAS displays the details of the transaction by showing its contents: an itemset $\{b, e\}$.

After gaining an insight about the distribution of data in the transaction database and selecting interesting data from the overview or the zoom-in view, users can then request iVAS to start the frequent set mining process to analyze the selected data for finding frequent sets of items. The results of this mining process—i.e., frequent sets of items—are displayed by iVAS in a two-dimensional space. The x-axis shows the domain items, and the y-axis shows the frequency. A frequent set of items consisting of k items (also known as a frequent k-itemset) is then represented by k circles, and these circles are linked by a horizontal line. For example, a frequent 2-itemset $\{a, d\}$ is represented by a horizontal line connecting two circles representing items a and d.

With this representation, users can easily visualize frequent itemsets and their frequencies. Note that, among all the frequent itemsets, it is not uncommon that multiple frequent itemsets may have the same frequency. A naïve representation is to have a band showing several frequent itemsets of the same frequency. However, such a representation would require a large amount of vertical space that may go beyond a single screen. In order to give users an overview of all the mined frequent itemsets on a single screen, a compressed representation is needed.

To reduce the amount of required vertical space, iVAS fills the last circle representing the last item in a frequent k-itemset. By doing so, if two itemsets X and Y having the same frequency such that X is a prefix of Y, then iVAS reduces the number of horizontal lines from two to one such that the last items of X and Y are filled. To elaborate, let X be a j-itemset and Y be a k-itemset such that $X \subset Y$ (where $j < k$). If X and Y have the same frequency, then X and Y are represented by a single horizontal line connecting k circles with the jth and the kth circles filled (and the remaining $k–2$ circles are unfilled). To a further extent, this compression technique is not confined to combining two horizontal lines (representing two itemsets that have the same frequency and are related by the prefix relationship) but multiple horizontal lines (representing several itemsets that have the same frequency and are related by the prefix relationship). Let us consider a concrete example with two itemsets $X = \{b, c\}$ and $Y = \{b, c, d\}$ both having the same frequency (say, 65%). Then, X can be represented by a horizontal line connecting an unfilled circle for item b and a filled circle for item c; Y can be represented by a horizontal line connecting two unfilled circles for items b & c and a filled circle for item d. Since $X \subset Y$, iVAS represents these two itemsets (as shown in Figure 3) by a horizontal line connecting three circles such that the circles for items c & d are filled indicating that c & d are the last items of the respective itemsets. In addition, one can also observe from Figure 3 that itemset $\{a, b, d, e\}$ and its prefix $\{a, b\}$ both share the same frequency of 60%.

Next, let us consider situations where two itemsets X and Y having the same frequency and sharing a common prefix but $X \not\subset Y$. In these situations, iVAS is unable to reduce the number of horizontal lines, but it can reduce the number of circles. To elaborate, let X be a j-itemset and Y be a k-itemset such that X and Y share the common prefix consisting of h items (where $h < j, k$). If X and Y have the same frequency, then X and Y are represented by a "fork": A horizontal line connecting j circles with the last circle filled and another horizontal line (which connects the last

Figure 3. The representation of some mined frequent itemsets in iVAS

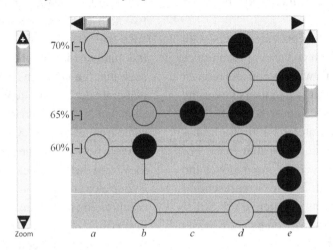

k–h items of Y with the last circle filled) "branching" from the *h*th circle of the first line. Here, to improve the legibility of graphs and to preserve graph aesthetics, iVAS reduces the number of edge crossings by using an orthogonality mechanism that limits edge crossings to a minimum. Specifically, bends for the "branch" occur only at 0° or 90° angles. This minimizes crossings, facilitating legibility and visual comprehension. Again, the compression technique can be applied to multiple itemsets sharing some common prefix and the same frequency. Let us consider a concrete example. Suppose X = {*a, b, d, e*} and Y = {*a, b, e*} having the same frequency (say, 60%). Then, X can be represented by a horizontal line connecting three unfilled circles for items *a, b* & *d* and a filled circle for item *e*; Y can be represented by a horizontal line connecting two unfilled circles for items *a* & *b* and a filled circle for item *e*. Since X and Y share the common prefix {*a, b*}, iVAS represents X and Y by a "fork" consisting of the horizontal line of X and another line containing the filled circle for item *e* "branching" from the unfilled circle for item *b*. If the common prefix {*a, b*} happens to be an itemset having the same frequency as X and Y, the circle for item *b* is then filled as shown in Figure 3.

Note that the aforementioned compression techniques help to reduce the number of horizontal lines as well as the number of circles to be displayed. However, for a large number of frequent itemsets, further reduction in the number of horizontal lines is needed so that the final results could all fit onto a single screen for the overview. To do so, iVAS projects all *p* horizontal lines representing multiple (≥ *p*) itemsets having the same frequency onto a single line (regardless whether or not they share any common prefix). The resulting horizontal line is a single line without any "branches", and it connects all the circles that can be found in the *p* horizontal lines. In this resulting line, a circle representing an item *x* is filled if it is filled in *any* of the *p* horizontal lines; a circle representing an item *x* is unfilled if it is unfilled in *all* of the *p* horizontal lines. For example, let us consider four itemsets {*a, b*}, {*a, b, d, e*}, {*a, b, e*} and {*b, d, e*} having the same frequency (say, 60%). Then, iVAS projects the horizontal lines representing these four frequent itemsets onto a single horizontal line connecting two unfilled circles (for items *a* and *d*) and two filled circles (for items *b* and *e*, which are the last items of these itemsets). Note that the resulting horizontal line represents a "virtual" itemset formed by projecting multiple itemsets of the

Figure 4. A representation of some mined frequent itemsets in iVAS, in which horizontal lines representing multiple itemsets of the same frequency are projected onto a single line

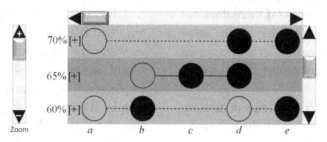

same frequency. To distinguish such a "virtual" itemset from the real one, iVAS uses a *dashed* horizontal line to represent the "virtual" itemset (the projection result) and uses a *solid* horizontal line to represent a real itemset. For example, in Figure 4, the solid horizontal line for frequency 65% represents two real itemsets {*b, c*} and {*b, c, d*}. The dashed horizontal line for frequency 70% does not represent a real itemset {*a, d, e*}; it represents the result of projecting two itemsets onto a single line.

Again, as iVAS tries to squeeze all the horizontal lines and fit them onto a single screen in the overview, users sometimes need to zoom in to get more detailed information. Hence, iVAS provides users with a *resolution slider*, which enables users to zoom in/out certain regions of the screen. When zooming out, users get an overview on one screen; when zooming in, users get the details split onto multiple screen space. To allow users to view the information across multiple screen space, iVAS provides users with (a) a *vertical scrollbar* for visualizing itemsets having different frequency values and (b) a *horizontal scrollbar* for visualizing different domain items within some itemsets. With the zoom-in view, users could obtain more details about the frequent itemsets mined from the transaction database.

With this zoom-in view or with the overview (i.e., the zoom-out view), iVAS provides users with interactive features to perform the following operations:

- Select some frequent itemsets of interest based on (a) the domain items within the itemsets and/or (b) the frequency values of the itemsets.
- Filter out the uninteresting frequent itemsets.

To perform the selection, users can draw a box to enclose interesting frequent itemsets in some regions of the screen (e.g., a region representing itemsets with very high frequency) for further analysis. Users can also click on the items (on the *x*-axis) and/or the frequency values (on the *y*-axis) to interactively select those interesting itemsets. By doing so, iVAS filters out the frequent itemsets that are uninteresting to users. For example, a store manager, who wants to put a promotion campaign on very frequently purchased collections of winter clothing, can specify that he wants to explore only those frequent itemsets having frequency ≥ 80% and containing a specific brand of winter clothing for further analysis.

In addition to allowing users to select interesting frequent itemsets based on the domain items and/or frequency, iVAS also provides users with an option to select frequent itemsets of certain cardinality (e.g., only show frequent 2-itemsets and 3-itemsets). This reduces the number of frequent itemsets to be shown, and thus enables users to focus on those interesting frequent itemsets. Besides showing frequent itemsets, iVAS also provides users with an option to visualize two other variants of frequent itemsets—namely, *closed frequent itemsets* and *maximal frequent itemsets*. A frequent itemset X is *closed* if there does not exist any proper superset of X having the same frequency as X; a frequent itemset Y is *maximal* if there does not exist any proper superset of Y that is also frequent.

Recall that, in order to fit all frequent itemsets in the overview, iVAS projects all the horizontal lines representing itemsets having the same frequency onto a single line. To reveal the details (i.e., the itemsets embedded within such a dashed line), iVAS allows users to interactively expand the line by clicking the [+] button. Once the line is expanded, users can view all horizontal lines representing real itemsets having such frequency. For example, by clicking the [+] buttons of all three lines shown in Figure 4 (representing the result of projecting itemsets of three distinct frequency values onto three different lines), users get Figure 3 (representing the mined frequent itemsets before projection). Conversely, clicking the [−] buttons in Figure 3 projects the itemsets that have the same frequency value onto a single line, which results in Figure 4.

Besides providing an overview and allowing users to zoom & filter, iVAS also provides users with details on demand. When users hover the mouse over a horizontal line or a circle, iVAS shows the contents (i.e., items within that frequent itemsets represented by circles on that line).

Application of iVAS in Mining Cellular Phone Call Records

In this section, we illustrate how our proposed iVAS can be applied to the VAST 2008 Mini-challenge (Grinstein et al., 2008) for visualizing and analyzing cellular phone call records that were collected over a period of 10 days in June 2006. The goal of this mini-challenge is to apply the visual analytic approach to help users (e.g., investigators) to understand this collection of phone call records and get some idea about the

social network of a specific caller (Caller 200 named Ferdinando Catalano).

Given this collection of phone call records, our proposed iVAS first gives a single-screen overview showing these $n = 9,834$ cellular phone call records made by $m \approx 400$ unique cellular phone callers (each caller can be uniquely identified by a caller ID) in a two-dimensional space. The x-axis shows the caller IDs, and the y-axis shows the phone call record IDs. Each record consists of two callers (Callers X and Y such that X called Y), which are represented by two circles. The circles are linked by a horizontal line. Then, users (e.g., investigators) can use the resolution slider of iVAS to change the display resolution so that they can zoom in to a certain region of the screen and get more details on that region. Then, as information is scattered across multiple screen space, users can use the vertical scrollbar to visualize different phone call records and the horizontal scrollbar to visualize different callers. As users are interested in a specific caller (Caller 200 named Ferdinando Catalano), they can interactively select Caller 200 by clicking the x-label for caller ID = 200. By doing so, iVAS highlights all 47 phone call records related to this caller (i.e., all 23 outgoing phone calls made by Caller 200 and all 24 incoming calls received by Caller 200), sends them for further analysis (e.g., data mining), and ignores the remaining $9,834 - 47 = 9,787$ records.

After applying the frequent set mining process to these 47 records, iVAS gives an overview of the mining results in a two-dimensional space. Similar to the overview of the phone call records, the x-axis of the overview of the mining results also shows the caller IDs. Unlike the y-axis of the overview of the phone call records (which shows the record IDs), the y-axis of the overview of the mining results shows the frequency. Here, the mining results are in the form of frequent 2-itemsets, which are indicated by five horizontal lines. Among them, four are solid lines indicating four real itemsets. Each of these lines connects two circles representing the caller who made the phone call and the caller who received the call. For example, one of them is the frequent itemset {Caller 5, Caller 200} with a frequency value of 14, which means that Callers 5 and 200 communicated with each other in 14 phone calls. Another frequent itemset is {Caller 1, Caller 200} with a frequency value of 9. The other two frequent itemsets have frequency values of 5 and 3. The fifth horizontal line shown by iVAS is a dashed one with a frequency value of 8, which indicates that more than one frequent itemset has a frequency of 8. Horizontal lines representing multiple itemsets are projected onto this single dashed line. By interactively clicking the [+] button, our proposed iVAS expands the dashed line and reveals to users the details that the two mined frequent itemsets {Caller 2, Caller 200} and {Caller 3, Caller 200} both have the same frequency value of 8.

For this VAST 2008 Mini-challenge on cellular phone call records, users were also given prior information as follows: "Close relatives and associate that Ferdinando Catalano would be calling include David Vidro, Juan Vidro, Jorge Vidro and Estaban Catalano. Ferdinando would call his brother, Estaban, most frequently. David Vidro coordinates most activities." Based on this prior information and the six mined frequent itemsets displayed by iVAS, users can induce that Caller 5 is highly likely to be Estaban Catalano (brother of Ferdinando—Caller 200) because these two callers communicated most frequently. Users can also induce that the next three frequent callers (in terms of communication with Caller 200)—namely, Callers 1, 2 and 3—are likely to be David Vidro, Juan Vidro and Jorge Vidro. In other words, by using our interactive visual analytic system iVAS, users can reveal the social network of Ferdinando Catalano (Caller 200).

Since data mining is supposed to be exploratory and be an iterative process, users can make use of iVAS to further discover more useful knowledge. For example, if users not only select records related to Caller 200 from the overview of phone call records but also select all 9,834 records

related to every caller for the frequent set mining process, then users can visualize more frequent itemsets. Among them, the 1-itemset {Caller 1} has the highest frequency of 313, which means that Caller 1 communicated 313 times (with 54 distinct callers): He made 24 calls (to 15 callers) and received 289 calls (from 51 callers). Based on this result and the prior information that David Vidro coordinated most activities, users can induce that Caller 1 is highly likely to be David Vidro.

As another example, let us consider a case where, after clicking Caller ID = 200 (which selects and highlights all the records related to Caller 200) from the overview of phone call records, users further refine their selection by drawing a box to select only the incoming calls received by Caller 200 (and ignore the outgoing calls made by Caller 200). The mining results on these 24 incoming calls, shown by iVAS, provide users with more details: Caller 200 received seven calls from Caller 5, six calls from Caller 1, five from Caller 3, four from Caller 2, and one call each from Callers 97 as well as 137. Alternatively, users can draw a box to refine his selection so that only those outgoing calls made by Caller 200 are sent to the data mining process. As such, iVAS analyzes these 23 outgoing calls and visualizes the results that Caller 200 called Caller 5 seven times, Callers 2 and 137 four times each, Callers 1 and 3 three times each, and Caller 97 twice.

Besides selecting phone call records based on the direction of calls (e.g., select only the incoming calls or only the outgoing calls), users can also select the records based on the day (e.g., select only the records for some specific date). For example, users can draw a box to select only those records captured on Day 1. Then, iVAS provides more details about Day 1: Callers 1, 2, 3 and 5 called Caller 200, who also returned calls to Callers 1 and 5. Similarly, users can also draw a box to select the records captured on each of the nine subsequent days for further analysis, and iVAS then returns the following details:

- On Day 2, Callers 1, 2, 3 and 5 communicated both ways with Caller 200, who also called Caller 137 but did not receive any phone calls from Caller 137.

- For the next five days (Days 3-7), Caller 200 continued to communicate with some of Callers 1, 2, 3 and 5.

- Caller 200 did not communicate with anyone on Day 8.

- On Days 9 and 10, communication patterns between Caller 200 and others were changed. Specifically, Caller 200 no longer communicated with his usual callers (e.g., Callers 1, 2, 3 and 5). Instead, he communicated with a new caller (e.g., he called Caller 97 twice on Day 9 and received a call from Caller 97 on Day 10).

To summarize, the detailed information provided by iVAS helps users (e.g., investigators) to visualize and analyze the *temporal behaviour* of these callers and their social network.

Application of iVAS in Mining Student Enrolment Databases

In the previous section, we illustrated how our proposed iVAS can be applicable for the visual analytics of cellular phone call records. In this section, let us illustrate the applicability of iVAS to another domain—namely, a student enrolment database. Here, each transaction in the database represents a collection of courses taken by a university student in an academic term. In a term, a student can take at least one course and at most six courses concurrently. Given such an enrolment database, iVAS shows an overview of the data distribution of student enrolment. This gives users (e.g., administrators, course instructors, etc.) an insight about the data distribution.

In the overview, the x-axis shows the course IDs, and the y-axis shows student IDs. Each transaction is denoted by either a circle (representing a student taking a single course) or a horizontal line connecting at least two and at most six circles (representing a student taking at least two and at most six courses). When users adjust the resolution slider to zoom in, they can get more details and/or can select and focus on only computer science courses. By vertically counting the number of circles for each course ID, users can obtain the exact number of students enrolled in each course. Even without precise counting, users can get an insight about the popularity of a course by observing whether there are many or just a few circles along the "vertical axis" for that course. If there are any courses of interest, users can select those courses by clicking their course IDs or by drawing a box enclosing those enrolment records of interest. Similarly, if there are any students of interest, users can select those students by clicking their student IDs or by drawing a box enclosing those enrolment records of interest. These enrolment records are then passed to the mining process for further analysis.

Once the frequent itemsets are found from the selected enrolment records, iVAS displays them in a two-dimensional space. The x-axis shows the course IDs, and the y-axis shows the frequency of the frequent itemsets. Each itemset is denoted by either a circle (representing a popular course) or a horizontal line connecting at least two and at most six circles (representing a set of popular courses taken concurrently by students). With the overview of the frequent sets (the output of the data mining process), users can automatically obtain the exact count of the students enrolled in a course without manually counting the number of circles along the "vertical axis" for that course in the overview of the enrolment records (the input of the data mining process).

For an enrolment database, it is not unusual that several combinations have the same frequency so that their corresponding horizontal lines are projected onto a single dashed one in the overview. To obtain the details, users need to expand such a line by clicking the [+] buttons. In such an expanded view, users (e.g., administrators, course instructors, etc.) can get answers to many questions, including the following:

- Which course is the most popular (i.e., 1-itemset with the highest frequency)?
- Which combination of courses is the most popular (i.e., k-itemset with the highest frequency)?
- What are some other popular combinations of courses (i.e., frequent k-itemsets)?
- Which combination of courses is the least popular (i.e., k-itemset with the lowest frequency)?

Answers to these questions help users to make intelligent administrative decisions such as the following:

- If users have resources to add an extra section of a course, which course should they add?
- If users need to reduce the offerings of courses, which courses should they reduce?
- When users schedule for exams, which courses should they avoid scheduling on the same day so as to reduce the chance of exam hardship?

For example, using the student enrolment data that we collected last academic term, users can observe the following: (a) COMP 4380 is the most popular course; (b) COMP 4300 is the least popular course; (c) {COMP 2150, COMP 3010}, {COMP 4350, COMP 4380, COMP 4580} and {COMP 4380, COMP 4550} are some other popular combinations of courses. Based on these observations, users may consider (a) offering an extra section of COMP 4380 if resource permits, (b) cancelling COMP 4300, and (c) spreading out the exam dates for COMP 4350, COMP 4380 and COMP 4580 as well as for the other popular combinations of courses.

Discussion: Other Applications of iVAS

So far, we have presented our interactive visual analytic system iVAS for two *data mining* applications: visual analytics on (a) cellular phone call records and (b) student enrolment records. In this section, we discuss applicability of iVAS to *text mining* as well as *web mining*.

For example, one can apply iVAS to visualize and analyze text databases consisting of large collections of documents from various sources like digital libraries, e-mail messages, news articles, references, research papers, and textbooks. Specifically, each document in the text database can be considered as a transaction. Each transaction consists of a set of keywords found in the text document. Then, users (say, readers of some text documents) can use iVAS to get an insight from the overview showing the distribution of keywords, select those keywords and/or documents of interest. After applying the text mining technique (specifically, keyword-based association analysis), iVAS helps users to visualize the mined associations in the form of terms/phrases that comprise sets of frequently occurring consecutive or closely located keywords. Among the mined keyword-based associations, some can be compound associations (e.g., domain-dependent terms or phrases like {"Barack", "Obama"}) while others can be non-compound associations (e.g., {"balance", "charges", "invoice", "tax", "total"}). The mined keyword-based associations help users to get a deep understanding of the text documents.

As another example, one can also apply iVAS to visualize and analyze web data. Note that the Web can be considered as a huge widely distributed global information service center for advertisements, consumer information, e-commerce, education, financial management, government, news, and other services. It also contains a rich collection of hyperlink information as well as web page access and usage information. Users (say, web service providers) can apply iVAS to conduct visual analytics on the web log data that contain web page access and usage information. Specifically, each transaction consists of the web pages visited by web surfers in a single session. Then, users can use iVAS to get an insight from the overview showing the distribution of web pages and select those pages of interest. After applying the web mining technique (specifically, web usage mining), iVAS helps users to visualize the mined web access patterns that consist of sets of frequently visited web pages. This helps users to discover web access patterns, allows users to identify potential clients, and thus enables users to enhance the quality of services provided to the web surfers.

FUTURE RESEARCH DIRECTIONS

So far, we have presented our interactive visual analytic system—iVAS—for exploratory or visual data mining. The system visualizes and analyzes the transactions in a traditional *static* database as well as the frequent itemsets mined from these database transactions. Due to advances in technology, large volumes of *data streams* (Gaber et al., 2005; Leung & Hao, 2009) can be easily generated at a rapid rate. In many real-life applications, technologies for visualizing and analyzing these *dynamic* streams of data are needed. As future work, we plan to extend our iVAS to visualize and analyze these streaming data as soon as they arrive.

Our iVAS visualizes and analyzes a traditional transaction database containing *precise* data such that the presence of an item in a transaction or the absence of an item from the transaction is definitely known. However, we are living in an uncertain world. There are situations (e.g., laboratory test results, medical diagnosis, etc.), in which we need to handle *uncertain data* (Leung et al., 2008c; Aggarwal & Yu, 2009). In these situations, the presence of an item in a transaction is *uncertain*. One can only express the *likelihood* of the occurrence of such an item or event, but one cannot

guarantee the absolute presence or absence of such an item or event. Hence, the second future research direction is to extend our proposed iVAS to handle uncertain data so that the resulting system will allow users to interactively visualize and analyze the uncertain data in the database as well as the frequent itemsets mined from these large volumes of uncertain data.

CONCLUSION

Many frequent set mining algorithms return the data analysis results in the form of a textual list of frequently occurring sets of items. This lengthy list can be difficult for the human user to comprehend. As suggested by the adage "a picture is worth a thousand words", it is desirable to use visualization techniques. In this chapter, we proposed an *interactive visual analytic system*—called *iVAS*—for effective visualization and advanced data analysis for various real-life data, text, and web mining applications. For both the input (i.e., the original data) and the output (i.e., the mined frequent sets) of the mining process, our iVAS gives the user an overview, allows the user to filter uninteresting information and to zoom in on the information of interest, and provides the user with details on demand.

REFERENCES

Aggarwal, C. C., & Yu, P. S. (2009). A survey of uncertain data algorithms and applications. *IEEE Transactions on Knowledge and Data Engineering, 21*(5), 609–623. doi:10.1109/TKDE.2008.190

Agrawal, R., Imieliński, T., & Swami, A. N. (1993). Mining association rules between sets of items in large databases. In P. Buneman & S. Jajodia (Eds.), *Proceedings of the 1993 ACM SIGMOD International Conference on Management of Data* (pp. 207-216). New York: ACM.

Agrawal, R., & Srikank, R. (1994). Fast algorithms for mining association rules in large databases. In J.B. Bocca, M. Jarke, & C. Zaniolo (Eds.), *Proceedings of the 20th International Conference on Very Large Data Bases* (pp. 487-499). San Francisco, CA: Morgan Kaufmann.

Ahlberg, C. (1996). Spotfire: An information exploration environment. *SIGMOD Record, 25*(4), 25–29. doi:10.1145/245882.245893

Ankerst, M., Elsen, C., Ester, M., & Kriegel, H.-P. (1999). Visual classification: An interactive approach to decision tree construction. In U. Fayyad, S. Chaudhuri, & D. Madigan (Eds.), *Proceedings of the Fifth ACM SIGKDD International Conference on Knowledge Discovery and Data Mining (KDD-99)* (pp. 392-396). New York: ACM.

Bayardo, R. J. (1998). Efficiently mining long patterns from databases. In L.M. Haas & A. Tiwary (Eds.), *Proceedings of the 1998 ACM SIGMOD International Conference on Management of Data* (pp. 85-93). New York: ACM.

Berchtold, S., Jagadish, H. V., & Ross, K. A. (1998). Independence diagrams: A technique for visual data mining. In R. Agrawal, P.E. Stolorz, & G. Piatetsky-Shapiro (Eds.), *Proceedings of the Fourth International Conference on Knowledge Discovery and Data Mining (KDD-98)* (pp. 139-143). Menlo Park, CA: AAAI Press.

Blanchard, J., Guillet, F., & Briand, H. (2007). Interactive visual exploration of association rules with rule-focusing methodology. *Knowledge and Information Systems, 13*(1), 43–75. doi:10.1007/s10115-006-0046-2

Cheng, H., & Han, J. (2009). Frequent itemsets and association rules. In Liu, L., & Özsu, M. T. (Eds.), *Encyclopedia of Database Systems* (pp. 1184–1187). New York: Springer.

Frawley, W. J., Piatetsky-Shapiro, G., & Matheus, C. J. (1991). Knowledge discovery in databases: An overview. In Piatetsky-Shapiro, G., & Frawley, W. J. (Eds.), *Knowledge Discovery in Databases* (pp. 1–30). Cambridge, MA: The MIT Press.

Gaber, M. M., Zaslavsky, A., & Krishnaswamy, S. (2005). Mining data streams: A review. *SIGMOD Record, 34*(2), 18–26. doi:10.1145/1083784.1083789

Grinstein, G., Plaisant, C., Laskowski, S., O'Connell, T., Scholtz, J., & Whiting, M. (2008). VAST 2008 Challenge: Introducing mini-challenges. In D. Ebert & T. Ertl (Eds.), *Proceedings of the 2008 IEEE Symposium on Visual Analytics Science and Technology (VAST)* (pp. 195-196). Piscataway, NJ: IEEE.

Han, J., & Cercone, N. (2000). AViz: A visualization system for discovering numeric association rules. In T. Terano, H. Liu, & A.L.P. Chen (Eds.), *Proceedings of the Fourth Pacific-Asia Conference on Knowledge Discovery and Data Mining (LNAI 1805*, pp. 269-280). Berlin, Germany: Springer.

Han, J., Cheng, H., Xin, D., & Yan, X. (2007). Frequent pattern mining: Current status and future directions. *Data Mining and Knowledge Discovery, 15*(1), 55–86. doi:10.1007/s10618-006-0059-1

Keim, D. A., & Kriegel, H.-P. (1996). Visualization techniques for mining large databases: A comparison. *IEEE Transactions on Knowledge and Data Engineering, 8*(6), 923–938. doi:10.1109/69.553159

Keim, D. A., Mansmann, F., Schneidewind, J., & Ziegler, H. (2006). Challenges in visual data analysis. In E. Banissi, R.A. Burkhard, A. Ursyn, J.J. Zhang, M. Bannatyne, C. Maple, A.J. Cowell, G.Y. Tian, & M. Hou (Eds.), *Proceedings of the 10th IEEE International Conference on Information Visualization* (pp. 9-16). Los Alamitos, CA: IEEE Computer Society.

Keim, D. A., Mansmann, F., Stoffel, A., & Ziegler, H. (2009). Visual analytics. In Liu, L., & Özsu, M. T. (Eds.), *Encyclopedia of Database Systems* (pp. 3341–3346). New York: Springer.

Koren, Y., & Harel, D. (2003) A two-way visualization method for clustered data. In L. Getoor, T.E. Senator, P. Domingos, & C. Faloutsos (Eds.), *Proceedings of the Ninth ACM SIGKDD International Conference on Knowledge Discovery and Data Mining* (*KDD-03*) (pp. 589-594). New York: ACM.

Lakshmanan, L. V. S., Leung, C. K.-S., & Ng, R. T. (2003). Efficient dynamic mining of constrained frequent sets. *ACM Transactions on Database Systems, 28*(4), 337–389. doi:10.1145/958942.958944

Leung, C. K.-S. (2009). Constraint-based association rule mining. In Wang, J. (Ed.), *Encyclopedia of Data Warehousing and Mining* (2nd ed., pp. 307–312). Hershey, PA: IGI Global.

Leung, C. K.-S., & Carmichael, C. L. (2009). FpViz: A visualizer for frequent pattern mining. In K. Puolamäki (Ed.), *Proceedings of the ACM SIGKDD Workshop on Visual Analytics and Knowledge Discovery: Integrating Automated Analysis with Interactive Exploration* (pp. 30-39). New York: ACM.

Leung, C. K.-S., & Hao, B. (2009). Mining of frequent itemsets from streams of uncertain data. In Y. Ioannidis, D. Lee, & R. Ng (Eds.), *Proceedings of the 25th IEEE International Conference on Data Engineering* (pp. 1663-1670). Los Alamitos, CA: IEEE Computer Society.

Leung, C. K.-S., Irani, P. P., & Carmichael, C. L. (2008a). FIsViz: A frequent itemset visualizer. In T. Washio, E. Suzuki, K.M. Ting, & A. Inokuchi (Eds.), *Proceedings of the 12th Pacific-Asia Conference on Knowledge Discovery and Data Mining* (*LNAI 5012,* pp. 644-652). Berlin, Germany: Springer.

Leung, C. K.-S., Irani, P. P., & Carmichael, C. L. (2008b). WiFIsViz: Effective visualization of frequent itemsets. In F. Giannotti, D. Gunopulos, F. Turini, C. Zaniolo, N. Ramakrishnan, & X. Wu (Eds.), *Proceedings of the Eighth IEEE International Conference on Data Mining* (pp. 875-880). Los Alamitos, CA: IEEE Computer Society.

Leung, C. K.-S., Khan, Q. I., Li, Z., & Hoque, T. (2007). CanTree: A canonical-order tree for incremental frequent-pattern mining. *Knowledge and Information Systems, 11*(3), 287–311. doi:10.1007/s10115-006-0032-8

Leung, C. K.-S., Mateo, M. A. F., & Brajczuk, D. A. (2008c). A tree-based approach for frequent pattern mining from uncertain data. In T. Washio, E. Suzuki, K.M. Ting, & A. Inokuchi (Eds.), *Proceedings of the 12th Pacific-Asia Conference on Knowledge Discovery and Data Mining* (*LNAI 5012,* pp. 653-661). Berlin, Germany: Springer.

Liu, B. (2009). Classification by association rule analysis. In Liu, L., & Özsu, M. T. (Eds.), *Encyclopedia of Database Systems* (pp. 335–340). New York: Springer.

Munzer, T., Kong, Q., Ng, R. T., Lee, J., Klawe, J., Radulovic, D., & Leung, C. K. (2005). *Visual mining of power sets with large alphabets. Technical report UBC CS TR-2005-25*. Vancouver, BC, Canada: Department of Computer Science, The University of British Columbia.

Pasquier, N., Bastide, Y., Taouil, R., & Lakhal, L. (1999). Discovering frequent closed itemsets for association rules. In C. Beeri & P. Buneman (Eds.), *Proceedings of the Seventh International Conference on Database Theory (LNCS 1540*, pp. 398-416). Berlin, Germany: Springer.

Pei, J., Han, J., Mortazavi-Asl, B., & Zhu, H. (2000). Mining access patterns efficiently from web logs. In T. Terano, H. Liu, & A.L.P. Chen (Eds.), *Proceedings of the Fourth Pacific-Asia Conference on Knowledge Discovery and Data Mining (LNAI 1805*, pp. 396-407). Berlin, Germany: Springer.

Schreck, T., Bernard, J., Tekušová, T., & Kohlhammer, J. (2008). Visual cluster analysis of trajectory data with interactive Kohonen Maps. In D. Ebert & T. Ertl (Eds.), *Proceedings of the 2008 IEEE Symposium on Visual Analytics Science and Technology (VAST)* (pp. 3-10). Piscataway, NJ: IEEE.

Stolte, C., Tang, D., & Hanrahan, P. (2002). Query, analysis, and visualization of hierarchically structured data using Polaris. In D. Hand, D. Keim, & R. Ng (Eds.), *Proceedings of the Eighth ACM SIGKDD International Conference on Knowledge Discovery and Data Mining (KDD-02)* (pp. 112-122). New York: ACM.

Thomas, J. J., & Cook, K. A. (Eds.). (2005). *Illuminating the Path: The Research and Development Agenda for Visual Analytics*. Los Alamitos, CA: IEEE Computer Society.

Yang, L. (2005). Pruning and visualizing generalized association rules in parallel coordinates. *IEEE Transactions on Knowledge and Data Engineering, 17*(1), 60–70. doi:10.1109/TKDE.2005.14

ADDITIONAL READING

Ankerst, M. (2009). Visual classification. In Liu, L., & Özsu, M. T. (Eds.), *Encyclopedia of Database Systems* (pp. 3352–3355). New York: Springer.

Bertini, E., & Lalanne, D. (2009). Surveying the complementary role of automatic data analysis and visualization in knowledge discovery. In K. Puolamäki (Ed.), *Proceedings of the ACM SIGKDD Workshop on Visual Analytics and Knowledge Discovery: Integrating Automated Analysis with Interactive Exploration* (pp. 12-20). New York: ACM.

Bruzzese, D., & Davino, C. (2008). Visual mining of association rules. In S.J. Simoff, M.H. Böhlen & A. Mazeika (Eds.), *Visual Data Mining: Theory, Techniques and Tools for Visual Analytics (LNCS 4404*, pp. 103-122). Berlin, Germany: Springer

Chen, C. (2004). *Information Visualization: Beyond the Horizon* (2nd ed.). London, UK: Springer.

Ebert, D., & Ertl, T. (Eds.). (2008). *Proceedings of the 2008 IEEE Symposium on Visual Analytics Science and Technology (VAST)*. Piscataway, NJ: IEEE.

Ebert, D. S., & Ertl, T. (Eds.). (2009). *Special issue on visual analytics, science and technology. Information Visualization, 8(1)*. Basingstoke, UK: Palgrave Macmillan.

Han, J., & Kamber, M. (2006). *Data Mining: Concepts and Techniques* (2nd ed.). San Francisco, CA: Morgan Kaufmann.

Kao, A., & Poteet, S. (Eds.). (2005). *Special issue on natural language processing and text mining. ACM SIGKDD Explorations, 7(1)*. New York: ACM.

Keim, D., & Schneidewind, J. (Eds.). (2007). *Special issue on visual analytics. ACM SIGKDD Explorations, 9(2)*. New York: ACM.

Keim, D. A., Mansmann, F., Schneidewind, J., Thomas, J., & Ziegler, H. (2008). Visual analytics: Scope and challenges. In S.J. Simoff, M.H. Böhlen & A. Mazeika (Eds.), *Visual Data Mining: Theory, Techniques and Tools for Visual Analytics* (*LNCS 4404*, pp. 76-90). Berlin, Germany: Springer.

Kielman, J., & Thomas, J. (Eds.). (2009). *Special issue on foundations and frontiers of visual analytics. Information Visualization, 8(4)*. Basingstoke, UK: Palgrave Macmillan.

Kovalerchuk, B., & Schwing, J. (Eds.). (2004). *Visual and Spatial Analysis: Advances in Data Mining, Reasoning, and Problem Solving*. Dordrecht, The Netherlands: Springer.

Leung, C. K.-S., & Carmichael, C. L. (2010). Exploring social networks: A frequent pattern visualization approach. In J. Zhan (Ed.), *Proceedings of the Second IEEE International Conference on Social Computing* (pp. 419-424). Los Alamitos, CA: IEEE Computer Society.

Liu, B. (2007). *Web Data Mining: Exploring Hyperlinks, Contents, and Usage Data*. Berlin, Germany: Springer.

Plaisant, C., Grinstein, G., & Scholtz, J. (2009). Special issue on visual-analytics evaluation. *IEEE Computer Graphics and Applications, 29*(3). Los Alamitos, CA: IEEE Computer Society.

Puolamäki, K., & Bertone, A. (Eds.). (2009). *Special issue on visual analytics and knowledge discovery. ACM SIGKDD Explorations, 11(2)*. New York: ACM.

Ribarsky, W., & Dill, J. (Eds.). (2007). *Proceedings of the 2007 IEEE Symposium on Visual Analytics Science and Technology* (*VAST*). Piscataway, NJ: IEEE.

Simoff, S. J., Böhlen, M. H., & Mazeika, A. (Eds.). (2008). *Visual Data Mining: Theory, Techniques and Tools for Visual Analytics (LNCS 4404)*. Berlin, Germany: Springer.

Sips, M. (2009). Visual clustering. In Liu, L., & Özsu, M. T. (Eds.), *Encyclopedia of Database Systems* (pp. 3355–3360). New York: Springer.

Spence, R. (2007). *Information Visualization: Design for Interaction* (2nd ed.). Harlow, UK: Prentice Hall.

Stasko, J., & van Wijk, J. J. (Eds.). (2009). *Proceedings of the 2009 IEEE Symposium on Visual Analytics Science and Technology* (*VAST*). Piscataway, NJ: IEEE.

Tan, P.-N., Steinbach, M., & Kumar, V. (2006). *Introduction to Data Mining*. Boston, MA: Addison-Wesley.

Ware, C. (2005). *Information Visualization: Perception for Design* (2nd ed.). San Francisco, CA: Morgan Kaufmann.

Wong, P. C., & Keim, D. (Eds.). (2006). *Proceedings of the 2006 IEEE Symposium on Visual Analytics Science and Technology* (*VAST*). Piscataway, NJ: IEEE.

Wong, P. C., & Thomas, J. (2004). Visual analytics. *IEEE Computer Graphics and Applications, 24*(5), 20–21. doi:10.1109/MCG.2004.39

Yang, L. (2008). Visual exploration of frequent itemsets and association rules. In S.J. Simoff, M.H. Böhlen & A. Mazeika (Eds.), *Visual Data Mining: Theory, Techniques and Tools for Visual Analytics* (*LNCS 4404*, pp. 60-75). Berlin, Germany: Springer.

Yang, L. (2009). Visual association rules. In Liu, L., & Özsu, M. T. (Eds.), *Encyclopedia of Database Systems* (pp. 3346–3352). New York: Springer.

KEY TERMS AND DEFINITIONS

Data Mining: *Data mining* refers to non-trivial extraction of implicit, previously unknown, and potentially useful information from data.

Database Transaction: A *database transaction* is a record, which can be uniquely identifiable by its transaction ID (or record ID), containing a set of co-occurring items or events in the domain of the database.

Frequent Itemset: A *frequent itemset* is a set of items having frequency exceeds or equals the user-specified minimum threshold.

Frequent Set Mining: *Frequent set mining* aims to search for implicit, previously unknown, and potentially useful sets of frequently co-occurring items from large volumes of data.

Itemset: An *itemset* is a set of items.

Text Mining: *Text mining* is the discovery of knowledge from text databases or document data-bases—which usually consist of semi-structured data—based on the extracted keywords, tags, or semantic information in the text.

Visual Analytics: *Visual analytics* is the science of analytical reasoning supported by interactive visual interfaces; it is also the new enabling and accessible analytic reasoning interactions supported by the combination of automated and visual analysis.

Web Mining: *Web mining* is a search from the World Wide Web (especially, from the webpage layout or semantic structure, hyperlink structure, and usage information) for useful knowledge such as web contents, web linkage structures, and web access patterns.

Chapter 14
Mammogram Mining Using Genetic Ant–Miner

K. Thangavel
Periyar University, India.

R. Roselin
Sri Sarada College for Women (Autonomous), India

ABSTRACT

Image mining deals with the extraction of implicit knowledge, image data relationship, or other patterns not explicitly stored in the images. It is an extension of data mining to image domain and an interdisciplinary endeavour. This chapter focuses on mammogram classification using genetic Ant-Miner. The key idea is to generate classifier for classifying mammograms as normal or abnormal using the proposed Genetic Ant-Miner algorithm. The Genetic Algorithm has been employed to optimize some of the ant parameters. A comparative analysis is performed in order to achieve the efficiency of the proposed algorithm. Further, the experimental results reveals that the improvement of the proposed Genetic Ant-Miner in the domain of Biomedical image Analysis.

DOI: 10.4018/978-1-60960-102-7.ch014

INTRODUCTION

A mammogram is an X- ray of the breast. Mammography is a specific type of imaging that uses low-dose x-ray system to examine breasts. A mammography examination called a mammogram is used to aid in the early detection and diagnosis of breast diseases.

Breast cancer is a cancer that starts in the breast, usually in the inner lining of the milk ducts or lobules. It occurs in both men and women, although male breast cancer is rare.

A lot of research has been focused on the development of algorithms for the automated classification of abnormal mammograms. These algorithms are based either on morphology and distribution features of Micro Classifications (MCs) extracted by radiologists or on computer-extracted image features (Baker, Kornguth, Iglehart & Floyd, 1996). There are two methods to extract image features. The first category accounts for morphology / shape features of individual MCs or of MC clusters, while the second category corresponds to texture features extracted from Regions of Interest (ROI) containing the MCs.

The performance of the Computer Aided Diagnosis schemes is differentiated with respect to the features investigated, the classifiers used and the data sets analyzed. The success of the morphological features-based schemes strongly depends on the robustness of the MCs segmentation algorithms (Veldkamp & Karssemeijer, 1996). Specifically, in the case of dense breast parenchyma abutting the MCs, classification is a challenging task due to difficulty in the segmentation process. The texture analysis approach seems to overcome this limitation as no segmentation stage is required. The rationale of using texture features is based on capturing changes in the texture of the tissue surrounding MCs.

Mining information and knowledge from large data-base has been recognized by many researchers as a key research topic in database system and machine learning. One of the data mining tasks gaining significant attention is the classification rules extraction from databases. The goal of this task is to assign each case (object, record, and instance) to one class, out of a set of predefined classes, based on the values of some attributes for the case. There are different classification algorithms used to extract relevant relationship in the data as decision trees which performing a successive partitioning of cases until all subsets belong to single class (Quinlan, 1987). Medical images have been classified by Osmar R. Zaiane, M.L Antonie and A. Coman (2002) using Association Rule based classifiers. Shuyan Wang, Mingquan Zhou and Guohua Geng (2005) proposed medical image classifier based on decision tree algorithm. The experimental results show the classification accuracy is around 69% to 80%. Walid Erray, and Hakim Hacid (2006) proposed a method that was able to take into account the costs in the automatic learning process using decision trees and got promising results.

Metaheuristics are generally applied to problems for which there is no satisfactory problem-specific algorithm or heuristic; or when it is not practical to implement such a method. Most commonly used metaheuristics are targeted to combinatorial optimization problems. The Ant-Miner algorithm is proposed by R. S. Parpinelli, H. S. Lopesand, A. Freitas (2002) applies an ant colony optimization heuristic to the classification task of data mining to discover an ordered list of classification rules. In a colony of social insects, such as ants, bees, wasps and termites, each insect usually performs its own tasks independently from other members of the colony. However, the tasks performed by different insects are related to each other in such a way that the colony, as a whole, is capable of solving complex problems through cooperation. Ant-Miner is interested in a particular behavior of real ants, namely the fact that they are capable of finding the shortest path between a food source and the nest without the use of visual information. As ant move, a certain amount of pheromone is dropped on the ground, marking the path with a trail of this substance. The more ants follow a given trail, the more attractive this trail becomes to be followed by other ants. This process can be described as a loop of positive feedback, in which the probability that an ant chooses a path is proportional to the number of ants that have already passed by that path.

This chapter attempts to apply Ant-Miner in mammogram processing and the Ant-Miner Parameters are optimized by using Genetic Algorithms.

METHODS AND MATERIALS

The Mammographic Image Analysis Society (MIAS) Database is used to perform the analysis of the efficiency of the proposed algorithm. The data is available at http://peipa.essex.ac.uk. The database contains 322 mammograms including normal, mass, and micro calcification cases. It indicates different classes of abnormalities such as calcification, well-defined circumscribed masses, speculated masses, ill-defines masses, architectural distortion, asymmetry and normal. For experimental analysis 300 mammograms are considered. The images are digitized at a size of 1024 X 1024 with 256 gray levels.

Digital Mammograms

Digital mammograms are among the most difficult medical images to be read due to their low contrast and differences in the types of tissues. Important visual clues of breast cancer include preliminary signs of masses and calcification clusters. Unfortunately, in the early stages of breast cancer, these signs are very subtle and varied in appearance, making diagnosis difficult, challenging even for specialists. This is the main reason for the development of classification systems to assist specialists in medical institutions. Due to the significance of an automated image categorization to help physicians and radiologists, much research

in the field of medical images classification has been done recently. With all this effort, there is still no widely used method for classifying medical images. This is due to the fact that the medical domain requires high accuracy and especially the rate of false negatives to be very low. In addition, another important factor that influences the success of classification methods is working in a team with medical specialists, which is desirable but often not achievable. Mammography alone cannot prove that a suspicious area is malignant or benign. To decide that, the tissue has to be removed for examination using breast biopsy techniques. A false positive detection may cause an unnecessary biopsy. Statistics show that only 20-30 percentages of breast biopsy cases are proved cancerous. In a false negative detection, an actual tumor remains undetected that could lead to higher costs or even to the cost of a human life. Here is the trade-off that appears in developing a classification system that could directly affect human life. Due to the significance of an automated image categorization to help physicians and radiologists, much research in the field of medical images classification has been done recently.

IMAGE PREPROCESSING

Since pre-processing is always necessary whenever the data to be made in noisy, inconsistent or incomplete environment and preprocessing significantly improves the efficiency of the data mining techniques, preprocessing of mammograms are necessitated. (Haralick, Shanmugam, & Dinstein, 1973)

To mine the mammogram two steps of data pre-processing are necessary.

- Image Cleaning
- Image Transformation

Image Cleaning

Images taken with both digital cameras and conventional film cameras will pick up noise from variety of sources. For computer vision, it is used to clear the noise and the isolated points that would tamper the data mining. The first step of mammogram mining is to use noise removing technique. This removes many noises and background Information. The most common means of removing the noise is to apply filter to the image. The following are the some of the commonly used filters.

- High Pass
- Low Pass
- Laplacian
- Median
- Sobel
- Roberts
- A filter in which you will modify the convolution kernel and
- User defined filter

Among the filters Median filter is used for mammogram preprocessing (Gonzalez and Woods, 1992).

Image Transformation

Data transformation in image domain can be considered as image enhancement. So the second step is to enhance the image. The purpose of image enhancement is to use special technique to improve the quality of image or change the image to other formats that are more suitable for processing afterwards. Usually there are two categories of image enhancement techniques: space domain and frequency domain. Histogram equalization technique is an algorithm of gray level enhancement performed in space domain. The distribution of the histogram of an image with low contrast will normally aggregate in a relatively small region. For images after equalization, the different

gray levels will have similar occurring rate. In the above situation, the entropy of the image is the largest and contains the most information. In this study, the widely used histogram equalization technique has been used to enhance the images (Acharya and Ray, 2005). Noise removal should be performed first in order not to enhance the noise simultaneously.

FEATURE EXTRACTION

Since the classification algorithm requires the classified data to be composed of feature vectors, data mining cannot be directly performed on the original image. The Gray Level Co-occurrence Matrix (GLCM) is a well-established robust statistical tool for extracting second order texture information from images (Dougherty, Kohavi & Sahami, 1995). The GLCM characterizes the spatial distribution of grey levels in an image. Specifically, an element in the GLCM, $P_{d,\theta}(i,j)$, represents the probability of occurrence of the pair of grey levels (i,j) separated by a distance d at direction θ. In this chapter, three GLCMs are computed, corresponding to three different directions ($\theta = 0°, 45°, 90°$) with one distance ($d = 1$ pixel). The 14 Haralick features are derived from each GLCM: Angular second moment, Contrast, Correlation, Variance, Inverse second different moment, Sum Average, Sum Variance, Sum Entropy, Entropy, Difference Variance, Difference Entropy, Measure of Correlation 1, Measure of Correlation 2, and Local Mean and tissue type is added as a fifteenth feature.

GLCM Construction

GLCM is a matrix S that contains the relative frequencies with which two pixels one with gray level value i and the other with gray level j - separated by distance d at a certain angle θ occur in the image. Given an image window W(x, y, c), for

Table 1.

Degree	Degree = 45° Distance = 1 **1 2 3 4**	Degree = 45° Distance = 2 **1 2 3 4**
1	3 3 0 0	3 1 0 0
2	3 2 0 1	1 1 0 0
3	0 0 0 1	0 0 0 1
4	1 1 0 1	1 1 0 0

each discrete values of d and θ the GLCM matrix $S(i, j, d, \theta)$ is defined as follows:

An entry in the matrix S gives the number of times gray level i is oriented with respect to gray level j such that where

$$W(x_1, y_1) = i \text{ and } W(x_2, y_2) = j$$

then

$$(x_2, y_2) = (x_1, y_1) + (d* \cos(\theta), d * \sin(\theta))$$

We use two different distances $d = \{1, 2\}$ and three different angles $\theta = \{0, 45, 90\}$. Here, angle representation is taken in clock wise direction.

Example:

Intensity matrix

$$\begin{pmatrix} 1 & 3 & 1 & 1 & 1 \\ 2 & 2 & 4 & 2 & 1 \\ 1 & 4 & 1 & 4 & 1 \\ 2 & 2 & 2 & 1 & 1 \\ 1 & 1 & 2 & 2 & 1 \end{pmatrix}$$

Different intensity values are 1, 2, 3 and 4.
GLCM for the above Intensity Matrix is shown in Table 1.

DISCRETIZATION

A discretization algorithm is applied in order to handle problems with real-valued attributes with classification. The term "cut-point" refers to a real value within the range of continuous values that divides the range into two intervals, one interval is less than or equal to the cutpoint and the other interval is greater than the cut-point. For example, a continuous interval [a, b] is partitioned into [a, c] and [c, b], where c is a cut-point. Cut-point is also known as split-point.

Discretization Process

A typical discretization process broadly consists of four steps: (1) sorting the continuous values of the feature to be discretized, (2) evaluating a cut-point for splitting or adjacent intervals for merging, (3) according to some criterion, splitting or merging intervals of continuous value, and (4) finally stopping at some point. After sorting, the next step in the discretization process is to find the best "cut-point" to split a range of continuous values or the best pair of adjacent intervals to merge. One typical evaluation function is to determine the correlation of a split or a merge with the class label. A stopping criterion specifies when to stop the discretization process. The number of inconsistencies caused by discretization — it should not be much higher than the number of inconsistencies of the original data before discretization. Two instances are considered inconsistent if they are the same in their attribute values except for their class labels.

Categories of Discretization Methods

Generally, the discretization methods can be categorised as: supervised or unsupervised. A distinction can be made dependent on whether the method takes class information into account to find proper intervals or not. Several discretization methods, such as equal width interval binning or equal frequency binning, do not make use of class membership information during the discretization process. These methods are referred to as unsupervised methods. In contrast, discretization methods that use class labels for carrying out discretization are referred to as supervised methods. Previous research indicated that supervised are better than unsupervised methods (Dougherty, Kohavi & Sahami, 1995).

Entropy Based Methods

It uses entropy based measures to evaluate candidate cut-points. This means that an entropy-based method will use the class information entropy of candidate partitions to select boundaries for discretization. Class information entropy is a measure of purity and it measures the amount of information which would be needed to specify to which class an instance belongs.

CLASSIFICATION OF MAMMOGRAMS

The major steps involved in mammogram classification using data mining technique are:

- Initially, region of interest of 300 mammograms (normal and abnormal) are taken by referring to the coordinate given in the MIAS database after applying preprocessing techniques.
- GLCM is constructed over the region.
- Haralick fourteen features are extracted forms a database for image mining.

- Rules are generated using classification algorithms.
- Ten fold cross validation is done to test the efficiency of the classifier.

C4.5 Algorithm

C4.5 is an algorithm used for inducing Classification Models, also called Decision Trees, from data. It is an extension to the ID3 algorithm.

Decision Tree

In the decision tree, each node corresponds to a non-categorical attribute and each arc to a possible value of that attribute. A leaf of the tree specifies the expected value of the categorical attribute for the records described by the path from the root to that leaf. Each node should be associated the non-categorical attribute which is most informative among the attributes not yet considered in the path from the root. This establishes what a "Good" decision tree is. Entropy is used to measure how informative is a node. This defines what we mean by "Good". This notion was introduced by Claude Shannon in Information Theory (Shannon, 1948, pp. 379-423 and 623-656).

ID3 Algorithm

The ID3 algorithm is used to build a decision tree (Quinlan 1987), given a set of non-categorical attributes C1, C2, ..., Cn, the categorical attribute W, and a training set T of records. C4.5 is an extension of ID3 that accounts for unavailable values, continuous attribute value ranges, pruning of decision trees, rule derivation, and so on.

Input

Let F be the set of features, W be the class attribute and S be training set

Figure 1. Analysis of rules generated by C4.5

Fold	Angle 0	Angle 45	Angle 90
Fold 1	No. Of. Rules – 20 TPR - 0.07 FPR - 0.00 ACC - 57% CDR - 13	No. Of. Rules – 18 TPR - 0.00 FPR - 0.00 ACC - 53% CDR - 16	No. Of. Rules – 11 TPR - 0.00 FPR - 0.00 ACC - 53% CDR - 14
Fold 2	No. Of. Rules – 32 TPR - 0.33 FPR - 0.00 ACC - 93% CDR - 15	No. Of. Rules – 15 TPR - 0.00 FPR - 0.00 ACC - 90% CDR - 4	No. Of. Rules – 26 TPR - 0.67 FPR - 0.00 ACC - 97% CDR - 23
Fold 3	No. Of. Rules – 19 TPR - 1.00 FPR - 0.32 ACC - 77% CDR - 11	No. Of. Rules – 12 TPR - 1.00 FPR - 0.68 ACC - 50% CDR - 18	No. Of. Rules – 15 TPR - 0.50 FPR - 0.00 ACC - 87% CDR - 13
Fold 4	No. Of. Rules – 22 TPR - 0 FPR - 0 ACC - 53% CDR - 14	No. Of. Rules – 14 TPR - 0.00 FPR - 0.00 ACC - 53% CDR - 14	No. Of. Rules – 18 TPR - 0.79 FPR - 0.00 ACC - 90% CDR - 16

Algorithm

- If S is empty return single node with value Failure
- If S consists of records all with the same value for the class attribute then return single node with that value.
- If F is empty, then return a single node with as value the most frequent of the values of the class attribute.
- Let D be the attribute with largest Gain(D, S) among the attributes in the feature set.
  Let $\{d_j$ where $j = 1, 2,..., m\}$ be the values of attribute D;
  Let $\{S_j$ where $j = 1, 2,..., m\}$ be the subsets of S consisting
  of records with value dj for attribute D;
  Return a tree with root labelled D and arcs labelled
  d1, d2,..., dm going respectively to the trees
    - Make a recursive call for (F-{D}, W, S1), (F-{D}, W, S2),.., (F-{D}, W, Sm);

The rules are generated using C4.5 for the derived features at angles 0^0, 45^0, 90^0 of co-occurrence

matrix. Ten fold cross validation is done. Figure 1 reports the analysis of rules generated by C4.5 with Number of Rules generated, TPR (True Positive Rate), FPR (False Positive Rate), ACC (Accuracy) and CDR (Classified under default class).

Ant-Miner Algorithm

Ant Colony Optimization (ACO) is a branch of newly developed swarm intelligence which is used for classification. Swarm intelligence is a field which studies "the emergent collective intelligence of groups of simple agents" (R. S. Parpinelli, H. S., Lopesand A., and A. Freitas 2002). In group of insects, which live in colonies, such as ants and bees, an individual can only do simple tasks on its own, while the colony's cooperative work is the main reason determining the intelligent behavior it shows. Most real ants are blind. However, each ant while it is walking, deposits a chemical substance on the ground called pheromone of a newly developed form of artificial intelligence called swarm intelligence.

ACO algorithms are based on the following ideas:

- Each path followed by an ant is associated with a candidate solution for a given problem.
- When an ant follows a path, the amount of pheromone deposited on that path is proportional to the quality of the corresponding solution for the target problem.

When an ant has to choose between two or more paths, the path(s) with a larger amount of pheromone have a greater probability of being chosen by the ant. (see Algorithm 1)

Pheromone Initialization

All cells in the pheromone table are initialized equally by the equation (1):

$$\tau_{ij}(t = o) = \frac{1}{\sum_{i=1}^{a} b_i} \qquad (1)$$

where a is the total number of attributes, and b_i is the number of possible values that can be taken on by attributes. The rule is constructed by the ant incrementally by adding one term at a time. The term selection is based on the probability as given by the equation(2).

$$P_{ij} = \frac{\eta_{ij}.\tau_{ij}(t)}{\sum_{i=1}^{a} x_i . \sum_{j=1}^{b_i} \left(\eta_{ij}.\tau_{ij}(t) \right)} \qquad (2)$$

where η_{ij} is the value of a problem-dependent heuristic function for a term. The higher the value of η_{ij} the more relevant for classification the term$_{ij}$ is, and so the higher its probability of being chosen. a is the total number of attributes. x_i is set to 1 if the attribute was not yet used by the current ant,

or to 0 otherwise. b_i is the number of values in the domain of the jth attribute.

Heuristic Value

In traditional ACO, a heuristic value is usually used in conjunction with the pheromone value to decide on the transitions to be made. In Ant-Miner, the heuristic value is taken to be an information theoretic measure for the quality of the term to be added to the rule. The quality here is measured in terms of the entropy for preferring this term to the others, and is given by the following equation (3).

$$H(W \mid A_i = V_{ij}) = -\sum_{W=1}^{K} (P(W \mid A_i = V_{ij}).Log_2 P(W \mid A_i = V_{ij})$$

$$(3)$$

where W is the class attribute (i.e., the attribute whose domain consists of the classes to be predicted).k is the number of classes. $P(w|A_i=V_{ij})$ is the empirical probability of observing class w conditional on having observed $A_i=V_{ij}$. The higher the value of $H(W|A_i = V_{ij})$, the more uniformly distributed the classes are and so, the smaller the probability that the current ant chooses to add term$_{ij}$ to its partial rule. The information-theoretic heuristic function is given in equation (4).

$$\eta_{ij} = \frac{Log_2 k - H(W \mid A_i = V_{ij})}{\sum_{i=1}^{a} x_i . \sum_{j=1}^{b_i} (Log_2 k - H(W \mid A_i = V_{ij}))}$$

$$(4)$$

where a, x_i, and b_i have the same meaning as in term selection equation. Immediately after the ant completes the construction of a rule, pruning is undertaken to increase the comprehensibility and accuracy of the rule. After the pruning step, the rule may be assigned a different predicted class based on the majority class in the cases covered

Algorithm 1. General description of ant-miner

```
/* 270 is the number of mammogram taken for training represents rows
15 includes (14 Haralick features + class attribute (Normal/Abnormal))
Training Set   =   {270 rows X 15}
/* TrainingSet Changed  -  Every time the main while loop is executed  some
of the row gets eliminated because of the rule generated or else the training
data is not sufficient enough to generate a rule. So a modification is done in
the while loop of original paper. */
While (TrainingSet Changed) and (TrainingSet > Max_uncovered _cases)
        t = 1  /*  Initializing the ant index */
        ct  = 1    /* Convergence test index */
        /* Pheromone Initialization * /
        Initialize Pheromone Using Equation [1]
        Repeat the following
                Initialize x(i) = 1 for  i represents the attribute index.
                R_t = {};
                While Usable term exists
                        Calculate Entropy for all attribute value pair using
Equation [3].
                        Calculate Heuristic Value for all attribute value
pair using Equation [4].
                        Calculate the Probability of all attribute value pair.
                        Select the term with highest probability.
                        Add the term to the rule R_t.
                        x(i) = 0;  /* i is the index of the attribute that is
added to the current rule  */
                End while
                Prune rule R_t based on the quality.
                Update the pheromone of all trails by increasing pheromone in
the trail followed by Ant_t using the Equation 6. and decreasing Pheromone in
the other details (simulating pheromone evaporation)
                        if (R_t is equal to R_{t-1}) then
                                ct  = ct + 1
                        else
                                ct  = 1;
                        end if
                        t = t + 1;
        until (t >= No_of _ants) or (j >= No_rules_coverg)
        Choose the best rule Rbest among all rules R_t constructed by all the
ants;
        Add rule R_best to DiscoveredRuleList;
        TrainingSet  = TrainingSet - { set of cases correctly covered by R_best}
End While
```

Figure 2 Analysis of rules generated by Ant-Miner

Fold	Angle 0	Angle 45	Angle 90
Fold 1	No. Of. Rules – 7 TPR - 1.00 FPR - 0.00 ACC - 100% CDR - 0	No. Of. Rules – 3 TPR - 0.00 FPR - 0.00 ACC - 53% CDR - 14	No. Of. Rules – 6 TPR - 1.00 FPR - 0.00 ACC - 100% CDR - 0
Fold 2	No. Of. Rules – 6 TPR - 1.00 FPR - 0.00 ACC - 100% CDR - 0	No. Of. Rules – 6 TPR - 1.00 FPR - 0.00 ACC - 100% CDR - 0	No. Of. Rules – 7 TPR - 1.00 FPR - 0.00 ACC - 100% CDR - 0
Fold 3	No. Of. Rules – 9 TPR - 1.00 FPR - 0.00 ACC - 100% CDR - 0	No. Of. Rules – 9 TPR - 1.00 FPR - 0.00 ACC - 100% CDR - 0	No. Of. Rules – 8 TPR - 1.00 FPR - 0.00 ACC - 100% CDR - 4
Fold 4	No. Of. Rules – 10 TPR - 1.00 FPR - 0.00 ACC - 100% CDR - 0	No. Of. Rules – 11 TPR - 1.00 FPR - 0.00 ACC - 100% CDR - 1	No. Of. Rules – 7 TPR - 1.00 FPR - 0.00 ACC - 100% CDR - 0

by the rule antecedent. The rule pruning procedure iteratively removes the term whose removal will cause a maximum increase in the quality of the rule. The quality of a rule is measured using the following equation (5).

$$Q = \frac{TP}{TP + FN} \cdot \frac{TN}{FP + TN} \qquad (5)$$

where *TP* (True Positives) is the number of cases covered by the rule that have the class predicted by the rule. *FP* (False Positives) is the number of cases covered by the rule that have a class different from the class predicted by the rule. *FN* (False Negatives) is the number of cases that are not covered by the rule but that have the class predicted by the rule. *TN* (True Negatives) is the number of cases that are not covered by the rule and that do not have the class predicted by the rule.

Pheromone Update Rule

After each ant completes the construction of its rule, pheromone updating is carried out as per the following equation (6).

$$\tau_{ij}(t + 1) = \tau_{ij}(t).Q, \forall ij \in R \qquad (6)$$

where *R* is the set of terms occurring in the rule constructed by the ant at iteration *t*. In Ant-Miner, pheromone evaporation is implemented in a somewhat indirect way. More precisely, the effect of pheromone evaporation for unused terms is achieved by normalizing the value of each pheromone t_{ij} This normalization is performed by dividing the value of each t_{ij} by the summation of all t_{ij}

Ant-Miner Parameter Setting

The following parameters used to achieve the results:

Number of Ants = 1000
Minimum cases per rule = 3
Maximum uncovered Cases = 5
Number of Rule Converge = 5

Figure 2 reports the analysis of rules generated by the Ant-Miner algorithm.

Figure 3. Decision Tree

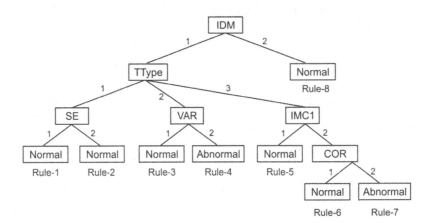

COMPARATIVE STUDY

The decision tree generated by C4.5 is given in Figure 3. The sample rules generated by C4.5 and Ant-Miner algorithms are given below.

Rules Generated With C4.5

Rule 1: IDM = 1 and TType = 1 and SE = 1: Normal
Rule 2: IDM = 1 and TType = 1 and SE = 2: Normal
Rule 3: IDM = 1 and TType = 2 and VAR = 1: Normal
Rule 4: IDM = 1 and TType = 2 and VAR = 2: Abnormal
Rule 5: IDM = 1 and TType = 3 and IMC1 = 2 and COR = 1: Normal
Rule 6: IDM = 1 and TType = 3 and IMC1 = 2 and COR = 2: Abnormal
Rule 7: IDM = 1 and TType = 3 and IMC1 = 1: Normal
Rule 8: IDM = 2: Normal

Angular Second Moment (ASM)
Contrast
Correlation (COR)
Variance (VAR)
Inverse Second Moment (IDM)

Local Mean (LM)
Sum Average (SA)
Sum Variance (SV)
Sum Entropy (SE)
Difference Entropy (DE)
Difference Variance (DV)
Information Measure of Correlation1 (IMC1)
Information Measure of Correlation2 (IMC2)
Local Mean (LM)
Tissue Type (TT)

Rules Generated With Ant-Miner

Rule 1: SE = 1 and COR = 1 and ENTROPY = 1 and DV = 1 and CONTRAST = 1 and SV = 2 and SA = 2 : Abnormal
Rule 2: ENTROPY = 1 and IMC2 = 1 : Normal

When comparing the results obtained by the both the algorithm the accuracy of Ant-Miner algorithm reaches 99% but in C4.5 it is 76%. Figure 4. give the comparative analysis of classification percentage of both algorithms.

Also the number of rules generated using Ant-Miner is less. Graphical representation of the number of rules generated by both algorithms is illustrated in Figure 5.

Figure 4. Analysis of Classification Percentage

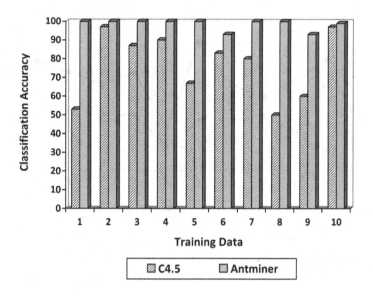

A ROC space is defined by FPR and TPR as *x* and *y* axes respectively, which depicts relative trade-offs between true positive (benefits) and false positive (costs). Each prediction result or one instance of confusion matrix represents one point in the ROC space. The best possible prediction method would yield a point in the upper left corner or coordinate (0,1) of the ROC space, representing 100% sensitivity (all true positives are found) and 100% specificity (no false positives are found). The (0,1) point is also called a perfect classification. The experimental results are plotted in the ROC space as in Figure 6. It is observed that AM has the good predicting ability than C4.5.

GENETIC ANT-MINER

The parameters used in the Ant-Miner algorithms are optimized using genetic algorithm with the aim of improving the accuracy by generating minimum number of rules in order to cover more patterns. The overall frame work is given in Figure 7.

GENETIC ALGORITHMS

As an optimization technique, Genetic Algorithms (GA) simultaneously examine and manipulate a set of possible solutions. The power of GA's comes from the fact that the technique is robust, and can deal successfully with a wide range of problem areas, including those which are difficult for other methods to solve. GA's are not guaranteed to find the global optimum solution to a problem, but they are generally good at finding "acceptably good" solutions to problems. Where specialized techniques exist for solving particular problems, they are likely to out-perform GA's in both speed and accuracy of the final result. Genetic Algorithms are good at exploring the solution space since they search from a set of designs and not from a single design. The GA starts with several alternative solutions to the optimization problem, which are considered as individuals in a population. These solutions are coded as binary strings, called chromosomes.

The initial population is constructed randomly. These individuals are evaluated using

Figure 5. Analysis of Rules generated

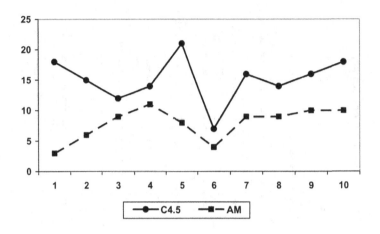

Figure 6. Plot of the Prediction in ROC space

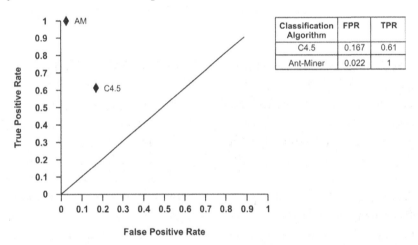

Classification Algorithm	FPR	TPR
C4.5	0.167	0.61
Ant-Miner	0.022	1

the partitioning-specific fitness function. The GA then uses these individuals to produce a new generation of hopefully better solutions. In each generation, two of the individuals are selected probabilistically as parents, with the selection probability proportional to their fitness. Crossover is performed on these individuals to generate two new individuals, called offspring, by exchanging parts of their structure. Thus each offspring inherits a combination of features from both parents. The next step is mutation. An incremental change is made to each member of the population, with a small probability. This ensures that the GA can explore new features that may not be in the population yet. It makes the entire search space reachable, despite the finite population size. Roulette Wheel parent selection method which is conceptually the simplest stochastic selection technique. The proposed generation replacement technique is based on replacing the most inferior member in a population by new offsprings. The genetic algorithm is given below

Figure 7. Genetic ant-miner

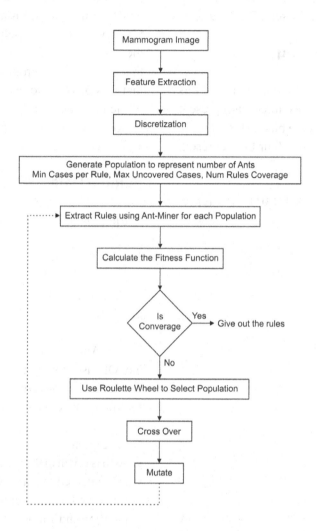

Algorithm

1. Encode Solution Space
2. (a) set pop size, max-gen, gen=0;
   (b) set crossover rate, mutation rate;
3. Initialize Population.
4. **While** max gen <= gen
   Evaluate Fitness
   For (i=1 to pop size)
   Select (mate1,mate2)
   if (rnd(0,1) < crossover rate)
   child = Crossover(mate1,mate2);
   if (rnd(0,1) < mutation rate)

   child = Mutation();
   Repair child if necessary
   End For
   Add offsprings to New Generation.
   gen = gen + 1
   End While
5. Return best chromosomes.

In this study, number of ants, minimum cases per rule, maximum uncovered cases and number of rule converge (numberOfAnts, minCasesPerRule, maxUncoveredCases, numRulesCoverge) are the parameters taken for optimization using genetic algorithm (Thangavel,K., Roselin,R., 2009)

Chromosome Encoding

Chromosome consists of 14 bits first two bits represent numberOfAnts, next three bits represent minCasesPerRule, next three bits represent max-UncoveredCases and the last four bits represent numRuleConverge.

Chromosome Sample : 01 001 011 0100 represents

Decoding

numberOfAnts - 200
minCasesPerRule - 3
maxUncoveredCases - 11
numRuleConverge - 6

Parameter Setting

Crossover Probability - 0.7
Mutation Rate - 0.001

The author's main goal is to find out minimum number of rules that classify maximum cases with high degree of accuracy so the fitness function is defined to maximize

$$F = a - cnr + nr/2$$

Where a represents accuracy, cnr denotes the cases not covered by the rules and nr is for number of rules.

COMPUTATIONAL RESULTS

Initially ten random populations are generated. The roulette wheel selection with the crossover probability of 0.7 and the mutation probability 0.001 are used for forming new generations. The fitness value for the populations is calculated using the above mentioned fitness function. By using this in the ten fold cross validation it is observed that it is possible to classify the suspicious area of the mammograms as normal or abnormal using only two rules for maximum folds with the 100% accuracy.

Sample Data

The population which has given the fittest value is

1 1 0 1 0 0 0 1 0 1 0 1

The decoded value for the chromosome is given by

No. Of Ants = 400
No. Of cases per Rule = 10
No. Of Rule Convergence = 3
Maximum Uncovered Cases = 10

The graphical representation of the population growth is given in the Figure 8. The highest fitness value expected is 2 as far as our fitness function is concerned. X axis represents individuals in the population and Y axis represents the fitness value.

COMPARATIVE STUDY

The results obtained using Ant-Miner is compared with Genetic optimized Ant-Miner algorithm. The result shows that the genetic optimized Ant-Miner parameter is able to produce minimum rules for classification with 100% accuracy. The average number of rules used is 5.7. The average default class used for classification is 1.6 with the accuracy of 94.7%. When the parameters are optimized it is possible to get 100% accuracy with 0.6 default class being used and the average number of rule

Figure 8. Population Growth

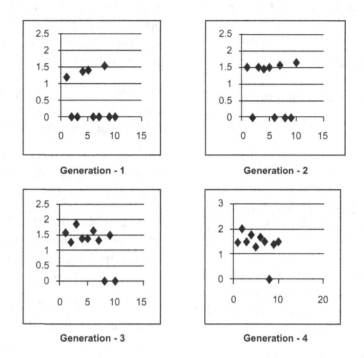

is 2 in the case of mammograms classification as normal and abnormal.

CONCLUSION

In this study, a data mining approach has been used to identify the abnormal mammograms. A classifier was derived from the Haralick's 14 features using C4.5 and Ant-Miner algorithms. It is reported that the classification accuracy of Ant-Miner produces 99% with TPR as 1.00 where as it is 76% in C4.5 with TPR as 0.61. Another observation made is the number of rules generated by the Ant-Miner algorithm is lesser than the number of rules generated by C4.5. Also the number of cases that are classified by the default case is less in Ant-Miner. Moreover C4.5 is a recursive algorithm but Ant-Miner is an iterative one so it is easy implement and maintain. Instead of assigning random values for Ant-Miner parameters

the application of genetic algorithm selects the parameter of good choice depends on the fitness function. In this study, the main emphasis is on getting minimum number of rules with greater accuracy and maximum rule coverage. The four parameters used in the Ant-Miner were optimized and used for obtaining rules in mammogram mining. Computational results showed that Ant-Miner is able to produce minimum set of rules that could classify maximum cases with greater accuracy.

FURTHER RESEARCH DIRECTION

Ant-Miner Performance is better when comparing to C4.5. Further study can be done using Ant-Miner to classify the suspicious region as benign or malignant. Instead of Haralick features other set features can be used for classification. Another difficulty encountered is Ant-Miner rules are not simple. Further study can be made by increasing the number of ants and to simplify the rules.

ACKNOWLEDGMENT

UGC Grant No. F-NO.34-105/2008 (SR) is gratefully acknowledged.

REFERENCES

Acharya & Ray. (2005). *Image Processing: Principles and Applications*. New York: Wiley-Interscience.

Baker, J. A., Kornguth, P. J., Lo, J. Y., & Floyd, C. E. (1996). Artificial neural network, improving the quality of breast biopsy recommendations. *Radiology*, (198): 131–135.

Breiman, F., & Olshen, S. (1984). *Classification and Decision Trees*. New York: Wadsworth.

Dougherty, J., Kohavi, R., & Sahami, M. (1995). Supervised and unsupervised discretization of continuous features. In: *Proceedings of the 12th international conference on machine learning*, (pp. 194—202). San Francisco: Morgan Kaufmann.

Gonzalez, R. C., & Woods, R. E. (1992). *Digital Image Processing*. Reading, MA: Addison-Wesley Publishing Co.

Haralick, R.M., Shanmugam, K. & Dinstein, I.(1973). Textural features for image classification. *IEEE Trans Syst Man Cybern SMC*, (3), 610--621.

Osmar, R., Zaïane, M.-L., & Coman, A. (2002). Mammography Classification by Association Rule-based Classifier. In *International Workshop on Multimedia Data Mining* (pp. 62-69), Edmonton, Alberta, Canada, (17-19 July).

Parpinelli, R. S., Lopesand, H. S., & Freitas, A. A. (2002). Data Mining with an Ant Colony Optimization Algorithm. *IEEE Transactions on Evolutionary Computation*, 6(4), 321–332. doi:10.1109/TEVC.2002.802452

Quinlan, J. R. (1987). Simplifying decision trees. *International Journal of Man-Machine Studies*, 27, 221–234. doi:10.1016/S0020-7373(87)80053-6

Shannon, C. E. (1948). A mathematical theory of communication. *The Bell System Technical Journal*, 27, 379–423.

Thangavel, K. & Roselin, R. (2009, November). Mammogram mining with genetic optimization of Ant-Miner parameters. *International journal of Recent Trends in Engineering, 2* (3).

Veldkamp, W. J. H., & Karssemeijer, N. (1996). Influence of segmentation on classification of microcalcifications in digital mammography. In *Proceedings of the 18th Annual International Conference of the IEEE Engineering in Medicine and Biology Society*, (October 31–November 3). Amsterdam, Netherlands: Institute of Electrical and Electronic Engineers, Inc.

Walker, R. F., Jackway, P., & Longstaff, I. D. (1995). Improving co-occurrence matrix feature discrimination. In *Proceedings of the 3rd Conference on Digital Image Computing: Techniques and Applications (DICTA '95)*, Brisbane, Australia, December 6–8. www.cancer.gov. (n.d.).

ADDITIONAL READING

American Cancer Society. (1998). *Cancer facts and figures*. Atlanta, GA: American Cancer Society.

Chan, H. P., Sahiner, B., Lam, K. L., Petrick, N., Helvie, M. A., & Goodsitt, M. (1998). Computerized analysis of mammographic microcalcifications in morphological and texture feature spaces. *Medical Physics*, (25): 2007–2019. doi:10.1118/1.598389

De Santo, M., Molinara, M., Tortorella, F., & Vento, M. (2003). Automatic classification of clustered microcalcifications by a multiple expert system. *Pattern Recognition*, (36): 1467–1477. doi:10.1016/S0031-3203(03)00004-9

Dhawan, AP., & Chitre, Y., & Kaiser-Bonasso. (1996). Analysis of mammographic microcalcifications using gray-level image structure features. *IEEE Transactions on Medical Imaging*, (15): 246–259. doi:10.1109/42.500063

Jiawei Han & Micheline Kamber. (2001). *Data Mining, Concepts and Techniques*. Morgan Kaufmann.

Kallergi, M. (2004). Computer-aided diagnosis of mammographic microcalcification clusters. *Medical Physics*, (31): 314–326. doi:10.1118/1.1637972

Kemal Polat & Salih Gü̈nes. (in press). A novel hybrid intelligent method based on C4.5 decision tree classifier and one-against-all approach for multi-class classification problems. *Expert Systems with Applications*.

Liu, H., Hussain, F., Tan, C.L., & Dash M. (2002). Discretization: An Enabling Technique, DMKD (6), 393—423.

Liu, Y., Zhang, D., & Lu, G. (2008). Region-based image retrieval with high-level semantics using decision tree learning. *Pattern Recognition*, (41): 2554–2570. doi:10.1016/j.patcog.2007.12.003

Majid, A. S., de Paredes, E. S., Doherty, R. D., Sharma, N. R., & Salvador, X. (2003). Missed breast carcinoma: pitfalls and pearls. *Radiographics*, (23): 881–895. doi:10.1148/rg.234025083

Markey, M. K., Lo, J. Y., & Floyd, C. E. (2002). Differences between computer-aided diagnosis of breast masses and that of calcifications. *Radiology*, (223): 489–493. doi:10.1148/radiol.2232011257

Markopoulos, C., Kouskos, E., Koufopoulos, K., Kyriakou, V., & Gogas, J. (2001). Use of artificial neural networks (computer analysis) in the diagnosis of microcalcifications on mammography. *European Journal of Radiology*, (39): 60–65. doi:10.1016/S0720-048X(00)00281-3

Papadopoulos, A., Fotiadis, D. I., & Likas, A. (2005). Characterization of clustered microcalcifications in digitized mammograms using neural networks and support vector machines. *Artificial Intelligence in Medicine*, (34): 141–150. doi:10.1016/j.artmed.2004.10.001

Paquerault, S., Yarusso, L. M., Papaioannou, J., Jiang, Y., & Nishikawa, R. M. (2004). Radial gradient-based segmentation of mammographic microcalcifications: observer evaluation and effect on CAD performance. *Medical Physics*, (31): 2648–2657. doi:10.1118/1.1767692

Quinlan, J. R. (1993). *C4.5: Programs for Machine Learning*. Morgan Kauffman.

Sampat, P. M., Markey, M. K., & Bovik, A. C. (2005). Computer-aided detection and diagnosis in mammography. In: Bovik AC, editor. Handbook of image and video processing. pp. 119- -1217 Academic Press, New York.

Thiele, D. L., Kimme-Smith, C., Johnson, T. D., McCombs, M., & Bassett, L. W. (1996). Using tissue texture surrounding calcification clusters to predict benign vs malignant outcomes. *Medical Physics*, (23): 549–555. doi:10.1118/1.597901

Veldkamp, W. J. H., Karssemeijer, N., Otten, J. D. M., & Hendriks, J. H. C. L. (2000). Automated classification of clustered microcalcifications into malignant and benign types. *Medical Physics*, (27): 2600–2608. doi:10.1118/1.1318221

KEY TERMS AND DEFINITIONS

Ant Colony Optimization: The ant colony optimization algorithm (ACO), is the simulation of ants food searching behaviour. Ant follows the pheromone deposited by the other ants to find out the shortest path to the food source. It is a probabilistic technique for solving computational problems which can be used for finding good paths through graphs.

Data Mining: Data mining is the process of extracting pattern from data. This mainly used for converting data into information.

Decision Tree: Decision tree is a tree where each node represents the attribute, arc represents value of the attribute and leaves represents the actual decision for the rule constructed from the root node, along the path to the leaf.

Discritization: It is the process of transforming continuous vales into discrete counter parts.

Entropy: Entropy is measure of uncertainty associated with a random variable. The entropy H of a discrete random variable X with possible values $\{x1, \quad x2, \ldots \quad xn\}$ is

$$Entropy = \sum_{i=1}^{n} \sum_{j=1}^{n} P(i,j) \ \log(P(i,j))$$

Heuristic: A heuristic is a function that ranks alternatives in a various search algorithm. Example: Entropy value can be used to rank the attributes.

Genetic Algorithm: A genetic algorithm is a search technique is used to find the approximate solution to optimization and search problems.

Chapter 15
Use of SciDBMaker as Tool for the Design of Specialized Biological Databases

Riadh Hammami
Université Laval, Canada

Ismail Fliss
Université Laval, Canada

ABSTRACT

The exponential growth of molecular biology research in recent decades has brought concomitant growth in the number and size of genomic and proteomic databases used to interpret experimental findings. Particularly, growth of protein sequence records created the need for smaller and manually annotated databases. Since scientists are continually developing new specific databases to enhance their understanding of biological processes, the authors created SciDBMaker to provide a tool for easy building of new specialized protein knowledge bases. This chapter also suggests best practices for specialized biological databases design, and provides examples for the implementation of these practices.

DOI: 10.4018/978-1-60960-102-7.ch015

INTRODUCTION

The exponential growth of research in molecular biology has brought concomitant proliferation of databases for stocking its findings. A variety of protein sequence databases exist. While all of these strive for completeness, the range of user interests is often beyond their scope. Large databases covering a broad range of domains tend to offer less detailed information than smaller, more specialized resources, often creating a need to combine data from many sources in order to obtain a complete picture. Scientific researchers are continually developing new specific databases to enhance their understanding of biological processes. In this chapter, we present the implementation of a new tool for protein data analysis. SciDBMaker is stand-alone software that allows the extraction of protein data from the Swiss-Prot database, sequence analysis comprising physicochemical profile calculations, homologous sequences search and multiple sequence alignments (Riadh Hammami, Zouhir, Naghmouchi, Ben Hamida, & Fliss, 2008). Furthermore, with its easy-to-use user interface, this software provides the opportunity to build more specialized protein databases from the universal protein sequence database Swiss-Prot. It compiles information with relative ease, updates and compares various data relevant to a given protein family and could solve the problem of dispersed biological search results. Using SciDBMaker, two databases were developed, namely BACTIBASE (R Hammami, Zouhir, Ben Hamida, & Fliss, 2007; Riadh Hammami, Zouhir, Le Lay, Ben Hamida, & Fliss, 2010) and PhytAMP (Riadh Hammami, Ben Hamida, Vergoten, & Fliss, 2009) and analyzed here as 'proof of concept'. Here, we share our knowledge in protein database development and provide advices that we hope are useful to people designing their own biological database.

BACKGROUND

Bioinformatics and computational biology methods are increasingly used to study biological systems and widely applied to facilitate collecting, organizing, and analyzing of large-scale of data in molecular biology. Biological databases appeared as invaluable method for managing these data and for making them accessible to scientific community. In this mold, molecular biological databases could contain either the result of large amounts of molecular biological experiments or manual extraction of literature data. Depending on the type of biological data that they enclose, these biodatabases fulfill different functions. Most molecular data are in the form of a biosequence of a DNA, RNA, or a protein molecule.

Dr. Dayhoff and her research group were pioneers in the development of computer methods for the analysis of protein sequences evolution. This led to the establishment in 1984 of the Protein Information Resource (PIR) as a resource to assist researchers in the identification and interpretation of protein sequence information (Wu et al., 2003). This has inspired Amos Bairoch in 1986 for the creation and public release of Swiss-Prot sequence database (Bairoch, 2000). The increasing quantities of nucleic acid sequence data being generated worldwide in 1980s created the need to the construction of nucleic acid sequence databases, notably GenBank (Benson, Karsch-Mizrachi, Lipman, Ostell, & Sayers, 2009), European Molecular Biology Laboratory Nucleotide Sequence Database (EMBL) (Hingamp, van den Broek, Stoesser, & Baker, 1999) and DNA Data Bank of Japan (DDBJ) (Tateno, Fukami-Kobayashi, Miyazaki, Sugawara, & Gojobori, 1998). Together, these databases form the International Nucleotide Sequence Database Collaboration (INSDC, http://www.insdc.org) which archives and makes publically available more than 80 million individual molecular sequences (Benson, et al., 2009). In 2002 PIR, along with its international partners, EBI (European Bioinformatics Institute) and

SIB (Swiss Institute of Bioinformatics), unified the PIR, Swiss-Prot, and TrEMBL databases by creating UniProt, a single worldwide database of protein sequence and function. Today, an important collection of biological databases are available in the public domain, spanning the worlds of sequence, family and structure of DNA, RNA and proteins, organisms, genomes, signaling and metabolic pathways, microarrays, biodiversity, and so on (Ellis & Attwood, 2001). Currently, there are many different types of biodatabases, including:

- **Bibliographic databases**: are considered as important information sources for bio-medical research and contain summary information taken from a variety of sources including journals, books, conference reports and patents. PubMed is one of the largest databases of life science abstracts with more than 19 million citations for biomedical articles from MEDLINE and life science journals (NCBI, 2002).
- **Taxonomy databases**: contain information classification and nomenclatural data on organisms. The National Center for Biotechnology Information (NCBI) hosts the NCBI Taxonomy database, which contains over 363 000 taxonomic nodes from living and extinct organisms.
- **Sequence databases**: store different types of sequences including individual genes, whole genomes, RNA, expressed sequence tags and proteins.
- **Structure databases**: The Protein Data Bank (PDB) was established in 1971 as a result of collaboration between the Research Collaboratory for Structural Bioinformatics (RCSB), the Macromolecular Structural Database (MSD-EBI) and the Protein Data Bank of Japan (PDBj) (Sussman et al., 1998). PDB is the single worldwide repository of information about the three-dimensional structures of proteins, nucleic acids and other biological macromolecules. PDB contains over 59 500 protein structures from X-ray crystallography, nuclear magnetic resonance (NMR), electron microscopy (EM), and theoretical modeling.
- **Genome/organism databases**: contain information on genes, gene location, gene nomenclature and links to sequence databases. At present, several gene-centric databases are available including Online Mendelian Inheritance in Man (OMIM) (Hamosh, Scott, Amberger, Bocchini, & McKusick, 2005), Human Genome Project (HGP), Mouse Genome Database (MGD) (Bult et al., 2010), FlyBase (Wilson, Goodman, Strelets, & The FlyBase Consortium, 2008), Saccharomyces Genome Database (SGD) (Engel et al., 2010), MaizeGDB (Lawrence, Dong, Polacco, Seigfried, & Brendel, 2004), etc.
- **Protein classification databases**: contain structural and functional classification of proteins. Of those, the CATH database is a hierarchical domain classification of protein structures taken from the Protein Data Bank (Cuff et al., 2009). Conversely, PANTHER database is a library of protein families and subfamilies indexed by function (Thomas et al., 2003).
- **Interaction databases**: store inter-relationships and interactions between DNA, RNA, proteins and many other chemical compounds.
- **Pathway databases**: are network representations of biological pathways that offer a different functional view from and complementary to sequence and structure databases (please see (Schaefer, 2004) for review).

Many of these web-based biological databases are interlinked and freely available to the scientific community. The high number of biological

Figure 1. Evolution of biological databases count in the NAR online Molecular Biology Database Collection

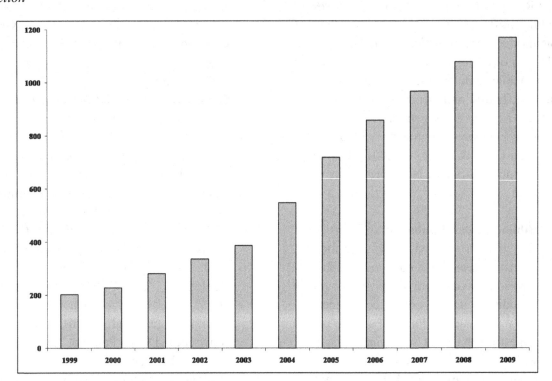

databases reflects essentially the type of data that they contain. Also, the diverse databases reflect the expertise and interests of the research groups that maintain them.

At present, hundreds of molecular biological databases exist. Different institutions and companies are implicated in the development and maintain of these data sources which vary widely in their content, formats and access methods (Köhler, 2004). Good starting points for finding relevant public databases are the annual Nucleic Acids Research database issue (Galperin & Cochrane, 2009), DBCat (Discala, Benigni, Barillot, & Vaysseix, 2000), the BioCatalog (Rodriguez-Tome, 1998), BioMed Central Databases, and the databases listed in the SRS server of the EBI (Zdobnov, Lopez, Apweiler, & Etzold, 2002). The Nucleic Acids Research (NAR) online Molecular Biology Database Collection is probably the most structured catalog for molecular biology databases

available so far with 1170 databases (Galperin & Cochrane, 2009). Figure 1 illustrates the annual growth of this collection with more than fivefold increasing in ten years. The inventory of molecular biology databases published in NAR is organized according to a pre-established hierarchy grouping together the databases according to a category list: Nucleotide Sequence, RNA sequence, Protein sequence, Structure, etc.

Today, databases continue to emerge from different research groups in a similar way. When such resources grow large enough, they are often posted on the Web for the benefit of the entire scientific community (Ellis & Attwood, 2001). This can be done with minimum initial expense for either hardware or software. A database must be accurate, verified, large enough and up-to-date as knowledge in its area of expertise grows. This growth must be oriented to meet the needs of the user community. Evolution of a database should

Figure 2. Exponential growth of UniProtKB/Swiss-Prot. Data obtained from the UniProt Web site

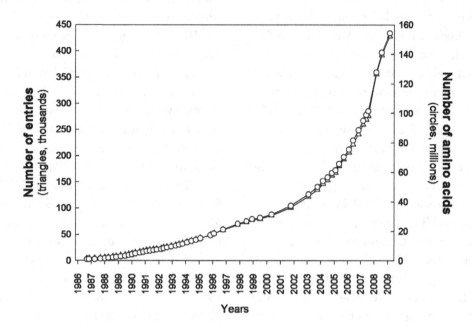

implicate data entry, checking, storage, retrieval, display and its associated tools analysis. The majority of biological databases started by storing their data in flat text files but evolved to use sophisticated database management systems to better serve their clientele.

SCIENTIFIC DATABASE MAKER, A COMPREHENSIVE TOOL FOR THE DESIGN OF SPECIALIZED BIOLOGICAL DATABASES

Why SciDBMaker?

The exponential growth of molecular biology research in recent decades has brought concomitant growth in the number and size of genomic and proteomic databases used to interpret experimental findings. The accumulation of genomic and proteic sequence data are best illustrated by the exponential growth of GenBank and UniProtKB/Swiss-Prot databases (Cavalcoli, 2001). As shown in Figure 2, the amount of information available

about proteins recorded in Swiss-Prot continues to increase at a rapid pace. UniProtKB/Swiss-Prot plays an ever more important role by providing a central resource on protein sequences and functional annotation for biologists and for scientists active in functional proteomics and genomics research.

The growth of protein sequence records created the need for smaller and manually annotated databases. A variety of protein sequence databases exist, ranging from simple sequence repositories to expertly curated universal databases that cover all species and in which the original sequence data are enhanced by manual addition of further information in each sequence record (Rolf Apweiler, Bairoch, & Wu, 2004). While all of these strive for completeness, the range of user interests is often beyond their scope. This may reflect the user's wish to combine different types of information or the inability of a single resource to contain the complete details of every relevant experiment. In addition, large databases with broad domains tend to offer less detailed information than smaller, more specialized, resources, with the result that data from many resources may need to be combined to provide a complete picture (Williams, Kersey, Pruess, & Apweiler, 2005). There is a clear need to gather, filter and critically evaluate this mass of information and store into smaller, more specialized, resources so that it can be used with greater efficiency. The development of a specialized database involves considerable resources and expertise. Since scientists are continually developing new specific databases to enhance their understanding of biological processes, we created SciDBMaker to provide a tool for easy building of new specialized protein knowledge bases (Riadh Hammami, et al., 2008). Scientific DataBase Maker is new stand-alone software for protein data analysis. The software interface allows successive steps for sequence manipulation, starting from user sequence search and homologous sequence retrieval from the UniProtKB/Swiss-Prot databank, followed by physicochemical profile calculations, multiple sequence alignments, phylogenic tree visualization and culminating in database export/building. All steps are performed in an interactive manner. Physical and chemical parameters, rarely found in public databases, provide a helpful tool for the analysis of a set of proteins and their calculation is achieved in a direct and interactive manner, with off-line access.

Data Collection, Annotation, Verification and Validation

The first step in database building should be data collection. Users may open files in Fasta or Swiss-Prot format, or import sequence entries from the UniProtKB/Swiss-Prot database. SciDBMaker uses Dbfetch to import entries online (Labarga, Valentin, Anderson, & Lopez, 2007). The tool is provided by the EBI for easy retrieval of entries from various databases. When sequences are loaded to the containers, SciDBMaker offers various methods for sequence analysis. To find similar sequences, the containers can be queried

with either proteins from the UniProtKB/Swis-sProt database or user-imported sequences, using the BLAST algorithm (Altschul et al., 1997). Then, sequences may be manually curated and annotated. Data annotation is a critical step in the development of specialized biological databases. Another verification/validation step may be used here: multiple sequence alignment (MSA). MSA is often used to assess sequence conservation/diversity, giving an important overview about homology between sequences. SciDBMaker offers an interactive use of CLUSTALW as tool for MSAs (M. A. Larkin et al., 2007). Generated trees may be used for a subsequent verification. These trees may be easily viewed using phylogenic tree visualization software such as TREEVIEW (Page, 1996). Thus, use of SciDBMaker would give a clearer picture about protein families.

Physicochemical Data Calculations/Predictions

When data collection and validation is completed, various physicochemical parameters may be calculated / predicted. Physicochemical properties and amino acid composition are useful to identify isomorphic relationships between proteins of the same family. SciDBMaker offers a rich set of physicochemical parameters such as amino acid composition (acidic, basic, hydrophobic, polar, absent and common amino acids), atomic composition, molecular weight (Patrickios & Yamasaki, 1995), theoretical pI (Bjellqvist, Basse, Olsen, & Celis, 1994; Patrickios & Yamasaki, 1995), extinction coefficient (Henryk, Russell, & Randolph, 1992), absorbance at 280 nm, estimated half-life in mammalian cells, yeast and E. coli (Bachmair, Finley, & Varshavsky, 1986; Gonda et al., 1989), instability index (Guruprasad, Reddy, & Pandit, 1990), aliphatic index (Ikai, 1980), grand average of hydropathicity (GRAVY) (Jack & Russell, 1982) and protein-binding potential (Boman index) (Radzeka & Wolfenden, 1988). Knowledge of physicochemical profile of a set of proteins may be exploited to identify subtle similarities between sequences and then evolutionary connections between these.

Generating Specialized Databases, How To

SciDBMaker contains 'Database Connector', a user-friendly interface, to enable interaction with database servers such (MySQL, Access, SQL server and Oracle). Thus, loaded data may be transferred easily to server as database. Few steps are sufficient to generate an SQL script with data content and running it at the server level. The Figure 3 shows a screen dump of 'Database Connector' with description of available commands.

The majority of scientific community use MySQL (http://www.mysql.com/) database server to store their databases. MySQL is the world's most popular open source database widely used among the web. Readers are invited to view a demonstration movie of SciDBMaker at the following website http://scidbmaker.pfba-lab-tun.org.

Application for The Design of Specialized Databases

BACTIBASE Database

BACTIBASE is an integrated open-access database designed for the characterization of bacterial antimicrobial peptides, commonly known

Figure 3. Screen dump of Database Connector. Available commands are: 'List bases': available databases list; 'List tables': available tables list, 'Open table': open requested table; 'Create requete': Generate a requete table for current document, before doing this, users should tape a name for the table; and 'Do requete': will execute this requete on the database server. After modifying data, users may save modification by pressing 'save' button

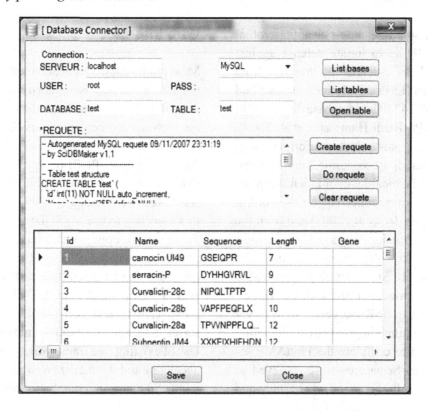

as bacteriocins (R Hammami, et al., 2007). The database provides a manually curated annotation of bacteriocin sequences which were collected from the UniProt database (R Apweiler, Bairoch, & Wu, 2007) and from the scientific literature using PubMed. All sequences were retrieved to SciDBMaker (Riadh Hammami, et al., 2008), validated and annotated. Various physicochemical parameters were calculated and resulted tables were then exported to MySQL server. BACTIBASE has been equipped with additional functions aimed at both casual and power users. These include incorporation of various tools for sequence analysis, such as homology search, multiple sequence alignments, Hidden Markov Models, molecular modeling and retrieval through 'Taxonomy Browser'. For further details about BACTIBASE, readers are invited to read the following papers (R Hammami, et al., 2007; Riadh Hammami, et al., 2010). The database is available at http://bactibase.pfba-lab-tun.org.

PhytAMP Database

Plants produce small cysteine-rich antimicrobial peptides (AMPs) as an innate defense against pathogens such as α-defensins, thionins, lipid transfer proteins (LTPs), cyclotides, snakins and hevein-like. PhytAMP is a database dedicated to these plant AMPs (Riadh Hammami, et al., 2009). The resource contains valuable information on these AMPs, including taxonomic, microbiological and physicochemical data. Antimicrobial plant peptide sequences were collected from the UniProt database (R Apweiler, et al., 2007) and from the scientific literature using PubMed. Microbiological information was collected from the literature by PubMed search. Since not all known AMPs sequences were present in the ExPASy (http://www.expasy.org/srs/) SRS server or NCBI server (http://www.ncbi.nlm.nih.gov/entrez/), literature search was used to complete the PhytAMP sequence database. Sequences were retrieved in SciDBMaker (Riadh Hammami, et al., 2008) and

curated and the resulting tables exported to the MySQL server. PhytAMP allows all plant AMP sequence information and physicochemical or biological data to be accessed via a user-friendly, web-based interface. The database can be queried using various criteria and retrieval of microbiological or physicochemical data, includes specific information on each peptide. A set of tools were provided for sequence analysis including and not limited to homology search, sequence alignments, structure prediction and hidden Markov models (Riadh Hammami, et al., 2009). The microbiological, physicochemical and structural proprieties thus provided should allow more comprehensive analysis of this group of antimicrobial peptides and enhance our understanding of plant defense biology. PhytAMP may be accessed free of charge at http://phytamp.pfba-lab-tun.org.

WHAT NEXT: WEB INTERFACE DESIGN AND TOOLS IMPLEMENTATION

Web Interface

Most public databases are connected to the Internet and can be accessed via web pages. Building web interface to database depends essentially on web server configuration. Various servers configuration are available, with LAMP (Linux Apache MySQL PHP) being the most popular. Our survey on databases published in Nucleic Acid Research database 2009 issue confirmed this tendency to use MySQL server, as shown in Table 1. Developing a web interface for a database require knowledge of at least two or more web programming language such as PHP, Perl, Ruby, ASP, Python, JavaScript, HTML. As shown in Table 2, PHP and Perl are the most preferred script languages by bioinformatics community. Use of existing free frameworks is good choice to accelerate and standardize web interface development. An increasing number of biology-oriented

Table 1. Survey on databases published in Nucleic Acid Research database 2009 issue

Server	count	%
MySQL	58	69.05
PostgreeSQL	15	17.86
Oracle	7	8.33
SQL server	3	3.57
XML	1	1.19
Total	84	100
Unknown	101	-

framework projects are developed and publicly available (such as BioPerl, BioPHP, BioPython, BioJava, BioRuby, etc...) (Dudley & Butte, 2009; Mangalam, 2002). A successful web-based interface should be user-friendly. Many databases provide hypertext links to entries in other databases. Thus, developers should provide stable database specific identifiers (accession numbers), which are generated when a new entry is added to the database. These accession numbers are used for interlinking database entries via web pages. To facilitate the development, maintain and growth of biological databases, developers should adopt generic approaches such as standard identifiers (accession numbers), naming conventions,

controlled vocabularies (ontology), adoption of standards for data representation and exchange, and the use of data warehousing technologies.

Which Tools May Use To Enhance My Database?

The incorporation of various tools for protein sequence analysis empowers databases and renders them more interactive. Among the methods used in the protein analysis pipeline are: protein sequence homology search [BLAST (Altschul, et al., 1997), FASTA (Pearson & Lipman, 1988) and SSEARCH (Pearson & Lipman, 1988)]; sequence similarity search [CLUSTALW (M. Larkin et

Table 2. Survey on databases published in Nucleic Acid Research database 2009 issue

Language	Count	%
PHP	26	36.62
Perl	24	33.80
JavaScript	7	9.86
Java	2	2.82
Ajax	1	1.41
ASP.NET	1	1.41
JSP	6	8.45
Adobe Flex	1	1.41
Python	2	2.82
Ruby	1	1.41
Total	71	100
Unknown	**131**	-

al., 2007), MUSCLE (Edgar, 2004), T-COFFEE (Notredame, Higgins, & Heringa, 2000), etc]; pattern and motif searches [HMMER (Durbin, Eddy, Krogh, & Mitchison, 1998), MEME (Bailey & Elkan, 1994), etc]; transmembrane helices prediction [TMHMM (Krogh, Larsson, von Heijne, & Sonnhammer, 2001)]; signal peptide prediction [SignalP (Dyrløv Bendtsen, Nielsen, von Heijne, & Brunak, 2004)]; secondary structure prediction [Jnet, etc]; homology modeling of protein 3D structures [MODELLER (Sali & Blundell, 1993)]. Other Bioinformatics features for protein analyses may be incorporated including and not limited to integrated 3D molecule viewer [Jmol, AstexViewer, and Chemis3D], hydrophobicity analyses, antigenicity analysis, protein charge analysis, reverse translation from protein to DNA, and proteolytic cleavage detection. Alternatively, bioinformatic free open source software analysis packages may be installed on the server and used for sequence analysis, with EMBOSS being the most popular (Rice, Longden, & Bleasby, 2000). When possible, developers may empower their databases using the popular sequence retrieval system (SRS), which is a keyword indexing and search system for biological databases (Moorhouse & Barry, 2005). The SRS system is a software package, currently distributed by BioWisdom Ltd. It is a widely used tool for cross-searching different biological databases (e.g., NCBI, SwissProt, and UniProt) and support diverse data formats, e.g., xml, flat file or relational format. Incorporating software tools for protein sequence analysis to database gives another angle of look to data and could allow a better understanding of biological systems.

Database developers should not neglect also to build a tool for data retrieval. This option is often required by users. Consequently, developers should provide a tool for the data retrieval from the database. Delivered data should set in a structured format to ease further automatic parsing and analysis. eXtensible Markup Language (XML) is presently becoming the standard for exchange of biological databases, and storing and querying different data sources using a XML database has several advantages (Achard, Vaysseix, & Barillot, 2001; Köhler, 2004). When the database become publicly available, logging users' queries and retrieved documents is invaluable to evaluate the performance of the database and its search engine. This may be easily done by adding a module to store a report on what was requested and what was returned. Therefore, learn from the users could be considered as an important tool to enhance databases. Developers should provide also statistics about their databases. In addition, statistical information may be built specifically when returning data after a search.

CONCLUSION

The exponential growth of molecular biology research in recent decades has brought concomitant growth in the number and size of genomic and proteomic databases used to interpret experimental findings. Particularly, growth of protein sequence records created the need for smaller and manually annotated databases. A variety of protein sequence databases exist, ranging from simple sequence repositories to expertly curated universal databases that cover all species and in which the original sequence data are enhanced by manual addition of further information in each sequence record. Large databases with broad domains tend to offer less detailed information than smaller, more specialized, resources, with the result that data from many resources may need to be combined to provide a complete picture. Since scientists are continually developing new specific databases to enhance their understanding of biological processes, we created SciDBMaker to provide a tool for easy building of new specialized protein knowledge bases. With its easy-to-use user interface, this software provides the opportunity to build more specialized protein databases from a universal protein sequence database such as Swiss-Prot.

Last decade, there has been a veritable explosion in specialized biological databases. In general, specialized databases give a very detailed and careful curation of the data by specialists in particular domains, and are considered as extremely valuable. Most of the developed databases are university based, and require time to grow up and become recognized as valuable research tools. To achieve this, curators play a critical role in validating, updating and maintaining data, and providing the best services to users. In turn, this requires an assured funding structure, and most of these databases try to attract funding for development and maintenance (Ellis & Attwood, 2001). In a world of hundreds of biological databases, the success of a database relies on data management technology for data integration. Thus, database developers should provide extensive assistance in the form of publicly accessible, machine processable documentation concerning the database schemas, contents, query interfaces, query languages (Jagadish & Olken, 2003). Adoption of such current technology by database developers was seen as an imperative issue.

REFERENCES

Achard, F., Vaysseix, G., & Barillot, E. (2001). XML, bioinformatics and data integration. [Review]. *Bioinformatics (Oxford, England)*, *17*(2), 115–125. doi:10.1093/bioinformatics/17.2.115

Altschul, S., Madden, T., Schaffer, A., Zhang, J., Zhang, Z., & Miller, W. (1997). Gapped BLAST and PSI-BLAST: a new generation of protein database search programs. *Nucleic Acids Research*, *25*(17), 3389–3402..doi:10.1093/nar/25.17.3389

Apweiler, R., Bairoch, A., & Wu, C. H. (2004). Protein sequence databases. [doi: DOI: 10.1016/j.cbpa.2003.12.004]. *Current Opinion in Chemical Biology, 8*(1), 76-80.

Apweiler, R., Bairoch, A., & Wu, H. (2007). The Universal Protein Resource (UniProt) Protein sequence databases. *Nucleic Acids Research, 35,* D193–D197.

Bachmair, A., Finley, D., & Varshavsky, A. (1986). In vivo half-life of a protein is a function of its amino-terminal residue. *Science, 234,* 179–186. doi:10.1126/science.3018930

Bailey, T., & Elkan, C. (1994). *Fitting a mixture model by expectation maximization to discover motifs in biopolymers.* Paper presented at the Proceedings of the Second International Conference on Intelligent Systems for Molecular Biology, Menlo Park, California.

Bairoch, A. (2000). Serendipity in bioinformatics, the tribulations of a Swiss bioinformatician through exciting times! *Bioinformatics (Oxford, England), 16*(1), 48–64..doi:10.1093/bioinformatics/16.1.48

Benson, D. A., Karsch-Mizrachi, I., Lipman, D. J., Ostell, J., & Sayers, E. W. (2009). GenBank. *Nucleic Acids Res, 37*(Database issue), D26-31. doi: gkn723 [pii] 10.1093/nar/gkn723

Bjellqvist, B., Basse, B., Olsen, E., & Celis, J. (1994). Reference points for comparisons of two-dimensional maps of proteins from different human cell types defined in a pH scale where isoelectric points correlate with polypeptide compositions. *Electrophoresis, 15,* 529–539. doi:10.1002/elps.1150150171

Bult, C. J., Kadin, J. A., Richardson, J. E., Blake, J. A., Eppig, J. T., & the Mouse Genome Database Group. (2010). The Mouse Genome Database: enhancements and updates. *Nucl. Acids Res., 38*(suppl_1), D586-592. doi: 10.1093/nar/gkp880

Cavalcoli, J. D. (2001). Genomic and Proteomic Databases: Large-Scale Analysis and Integration of Data. [doi: DOI: 10.1016/S1050-1738(01)00089-5]. *Trends in Cardiovascular Medicine, 11*(2), 76-81.

Cuff, A., Redfern, O. C., Greene, L., Sillitoe, I., Lewis, T., & Dibley, M. (2009)... *The CATH Hierarchy Revisited Structural Divergence in Domain Superfamilies and the Continuity of Fold Space.*, *17*(8), 1051–1062.

Discala, C., Benigni, X., Barillot, E., & Vaysseix, G. (2000). DBcat: a catalog of 500 biological databases. *Nucleic Acids Research, 28*(1), 8–9.. doi:10.1093/nar/28.1.8

Dudley, J. T., & Butte, A. J. (2009). A Quick Guide for Developing Effective Bioinformatics Programming Skills. *PLoS Computational Biology, 5*(12), e1000589. doi:10.1371/journal.pcbi.1000589

Durbin, R., Eddy, S., Krogh, A., & Mitchison, G. (1998). *Biological Sequence Analysis: Probabilistic Models of Proteins and Nucleic Acids.* Cambridge, UK: Cambridge University Press. doi:10.1017/CBO9780511790492

Dyrløv Bendtsen, J., Nielsen, H., von Heijne, G., & Brunak, S. (2004). Improved Prediction of Signal Peptides: SignalP 3.0. [doi: DOI: 10.1016/j.jmb.2004.05.028]. *Journal of Molecular Biology, 340*(4), 783-795.

Edgar, R. C. (2004). MUSCLE: multiple sequence alignment with high accuracy and high throughput. *Nucleic Acids Research, 32*(5), 1792–1797.. doi:10.1093/nar/gkh340

Ellis, L. B. M., & Attwood, T. K. (2001). Molecular biology databases: today and tomorrow. [doi: DOI: 10.1016/S1359-6446(01)01802-5]. *Drug Discovery Today, 6*(10), 509-513.

Engel, S. R., Balakrishnan, R., Binkley, G., Christie, K. R., Costanzo, M. C., Dwight, S. S., et al. (2010). Saccharomyces Genome Database provides mutant phenotype data. *Nucl. Acids Res., 38*(suppl_1), D433-436. doi: 10.1093/nar/gkp917

Galperin, M. Y., & Cochrane, G. R. (2009). Nucleic Acids Research annual Database Issue and the NAR online Molecular Biology Database Collection in 2009. *Nucl. Acids Res., 37*(suppl_1), D1-4. doi: 10.1093/nar/gkn942

Gonda, D., Bachmair, A., Wunning, I., Tobias, J., Lane, W., & Varshavsky, A. (1989). Universality and structure of the N-end rule. *The Journal of Biological Chemistry, 264*, 16700–16712.

Guruprasad, K., Reddy, B., & Pandit, M. (1990). Correlation between stability of a protein and its dipeptide composition: a novel approach for predicting in vivo stability of a protein from its primary sequence. *Protein Engineering, 4*, 155–161. doi:10.1093/protein/4.2.155

Hammami, R., Ben Hamida, J., Vergoten, G., & Fliss, I. (2009). PhytAMP: a database dedicated to antimicrobial plant peptides. *Nucl. Acids Res., 37*(suppl_1), D963-968. doi: 10.1093/nar/gkn655

Hammami, R., Zouhir, A., Ben Hamida, J., & Fliss, I. (2007). BACTIBASE: a new web-accessible database for bacteriocin characterization. *BMC Microbiology, 7*, 89. doi:10.1186/1471-2180-7-89

Hammami, R., Zouhir, A., Le Lay, C., Ben Hamida, J., & Fliss, I. (2010). BACTIBASE second release: a database and tool platform for bacteriocin characterization. *BMC Microbiology, 10*(1), 22. doi:10.1186/1471-2180-10-22

Hammami, R., Zouhir, A., Naghmouchi, K., Ben Hamida, J., & Fliss, I. (2008). SciDBMaker: new software for computer-aided design of specialized biological databases. *BMC Bioinformatics, 9*(1), 121. doi:10.1186/1471-2105-9-121

Hamosh, A., Scott, A. F., Amberger, J. S., Bocchini, C. A., & McKusick, V. A. (2005). Online Mendelian Inheritance in Man (OMIM), a knowledgebase of human genes and genetic disorders. *Nucl. Acids Res., 33*(suppl_1), D514-517. doi: 10.1093/nar/gki033

Henryk, M., Russell, M., & Randolph, V. (1992). Statistical determination of the average values of the extinction coefficients of tryptophan and tyrosine in native proteins. *Analytical Biochemistry, 200*, 74–80. doi:10.1016/0003-2697(92)90279-G

Hingamp, P., van den Broek, A., Stoesser, G., & Baker, W. (1999). The EMBL nucleotide sequence database. [10.1385/MB:12:3:255]. *Molecular Biotechnology, 12*(3), 255-267.

Ikai, A. (1980). Thermostability and aliphatic index of globular proteins. *Journal of Biochemistry, 88*, 1895–1898.

Jack, K., & Russell, F. (1982). A simple method for displaying the hydropathic character of a protein. *Journal of Molecular Biology, 157*, 105–132. doi:10.1016/0022-2836(82)90515-0

Jagadish, H. V., & Olken, F. (2003). Database Management for Life Science Research: Summary Report of the Workshop on Data Management for Molecular and Cell Biology at the National Library of Medicine, Bethesda, Maryland, February 2–3, 2003. *OMICS: A Journal of Integrative Biology, 7*(1), 131-137. doi: doi:10.1089/153623103322006797

Köhler, J. (2004). Integration of life science databases. [doi: DOI: 10.1016/S1741-8364(04)02392-3]. *Drug Discovery Today: BIOSILICO, 2*(2), 61-69.

Krogh, A., Larsson, B., von Heijne, G., & Sonnhammer, E. L. L. (2001). Predicting transmembrane protein topology with a hidden markov model: application to complete genomes. [doi: DOI: 10.1006/jmbi.2000.4315]. *Journal of Molecular Biology, 305*(3), 567-580.

Labarga, A., Valentin, F., Anderson, M., & Lopez, R. (2007). Web Services at the European Bioinformatics Institute. *Nucl. Acids Res., 35*(suppl_2), W6-11. doi: 10.1093/nar/gkm291

Larkin, M., Blackshields, G., Brown, N., Chenna, R., McGettigan, P., & McWilliam, H. (2007). ClustalW and ClustalX version 2.0. *Bioinformatics (Oxford, England), 23*(21), 2947–2948. doi:10.1093/bioinformatics/btm404

Larkin, M. A., Blackshields, G., Brown, N. P., Chenna, R., McGettigan, P. A., & McWilliam, H. (2007). Clustal W and Clustal X version 2.0. *Bioinformatics (Oxford, England), 23*(21), 2947–2948..doi:10.1093/bioinformatics/btm404

Lawrence, C. J., Dong, O. F., Polacco, M. L., Seigfried, T. E., & Brendel, V. (2004). MaizeGDB, the community database for maize genetics and genomics. [Article]. *Nucleic Acids Research, 32*, D393–D397..doi:10.1093/nar/gkh011

Mangalam, H. (2002). The Bio* toolkits -- a brief overview. *Briefings in Bioinformatics, 3*(3), 296–302..doi:10.1093/bib/3.3.296

Moorhouse, M., & Barry, P. (2005). *The Sequence Retrieval System* (pp. 297–301). Bioinformatics Biocomputing and Perl.

NCBI. (2002, 01/03/2010). What's the Difference Between MEDLINE® and PubMed®. *Fact Sheet* Retrieved 30/03/2010, from http://www.nlm.nih.gov/pubs/factsheets/dif_med_pub.html

Notredame, C., Higgins, D. G., & Heringa, J. (2000). T-coffee: a novel method for fast and accurate multiple sequence alignment. [doi: DOI: 10.1006/jmbi.2000.4042]. *Journal of Molecular Biology, 302*(1), 205-217.

Page, R. D. (1996). TreeView: an application to display phylogenetic trees on personal computers. *Computer Applications in the Biosciences, 12*(4), 357–358.

Patrickios, C., & Yamasaki, E. (1995). Polypeptide amino acid composition and isoelectric point. *Analytical Biochemistry, 231*, 82–91. doi:10.1006/abio.1995.1506

Pearson, W. R., & Lipman, D. J. (1988). Improved tools for biological sequence comparison. *Proceedings of the National Academy of Sciences of the United States of America, 85*(8), 2444–2448. doi:10.1073/pnas.85.8.2444

Radzeka, A., & Wolfenden, R. (1988). Comparing the polarities of amino acids: side-chain distribution coefficients between vapor phase, cyclohexane, 1-octanol and neutral aqueous solution. *Biochemistry, 27*, 1664–1670. doi:10.1021/bi00405a042

Rice, P., Longden, I., & Bleasby, A. (2000). EMBOSS: the European Molecular Biology Open Software Suite. *Trends Genet, 16*(6), 276-277. doi: S0168-9525(00)02024-2 [pii]

Rodriguez-Tome, P. (1998). The BioCatalog. *Bioinformatics (Oxford, England), 14*(5), 469–470.. doi:10.1093/bioinformatics/14.5.469

Sali, A., & Blundell, T. L. (1993). Comparative protein modelling by satisfaction of spatial restraints. *J Mol Biol, 234*(3), 779-815. doi: S0022-2836(83)71626-8 [pii] 10.1006/jmbi.1993.1626

Schaefer, C. F. (2004). Pathway Databases. *Annals of the New York Academy of Sciences, 1020*(The Applications of Bioinformatics in Cancer Detection), 77-91.

Sussman, J. L., Lin, D., Jiang, J., Manning, N. O., Prilusky, J., Ritter, O., et al. (1998). Protein Data Bank (PDB): Database of Three-Dimensional Structural Information of Biological Macromolecules. *Acta Crystallographica Section D, 54*(6 Part 1), 1078-1084. doi: doi:10.1107/S0907444998009378

Tateno, Y., Fukami-Kobayashi, K., Miyazaki, S., Sugawara, H., & Gojobori, T. (1998). DNA Data Bank of Japan at work on genome sequence data. *Nucleic Acids Research, 26*(1), 16–20.. doi:10.1093/nar/26.1.16

Thomas, P. D., Campbell, M. J., Kejariwal, A., Mi, H., Karlak, B., & Daverman, R. (2003). PANTHER: A Library of Protein Families and Subfamilies Indexed by Function. *Genome Research, 13*(9), 2129–2141..doi:10.1101/gr.772403

Williams, A. L., Kersey, P. J., Pruess, M., & Apweiler, R. (2005). Biological Databases: Infrastructure, Content and Integration. In Francisco Azuaje, J. D. (Ed.), *Data Analysis and Visualization in Genomics and Proteomics* (pp. 11–28). doi:10.1002/0470094419.ch2

Wilson, R. J., Goodman, J. L., Strelets, V. B., & The FlyBase Consortium. (2008). FlyBase: integration and improvements to query tools. *Nucl. Acids Res., 36*(suppl_1), D588-593. doi: 10.1093/nar/gkm930

Wu, C. H., Yeh, L.-S. L., Huang, H., Arminski, L., Castro-Alvear, J., & Chen, Y. (2003). The Protein Information Resource. *Nucleic Acids Research, 31*(1), 345–347..doi:10.1093/nar/gkg040

Zdobnov, E. M., Lopez, R., Apweiler, R., & Etzold, T. (2002). The EBI SRS server--recent developments. *Bioinformatics (Oxford, England), 18*(2), 368–373..doi:10.1093/bioinformatics/18.2.368

KEY TERMS AND DEFINITIONS

Bioinformatics and Computational Biology: the science of managing, analysis, modeling, simulation and optimization of biological systems using advanced computing techniques.

Biological Pathways: a pathway is a causal sequence of molecular interactions or reactions forming mostly a network.

Data Warehousing: the process of designing, building, and maintaining a data warehouse system. The latter may be defined as a database constructed to allow efficient querying of the data it contains, possibly constructed from different primary data sources.

Fasta Format: a text-based format for representing either nucleic acid or protein sequences, in which base pairs or protein residues are represented using single-letter codes.

Genome: a full genetic complement of a cell or an organism including its DNA and RNA.

Genomics: the study of all the genes and how they interact with each other and the environment.

Hidden Markov Models (HMM): a popular statistical tool for modeling a wide range of sequential data. In bioinformatics, HMM based approaches have been applied to biological sequence analysis, as gene finding and protein family characterization.

Molecular Modeling: the science (or art) of representing molecular structures numerically and simulating their behavior with the equations of quantum and classical physics.

Multiple Sequence Alignment (MSA): refers to the process of aligning three or more biological sequences (protein, DNA, or RNA) to identify similarities between them.

Ontology: a system for representing complex information (concepts, relations, attributes, constraints, objects, values) that can be manipulated by a computer program.

Phylogenic Tree: a graphical representation of the evolutionary relationship between taxonomic groups based upon similarities and differences in their physical and/or genetic characteristics.

Proteomics: the systematic study of the entire complement of proteins (proteome) in a cell, tissue or organism.

Sequence Annotation: may be defined as the biological evaluation and explanation of a specific region on a nucleic acid or protein sequence that includes, but is not limited to, gene transcripts. Any feature that can be anchored to the sequence - for example, a mutation, a cut site, a start or stop signal, transcription factor binding site, or probe or primer binding site - is an annotation.

Sequence Homology: refers to the degree of similarity between biological sequences.

SQL Script: a text file containing SQL statements that can be executed in the database server.

Swiss-Prot Format: a text-based format for representing proteins with high level of annotations (such as the description of the function of a protein, its domain structure, post-translational modifications, variants, etc)

XML (eXtensible Markup Language): a web-dedicated data exchange language developed by the World Wide Web Consortium (W3C). In bioinformatics, XML is increasingly used within the last few years, and several XML based data formats have been developed (please see for(Achard, et al., 2001) review).

Chapter 16
Interactive Visualization Tool for Analysis of Large Image Databases

Anca Doloc-Mihu
Emory University, USA

ABSTRACT

Navigation and interaction are essential features for an interface that is built as a help tool for analyzing large image databases. A tool for actively searching for information in large image databases is called an Image Retrieval System, or its more advanced version is called an Adaptive Image Retrieval System (AIRS). In an Adaptive Image Retrieval System (AIRS) the user-system interaction is built through an interface that allows the relevance feedback process to take place. In this chapter, the author identifies two types of users for an AIRS: a user who seeks images whom the author refers to as an end-user, and a user who designs and researches the collection and the retrieval systems whom the author refers to as a researcher-user. In this context, she describes a new interactive multiple views interface for an AIRS (Doloc-Mihu, 2007), in which each view illustrates the relationships between the images from the collection by using visual attributes (colors, shapes, proximities). With such views, the interface allows the user (both end-user and researcher-user) a more effective interaction with the system, which, further, helps during the analysis of the image collection. The author's qualitative evaluation of these multiple views in AIRS shows that each view has its own limitations and benefits. However, together, the views offer complementary information that helps the user in improving his or her search effectiveness.

DOI: 10.4018/978-1-60960-102-7.ch016

INTRODUCTION

This chapter focuses on visualization techniques used by Web-based Adaptive Image Retrieval Systems to allow different users to efficiently navigate, search and analyze large image databases.

In a Web-based Adaptive Retrieval System, the goal is to answer as fast and accurate as possible with data (documents, images) that meet the user's request. Recent advances in Internet technology require the development of advanced Web-based tools for efficiently accessing images from tremendously large, and continuously growing, image collections. One such tool for actively searching for information is an Image Retrieval System. The aim of an Image Retrieval System is to retrieve images that are relevant to the user's request from a large image collection. In this task, the visualization component of the system is responsible for conveying this information to the user, which makes it a key component of the retrieval system.

An Adaptive Image Retrieval System (AIRS) consists of several components, one for each of the following tasks: processing, indexing, retrieval, learning, fusion, and visualization. An Adaptive Image Retrieval System is an Image Retrieval System that is able to automatically adapt to the user's needs. This adaptation could be performed in the system by using a learning component. The adaptive (learning) component is used in an image retrieval system as a solution to address the semantic gap problem, which is the difference between what the retrieval system can distinguish (low-level features describing the images) and what people perceive from images (high-level semantic concepts given as query images). Again, this information must be properly conveyed by the system to the user via its visualization component.

A variety of Image Retrieval Systems have been developed during the past decade of research, all having the same goal: to return images that are similar to the query according to the user's perception. These systems rely on different approaches for representing the contents of the image collection(s), such as content-based features (color, shape, texture, and layout), keywords, or both. For searching the collection, the user may specify either feature representations of images or entire image(s), called query-by-example approach, or both. The closeness between images (image semantics) is determined by the specific query that the user is asking. The process of query formulation is a ``conversational'' activity between the user and the system during which the meaning of an image is created (Santini, Gupta, & Ramesh, 1999). This user-system interaction process takes place through the visualization component or the system's interface. However, many of these image retrieval systems focus on improving the performance of their retrieval component and disregard the special custom visualization needs of a user, who is the main beneficiary of the system.

The research presented in this chapter describes several visualization techniques for two types of users of an AIRS: a user who seeks images whom we refer to as an end-user, and a user who designs and researches the collection and the retrieval systems whom we refer to as a researcher-user. The focus of this chapter is on interfaces that include multiple views, in which each view illustrates different relations between images at different levels of detail and can be selected by the users according to their informational needs. With such views, the interface allows user (end-user or researcher-user) more effective interaction with the system; by seeing more information about the request sent to the system as well as by better understanding of the results, the user is able to refine his/her query iteratively, which further improves significantly the retrieval results. We make a direct correspondence between the types of information needed by the different types of users and the visual information that is displayed for them. This correspondence will help us build an interface that reflects only as much detail as necessary for the user to get the appropriate content information that will help throughout the searching process.

It is known that the existing AIRSs are facing different problems, like the existing gap between concepts and representations, user subjectivity, etc. An interface tool such as the one we present in this work (Doloc-Mihu, Raghavan, Karnatapu, & Chu, 2005) can offer support in designing the retrieval system by helping the researcher-user understand the retrieval system, as well as the database with all existing relationships between the images. Therefore, it acts as a tool for image data exploration and analysis. Also, this interface allows user more interaction with the system by seeing more information about the request she or he sends to the system. Therefore, it can be used as a help tool for query formulation. For short, our visual interface supports retrieval and learning, as well as browsing, which makes it suitable for an Adaptive Image Retrieval System.

BACKGROUND

It is essential for an image retrieval system to communicate the information to users in the best possible way for the user to understand it. In this context, Croft (1995) pointed out that interfaces for image retrieval systems should support features like query formulation, feedback, and presentation of retrieved information. At the same time, "image retrieval systems must support users in locating the images want, quickly and easily" (Rodden, 2002).

There are many proposed interfaces for introducing the query: annotation based, selection of features and/or objects from provided lists, sketching the image, and selecting typical images of interest called query by example (see (Baeza-Yates, & Ribeiro-Neto, 1999; Rodden, 2002)). One way to present the results to the user is by visualizing the projections of images into a 2D or 3D space, where similar images are positioned closer to each other. Some systems proposed to organize images

into hierarchies (e.g., self-organizing maps (Kohonen, 1998) used in PicSOM). In these systems navigation through the data is restrictive because images are positioned at certain fixed distance in tree-like grids.

Pecenovic, Do, Vetterli, & Pu (2000) proposed a visualization approach based on the idea that dynamic and interactive visualizations of data combined with search by queries will help the user to retrieve the desired information. Rubner, Tomasi, & Guibas (1998b) have proposed to use a low-level content based similarity metric to create visualizations of sets of images. Thumbnails of the images are placed by using the multidimensional scaling (MDS) method (Shepard, 1962) on the display such that the distances on the screen reflect the real distances between the images as much as possible. Experiments (Pecenovic, Do, Vetterli, & Pu, 2000) show that users preferred the results displayed into 2D maps over the ones displayed in lists, with faster results achieved in the 2D maps layouts (Rubner, Tomasi, & Guibas, 1998a).

Recently, researchers (e.g., (Walker, Rummel, & Koedinger, 2009; Doloc-Mihu, 2007)) include in their systems an adaptive component, which has the role of automatically adapting the system to the specific user informational need. In our system (Doloc-Mihu, 2007), the adaptive component is based on supervised learning algorithms, which is combined with the relevance feedback method. Our AIRS uses the relevance feedback method as a solution for reducing the existing gap between the high-level semantic concepts existing in user's mind and expressed as queries, and the low-level features describing the images. Like many image retrieval systems, the system uses a query by example (QBE) approach, in which the query consists of a set of images (represented by color histograms) from the image database.

Motivation. Usually, the user-system interaction is built through an interface that allows the relevance feedback process to take place. Most image retrieval systems simply display the result list of images (or their thumbnails) to the user in a 2D grid (Veltkamp, & Tanase, 2000), without including any information about the relationships between images. This is referred to in this paper as the list view. However, an AIRS stores and manages different types of information about an image database such as images, their similarities, and their feature representations. As a result, there is a need for different views that display the information at different levels of detail and can be selected by different users according to their needs.

Enhancing the visualization of the query result is a valuable way of helping the user to satisfy their information needs. Therefore, there is a need for general purpose user interfaces for visual information retrieval that should include features like query refinement from examples. The interfaces should also include similarity display of the visual examples and of the results, and easy handling of the visual content. That is, there is a need for query refinement interfaces, which should allow iterative query refinement by relevance feedback from user in a perceptive way.

However, an interface has to provide only as much detail as necessary for the user to get the appropriate content information that will help throughout the searching process. Content information can help user understand new (or not seen) images by inferring the similarities between these images and the old (known, seen) images. By navigating through the visual information, the user can improve her or his mental image about the existing relationships between the data reflected in the query, which, in turn, will help the retrieval system to return results that better satisfy the user's request. In this context, a major challenge is how to visualize the relationships between images in order to make the contents of the digital libraries more accessible and manageable to users.

Another challenge in Image Retrieval is the user subjectivity. It is known that there are significant differences between the rankings produced for different users or even between two runs by the same user at different times for the same initial query.

In order to have an efficient and effective Web-based Adaptive Image Retrieval System, we need to have an interface capable to offer enough information to help user in his/her search. As stated in (Loupy, & Bellot, 2000), "human-system interaction (i.e., interface design and usage) should be taken into account. A system could receive a very high rating when it is evaluated by using precision/recall measures, but it might by not usable by users due to its efficiency or interface design." The needs discussed above motivate us to study different views for an interface for our AIRS system. Next, we briefly present the layouts of the views that we implemented so far in the system.

Layouts and algorithms. Our interface includes four types of views, each based on a certain layout and algorithm.

Kamada-Kawai (KK) (Kamada, & Kawai, 1989). Based on given distances between any two images from the database, the algorithm builds a general undirected weighted graph, where the length of an edge equals to the Euclidean distance between the two points, which in our system represent two images.

Force-Directed (FD) (Fruchterman, & Reingold, 1991). This algorithm builds an undirected graph with uniform edge lengths (no weights) for a multidimensional vector dataset. The method distributes the points evenly in the frame, with a nice spread layout.

Cluster. For clustering the result list of images, we use the K-means clustering algorithm (Lloyd, 1957), which groups them into k clusters, such that each image belongs to the cluster with the nearest mean. The algorithm splits the display surface into k parts, in which the group of points pertaining to the images from the respective cluster are displayed together very close to each other.

Parallel Coordinates (PC) (Inselberg, 1997). The algorithm provides a very simple representation of high dimensional vectors on a plane. A parallel coordinates visualization assigns one vertical axis to each feature (color in our case). All axes are parallel to each other, and equally spaced horizontally. Each feature is plotted on its own axis by using its frequency value, and the points from the adjacent axes are connected by straight lines. Thus, a point in a N- dimensional space becomes a polygonal line with N-1 lines connecting the N color frequencies. The order in which the axes are drawn is arbitrary. Thus, different orders can produce different representations. Next, we introduce our AIRS interface.

MULTIPLE VIEWS INTERFACE

An AIRS contains different types of information about an image database such as images, their similarities, and their feature representations. In addition, an AIRS is used by a person interested in finding images and/or information contained within a group of images from the database. Therefore, an AIRS should have an interface capable of handling all of these characteristics.

Inspired by the work done by Pecenovic and Rubner (Pecenovic, Do, Vetterli, & Pu, 2000; Rubner, Tomasi, & Guibas, 1998a) we build a multiple-view interface for our AIRS that provides four types of views: list view, graph views, cluster view, and histogram views, and where each view type presents a certain type of information. Whereas the list and histogram views display retrieval output in a traditional way, one displaying images and the other displaying feature (here, color) representations of these images, the graph and cluster views display structural representations of these images. Besides the views used by Pecenovic and Rubner we add the histogram views to our interface because we identify two types of users for our system: end-user and researcher-user. Each type of user has different needs which the system tries to satisfy by providing more detailed information about the database. For this, in the following we are identifying the need or the features that an interface for a Web-based AIRS should include, and then we present a multiple view interface that addresses them.

Necessary Interface Characteristics

We identify the "need", i.e. the requirements one should considerate when building an AIRS interface, as being given by the following four issues: the types of users, the types of information, the query formulation to allow for adaptation, and the general characteristics.

Different types of users. An AIRS is mainly used by two types of users, a user who seeks images whom we refer to as an end-user, and a user who designs and researches the database and the retrieval system whom we refer to as a researcher-user.

Different types of information. As both types of users seek for image information, their levels of information need differ. For example, the end-user searches for images as pictures (e.g., a person searching for images on the Internet), whereas a researcher needs detailed information about the representations of the images and the system (e.g., a person whose job is to maintain a digital image collection). That is, the end-user might be satisfied by a list view that includes the images themselves or their thumbnails, but the researcher-user needs views that include different relationships between images and/or image processing details.

As a result, there is a need for views that display the information at different levels of detail and can be selected by the users according to their needs. For this, we make a direct correspondence between the types of information needed by the different types of users and the visual information that is displayed for them.

First, the end-user who searches for a better query can use a list view or a graph view. Whereas the former ignores to display any existing relations between images, the latter is based on these relations. Actually, experiments (Pecenovic, Do, Vetterli, & Pu, 2000; Rubner, Tomasi, & Guibas, 1998b) show that users prefer the results displayed into graphs over the ones displayed in list views. Then, the designer or the researcher-user is a user that works effectively with the retrieval system

Figure 1. Conceptual views

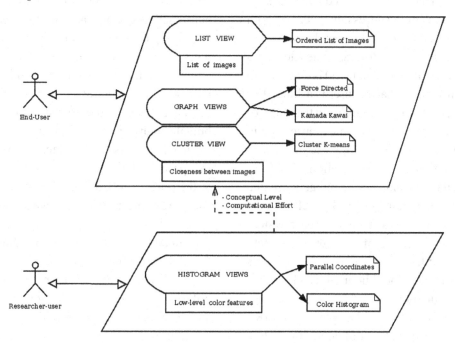

or with the image database. Therefore, an interface that provides detailed and accurate content information (such as histogram views) about the database and the retrieval process will facilitate this user's needs. Note that the researcher will try to see these images through the computer's ``eyes'', i.e. at the image processing level of detail.

Figure 1 illustrates the conceptual levels of our views and their corresponding types of users. Each view type is attached to a brief description of its layout, and the kind of algorithms used to build it. Our views are aimed at users with different informational needs, each type of need being satisfied by a particular view. In our vision, the AIRS interface acts as a researcher's tool or an end-user's tool depending on how the user defines him/herself at the moment of search. The interface allows users to switch between the multiple views at each step, and the choice depends on how much effort a user wants to put into this search process.

In Figure 1, our multiple views are organized hierarchically according to the level of information that they display. For example, if one makes

an analogy with a document organization, then at the top of the hierarchy is the list display, which provides a general overview (or contents) of the document. The graph views follow in the hierarchy, and act like an abstract by displaying the relationships between the images from the result list. The histogram views, which display detailed information about the image representations, are at the bottom of the hierarchy and correspond to the content of the document.

However, if we look at these layouts from another point of view, both list and histogram views are detailed and accurate layouts, because they display the information "as is" without considering any relationships between the images. On the other hand, graph displays are abstract (structured) and approximate layouts since they symbolize images and their relationships. Note that graph views display more information than the list views and less than the histogram views. Therefore, they can act as a bridge between the two conceptual levels and help user provide more clear requests, which in turn, will help the retrieval system to better satisfy user's needs. In this case, the graph views could address the needs of both types of users, end-user and research-user.

Query Formulation Process. The closeness between images (image semantics) is determined by the specific query that the user is asking. The meaning depends on the whole distribution of images in the database and on the metric used in the querying process. Therefore, the process of query formulation is a ``conversational'' activity during which the meaning of an image is created (Santini, Gupta, & Jain, 1999). By defining the meaning of an image as a result of the user-system interaction, the interface of the retrieval system becomes one of the most important components of the system, and should be used as a help tool for query formulation.

In very general terms, the role of an AIRS interface is to focus the user attention on certain relations between images that, given the current meaning, are relevant. The system interface could do this by displaying the relations between images according to the similarity criterion used to define the ``meaning'' or semantics of an image. The full meaning of an image depends not only on the image data, but also on the interpretation, i.e., the user perception of the image. Therefore, the query formulation should be seen as a process in which meaning is created through the interaction of the user and the images.

General Interface Characteristics. While we want to display more useful information for the user to be able to better satisfy his or her needs, we also want to keep the display as **simple** as possible. The reason is that a simple visual interface is always easier and faster to read than a more complex one. For this, in next section, we study the views with their benefits and limitations, in a concrete case.

Adaptive learning techniques are successfully applied to information retrieval systems. An AIRS is based on the relevance feedback method. By using a relevance feedback approach, the system tries to reduce the existing gap between the high-

level semantic concepts existing in user's mind and expressed as queries, and the low-level features describing the images. Many image retrieval systems use a query by example (QBE) approach, in which the query consists of a set of images (here, represented by color histograms) from the image database. Usually, the user-system interaction is built through an interface that allows the relevance feedback process to take place. However, during this process there is more information available to the retrieval system that is not revealed to the user via the interface. We believe that this information, if shown in a simple, meaningful way, can significantly help the user in building the query from his/her mind.

Note that in this chapter we are interested only in those characteristics that are specific to an interface for a Web-based AIRS used by a research-user (and an end-user) for the difficult task of analysis or image mining in very large image databases. In addition to these system specific characteristics mentioned in this section, of course, the AIRS interface should include, like any Web-based well constructed interface, several other general characteristics such as consistency of data display, flexibility for user control, compatibility with system information, etc. (complete guidelines given in (Shneiderman, & Plaisant, 2004, pp.63)), and should consider several usability factors (Lauesen, 2005, pp.24).

Multiple Views Interface

In this section, we describe an interface for the AIRS, proposed in (Doloc-Mihu, Raghavan, Karnatapu, & Chu, 2005; Doloc-Mihu, 2007), that includes multiple views and complies with the requirements given by the characteristics of the AIRS system, which we presented in previous section.

Interface Description. Figure 2 illustrates the interface before the user submits a query to the retrieval system. Precisely, it shows the user selection of the type of display for the search results.

Figure 2. Multiple views interface for AIRS (Doloc-Mihu, 2007). It shows the selection of the results displaying methods

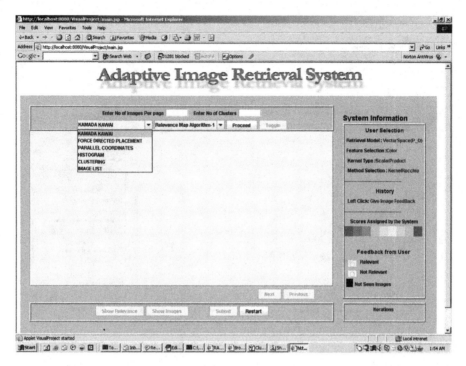

At the very beginning of the search, the user has to select the retrieval method he/she desires to use, and the learning algorithm the system will be using. These can be chosen from drop down lists, and are shown on our figure, on the left side panel as "User Selection".

In this AIRS interface, the screen surface is split into four main parts, as follows: The main section, which occupies the biggest surface of the screen (light grey color in Figure 2), displays the image information (result list) in the view with the layout selected by user. This section is surrounded at the top and bottom by two separate sections each containing buttons, text fields and selection lists, which allow user to input his/her display preferences and start querying the system. The "System Information" section on the left displays useful information for the user, such as his/her selection and system information, i.e., this is a "help" display that presents the history of the system.

As illustrated in Figure 2, there are six views available to the user for displaying the search results, images and/or information about them. The user can select to have the interface display the retrieval results in one (Figure 3, KK graph view) or multiple views (e.g., Figure 4, KK graph view and PC histogram view). Once the user makes his/her choices, by pressing the "Proceed" button he/she can start the search performed by the retrieval system. As the user presses "Submit" button, the system returns a new ranking of the whole image database, to which we refer to as the result list. Then, the system splits the new result list into several sublists and displays each sublist on a separate page display. The user must introduce the desired number of images to be shown per page display. Figure 3 illustrates a page display of twenty images in a graph view. The "Next" and "Previous" buttons for each display allow user to navigate through the results list page by page (Figure 3).

Figure 3. Graph view (Kamada-Kawai, 1989). Displays to 20 images with their relevance and feedback information

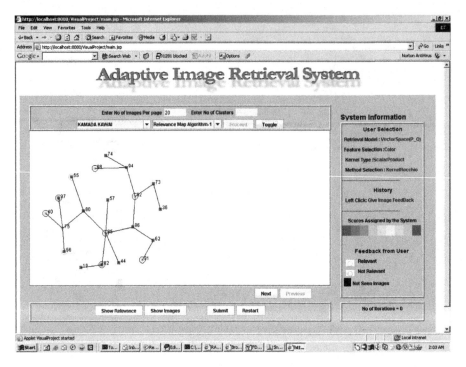

Figure 4. Choice of two views: Kamada-Kawai graph view and Parallel Coordinates histogram view. Both display the information for the same set of 20 result images after feedback

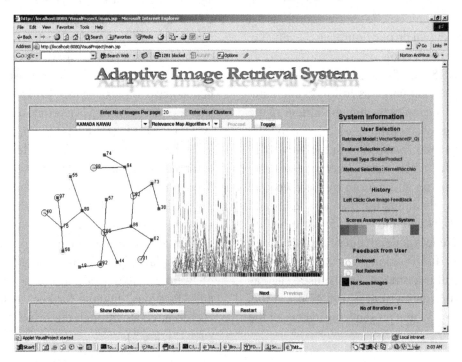

On each view of the proposed interface, each image is mapped to a node, which is depicted as a small rectangle, on the visualization map (Figure 3). The name of each image is also displayed next to each node (names are for example, "73. jpg" displayed as "73"). The relationships between images are reflected by the spatial arrangements and by the colors of these nodes on the map. Any node in the visualization can be selected (click on the image point/rectangle), causing the image that it refers to, to be returned in a window, in which the user can enter his or her feedback (relevant or non-relevant).

Our interface includes six views: a standard list view, also called grid view in the literature (Rodden, 2002), two graphs views, a clustering view, and two histogram views. The user can switch at any moment between these different displays by pressing the "Toggle" button.

- *List view.* The list view is currently used by most of the image retrieval systems (Rodden, 2002; Cox, Miller, Minka, Papathomas, & Yianilos, 2000; Campbell, 2000; Combs, & Bederson, 1999). This view displays all images or their thumbnails, without any inside information about the relationships between images.
- *Cluster view.* The cluster view displays the rectangles associated with the images in groups or clusters, such that images within a group are considered as similar to each other, and images from two groups are considered not similar. This view resembles the graph view, but image rectangles are not connected by any lines.
- *Graph views.* The graph views denote the images as small rectangles on a 2D plane, based on distances between images, with the closest two images connected through an edge by using KK or FD algorithm. Each such rectangle has dynamic coordinates (that change from an iteration to the next iteration) and an action associated

with it. When the mouse passes over the image rectangle, a left click on the colored rectangle pops-up a window for user feedback of the respective image.

- *Histogram views.* The histogram views, where we include the histogram and the parallel coordinates views, present the image at a low-level, at the feature representation (colors, here) level. By relying on the features representing the images, these layouts display very detailed and accurate views of the relationships between images.

These views are presented in detail in our previous work (Doloc-Mihu, 2007). Next, we present the information visualized through these views.

Visualizing Relationships between Images. A way to reduce the gap between the user's high-level concepts (queries) and the system's low-level knowledge is to help the user understand and perform better query search. For this, association of color, shape and proximity can be used to increase the amount of information to display. Since users perceive these visual attributes very easily, they can be used together to communicate more information to the user faster. Therefore, by associating these visual attributes we can display both relevance judgments, given by the system and by the user, of an image with respect to a query.

In our interface, we represent the similarity information between images from the result list at each feedback step by using color, shape, and position attributes. By positioning the images (their associated points or rectangles) in a meaningful way on the screen, the user can get a feeling of their closeness with respect to the given query. As a result, we get a spatial arrangement of images based on correlations between them (Figure 3). In the following, we describe how we associate relevance assessments to visual elements in our interface.

Shape *symbolizes the relevance provider.* In AIRS, we deal with two types of relevances: one coming from the user as feedback, and the other one coming from the system as a result of the retrieval process. To differentiate between the two providers we use circles for the user and rectangles for the system (for e.g., nodes 73 and 37 in Figure 3 reflect both types of relevances).

Color *symbolizes the relevance attribute.* Our interface reflects the degree of relevance for each relevance provider separately, by using color, as follows:

- *"Temperature" like colormap for system relevance.* Our display is a 2D plane where small colored rectangles, that symbolize images, are filled with a color that symbolizes the image's relevance to the query, given by the system. For the first display, all images are "not relevant" and are displayed with the same color (i.e., black). Then, the color of the rectangle is dynamically determined by the system at each feedback step based on the image's rank in the results' list. Therefore, the colors of the rectangles act as a relevance color map returned by the system. Note that some images might share the same color (for e.g., nodes 55 and 94 in Figure 3), which means that the retrieval system ranked them very close to each other with respect to the given query.

- *Green/brown colors for user relevance.* Initially, all images are in a random order as there is no feedback from the user (no circle surrounding the rectangle). Once the user gives feedback on an image, his or her relevance is illustrated as a circle surrounding the image rectangle. A brown circle shows a non-relevant image, whereas a green one stands for a relevant image (e.g., nodes 37, and 73 in Figure 3, respectively). Therefore, we represent the user relevance of each image to a given request by using color.

Position *(edges) symbolizes proximities between images.* The display distances are based on the similarities between images and not on the user's query. To display the images on a plane, algorithms for placement of points on a plane are used (Force-Directed and Kamada-Kawai algorithms), based on Euclidian distances between the images. Both algorithms build a MST (minimum spanning tree) for a set of given points and displays them on the screen (see Figure 3). Therefore, both layouts use edges to show the closeness between two images. While in Kamada-Kawai graph the length of an edge shows the closeness between the two images (the shorter the edge, the closer the two images), in Force-Directed graph the length of an edge has no particular significance, as it is calculated by the algorithm such that the images (their points on the screen) are nicely spread, without overlapping.

To summarize, we represent the relevance of each image to a given request by using its color and its arrangement on the plane. Further, we distinguish the different relevances by using different shapes, such as a rectangle for the system relevance resulting from the learning process and a circle for user's preference. By doing this, the user can see the differences (if any) between the two (system's relevance versus his or her own relevance). In other words, the association of the visual attributes can suggest an image as being relevant to user's query in two ways: as found by the retrieval system, and, in the same time, as being not seen by user or seen by him/her with its corresponding feedback. Next, we describe how to obtain the colors for the rectangles.

Building the Colormap. We use a temperature map display to present to the user the system ranking of images according to his or her feedback. For this, we use 9 colors, ranging from red (as a most relevant image) to pastel-pink and white for less relevant images, and from pastel-blue for the non-relevant images with a higher rank to blue for the non-relevant images with lower rank (shown in the right panel of Figure 2).

At each feedback step, the system reads all ranking (ordered) values returned by the system. The idea is to divide their range interval (the [max *Rank*, min *Rank*] interval) in sub-intervals and to assign the colors within these sub-intervals. There are two ways to assign the colors. The first method splits the ranking interval into pages, and then each page is considered to be a full colormap that is further divided into 9 equal sub-intervals. The second method divides the ranking interval into 9 equal sub-intervals to which the colors are assigned, and then each sub-interval is split into pages. Note that the only difference between the two algorithms lies in the number of images the system considers while assigning the colors. The user can choose either algorithm by selecting the corresponding name from the algorithm list with two choices "Relevance Map Algorithm1" or "Relevance Map Algorithm2" (see Figure 2).

Several text retrieval systems use the spatial proximity to communicate to user the similarity/dissimilarity between documents, like (Leuski & Allan, 2000), for example. However, very few image retrieval systems support this kind of feature. Systems like (Rubner, Tomasi, & Guibas, 1998a; Rodden, 2002), El Nino (Santini & Jain, 2000), PicSOM (Oja, Laaksonen, Koskela, & Brandt, 1999) use PCA, MDS or SOM methods for showing the proximity between images, but none of them uses the force directed graphs that it is used by Doloc-Mihu (2007). Moreover, the latter associates color, shape and proximity attributes to communicate more information about images to user.

Discussion on the Multiple Views AIRS Interface. All views reflect semantic information at different levels of abstraction through a visual layout. To help the user, this visual layout must be easily readable. The more crowded a display is, the more difficult it is for a user to distinguish between the points and to select the desired images for feedback.

Herman et al. (2000) pointed out some existing visualization problems, encountered especially when dealing with graphs, such as planarity, predictability, time complexity, density, overlapping, and the size of the image list to be displayed. We do not address these layout problems here, but we simply identify which of them exist in our views. Additionally, we try to understand how this interface helps the user in building a better query, and what differences exist between the multiple views.

In our example views, we noticed the following factors that influence the crowdedness of our layouts: overlapping colors, overlapping edges, crossing edges, number of images per page, and the number of features per page for the histogram views. Next, we compare our views along these factors (Doloc-Mihu, 2007).

Overlapping colors. Notice that in our example this factor does not appear in the histogram and list views, it can sometimes occur in the FD graph view, and it can happen in KK, cluster, and PC views quite frequently. In the latter, we can have two or more images within the same relevance interval, i.e., with the same color, which makes it difficult for the user to say which line (or rectangle) pertains to which of these images.

Overlapping edges. There may be some overlapping edges in KK graph view and more often in PC view between different string lines (or images). In the PC view, the overlapping edges is a desired factor, but it makes the layout not readable if the number of images is too big. This is not an issue for the list, histogram and cluster views, as they do not include edges.

Crossing edges. This factor is not an issue for the list, cluster, and the histogram displays, but the PC view is based on it for comparing images. While both graph algorithms display the same MST, when comparing them, one can easily notice that KK displays edges without too much distortion, while FD does have a nice display without any edge weight consideration (DOloc-Mihu, 2007), but with more spread nodes and less crossing edges. Although KK algorithm reproduces the real closeness between images as the shortest path between them, this information might be difficult to read due to the number of the crossing edges.

Number of images. Another reason for a crowded display is the number of the displayed images. Whereas all views depend on this factor, their maximum limits differ. Out of all views the PC view requires the smallest number of images for a nice layout. This happens maybe due to the nature of the image histograms. We also found that a list view can display maximum around 200 images per page. The histogram view showed a similar limitation. However, the graph and cluster views seem to be able to display many images per page (we tried successfully with a maximum of 1000 images).

Number of features (colors). This factor is characteristic only to the histogram views (Figure 4), as the other views do not display images at the feature level. We notice that there is a trade-off between the user and the system desired number of features (colors). Whereas a small number is not enough for representing an image due to loosing the discrimination power, it will be easier for user to see its representation. Also, as colors are displayed quite small due to the window size limitation, a larger number of colors will result in an even more crowded display. This shows that there is a trade-off between the user visual limitation and the computer visual limitation.

Why Multiple Views Interface for an AIRS? As we can see from the above discussion, each view presents problems and benefits. But the limitations posed by one view can be compensated by another view, i.e., the views offer complementary information from which the user can benefit.

By displaying both images and different statistics for these images, our interface aims to be a better tool for user to give feedback. By bringing up the information from all previous steps, the interface helps user to decide the next step in query building. Based on the new and old information the user is able to decide how to change the query in order to satisfy his or her need. At each retrieval step, the re-organization needed

relative to a subsequent user interaction involves the whole database. Some images will disappear from the display, and some will appear. But, the views display the relevances (given by the user and by the system) by using visual attributes that help the user understand the relationships between the images.

To build an AIRS is a difficult task by itself. Thus, if we can provide a tool to help user understand the system problems and limitations (and communicate them to the user), it will be like a next step in a further improvement of the system. It is known that the existing AIRSs are facing different problems, like the existing gap between concepts and representations, user subjectivity, etc. Therefore, an interface tool such as the one we propose can offer support in designing the system. This type of interface can help user understand the retrieval system, as well as the database with all existing relationships between the images. Therefore, it acts as a tool for image data exploration and analysis.

CONCLUSION

In this chapter, we have described an interactive multiple views interface for a Web-based AIRS, in which each view displays different information required by users according to their informational needs (end-user or researcher-user). The users of the proposed interface have an active role in exploring the semantics of an image. For a better user-system interaction, the views of the interface are dynamically clickable.

Our interface illustrates different relations between images by using visual attributes (colors, shape, and proximities). With such views, the user can see the relationships between images, as well as better understand the results, and how to refine the query iteratively. The interface allows user more interaction with the system by seeing more information about the request she or he sends to the system. Therefore, it can be used as a help tool for query formulation. For short, our interface supports retrieval and learning, as well as browsing, which makes it suitable for an Adaptive Image Retrieval System.

The qualitative evaluation of these multiple views (Doloc-Mihu, 2007) in an AIRS shows that all views present limitations and benefits. However, the views offer complementary information that helps user in his or her search. Our work in progress deals with scalability issues posed by each view. Also, we are investigating other types of views that could bring new types of information about the images to the user.

The study presented in this chapter provides a framework within which future experiments can be carried out to understand how well the views are deployed. Future work includes evaluation of the visual interface in the query formulation process. Additional user studies are necessary to establish the usability of the multiple views and for further improvements of the interface.

REFERENCES

Baeza-Yates, R., & Ribeiro-Neto, B. (1999). *Modern Information Retrieval*. New York: Addison-Wesley.

Campbell, I. (2000). Interactive evaluation of the Ostensive Model using a new test collection of images with multiple relevance assessments. *Journal of Information Retrieval, 2*(1), 85–112.

Combs, T. T. A., & Bederson, B. B. (1999). Does zooming improve image browsing? In *Proceedings of Digital Libraries* (pp. 130–137). New York: Association of Computing Machinery.

Cox, I. J., Miller, M. L., Minka, T. P., Papathomas, T. V., & Yianilos, P. N. (2000). The Bayesian Image Retrieval System, PicHunter: Theory, implementation, and psychophysical experiments. *IEEE Transactions on Image Processing, 9*(1), 20–37. doi:10.1109/83.817596

Croft, W. B. (1995). What do people want from information retrieval? *D-Lib Magazine.*

de Loupy, C., & Bellot, P. (2000). Evaluation of document retrieval systems and query difficulty. In *Using Evaluation within HLT Programs: Results and Trends*, Athens, Greece, (pp. 34-40).

Del Bimbo, A. (2001). *Visual Information Retrieval*. San Francisco, CA: Morgan Kaufmann Publishers, Inc.

Doloc-Mihu, A. (2007). *Adaptive Image Retrieval System: Similarity modeling, Learning, Fusion, and Visualization*. Doctoral dissertation, University of Louisiana at Lafayette, Louisiana.

Doloc-Mihu, A., Raghavan, V., Karnatapu, S., & Chu, C. H. H. (2005). Interface for visualization of image database in Adaptive Image Retrieval Systems. In *Visualization and Data Analysis (VDA05), Proceedings of SPIE-IS&T Electronic Imaging, SPIE* (vol.5669, pp. 382-393).

Fruchterman, T.M.J., & Reingold, E.M. (1991). Graph drawing by Force-directed Placement. *software - Practice and Experience, 21*, 1129-1164.

Herman, I., Melancon, G., & Marshall, M. S. (2000). Graph visualization and navigation in Information Visualization: a survey. *IEEE Transactions on Visualization and Computer Graphics, 6*, 1–21. doi:10.1109/2945.841119

Inselberg, A. (1997). Multidimensional detective. In *IEEE Symposium of Information Visualization*, (pp.100-107). Washington, DC: IEEE Computer Society.

Kamada, T., & Kawai, S. (1989). An algorithm for drawing general undirected graphs. *Information Processing Letters, 31*, 7–15. doi:10.1016/0020-0190(89)90102-6

Kohonen, T. (1998). Self-Organization of very large document collections: State of the art. In *Proceedings of the 8th International Conference on Artificial Neural Networks, ICANN'98*, (vol. 1, pp. 65-74).

Lauesen, S. (2005). *User interface design – A software engineering perspective*. Harlow, UK: Addison-Wesley.

Leuski, A., & Allan, J. (2000). Improving interactive retrieval by combining ranked lists and clustering. In *Proceedings of RIAO,* (pp. 665-681).

Lloyd, S. P. (1957). Least square quantization in PCM. *IEEE Transactions on Information Theory*, *28*(2), 129–137. doi:10.1109/TIT.1982.1056489

Oja, E., Laaksonen, J., Koskela, M., & Brandt, S. (1999). Self-Organizing Maps for Content-based Image Database Retrieval. In *Kohonen Maps* (pp. 349–362). Amsterdam: Elsevier. doi:10.1016/B978-044450270-4/50028-0

Pecenovic, Z., Do, M. N., Vetterli, M., & Pu, P. (2000). Integrated browsing and searching of large image collections. In *Proceedings of the 4th Intl. Conf. on Visual Information Systems (VISUAL)*, (pp.279-289).

Rodden, K. (2002). *Evaluating similarity-based visualizations as interfaces for image browsing*. Doctoral dissertation, University of Cambridge, Cambridge, UK.

Rubner, Y., Tomasi, C., & Guibas, L. J. (1998a). Adaptive color-image embeddings for database navigation. In *Proceedings of the Asian Conference on Computer Vision*, (pp. 104-111). Washington, DC: IEEE.

Rubner, Y., Tomasi, C., & Guibas, L. J. (1998b). A metric for distributions with applications to image databases. In *Proceedings of the 6th IEEE International Conference on Computer Vision*, (pp.59-66).

Santini, S., Gupta, A., & Jain, R. (1999). A user interface for emergent semantics in image databases. In *Proceedings of the 8th IFIP Working Conference on Database Semantics (DS-8)*, (pp.123-143).

Santini, S., & Jain, R. (2000). Integrated browsing and querying for image databases. *IEEE MultiMedia*, *7*(3), 26–39. doi:10.1109/93.879766

Shepard, R. N. (1962). The analysis of proximities: Multidimensional scaling with an unknown distance function. *Psychometrika*, *27*, 125–140. doi:10.1007/BF02289630

Shneiderman, B., & Plaisant, C. (2004). *Designing the user interface. University of Maryland*. College Park, MD: Addison-Wesley.

Veltkamp, R. C., & Tanase, M. (2000). *Content-Based Image Retrieval Systems: A survey*. Ultrecht University, UU-CS-2000-34. Retrieved from http://www.aa-lab.cs.uu.nl/cbirsurvey/cbir-survey/

Walker, E., Rummel, N., & Koedinger, K. R. (2009). A research framework for providing adaptive collaborative learning support. *User Modeling and User-Adapted Interaction*, *19*(5), 387–431. doi:10.1007/s11257-009-9069-1

Wikipedia. (2010). *Information visualization*. Retrieved January 17, 2010, from http://en.wikipedia.org/wiki/Information_visualization#cite_note-MF08-0

KEY TERMS AND DEFINITIONS

Adaptive Image Retrieval System: An image retrieval system that is able to automatically adapt to the user's informational needs.

Content-Based Image Retrieval: (CBIR), also known as **Content-Based Visual Information Retrieval (CBVIR)**: Similar to image retrieval for the case when the search will be entirely based on the actual contents of the image, which can be derived from the image itself, such as colors, shapes, textures, and so on.

Image Retrieval System: A software tool used to perform the image retrieval task, which is browsing, searching and retrieving images from a large database of digital images.

Image Retrieval: Science of searching and retrieving images from a large database of digital images (Del Bimbo, 2001).

Information Visualization: The interdisciplinary study of "the visual representation of large-scale collections of non-numerical information, such as files and lines of code in software systems, library and bibliographic databases, networks of relations on the internet, and so forth" (Wikipedia, 2010).

Interactivity: Characteristics of a software tool, which accepts and responds to input from humans—for example, data or commands. Interactive software includes most popular programs, such as word processors or spreadsheet applications. This interactivity is achieved in an image retrieval system via an interface.

Relevance Feedback: An interactive technique, in which the user judges the search results after each step and then the system uses this feedback information to come up with results that will better satisfy the user's informational needs. This is a feature of some information retrieval and some image retrieval systems.

Chapter 17
Supercomputers and Supercomputing

Jeffrey Scott Cook
Arkansas State University, USA

ABSTRACT

What is a Supercomputer? A Supercomputer is defined as the fastest type of computer used for specialized applications that require a massive number of mathematical calculations. The term "supercomputer" was coined in 1929 by the New York World, referring to tabulators manufactured by IBM. To modern computer users, these tabulators would probably appear awkward, slow, and cumbersome to use, but at the time, they represented the cutting edge of technology. This continues to be true of supercomputers today, which harness immense processing power so that they are incredibly fast, sophisticated, and powerful.

INTRODUCTION

The primary use for supercomputers is in scientific computing, which requires high-powered computers to perform complex calculations. Scientific organizations boast supercomputers the size of rooms for the purpose of performing calculations, rendering complex formulas, and performing other tasks which require a formidable amount of computer power.

Design

Supercomputers tradionally gained their speed over conventional computers through the use of innovative designs that allow them to perform many tasks in parallel, as well as complex detail engineering. They tend to be specialized for certain types of computation, usually numerical calculations, and perform poorly at more general computing tasks. Their memory hierarchy is very carefully designed to ensure the processor is kept

DOI: 10.4018/978-1-60960-102-7.ch017

fed with data and instructions at all times—in fact, much of the performance difference between slower computers and supercomputers is due to the memory hierarchy design and componentry. Their I/O systems tend to be designed to support high bandwidth, with latency less of an issue, because supercomputers are not used for transaction processing.

Supercomputer Challenges and Technologies

- A supercomputer generates heat and must be cooled. Cooling most supercomputers is a major High Voltage Alternating Current problem.
- Information cannot move faster than the speed of light between two parts of a supercomputer. For this reason, a supercomputer that is many meters across must have latencies between its components measured at least in the tens of nanoseconds. Seymour Cray's Cray supercomputer designs attempted to keep cable runs as short as possible for this reason.
- Supercomputers consume and produce massive amounts of data in a very short period of time. Much work is needed to ensure that this information can be transferred quickly and stored/retrieved correctly. Technologies developed for supercomputers include:
  - Vector processing
  - Liquid cooling
  - NUMA (Non-Uniform Memory Access)
  - Striped disks (the first instance of what was later called RAID, Redundant Array of Independent Disks)
  - Parallel file systems

In many cases, a supercomputer is custom-assembled, utilizing elements from a range of computer manufacturers and tailored for its intended use. Most supercomputers run on a Linux® or Unix® operating system, as these operating systems are extremely flexible, stable, and efficient.

Supercomputers typically have multiple processors and a variety of other technological tricks to ensure that they run smoothly. One of the biggest concerns with running a supercomputer is cooling. As one might imagine, supercomputers get extremely hot as they run, requiring complex cooling systems to ensure that no part of the computer fails. Many of these cooling systems take advantage of liquid gases, which can get extremely cold. Danish company Dynamics has invented the coolest (in both senses) CPU cooler ever. It achieves this not with boring old moving air, or even dull H2O. No, the LM10 uses liquid metal: Think T1000 in your PC. Danamics claims that the cooler is more efficient than just pumping water over the components. (Danamics Technology, 2010) Unfortunately, the site only mentions "liquid metal" and not any specific kind of metal. Chemistry tells us that there are five metallic elements which are liquid at room temperature:

Rubidium (melting point 39 °C, 102 °F)
Francium (27 °C, 81 °F)
Mercury (−39 °C, −38 °F)
Caesium (28 °C, 83 °F)
Gallium (30 °C, 86 °F)

For cooling purposes, it looks like mercury would be best suited as it can get colder without solidifying. (Danamics Technology, 2010). Can anybody tell us if liquid metal is both a better conductor of heat and also more able to suck up and store that heat?

The actual pump mechanism is interesting, too. Instead of propellers or impellers, the metal is moved by electromagnetic induction. Danamics Corporation claims, again without details, that its "patent pending multi-string electromagnetic pump" will use a lot less power than conventional electromagnetic pumps. (Danamics Technology, 2010).

Another issue is the speed at which information can be transferred or written to a storage device, as the speed of data transfer will limit the supercomputer's performance.

The chief difference between a supercomputer and a mainframe is that a supercomputer channels all its power into executing a few programs as fast as possible, whereas a mainframe uses its power to execute many programs concurrently.

Special Purpose Supercomputers

Special-purpose supercomputers are high-performance computing devices with a hardware architecture dedicated to a single problem. This allows the use of specially programmed Field-programmable gate array chips or even custom Very Large Scale Integration (VLSI) chips, allowing higher price/performance ratios by sacrificing generality. They are used for applications such as astrophysics computation and brute-force code breaking. Historically a new special-purpose supercomputer has occasionally been faster than the world's fastest general-purpose supercomputer, by some measure. For example, GRAPE-6 was faster than the Earth Simulator in 2002 for a particular special set of problems.

Examples of Special-Purpose Supercomputers:

- Belle, Deep Blue, and Hydra, for playing chess (Wapedia, 2010)
- Reconfigurable computing machines or parts (Wapedia, 2010)
- GRAPE, for astrophysics and molecular dynamics (Wapedia, 2010)
- MDGRAPE-3, for protein structure computation (Wapedia, 2010)
- D.E. Shaw Research Anton, for simulating molecular dynamics (Wapedia, 2010)

The National Security Agency (NSA) J.I.Nelson (Nelson, 2010) supercomputer center contains the largest accumulation of computer power in any one building on Earth. One Cray Triton supercomputer at the facility can handle 64 billion instructions per second. The National Aeronautics and Space Administration (NASA) boasts it's supercomputer named "Columbia" which is comprised of an integrated cluster of 20 interconnected SGI® Altix® 512-processor systems, for a total of 10,240 Intel® Itanium® 2 processors, Columbia (named after the Columbia shuttle disaster) was built and installed at the National Aeronautics and Space Administration (NASA) Advanced Supercomputing facility at Ames, Iowa in less than 120 days. (Dunbar, 2009).

Supercomputers are very expensive and are employed for specialized applications that require immense amounts of mathematical calculations. Supercomputers are called upon to perform the most compute-intensive tasks of modern times. As supercomputers have developed in the last 30 years, so have the tasks they typically perform. Modeling of real world complex systems such as fluid dynamics, weather patterns, seismic activity prediction, and nuclear explosion dynamics represent the most modern adaptations of supercomputers. Other tasks include human genome sequencing, credit card transaction processing, and the design and testing of modern aircraft. With the incredibly large amounts of data being produced daily and retrieval of data from data bases makes the need for supercomputers in high demand.

Today's fastest supercomputers include IBM's Blue Gene and ASCI Purple, SCC's Beowulf, and Cray's SV2. These supercomputers are usually designed to carry out specific tasks. For example, IBM's ASCI Purple is a $250 million supercomputer built for the Department of Energy (DOE). This computer, with a peak speed of 467 teraflops, is used to simulate aging and the operation of nuclear weapons.

A Brief Look at Measuring Supercomputer Speed

Processing speeds supercomputer computational power is rated in FLOPS (Floating Point Operations Per Second). The first commercially available supercomputers reached speeds of 10 to 100 million FLOPS (Super Computers, 2009). The next generation of supercomputers (some of which are presently in the early stages of development) is predicted to break the petaflop level. This would represent computing power more than 1,000 times faster than a teraflop machine. To put these processing speeds in perspective, a relatively old supercomputer such as the Cray C90 (built in the mid to late 1990s) has a processing speed of only 8 gigaflops. It can solve a problem, which takes a personal computer a few hours, in .002 seconds!

Supercomputer Architecture

Supercomputer design varies from model to model. Generally, there are vector computers and parallel computers. Vector computers use a very fast data "pipeline" to move data from components and memory in the computer to a central processor. Parallel computers use multiple processors, each with their own memory banks, to 'split up' data intensive tasks. A good analogy to contrast vector and parallel computers is that a vector computer could be represented as a single person solving a series of 20 math problems in consecutive order; while a parallel computer could be represented as 20 people, each solving one math problem in the series. Even if the single person (vector) were a master mathematician, 20 people would be able to finish the series much quicker.

Other major differences between vector and parallel processors include how data is handled and how each machine allocates memory. A vector machine is usually a single super-fast processor with the entire computer's memory allocated to its operation. A parallel machine has multiple processors, each with its own memory. Vector machines

are easier to program, while parallel machines, with data from multiple processors (in some cases greater than 10,000 processors), can be tricky to orchestrate. To continue the analogy, 20 people working together (parallel) could have trouble with communication of data between them, whereas a single person (vector) would entirely avoid these communication complexities. Recently, parallel vector computers have been developed to take advantage of both designs.

Vector Computers

A vector computer or vector processor is a machine designed to efficiently handle arithmetic operations on elements of arrays, called vectors. Such machines are especially useful in high-performance scientific computing, where matrix and vector arithmetic are quite common. The Cray Y-MP and the Convex C3880 are two examples of vector processors used today.

Parallel Computers: Parallel computing is a form of computation in which many calculations are carried out simultaneously, operating on the principle that large problems can often be divided into smaller ones, which are then solved concurrently ("in parallel"). There are several different forms of parallel computing: bit-level, instruction level, data, and task parallelism.

Bit-Level: is a form of parallel computing based on increasing processor word size. From the advent of very-large-scale integration (VLSI) computer chip fabrication technology in the 1970s until about 1986, advancements in computer architecture were done by increasing bit-level parallelism Increasing the word size reduces the number of instructions the processor must execute in order to perform an operation on variables whose sizes are greater than the length of the word. (For example, consider a case where an 8-bit processor must add two 16-bit integers. The processor must first add the 8 lower-order bits from each integer, and then add the 8 higher-order bits, requiring two instructions to complete a single operation.

A 16-bit processor would be able to complete the operation with single instruction).

Instruction Level: is a measure of how many of the operations in a computer program can be performed simultaneously.

Data Parallelism: (also known as loop-level parallelism) is a form of parallelization of computing across multiple processors in parallel computing environments. Data parallelism focuses on distributing the data across different parallel computing nodes. It contrasts to task parallelism as another form of parallelism.

Task Parallelism: (also known as **function parallelism** and **control parallelism**) is a form of parallelization of computer code across multiple processors in parallel computing environments. Task parallelism focuses on distributing execution processes (threads) across different parallel computing nodes. It contrasts to data parallelism as another form of parallelism.

Parallelism has been employed for many years, mainly in high-performance computing, but interest in it has grown lately due to the physical constraints preventing frequency scaling. As power consumption (and consequently heat generation) by computers has become a concern in recent years, parallel computing has become the dominant paradigm in computer architecture, mainly in the form of multicore processors.

Data-Intensive Supercomputing or DISK

Google and its competitors have created a new class of large-scale computer systems to support Internet search. These "Data-Intensive Super Computing" (DISC) systems differ from conventional supercomputers in their focus on data: they acquire and maintain continually changing data sets, in addition to performing large-scale computations over the data.

As we discussed earlier, the massive amounts of data arising from such diverse sources as telescope imagery, medical records, online transaction records, and web pages, DISC systems have the potential to achieve major advances in science, health care, business efficiencies, and information access. DISC opens up many important research topics in system design, resource management, programming models, parallel algorithms, and applications. The following applications come from very different fields, but they share in common the central role of data in their computation (Grider et al., 2010).

1. **Web search without language barriers.** The user can type a query in any (human) language. The engine retrieves relevant documents from across the worldwide web in all languages and translates them into the user's preferred language. Key to the translation is the creation of sophisticated statistical language models and translation algorithms. The language model must be continuously updated by crawling the web for new and modified documents and recomputing the model. By this means, the translation engine will be updated to track newly created word patterns and idioms, such as "improvised explosive devices."

    Google already demonstrated the value of applying massive amounts of computation to language translation in the 2005 National Institute of Standards and Technology (NIST) machine translation competition. They won all four categories of the competition in the first year they entered, translating Arabic to English and Chinese to English. Their approach was purely statistical. They trained their program using, among other things, multilingual United Nations documents comprising over 200 billion words, as well as English-language documents comprising over one trillion words. No one in their machine translation group knew either Chinese or Arabic. During the competition, they applied the collective power of 1000 processors to perform the translation.

2. **Inferring biological function from genomic sequences**. Increasingly, computational biology involves comparing genomic data from different species and from different organisms of the same species to determine how information is encoded in DNA. Ever larger data sets are being collected as new sequences are discovered, and new forms of derived data are computed. The National Center for Biotechnology Innovation (NCBI) maintains the Embank database of nucleotide sequences, which has been doubling in size every 10 months. As of August, 2006, it contained over 65 billion nucleotide bases from more than 100,000 distinct organisms (Adams, 2008). Although the total volume of data is less than one terabyte, the computations performed are very demanding. In addition, the amount of genetic information available to researchers will increase rapidly once it becomes feasible to sequence the DNA of individual organisms, for example to enable pharmacogenomics, predicting a patient's response to different drugs based on his or her genetic makeup.

3. **Predicting and modeling the effects of earthquakes**. Scientists are creating increasingly detailed and accurate finite-element meshes representing the geological properties of the earth's crust, enabling them to model the effect of a geological disturbance and the probabilities of earthquakes occurring in different regions of the world. These models are continually updated as actual earthquake data are analyzed and as more sophisticated modeling techniques are devised. The models are an important shared resource among geologists, computational scientists, and civil engineers. Discovering new astronomical phenomena from telescope imagery data. Massive amounts of imagery data are collected daily and additional results are derived from computation applied to that data. Providing this information in the form of a shared global database would reduce the redundant storage and computation required to maintain separate copies.

4. **Synthesizing realistic graphic animations**. The system stores large amounts of motion capture data and uses this to generate high quality animations. Over time, the motion data can be expanded and refined by capturing more subjects performing more tasks, yielding richer and more realistic animations.

5. **Understanding the spatial and temporal patterns of brain behavior based on Magnetic Risidual Imagery data.** Information from multiple data sets, measured on different subjects and at different time periods, can be jointly analyzed to better understand how brains function. This data must be updated regularly as new measurements are made. These and many other tasks have the properties that they involve collecting and maintaining very large data sets and applying vast amounts of computational power to the data.

An increasing number of data-intensive computational problems are arising as technology for capturing and storing data becomes more widespread and economical, and as the web provides a mechanism to retrieve data from all around the world. Quite importantly, the relevant data sets are not static. They must be updated on a regular basis, and new data derived from computations over the raw information should be updated and saved. By engaging the academic research community in these issues, we can more systematically and in a more open forum explore fundamental aspects of a societally important style of computing.

Top Super Computers on Earth

1. Blue Gene/L: Lawrence Livermore National Laboratory

Blue Gene/L is currently the fastest supercomputer in the world peaking at 478.2 Teraflops by using 65,536 (processors and runs a scaled down version of Linux (Lawrence Livermore, 2009). It is a collaborative project among IBM, Lawrence Livermore Labs, and the United States Department of Energy and uses a cell-based design which gives it a saleable architecture that can be expanded by adding more building blocks without worry of introducing bottlenecks as the machine scales up. Recently, Blue Gene/L was in the news when scientists ran a cortical simulator as complex as half of a mouse brain which is thought to have about eight million neurons with each one having up to 8,000 connections with other nerve fibers. When not mimicking half of a rodent's brain, Blue Gene/L is being used mainly to simulate biochemical processes involving proteins.

2. Red Storm: Sandia National Laboratories

Red Storm is a parallel processing supercomputer designed by Cray and Sandia Laboratories to perform simulated testing on nuclear weapons stockpiling which includes designing replacement components, virtual testing of components under different conditions, and assisting in testing of weapons engineering and weapons physics. Red Storm consists of 12,960 AMD Opteron computer nodes and can peak at 124.42 Teraflops and uses a lightweight Linux Operating System which consists of only the minimum features needed to support Red Storm's applications. (Top 500 Supercomputers, 2010)

3. BGW (Blue Gene/W): IBM Thomas J. Watson Research Center

Blue Gene/W or BGW, can be found in IBM's Thomas J. Watson Research Center and can reach a peak of 114 Teraflops by using 20 refrigerator sized racks that each consists of 1024 nodes. Every node contains two 700 MHz power 440 processors and 512 MB of memory. Blue Gene/W main priority is to perform production science computations including biological simulations, protein folding and other projects created by worldwide IBM scientists.

4. ASC Purple: Lawrence Livermore National Laboratory

ASC Purple came about through collaboration between Lawrence Livermore Labs and IBM. Its peak of 100 Teraflops comes from a redundant ring of 196 IBM Power5 SMP servers which contain a total of 12,544 microprocessors with 50 terabytes of total memory and 2 petabytes of storage disk capacity. ASC Purple is currently being used to conduct nuclear weapons performance simulations which normally would be tested in underground nuclear detonations.

5. BGW (Blue Gene/W): IBM Thomas J. Watson Research Center

Blue Gene/W or BGW, can be found in IBM's Thomas J. Watson Research Center and can reach a peak of 114 Teraflops by using 20 refrigerator sized racks that each consists of 1024 nodes. Every node contains two 700 MHz power 440 processors and 512 MB of memory. Blue Gene/W main priority is to perform production science computations including biological simulations.

6. MareNostrum: Barcelona Supercomputing Center

MareNostrum is currently the most powerful supercomputer in Europe which consists of 10,240 processors that can peak at 94.21 Teraflops. Its 2,560 JS21 blade computing nodes take up a space of about half a basketball court (120 mÂ²) and are installed in the Barcelona Supercomputing Center in Barcelona, Spain. MareNostrum is currently being used for a variety of applications which includes human genome research, weather forecasting, and drug research. (Nostrum, 2010)

7. Thunderbird: Sandia National Laboratories

Thunderbird is an 8960-processor Linux cluster developed by Dell, Inc. and currently resides at Sandia National Laboratories, a National Nuclear Security Administration lab, located in Albuquerque NM. It is considered to be a capacity cluster suited to perform many mid-sized tasks rather than a single huge task. Thunderbird's 53.0 Teraflops have placed it at number 6 on the Top 500 fastest computers list and it is currently used in performing weapons simulations, scale-to-device modeling of radiation effects on semiconductor electronics, and weapon-response safety in extreme thermal and impact environments.

8. Tera-10

Built by Bull SA for France's Atomic Energy Commission), the Tera-10 is currently ranked number 7 on the Top 500 list of fastest computers in the world. The Tera-10 consists of 544 of Bull's Nova Scale 6160 servers with each one featuring eight Dual-Core Intel Itanium processors and runs at about 42.9 Teraflops. It uses Linux as an operating system and is used for nuclear testing simulations.

9. Red Diamond

Red Diamond located in Fayetteville, Arkansas at University of Arkansas (UA) is a Diamond in the rough. The Star of Arkansas supercomputer (Figure 1 and Figure 2) is built from 157 computer nodes, each with dual quad-core Xeon E5430 processors, 2x6MB cache, 2.66GHz, 1333FSB. There are a total of 1,256 cores and each core has 2GB of memory. Performance on supercomputers is measured in "flops," or floating point operations per second. The theoretical peak performance of Star is 13.36Tflops, or 13.36 trillion floating point operations each second.

Funding for Red Diamond was supplied through a Major Research Instrumentation Grant (#0421099) from the National Science Foundation (NSF) and additional support from the University of Arkansas (UA).

Operating Systems

Supercomputers predominantly run some variant of Linux or UNIX. Linux has been the most popular operating system since 2004 Supercomputer operating systems, today most often variants of Linux or UNIX, are every bit as complex as those for smaller machines, if not more so. Their user interfaces tend to be less developed, however, as the OS developers have limited programming resources to spend on non-essential parts of the OS (i.e., parts not directly contributing to the optimal utilization of the machine's hardware). This stems from the fact that because these computers, often priced at millions of dollars, are sold to a very small market, their R&D budgets are often limited. This section is about operating systems that use the Linux kernel.

Filiations of Unix and Unix-like systems Unix (officially trademarked as UNIXÂ®, sometimes also written as or Â® with small caps) is a computer operating system originally developed in 1969 by a group of AT&T employees at Bell Labs that included Ken Thompson, Dennis Ritchie and

Figure 1.

Douglas McIlroy. An operating system (OS) is software that manages computer resources and provides programmers with an interface used to access those resources. Interestingly this has been a continuing trend throughout the supercomputer industry, with former technology leaders such as Silicon Graphics taking a back seat to such companies as AMD and NVIDIA, who have been able to produce cheap, feature-rich, high-performance, and innovative products due to the vast number of consumers driving their R&D. The American multinational Nvidia Corporation specializes in the manufacture of graphics-processor technologies for workstations, desktop computers, and handheld devices.

Historically, until the early-to-mid-1980s, supercomputers usually sacrificed instruction set compatibility and code portability for performance (processing and memory access speed). For the most part, supercomputers to this time (unlike high-end mainframes) had vastly different operating systems. The Cray-1 alone had at least six different proprietary OSs largely unknown to the general computing community. Similarly different and incompatible vectorizing and parallelizing compilers for Fortran existed. This trend would have continued with the ETA-10 were it not for the initial instruction set compatibility between the Cray-1 and the Cray X-MP, and the adoption of UNIX operating system variants (such as Cray's Unicos and today's Linux.)

An instruction set is (a list of) all instructions, and all their variations, that a processor can execute. Fortran (previously FORTRAN) is a general-purpose, procedural, imperative programming language that is especially suited to numeric computation and scientific computing. The ETA-10 was a line of supercomputers manufactured by ETA Systems (a spin-off division of CDC) in the 1980s and which implemented the instruction set of the CDC Cyber 205. UNICOS is the Unix successor of the Cray Operating System (COS) for Cray supercomputers.

Software Tools

Software tools for distributed processing include standard APIs. An Application Programming In-

Figure 2.

terface (API) is a set of definitions of the ways in which one piece of computer software communicates with another such as MPI. Message Passing Interface (MPI) is a computer communications protocol. It is a de facto standard for communication among the nodes running a parallel program on a distributed memory system. Parallel Virtual Machine (PVM) is a software tool for parallel networking of computers. It is designed to allow a network of heterogeneous machines to be used as a single distributed parallel processor and open source-based software solutions such as Beowulf and open Mosix which facilitate the creation of a sort of "virtual supercomputer" from a collection of ordinary workstations or servers.

Technology like Rendezvous paves the way for the creation of ad hoc computer clusters. An example of this is the distributed rendering function in Apple's Shake compositing application. Computers running the Shake software merely need to be in proximity to each other, in networking terms, to automatically discover and use each other's resources. While no one has yet built an ad hoc computer cluster that rivals even yesteryear's supercomputers, the line between desktop, or even laptop, and supercomputer is beginning to blur, and

is likely to continue to blur as built-in support for parallelism and distributed processing increases in mainstream desktop operating systems.

Supercomputing Data Mining

Supercomputing is today used for high performance data mining and data intensive computing of large and distributed data sets. According to Wikipedia (2009), supercomputers or HPC (High Performance Computing) are used for highly calculation-intensive tasks such as problems involving quantum mechanical physics, weather forecasting, global warming, molecular modeling, and physical simulations.

Segall, Zhang and Pierce (2009) discusses background of supercomputing data mining such as Sanchez (1996) and Grossman (2006) that are as discussed below. Sanchez (1996) cited the importance of supercomputing data mining by stating "Data mining with these big, super-fast computers is a hot topic in business, medicine and research because data mining means creating new knowledge from vast quantities of information, just like searching for tiny bits of gold in a stream bed".

Grossman (2006) as Director of the National Center for Data Mining at the University of Illinois at Chicago cited in a report of funding acknowledgements several funded proposals by the National Science Foundation (NSF) such as a proposal entitled "Developing software tools and network services for mining remote and distributed data over high performance networks" and another proposal entitled "Tera Mining: A test bed for distributed data mining over high performance SONET and Lambda Networks."

Segall, Zhang, and Pierce (2009) illustrates the visualization of supercomputing for two selected software of Avizo® by Visualization Science Group and JMP® Genomics from SAS Institute. According to Segall, Zhang, and Pierce (2009), "both software are used for supercomputing data mining at the University of Minnesota Supercomputing Institute for Advanced Computation Research. Avizo® is 3-D visualization software for scientific and industrial data that can process very large datasets at interactive speed. JMP® Genomics from SAS is used for discovering the biological patterns in genomics data."

CONCLUSION

Simply put, a supercomputer consists of several computers to form a cluster with a main terminal that is networked through a router or switch hub. Installed is cluster management service and communication software on the computer that will serve as the master computer in the cluster. The Message Passing Interface (MPI) is stable and easy-to-use software for this task. The MPI software allows each computer in the cluster to be assigned a unique address on the network cluster for identification. All of the computers in the cluster must have the same operating system. Windows 2000 professional or Windows NT® are considered to be a reliable OS. Usually supercomputers run on a Linux® or Unix® platform which

is found to be the steadiest operating systems for the task at hand.

REFERENCES

Danamics Technology. (2010). Retrieved April 20th, 2010. From http://www.danamics.dk/technology.html

Dunbar, J. (2009, July 13th). Retrieved April 14 2010 from http://www.nas.nasa.gov/About/Projects/Columbia/columbia.html

Grider, G., Nunez, J., Bent, J., Wingate, M., Torrez, A., Chen, H. B., et al. (n.d.). *File Systems for the World's Fastest Computer*. Retrieved April 13th 2010 from http://www.pdsi-scidac.org/events/PDSW09/resources/LANL.pdf

Grossman, R. (2006). *National Center for Data Mining: Funding Acknowledgements*. University of Illinois at Chicago, Chicago. Retrieved from http://www.ncdm.uic.edu/grantAcknowledgement.html

Johansson, J. (2006). *Introduction to High Speed Computing*. University of Alberta, Alberta, Canada. Retrieved May 4, 2010 from http://www.ualberta.ca/CNS/RESEARCH/Courses/2006/HPCWorkshop/AICT0603.IntroToHPC.pdf

Lawrence Livermore National Laboratory. (2008). *Advanced Simulation and Computing Purple, 100 teraFLOPS Dedicated to Capability Computing*. Retrieved April 22nd from https://asc.llnl.gov/computing_resources/purple/

Lawrence Livermore National Laboratory. (2009). *Advanced Simulation and Computing, On the Path to Predictive Simulation*. Retrieved on May 4 2010. https://asc.llnl.gov/computing_resources/bluegenel/

Nelson, J. I. (n.d.). Retrieved April 17th 2010 from http://www.nerdylorrin.net/jerry/politics/Warrantless/WarrantlessFACTS.html

Nostrum, N. (n.d.). Retrieved on April 15th, 2010 at http://www.bsc.es/plantillaA.php?cat_id=5

Philips, J. (2010). *Sandia National Laboratories*. Retrieved April 10th, 2010 from http://www.sandia.gov/ASC/redstorm.html

Sanchez, E. (1996). Speedier: Penn researchers to link supercomputers to community problems. *Compass*, *43*(4), 14. Retrieved from http://www.upenn.edu/pennnews/features/1996/091796/research.

Segall, R. S., Zhang, Q., & Pierce, R. M. (2009). Visualization by Supercomputing Data Mining. In *Proceedings of the 4th INFORMS Workshop on Data Mining and System Informatics*, San Diego, CA, October 10.

Supercomputers. (2009). Retrieved April 20th 2010 from http://www.computerbasicsguide.com/basics/supercomputers.html

Top 500 Supercomputers. (n.d.). Retrieved April 17th, 2010 from http://www.top500.org/system/7466

Top 500 Supercomputing Sites. (n.d.). Retrieved May 4, 2010 from http://www.top500.org/list/2009/11/100

Top 7 Most Powerful Supercomputers in the World. (2007). In *The Last Laugh Depot, Saung Thamar*. Retrieved April 15th, 2010 from http://saungthamar.multiply.com/journal/item/81

Wapedia Supercomputer. (2010). Retrieved on April 14th 2010 from http://wapedia.mobi/en/Supercomputer

Wikipedia. (2009). *Supercomputers*. Retrieved May 19, 2009 from BookRags.com: http://www.bookrags.com/wiki/Supercomputer

Wikipedia. (2010). Retrieved April 27 2010 from http://en.wikipedia.org/wiki/Supercomputer

KEY TERMS AND DEFINITIONS

Cluster: A type of multiprocessor or architecture in which there is a hierarchy of the units of replication. At the lowest level, "processors" are replicated to form a "cluster". The cluster consists of M processors and a shared switching network that provides communication among the processors and access to a shared local memory. At the next higher level, the clusters are replicated. A clustered "system" consists of N clusters interconnected through a global network that allows communication among the clusters and access to a global memory that is shared among the cluster. The purpose of clustering is to reduce conflicts in accessing shared resources, whether these resources are the communication network or the storage system.

Computing Nodes: A node is any device connected to a computer network. Nodes can be computers, personal digital assistants (PDAs), cell phones, or various other network appliances. On an IP network, a node is any device with an IP address.

Data Parallelism: (also known as loop-level parallelism) is a form of parallelization of computing across multiple processors in parallel computing environments. Data parallelism focuses on distributing the data across different parallel computing nodes. It contrasts to task parallelism as another form of parallelism.

Deep Blue: A super computer developed by researchers at IBM to explore the use of parallel processing to solve complex computing problems. It is known as the first computer to beat the current chess World Grand Master.

Distributed Processing: Processing on a number of networked computers that do not share main memory. One typically infers the computers are of different relative power and function. An example is a supercomputer, a mini-computer, and a workstation all providing computation for a single application in such a way that the process is distributed appropriately over all the vehicles.

FPGA Chips: Short for Field-Programmable Gate Array, a type of logic chip that can be programmed. An FPGA is similar to a PLD, but whereas PLDs are generally limited to hundreds of gates, FPGAs support thousands of gates. They are especially popular for prototyping integrated circuit designs. Once the design is set, hardwired chips are produced for faster performance.

Flops: Floating point operations per second; a measure of memory access performance, equal to the rate at which a machine can perform single-precision floating-point calculations.

Frequency Scaling: Frequency scaling (also known as frequency ramping) is, in computer architecture, the technique of ramping a processor's frequency so as to achieve performance gains.

Local Disk Space: Disk space attached to an individual processor (CPU) in a multiprocessor system. On CTC's IBM SP, each node's local disk space is used as scratch space for running jobs, because access to it is much faster than access to the shared file system, AFS.

Compilation of References

Abbassi, Z., & Mirrokni, V. S. (2007). A recommender system based on local random walks and spectral methods. In WebKDD/SNAKDD '07: Proceedings of the 9th WebKDD and 1st SNAKDD 2007 workshop on Web mining and social network analysis (pp. 102-108). New York, NY, USA.

Aberer, K., & Wu, J. (2004). Using siterank for p2p web retrieval. Technical report. Swiss Fed. Institute of Technology.

Abraham, R., Simha, J. B., & Iyengar, S. S. (2007). Medical Data mining with a new algorithm for feature selection and Naïve Bayesian Classifier. In *Proceedings of IEEE International Conference on Information Technology*, (pp. 44-49).

Achard, F., Vaysseix, G., & Barillot, E. (2001). XML, bioinformatics and data integration. [Review]. *Bioinformatics (Oxford, England)*, *17*(2), 115–125. doi:10.1093/bioinformatics/17.2.115

Acharya & Ray. (2005). *Image Processing: Principles and Applications*. New York: Wiley-Interscience.

Acs, Z. j., & Audretsch, D. B. (1989). Patents as a measure of innovative activity. *Kyklos*, *42*(2), 171–180. doi:10.1111/j.1467-6435.1989.tb00186.x

Adamic, L. A., & Adar, E. (2007). Friends and Neighbors on the Web. *Social Networks*, *25*, 211–230. doi:10.1016/S0378-8733(03)00009-1

Afifi, A. A., & Azen, S. P. (1972). *Statistical Analysis: A computer oriented approach*. New York: Academic Press, Inc.

Aggarwal, C. C., & Yu, P. S. (2005). An effective and efficient algorithm for high-dimensional outlier detection. *The VLDB Journal*, *14*, 211–221. doi:10.1007/s00778-004-0125-5

Aggarwal, C. C., & Yu, P. S. (Eds.). (2008). *Privacy-Preserving Data Mining Models and Algorithms*. Berlin: Springer.

Aggarwal, C. C., & Yu, P. S. (2009). A survey of uncertain data algorithms and applications. *IEEE Transactions on Knowledge and Data Engineering*, *21*(5), 609–623. doi:10.1109/TKDE.2008.190

Aggarwal, C. C., & Yu, P. S. (2001). Outlier detection for high dimensional data. In *ACM SIGMOD International Conference on Management of Data* (pp.37-46).

Agrawal, R., & Srikank, R. (1994). Fast algorithms for mining association rules in large databases. In J.B. Bocca, M. Jarke, & C. Zaniolo (Eds.), *Proceedings of the 20th International Conference on Very Large Data Bases* (pp. 487-499). San Francisco, CA: Morgan Kaufmann.

Agrawal, R., Gehrke, J., Gunopulos, D., & Raghavan, P. (1998). Automatic subspace Clustering of high dimensional data for data mining applications. In *Proceedings of the ACM SIGMOD International Conference on Management of Data*, (pp. 94-105), Seattle, WA.

DOI: 10.4018/978-1-60960-102-7.chcrf

Agrawal, R., Gunopulos, D., & Leymann, F. (1998). Mining Process Models from Workflow Logs. In *Proceedings of Sixth International Conference on Extending Database Technology*, (pp. 469–483).

Agrawal, R., Imieliński, T., & Swami, A. N. (1993). Mining association rules between sets of items in large databases. In P. Buneman & S. Jajodia (Eds.), *Proceedings of the 1993 ACM SIGMOD International Conference on Management of Data* (pp. 207-216). New York: ACM.

Aha, D. W., & Bankert, R. L. (1995). A Comparative Evaluation of Sequential Feature Selection Algorithms. In *Proceedings of the Fifth International Workshop on Artificial Intelligence and Statistics*, (pp. 199-206), Florida, USA.

Ahlberg, C. (1996). Spotfire: An information exploration environment. *SIGMOD Record*, *25*(4), 25–29. doi:10.1145/245882.245893

Alagambigai, P., & Thangavel, K. (2009). Feature Selection for Visual Clustering, In *Proceedings of International Conference on Advances in Recent Technologies in Communication and Computing, IEEE Computer Society*, (pp.498-502).

Alagambigai, P., Thangavel, K., & Karthikeyani Vishalakshi, N. (2009). Entropy Weighting Feature Selection for Interactive Visual Clustering. In *Proceedings of 4th International Conference on Artificial Intelligence*, (pp. 545-557).

Alba, E., Aldana, J. F., & Troya, J. M. (1993). Fully automatic ANN design: A genetic approach. In *Proc. Int. Workshop Artificial Neural Networks (IWANN'93)*, (LNCS 686, pp. 399-404). Berlin: Springer-Verlag.

Almeida, J. A. S., Barbosa, L. M. S., Pais, A. A. C. C., & Formosinho, S. J. (2007). Improving hierarchical cluster analysis: A new method with outlier detection and automatic clustering. *Chemometrics and Intelligent Laboratory Systems*, *87*, 208–217. doi:10.1016/j.chemolab.2007.01.005

Almuallim, H., & Dietterich, T. G. (1991). Learning with many irrelevant features. In *Proceedings of the Ninth Nat. Conf. on Artificial Intelligence,* (pp. 547-552), Anaheim, CA. Cambridge, MA: MIT Press.

Altschul, S., Madden, T., Schaffer, A., Zhang, J., Zhang, Z., & Miller, W. (1997). Gapped BLAST and PSI-BLAST: a new generation of protein database search programs. *Nucleic Acids Research, 25*(17), 3389–3402..doi:10.1093/nar/25.17.3389

Andersen, R., Chung, F., & Lang, K. (2007). Local partitioning for directed graphs using PageRank. WAW2007 [Springer-Verlag.]. *Lecture Notes in Computer Science, 4863*, 166–178. doi:10.1007/978-3-540-77004-6_13

Anderson, E. W. (1994). Cross-category variation in customer satisfaction and retention. *Marketing Letters, 5*(January), 19–30. doi:10.1007/BF00993955

Anderson, E. W., Fornell, C., & Lehmann, D. (1994). Customer satisfaction, market share and profitability: Findings from Sweden. *Journal of Marketing, 58*(July), 63–66.

Anderson, E. W., & Sullivan, M. (1993). The antecedents and consequences of customer satisfaction for firms. *Science, 12*(2), 125–143.

Anderson, R. E. (1973). Consumer dissatisfaction: The effect of disconfirmed expectancy on perceived product performance. *JMR, Journal of Marketing Research, 10*(February), 38–44. doi:10.2307/3149407

Andrew, J. N. (2009). Measuring knowledge spillovers: What patents, licenses and publications reveal about innovation diffusion. *Research Policy, 38*(6), 994–1005. doi:10.1016/j.respol.2009.01.023

Andrew, K. (2001). Rough Set Theory: A Data Mining Tool for Semiconductor Manufacturing. *IEEE Transactions on Electronics Packaging Manufacturing, 24*(1).

Angiulli, F., & Fassetti, F. (2010). Distance-based outlier queries in data streams: the novel task and algorithms. *Data Mining and Knowledge Discovery, 20*(2), 290–324. doi:10.1007/s10618-009-0159-9

Angiulli, F., & Pizzuti, C. (2005). Outlier mining in large high-dimensional data Sets. *IEEE Transactions on Knowledge and Data Engineering, 17*(2), 203–215. doi:10.1109/TKDE.2005.31

Angiulli, F., & Pizzuti, C. (2002). Fast outlier detection in high dimensional spaces. In *the sixth European conference on the principles of data mining and knowledge discovery*, (pp.15-26).

Ankerst, M., Elsen, C., Ester, M., & Kriegel, H.-P. (1999). Visual classification: An interactive approach to decision tree construction. In U. Fayyad, S. Chaudhuri, & D. Madigan (Eds.), *Proceedings of the Fifth ACM SIGKDD International Conference on Knowledge Discovery and Data Mining (KDD-99)* (pp. 392-396). New York: ACM.

Antoniou, G., & van Harmelen, F. (2008). *A Semantic Web Primer*. Cambridge, MA: Massachusetts Institute of Technology.

Antons, C. M., & Maltz, E. N. (2006). Expanding the role of Institutional Research at small private universities: A case study in Enrollment Management using Data Mining. *New Directions for Institutional Research, 131*(Fall), 69–81. doi:10.1002/ir.188

Applied Analytics Using SAS Enterprise Miner (AAEM) 5.3: Course Notes (2009).

Apweiler, R., Bairoch, A., & Wu, H. (2007). The Universal Protein Resource (UniProt) Protein sequence databases. *Nucleic Acids Research, 35*, D193–D197.

Apweiler, R., Bairoch, A., & Wu, C. H. (2004). Protein sequence databases. [doi: DOI: 10.1016/j.cbpa.2003.12.004]. *Current Opinion in Chemical Biology, 8*(1), 76-80.

Archibugi, D., & Pianta, M. (1996). Measuring technological change through patents and innovation surveys. *Technovation, 16*(9), 451–468. doi:10.1016/0166-4972(96)00031-4

Ashton, W. B., & Sen, R. K. (1988). Using patent information in technology business planning I. *Research-Technology Management, 31*(6), 42–46.

Assent, I., Krieger, R., Muller, E., & Seidl, T. (2007). Subspace outlier mining in large multimedia databases. In *Dagstuhl Seminar Proceedings on Parallel Universes and Local Patterns*.

Asuncion, A., & Newman, D. J. (2007). *UCI Machine Learning Repository*. Retrieved from http://www.ics.uci.edu/~mlearn/MLRepository.html. Irvine, CA: University of California, School of Information and Computer Science.

Avrachenkov, K., Dobrynin, V., Nemirovsky, D., Pham, S. K., & Smirnova, E. (2008). Pagerank based clustering of hypertext document collections. In SIGIR '08: Proceedings of the 31st annual international ACM SIGIR conference on Research and development in information retrieval (pp. 873-874), New York, NY, USA.

Bachmair, A., Finley, D., & Varshavsky, A. (1986). In vivo half-life of a protein is a function of its amino-terminal residue. *Science, 234*, 179–186. doi:10.1126/science.3018930

Baeza-Yates, R., & Ribeiro-Neto, B. (1999). *Modern Information Retrieval*. Boston: Addison-Wesley.

Baeza-Yates, R., & Ribeiro-Neto, B. (1999). *Modern Information Retrieval*. New York: Addison-Wesley.

Bailey, T., & Elkan, C. (1994). *Fitting a mixture model by expectation maximization to discover motifs in biopolymers*. Paper presented at the Proceedings of the Second International Conference on Intelligent Systems for Molecular Biology, Menlo Park, California.

Bairoch, A. (2000). Serendipity in bioinformatics, the tribulations of a Swiss bioinformatician through exciting times! *Bioinformatics (Oxford, England), 16*(1), 48–64.. doi:10.1093/bioinformatics/16.1.48

Baker, J. A., Kornguth, P. J., Lo, J. Y., & Floyd, C. E. (1996). Artificial neural network, improving the quality of breast biopsy recommendations. *Radiology*, (198): 131–135.

Barnett, V., & Lewis, T. (1994). *Outliers in Statistical Data*. New York: Wiley.

Basili, R., Cammisa, M., & Donati, E. (2005). RitroveRAI: A web application for semantic indexing and hyperlinking of multimedia news. In *Fourth International Semantic Web Conference 2005 (ISWC 2005), LNCS 3729 (pp. 97-111)*, Galway, Ireland. Berlin: Springer.

Battiti, R. (1994). Using mutual information for selecting features in supervised neural net learning. *IEEE Transactions on Neural Networks*, 537. doi:10.1109/72.298224

Bay, S., & Schwabacher, M. (2003). Mining distance-based outliers in near linear time with randomization and a simple pruning rule. In *ACM SIGKDD* (pp. 29-38).

Bayardo, R. J. (1998). Efficiently mining long patterns from databases. In L.M. Haas & A. Tiwary (Eds.), *Proceedings of the 1998 ACM SIGMOD International Conference on Management of Data* (pp. 85-93). New York: ACM.

Belew, R., McInerney, J., & Schraudolph, N. (1991). Evolving networks: using the genetic algorithm with connectionist learning. In *Proceedings of the Second Artificial Life Conference*, (pp. 511-547). New York: Addison-Wesley.

Bello, R., Nowe, A., Caballero, Y., Gomez, Y., & Vrancx, P. (2005). A model based on ant colony system and rough set theory to feature selection. In *Proceedings of the 2005 conference on Genetic and evolutionary computation*, Washington DC.

Ben-Gal, I. (2005). Outlier Detection. In Maimon, O., & Rockack, L. (Eds.), *Data Mining and Knowledge Discovery Handbook: A Complete Guide for Practitioners and Researchers* (pp. 1–16). Amsterdam: Kluwer Academic Publishers. doi:10.1007/0-387-25465-X_7

Benson, D. A., Karsch-Mizrachi, I., Lipman, D. J., Ostell, J., & Sayers, E. W. (2009). GenBank. *Nucleic Acids Res, 37*(Database issue), D26-31. doi: gkn723 [pii] 10.1093/nar/gkn723

Bentley, J. L. (1975). Multidimensional binary search trees used for associative searching. *Communications of the ACM, 18*(9), 509–517. doi:10.1145/361002.361007

Berchtold, S., Jagadish, H. V., & Ross, K. A. (1998). Independence diagrams: A technique for visual data mining. In R. Agrawal, P.E. Stolorz, & G. Piatetsky-Shapiro (Eds.), *Proceedings of the Fourth International Conference on Knowledge Discovery and Data Mining (KDD-98)* (pp. 139-143). Menlo Park, CA: AAAI Press.

Berchtold, S., Keim, D., & Kreigel, H. P. (1996). The X-tree: an index structure for high-dimensional data. In *the 22ⁿᵈ International Conference on Very Large Databases*, (pp. 28-39).

Bergman, M. (2001, August). The deep Web:Surfacing hidden value. BrightPlanet. *Journal of Electronic Publishing, 7*(1). Retrieved from http://beta.bright-planet.com/deepcontent/tutorials/DeepWeb/index.asp. doi:10.3998/3336451.0007.104

Berners-Lee, T., Hendler, J., & Ora, L. (2001). The Semantic Web. *Scientific American, 284*(5), 34. doi:10.1038/scientificamerican0501-34

Berson, A., & Smith, S. J. (1997). *Data Warehousing, Data Mining and Olap*. New York: McGraw-Hill.

Berson, A., Smith, S., & Thearling, K. (2000). *Building Data Mining Applications for CRM*. New York: McGraw-Hill Professional.

Beyer, K., Goldstein, J., Ramakrishnan, R., & Shaft, U. (1999). When is nearest neighbor meaningful? In *the 7ᵗʰ International Conference on Database Theory* (pp. 217-235).

Bianchi, L. M. (2009). Databases and Data Mining. *Computer, Information and Society*. York University. Retrieved November 10, 2009 from http://www.yorku.ca/lbianchi/nats1700/lecture14.html

Bigi, B., Brun, A., Haton, J.-P., Smaïli, K., & Zitouni, I. (2001) A comparative study of topic identification on newspaper and e-mail. In *Proceedings of String Processing and Information Retrieval Conference (SPIRE2001)*, (pp. 238).

Bird, C., Gourley, A., Devanbu, P., Gertz, M., & Swaminathan, A. (2006). Mining email social networks in postgres. In *MSR '06: Proceedings of the 2006 international workshop on Mining software repositories*, (pp. 185-186). New York: ACM Press.

Bjellqvist, B., Basse, B., Olsen, E., & Celis, J. (1994). Reference points for comparisons of two-dimensional maps of proteins from different human cell types defined in a pH scale where isoelectric points correlate with polypeptide compositions. *Electrophoresis*, *15*, 529–539. doi:10.1002/elps.1150150171

Blanchard, J., Guillet, F., & Briand, H. (2007). Interactive visual exploration of association rules with rule-focusing methodology. *Knowledge and Information Systems*, *13*(1), 43–75. doi:10.1007/s10115-006-0046-2

Blum, A. L., & Rivest, R. L. (1992). Training a 3-node neural networks is NP-complete. *Neural Networks*, (5): 117–127. doi:10.1016/S0893-6080(05)80010-3

Blum, A. L., & Langley, P. (1997). Selection of relevant features and examples in machine learning. *Artificial Intelligence*, *97*(1-2), 245–271. doi:10.1016/S0004-3702(97)00063-5

Boriah, S., Chandola, V., & Kumar, V. (2008). Similarity measures for categorical data: a comparative evaluation. In *SIAM International Conference on Data Mining*, (pp. 243-254).

Bosworth, D. L. (1984). Foreign patent flows to and from the United Kingdom. *Research Policy*, *13*(2), 115–124. doi:10.1016/0048-7333(84)90010-6

Boudjeloud, L., & Poulet, F. (2005). Visual Interactive Evolutionary Algorithm for High Dimensional Data Clustering and Outlier Detection. In Carbonell, J. G., & Siekmann, J. (Eds.), *Advances in Knowledge Discovery and Data Mining* (pp. 426–431). Berlin: Springer Berlin. doi:10.1007/11430919_50

Bozsak, E., Ehrig, M., Handschuh, S., Hotho, A., Maedche, A., Motik, B., et al. (2002). Kaon - towards a large scale Semantic Web. In *Third International Conference on E-Commerce and Web Technology, EC-Web 2002* (pp.304–313), Aix-en-Provence, France.

Breese, J., Heckerman, D., & Kadie, C. (1998). Empirical analysis of predictive algorithms for collaborative filtering. In *Proceedings of the Uncertainty in Artificial Intelligence Conference*, (pp. 43–52).

Breiman, L., Friedman, J. H., Olshen, R. A., & Stone, C. J. (1984). *Classification and Regression trees*. Belmont, CA: Wadsworth, Inc.

Breiman, F., & Olshen, S. (1984). *Classification and Decision Trees*. New York: Wadsworth.

Breitzman, A., & Thomas, P. (2002). Using patent citation analysis to target/value M&A candidates. *Research technology management*, *45*(5), 28-36.

Breunig, M., Kriegel, H., Ng, R., & Sander, J. (2000). LOF: Identifying density-based local outliers. In the *ACM SIGMOD International Conference on Management of Data* (pp.93-104).

Brin, S. (1998). The anatomy of a largescale hypertextual web search engine. In Computer Networks and ISDN Systems (pp. 107-117).

Broder, A. Z., Lempel, R., Maghoul, F., & Pedersen, J. (2004). Efficient PageRank approximation via graph aggregation. In WWW Alt. '04: Proceedings of the 13th international World Wide Web conference on Alternate track papers & posters (pp. 484-485), New York, NY, USA.

Buitelaar, P., Cimiano, P., Frank, A., Hartung, M., & Racioppa, S. (2008). Ontology-based information extraction and integration from heterogeneous data sources. *International Journal of Human-Computer Studies*, *66*(11), 759–788. doi:10.1016/j.ijhcs.2008.07.007

Bult, C. J., Kadin, J. A., Richardson, J. E., Blake, J. A., Eppig, J. T., & the Mouse Genome Database Group. (2010). The Mouse Genome Database: enhancements and updates. *Nucl. Acids Res., 38*(suppl_1), D586-592. doi: 10.1093/nar/gkp880

Campbell, I. (2000). Interactive evaluation of the Ostensive Model using a new test collection of images with multiple relevance assessments. *Journal of Information Retrieval, 2*(1), 85–112.

Campbell, J. D. (2008). *Analysis of Institutional Data in Predicting Student Retention Utilizing Knowledge Discovery and Statistical Techniques.* Unpublished doctoral dissertation, Northern Arizona University.

Cantú-Paz, E., & Kamath, C. (2005). An Empirical Comparison of Combinatios of Evolutionary Algorithms and Neural Networks for Classification Problems. *IEEE Transactions on Systems, Man, and Cybernetics. Part B, Cybernetics*, 915–927. doi:10.1109/TSMCB.2005.847740

Card, S. K., Shneiderman, B., & Mackinlay, J. D. (1999). *Readings in information visualization: using vision to think.* San Francisco: Morgan Kaufmann.

Cardozo, R. N. (1965). An experimental study of customer effort, expectations, and satisfaction. *JMR, Journal of Marketing Research, 2*(August), 244–249. doi:10.2307/3150182

Cavalcoli, J. D. (2001). Genomic and Proteomic Databases: Large-Scale Analysis and Integration of Data. [doi: DOI: 10.1016/S1050-1738(01)00089-5]. *Trends in Cardiovascular Medicine, 11*(2), 76-81.

Ceglar, A., Roddick, J. F., & Powers, D. M. W. (2007). CURIO: A fast outlier and outlier cluster detection algorithm for large datasets. In Ong, K. L., Li, W., & Gao, J. (Ed.), *Conferences in Research and Practice in Information Technology, Vol. 84, The Second International Workshop on Integrating AI and Data Mining.* Gold Coast, Australia: Australian Computer Society, Inc.

Chakrabarti, S. (2003). *Mining the Web: Discovering Knowledge from Hypertext Data.* San Francisco, CA: Morgan Kaufmann Publications/Elsevier.

Chakrabarti, D., & Faloutsos, C. (2006). Graph Mining: Laws, Generators, and Algorithms. *ACM Computing Surveys, 38*(1).

Chakrabarti, S. (2003). *Mining the Web: Discovering Knowledge from Hypertext Data.* San Francisco: Morgan Kaufmann Publishers.

Chandola, V., Banerjee, A., & Kumar, V. (2009). Anomaly Detection: A Survey. *ACM Computing Surveys, 41*(3), 15:1-15:58.

Chaudhary, A., Szalay, A. S., Szalay Er, S., & Moore, A. W. (2002). Very fast outlier detection in large multidimensional data sets. In *ACM SIGMOD Workshop in Research Issues in Data Mining and Knowledge Discovery* (pp. 45-52).

Chen, K., & Liu, L. (2004). VISTA - Validating and Refining Clusters via Visualization. *Information Visualization, 4*, 257–270. doi:10.1057/palgrave.ivs.9500076

Chen, K., & Liu, L. (2006). iVIBRATE: Interactive Visualization-Based Framework for Clustering Large Datasets. *ACM Transactions on Information Systems, 24*, 245–294. doi:10.1145/1148020.1148024

Chen, Z., Menzies, T., Port, D., & Boehm, B. (2005). Finding the right data for software cost modeling. *IEEE Software, 22*, 38–46. doi:10.1109/MS.2005.151

Chen, M. S., Han, J., & Chu, Y. P. S. (1996). Data Mining: An Overview from a Database Perspective. *IEEE Transactions on Knowledge and Data Engineering, 8*(6), 866–883. doi:10.1109/69.553155

Chen, Q. (2008). The effect of patent laws on invention rates: Evidence from cross-country panels. *Journal of Comparative Economics, 36*(4), 694–704. doi:10.1016/j.jce.2008.05.004

Chen, A. (2004, 7/5/2004). Semantic Web is 2 steps closer. *eweek.com* 21(27), 46.

Chen, K., & Liu, H. (1999). Towards an evolutionary algorithm: Comparison of two feature selection algorithms. In *Proceedings of Congress on Evolutionary Computation.*

Cheng, H., & Han, J. (2009). Frequent itemsets and association rules. In Liu, L., & Özsu, M. T. (Eds.), *Encyclopedia of Database Systems* (pp. 1184–1187). New York: Springer.

Cheng, Y., & Church, G. M. (2000). Biclustering of expression data. In *Proceedings. of the eighth International Conference on Intelligent Systems for Molecular Biology*, (pp. 93–103).

Chi, C.-C., Kuo, C.-H., & Lu, M.-Y. % Tsao, N-L. (2008). Concept-based pages recommendation by using cluster algorithm. In *Proceedings of Eighth IEEE International Conference on Advanced Learning Technologies*, 1–5 July, Santander, Spain, (pp.298–300).

Chikhi, N.F., Rothenburger, B., & AussenacGilles, N. (2008). Combining link and content information for scientific topics discovery. IEEE International Conference on Tools with Artificial Intelligence (pp. 211-214). Dayton, OH, USA.

Chiu, Y. J., & Chen, Y. W. (2007). Using AHP in patent valuation. *Mathematical and Computer Modelling, 46*(7-8), 1054–1062. doi:10.1016/j.mcm.2007.03.009

Choy, C., Kim, S., & Park, Y. (2007). A patent-based cross impact analysis for Quantitative estimation of technological impact: the case of information and Communication technology. *Technological Forecasting and Social Change, 74*(8), 1296–1314. doi:10.1016/j.techfore.2006.10.008

Churchill, G. A. J., & Surprenant, C. (1982). An investigation into the determinants of consumer satisfaction. *JMR, Journal of Marketing Research, 19*, 491–504. doi:10.2307/3151722

Ciesielski, K., & Klopotek, M. A. (2006). Text data clustering by contextual graphs. In Todorovski, L., Lavrac, N., & Jantke, K. P. (Eds.), *Discovery Science (DS2006), LNAI 4265* (pp. 65–76). Barcelona, Spain: SpringerVerlag. doi:10.1007/11893318_10

Ciesielski, K., & Klopotek, M. A. (2007). Towards adaptive web mining: Histograms and contexts in text data clustering. In M.R. Berthold and J. ShaweTaylor, editors, Intelligent Data Analysis (IDA2007), LNCS 4723 (pp. 284-295). SpringerVerlag. Ljubljana, Slovenia.

Claypool, M., Le, P., Wased, M., & Brown, D. (2001). Implicit Interest Indicators. In *Proceedings of sixth international conference on Intelligent User Interfaces* (pp. 33–40). New York: ACM Press. doi:10.1145/359784.359836

Cohn, D., & Hofmann, T. (2001). The missing link a probabilistic model of document content and hypertext connectivity. In *Advances in Neural Information Processing Systems* (*Vol. 13*). The MIT Press.

Combs, T. T. A., & Bederson, B. B. (1999). Does zooming improve image browsing? In *Proceedings of Digital Libraries* (pp. 130–137). New York: Association of Computing Machinery.

Cook, D. R., Buja, A., Cabrea, J., & Harley, H. (1995). Grand Tour and Projection pursuit. *Journal of Computational and Graphical Statistics, 23*, 155–172. doi:10.2307/1390844

Cox, I. J., Miller, M. L., Minka, T. P., Papathomas, T. V., & Yianilos, P. N. (2000). The Bayesian Image Retrieval System, PicHunter: Theory, implementation, and psychophysical experiments. *IEEE Transactions on Image Processing, 9*(1), 20–37. doi:10.1109/83.817596

Crescenzi, V., Mecca, G., & Merialdo, P. (2001). *ROADRUNNER: Towards Automatic Data Extraction from Large Web Sites*. Paper presented at the 27th International Conference on Very Large Databases, Rome, Italy.

Croft, W. B. (1995). What do people want from information retrieval? *D-Lib Magazine*.

Cuff, A., Redfern, O. C., Greene, L., Sillitoe, I., Lewis, T., & Dibley, M. (2009)... *The CATH Hierarchy Revisited Structural Divergence in Domain Superfamilies and the Continuity of Fold Space., 17*(8), 1051–1062.

Daconta, M. C., Obrst, L. J., & Smith, K. T. (2003). *The Semantic Web: A Guide to the Future of XML, Web Services, and Knowledge Management*. Chichester, UK: Wiley.

Danamics Technology. (2010). Retrieved April 20th, 2010. From http://www.danamics.dk/technology.html

Das, K., & Schneider, J. (2007). Detecting anomalous records in categorical datasets. In *the 13th ACM SIGKDD International Conference on Knowledge Discovery and Data Mining* (pp. 220-229), San Jose, USA.

DasGupta, B. & Schnitger, G. (1992). *Efficient approximation with neural networks: A comparison of gate functions*. Dep. Comput. Sci., Pennsylvania State Univ., University Park, Tech. Rep.

Dash, M., & Liu, H. (1997). Feature selection methods for classifications. *Intelligent Data Analysis: An International Journal, 1*(3).

Dash, M., Liu, H., & Motoda, H. (2000). Consistency based Feature Selection. In *Proceedings of Pacific-Asia Conf. on Knowledge Discovery and Data Mining (PAKDD)*, (pp. 98–109).

Davis, C. M., Hardin, J. M., Bohannon, T., & Oglesby, J. (2008). Data Mining applications in higher Education. In K. D. Lawrence, S. Kudyba & R. K, Klimberg (Eds.) *Data Mining Methods and Applications* (pp. 123-147). Boca Raton, FL: Auerbach Publications.

Day, A. (2004). Data Warehouses. *American City and County, 119*(1), 18.

de Castro, L. N., & Timmis, J. (2002). *Artificial Immune Systems: A New Computational Intelligence Approach*. Springer Verlag.

de Castro, P. A. D., de França, F. O., Ferreira, H. M., & Von Zuben, F. J. (2007). Applying Biclustering to Perform Collaborative Filtering. In *Seventh IEEE International Conference on Intelligent Systems Design and Applications*, (pp. 421-426).

de Loupy, C., & Bellot, P. (2000). Evaluation of document retrieval systems and query difficulty. In *Using Evaluation within HLT Programs: Results and Trends*, Athens, Greece, (pp. 34-40).

Decker, S., van Harmelen, F., Broekstra, J., Erdmann, M., Fensel, D., & Horrocks, I. (2000). The Semantic Web: The Roles of XML and RDF. *IEEE Internet Computing, 4*(5), 63–74. doi:10.1109/4236.877487

Del Bimbo, A. (2001). *Visual Information Retrieval*. San Francisco, CA: Morgan Kaufmann Publishers, Inc.

DesJardins, M., MacGlashan, J., & Ferraioli, J. (2007). *Interactive Visual Clustering* (pp. 361–364). Intelligent User Interfaces.

Devaney, M., & Ram, A. (1997). Efficient Feature Selection in conceptual Clustering. In *Proceedings of the 14th International Conference on Machine Learning*, (pp.92-97). San Francisco: Morgan Kaufmann, http://cc.gatech.edu/aimosaic/students/markd/papers/icml-97/icml-97.pdf

Dietterich, T. G. (1998). Approximate statistical tests for comparing supervised classification learning algorithms. *Neural Computation, 10*(7), 1895–1924. doi:10.1162/089976698300017197

Ding, L., Kolari, P., Ding, Z., Avancha, S., Finin, T., & Joshi, A. (2007). Using ontologies in the Semantic Web: A survey. In Sharman, R., Kishmore, R., & Ramesh, R. (Eds.), *Ontologies: A handbook of Principles, Concepts and Applications in Information Systems* (*Vol. 14*, pp. 79–113). Berlin: Springer-Verlag.

Discala, C., Benigni, X., Barillot, E., & Vaysseix, G. (2000). DBcat: a catalog of 500 biological databases. *Nucleic Acids Research, 28*(1), 8–9..doi:10.1093/nar/28.1.8

Doloc-Mihu, A. (2007). *Adaptive Image Retrieval System: Similarity modeling, Learning, Fusion, and Visualization*. Doctoral dissertation, University of Louisiana at Lafayette, Louisiana.

Doloc-Mihu, A., Raghavan, V., Karnatapu, S., & Chu, C. H. H. (2005). Interface for visualization of image database in Adaptive Image Retrieval Systems. In *Visualization and Data Analysis (VDA05), Proceedings of SPIE-IS&T Electronic Imaging, SPIE* (vol.5669, pp. 382-393).

Domeniconi, C., Papadopoulos, P., Gunopulos, D., & Ma, S. (2004). Subspace Clustering of High Dimensional Data. In *Proc. SIAM Int'l Conf. Data Mining*, (pp.31-35).

Domingos, P. (2005). Mining Social Networks for Viral Marketing. *IEEE Intelligent Systems, 20*(1), 80–82.

Dong, L., Xiao, D., Liang, Y., & Liu, Y. (2008). Rough set and fuzzy wavelet neural network integrated with least square weighted fusion algorithm based fault diagnosis research for power transformers. *Electric Power Systems Research, 78*(1), 129–136. doi:10.1016/j.epsr.2006.12.013

Dougherty, J., Kohavi, R., & Sahami, M. (1995). Supervised and unsupervised discretization of continuous features. In: *Proceedings of the 12th international conference on machine learning,* (pp. 194—202). San Francisco: Morgan Kaufmann.

Doumpos, M., Marinakis, Y., Marinaki, M., & Zopounidis, C. (2009). An evolutionary approach to construction of outranking models for multicriteria classification: The case of the ELECTRE TRI method. *European Journal of Operational Research, 199*(2), 496–505. doi:10.1016/j.ejor.2008.11.035

Draper, D., Halevy, A. Y., & Weld, D. S. (2001). The nimble xml data integration system. In *17th International Conference on Data Engineering(ICDE 01),* (pp. 155–160).

Duan, L., Xu, L., Liu, Y., & Lee, J. (2009). Cluster-based outlier detection. *Annals of Operations Research, 168,* 151–168. doi:10.1007/s10479-008-0371-9

Duch, H. (2006). Filter methods. In Guyon, I., Gunn, S., Nikravesh, M., & Zadeh, L. (Eds.), *Feature extraction, foundations and applications: Studies in Fuzziness and Soft Computing* (pp. 89–118). Berlin: Physica-Verlag, Springer.

Duda, R. O., Hart, P. E., & Stork, D. G. (2001). *Pattern Classification* (2nd ed.). New York: John Wiley & Sons.

Dudley, J. T., & Butte, A. J. (2009). A Quick Guide for Developing Effective Bioinformatics Programming Skills. *PLoS Computational Biology, 5*(12), e1000589. doi:10.1371/journal.pcbi.1000589

Duguet, E., & Macgarvie, M. (2005). How well do patent citations measure flows of Technology? Evidence from French innovation surveys. *Economics of Innovation and New Technology, 14*(5), 375–393. doi:10.1080/1043859042000307347

Dunbar, J. (2009, July 13th). Retrieved April 14 2010 from http://www.nas.nasa.gov/About/Projects/Columbia/columbia.html

Durbin, R., Eddy, S., Krogh, A., & Mitchison, G. (1998). *Biological Sequence Analysis: Probabilistic Models of Proteins and Nucleic Acids.* Cambridge, UK: Cambridge University Press. doi:10.1017/CBO9780511790492

Dy, J. G., & Broadly, E. C. (2004). Feature Selection for unsupervised learning. *Journal of Machine Learning Research, 5,* 845–889.

Dy, J. G., & Broadly, E. C. (2000). Interactive Visualization and Feature selection for Unsupervised Data. In *Proceedings of 6th ACM SIGKDD International Conference on Knowledge Discovery and data Mining,* (pp.360-364). New York: ACM Press.

Dy, J. G., & Brodley, C. E. (2000). Feature Subset Selection and Order Identification for Unsupervised Learning. In *Proceedings of the Seventeenth International Conference on Machine Learning,* (pp. 247-254), Stanford University, CA.

Dy, J. G., & Brodley, C. E. (2000a). Visualization and interactive feature selection for unsupervised data. In *Proceedings of the 6th ACM SIGKDD International Conference on Knowledge Discovery & Data Mining (KDD-00),* (pp. 360-364).

Dyrløv Bendtsen, J., Nielsen, H., von Heijne, G., & Brunak, S. (2004). Improved Prediction of Signal Peptides: SignalP 3.0. [doi: DOI: 10.1016/j.jmb.2004.05.028]. *Journal of Molecular Biology, 340*(4), 783-795.

Dzbor, M., Motta, E., & Stutt, A. (2005). Achieving higher level learning through adaptable Semantic Web applications. *International Journal of Knowledge and Learning, 1*(1/2), 25–43. doi:10.1504/IJKL.2005.006249

Dzbor, M., & Motta, E. (2006). Study on integrating semantic applications with magpie. In Euzenat, J., & Domingue, J. (Eds.), *AIMSA 2006, LNAI 4183* (pp. 66–76).

Dzbor, M., Domingue, J., & Motta, E. (2003). Magpie: Towards a Semantic Web browser. In *International Semantic Web Conference 2003 (ISWC 2003).*

Edgar, R. C. (2004). MUSCLE: multiple sequence alignment with high accuracy and high throughput. *Nucleic Acids Research, 32*(5), 1792–1797..doi:10.1093/nar/gkh340

Efron, B., & Tibshirani, R. J. (1993). *An Introduction to Bootstrap*. New York: Chapman & Hall.

Einhorn, H. J., & Hogarth, R. M. (1981). Behavioral decision theory: Processes of judgement and choice. *Annual Review of Psychology, 32*, 53–88. doi:10.1146/annurev.ps.32.020181.000413

Eirinaki, M., & Vazirgiannis, M. (2003). Web Mining for Web Personalization. *ACM Transactions on Internet Technology, 3*(1), 1–27. doi:10.1145/643477.643478

Eiron, N., & McCurley, K. S. (2003). Analysis of anchor text for web search. In SIGIR '03: Proceedings of the 26th annual international ACM SIGIR conference on Research and development in informaion retrieval (pp. 459-460). New York, NY, USA.

Eiron, N., McCurley, K. S., & Tomlin, J. A. (2004). Ranking the web frontier. In WWW '04: Proceedings of the 13th international conference on World Wide Web, (pp. 309-318). ACM Press. New York, NY, USA.

Ellis, L. B. M., & Attwood, T. K. (2001). Molecular biology databases: today and tomorrow. [doi: DOI: 10.1016/S1359-6446(01)01802-5]. *Drug Discovery Today, 6*(10), 509-513.

Embley, D., Tao, C., & Liddle, S. (2005). Automating the extraction of data from html tables with unknown structure. *Data & Knowledge Engineering, 54*(1), 3–28. doi:10.1016/j.datak.2004.10.004

Engel, S. R., Balakrishnan, R., Binkley, G., Christie, K. R., Costanzo, M. C., Dwight, S. S., et al. (2010). Saccharomyces Genome Database provides mutant phenotype data. *Nucl. Acids Res., 38*(suppl_1), D433-436. doi:10.1093/nar/gkp917

Enterprise Miner, S. A. S. (2006). *SAS Enterprise Miner software, Version 5.2 of the SAS System for Windows*. Cary, NC: SAS Institute Inc.

Ester, M., Kriegel, H. P., Sander, J., & Xu, X. (1996). A density-based algorithm for discovering clusters in large spatial databases. In *ACM SIGKDD International Conference on Knowledge Discovery and Data Mining* (pp. 226-231).

Etzioni, O., Banko, M., Soderland, S., & Weld, D. S. (2008). Open information extraction from the web. *Communications of the ACM, 51*(12), 68–74. doi:10.1145/1409360.1409378

Euzenat, J., & Shvaiko, P. (2007). *Ontology Matching*. Berlin: Springer-Verlag.

Fahlman, S. (1988). Faster-learning variantions of back-propagation: An empirical study. In D.S. Touretzky, G. Hinton, T. Sejnowski, (Eds.), *Proceedings of the 1988 Connectionist Models Summer School*, (pp. 38-51). San Mateo, CA: Morgan Kaufmann.

Fawcett, T., & Provost, F. (1999). Activity monitoring: noticing interesting changes in behavior. In S. Chaudhuri, & D. Madigan, (Ed.), *5th ACM SIGKDD International Conference on Knowledge Discovery and Data Mining (KDD)*, (pp. 53-62).

Fayyad, U., Piatetsky-Shapiro, G., & Smyth, P. (1996). From data mining to knowledge discovery in databases. *AI Magazine, 17*, 37–54.

Feldman, R., & Sanger, J. (2007). *The Text Mining Handbook: Advanced Approaches in Analyzing unstructured Data*. New York: Cambridge University Press.

Fogaras, D. I., & Racz, B. (2004). Towards scaling fully personalized PageRank. In Proceedings WAW 2004, (pp. 105-117).

Foglia, P. (2007). Patentability search strategies and the reformed IPC: A patent office perspective. *World Patent Information, 29*(1), 33–53. doi:10.1016/j.wpi.2006.08.002

Foong, D. L. Y. (2002). A Visualization-Driven Approach for Strategic Knowledge Discovery. In Fayyad, U. (Ed.), *Information Visualization in Data Mining and Knowledge Discovery*. San Fransisco, CA: Morgan Kaufmann.

Frawley, W. J., Piatetsky-Shapiro, G., & Matheus, C. J. (1991). Knowledge discovery in databases: An overview. In Piatetsky-Shapiro, G., & Frawley, W. J. (Eds.), *Knowledge Discovery in Databases* (pp. 1–30). Cambridge, MA: The MIT Press.

Fritzke, B. (1997). A selforganizing network that can follow nonstationary distributions. In ICANN '97: Proceedings of the 7th International Conference on Artificial Neural Networks, (pp. 613-618). SpringerVerlag.

Fruchterman, T.M.J., & Reingold, E.M. (1991). Graph drawing by Force-directed Placement. *software - Practice and Experience, 21*, 1129-1164.

Fu, F., Chen, X., Liu, L., & Wang, L. (2007). Social dilemmas in an online social network: the structure and evolution of cooperation. *Physics Letters. [Part A], 371*, 58–64. doi:10.1016/j.physleta.2007.05.116

Fu, Y., Sandhu, K., & Shih, M. (1999). Fast Clustering of Web Users Based on Navigation Patterns. In *Proceedings of World Multiconference on Systemics, Cybernetics and Informatics (SCI/ISAS'99), (5)*, 560-567.

Gaber, M. M., Zaslavsky, A., & Krishnaswamy, S. (2005). Mining data streams: A review. *SIGMOD Record, 34*(2), 18–26. doi:10.1145/1083784.1083789

Galperin, M. Y., & Cochrane, G. R. (2009). Nucleic Acids Research annual Database Issue and the NAR online Molecular Biology Database Collection in 2009. *Nucl. Acids Res., 37*(suppl_1), D1-4. doi: 10.1093/nar/gkn942

Gao, J., Cheng, H., & Tan, P. N. (2006). Semi-supervised outlier detection. In *the ACM SIGAC Symposium on applied computing* (pp. 635-636). New York: ACM Press.

Gaudreault, J., Frayret, J. M., & Pesant, G. (2009). Distributed search for supply chain coordination. *Computers in Industry, 60*(6), 441–451. doi:10.1016/j.compind.2009.02.006

Gelle, E., & Karhu, K. (2003). Information quality for strategic technology planning. *Industrial Management & Data Systems, 103*(8), 633–643. doi:10.1108/02635570310497675

Geyer-Schulz, A., & Hahsler, M. (July 2002). Evaluation of Recommender Algorithms for an Internet Information Broker based on Simple Association Rules and on the Repeat-Buying Theory, In B. Masand, M. Spiliopoulou, J. Srivastava, O. Zaïane, (Eds.), *Proceedings of WEBKDD'2002* (pp. 100-114). Edmonton: Canada.

Ghoting, A., Otey, M. E., & Parthasarathy, S. (2004). LOADED: link-based outlier and anomaly detecting in evolving data sets. In *International Conference on Data Mining* (pp. 387-390).

Ghoting, A., Parthasarathy, S., & Otey, M. (2006). Fast Mining of distance-based outliers in high-dimensional datasets. In *SIAM International Conference on Data Mining (SDM'06), (pp. 608-612). Bethesda, MA: SIAM.

Gibson, D., Kleinberg, J., & Raghavan, P. (1998). Inferring web communities from link topology. In HYPERTEXT '98: Proceedings of the ninth ACM conference on Hypertext and hypermedia: links, objects, time and space--structure in hypermedia systems, (pp. 225-234). ACM. New York, NY, USA.

Ginarte, J. C., & Park, W. G. (1997). Determinants of patent rights: A cross-national study. *Research Policy, 26*(3), 283–301. doi:10.1016/S0048-7333(97)00022-X

Gleich, D., Zhukov, L., & Berkhin, P. (2004). *Fast parallel PageRank: A linear system approach. Technical report*, Yahoo!Research Labs.

Goldberg, D., Nichols, D., Oki, B. M., & Terry, D. (1992). Using Collaborative Filtering to Weave an Information Tapestry. *Communications of the ACM, 35*(12), 61–70. doi:10.1145/138859.138867

Gomez-Perez, A., Fernando-Lopez, M., & Corcho, O. (2004). *Ontological Engineering: with examples from the areas of Knowledge Management, e-Commerce and the Semantic Web*. London: Springer-Verlag.

Gonda, D., Bachmair, A., Wunning, I., Tobias, J., Lane, W., & Varshavsky, A. (1989). Universality and structure of the N-end rule. *The Journal of Biological Chemistry, 264*, 16700–16712.

Gonzalez, R. C., & Woods, R. E. (1992). *Digital Image Processing*. Reading, MA: Addison-Wesley Publishing Co.

Goth, G. (2008). Are Social Networking Growing Up? *IEEE Distributed Systems Online, 9*(2), 3. doi:10.1109/MDSO.2008.4

Graham, S., & Mowery, D. C. (2003). Intellectual property protection in the software industry. In Cohen, W., & Merrill, S. (Eds.), *Patents in the knowledge-based economy: proceedings of the science, technology and economic policy board*. Washington, DC: National academies press.

Greenidge, C. A. (2009). *SEMWAP: An Ontology-Based Information Extraction Framework for Semantic Web Applications*. Unpublished doctoral dissertation, University of the West Indies, Cave Hill, Barbados.

Greenwood, G. W. (1997). Training partially recurrent neural networks using evolutionary strategies. *IEEE Transactions on Speech and Audio Processing, 5*, 192–194. doi:10.1109/89.554781

Grider, G., Nunez, J., Bent, J., Wingate, M., Torrez, A., Chen, H. B., et al. (n.d.). *File Systems for the World's Fastest Computer*. Retrieved April 13th 2010 from http://www.pdsi-scidac.org/events/PDSW09/resources/LANL.pdf

Grigori, D., Casati, F., Dayal, U., & Shan, M. (2001). Improving Business Process Quality through Exception Understanding, Prediction, and Prevention. In *Proceedings of 27th International Conference on Very Large Data Bases (VLDB'01)*, (pp. 159–168).

Grinstein, G., Plaisant, C., Laskowski, S., O'Connell, T., Scholtz, J., & Whiting, M. (2008). VAST 2008 Challenge: Introducing mini-challenges. In D. Ebert & T. Ertl (Eds.), *Proceedings of the 2008 IEEE Symposium on Visual Analytics Science and Technology (VAST)* (pp. 195-196). Piscataway, NJ: IEEE.

Grossman, R. (2006). *National Center for Data Mining: Funding Acknowledgements*. University of Illinois at Chicago, Chicago. Retrieved from http://www.ncdm.uic.edu/grantAcknowledgement.html

Guha, G. Rastogi., R. & Shim, K. (1998). CURE: An efficient clustering algorithm for large databases. In *Proc. of the ACM SIGMOD*, (pp.73-84).

Guha, S., Rastogi, R., & Kyuseok, S. (1999). ROCK: A robust clustering algorithm for categorical attributes. In *International Conference on Data Engineering (ICDE'99)* (pp. 512-521).

Guruprasad, K., Reddy, B., & Pandit, M. (1990). Correlation between stability of a protein and its dipeptide composition: a novel approach for predicting in vivo stability of a protein from its primary sequence. *Protein Engineering, 4*, 155–161. doi:10.1093/protein/4.2.155

Gutierrez, J. M. P., & Gregori, J. F. (2008). *Clustering techniques applied to outlier detection of financial market series using a moving window filtering algorithm*. Unpublished working paper series, No. 948, European Central Bank, Frankfurt, Germany.

Gyongyi, Z. GarciaMolina, H., & Pedersen, J. (2004). Combating web spam with trustrank. Technical Report 200417. Stanford InfoLab.

Hammami, R., Zouhir, A., Ben Hamida, J., & Fliss, I. (2007). BACTIBASE: a new web-accessible database for bacteriocin characterization. *BMC Microbiology, 7*, 89. doi:10.1186/1471-2180-7-89

Hammami, R., Zouhir, A., Le Lay, C., Ben Hamida, J., & Fliss, I. (2010). BACTIBASE second release: a database and tool platform for bacteriocin characterization. *BMC Microbiology, 10*(1), 22. doi:10.1186/1471-2180-10-22

Hammami, R., Zouhir, A., Naghmouchi, K., Ben Hamida, J., & Fliss, I. (2008). SciDBMaker: new software for computer-aided design of specialized biological databases. *BMC Bioinformatics, 9*(1), 121. doi:10.1186/1471-2105-9-121

Hammami, R., Ben Hamida, J., Vergoten, G., & Fliss, I. (2009). PhytAMP: a database dedicated to antimicrobial plant peptides. *Nucl. Acids Res., 37*(suppl_1), D963-968. doi: 10.1093/nar/gkn655

Hammouda, K. M., & Kamel, M. S. (2004). Efficient phrase-based document indexing for Web document clustering. *IEEE Transactions on Knowledge and Data Engineering, 16*(10), 1279–1296. doi:10.1109/TKDE.2004.58

Hamosh, A., Scott, A. F., Amberger, J. S., Bocchini, C. A., & McKusick, V. A. (2005). Online Mendelian Inheritance in Man (OMIM), a knowledgebase of human genes and genetic disorders. *Nucl. Acids Res., 33*(suppl_1), D514-517. doi: 10.1093/nar/gki033

Han, J., & Kamber, M. (2000). *Data Mining: Concepts and Techniques.* San Francisco: Morgan Kaufman Publishers.

Han, J., Cheng, H., Xin, D., & Yan, X. (2007). Frequent pattern mining: Current status and future directions. *Data Mining and Knowledge Discovery, 15*(1), 55–86. doi:10.1007/s10618-006-0059-1

Han, J., & Cercone, N. (2000). AViz: A visualization system for discovering numeric association rules. In T. Terano, H. Liu, & A.L.P. Chen (Eds.), *Proceedings of the Fourth Pacific-Asia Conference on Knowledge Discovery and Data Mining* (*LNAI 1805*, pp. 269-280). Berlin, Germany: Springer.

Haralick, R.M., Shanmugam, K. & Dinstein, I.(1973). Textural features for image classification. *IEEE Trans Syst Man Cybern SMC,* (3), 610--621.

Harkins, S., He, H., Williams, G. J., & Baxter, R. A. (2002). Outlier detection using replicator neural networks. In Y. Kambayashi, W. Winiwarter & M. Arikawa (Ed.), *the 4ᵗʰ International Conference on Data Warehousing and Knowledge Discovery (DaWak '02),* LNCS, Vol. 2454 (pp. 170-180). Aixen-Provence, France: Springer.

Harold, E. R. (2003). *Processing XML with Java: A guide to SAX, DOM, JDOM, JAXP and TrAX.* Boston: Addison-Wesley.

Harp, S. A., Samad, T., & Guha, A. (1989) Toward the genetic synthesis of neural networks. In J.D. Schafer, (Ed.), *Proc. 3rd Int. Conf. Genetic Algorithms and Their Applications,* (pp. 360-369). San Mateo, CA: Morgan Kaufmann.

Hassell, J., Aleman-Meza, B., & Arpinar, I. B. (2006). *Ontology-Driven Automatic Entity Disambiguation in Unstructured Text.* Paper presented at the ISWC 2006, Athens, GA, USA.

Hastie, T., Tibshirani, R., & Friedman, J. H. (2001). *The Elements of Statistical Learning: data mining, inference, and prediction.* New York: Springer. Retrieved from Http://eric.univ-lyon2.fr/~ricco/tanagra/en/tanagra.html.

Hausman, J., & Leonard, G. K. (2006). Real options and patent damages: the legal treatment of non-infringing alternatives, and incentives to innovate. *Journal of Economic Surveys, 20*(4), 493–512. doi:10.1111/j.1467-6419.2006.00258.x

Hawkins, D. (1980). *Identification of Outliers.* London: Chapman and Hall.

Haykin, S. (1999). *Neural Networks* (2nd ed.). Englewood Cliffs, NJ: Prentice Hall.

He, Z., Xu, X., & Deng, S. (2003). Discovering cluster-based local outliers. *Pattern Recognition Letters, 24,* 1641–1650. doi:10.1016/S0167-8655(03)00003-5

He, Z., Xu, X., & Deng, S. (2006). A fast greedy algorithm for outlier mining. In *PAKDD '06* (pp. 567-576).

Heckerman, D., Mannila, H., Pregibon, D., & Uthurusamy, R. (1997). *Proceedings of the Third International Conference on Knowledge Discovery and Data Mining.* Menlo Park, CA: AAAI press.

Heer, J., & Boyd, D. (2005) Vizster: Visualizing Online Social Network. In *Proceedings of 2005 IEEE Symposium,* (pp.32-39).

Helpman, E. (1993). Innovation, imitation, and intellectual property rights. *Econometrica, 61*(6), 1247–1280. doi:10.2307/2951642

Henryk, M., Russell, M., & Randolph, V. (1992). Statistical determination of the average values of the extinction coefficients of tryptophan and tyrosine in native proteins. *Analytical Biochemistry, 200,* 74–80. doi:10.1016/0003-2697(92)90279-G

Hepp, M. (2007). Possible ontologies: How reality constrains the development of relevant ontologies. *IEEE Internet Computing*, *11*(1), 90–96. doi:10.1109/MIC.2007.20

Hereof, D., & Hoisl, K. (2007). Institutionalized incentives for ingenuity-patent value and the german employees. *Inventions Act. Research Policy*, *36*(8), 1143–1162.

Hereof, D., Schererc, F. M., & Vopel, K. (2003). Citations, family size, opposition and the value of patent rights. *Research Policy*, *32*(8), 1343–1363. doi:10.1016/S0048-7333(02)00124-5

Herman, I., Melancon, G., & Marshall, M. S. (2000). Graph visualization and navigation in Information Visualization: a survey. *IEEE Transactions on Visualization and Computer Graphics*, *6*, 1–21. doi:10.1109/2945.841119

Herrera, F., Hervás, C., Otero, J., & Sánchez, L. (2004). Un estudio empírico preliminar sobre los tests estadísticos más habituales en el aprendizaje automático. In Giraldez, R., Riquelme, J. C., & Aguilar, J. S. (Eds.), *Tendencias de la Minería de Datos en España, Red Española de Minería de Datos y Aprendizaje (TIC2002-11124-E)* (pp. 403–412).

Herzog, S. (2006). Estimating student retention and degree-completion time: Decision Trees and Neural Networks vis-à-vis Regression. *New Directions for Institutional Research*, *131*(Fall), 17–33. doi:10.1002/ir.185

Hingamp, P., van den Broek, A., Stoesser, G., & Baker, W. (1999). The EMBL nucleotide sequence database. [10.1385/MB:12:3:255]. *Molecular Biotechnology*, *12*(3), 255-267.

Hinnerburg, A., Keim, D., & Wawryniuk, M. (1999). HD-Eye: Visual Mining of High – Dimensional Data. *IEEE Computer Graphics and Applications*, *19*(5), 22–31. doi:10.1109/38.788795

Hirschey, M., & Richardson, V. J. (2001). Valuation effects of patent quality: A Comparison for Japanese and US firms. *Pacific-Basin Finance Journal*, *9*(1), 65–82. doi:10.1016/S0927-538X(00)00038-X

Hirschey, M., & Richardson, V. J. (2004). Are scientific indicators of patent quality Useful to investors? *Journal of Empirical Finance*, *11*(1), 91–107. doi:10.1016/j.jempfin.2003.01.001

Hodge, V., & Austin, J. (2004). A survey of outlier detection methodologies. *Artificial Intelligence Review*, *22*(2), 85–126. doi:10.1023/B:AIRE.0000045502.10941.a9

Holzinger, W., Krupl, B., & Herzog, M. (2006). Using ontologies for extracting product features from web pages. In *ISWC 2006,* LNCS, Athens, GA, USA.

Hong, S. J. (1997). Use of contextual information for feature ranking and discretization. *IEEE Transactions on Knowledge and Data Engineering*, *9*(5), 718–730. doi:10.1109/69.634751

Horn, R. (1994). *Topics in Matrix Analysis*. Cambridge, UK: Cambridge University Press.

Horrocks, I., Parsia, B., Patel-Schneider, P., & Hendler, J. (2005). Semantic Web architecture: Stack or two towers? In *Principles and Practice of Semantic Web Reasoning* (pp. 37–41). PPSWR. doi:10.1007/11552222_4

Hu, W., & Qu, Y. (2007). Discovering simple mappings between relational database schemas and ontologies. In K. Aberer (Ed.), *International Semantic Web Conference, LNCS Vol. 4825*, Busan, Korea. Berlin: Springer.

Huang, Z., Zeng, D., & Chen, H. (2007). A comparison of collaborative filtering recommendation algorithms for ecommerce. *IEEE Intelligent Systems*, *22*(5), 68–78. doi:10.1109/MIS.2007.4338497

Huang, C. C., & Tseng, T. L. (2004). Rough set approach to case-based reasoning application. *Expert Systems with Applications*, *26*(3), 369–385. doi:10.1016/j.eswa.2003.09.008

Huang, C. C., Fan, Y. N., Tseng, T. L., Lee, C. H., & Huang, H. F. (2008). A hybrid data mining approach to quality assurance of manufacturing process. *IEEE International Conference on Fuzzy Systems.*

Hui, Z., Bin, P., Ke, X., & Hui, W. (2006). An efficient algorithm for clustering search engine results. In *2006 International Conference on Computational Intelligence and Security*, November, Guangzhou, China, (pp. 1429–1434).

Hunter, A. (2001). Data Mining. *Knowledge Management*, (July/August). Retrieved November 19, 2009 from http://www.cs.ucl.ac.uk/staff/a.hunter/tradepress/

Hwang, C.-S., & Chen, Y.-P. (2006). Fuzzy Collaborative Filtering for Web Page Prediction. In *Proceedings of JCIS Advanced Intelligent Systems Research*, (pp. 11-16).

Hwang, M. W., Choi, J. Y., & Park, J. (1997). Evolutionary projection neural networks. In *Proc. 1997 IEEE Int. Conf. Evolutionary Computation, ICEC'97*, (pp. 667-671).

IBM. (2002). *Using Intelligent Miner for Data*. Armonk, NY: IBM Corporation.

Ikai, A. (1980). Thermostability and aliphatic index of globular proteins. *Journal of Biochemistry, 88*, 1895–1898.

Imhoff, C., Galemmo, N., & Geiger, J. G. (2003). *Mastering Data Warehouse Design: Relational and Dimensional Techniques*. New York: John Wiley & Sons.

Inbarani, H., & Thangavel, K. (2009). Mining and Analysis of Clickstream Patterns. In *Foundations of Computational, Intelligence - Data Mining, Studies in Computational Intelligence* (pp. 3–27). Berlin: Springer.

Inbarani, H., Thangavel, K. & Pethalakshmi.(2007). A Rough Set Based Feature Selection for web usage mining. In *Proceedings of the International Conference on Computational Intelligence and Multimedia Applications* (ICCIMA 2007),1, (pp. 33-38).

Inmon, W. H. (2002). *Building the Data Warehouse* (3rd ed.). New York: John Wiley & Sons.

Inselberg, A. (1997). Multidimensional detective. In *IEEE Symposium of Information Visualization*, (pp.100-107). Washington, DC: IEEE Computer Society.

Isaac, A., van der Meij, L., Schlobach, S., & Wang, S. (2007). An empirical study of instance-based ontology matching. In K. Aberer (Ed.), *International Semantic Web Conference, Vol. 4825*, pp. 253–266, Busan, Korea.

Jack, K., & Russell, F. (1982). A simple method for displaying the hydropathic character of a protein. *Journal of Molecular Biology, 157*, 105–132. doi:10.1016/0022-2836(82)90515-0

Jagadish, H. V., & Olken, F. (2003). Database Management for Life Science Research: Summary Report of the Workshop on Data Management for Molecular and Cell Biology at the National Library of Medicine, Bethesda, Maryland, February 2–3, 2003. *OMICS: A Journal of Integrative Biology, 7*(1), 131-137. doi: doi:10.1089/153623103322006797

Jain, A. K., Murty, M. N., & Flynn, P. J. (1999). Data Clustering: A Review. *ACM Computing Surveys*, 264–323. doi:10.1145/331499.331504

Jenamani, M., Mohapatra, P. K. J., & Ghose, S. (2002). Online Customized Index Synthesis in Commercial Web Sites. *IEEE Intelligent Systems*, 20–27. doi:10.1109/MIS.2002.1134358

Jensen, R., & Shen, Q. (2007). Fuzzy-Rough Sets Assisted Attribute Selection. *IEEE Transactions on Fuzzy Systems, 15*(1), 73–89. doi:10.1109/TFUZZ.2006.889761

Jensen, D., & Neville, J. (2002). *Data mining in social networks*. National Academy of Sciences Symposium on Dynamic Social Network Analysis.

Jerzy, W. G. (1988). Knowledge acquisition under uncertainty — a rough set approach. *Journal of Intelligent & Robotic Systems, 1*(1), 3–16. doi:10.1007/BF00437317

Jiang, M. F., Tseng, S. S., & Su, C. M. (2001). Two-phase clustering process for outliers detection. *Pattern Recognition Letters, 22*, 691–700. doi:10.1016/S0167-8655(00)00131-8

Jiang, D., Tang, C., & Zhang, A. (2004). Cluster analysis for gene expression data: a survey. *IEEE Transactions on Knowledge and Data Engineering, 16*(11), 1370–1386. doi:10.1109/TKDE.2004.68

Jiang, D., Tang, C., & Zhang, A. (2004). Cluster Analysis for Gene Expression Data: A Survey. *IEEE Transactions on Knowledge and Data Engineering, 11*(16), 1370–1386. doi:10.1109/TKDE.2004.68

Jin, W., Tung, A. K. H., & Han, J. (2001). Mining top-n local outliers in large databases. In *KDD '01* (pp. 293-298).

Jin, Y. Z., Matsuo, Y., & Ishizuka, M. (2007). Extracting social networks among various entities on the web. In *Proceedings of the Fourth European Semantic Web Conference* (pp. 251-266). Berlin: Springer.

Jing, L., & Michael, K., Ng., & Huang, J. Z. (2007). An Entropy Weighting k-Means Algorithm for Subspace Clustering of High-Dimensional Sparse Data. *IEEE Transactions on Knowledge and Data Engineering*, *19*(8), 1026–1041. doi:10.1109/TKDE.2007.1048

Johansson, J. (2006). *Introduction to High Speed Computing*. University of Alberta, Alberta, Canada. Retrieved May 4, 2010 from http://www.ualberta.ca/CNS/RESEARCH/Courses/2006/HPCWorkshop/AICT0603.IntroToHPC.pdf

John, G. H., Kohavi, R., & Pfleger, K. (1994). Irrelevant Features and the Subset Selection Problem. In *Proceedings of the 11th Int. Conf. on Machine Learning*.

Jouve, P., & Nicoloyannis, N. (2005). A filter feature selection method for clustering, In *ISMIS*, (pp. 583-593). Berlin: Springer.

Jurafsky, D., & Martin, J. H. (2009). *Speech and Language Processing: An Introduction to Natural Language Processing, Computational Linguistics, and Speech Recognition* (2nd ed.). Upper Saddle River, NJ: Pearson, Prentice Hall.

Kalfoglou, Y., Alani, H., Schorlemmer, M., & Walton, C. (2004). *On the emergent Semantic Web and overlooked issues*. Paper presented at the 3rd International Semantic Web Conference (ISWC'04).

Kamada, T., & Kawai, S. (1989). An algorithm for drawing general undirected graphs. *Information Processing Letters*, *31*, 7–15. doi:10.1016/0020-0190(89)90102-6

Kamien, M. I., Tauman, Y., & Zang, I. (1988). Optimal license fees for a new product. *Mathematical Social Sciences*, *16*(1), 77–106. doi:10.1016/0165-4896(88)90006-6

Kamvar, S. D., Haveliwala, T., Manning, C., & Golub, G. (2003). *Exploiting the block structure of the web for computing PageRank. Technical report*. Stanford University.

Kamvar, S.D., Schlosser, M.T., & GarciaMolina, H. (2003). The eigentrust algorithm for reputation management in p2p networks. In Proceedings of the Twelfth International World Wide Web Conference, (pp. 640-651). ACM Press.

Kandogan, E. (2001). Visualizing Multi-dimensional Clusters, Trends and outliers using star co-ordinates. In *Proceedings of ACM KDD*, (pp. 107-116).

Kaur, H., & Wasan, S. K. (2009). An Integrated Approach in Medical Decision Making for Eliciting Knowledge, Web-based Applications in Health Care & Biomedicine. In Lazakidou, A. (Ed.), *Annals of Information System (AoIS)*. Berlin: Springer.

Kaur, H., Wasan, S. K., Al-Hegami, A. S., & Bhatnagar, V. (2006). *A Unified Approach for Discovery of Interesting Association Rules in Medical Databases, Advances in Data Mining*, (LNAI 4065, pp. 53-63). Berlin: Springer-Verlag.

Keim, D. A. (2002). Information visualization and Visual Data mining. *IEEE Transactions on Visualization and Computer Graphics*, *7*(1), 1–8. doi:10.1109/2945.981847

Keim, D. A., Panse, C., Sips, M., & North, S. C. (2004). Visual data mining in large geospatial point sets. *IEEE Computer Graphics and Applications*, *24*, 36–44. doi:10.1109/MCG.2004.41

Keim, D. A., & Kriegel, H.-P. (1996). Visualization techniques for mining large databases: A comparison. *IEEE Transactions on Knowledge and Data Engineering*, *8*(6), 923–938. doi:10.1109/69.553159

Keim, D., & Ward, M. (2007). Visualization. In Berthold, M., & Hand, D. J. (Eds.), *Intelligent Data Analysis: An Introduction* (pp. 403–429). Berlin: Springer.

Keim, D. A., Mansmann, F., Stoffel, A., & Ziegler, H. (2009). Visual analytics. In Liu, L., & Özsu, M. T. (Eds.), *Encyclopedia of Database Systems* (pp. 3341–3346). New York: Springer.

Keim, D. A., Mansmann, F., Schneidewind, J., & Ziegler, H. (2006). Challenges in visual data analysis. In E. Banissi, R.A. Burkhard, A. Ursyn, J.J. Zhang, M. Bannatyne, C. Maple, A.J. Cowell, G.Y. Tian, & M. Hou (Eds.), *Proceedings of the 10th IEEE International Conference on Information Visualization* (pp. 9-16). Los Alamitos, CA: IEEE Computer Society.

Kenneth, A. F., Scharfstein, D. S., & Stein, J. C. (1993). Risk management: coordinating corporate investment and financing policies. *The Journal of Finance, 48*(5), 1629–1658. doi:10.2307/2329062

Kim, W. (2003). A Taxonomy of Dirty Data. *Data Mining and Knowledge Discovery, 7*, 81–99. doi:10.1023/A:1021564703268

Kim, W. (1990). *Introduction to Object-Oriented Databases.* Cambridge, MA: MIT Press.

Kim, J.-H., Choi, S.-S., & Moon, B.-R. (2005). Normalization for neural network in genetic search. In *Genetic and Evolutionary Computation Conference*, (pp. 1-10).

Kim, Y., Street, W., & Menczer, F. (2000). Feature selection for unsupervised learning via evolutionary search. In *Proceedings of the Sixth ACM SIGKDD International Conference on Knowledge Discovery and Data Mining*, (pp. 365–369).

Kimball, R., & Ross, M. (2002). *The Data Warehouse Toolkit: The Complete Guide to Dimensional Modeling* (2nd ed.). New York: John Wiley & Sons.

Kira, K., & Rendell, L. (1992). The feature selection problem: traditional methods and a new algorithm. In *Tenth National conf. on AI*, (pp.129-134). Cambridge, MA: MIT Press.

Kirsopp, C., & Shepperd, M. (2002). Case and Feature Subset Selection in Case Based Software Project Effort Prediction. In *Proceedings of 22nd SGAI Int'l Conf. Knowledge Based Systems and Applied Artificial Intelligence.*

Kitano, H. (1990). Designing neural networks using genetic algorithms with graph generation system. *Complex Systems, 4*, 461–476.

Kleinberg, J. (1999). Authoritative sources in a hyperlinked environment. In Journal of the ACM, 46 (pp. 604632).

Klopotek, M., Wierzchon, S., Ciesielski, K., Draminski, M., & Czerski, D. (2007). *Conceptual Maps of Document Collections in Internet and Intranet. Coping with the Technological Challenge.* Warszawa, Poland: IPI PAN Publishing House.

Knight, H. (2001). *Patent strategy for researchers and research managers. New York.* Jackson: Wiley.

Knorr, E., Ng, R., & Tucakov, V. (2000). Distance-based outliers: algorithms and applications. *The VLDB Journal, 8*, 237–253. doi:10.1007/s007780050006

Knorr, E., & Ng, R. (1998). Algorithms for mining distance-based outliers in large data sets. In *the 24th International conference on Very Large Databases (VLDB)*, (pp. 392-403).

Kohavi, R., & John, G. H. (1997). Wrappers for Feature Subset Selection. *Artificial Intelligence, 97*(1-2), 273–324. doi:10.1016/S0004-3702(97)00043-X

Köhler, J. (2004). Integration of life science databases. [doi: DOI: 10.1016/S1741-8364(04)02392-3]. *Drug Discovery Today: BIOSILICO, 2*(2), 61-69.

Kohlschtter, C., Chirita, R., & Nejdl, W. (2006). Efficient parallel computation of PageRank. In Proc. of the 28th European Conference on Information Retrieval.

Kohonen, T., Kaski, S., Somervuo, P., Lagus, K., Oja, M., & Paatero, V. (2003). *Selforganization of very large document collections. Technical report.* Helsinki, Finland: University of Technology.

Kohonen, T. (1998). Self-Organization of very large document collections: State of the art. In *Proceedings of the 8th International Conference on Artificial Neural Networks, ICANN'98*, (vol. 1, pp. 65-74).

Kolaczyk, E. D. (2009). *Statistical analysis of network data: methods and models.* Springer.

Kononenko, I. (1994). Estimating attributes: analysis and extensions of Relief. In De Raedt, L., & Bergadano, F. (Eds.), *Machine Learning: ECML-94* (pp. 171–182). Berlin: Springer Verlag.

Kononenko, I., Bratko, I., & Kukar, I. (1998). Application of machine learning to medical diagnosis. In Michalski, R. S., Bratko, I., & Kubat, M. (Eds.), *Machine Learning and Data Mining: Methods and Applications* (pp. 389–408). Chichester, UK: Wiley.

Kononenko, I. (1995). On biases in estimating multi-valued attributes. In *Proceedings of the International Joint Conference on Artificial Intelligence (IJCAI'95)*, (pp. 1034–1040). San Francisco: Morgan Kaufmann

Kopak, R. W. (1999). *Functional link typing in hypertext. ACM Computing Surveys.* New York, NY, USA: ACM Press.

Koren, Y., & Harel, D. (2003) A two-way visualization method for clustered data. In L. Getoor, T.E. Senator, P. Domingos, & C. Faloutsos (Eds.), *Proceedings of the Ninth ACM SIGKDD International Conference on Knowledge Discovery and Data Mining* (*KDD-03*) (pp. 589-594). New York: ACM.

Koufakou, A., & Georgiopoulos, M. (2010). A fast outlier detection strategy for distributed high-dimensional data sets with mixed attributes. *Data Mining and Knowledge Discovery, 20*(2), 259–289. doi:10.1007/s10618-009-0148-z

Koufakou, A., Ortiz, E. G., Georgiopoulos, M., Anagnostopoulos, G. C., & Reynolds, K. M. (2007). A Scalable and Efficient Outlier Detection Strategy for Categorical Data. In *the 19ᵗʰ IEEE International Conference on Tools with Artificial Intelligence,* (pp. 210-217).

Koza, J. R. (1992). *Genetic Programming: On the Programming of Computers by Means of Natural Selection.* Cambridge, MA: MIT Press.

Krishnapuram, B., Harternink, A. J., Carin, L., & Figueiredo, M. A. T. (2004). A bayesian approach to joint feature selection and classifier design. *IEEE Transactions on Pattern Analysis and Machine Intelligence*, 1105–1111. doi:10.1109/TPAMI.2004.55

Krogh, A., Larsson, B., von Heijne, G., & Sonnhammer, E. L. L. (2001). Predicting transmembrane protein topology with a hidden markov model: application to complete genomes. [doi: DOI: 10.1006/jmbi.2000.4315]. *Journal of Molecular Biology, 305*(3), 567-580.

Kuijk, Ad. J.G. van & Lobeck, M. A. (1984). A model title page for patent specifications. *World Patent Information, 6*(1), 24–31. doi:10.1016/0172-2190(84)90020-6

Kurucz, M., Benczúr, A. A., Csalogány, K., & Lukács, L. (2009). Spectral Clustering in Social Networks, In *Proceedings of WebKDD/SNA-KDD 2007* (pp. 1–20).

Labarga, A., Valentin, F., Anderson, M., & Lopez, R. (2007). Web Services at the European Bioinformatics Institute. *Nucl. Acids Res., 35*(suppl_2), W6-11. doi: 10.1093/nar/gkm291

Lacy, L. W. (2005). *OWL: Representing Information Using the Web Ontology Language*. Bloomington, IN: Trafford Publishing.

Ladley, J. (March 2007). Beyond the Data Warehouse: A Fresh Look. *DM Review Online*. Available at http://dmreview.com

Laender, A. H. F., Ribeiro-Neto, B. A., da Silva, A. S., & Teixeira, J. S. (2002). A Brief Survey of Web Data Extraction Tools. *SIGMOD Record, 31*(2), 84–93. doi:10.1145/565117.565137

Lahiri, M., & Berger-Wolf, T. Y. (2008). Mining Periodic Behavior in Dynamic Social Networks. In *Proceedings of Eighth IEEE International Conference on Data Mining* (pp. 373-382).

Lai, K. K., & Wu, S. J. (2005). Using the patent co-citation approach to establish a new patent classification system. *Information Processing & Management, 41*(2), 313–330. doi:10.1016/j.ipm.2003.11.004

Lai, Y. H., & Che, H. C. (2009). Modeling patent legal value by Extension Neural Network. *Expert Systems with Applications*, *36*(7), 10520–10528. doi:10.1016/j.eswa.2009.01.027

Lakshmanan, L. V. S., Leung, C. K.-S., & Ng, R. T. (2003). Efficient dynamic mining of constrained frequent sets. *ACM Transactions on Database Systems*, *28*(4), 337–389. doi:10.1145/958942.958944

Langley, P. (1994). Selection of relevant features in machine learning, In *Proceedings of the AAAI Fall Symposium on Relevance*. New Orleans: AAAI Press.

Langville, A., & Meyer, C. D. (2006). *Google's Pagerank and Beyond: The Science of Search Engine Rankings*. Princeton, Oxford: Princeton University Press.

Lanjouw, J. O., & Schankerman, M. (2001). Characteristics of Patent Litigation: A Window on Competition. *The Rand Journal of Economics*, *32*(1), 129–151. doi:10.2307/2696401

Larkin, M., Blackshields, G., Brown, N., Chenna, R., McGettigan, P., & McWilliam, H. (2007). ClustalW and ClustalX version 2.0. *Bioinformatics (Oxford, England)*, *23*(21), 2947–2948. doi:10.1093/bioinformatics/btm404

Larose, D. T. (2004). *Discovering Knowledge in Data: An Introduction to Data Mining*. New York: Wiley-Interscience.

Lauesen, S. (2005). *User interface design – A software engineering perspective*. Harlow, UK: Addison-Wesley.

Lauw, H., Lim, E.-P., Pang, H., & Tan, T.-T. (2005). Social network discovery by mining spatio-temporal events. *Computational & Mathematical Organization Theory*, *11*(2), 97–118. doi:10.1007/s10588-005-3939-9

Lawrence, C. J., Dong, O. F., Polacco, M. L., Seigfried, T. E., & Brendel, V. (2004). MaizeGDB, the community database for maize genetics and genomics. [Article]. *Nucleic Acids Research*, *32*, D393–D397..doi:10.1093/nar/gkh011

Lawrence Livermore National Laboratory. (2008). *Advanced Simulation and Computing Purple, 100 teraFLOPS Dedicated to Capability Computing*. Retrieved April 22nd from https://asc.llnl.gov/computing_resources/purple/

Lawrence Livermore National Laboratory. (2009). *Advanced Simulation and Computing, On the Path to Predictive Simulation*. Retrieved on May 4 2010. https://asc.llnl.gov/computing_resources/bluegenel/

Lazarevic, A., & Kumar, V. (2005). Feature bagging for outlier detection. In *KDD'05* (pp. 157-166).

Lazarevic, A., Ertoz, L., Kumar, V., Ozgur, A., & Srivastava, J. (2003). A comparative study of Anomaly detection schemes in network intrusion detection. In *SIAM International Conference on Data Mining*.

Lee, H.-T., Leonard, D., Wang, X., & Loguinov, D. (2008). Scaling to 6 billion pages and beyond. In *WWW2008*. Beijing, China: Irlbot.

Lempel, R., & Moran, S. (2000). The stochastic approach for linkstructure analysis (salsa) and the tkc effect. In Proceedings of the Ninth International Conference on the World Wide Web.

Leskovec, J., Adamic, L. A., & Huberman, B. A. (2007). The dynamics of viral marketing. *ACM Transactions on the Web*, *1*(1), 1–39. doi:10.1145/1232722.1232727

Leung, C. K.-S., Khan, Q. I., Li, Z., & Hoque, T. (2007). CanTree: A canonical-order tree for incremental frequent-pattern mining. *Knowledge and Information Systems*, *11*(3), 287–311. doi:10.1007/s10115-006-0032-8

Leung, C. K.-S. (2009). Constraint-based association rule mining. In Wang, J. (Ed.), *Encyclopedia of Data Warehousing and Mining* (2nd ed., pp. 307–312). Hershey, PA: IGI Global.

Leung, C. K.-S., & Carmichael, C. L. (2009). FpViz: A visualizer for frequent pattern mining. In K. Puolamäki (Ed.), *Proceedings of the ACM SIGKDD Workshop on Visual Analytics and Knowledge Discovery: Integrating Automated Analysis with Interactive Exploration* (pp. 30-39). New York: ACM.

Leung, C. K.-S., & Hao, B. (2009). Mining of frequent itemsets from streams of uncertain data. In Y. Ioannidis, D. Lee, & R. Ng (Eds.), *Proceedings of the 25th IEEE International Conference on Data Engineering* (pp. 1663-1670). Los Alamitos, CA: IEEE Computer Society.

Leung, C. K.-S., Irani, P. P., & Carmichael, C. L. (2008a). FIsViz: A frequent itemset visualizer. In T. Washio, E. Suzuki, K.M. Ting, & A. Inokuchi (Eds.), *Proceedings of the 12th Pacific-Asia Conference on Knowledge Discovery and Data Mining* (*LNAI 5012,* pp. 644-652). Berlin, Germany: Springer.

Leung, C. K.-S., Irani, P. P., & Carmichael, C. L. (2008b). WiFIsViz: Effective visualization of frequent itemsets. In F. Giannotti, D. Gunopulos, F. Turini, C. Zaniolo, N. Ramakrishnan, & X. Wu (Eds.), *Proceedings of the Eighth IEEE International Conference on Data Mining* (pp. 875-880). Los Alamitos, CA: IEEE Computer Society.

Leung, C. K.-S., Mateo, M. A. F., & Brajczuk, D. A. (2008c). A tree-based approach for frequent pattern mining from uncertain data. In T. Washio, E. Suzuki, K.M. Ting, & A. Inokuchi (Eds.), *Proceedings of the 12th Pacific-Asia Conference on Knowledge Discovery and Data Mining* (*LNAI 5012,* pp. 653-661). Berlin, Germany: Springer.

Leuski, A., & Allan, J. (2000). Improving interactive retrieval by combining ranked lists and clustering. In *Proceedings of RIAO,* (pp. 665-681).

Levine, L. O. (1987). Patent activity by date of application — Estimating recent applications in the U.S. patent system. *World Patent Information, 9*(3), 137-139.

Levitas, E. F., McFadyen, M. A., & Loree, D. (2006). Survival and the introduction of new technology: a patent analysis in the integrated circuit industry. *Journal of Engineering and Technology Management, 23*(3), 182–201. doi:10.1016/j.jengtecman.2006.06.008

Li, H.-Y., Xie, C.-S., & Liu, Y. (2007). A new method of pefetching I/O requests. In *International Conference on Networking, Architecture and Storage*, July, Guilin, China, (pp. 217–224).

Li, K., & Teng, G. (2006). Unsupervised SVM based on p-kernels for anomaly detection. In *the IEEE International Conference on Innovative Computing, Information and Control* (pp. 59-62), Beijing, China.

Liang, W. Y., & Huang, C. C. (2006). Agent-based demand forecast in multi-echelon supply chain. *Decision Support Systems, 42*(1), 390–407. doi:10.1016/j.dss.2005.01.009

Lingras, P., Hogo, M., Snorek, M., & West, C. (2005). Temporal analysis of clusters of supermarket customers: conventional versus interval set approach. *Information Sciences, 172*(1-2), 215–240. doi:10.1016/j.ins.2004.12.007

Liu, H., & Motoda, H. (1998). *Feature Selection for Knowledge Discovery and Data Mining.* Norwell, MA: Kluwer Academic Publishers.

Liu, H., & Yu, L. (2005). Towards integrating feature selection algorithm for classification and clustering. *IEEE Transactions on Knowledge and Data Engineering, 17*(4), 491–502. doi:10.1109/TKDE.2005.66

Liu, S., & Shyu, J. (1997). Strategic planning for technology development with patent analysis. *International Journal of Technology Management, 13*(5-6), 661–680. doi:10.1504/IJTM.1997.001689

Liu, H., & Keselj, V. (2007). Combined mining of Web server logs and web contents for classifying user navigation patterns and predicting users' future requests. *Data & Knowledge Engineering, 2*(61), 304–330. doi:10.1016/j.datak.2006.06.001

Liu, B. (2009). Classification by association rule analysis. In Liu, L., & Özsu, M. T. (Eds.), *Encyclopedia of Database Systems* (pp. 335–340). New York: Springer.

Liu, H., & Setiono, R. (1996) A probabilistic approach to feature selection - a filter solution. In *Proceedings of the Thirteenth International Conference on Machine Learning (ICML),* (pp. 319–327). San Francisco, CA: Morgan Kaufmann Publishers.

Liu, H., Motoda, H., & Yu, L. (2002). Feature selection with selective sampling. In *Proceedings of the Nineteenth International Conference on Machine Learning,* (pp. 395–402).

Liu, J.-G., & Wu, W.-P. (2004). Web Usage Mining For Electronic Business Applications. In *Proceedings of the Third International Conference on Machine Learning and Cybernetics,* Shanghai, (2), 1314-1318.

Lloyd, S. P. (1957). Least square quantization in PCM. *IEEE Transactions on Information Theory, 28*(2), 129–137. doi:10.1109/TIT.1982.1056489

Makarov, M. (2004). The process of reforming the International Patent Classification. *World Patent Information, 26*(2), 137-141.

Malcolm, J. B., & Michael, J. P. (2001). Variable precision rough set theory and data discretisation: an application to corporate failure prediction. *Omega, 29*(6), 561–576. doi:10.1016/S0305-0483(01)00045-7

Manaskasemsak, B., & Rungsawang, A. (2004). Parallel PageRank computation on a gigabit pc cluster. In AINA '04: Proceedings of the 18th International Conference on Advanced Information Networking and Applications, page 273. IEEE Computer Society. Washington, DC, USA.

Mangalam, H. (2002). The Bio* toolkits -- a brief overview. *Briefings in Bioinformatics, 3*(3), 296–302..doi:10.1093/bib/3.3.296

Manning, Ch. D., & Raghavan, P. (2009). *Schütze, H. An Introduction to Information Retrieval.* Cambridge: Cambridge University Press.

Manning, C. D., Raghavan, P., & Schutze, H. (2008). *Introduction to Information Retrieval.* Cambridge, UK: Cambridge University Press.

Manning, C. D., & Schutze, H. (1999). *Foundations of Statistical Natural Language Processing.* Cambridge, MA: MIT Press.

Mariani, M., & Romanelli, M. (2007). Stacking" and "picking" inventions: The patenting behavior of European inventors. *Research Policy, 36*(8), 1128–1142. doi:10.1016/j.respol.2007.07.009

Markou, M., & Singh, S. (2003a). Novelty detection: A review – Part 1: Statistical approaches. *Signal Processing, 83*(12), 2481–2497. doi:10.1016/j.sigpro.2003.07.018

Markou, M., & Singh, S. (2003b). Novelty detection: A review – Part 2: Neural network based approaches. *Signal Processing, 83*(12), 2499–2521. doi:10.1016/j.sigpro.2003.07.019

Marshall, S. J., & Harrison, R. F. (1991). Optimization and training of feedforward neural networks by genetic algorithms. In *Proceedings of the Second International Conference on Artificial Neural Networks and Genetic Algorithms,* (pp. 39-43). Berlin: Springer-Verlag.

Matsuo, Y., Tomobe, H., & Nishimura, T. (2007). Robust Estimation of Google Counts for Social Network Extraction. In *Proceedings of Twenty Second Conference on Artificial Intelligence* (pp. 1395-1401).

McBurney, P., & Ohsawa, Y. (2003). *Chance discovery, Advanced Information Processing.* Berlin: Springer.

Merrill, J. W. L., & Port, R. F. (1991). Fractally configured neural networks. *Neural Networks, 4*(1), 53–60. doi:10.1016/0893-6080(91)90031-Y

Merz, C. J., & Murphy, P. M. (1998). *UCI Repository of Machine Learning Databases.* Irvine, CA: University of California. Retrieved from http://www.ics.uci.eedu/~mlearn/

Miller, A. (2002). *Subset Selection in Regression.* Boca Raton, FL: Chapman & Hall/CRC.

Miller, G. F., Todd, P. M., & Hedge, S. U. (1989) Designing neural networks using genetic algorithms. In *Proceedings of the Third International Conference on Genetic algorithms,* (pp. 379-384). San Mateo, CA: Morgan Kaufmann.

Mishne, G. (2007). Using Blog Properties to Improve Retrieval. In *Proceedings of International Conference on Weblogs and Social Media (ICWSM 2007),* Boulder, CO.

Mitra, P., Murthy, P. A., & Pal, S. K. (2002). Unsupervised feature selection using feature similarity. *IEEE Transactions on Pattern Analysis and Machine Intelligence, 24*(3), 301–312. doi:10.1109/34.990133

Mittal, V., & Kamakura, W. (2001). Satisfaction, repurchase intention, and repurchase behavior: Investigating the moderating effect of customer characteristics. *JMR, Journal of Marketing Research, 38*(February), 131–142. doi:10.1509/jmkr.38.1.131.18832

Mittal, V., Ross, W. J., & Baldasare, P. (1998). The asymmetric impact of negative and positive attribute-level performance on overall satisfaction and repurchase intentions. *Journal of Marketing, 62*(January), 33–47. doi:10.2307/1251801

Mobasher, B. (2002). Discovery and Evaluation of Aggregate Usage Profiles for Web Personalization. *Data Mining and Knowledge Discovery, 6*, 61–82. doi:10.1023/A:1013232803866

Mobasher, B., Cooley, R., & Srivastava, J. (1999). Creating adaptive web sites through usage-based clustering of urls. In *IEEE Knowledge and Data Engineering Workshop (KDEX'99)*, (pp. 19-25).

Mogee, M. E. (1991). Using patent data for technology analysis and planning. *Research-Technology Management, 34*(4), 43–49.

Montana, D. J. (1995). Strongly typed genetic programming. *Evolutionary Computation, 3*(2), 199–200. doi:10.1162/evco.1995.3.2.199

Moorhouse, M., & Barry, P. (2005). *The Sequence Retrieval System* (pp. 297–301). Bioinformatics Biocomputing and Perl.

Moustakis, V., & Charissis, G. (1999). Machine learning and medical decision making. In *Proceedings of Workshop on Machine Learning in Medical applications, Advance Course in Artificial Intelligence- ACAI99*, Chania, Greece, (pp. 1-19).

Muller, E., Assent, I., Steinhausen, U., & Seidl, T. (2008). OutRank: Ranking outliers in high dimensional data. In *IEEE ICDE 2008 Workshops: The 3rd International Workshop on Self-managing Database Systems (SMDB)*, (pp. 600-603), Cancún, México.

Munzer, T., Kong, Q., Ng, R. T., Lee, J., Klawe, J., Radulovic, D., & Leung, C. K. (2005). *Visual mining of power sets with large alphabets. Technical report UBC CS TR-2005-25*. Vancouver, BC, Canada: Department of Computer Science, The University of British Columbia.

Naisbitt, J. (1984). *Megatrends*. New York: Grand Central Publishing.

Narendra, P. M., & Fukunaga, K. (1977). A Branch and Bound Algorithm for Feature Subset Selection. *IEEE Transactions on Computers*, 917–922. doi:10.1109/TC.1977.1674939

Nasraoui, O., Soliman, M., Saka, E., Badia, A., & Germain, R. (2008). A web usage mining framework for mining evolving user profiles in dynamic websites. *IEEE Transactions on Knowledge and Data Engineering, 2*(20), 202–215. doi:10.1109/TKDE.2007.190667

Nasraoui, O., & Petenes, C. (2003). Combining Web Usage Mining and Fuzzy Inference for Web site Personalization. In *proceedings of WebKDD workshop*, (pp. 37-46).

NCBI. (2002, 01/03/2010). What's the Difference Between MEDLINE® and PubMed®. *Fact Sheet* Retrieved 30/03/2010, from http://www.nlm.nih.gov/pubs/factsheets/dif_med_pub.html

Nelson, J. I. (n.d.). Retrieved April 17th 2010 from http://www.nerdylorrin.net/jerry/politics/Warrantless/WarrantlessFACTS.html

Niu, K., Huang, C., Zhang, S., & Chen, J. (2007). ODDC: Outlier detection using distance distribution clustering. In Washio, T. (Eds.), *PAKDD 2007 Workshops: Emerging Technologies in Knowledge Discovery and Data Mining, 4819* (pp. 332–343). Berlin: Springer. doi:10.1007/978-3-540-77018-3_34

Nolfi, S., & Parisi, D. (2002). Evolution of Artificial Neural Networks. In *Handbook of brain theory and neural networks* (2nd ed., pp. 418–421). Cambridge, MA: MIT Press.

Nostrum, N. (n.d.). Retrieved on April 15th, 2010 at http://www.bsc.es/plantillaA.php?cat_id=5

Notredame, C., Higgins, D. G., & Heringa, J. (2000). T-coffee: a novel method for fast and accurate multiple sequence alignment. [doi: DOI: 10.1006/jmbi.2000.4042]. *Journal of Molecular Biology, 302*(1), 205-217.

Nowson, S., & Oberlander, J. (2007). Identifying More Bloggers: Towards large scale personality classification of personal weblogs. In *Proceedings of International Conference on Weblogs and Social Media (2007)*, Boulder, CO.

Noy, N. F., Ferguson, R. W., & Musen, M. A. (2000). The knowledge model of Protégé-2000: Combining interoperability and flexibility. In: Dieng, R., Corby, O. (eds), *12th International Conference in Knowledge Engineering and Knowledge Management (EKAW'00)*, Juan-Les-Pins, France, (pp. 17-32).

Oja, E., Laaksonen, J., Koskela, M., & Brandt, S. (1999). Self-Organizing Maps for Content-based Image Database Retrieval. In *Kohonen Maps* (pp. 349–362). Amsterdam: Elsevier. doi:10.1016/B978-044450270-4/50028-0

Olinsky, A., Kennedy, K., & Kennedy, B. (2010). *Assessing Gradient Boosting in the Reduction of Misclassification Error in the Prediction of Success of Actuarial Majors*. NEDSI 2010 Proceedings, March 2010.

Oliver, R. L. (1993). Cognitive, affective and attribute bases of the satisfaction response. *The Journal of Consumer Research, 20*, 418–430. doi:10.1086/209358

Oliver, R. L. (1997). *Satisfaction: A Behavioral Perspective on the Consumer*. New York: McGraw-Hill.

Osmar, R., Zaïane, M.-L., & Coman, A. (2002). Mammography Classification by Association Rule-based Classifier. In *International Workshop on Multimedia Data Mining* (pp. 62-69), Edmonton, Alberta, Canada, (17-19 July).

Paci, R., & Sassu, A. (1997). International patents and national technological specialization. *Technovation, 17*(10), 25-38.

Page, R. D. (1996). TreeView: an application to display phylogenetic trees on personal computers. *Computer Applications in the Biosciences, 12*(4), 357–358.

Palace, B. (1996). What is Data Mining. *Data Mining Technology Note prepared for Management 274A Anderson Graduate School of Management at UCLA*. Retrieved November 15, 2009 from http://www.anderson.ucla.edu/faculty/jason.frand/teacher/technologies/palace/datamining.htm

Pallis, G., Angelis, L., & Vakali, A. (2007). Validation and interpretation of web users' sessions clusters. *Information Processing & Management, 5*(43), 1348–1367. doi:10.1016/j.ipm.2006.10.010

Pallis, G., & Vakali, A. (2006). Insight and perspectives for content delivery networks. *Communications of the ACM, 1*(49), 101–106. doi:10.1145/1107458.1107462

Papadimitriou, S., Kitawaga, H., Gibbons, P., & Faloutsos, C. (2003). LOCI: Fast outlier detection using the local correlation integral. In *International Conference on Data Engineering*, (pp. 315-326).

Park, Y., & Park, G. (2004). A new method for technology valuation in monetary legal value: procedure and application. *Technovation, 24*(5), 387–394. doi:10.1016/S0166-4972(02)00099-8

Parpinelli, R. S., Lopesand, H. S., & Freitas, A. A. (2002). Data Mining with an Ant Colony Optimization Algorithm. *IEEE Transactions on Evolutionary Computation, 6*(4), 321–332. doi:10.1109/TEVC.2002.802452

Parsons, J., Ralph, P., & Gallagher, K. (2004). Using Viewing Time to Infer User Preference in Recommender Systems. In *Proceedings of AAAI Workshop on Semantic Web Personalization*, (pp. 52-63).

Pasquier, N., Bastide, Y., Taouil, R., & Lakhal, L. (1999). Discovering frequent closed itemsets for association rules. In C. Beeri & P. Buneman (Eds.), *Proceedings of the Seventh International Conference on Database Theory (LNCS 1540*, pp. 398-416). Berlin, Germany: Springer.

Patcha, A., & Park, J. M. (2007). An overview of anomaly detection techniques: Existing solutions and latest technological trends. *Computer Networks, 51*, 3448–3470. doi:10.1016/j.comnet.2007.02.001

Patrickios, C., & Yamasaki, E. (1995). Polypeptide amino acid composition and isoelectric point. *Analytical Biochemistry, 231*, 82–91. doi:10.1006/abio.1995.1506

Pawlak, Z. (1991). *Rough sets Theoretical aspects of reasoning about data.* Dordrecht: Kluwer Academic Publishers.

Pawlak, Z. (1997). Rough set approach to knowledge-based decision. *European Journal of Operational Research, 99*(1), 48–57. doi:10.1016/S0377-2217(96)00382-7

Pawlak, Z. (1982). Rough sets. *International journal of computer and information sciences, 11*(5), 341-356.

Pearson, W. R., & Lipman, D. J. (1988). Improved tools for biological sequence comparison. *Proceedings of the National Academy of Sciences of the United States of America, 85*(8), 2444–2448. doi:10.1073/pnas.85.8.2444

Pecenovic, Z., Do, M. N., Vetterli, M., & Pu, P. (2000). Integrated browsing and searching of large image collections. In *Proceedings of the 4th Intl. Conf. on Visual Information Systems (VISUAL),* (pp.279-289).

Pechinizkiy, M., Tsymbal, A., & Puuronen, S. (2004). PCA-based Feature Transformations for Classification: Issues in Medical Diagnostics. In R. Long (Eds.), *Proc of 17th IEEE Symposium on Computer-Based Medical Systems,* Bethesda, MD, (pp. 535-540).

Peeters, G., & Czapinski, J. (1990). Positive-negative asymmetry in evaluations: The distinction between affective and informational negativity effect. *European Review of Social Psychology, 1,* 33–60. doi:10.1080/14792779108401856

Pei, J., Han, J., Mortazavi-Asl, B., & Zhu, H. (2000). Mining access patterns efficiently from web logs. In T. Terano, H. Liu, & A.L.P. Chen (Eds.), *Proceedings of the Fourth Pacific-Asia Conference on Knowledge Discovery and Data Mining (LNAI 1805,* pp. 396-407). Berlin, Germany: Springer.

Penrose, E. (1951). *The Economic of the International Patent System.* Baltimore, MD: John Hopkins Press.

Perkowitz, M., & Etzioni, O. (2000). Towards adaptive web sites: conceptual framework and case study. *Artificial Intelligence, 118,* 245–275. doi:10.1016/S0004-3702(99)00098-3

Peter, H., & Greenidge, C. A. (2005). Data Warehousing Search Engine. In Wang, J. (Ed.), *Encyclopedia of Data Warehousing and Mining (Vol. 1,* pp. 328–333). Hershey, PA: Idea Group Publishing.

Peter, H. & Greenidge, C.A. (2009). Validation of an ontology-based Framework for the Semantic Web. (*Journal of Web Semantics*).

Petridou, S. G., Koutsonikola, V. A., Vakali, A. I., & Papadimitriou, G. I. (2008). Time Aware Web Users Clustering. *IEEE Transactions on Knowledge and Data Engineering, 5*(20), 653–667. doi:10.1109/TKDE.2007.190741

Philips, J. (2010). *Sandia National Laboratories.* Retrieved April 10th, 2010 from http://www.sandia.gov/ASC/redstorm.html

Powers, S. (2003). *Practical RDF.* Sebastopol, CA: O'Reilly Media.

Predki, B., Słowiński, R., Stefanowski, J., Susmaga, R., & Wilk, S. (2008). ROSE - Software Implementation of the Rough Set Theory. *Lecture Notes in Computer Science, 1424,* 605–608. doi:10.1007/3-540-69115-4_85

Predki, B., Słowiński, R., Stefanowski, J., Susmaga, R., & Wilk, S. (2008). ROSE - Software Implementation of the Rough Set Theory. *LNCS, 1424,* 605–608.

Qian, Y., Liang, J., & Dang, C. (2008). Converse approximation and rule extraction from decision tables in rough set theory. *Computers & Mathematics with Applications (Oxford, England), 55*(8), 1754–1765. doi:10.1016/j.camwa.2007.08.031

Quan, D., Huynh, D., & Karger, D. R. (2003). Haystack: A platform for authoring end user Semantic Web applications. In *12th International WWW Conference 2003.*

Quinlan, J. R. (1993). *Programs for Machine Learning.* Los Altos, CA: Morgan Kaufmann.

Quinlan, J. R. (1993). *C4.5: Programs for Machine Learning.* San Francisco: Morgan Kaufmann.

Quinlan, J. R. (1987). Simplifying decision trees. *International Journal of Man-Machine Studies, 27,* 221–234. doi:10.1016/S0020-7373(87)80053-6

Rabuñal, J. R., & Dorado, J. (2005). *Artificial Neural Networks in Real-Life Applications.* Hershey, PA: Idea Group Inc.

Rabuñal, J. R., Dorado, J., Pazos, A., Pereira, J., & Rivero, D. (2004). A New Approach to the Extraction of ANN Rules and to Their Generalization Capacity Through GP. *Neural Computation, 16*(7), 1483–1523. doi:10.1162/089976604323057461

Rabuñal, J.R., Dorado, J., Puertas, J., Pazos, A., Santos, A. & Rivero, D. (2003). Prediction and Modelling of the Rainfall-Runoff Transformation of a Typical Urban Basin using ANN and GP. *Applied Artificial Intelligence.*

Radzeka, A., & Wolfenden, R. (1988). Comparing the polarities of amino acids: side-chain distribution coefficients between vapor phase, cyclohexane, 1-octanol and neutral aqueous solution. *Biochemistry, 27,* 1664–1670. doi:10.1021/bi00405a042

Ramaswami, S., Rastogi, R., & Shim, K. (2000). Efficient Algorithms for Mining Outliers from Large Data Sets. In *ACM SIGMOD International Conference on Management of Data,* (pp. 427-438). New York: ACM Press.

Reed, R. (1993). Pruning algorithms – a survey. *IEEE Transactions on Neural Networks, 4*(5), 740–747. doi:10.1109/72.248452

Reitzig, M. (2004). Improving patent valuations for management purposes – Validating new indicators by analyzing application rationales. *Research Policy, 33*(6-7), 939–957. doi:10.1016/j.respol.2004.02.004

Resnick, P., Iacovou, N., Suchak, M., Bergstrom, P., & Riedl, J. (1994). Grouplens: An open architecture for collaborative filtering on netnews. In *Proceedings of the Computer Supported Collaborative Work Conference,* (pp. 175–186).

Rice, P., Longden, I., & Bleasby, A. (2000). EMBOSS: the European Molecular Biology Open Software Suite. *Trends Genet, 16*(6), 276-277. doi:S0168-9525(00)02024-2 [pii]

Richards, G., Rayward-Smith, V. J., Sonksen, P. H., Carey, S., & Weng, C. (2001). Data mining for indicators of early mortality in a database of clinical records. *Artificial Intelligence in Medicine, 22,* 215–231. doi:10.1016/S0933-3657(00)00110-X

Richardson, M., & Domingos, P. (2002). The intelligent surfer: Probabilistic combination of link and content information in PageRank. In Advances in Neural Information Processing Systems 14 (pp. 14411448). Cambridge, MA: MIT Press. Department of Computer Science and Engineering, University of Washington, USA.

Richardson, M., & Domingos, P. (2002). Mining Knowledge-Sharing Sites for Viral Marketing. In *Proceedings of 8th ACM SIGKDD International Conference on Knowledge Discovery and Data Mining,* (pp. 61-70).

Rivero, D., Rabuñal, J. R., Dorado, J., & Pazos, A. (2005). *Time Series Forecast with Anticipation using Genetic Programming* (pp. 968–975). IWANN.

Rivero, D., Rabuñal, J. R., Dorado, J., & Pazos, A. (2004). Using Genetic Programming for Character Discrimination in Damaged Documents. In *Applications of Evolutionary Computing, EvoWorkshops2004: EvoBIO, EvoCOMNET, EvoHOT, EvoIASP, EvoMUSART, EvoSTOC (Conference proceedings),* (pp. 349-358).

Robnik-Šikonja, M., & Kononenko, I. (2003). Theoretical and empirical analysis of ReliefF and RReliefF. *Machine Learning Journal, 53,* 23–69. doi:10.1023/A:1025667309714

Robnik-Šikonja, M., & Vanhoof, K. (2007). Evaluation of ordinal attributes at value level. *Data Mining and Knowledge Discovery, 14,* 225–243. doi:10.1007/s10618-006-0048-4

Rodden, K. (2002). *Evaluating similarity-based visualizations as interfaces for image browsing.* Doctoral dissertation, University of Cambridge, Cambridge, UK.

Rodriguez-Tome, P. (1998). The BioCatalog. *Bioinformatics (Oxford, England), 14*(5), 469–470..doi:10.1093/bioinformatics/14.5.469

Ross, M. (2006, Oct.). Four Fixes Refurbish Legacy Data Warehouses. *Intelligent Enterprise, 9*(10), 43–45. Available at http://www.intelligententerprise.com.

Rubner, Y., Tomasi, C., & Guibas, L. J. (1998a). Adaptive color-image embeddings for database navigation. In *Proceedings of the Asian Conference on Computer Vision,* (pp. 104-111). Washington, DC: IEEE.

Rubner, Y., Tomasi, C., & Guibas, L. J. (1998b). A metric for distributions with applications to image databases. In *Proceedings of the 6th IEEE International Conference on Computer Vision,* (pp.59-66).

Rumelhart, D. E., Hinton, G. E., & Williams, R. J. (1986). Learning internal representations by error propagation. In Rumelhart, D. E., & McClelland, J. L. (Eds.), *Parallel Distributed Processing: Explorations in the Microstructures of Cognition* (pp. 318–362). Cambridge, MA: MIT Press.

Rupprecht, K. (1994). CD-ROMs for publication of patents: A critical review. *World Patent Information, 16*(4), 216–219. doi:10.1016/0172-2190(94)90006-X

Russell, S., & Norvig, P. (2003). *Artificial Intelligence: A Modern Approach* (2nd ed.). Upper Saddle River, NJ: Prentice Hall.

Saiki, T., Akano, Y., Watanabe, C., & Tou, Y. (2006). A new dimension of potential resources in innovation: A wider scope of patent claims can lead to new functionality development. *Technovation, 26*(7), 796–806. doi:10.1016/j.technovation.2005.06.002

Sali, A., & Blundell, T. L. (1993). Comparative protein modelling by satisfaction of spatial restraints. *J Mol Biol, 234*(3), 779-815. doi:S0022-2836(83)71626-8 [pii] 10.1006/jmbi.1993.1626

Sanchez, E. (1996). Speedier: Penn researchers to link supercomputers to community problems. *Compass, 43*(4), 14. Retrieved from http://www.upenn.edu/pennnews/features/1996/091796/research.

Sankaralingam, K., Sethumadhavan, S., & Browne, J. C. (2003). Distributed PageRank for p2p systems. In Proc. of the 12th IEEE Intl. Symp. on High Performance Distributed Computing (HPDC).

Santini, S., & Jain, R. (2000). Integrated browsing and querying for image databases. *IEEE MultiMedia, 7*(3), 26–39. doi:10.1109/93.879766

Santini, S., Gupta, A., & Jain, R. (1999). A user interface for emergent semantics in image databases. In *Proceedings of the 8th IFIP Working Conference on Database Semantics (DS-8),* (pp.123-143).

Sarukkai, R. R. (2000). Link Prediction and Path Analysis Using Markov Chains. In *Proceedings of the 9th International World Wide Web Conference on Computer networks,* (pp. 377-386). Amsterdam: North-Holland Publishing.

Sarwar, B., Karypis, G., Konstan, J., & Riedl, J. (2001). Item-based collaborative filtering recommendation algorithms. In *Proceedings of the WWW Conference,* (pp. 285–295).

SAS. (n.d.). *Data mining with SAS® Enterprise Miner™.* Retrieved November 19, 2009 from http://www.sas.com/technologies/analytics/ datamining/miner/

Sayal, M., Casati, F., Dayal, U., & Shan, M. (2002). Business Process Cockpit. In *Proceedings of 28th International Conference on Very Large Data Bases (VLDB'02),* (pp. 880–883).

Schaefer, C. F. (2004). Pathway Databases. *Annals of the New York Academy of Sciences, 1020*(The Applications of Bioinformatics in Cancer Detection), 77-91.

Scholkpof, B., Williamson, R., Smola, A., Taylor, J. S., & Platt, J. (1999). Support vector method for novelty detection. In *the Advances in Neural Information Processing Systems (NIPS),* (pp.582-588). Cambridge, MA: MIT Press.

Schoop, M., De Moor, A., & Dietz, J. L. (2006). The pragmatic web: A manifesto. *Communications of the ACM, 49*(5), 75–76. doi:10.1145/1125944.1125979

Schreck, T., Bernard, J., Tekušová, T., & Kohlhammer, J. (2008). Visual cluster analysis of trajectory data with interactive Kohonen Maps. In D. Ebert & T. Ertl (Eds.), *Proceedings of the 2008 IEEE Symposium on Visual Analytics Science and Technology* (*VAST*) (pp. 3-10). Piscataway, NJ: IEEE.

Schreiber, G., & Aroyo, L. (2008). Principles for knowledge engineering on the web. In *16th International Conference on Knowledge Engineering: Practice and Patterns*, LNAI, Acitrezza, Italy. Berlin: Springer-Verlag.

Schumacher, P., Olinsky, A., & Quinn, J. (in press). A comparison of Logistic Regression, Neural Networks, and Classification Trees predicting success of actuarial students. *Journal of Education for Business*.

Schwartz, E. (2003). Data Warehouses Get Active. *InfoWorld, 25*(48), 12–13.

Scott, J. (2000). *Social Network Analysis: A Handbook* (2nd ed.). New York: Sage Publications.

Segall, R. S., Zhang, Q., & Pierce, R. M. (2009). Visualization by Supercomputing Data Mining. In *Proceedings of the 4th INFORMS Workshop on Data Mining and System Informatics*, San Diego, CA, October 10.

Sethi, V., & King, R. (1999). Nonlinear and noncompensatory models in user information satisfaction measurement. *Information Systems Research, 10*(1), 87–96. doi:10.1287/isre.10.1.87

Shadbolt, N., Berners-Lee, T., & Hall, W. (2006). The Semantic Web revisited. *IEEE Intelligent Systems, 21*(3), 96–101. doi:10.1109/MIS.2006.62

Shah, U., Finin, T., Joshi, A., Cost, R. S., & Mayfield, J. (2002). *Information Retrieval on the Semantic Web.* Paper presented at the Tenth International Conference on Information and Knowledge Management (CIKM 2002), McLean, VA.

Shannon, C. E. (1948). A mathematical theory of communication. *The Bell System Technical Journal, 27*, 379–423.

Shchekotykhin, K., Jannach, D., Friedrich, G., & Kozeruk, O. (2007). Allright: Automatic ontology instantiation from tabular web documents. In K. Aberer (Ed.), *International Semantic Web Conference*, (LNCS 4825, pp. 466–479), Busan, Korea, Berlin: Springer.

Shen, L., Francis, E., Tay, H., Qu, L., & Shen, Y. (2000). Fault diagnosis using Rough Sets Theory. *Computers in Industry, 43*(1), 61–72. doi:10.1016/S0166-3615(00)00050-6

Shen, W., DeRose, P., McCann, R., Doan, A., & Ramakrishnan, R. (2008). Toward best-effort information extraction. In *ACM SIGMOD International Conference on the Management of Data,* Vancouver, Canada

Sheng, Q., Moreau, Y., & De Moor, B. (2003). Biclustering micrarray data by Gibbs sampling. *Journal of Bioinformatics, 19*(2), 196–205.

Shepard, R. N. (1962). The analysis of proximities: Multidimensional scaling with an unknown distance function. *Psychometrika, 27*, 125–140. doi:10.1007/BF02289630

Shi, S., Yu, J., Yang, G., & Wang, D. (2003). Distributed page ranking in structured p2p networks. Parallel Processing, International Conference.

Shneiderman, B., & Plaisant, C. (2004). *Designing the user interface. University of Maryland.* College Park, MD: Addison-Wesley.

Shyng, J. Y., Wang, F. K., Tzeng, G. H., & Wu, K. S. (2005). Rough set theory in analyzing the attributes of combination values for the insurance market. *Expert Systems with Applications, 32*(1), 56–64. doi:10.1016/j.eswa.2005.11.002

Silverberg, G., & Verspagenb, B. (2007). The size distribution of innovations Revisited: An application of extreme value statistics to citation and value Measures of patent significance. *Journal of Econometrics, 139*(2), 318–339. doi:10.1016/j.jeconom.2006.10.017

Simoudis, E., Han, J., & Fayyad, U. (1996). In *Proceedings of the Second International Conference on Knowledge Discovery and Data Mining.* Menlo Park, CA: AAAI press.

Singh, L., Beard, M., Getoor, L., & Blake, M. B. (2007). Visual mining of multi-modal social networks at different abstraction levels. In *Proceedings of 11th International Conference Information Visualization (IV '07)*, (pp. 672-679).

Sithirasenan, E., & Muthukkumarasamy, V. (2008). Substantiating security threats using group outlier detection techniques. In *IEEE GLOBECOM*, (pp. 2179-2184).

Skalak, D., & Rissland, E. (1990). Inductive learning in a mixed paradigm setting. In *the 8th National Conference on Artificial Intelligence*, (pp. 840-847). Boston: AAAI Press / MIT Press.

Smith, R., & Schumacher, P. (2005). Predicting success for actuarial students in undergraduate mathematics courses. *College Student Journal*, (39): 165–177.

Smith, R., & Schumacher, P. (2006). Academic attributes of college freshmen that lead to success in actuarial studies in a business college. *Journal of Education for Business*, (81): 256–260. doi:10.3200/JOEB.81.5.256-260

Song, Q., & Shepperd, M. (2006). Mining web browsing patterns for E-commerce. *Computers in Industry*, 622–630. doi:10.1016/j.compind.2005.11.006

Soong, J. W. (2005). *Patent Damage Strategies and The Enterprise License: Constructive Notice, Actual Notice, No Notice*, Duke L. & Tech. Rev. 0002.

Sourina, O., & Liu, D. (2004). Visual interactive 3-dimensional clustering with implicit functions. *Proceedings. of the IEEE Conference on Cybernetics and Intelligent Systems*, *1*(1-3), 382–386.

Spence, R. (2000). *Information visualization: design for interaction*. Reading, MA: Addison Wesley.

Spreng, R. A., McKensey, S., & Olshavsky, R. (1996). A reexamination of the determinants of consumer satisfaction. *Journal of Marketing*, *60*(July), 15–32. doi:10.2307/1251839

SPSS. (2006). *15.0 Command Syntax Reference*. Chicago: SPSS Inc.

Srinivasa, N., & Medasani, S. (2004). Active fuzzy clustering for collaborative filtering. In *Proceedings of IEEE International Conference on Fuzzy Systems*, July, Budapest, Hungary, (pp. 1607–1702).

Staab, S., Domingos, P., Mike, P., Golbeck, J., Ding, L., & Finin, T. (2005). Social Networks Applied. *IEEE Intelligent Systems*, *20*, 80–93. doi:10.1109/MIS.2005.16

Stembridge & Corish. (2004). Patent data mining and effective patent portfolio management. *Intellectual Asset Management*, *8*, 30–35.

Stolte, C., Tang, D., & Hanrahan, P. (2002). Query, analysis, and visualization of hierarchically structured data using Polaris. In D. Hand, D. Keim, & R. Ng (Eds.), *Proceedings of the Eighth ACM SIGKDD International Conference on Knowledge Discovery and Data Mining (KDD-02)* (pp. 112-122). New York: ACM.

Stone, M. (1978). Cross-validation: A review. *Matemastische Operationsforschung Statischen. Serie Statistics*, *9*, 127–139.

Sullivan, D. (2000). *Search Engines Review Chart*. Retrieved June 10, 2002, from http://searchenginewatch.com

Sumathi & Sivanandam. (2006). *Introduction to Data Mining and Its Applications*. Berlin: Springer-Verlag.

Supercomputers. (2009). Retrieved April 20th 2010 from http://www.computerbasicsguide.com/basics/supercomputers.html

Sussman, J. L., Lin, D., Jiang, J., Manning, N. O., Prilusky, J., Ritter, O., et al. (1998). Protein Data Bank (PDB): Database of Three-Dimensional Structural Information of Biological Macromolecules. *Acta Crystallographica Section D*, *54*(6 Part 1), 1078-1084. doi: doi:10.1107/S0907444998009378

Sutton, R. S. (1986). Two problems with backpropagation and other steepest-descent learning procedure for networks. In *Proc. 8th Annual Conf. Cognitive Science Society*, (pp. 823-831). Hillsdale, NJ: Erlbaum.

Suzuki, E., & Zytkow, J. (2000). Unified algorithm for undirected discovery of exception rules. In *PKDD '00*, (pp. 169-180).

Sydow, M. (2005). Approximation quality of the rbs ranking algorithm. In Intelligent. *Information Systems, 2005*, 289–296.

Szymanski, D. M., & Henard, D. (2001). Consumer satisfaction: A meta-analysis of the empirical evidence. *Journal of the Academy of Marketing Science, 29*(1), 16–35.

Tan, X., Yao, M., & Xu, M. (2006). An Effective Technique for Personalization Recommendation Based on Access Sequential Patterns. In *IEEE Proceedings of Asia-pacific conference on Services computing*.

Tang, J., Zhang, J., Yao, L., & Li, J. (2008). Extraction and Mining of an Academic Social Network. In. *Proceedings of World Wide Web Conference, 2008*, 1193–1194.

Tang, C., Zhang, L., Zhang, I., & Ramanathan, M. (2001). Interrelated two-way clustering: an unsupervised approach for gene expression data analysis. In *Proceedings of the 2nd IEEE Int. Symposium on Bioinformatics and Bioengineering*, (pp. 41–48).

Tao, Y., Xiao, X., & Zhou, S. (2006). Mining distance-based outliers from large databases in any metric space. In *the 12th ACM SIGKDD International Conference on Knowledge Discovery and Data Mining* (394-403). Philadelphia: ACM Press.

Tateno, Y., Fukami-Kobayashi, K., Miyazaki, S., Sugawara, H., & Gojobori, T. (1998). DNA Data Bank of Japan at work on genome sequence data. *Nucleic Acids Research, 26*(1), 16–20..doi:10.1093/nar/26.1.16

Taylor, C. T., & Silberston, Z. A. (1973). *The Economic Impact of the Patent Systems: a Study of the British Experience*. London: Cambridge University Press.

Thangavel, K. & Roselin, R. (2009, November). Mammogram mining with genetic optimization of Ant-Miner parameters. *International journal of Recent Trends in Engineering, 2* (3).

Thangavel, K., Alagambigai, P., & Devakumari, D. (2009). Improved Visual Clustering through Unsupervised Dimensionality Reduction, Goebel, R., Siekmann, J. & Wahlster, W. (Ed.), *Rough Sets, Fuzzy Sets, Data Mining and Granular Computing, (LNCS 5908)*, (pp. 439-446). Berlin: Springer.

The Gale Group Inc. (2002). Data Mining and Walmart. In *Computer Sciences, Encyclopedia.com*. Retrieved November 20, 2009 from: http://www.encyclopedia.com/doc/1G2-3401200510.html

Thomas, J. J., & Cook, K. A. (Eds.). (2005). *Illuminating the Path: The Research and Development Agenda for Visual Analytics*. Los Alamitos, CA: IEEE Computer Society.

Thomas, P. D., Campbell, M. J., Kejariwal, A., Mi, H., Karlak, B., & Daverman, R. (2003). PANTHER: A Library of Protein Families and Subfamilies Indexed by Function. *Genome Research, 13*(9), 2129–2141..doi:10.1101/gr.772403

Thuraisingham, B. (1999). *DataMining: Technologies, Techniques, Tools and Trends* (pp. 42–48). Boca Raton, FL: CRC press.

Ting, H. (2008). Web Mining Techniques for On-line Social Networks Analysis, In *Proceedings of International Conference on Service Systems and Service Managemen*, (pp. 1-5).

Top 500 Supercomputers. (n.d.). Retrieved April 17th, 2010 from http://www.top500.org/system/7466

Top 500 Supercomputing Sites. (n.d.). Retrieved May 4, 2010 from http://www.top500.org/list/2009/11/100

Top 7 Most Powerful Supercomputers in the World. (2007). In *The Last Laugh Depot, Saung Thamar*. Retrieved April 15th, 2010 from http://saungthamar.multiply.com/journal/item/81

Torgo, L., & Ribeiro, R. (2003). Predicting outliers. In Lavrac, N., Gamberger, D., Todorovski, L., & Blockeel, H. (Eds.), *Principles of Data Mining and Knowledge Discovery, LNAI 2838* (pp. 447–458). Springer.

Tory, M., & Moller, T. (2004). Human Factors in Visualization Research. *IEEE Transactions on Visualization and Computer Graphics*, *10*(1), 72–84. doi:10.1109/TVCG.2004.1260759

Tse, D. K., & Wilton, P. (1988). Models of consumer satisfaction formation: An extension. *JMR, Journal of Marketing Research*, *25*(May), 204–212. doi:10.2307/3172652

Tseng, T. L., & Huang, C. C. (2007). Rough set-based approach to feature selection in customer relationship management. *Omega*, *35*(4), 365–383. doi:10.1016/j.omega.2005.07.006

Tseng, T. L., Jothishankar, M. C., & Wu, T. T. (2004). Quality control problem in printed circuit board manufacturing—An extended rough set theory approach. *Journal of Manufacturing Systems*, *23*(1), 56–72. doi:10.1016/S0278-6125(04)80007-4

Tseng, B. L., Tatemura, J., & Wu, Y. (2005). Tomographic Clustering to Visualize Blog Communities as Mountain Views. In *Proceedings of World Wide Web Conference 2005*.

Turney, P., Whitley, D., & Anderson, R. (1996). Special issue on the baldwinian effect. *Evolutionary Computation*, *4*(3), 213–329.

United States General Accounting Office. (2004). *Computer-Assisted Passenger Prescreening System Faces Significant Implementation Challenges*. Report to Congressional Committees, GAO, Report GAO-04-385, Washington DC 20548. Retrieved November 10, 2009 from http://www.gao.gov/new.items/d04385.pdf

van der Aalst, W., Weijters, A., & Maruster, L. (2004a). Workflow Mining: Discovering Process Models from Event Logs. *IEEE Transactions on Knowledge and Data Engineering*, *16*(9), 1128–1142. doi:10.1109/TKDE.2004.47

van der Aalst, W., & Song, M. (2004b). Mining Social Networks: Uncovering Interaction Patterns in Business Processes. In *Proceedings of International Conference on Business Process Management*, (pp. 244–260).

Van Trieste, S., & Vis, W. (2007). Valuing patents on cost-reducing technology: A case study. *International Journal of Production Economics*, *105*(1), 282–292. doi:10.1016/j.ijpe.2006.04.019

Vandamme, J. P., Meskens, N., & Superby, J. F. (2007). Predicting academic performance by Data Mining methods. *Education Economics*, *15*(4), 405–419. doi:10.1080/09645290701409939

Varshavsky, R., Gottlieb, A., Linial, M., & Horn, D. (2006). Novel unsupervised feature filtering of biological data. *Bioinformatics (Oxford, England)*, *22*(14), 507–513. doi:10.1093/bioinformatics/btl214

Vayshavsky, R., Gottlieb, A., Linial, M., & Horn, D. (2004). Noval Unsupervised Feature Filtering of Biological Data. In *Text Mining and Information Extraction* (pp. 1–7). Oxford, UK: Oxford University Press.

Veldkamp, W. J. H., & Karssemeijer, N. (1996). Influence of segmentation on classification of microcalcifications in digital mammography. In *Proceedings of the 18th Annual International Conference of the IEEE Engineering in Medicine and Biology Society*, (October 31–November 3). Amsterdam, Netherlands: Institute of Electrical and Electronic Engineers, Inc.

Veltkamp, R. C., & Tanase, M. (2000). *Content-Based Image Retrieval Systems: A survey*. Ultrecht University, UU-CS-2000-34. Retrieved from http://www.aa-lab.cs.uu.nl/cbirsurvey/cbir-survey/

Verhaegen, P. A., D'hondt, J., Vertommen, J., Dewulf, S., & Duflou, J. R. (2009). Relating properties and functions from patents to TRIZ trends. [Design Synthesis]. *CIRP Journal of Manufacturing Science and Technology*, *1*(3), 126–130. doi:10.1016/j.cirpj.2008.09.010

Von Wartburg, I., Teichert, T., & Rost, K. (2005). Inventive progress measured by Multi-stage patent citation analysis. *Research Policy*, *34*(10), 1591–1607. doi:10.1016/j.respol.2005.08.001

Walker, E., Rummel, N., & Koedinger, K. R. (2009). A research framework for providing adaptive collaborative learning support. *User Modeling and User-Adapted Interaction, 19*(5), 387–431. doi:10.1007/s11257-009-9069-1

Walker, R. F., Jackway, P., & Longstaff, I. D. (1995). Improving co-occurrence matrix feature discrimination. In *Proceedings of the 3rd Conference on Digital Image Computing: Techniques and Applications (DICTA '95)*, Brisbane, Australia, December 6–8. www.cancer.gov. (n.d.).

Wall, M., Rechtsteiner, A., & Rocha, L. (2003). Singular value Decomposition and Principal Component Analysis. In Berrar, D., Dubitzky, W., & Granzow, M. (Eds.), *A Practical approach to Microarray Data Analysis* (pp. 91–109). Amsterdam: Kluwer. doi:10.1007/0-306-47815-3_5

Wang, Q. H., & Li, J. R. (2004). A rough set-based fault ranking prototype system for fault diagnosis. *Engineering Applications of Artificial Intelligence, 17*(8), 909–917. doi:10.1016/j.engappai.2004.08.013

Wang, J., & Lochovsky, F. H. (2003). Data extraction and label assignment for Web databases. *WWW 2003 Conference*, Budapest, Hungary.

Wang, Y., & DeWitt, D. J. (2004). Computing PageRank in a distributed internet search system. In VLDB '04: Proceedings of the Thirtieth international conference on Very large data bases (pp. 420-431). VLDB Endowment.

Wapedia Supercomputer. (2010). Retrieved on April 14th 2010 from http://wapedia.mobi/en/Supercomputer

Wasserman, S., & Faust, K. (1994). *Social Network Analysis: Methods and Applications*. Cambridge: Cambridge University Press.

Wiess, G., & Provost, F. (2001). *The Effect of Class Distribution on Classifier Learning: An Empirical Study*. Unpublished Technical Report ML-TR-44, Department of Computer Science, Rutgers University.

Wikipedia. (2009). *Supercomputers*. Retrieved May 19, 2009 from BookRags.com: http://www.bookrags.com/wiki/Supercomputer

Wikipedia. (2010). *Information visualization*. Retrieved January 17, 2010, from http://en.wikipedia.org/wiki/Information_visualization#cite_note-MF08-0

Wikipedia. (2010). Retrieved April 27 2010 from http://en.wikipedia.org/wiki/Supercomputer

Williams, A. L., Kersey, P. J., Pruess, M., & Apweiler, R. (2005). Biological Databases: Infrastructure, Content and Integration. In Francisco Azuaje, J. D. (Ed.), *Data Analysis and Visualization in Genomics and Proteomics* (pp. 11–28). doi:10.1002/0470094419.ch2

Wilson, R. J., Goodman, J. L., Strelets, V. B., & The FlyBase Consortium. (2008). FlyBase: integration and improvements to query tools. *Nucl. Acids Res., 36*(suppl_1), D588-593. doi: 10.1093/nar/gkm930

Witten, I. H., & Frank, E. (2005). *Data Mining Practical Machine Learning Tools and Techniques*. San Fransisco, CA: Morgan Kaufmann.

Wong, T.-l., & Lam, W. (2009). An unsupervised method for joint information extraction and feature mining across different web sites. *Data & Knowledge Engineering, 68*(1), 107–125. doi:10.1016/j.datak.2008.08.009

Wong, P. C. (1999). Visual Data Mining. *IEEE Computer Graphics and Applications, 19*(5), 20–21. doi:10.1109/MCG.1999.788794

Wu, C. H., Yeh, L.-S. L., Huang, H., Arminski, L., Castro-Alvear, J., & Chen, Y. (2003). The Protein Information Resource. *Nucleic Acids Research, 31*(1), 345–347.. doi:10.1093/nar/gkg040

Xiao, H., & Zhang, X. (2008). Comparison studies on classification for remote sensing image based on data mining method. *WSES Transactions on Computers, 7*(5), 552–558.

Xiao, J., Zhang, Y., Jia, X., & Li, T. (2001). Measuring Similarity of Interests for Clustering web-Users. In *Proceedings Of the 12th Australian Database Conference*, (pp. 107-114).

Xu, G. (2008). *Web Mining Techniques for Recommendation and Personalization*. Ph.D thesis.

Yang, L. (2005). Pruning and visualizing generalized association rules in parallel coordinates. *IEEE Transactions on Knowledge and Data Engineering, 17*(1), 60–70. doi:10.1109/TKDE.2005.14

Yang, C. C., & Ng, T. D. (2007). Terrorism and Crime Related Weblog Social Network: Link, Content Analysis and Information Visualization. In *Proceedings of IEEE International Conference on Intelligence and Security Informatics,* (pp. 55–58).

Yang, W.-S., Dia, J.-B., Cheng, H.-C., & Lin, H.-T. (2006). Mining social networks for targeted advertising. In *Proceedings of the 39th Annual Hawaii International Conference on System Science (HICSS '06),* (vol. 6, pp. 137a).

Yang, X., Latecki, L. J., & Pokrajac, D. (2008). Outlier detection with globally optimal exemplar-based GMM. In *SIAM International Conference on Data Mining (SDM'08)* (pp. 145-154).

Yao, X. (1999). `Evolving artificial neural networks. *Proceedings of the IEEE, 87*(9), 1423–1447. doi:10.1109/5.784219

Yao, X., & Liu, Y. (1998). Toward designing artificial neural networks by evolution. *Applied Mathematics and Computation, 91*(1), 83–90. doi:10.1016/S0096-3003(97)10005-4

Yi, Y. (1991). A critical review of consumer satisfaction. In Zeithaml, V. A. (Ed.), *Review of Marketing* (pp. 68–123). Chicago: American Marketing Association.

Yu, L., & Liu, H. (2004). Efficient feature selection via analysis of relevance and redundancy. *Journal of Machine Learning Research, 5,* 1205–1224.

Yu, L., & Liu, H. (2003). Feature selection for high-dimensional data: A fast correlation-based filter solution. In *Proceedings of the 12th International Conference on Machine Learning (ICML-03),* Washington, DC, (pp. 856–863). San Francisco, CA, Morgan Kaufmann.

Zadeh, P. M., & Moshkenani, M. S. (2008). Mining Social Network for Semantic Advertisement. In *Proceedings of Third International Conference on Convergence and Hybrid Information Technology,* (pp. 611-618).

Zaihrayeu, I., Sun, L., Giunchiglia, F., Pan, W., Ju, Q., Chi, M., & Huang, X. (2007). From web directories to ontologies: Natural language processing challenges. In *ISWC/ASWC 2007, LCNS 4825, Busan, Korea.* Berlin: Springer-Verlag.

Zdobnov, E. M., Lopez, R., Apweiler, R., & Etzold, T. (2002). The EBI SRS server--recent developments. *Bioinformatics (Oxford, England), 18*(2), 368–373.. doi:10.1093/bioinformatics/18.2.368

Zhang, L., Zhang, K., & Li, C. (2008). *A topical PageRank based algorithm for recommender systems* (pp. 713–714). In SIGIR.

Zhang, J., & Wang, H. (2006). Detecting outlying subspaces for high-dimensional data: the new task, algorithms, and performance. *Knowledge and Information Systems, 10*(3), 333–355. doi:10.1007/s10115-006-0020-z

Zhang, Y., Yang, S., & Wang, Y. (2008). LDBOD: A novel distribution based outlier detector. *Pattern Recognition Letters, 29,* 967–976. doi:10.1016/j.patrec.2008.01.019

Zhang, Z., Shi, Y., & Gao, G. (2009). A rough set-based multiple criteria linear programming approach for the medical diagnosis and prognosis. *Expert Systems with Applications, 36*(5), 8932–8937. doi:10.1016/j.eswa.2008.11.007

Zhang, T., Ramakrishnan, R., & Livny, M. (1996). Birch: An efficient data clustering method for very large databases. In *the ACM SIGMOD International Conference on Management of Data* (pp. 103-114), Montreal, Canada: ACM Press.

Zheng, Z., Srihari, R., & Srihari, S. (2003). A feature selection framework for text filtering. In *Proceedings of Third IEEE International Conference on Data Mining (ICDM),* November 19-22, (pp. 705- 708).

Zhou, L., Ding, J., Wang, Y., Cheng, B., & Cao, F. (2009). The Social Network Mining of BBS. *Journal of Networks*, *4*(4), 298–305. doi:10.4304/jnw.4.4.298-305

Zhou, D., Councill, I., Zha, H., & Giles, C. (2007) Discovering Temporal Communities from Social Network Documents. In *Proceedings of 7th IEEE International Conference on Data Mining (ICDM 2007)*, (pp. 745-750).

Zhu, X., & Goldberg, A. (2009). *Introduction to Semi-Supervised Learning*. San Francisco: Morgan and Claypool Publishers.

Zhu, C., Kitagawa, H., & Faloutsos, C. (2005). Example-based robust outlier detection in high dimensional datasets. In *the IEEE International Conference on Data Mining (ICDM'05)*, (pp. 829-832).

Zhu, J., Hong, J., & Hughes, J. G. (2002). Using markov models for web site link prediction. In HYPERTEXT '02: Proceedings of the thirteenth ACM conference on Hypertext and hypermedia, (pp. 169-170). ACM Press. New York, NY, USA.

Zhu, Y., & Li, X. (2005). Distributed PageRank computation based on iterative aggregationdisaggregation methods. In Proc. of the 14th ACM international conference on Information and knowledge management (pp. 578-585).

Ziarko, W. P., & Van Rijsbergen, C. J. (1994). *Rough Sets, Fuzzy sets and Knowledge Discovery*. New York: Springer-Verlag.

Zillman, M. P. (2005). *Deep Web research 2005*. Retrieved from http://www.llrx.com/features/deepweb2005.htm

About the Contributors

Qingyu Zhang received his Ph.D. in Manufacturing Management and Engineering from the College of Business Administration of the University of Toledo. He is a Certified Fellow in Production and Inventory Management (CFPIM) by APICS. He is also certified MCSD, MCSE, and MCDBA by Microsoft. He is an associate professor at Arkansas State University. He has published in *European Journal of Operational Research, International Journal of Production Research, Journal of Operations Management, International Journal of Production Economics, Kybernetes: International Journal of Systems and Cybernetics, Industrial Management & Data Systems, International Journal of Operations and Production Management, International Journal of Logistics Management, Journal of Systems Science and Systems Engineering, International Journal of Product Development, International Journal of Quality and Reliability Management, European Journal of Innovation Management,* and *International Journal of Information Technology and Decision Making.* Dr. Zhang's research interests are supply chain management, value chain flexibility, e-commerce, product development, and data mining. He serves on the Editorial Boards of *Journal of Computer Information Systems, Information Resource Management Journal, International Journal of Data Analysis Techniques and Strategy,* and *International Journal of Information Technology Project Management.*

Richard S. Segall is associate professor of computer & information technology at Arkansas State University. He holds BS and MS in mathematics, MS in operations research and statistics from Rensselaer Polytechnic Institute, and PhD in operations research form University of Massachusetts at Amherst. His publications have appeared in journals including *International Journal of Information Technology and Decision Making, Applied Mathematical Modeling, Kybernetes: International Journal of Systems and Cybernetics,* and *Journal of the Operational Research Society.* He has book chapters in *Encyclopedia of Data Warehousing and Mining, Handbook of Computational Intelligence in Manufacturing and Production Management,* and *Handbook of Research on Text and Web Mining Technologies.* His research interests include data mining, text mining, web mining, database management, and mathematical modeling, and have been funded by U.S. Air Force, NASA, Arkansas Biosciences Institute, and Arkansas Science & Technology Authority. He is a member of the Editorial Board of the *International Journal of Data Mining, Modeling and Management,* the Program Committees of the *13th and 14th World Multi-Conference on Systemics, Cybernetics and Informatics,* and Local Arrangements Chair of the *2010 MidSouth Computational Biology & Bioinformatics Society Conference.*

Mei Cao is an Assistant Professor at the University of Wisconsin-Superior. She received her Ph.D. in Manufacturing Management and Engineering from the College of Business Administration of the

University of Toledo. She has publications in various academic journals such as *European Journal of Operational Research, International Journal of Production Research, International Journal of Operations and Production Management, Journal of Systems Science and Systems Engineering, Information & Management, Industrial Management & Data Systems, International Journal of Product Development, International Journal of Services Technology and Management.* She serves on the editorial boards of *International Journal of Operations Research and Information Systems,* and *International Journal of Information Technology Project Management.* She received Distinguished Paper Award by McGraw-Hill/Irwin at the *Midwest Business Administration Association Annual Meeting* in Chicago in 2004. Her research interests include Supply Chain Management, Transportation and Logistics, Flexibility, and Inter-Organizational Information Systems. Her research has been funded by the *National Center for Freight and Infrastructure Research and Education (CFIRE)* and *Midwest Regional University Transportation Center (MRUTC)* under the sponsorship of the Department of Transportation.

* * *

P. Alagambigai has received M. Phil degree in the area of Computer Networks from Mother Teresa Women's university. Currently she is working as Assistant Professor in the Department of Computer Applications, Easwari Engineering College, Chennai, India. She has published 12 research publications in various National and Inter National Journals. Her research interests include Data Mining and Visual Data Mining.

M. Afshar Alam is a Professor in Computer Science and also Dean, Faculty of Management and Information Technology at the Hamdard University, New Delhi, India. In 1997-2000 he founded the Department of Computer Science, Hamdard University. He was also founder of Computer Centre at Hamdard University. He received his Master degree in Computer Science from the Aligarh Muslim University, Aligarh and Ph.D. from Jamia Millia Islamia University, New Delhi. His research interests include Fuzzy logic, Software Engineering and Bioinformatics. He is the author of a book on Software re-engineering and over 50 publications in International/ National journals and conference. He is a member of expert committee AICTE, DST, UGC and Ministry of Human Resource Development (MHRD).

Gopalasamy Athithan received his B.E (Hons) degree in electronics and communications engineering in 1981 from the Coimbatore Institute of Technology, Coimbatore, Tamilnadu. He received his Ph.D. degree in physics in 1997 from the Indian Institute of Technology, Bombay. He worked in IGCAR for six years in computer graphics and modeling of crystal structures. In October 1988 he joined ANURAG, Hyderabad where he continued his work on computer graphics besides taking up projects on parallel processing and neural networks. Since June 2000 he is with the Centre for Artificial Intelligence and Robotics working on the development information security solutions among other things. He has published about twenty papers in archived journals and twenty papers in national and international conferences. Dr. Athithan was selected as a *young associate* of the Indian Academy of Sciences in 1989. He received the *Scientist of the Year* award from the Defense Research and Development Organization (DRDO) for the year 1998. Along with his team, he received the *Agni Award for Excellence in Self-Reliance* for the year 2008 from DRDO.

Christopher L. Carmichael received his B.C.Sc. (Honours) degree, with major in computer science and minor in mathematics, from The University of Manitoba, Winnipeg, MB, Canada. Before that, he earned his diploma in mechanical engineering technology from Red River College, Winnipeg, MB, Canada, and spent a long career in designing and programming commercial control systems for building heating/air conditioning ventilation systems. Currently, he is pursuing his thesis-based M.Sc. degree program in computer science at The University of Manitoba under the academic supervision of Dr. Carson K.-S. Leung. Mr. Carmichael enjoys conducting research in the areas of data mining, data visualization, and visual analytics.

Ritu Chauhan is currently studying at the Hamdard University at New Delhi towards a Ph.D. in Spatial Data Mining; concentrating on clustering data mining under the supervision of Dr. Harleen Kaur. She previously gained a M.Sc. degree in Computer Science at the Hamdard University, New Delhi.

Krzysztof Ciesielski is currently an Assistant Professor at the Institute of Computer Science. He also works as a Data Mining Expert for Stat Consulting Ltd. He received MSc degree (2003) in computer science from Warsaw University, Poland, and BSc degree in mathematics (1998) from the same university. In January 2008 he received PhD degree (cum laude) from the Institute of Computer Science, Polish Academy of Sciences. His major research interests include: social network analysis, recommender systems, text and web mining, high dimensional data clustering and classification. He participated in many research projects concerning these topics. He is an author or co-author of more than 30 scientific publications in national and international journals and conference proceedings.

Jeffrey Scott Cook worked for the Microsoft Corporation in the development of Windows 2000 and Windows Version XP as a Beta Tester. Jeffrey Scott Cook has spent 9 years in the United States Army where he specialized in nuclear, biological and chemical warfare agents. He also specialized in computer systems and foreign languages. He currently holds a patent in Aerospace-design recently adopted by Boeing Aerospace Corporation along with several software development patents. He is currently working on a book that deals with the register of Windows 2000 and Windows XP. He is currently a research writer and he has served 5 years on the Republican National Committee of The United States House of Representatives and plans to run again in November. Jeffrey Scott Cook is currently in Cambridge's book of Who's Who for influential people.

Dariusz Czerski holds the position of an Assistant Professor at the Institute of Computer Science. He received BSc degree and MSc degree in computer science from the University of Podlasie, Poland. In 2010 he received PhD degree from the Institute of Computer Science, Polish Academy of Sciences. His major research interests include: recommender systems, text and web mining, search engine design and construction, high dimensional data clustering and classification. He participated in many research projects concerning these topics. He is an author or co-author of more than 10 scientific publications.

Anca Doloc-Mihu received her Ph.D. degree in Computer Science at the University of Louisiana at Lafayette (USA) in May 2007. Currently, she is a postdoctoral fellow at Emory University (USA), in the Department of Biology. Her research interests include data mining methods for analysis and visualization of large non-textual data collections, such as electrophysiology recordings, images, video and sound.

Julian Dorado was born in A Coruña, on July 30ᵗʰ 1970. He obtained his MS degree in Computer Science at the University of A Coruña, A Coruña, Spain in 1994 and his PhD degree in Computer Science at the same university in 1999. He also obtained a MS in Biology at the University of A Coruña in 2004. He is Senior Lecturer at the Faculty of Computer Science of the University of A Coruña. He has headed different research projects for the university, the regional and national government. He is author or co-author of over 90 contributions to the most important conferences and he is also author or co-author of over 40 papers in different journals. He is the co-editor of the Encyclopaedia of Artificial Intelligence, Information Science Reference, 2008. His research interest is focused on artificial embryogeny, genetic algorithms, genetic programming, artificial neural networks and bioinformatics.

Mchał Dramiński is currently an Assistant Professor at the Institute of Computer Science. He received MSc degree in computer science from Warsaw University of Technology, Poland, and his PhD degree from the Institute of Computer Science, Polish Academy of Sciences. His major research interests include: recommender systems, text and web mining, search engines, bio-informatics, micro-array analysis, high dimensional data clustering and classification for low-count samples. He participated in many research projects concerning these topics. He is an author or co-author of more than 30 scientific publications in national and international journals and conference proceedings.

Ismail Fliss obtained his doctorate in veterinary medicine in 1999 from the National School of Veterinary medicine, Tunis, Tunisia. He undertook a PhD in food science and technology at Laval University. In 1996, he completed a postdoctoral fellowship at the Canadian Food Inspection Agency, Ottawa. Dr. Fliss is currently a full professor in the Department of Food Science and Nutrition at Laval University. He is recognized worldwide for its work on the identification, purification and use in different sectors (food, medical and veterinary) of bacteriocins of lactic acid bacteria as natural antimicrobials.

Charles Greenidge has served in various capacities during the period 1998-2010 as part-time lecturer/tutor/demonstrator in the department of Computer Science, Mathematics and Physics at the University of the West Indies (UWI). He has also taught computer studies at the Barbados Community College. He holds B.Sc and M.Phil degrees in computer science, and recently earned the Ph.D in 2009 for studies related to the Semantic Web. His developer skill set includes the C, C++, Java and Perl programming languages. His current research interests span topics related to the convergence of Artificial Intelligence, Natural Language Processing, Web databases and the Semantic Web.

Riadh Hammami received his BSc in Biology from the University of Tunis El Manar (2001). He did a Master's degree in Biochemistry (2004) at the same University in the laboratory of Dr. Mohamed El Ayeb (Institute Pasteur in Tunis). He received a Joint Doctorate in Biology (2009) from the University of Tunis El Manar (in the laboratory of Dr. Jeannette Ben Hamida) and University of Lille1 - Sciences & Technologies (under supervision of Dr. Gérard Vergoten). After completing his Ph.D., Dr. Hammami started his post-doctoral training with Dr. Ismail Fliss and Dr. Julie Jean at the Department of Food Science and Nutrition, Laval University. His research interests focus on bioinformatics and biochemistry of antimicrobial peptides.

Chun-Che Huang received the Ph.D. degree in Industrial Engineering from the University of Iowa, Iowa City, and the M.S. degree in Operations Research from Columbia University, New York. He is a

Professor in the Department of Information Management, National Chi Nan University, Taiwan and directs the Laboratory of Intelligent Systems and Knowledge Management (the ISKM Lab.). He is interested in intelligent systems, knowledge management, and concurrent engineering. He has published research papers in journals sponsored by various societies.

H. Hannah Inbarani is currently working an associate professor, Department of Computer science, Periyar Uinversity, Salem, India. She received M.sc degree in Computer science from Bharathidasan University, Trichy, India in 1991, M.Phil degree from M.S University, Tirunelveli, India in 2001 and M. Tech Degree from AAI deemed University, Allahabad, India in 2005. Her research interest lies in Rough sets, Fuzzy systems, Internet Technologies, Swarm Intelligence and Web mining. She has published five research papers in the areas like web usage mining, roughsets and ant clustering in reputed International journals.

Harleen Kaur gained her Ph.D. in Computer Science from Jamia Millia Islamia University, New Delhi, India on the topic of Applications of Data Mining techniques in Health care Management. She graduated from the University of Delhi, New Delhi. She has previously served as a Lecturer in Computer Science, University of Delhi. Currently, she is an Assistant Professor at the Department of Computer Science, Hamdard University. She has published numerous research articles in refereed international journals and conference proceedings and books. She is a member of several international bodies. Her main research interests are in the fields of Data analysis with applications to medical databases, Medical decision making, Fuzzy logic, Bayesian networks and visualization.

Mieczysław A. Kłopotek holds the position of a professor at the Institute of Computer Science, Polish Academy of Sciences, Warszawa, Poland and of the Chair of Artificial Intelligence Department at the University of Podlasie, Siedlce Poland. He obtained M.Sc. Eng. and PhD. in computer science from the Dresden University of Technology, Germany (in 1983 and 1984 resp.). He was granted the Dr. Eng. Habil. degree in computer science by the Institute of Computer Science, Polish Academy of Sciences, Warszawa, Poland (1998) and the Scientific Title of Professor of Technical Sciences by the President of the Republic of Poland (2009). His fields of interest include artificial intelligence, reasoning, decision-making theory, machine learning, managing uncertainty in knowledge-based systems, Bayesian networks, Dempster-Shafer's theory of evidence, programming on the Internet, computer vision. He published over 250 papers in national and international conference proceedings and journals, as well as 4 monographs and 18 book chapters.

Carson K.-S. Leung received his B.Sc. (Honours), M.Sc., and Ph.D. degrees, all in computer science, from The University of British Columbia, Vancouver, BC, Canada. Currently, he is an Associate Professor in Department of Computer Science at The University of Manitoba, Winnipeg, MB, Canada. His research interests include the areas of databases, data mining, data warehousing, data visualization, and visual analytics. His work has been published in refereed international journals and conferences such as *ACM Transactions on Database Systems*, IEEE International Conference on Data Engineering (ICDE), IEEE International Conference on Data Mining (ICDM), and Pacific-Asia Conference on Knowledge Discovery and Data Mining (PAKDD). In recent years, he has served as a Program Committee member for conferences like European Conference on Machine Learning and Principles and

Practice of Knowledge Discovery in Databases (ECML/PKDD) and an Organizing Committee member for conferences like ACM SIGMOD International Conference on Management of Data.

Hao-Syuan Lin is currently a graduate student in the MBA program at National Chi Nan University, Taiwan. His research interest includes but not limited to intelligent information systems and patent development and management. He has published two refereed conference papers in the Management Information System (MIS) area sponsored by the Chinese Society of Information Management in Taiwan.

Roberto Marmo received a PhD in Electronic and Computer Engineering from the University of Pavia (Italy) in 2005. Currently, he is a Researcher and Contract Professor at the University of Pavia and University of Insubria - Como. His research interests are focused on information visualization, social networks, visual data mining. He has been involved in projects regarding application of social and business social networks. Author of four books in Italian language about networks Facebook, LinkedIn, Viadeo. Web site http://vision.unipv.it

M Narasimha Murty received his Ph.D. from the Indian Institute of Science, Bangalore, India in 1982. He is a professor in the Department of Computer Science and Automation at the Indian Institute of Science, Bangalore. He has guided 18 Ph.D. students in the areas of Pattern Recognition and Data Mining. He has published around 120 papers in various journals and conference proceedings in these areas. He worked on Indo-US projects and visited Michigan State University, East Lansing, USA and University of Dauphine, Paris. He is currently interested in Pattern Clustering.

Alan Olinsky is a professor of mathematics and computer information systems at Bryant University. He earned his PhD in Management Science from the University of Rhode Island and holds an MS in Mathematics Education and a BBA in Public Accounting from Hofstra University. His research interests include statistics, management science, and data mining. He has published articles on these topics in professional journals including the *Journal of American Academy of Business, Journal of Mathematical Education in Science and Technology, European Journal Of Operational Research, Interfaces,* and *Advances In Business And Management Forecasting.* He is president of the Rhode Island Chapter of the American Statistical Association and a member of the Northeast Decision Sciences Institute. In addition to his research interests, Dr. Olinsky is committed to pedagogical issues at Bryant University as well as on a national scale. He currently teaches courses in multivariate statistics, spreadsheet modeling, and management science. He also has appeared several times as an expert witness in statistical matters at hearings and trials.

Alejandro Pazos was born in Padron on November 20th, 1959. (M-92). He obtained his MS degree in Medicine and Surgery in 1987 at the USC, Santiago de Compostela, Spain. He also has a PhD degree in Medicine obtained at the UCM, Madrid, Spain in 1996, an Ms degree in Computer Science obtained at the UPM, Madrid, Spain, in 1989 and a PhD degree in Computer Science at the UPM, Madrid, Spain, obtained in 1990. He is currently a Professor at the Faculty of Computer Science of the University of A Coruña since 1999, A Coruña, Spain. He is also the head of the department of Information and Communication Technologies at the same university. He has headed several research projects for regional, national and international administrations. He is author or co-author of more than 60 papers in different journals and more than 160 papers in different conferences. His main research interests are biomedical computer systems, artificial neural networks and artificial intelligence in medicine. Dr. Pazos is also affiliated to INNS, ACM and IAKE. He has also worked as a consultant of the Spanish Ministry of Defence. He has worked as a representative of the Science and Technology Ministry of Spain and the Galician regional Research and Development plan.

Hadrian Peter holds the B.Sc and M.Sc in Mathematics, and the MS and PhD in Computer Science. He is currently a Senior Lecturer in Computer Science at the University of the West Indies. He has over 30 years of teaching experience in several areas of Computer Science / IT including: Database Systems, Operating Systems, Software Engineering, Artificial Intelligence, Compilers, Data Structures, C, C++, FoxPro, PL/1, Java. His research activities span the areas of Formal Specification and Object-Oriented Design, Neural Networks/Artificial Intelligence (with applications to Medical Diagnosis), Data Ware-housing and, more recently, the Semantic Web. He has supervised several graduate students and also serves as a member of the editorial board of the International Journal of Data Mining, Modelling and Management (IJDMMM).

John Quinn is a Professor of Mathematics at Bryant University and has been teaching there since 1991. Prior to teaching, Professor Quinn was a mechanical engineer at the Naval Underwater Systems Center (now the Naval Undersea Warfare Center) in Newport, R.I. He received his Sc.B. degree from Brown University in 1978, and his M.S. and Ph.D. degrees from Harvard University in 1987 and 1991, respectively. Professor Quinn has had articles published in multiple areas. He has done previous research in mathematical programming methods and computable general equilibrium models in economics. He currently does research in data mining applications and simulation models.

Juan Ramon Rabuñal was born in Arteixo on January 21st, 1973. He obtained his BSc degree in Computer Science in 1996, the MS degree in Computer Science in 1999 and the PhD degree in Computer Science in 2002, all of them at the University of A Coruña, A Coruña, Spain. He also obtained a PhD degree in Civil Engineering in 2008 at the same university. Nowadays, he shares his time between his lecturer position at the Faculty of Computer Science of the University of A Coruña and the direction of the Center of Technological Innovations in Construction and Civil Engineering. He has also headed several research projects for the university, the regional government as well as the national government. His main research interests are artificial neural networks, genetic programming, genetic algorithms and artificial intelligence in civil engineering.

Daniel Rivero was born in A Coruña on January, 30th 1978. He obtained his MS degree in Computer Science at the University of A Coruña, A Coruña, Spain in 2001 and the PhD degree in Computer Science in 2007 at the same University. He is currently assistant professor at the Faculty of Computer Science of the University of A Coruña. Before he got that academic position, he has received different research grants from different administrations for more than four years. His main research interests are artificial neural networks, genetic algorithms, genetic programming, adaptative systems.

Marko Robnik-Šikonja received his Ph.D. in 2001 in computer science from University of Ljubljana, Slovenia. He is an Assistant Professor at University of Ljubljana, Faculty of Computer and Information Science. His research interests include machine learning, data mining, knowledge discovery, cognitive modeling, and practical applications. He is (co)author of more than 40 publications in journals and international conferences. He is editorial board member of Journal of Data Mining, Modelling and Management.

R. Roselin, has received M. Phil degree in the area of Data Compression from Mother Teresa Women's university in May 2001. Currently she has been working as Assistant Professor in the Department of Computer Science, Sri Sarada College for Women (Autonomous), Salem – 16, India since June 2001. She is doing research in the field of mammogram image mining. Her research interests include Data Mining and Pattern recognition.

Phyllis A. Schumacher is a professor of mathematics at Bryant University. She earned her PhD in Statistics from the University of Connecticut and also holds an MS and BA in Mathematics from the University of Rhode Island. She is a member of the American Statistical Association and is a past President and Vice-President of the RI Chapter. Her research interests include issues in mathematics education, application of statistics to psychology and gender issues in mathematics, and technology. She has published articles on these topics in professional journals on psychology, and mathematics and business education including *Computers in Human Behavior, The Journal of Education for Business, and Primus*. Dr. Schumacher currently is teaching Actuarial Statistics and advises actuarial majors at Bryant. She also is active in the K-16 educational arena and has worked on two federal grants where she served as a mentor to middle and high school mathematics teachers in RI.

N N R Ranga Suri received his Bachelors and Masters Degrees in Computer Science and Engineering in 1998 and 2003 respectively. He has been working as a scientist with the Centre for Artificial Intelligence and Robotics, Bangalore for the past 10 years. He has currently registered for PhD at the Indian Institute of Science, Bangalore. His present research work includes the development of Data Mining based methods for Information Security. He has published around 6 papers in various national and international conferences.

K. Thangavel has received Ph.D degree in the area of Optimization Algorithms from The Gandhigram Rural Institute-Deemed University, Gandhigram, Tamilnadu, India in 1999. Currently he is working as Professor and Head in the Department of Computer Science, Periyar University, Salem, Tamilnadu, India. He has published more than 125 research publications in various National and Inter National Journals. He has edited three books published by Narosa Publishers New Delhi, India. He has successfully guided for 5 Ph. D and 10 M. Phil scholars. More than 15 Ph.D scholars are pursuing under his research supervision. His research interests include Data Mining, Digital Medical Image Processing, Soft Computing, Mobile Computing and Bio-informatics. He is a life member of Operational Research Society of India and member of the research group in Rough set Society. He has organized three National Conferences, three National Seminars, five Research workshops and two 21 day UGC refresher progrmmes. He is reviver for leading publishers such as Elsevier, Springer, Taylor and Francis.

Tzu-Liang (Bill) Tseng is Associate Professor of Industrial, Manufacturing and Systems Engineering at University of Taxes at El Paso. He received his M.S. degree in Industrial Engineering from the University of Wisconsin at Madison in 1995 and Ph.D in Industrial Engineering from the University of Iowa, Iowa City in 1999. Dr. Tseng delivered research results to many refereed journals such as IEEE Transactions, IIE Transaction, International Journal of Production Research, Journal of Manufacturing

Systems and International Journal of Management Science, OMEGA and others (over 100 refereed publication). He has been serving as principle invigorator of several research projects funded by NSF, NASA, DoEd, and KSEF. He is currently serving as an editor of Journal of Computer Standards & Interfaces.

Koen Vanhoof's major research interests lie in the areas of data mining, statistics, knowledge engineering and modeling, computational intelligence methods, decision support systems and soft computing applications to information management, marketing and finance, mobility and traffic safety. He has authored and/or co-authored over 40 peer-reviewed journal articles and about 6 book chapters and 60 conference papers on his research topics. He is co-editor of the International Journal of Information Theory and Applications. He has been appointed as a guest professor in Jagilionski University (Krakow, Poland), University of Antwerp (Belgium), University of Maastricht (Netherlands), University of Economics (Sofia, Bulgary), Technical University (St. Petersburg, Russia) , Academy of Economics (Wroclaw , Poland) and Erasmus University (Rotterdam,Netherlands). Currently he is vice-dean of research at the Faculty of Applied Economics and project leader of the Data mining research group at University of Hasselt.

Sławomir T. Wierzchoń received MSc (1974) and PhD degree in computer science (1979) from Technical University of Warsaw, Poland. He holds Doctor of Science (Habilitation) degree in computer science from the Polish Academy of Science (1997). In June 2003 he received the title of Professor from the President of Poland. Currently Full Professor at the Institute of Computer Science of Polish Academy of Sciences. Also Full Professor and Head of Computational Intelligence Department at the University of Gdansk. Main research areas are: biologically inspired computation, artificial intelligence, especially management of uncertainty, expert systems and machine learning, intelligent information systems. He authored and coauthored more than 200 scientific publications in national and international journals and conference proceedings. He cooperated with medical centers in the area of statistical analysis and knowledge discovery in databases. Participated and participates in national and international research projects, recently concerning construction of document map based internet search engines.

Tri Kurniawan Wijaya is a faculty member of the Department of Computer Science, Sekolah Tinggi Teknik Surabaya, Indonesia. His primary research interests are including data mining, machine learning, and intelligent system. He has published articles in conferences, newsletter, and peer-reviewed journals and also has done several projects involving information system area, intelligent scheduling and general game playing. Besides doing his research, he also enjoys working as a Lego Mindstorms Robotics trainer in Robokidz Computer Learning Center, Surabaya, Indonesia. He and his team won national robotic competitions for the last three years and became their country's representative in the world robotic competitions for Lego Mindstorms.

Index